Computer Science Companion

Fifth Edition
2020-2021

by
William T. Verts, Ph.D.
University of Massachusetts at Amherst
verts@cs.umass.edu
http://www.cs.umass.edu/~verts/

Kendall Hunt
publishing company

Illustrations and graphs throughout text created by William T. Verts, Ph.D.

www.kendallhunt.com
Send all inquiries to:
4050 Westmark Drive
Dubuque, IA 52004-1840

Printed in the United States of America

Table of Contents (Coarse)

Table of Contents (Coarse)

Table of Contents (Fine)

The Rest of this Page Left Intentionally Blank. Mostly.
Make Notes Here, or Doodle Something.

1: *Introduction*

This book is a reference manual for a number of topics that I have covered in my computer science classes. For the past ten years I have taught four distinct courses per academic year: computer literacy, problem solving with the Internet, programming in Python, and representing, storing, and retrieving information. While I wrote my own textbooks for the computer literacy and representing information courses, and have used someone else's textbook for the programming course, it became clear to me that I needed a general reference work, and *not* a textbook, that applies to all of these courses. There are several lectures I have given identically in more than one course; rather than duplicate the material each time, this reference manual becomes a single resource for all the students. It was designed from the outset to be their companion in their studies. Also, many students have taken several of my courses (sometimes concurrently), and they deserve a reference that applies universally. Finally, I need a "one-stop shopping" resource like this for a lot of my own work.

A large amount of the material in this book was originally in my Computer Literacy Workbook up through the 20TH edition (2013-2014 printing). That book was printed in three separate volumes, and a lot of reference material was duplicated at the end of each volume. By extracting that material into its own unique volume, and adding extensive amounts of new material, it made the textbook for the computer literacy course considerably smaller (and correspondingly cheaper), while simultaneously creating a more general reference for the other courses.

As a result, *no single course*, whether taught by me or by anyone else, will draw upon all the material in this book. Each course will engage with some subset of the material, some more than others, and with a certain degree of overlap with the requirements of the other courses. Students taking several computer science courses will be exposed to a greater amount of material relative to those who take only one course, and those students would not then have to buy a new reference book for each course.

I've tried to make this book "browse-able" as well. If you have any interest in math, web design, practical computation, geometry, programming, etc., you will find something of interest just by opening the book at random. However, no single topic will be covered in its entirety; in each case there is just enough theory and just enough practice to get students started on explorations of their own. Trying to cover all of the topics mentioned in this book thoroughly and completely would result in a massive tome twenty times the size of what is currently here. You don't want to have to wade through all that, and I don't want to write it.

The Editions

The second edition fixed some minor errors in the first edition, added more reference tables, and expanded the material on programming for both JavaScript and Python (particularly for Python). The third edition added a lot more reference pages, including universal calendars, manuals for the JavaScript and Python programming languages, and reorganizes the layout of the programming chapters. It fixed even more annoying mistakes from the earlier versions. The revised third edition added <u>no</u> new pages, but only corrected minor errors, added a little new material, and had modifications to take advantage of color printing.

The fourth and fifth editions both added a considerable amount of new material, particularly in the Web, Python, Graphics, and Sound chapters. The section on Python programming has been cleaned up a lot, and mistakes fixed. Increased treatment of graphics include a description of how to implement a simple but fairly complete graphics system in Python that does not depend on anyone's third-party libraries. Specifically, a programmer can now create industry-standard `.BMP` graphics files, as well as `.WAV` audio files with just the tools in this book.

Throughout this book much of the material, particularly the programming examples, are items developed by me alone. I wrote all the actual runnable code in HTML, JavaScript, Python, and Pascal that is included in the book, and all the recipes in the eponymous chapter are either my own creations or are from family lore. All tables and graphics in this book are things I created personally, sometimes with a spreadsheet but often with my own custom software; no images were "borrowed" from elsewhere.

However, by necessity frequent reference is also made to a number of software packages, file formats, data sources, and algorithms developed by individuals other than myself, or by commercial entities. Credit is given when I know who created or designed the first instance of an algorithm or idea, along with the year that they developed the idea. In addition, many tables of data are so widely available publically that proper attribution is impossible. Mathematical topics are widely known to and discussed by multiple sources, and may have originally been developed decades or even centuries before now, well before the advent of electronic computing.

Otherwise, all trademarks used herein are owned by their respective companies. Any omissions are unintentional. No commercial endorsements are implied or are to be inferred.

It should be noted that a number of tables and references will, sooner or later, go out of date. Web domains and defined colors will change, hardware will improve, programming languages will go in and out of favor, and software will be updated. I've tried to make all the material in this edition as correct as possible, but it is inevitable that there will be some things that are obsolete or simply flat-out wrong when you first encounter the book. Any mistakes are mine and mine alone.

Personal Statement 2020

As I write this introduction for the 5TH Edition in the summer of 2020, I am also preparing to retire from the University at which I have worked as faculty for the past 30 years and as a graduate student for 10 years before that. The current and unresolved COVID-19 pandemic, along with some personal reasons, have led me to this decision a couple of years before I anticipated doing so.

This may be the last edition of the *Companion*, so I have been working this summer to include as much relevant material as I can, and at the same time reduce as many errors as possible (including a really embarrassing typo that has been present since the very first edition). I will be teaching during academic year 2020-2021 in a post-retirement appointment; as it is still unclear whether I will be continuing in that appointment afterwards it is also uncertain if I will have a need for further editions of this book, although any subsequent mistakes I find will annoy the heck out of me. If the faculty who take over my classes after I've completely retired have any need for updates I'll probably make them, although it may be from the beach in Bora Bora.

My sincerest thanks go out to Alfred Hough and Matthew Frain for their invaluable assistance in cleaning up the section on accuracy versus precision. I appreciate all you've done to keep me honest, guys. Also, thanks to my wife Catherine and daughter RJ, mostly for putting up with me over the years with good humor, and a certain bemusement, during my episodes of writing, coding, and mumbling under my breath about convex hulls, color models, bitmaps, and saucepans.

2: *Physical Quantities*

This first section contains conversion tables between units of length, area, volume, mass, and time, including some odd conversions between the US measurement system and the metric system. It also contains information about calendars and temperature. Finally, there is a periodic table of the elements as well as tables of the elements sorted by atomic number and atomic mass.

The units chosen for inclusion are not comprehensive; there are a lot more conversion factors than what are presented here. However, those shown here represent many of the most common units encountered in day-to-day transactions.

Units of Length, Area, and Volume

			Linear					
		cm per...	Inches per...	Feet per...	Yards per...	Meters per...	Km per...	Miles per...
...Linear	cm	1	0.393700787	0.0328084	0.010936133	0.01	0.00001	6.21371E-06
	Inch	2.54	1	0.0833333	0.027777778	0.0254	2.54E-05	1.57828E-05
	Foot	30.48	12	1	0.333333333	0.3048	0.000305	0.000189394
	Yard	91.44	36	3	1	0.9144	0.000914	0.000568182
	Meter	100	39.37007874	3.2808399	1.093613298	1	0.001	0.000621371
	Km	100000	39370.07874	3280.8399	1093.613298	1000	1	0.621371192
	Mile	160934.4	63360	5280	1760	1609.344	1.609344	1

			Square					
		cm per...	Inches per...	Feet per...	Yards per...	Meters per...	Km per...	Miles per...
...Square	cm	1	0.15500031	0.0010764	0.000119599	0.0001	1E-10	3.86102E-11
	Inch	6.4516	1	0.0069444	0.000771605	0.00064516	6.45E-10	2.49098E-10
	Foot	929.0304	144	1	0.111111111	0.09290304	9.29E-08	3.58701E-08
	Yard	8361.2736	1296	9	1	0.83612736	8.36E-07	3.22831E-07
	Meter	10000	1550.0031	10.76391	1.195990046	1	0.000001	3.86102E-07
	Km	10000000000	1550003100	10763910	1195990.046	1000000	1	0.386102159
	Mile	25899881103	4014489600	27878400	3097600	2589988.11	2.589988	1

			Cubic					
		cm per...	Inches per...	Feet per...	Yards per...	Meters per...	Km per...	Miles per...
...Cubic	cm	1	0.061023744	3.531E-05	1.30795E-06	0.000001	1E-15	2.39913E-16
	Inch	16.387064	1	0.0005787	2.14335E-05	1.63871E-05	1.64E-14	3.93147E-15
	Foot	28316.84659	1728	1	0.037037037	0.028316847	2.83E-11	6.79357E-12
	Yard	764554.858	46656	27	1	0.764554858	7.65E-10	1.83426E-10
	Meter	1000000	61023.74409	35.314667	1.307950619	1	1E-09	2.39913E-10
	Km	1E+15	6.10237E+13	3.531E+10	1307950619	1000000000	1	0.239912759
	Mile	4.16818E+15	2.54358E+14	1.472E+11	5451776000	4168181825	4.168182	1

Units of Mass and Weight

	Grams per...	Ounces per...	Pounds per...	Kilograms per...	Short Tons per...	Metric Tons per...
...Gram	1	0.035273962	0.002204623	0.001	1.10231E-06	0.000001
...Ounce	28.34952313	1	0.0625	0.028349523	0.00003125	2.83495E-05
...Pound	453.59237	16	1	0.45359237	0.0005	0.000453592
...Kilogram	1000	35.27396195	2.204622622	1	0.001102311	0.001
...Short Ton	907184.74	32000	2000	907.18474	1	0.90718474
...Metric Ton	1000000	35273.96195	2204.622622	1000	1.102311311	1

To someone who has grown up in a metric environment a ***metric ton*** means 1000 kilograms, which is about 2205 pounds. To most Americans a ton is 2000 pounds, also called a ***short ton***. There is also a ***long ton***, weighing 2240 pounds. Which one is correct? They all are! Which one you use depends on the context of the problem, so be careful!

Distances in 64^{THS} of an Inch, plus Millimeters

N/64	GCD	Decimal	mm	N/64	GCD	Decimal	mm
1/64	1/64	0.015625	0.396875	33/64	33/64	0.515625	13.096875
2/64	1/32	0.031250	0.793750	34/64	17/32	0.531250	13.493750
3/64	3/64	0.046875	1.190625	35/64	35/64	0.546875	13.890625
4/64	1/16	0.062500	1.587500	36/64	9/16	0.562500	14.287500
5/64	5/64	0.078125	1.984375	37/64	37/64	0.578125	14.684375
6/64	3/32	0.093750	2.381250	38/64	19/32	0.593750	15.081250
7/64	7/64	0.109375	2.778125	39/64	39/64	0.609375	15.478125
8/64	1/8	0.125000	3.175000	40/64	5/8	0.625000	15.875000
9/64	9/64	0.140625	3.571875	41/64	41/64	0.640625	16.271875
10/64	5/32	0.156250	3.968750	42/64	21/32	0.656250	16.668750
11/64	11/64	0.171875	4.365625	43/64	43/64	0.671875	17.065625
12/64	3/16	0.187500	4.762500	44/64	11/16	0.687500	17.462500
13/64	13/64	0.203125	5.159375	45/64	45/64	0.703125	17.859375
14/64	7/32	0.218750	5.556250	46/64	23/32	0.718750	18.256250
15/64	15/64	0.234375	5.953125	47/64	47/64	0.734375	18.653125
16/64	1/4	0.250000	6.350000	48/64	3/4	0.750000	19.050000
17/64	17/64	0.265625	6.746875	49/64	49/64	0.765625	19.446875
18/64	9/32	0.281250	7.143750	50/64	25/32	0.781250	19.843750
19/64	19/64	0.296875	7.540625	51/64	51/64	0.796875	20.240625
20/64	5/16	0.312500	7.937500	52/64	13/16	0.812500	20.637500
21/64	21/64	0.328125	8.334375	53/64	53/64	0.828125	21.034375
22/64	11/32	0.343750	8.731250	54/64	27/32	0.843750	21.431250
23/64	23/64	0.359375	9.128125	55/64	55/64	0.859375	21.828125
24/64	3/8	0.375000	9.525000	56/64	7/8	0.875000	22.225000
25/64	25/64	0.390625	9.921875	57/64	57/64	0.890625	22.621875
26/64	13/32	0.406250	10.318750	58/64	29/32	0.906250	23.018750
27/64	27/64	0.421875	10.715625	59/64	59/64	0.921875	23.415625
28/64	7/16	0.437500	11.112500	60/64	15/16	0.937500	23.812500
29/64	29/64	0.453125	11.509375	61/64	61/64	0.953125	24.209375
30/64	15/32	0.468750	11.906250	62/64	31/32	0.968750	24.606250
31/64	31/64	0.484375	12.303125	63/64	63/64	0.984375	25.003125
32/64	1/2	0.500000	12.700000	64/64	1/1	1.000000	25.400000

This table is primarily the conversion between fractions in 64^{THS} and their decimal equivalents, regardless of any underlying units, but when those values are treated as inches it makes sense to show the equivalent value in millimeters as well. Woodworkers may find this table useful, as drill bits, wrenches, and plywood thicknesses are often in multiples of 1/64TH of an inch.

Distances in terms of the Speed-Of-Light

Speed of Light (in Vacuum)	Meters/Second	Km/Second	Miles/Second	Inches/ns
	299,792,458	299,792	186,282.3971	11.8

	Meters per…	Km per…	Miles per…
…Light Year	9,460,730,472,580,800	9,460,730,472,581	5,878,625,373,184
…Light Day	25,902,068,371,200	25,902,068,371	16,094,799,105
…Light Hour	1,079,252,848,800	1,079,252,849	670,616,629
…Light Minute	17,987,547,480	17,987,547	11,176,944
…Light Second	299,792,458	299,792	186,282

	1 Parsec =	1 Astronomical Unit =
Meters	3.08567758E+16	149,597,870,700
Miles	1.9173512E+13	92,955,807
A.U.	206264.81	1
Light Years	3.2615638	0.000015812507
Parsecs	1	0.0000048481368

Stellar Distances

Star	Parsecs	Light Years	Miles	Kilometers
Sun	0	0	0	0
Proxima Centauri	1.3009±0.0005	4.243±0.0017	2.494E+13 ± 9.994E+09	4.014E+13 ± 1.608E+10
Alpha Centauri	1.3385±0.0021	4.366±0.007	2.567E+13 ± 4.115E+10	4.131E+13 ± 6.623E+10
Barnard's Star	1.8335±0.001	5.98±0.003	3.515E+13 ± 1.764E+10	5.658E+13 ± 2.838E+10
Luhman 16	2.020±0.019	6.588±0.062	3.873E+13 ± 3.645E+11	6.233E+13 ± 5.866E+11
WISE 0855-0714	2.20	7.175	4.218E+13 ± 0.000E+00	6.788E+13 ± 0.000E+00
Wolf 359	2.386±0.012	7.78±0.04	4.574E+13 ± 2.351E+11	7.360E+13 ± 3.784E+11
Lalande 21185	2.547±0.004	8.307±0.014	4.883E+13 ± 8.230E+10	7.859E+13 ± 1.325E+11
Sirius	2.637±0.011	8.6±0.04	5.056E+13 ± 2.351E+11	8.136E+13 ± 3.784E+11
Luyten 726-8	2.676±0.019	8.73±0.06	5.132E+13 ± 3.527E+11	8.259E+13 ± 5.676E+11
Ross 154	2.97±0.018	9.69±0.06	5.696E+13 ± 3.527E+11	9.167E+13 ± 5.676E+11
Ross 248	3.16±0.01	10.30±0.04	6.055E+13 ± 2.351E+11	9.745E+13 ± 3.784E+11
Epsilon Eridani	3.216±0.002	10.489±0.005	6.166E+13 ± 2.939E+10	9.923E+13 ± 4.730E+10

Note: the columns for Miles and Kilometers were calculated directly from the Light Years column, and are way more precise than is truly justifiable. These columns have been included to give a general sense of the magnitudes involved, but should not be trusted beyond two significant figures. For example, the distance to Proxima Centauri should be interpreted as "about 25 trillion miles, plus or minus about 10 billion miles" rather than as the values shown in the table.

Planetary Masses, Radii, and Acceleration due to Gravity

	Mass (Kg)	Radius		Acceleration due to Gravity			
		Km	Miles	m/s²	(km/hr)/s	ft/s²	mph/s
Mercury	3.3022E+23	2,439.7	1,516.0	3.70000	13.32000	12.13911	8.27666
Venus	4.8676E+24	6,051.8	3,760.4	8.87000	31.93200	29.10105	19.84162
Earth (minimum)	5.9722E+24	6,352.8	3,947.4	9.76390	35.15004	32.03379	21.84122
Earth (equatorial)		6,378.1	3,963.2	9.78033	35.20919	32.08770	21.87798
Earth (average)		6,371.0	3,958.8	9.80665	35.30394	32.17405	21.93685
Earth (maximum)		6,384.4	3,967.1	9.82500	35.37000	32.23425	21.97790
Mars	6.4185E+23	3,389.5	2,106.1	3.71100	13.35960	12.17520	8.30127
Jupiter*	1.8986E+27	69,911.0	43,440.7	24.79000	89.24400	81.33202	55.45365
Saturn*	5.6846E+26	58,232.0	36,183.7	10.44000	37.58400	34.25197	23.35361
Uranus*	8.6810E+25	25,362.0	15,759.2	8.69000	31.28400	28.51050	19.43898
Neptune*	1.0243E+26	24,622.0	15,299.4	11.15000	40.14000	36.58136	24.94184
Pluto	1.3050E+22	1,184.0	735.7	0.65500	2.35800	2.14895	1.46519

Precision of results is arbitrarily high in most cases, and should not be taken as absolute.

* Gas Giants are considerably flatter at their poles than at their equators, thus Radii and Acceleration are shown as averages.

Odd Conversions and Constants

Acres per Square Mile	640
Square Yards per Acre	4840
Square Meters per Hectare	10000
Acres per Hectare	2.4710538

US teaspoons per US Tablespoon	3
US Tablespoons per US Cup	16
US Cups per US Pint	2
US Pints per US Quart	2
Quarts per US Gallon	4
Cubic Inches per US Gallon	231
Cubic Feet per Acre-Foot	43560
US Gallons per Acre-Foot	325851.429
Cubic cm per Liter	1000
Liters per US Gallon	3.785411784

United States Coins		Composition	Weight	Diameter		Thickness	
(Simple exact values highlighted)			g	in	mm	in	mm
Penny	1864-1942, 1944-1982	95% Cu, 5% Zn or Zn/Sn	3.110	0.750	19.05	0.0598	1.52
	1943	99% Steel, 1% Zn	2.720				
	1982-present	2.5% Cu, 97.5% Zn	2.500				
Nickel		75% Cu, 25% Ni	5.000	0.835	21.21	0.0768	1.95
Dime		91.67% Cu, 8.33% Ni	2.268	0.705	17.91	0.0531	1.35
Quarter		91.67% Cu, 8.33% Ni	5.670	0.955	24.26	0.0689	1.75
Half Dollar		91.67% Cu, 8.33% Ni	11.340	1.205	30.61	0.0846	2.15
Presidential/Sacajawea Dollar		88.5% Cu, 6% Zn, 3.5% Mn, 2% Ni	8.100	1.043	26.49	0.0787	2.00

Temperature

	Kelvin	Celsius	Fahrenheit
Absolute Zero	0	-273.15	-459.67
Fahrenheit/Celsius Equal	233.15	-40	-40
Freezing Point of Water	273.15	0	32
Body Heat (typical)	310.15	37	98.6
Boiling Point of Water	373.15	100	212
Photosphere of Sun	5778	5504	9939

Absolute Zero (°K) is the point at which all molecular motion stops.

To convert from Kelvin to Celsius, compute: $°C = °K - 273.15$.

To convert from Celsius to Kelvin, compute: $°K = °C + 273.15$.

To convert from Celsius to Fahrenheit, compute: $°F = °C \times 1.8 + 32$

Alternatively, compute: $°F = °C \times 9 \div 5 + 32$

To convert from Fahrenheit to Celsius, compute: $°C = (°F - 32) / 1.8$

Alternatively, compute: $°C = (°F - 32) \times 5 \div 9$

Units of Time

	Nanoseconds (ns) per...	Microseconds (μs) per...	Milliseconds (ms) per...	Seconds per...
...ns	1	0.001	0.000001	0.000000001
...μs	1,000	1	0.001	0.000001
...ms	1,000,000	1,000	1	0.001
...Second	1,000,000,000	1,000,000	1,000	1
...Minute	60,000,000,000	60,000,000	60,000	60
...Hour	3,600,000,000,000	3,600,000,000	3,600,000	3,600
...Day	86,400,000,000,000	86,400,000,000	86,400,000	86,400
...Year	31,557,600,000,000,000	31,557,600,000,000	31,557,600,000	31,557,600

	Minutes per...	Hours per...	Days per...	Years per...
...ns	0.0000000000166667	0.0000000000002778	0.0000000000000116	0.000000000000000032
...μs	0.0000000166666667	0.0000000002777778	0.0000000000115741	0.000000000000031688
...ms	0.0000166666666667	0.0000002777777778	0.0000000115740741	0.000000000031688088
...Second	0.0166666666666667	0.0002777777777778	0.0000115740740741	0.000000031688087814
...Minute	1	0.0166666666666667	0.0006944444444444	0.000001901285268842
...Hour	60	1	0.0416666666666667	0.000114077116130504
...Day	1,440	24	1	0.002737850787132100
...Year	525,960	8,766	365.25	1

Calendar Definitions

The **_mean tropical year_** (time for the Earth to go around the sun relative to the seasons) on January 1, 2000 was 365.2421897 days.

The **_sidereal year_** (time for the Earth to go around the sun relative to the fixed stars) on January 1, 2000 was 365.256363004 days.

The average length of a **_solar year_** as defined by the Gregorian calendar is 365.2425 days.

The **_Julian calendar_** (itself a reform of the older Roman calendar and used from 46 B.C.E. to 1582 C.E.) used a year length of 365.25 days, which caused the calendar to drift relative to the seasons. This drift was approximately three days every 400 years.

Month	Days in Month
January	31
February	28 or 29
March	31
April	30
May	31
June	30
July	31
August	31
September	30
October	31
November	30
December	31

Not to be confused with the Julian calendar, the **_Julian Day_** is the number of days since January 1, 4713 BCE. January 1, 2000 was Julian Day 2451545.

The **_Gregorian calendar_**, which had a better method of computing leap years than the Julian calendar, was first applied in October 1582. To correct the calendar drift that had occurred by that time, October 4, 1582 was followed directly by October 15. Adoption of the new calendar was neither immediate nor universal: some countries did not adopt it until the 20TH Century.

The Gregorian calendar reform was in part to compute the correct **_date of Easter_**, defined as the first Sunday after the full moon after the Spring Equinox in March. The proper dates are defined more by religion than by astronomy, so the date of Easter can range from March 22 through April 25.

In the Gregorian calendar, **_leap years_**, where February has 29 days instead of 28 days, are years evenly divisible by 4, except for century years, except for century years evenly divisible by 400. That is, years 1700, 1800, 1900, 2100, 2200, and 2300 were not leap years, but 2000 was a leap year, and 2400 will be a leap year as well.

In Microsoft Excel, however, year 1900 is considered a leap year. This is to remain compatible with earlier Lotus 1-2-3 spreadsheets where the original bug was introduced.

The **_Y2K problem_** (or **_Millennium Bug_**) was due to a lot of software written in the mid to late 20TH Century that implemented years as two digits instead of four (so the year 1969 would be represented as **69**, for example). The worry was that when January 1, 2000 occurred, the date **00** would be interpreted as 1900 instead of 2000. Due to lengthy and expensive software overhauls, the problem was largely avoided.

In UNIX, dates are measured as the number of seconds since midnight on January 1, 1970, and are stored in a 32-bit signed integer. The maximum value will be reached on January 19, 2038. As with Y2K, steps are being taken now to avoid or reduce the **_Year 2038 problem_**.

The Gregorian Calendar

In the Gregorian calendar system, there are only 14 unique yearly calendars: there are seven possibilities for which day of the week applies to January 1ST, and February has either 28 days (in normal years) or 29 days (in leap years). Once those two things are known, the rest of the days can be computed deterministically. The table below shows which years between 1900 and 2099 use each of the 14 possible calendars.

Calendar	January 1ST	Leap Year?	Years between 1900-2099 that use this Calendar
1	Sunday	NO	1905 1911 1922 1933 1939 1950 1961 1967 1978 1989 1995 2006 2017 2023 2034 2045 2051 2062 2073 2079 2090
2	Monday	NO	1900 1906 1917 1923 1934 1945 1951 1962 1973 1979 1990 2001 2007 2018 2029 2035 2046 2057 2063 2074 2085 2091
3	Tuesday	NO	1901 1907 1918 1929 1935 1946 1957 1963 1974 1985 1991 2002 2013 2019 2030 2041 2047 2058 2069 2075 2086 2097
4	Wednesday	NO	1902 1913 1919 1930 1941 1947 1958 1969 1975 1986 1997 2003 2014 2025 2031 2042 2053 2059 2070 2081 2087 2098
5	Thursday	NO	1903 1914 1925 1931 1942 1953 1959 1970 1981 1987 1998 2009 2015 2026 2037 2043 2054 2065 2071 2082 2093 2099
6	Friday	NO	1909 1915 1926 1937 1943 1954 1965 1971 1982 1993 1999 2010 2021 2027 2038 2049 2055 2066 2077 2083 2094
7	Saturday	NO	1910 1921 1927 1938 1949 1955 1966 1977 1983 1994 2005 2011 2022 2033 2039 2050 2061 2067 2078 2089 2095
8	Sunday	YES	1928 1956 1984 2012 2040 2068 2096
9	Monday	YES	1912 1940 1968 1996 2024 2052 2080
10	Tuesday	YES	1924 1952 1980 2008 2036 2064 2092
11	Wednesday	YES	1908 1936 1964 1992 2020 2048 2076
12	Thursday	YES	1920 1948 1976 2004 2032 2060 2088
13	Friday	YES	1904 1932 1960 1988 2016 2044 2072
14	Saturday	YES	1916 1944 1972 2000 2028 2056 2084

On the following two pages are an index of years from 1583 (the first full year to use the Gregorian calendar) up through 2142, and the number of the calendar that applies to each year. For example, the entry for 2020 is 11, which indicates that year 2020 uses calendar 11 (January 1ST is on Wednesday, and it is a leap year). Once the calendar number is known, the actual yearly calendar can be looked up on the five pages that follow the index.

Calendar Indexes, 1583-1862

Year	#	Year	#	Year	#	Year	#	Year	#	Year	#	Year	#
1583	7	1623	1	1663	2	1703	2	1743	3	1783	4	1823	4
1584	8	1624	9	1664	10	1704	10	1744	11	1784	12	1824	12
1585	3	1625	4	1665	5	1705	5	1745	6	1785	7	1825	7
1586	4	1626	5	1666	6	1706	6	1746	7	1786	1	1826	1
1587	5	1627	6	1667	7	1707	7	1747	1	1787	2	1827	2
1588	13	1628	14	1668	8	1708	8	1748	9	1788	10	1828	10
1589	1	1629	2	1669	3	1709	3	1749	4	1789	5	1829	5
1590	2	1630	3	1670	4	1710	4	1750	5	1790	6	1830	6
1591	3	1631	4	1671	5	1711	5	1751	6	1791	7	1831	7
1592	11	1632	12	1672	13	1712	13	1752	14	1792	8	1832	8
1593	6	1633	7	1673	1	1713	1	1753	2	1793	3	1833	3
1594	7	1634	1	1674	2	1714	2	1754	3	1794	4	1834	4
1595	1	1635	2	1675	3	1715	3	1755	4	1795	5	1835	5
1596	9	1636	10	1676	11	1716	11	1756	12	1796	13	1836	13
1597	4	1637	5	1677	6	1717	6	1757	7	1797	1	1837	1
1598	5	1638	6	1678	7	1718	7	1758	1	1798	2	1838	2
1599	6	1639	7	1679	1	1719	1	1759	2	1799	3	1839	3
1600	14	1640	8	1680	9	1720	9	1760	10	1800	4	1840	11
1601	2	1641	3	1681	4	1721	4	1761	5	1801	5	1841	6
1602	3	1642	4	1682	5	1722	5	1762	6	1802	6	1842	7
1603	4	1643	5	1683	6	1723	6	1763	7	1803	7	1843	1
1604	12	1644	13	1684	14	1724	14	1764	8	1804	8	1844	9
1605	7	1645	1	1685	2	1725	2	1765	3	1805	3	1845	4
1606	1	1646	2	1686	3	1726	3	1766	4	1806	4	1846	5
1607	2	1647	3	1687	4	1727	4	1767	5	1807	5	1847	6
1608	10	1648	11	1688	12	1728	12	1768	13	1808	13	1848	14
1609	5	1649	6	1689	7	1729	7	1769	1	1809	1	1849	2
1610	6	1650	7	1690	1	1730	1	1770	2	1810	2	1850	3
1611	7	1651	1	1691	2	1731	2	1771	3	1811	3	1851	4
1612	8	1652	9	1692	10	1732	10	1772	11	1812	11	1852	12
1613	3	1653	4	1693	5	1733	5	1773	6	1813	6	1853	7
1614	4	1654	5	1694	6	1734	6	1774	7	1814	7	1854	1
1615	5	1655	6	1695	7	1735	7	1775	1	1815	1	1855	2
1616	13	1656	14	1696	8	1736	8	1776	9	1816	9	1856	10
1617	1	1657	2	1697	3	1737	3	1777	4	1817	4	1857	5
1618	2	1658	3	1698	4	1738	4	1778	5	1818	5	1858	6
1619	3	1659	4	1699	5	1739	5	1779	6	1819	6	1859	7
1620	11	1660	12	1700	6	1740	13	1780	14	1820	14	1860	8
1621	6	1661	7	1701	7	1741	1	1781	2	1821	2	1861	3
1622	7	1662	1	1702	1	1742	2	1782	3	1822	3	1862	4

Calendar Indexes, 1863-2142

Year	#	Year	#	Year	#	Year	#	Year	#	Year	#	Year	#
1863	5	1903	5	1943	6	1983	7	2023	1	2063	2	2103	2
1864	13	1904	13	1944	14	1984	8	2024	9	2064	10	2104	10
1865	1	1905	1	1945	2	1985	3	2025	4	2065	5	2105	5
1866	2	1906	2	1946	3	1986	4	2026	5	2066	6	2106	6
1867	3	1907	3	1947	4	1987	5	2027	6	2067	7	2107	7
1868	11	1908	11	1948	12	1988	13	2028	14	2068	8	2108	8
1869	6	1909	6	1949	7	1989	1	2029	2	2069	3	2109	3
1870	7	1910	7	1950	1	1990	2	2030	3	2070	4	2110	4
1871	1	1911	1	1951	2	1991	3	2031	4	2071	5	2111	5
1872	9	1912	9	1952	10	1992	11	2032	12	2072	13	2112	13
1873	4	1913	4	1953	5	1993	6	2033	7	2073	1	2113	1
1874	5	1914	5	1954	6	1994	7	2034	1	2074	2	2114	2
1875	6	1915	6	1955	7	1995	1	2035	2	2075	3	2115	3
1876	14	1916	14	1956	8	1996	9	2036	10	2076	11	2116	11
1877	2	1917	2	1957	3	1997	4	2037	5	2077	6	2117	6
1878	3	1918	3	1958	4	1998	5	2038	6	2078	7	2118	7
1879	4	1919	4	1959	5	1999	6	2039	7	2079	1	2119	1
1880	12	1920	12	1960	13	2000	14	2040	8	2080	9	2120	9
1881	7	1921	7	1961	1	2001	2	2041	3	2081	4	2121	4
1882	1	1922	1	1962	2	2002	3	2042	4	2082	5	2122	5
1883	2	1923	2	1963	3	2003	4	2043	5	2083	6	2123	6
1884	10	1924	10	1964	11	2004	12	2044	13	2084	14	2124	14
1885	5	1925	5	1965	6	2005	7	2045	1	2085	2	2125	2
1886	6	1926	6	1966	7	2006	1	2046	2	2086	3	2126	3
1887	7	1927	7	1967	1	2007	2	2047	3	2087	4	2127	4
1888	8	1928	8	1968	9	2008	10	2048	11	2088	12	2128	12
1889	3	1929	3	1969	4	2009	5	2049	6	2089	7	2129	7
1890	4	1930	4	1970	5	2010	6	2050	7	2090	1	2130	1
1891	5	1931	5	1971	6	2011	7	2051	1	2091	2	2131	2
1892	13	1932	13	1972	14	2012	8	2052	9	2092	10	2132	10
1893	1	1933	1	1973	2	2013	3	2053	4	2093	5	2133	5
1894	2	1934	2	1974	3	2014	4	2054	5	2094	6	2134	6
1895	3	1935	3	1975	4	2015	5	2055	6	2095	7	2135	7
1896	11	1936	11	1976	12	2016	13	2056	14	2096	8	2136	8
1897	6	1937	6	1977	7	2017	1	2057	2	2097	3	2137	3
1898	7	1938	7	1978	1	2018	2	2058	3	2098	4	2138	4
1899	1	1939	1	1979	2	2019	3	2059	4	2099	5	2139	5
1900	2	1940	9	1980	10	2020	11	2060	12	2100	6	2140	13
1901	3	1941	4	1981	5	2021	6	2061	7	2101	7	2141	1
1902	4	1942	5	1982	6	2022	7	2062	1	2102	1	2142	2

Calendars 1-3

Calendar #1

	Su	Mo	Tu	We	Th	Fr	Sa
	1	2	3	4	5	6	7
	8	9	10	11	12	13	14
J	15	16	17	18	19	20	21
	22	23	24	25	26	27	28
	29	30	31	1	2	3	4
	5	6	7	8	9	10	11
F	12	13	14	15	16	17	18
	19	20	21	22	23	24	25
	26	27	28	1	2	3	4
	5	6	7	8	9	10	11
M	12	13	14	15	16	17	18
	19	20	21	22	23	24	25
	26	27	28	29	30	31	1
	2	3	4	5	6	7	8
A	9	10	11	12	13	14	15
	16	17	18	19	20	21	22
	23	24	25	26	27	28	29
	30	1	2	3	4	5	6
	7	8	9	10	11	12	13
M	14	15	16	17	18	19	20
	21	22	23	24	25	26	27
	28	29	30	31	1	2	3
	4	5	6	7	8	9	10
J	11	12	13	14	15	16	17
	18	19	20	21	22	23	24
	25	26	27	28	29	30	1
	2	3	4	5	6	7	8
J	9	10	11	12	13	14	15
	16	17	18	19	20	21	22
	23	24	25	26	27	28	29
	30	31	1	2	3	4	5
	6	7	8	9	10	11	12
A	13	14	15	16	17	18	19
	20	21	22	23	24	25	26
	27	28	29	30	31	1	2
	3	4	5	6	7	8	9
S	10	11	12	13	14	15	16
	17	18	19	20	21	22	23
	24	25	26	27	28	29	30
	1	2	3	4	5	6	7
	8	9	10	11	12	13	14
O	15	16	17	18	19	20	21
	22	23	24	25	26	27	28
	29	30	31	1	2	3	4
	5	6	7	8	9	10	11
N	12	13	14	15	16	17	18
	19	20	21	22	23	24	25
	26	27	28	29	30	1	2
	3	4	5	6	7	8	9
D	10	11	12	13	14	15	16
	17	18	19	20	21	22	23
	24	25	26	27	28	29	30
	31						

Calendar #2

	Su	Mo	Tu	We	Th	Fr	Sa
		1	2	3	4	5	6
	7	8	9	10	11	12	13
J	14	15	16	17	18	19	20
	21	22	23	24	25	26	27
	28	29	30	31	1	2	3
	4	5	6	7	8	9	10
F	11	12	13	14	15	16	17
	18	19	20	21	22	23	24
	25	26	27	28	1	2	3
	4	5	6	7	8	9	10
M	11	12	13	14	15	16	17
	18	19	20	21	22	23	24
	25	26	27	28	29	30	31
	1	2	3	4	5	6	7
A	8	9	10	11	12	13	14
	15	16	17	18	19	20	21
	22	23	24	25	26	27	28
	29	30	1	2	3	4	5
	6	7	8	9	10	11	12
M	13	14	15	16	17	18	19
	20	21	22	23	24	25	26
	27	28	29	30	31	1	2
	3	4	5	6	7	8	9
J	10	11	12	13	14	15	16
	17	18	19	20	21	22	23
	24	25	26	27	28	29	30
	1	2	3	4	5	6	7
J	8	9	10	11	12	13	14
	15	16	17	18	19	20	21
	22	23	24	25	26	27	28
	29	30	31	1	2	3	4
	5	6	7	8	9	10	11
A	12	13	14	15	16	17	18
	19	20	21	22	23	24	25
	26	27	28	29	30	31	1
	2	3	4	5	6	7	8
S	9	10	11	12	13	14	15
	16	17	18	19	20	21	22
	23	24	25	26	27	28	29
	30	1	2	3	4	5	6
	7	8	9	10	11	12	13
O	14	15	16	17	18	19	20
	21	22	23	24	25	26	27
	28	29	30	31	1	2	3
	4	5	6	7	8	9	10
N	11	12	13	14	15	16	17
	18	19	20	21	22	23	24
	25	26	27	28	29	30	1
	2	3	4	5	6	7	8
D	9	10	11	12	13	14	15
	16	17	18	19	20	21	22
	23	24	25	26	27	28	29
	30	31					

Calendar #3

	Su	Mo	Tu	We	Th	Fr	Sa
			1	2	3	4	5
	6	7	8	9	10	11	12
J	13	14	15	16	17	18	19
	20	21	22	23	24	25	26
	27	28	29	30	31	1	2
	3	4	5	6	7	8	9
F	10	11	12	13	14	15	16
	17	18	19	20	21	22	23
	24	25	26	27	28	1	2
	3	4	5	6	7	8	9
M	10	11	12	13	14	15	16
	17	18	19	20	21	22	23
	24	25	26	27	28	29	30
	31	1	2	3	4	5	6
	7	8	9	10	11	12	13
A	14	15	16	17	18	19	20
	21	22	23	24	25	26	27
	28	29	30	1	2	3	4
	5	6	7	8	9	10	11
M	12	13	14	15	16	17	18
	19	20	21	22	23	24	25
	26	27	28	29	30	31	1
	2	3	4	5	6	7	8
J	9	10	11	12	13	14	15
	16	17	18	19	20	21	22
	23	24	25	26	27	28	29
	30	1	2	3	4	5	6
	7	8	9	10	11	12	13
J	14	15	16	17	18	19	20
	21	22	23	24	25	26	27
	28	29	30	31	1	2	3
	4	5	6	7	8	9	10
A	11	12	13	14	15	16	17
	18	19	20	21	22	23	24
	25	26	27	28	29	30	31
	1	2	3	4	5	6	7
	8	9	10	11	12	13	14
S	15	16	17	18	19	20	21
	22	23	24	25	26	27	28
	29	30	1	2	3	4	5
	6	7	8	9	10	11	12
O	13	14	15	16	17	18	19
	20	21	22	23	24	25	26
	27	28	29	30	31	1	2
	3	4	5	6	7	8	9
N	10	11	12	13	14	15	16
	17	18	19	20	21	22	23
	24	25	26	27	28	29	30
	1	2	3	4	5	6	7
D	8	9	10	11	12	13	14
	15	16	17	18	19	20	21
	22	23	24	25	26	27	28
	29	30	31				

Calendars 4-6

Calendar #4

	Su	Mo	Tu	We	Th	Fr	Sa
				1	2	3	4
	5	6	7	8	9	10	11
J	12	13	14	15	16	17	18
	19	20	21	22	23	24	25
	26	27	28	29	30	31	1
	2	3	4	5	6	7	8
F	9	10	11	12	13	14	15
	16	17	18	19	20	21	22
	23	24	25	26	27	28	1
	2	3	4	5	6	7	8
M	9	10	11	12	13	14	15
	16	17	18	19	20	21	22
	23	24	25	26	27	28	29
	30	31	1	2	3	4	5
	6	7	8	9	10	11	12
A	13	14	15	16	17	18	19
	20	21	22	23	24	25	26
	27	28	29	30	1	2	3
	4	5	6	7	8	9	10
M	11	12	13	14	15	16	17
	18	19	20	21	22	23	24
	25	26	27	28	29	30	31
	1	2	3	4	5	6	7
J	8	9	10	11	12	13	14
	15	16	17	18	19	20	21
	22	23	24	25	26	27	28
	29	30	1	2	3	4	5
	6	7	8	9	10	11	12
J	13	14	15	16	17	18	19
	20	21	22	23	24	25	26
	27	28	29	30	31	1	2
	3	4	5	6	7	8	9
A	10	11	12	13	14	15	16
	17	18	19	20	21	22	23
	24	25	26	27	28	29	30
	31	1	2	3	4	5	6
	7	8	9	10	11	12	13
S	14	15	16	17	18	19	20
	21	22	23	24	25	26	27
	28	29	30	1	2	3	4
	5	6	7	8	9	10	11
O	12	13	14	15	16	17	18
	19	20	21	22	23	24	25
	26	27	28	29	30	31	1
	2	3	4	5	6	7	8
N	9	10	11	12	13	14	15
	16	17	18	19	20	21	22
	23	24	25	26	27	28	29
	30	1	2	3	4	5	6
	7	8	9	10	11	12	13
D	14	15	16	17	18	19	20
	21	22	23	24	25	26	27
	28	29	30	31			

Calendar #5

	Su	Mo	Tu	We	Th	Fr	Sa
				1	2	3	
	4	5	6	7	8	9	10
J	11	12	13	14	15	16	17
	18	19	20	21	22	23	24
	25	26	27	28	29	30	31
	1	2	3	4	5	6	7
F	8	9	10	11	12	13	14
	15	16	17	18	19	20	21
	22	23	24	25	26	27	28
	1	2	3	4	5	6	7
M	8	9	10	11	12	13	14
	15	16	17	18	19	20	21
	22	23	24	25	26	27	28
	29	30	31	1	2	3	4
	5	6	7	8	9	10	11
A	12	13	14	15	16	17	18
	19	20	21	22	23	24	25
	26	27	28	29	30	1	2
	3	4	5	6	7	8	9
M	10	11	12	13	14	15	16
	17	18	19	20	21	22	23
	24	25	26	27	28	29	30
	31	1	2	3	4	5	6
	7	8	9	10	11	12	13
J	14	15	16	17	18	19	20
	21	22	23	24	25	26	27
	28	29	30	1	2	3	4
	5	6	7	8	9	10	11
J	12	13	14	15	16	17	18
	19	20	21	22	23	24	25
	26	27	28	29	30	31	1
	2	3	4	5	6	7	8
A	9	10	11	12	13	14	15
	16	17	18	19	20	21	22
	23	24	25	26	27	28	29
	30	31	1	2	3	4	5
	6	7	8	9	10	11	12
S	13	14	15	16	17	18	19
	20	21	22	23	24	25	26
	27	28	29	30	1	2	3
	4	5	6	7	8	9	10
O	11	12	13	14	15	16	17
	18	19	20	21	22	23	24
	25	26	27	28	29	30	31
	1	2	3	4	5	6	7
N	8	9	10	11	12	13	14
	15	16	17	18	19	20	21
	22	23	24	25	26	27	28
	29	30	1	2	3	4	5
	6	7	8	9	10	11	12
D	13	14	15	16	17	18	19
	20	21	22	23	24	25	26
	27	28	29	30	31		

Calendar #6

	Su	Mo	Tu	We	Th	Fr	Sa
						1	2
	3	4	5	6	7	8	9
J	10	11	12	13	14	15	16
	17	18	19	20	21	22	23
	24	25	26	27	28	29	30
	31	1	2	3	4	5	6
	7	8	9	10	11	12	13
F	14	15	16	17	18	19	20
	21	22	23	24	25	26	27
	28	1	2	3	4	5	6
	7	8	9	10	11	12	13
M	14	15	16	17	18	19	20
	21	22	23	24	25	26	27
	28	29	30	31	1	2	3
	4	5	6	7	8	9	10
A	11	12	13	14	15	16	17
	18	19	20	21	22	23	24
	25	26	27	28	29	30	1
	2	3	4	5	6	7	8
M	9	10	11	12	13	14	15
	16	17	18	19	20	21	22
	23	24	25	26	27	28	29
	30	31	1	2	3	4	5
	6	7	8	9	10	11	12
J	13	14	15	16	17	18	19
	20	21	22	23	24	25	26
	27	28	29	30	1	2	3
	4	5	6	7	8	9	10
J	11	12	13	14	15	16	17
	18	19	20	21	22	23	24
	25	26	27	28	29	30	31
	1	2	3	4	5	6	7
A	8	9	10	11	12	13	14
	15	16	17	18	19	20	21
	22	23	24	25	26	27	28
	29	30	31	1	2	3	4
	5	6	7	8	9	10	11
S	12	13	14	15	16	17	18
	19	20	21	22	23	24	25
	26	27	28	29	30	1	2
	3	4	5	6	7	8	9
O	10	11	12	13	14	15	16
	17	18	19	20	21	22	23
	24	25	26	27	28	29	30
	31	1	2	3	4	5	6
	7	8	9	10	11	12	13
N	14	15	16	17	18	19	20
	21	22	23	24	25	26	27
	28	29	30	1	2	3	4
	5	6	7	8	9	10	11
D	12	13	14	15	16	17	18
	19	20	21	22	23	24	25
	26	27	28	29	30	31	

Calendars 7-9

Calendar #7

Mo	Su	Mo	Tu	We	Th	Fr	Sa
							1
J	2	3	4	5	6	7	8
	9	10	11	12	13	14	15
	16	17	18	19	20	21	22
	23	24	25	26	27	28	29
	30	31	1	2	3	4	5
F	6	7	8	9	10	11	12
	13	14	15	16	17	18	19
	20	21	22	23	24	25	26
	27	28	1	2	3	4	5
M	6	7	8	9	10	11	12
	13	14	15	16	17	18	19
	20	21	22	23	24	25	26
	27	28	29	30	31	1	2
A	3	4	5	6	7	8	9
	10	11	12	13	14	15	16
	17	18	19	20	21	22	23
	24	25	26	27	28	29	30
M	1	2	3	4	5	6	7
	8	9	10	11	12	13	14
	15	16	17	18	19	20	21
	22	23	24	25	26	27	28
	29	30	31	1	2	3	4
J	5	6	7	8	9	10	11
	12	13	14	15	16	17	18
	19	20	21	22	23	24	25
	26	27	28	29	30	1	2
J	3	4	5	6	7	8	9
	10	11	12	13	14	15	16
	17	18	19	20	21	22	23
	24	25	26	27	28	29	30
	31	1	2	3	4	5	6
A	7	8	9	10	11	12	13
	14	15	16	17	18	19	20
	21	22	23	24	25	26	27
	28	29	30	31	1	2	3
S	4	5	6	7	8	9	10
	11	12	13	14	15	16	17
	18	19	20	21	22	23	24
	25	26	27	28	29	30	1
O	2	3	4	5	6	7	8
	9	10	11	12	13	14	15
	16	17	18	19	20	21	22
	23	24	25	26	27	28	29
	30	31	1	2	3	4	5
N	6	7	8	9	10	11	12
	13	14	15	16	17	18	19
	20	21	22	23	24	25	26
	27	28	29	30	1	2	3
D	4	5	6	7	8	9	10
	11	12	13	14	15	16	17
	18	19	20	21	22	23	24
	25	26	27	28	29	30	31

Calendar #8

Mo	Su	Mo	Tu	We	Th	Fr	Sa
	1	2	3	4	5	6	7
J	8	9	10	11	12	13	14
	15	16	17	18	19	20	21
	22	23	24	25	26	27	28
	29	30	31	1	2	3	4
F	5	6	7	8	9	10	11
	12	13	14	15	16	17	18
	19	20	21	22	23	24	25
	26	27	28	29	1	2	3
M	4	5	6	7	8	9	10
	11	12	13	14	15	16	17
	18	19	20	21	22	23	24
	25	26	27	28	29	30	31
A	1	2	3	4	5	6	7
	8	9	10	11	12	13	14
	15	16	17	18	19	20	21
	22	23	24	25	26	27	28
	29	30	1	2	3	4	5
M	6	7	8	9	10	11	12
	13	14	15	16	17	18	19
	20	21	22	23	24	25	26
	27	28	29	30	31	1	2
J	3	4	5	6	7	8	9
	10	11	12	13	14	15	16
	17	18	19	20	21	22	23
	24	25	26	27	28	29	30
	1	2	3	4	5	6	7
J	8	9	10	11	12	13	14
	15	16	17	18	19	20	21
	22	23	24	25	26	27	28
	29	30	31	1	2	3	4
A	5	6	7	8	9	10	11
	12	13	14	15	16	17	18
	19	20	21	22	23	24	25
	26	27	28	29	30	31	1
S	2	3	4	5	6	7	8
	9	10	11	12	13	14	15
	16	17	18	19	20	21	22
	23	24	25	26	27	28	29
	30	1	2	3	4	5	6
O	7	8	9	10	11	12	13
	14	15	16	17	18	19	20
	21	22	23	24	25	26	27
	28	29	30	31	1	2	3
N	4	5	6	7	8	9	10
	11	12	13	14	15	16	17
	18	19	20	21	22	23	24
	25	26	27	28	29	30	1
D	2	3	4	5	6	7	8
	9	10	11	12	13	14	15
	16	17	18	19	20	21	22
	23	24	25	26	27	28	29
	30	31					

Calendar #9

Mo	Su	Mo	Tu	We	Th	Fr	Sa
		1	2	3	4	5	6
J	7	8	9	10	11	12	13
	14	15	16	17	18	19	20
	21	22	23	24	25	26	27
	28	29	30	31	1	2	3
F	4	5	6	7	8	9	10
	11	12	13	14	15	16	17
	18	19	20	21	22	23	24
	25	26	27	28	29	1	2
M	3	4	5	6	7	8	9
	10	11	12	13	14	15	16
	17	18	19	20	21	22	23
	24	25	26	27	28	29	30
	31	1	2	3	4	5	6
A	7	8	9	10	11	12	13
	14	15	16	17	18	19	20
	21	22	23	24	25	26	27
	28	29	30	1	2	3	4
M	5	6	7	8	9	10	11
	12	13	14	15	16	17	18
	19	20	21	22	23	24	25
	26	27	28	29	30	31	1
J	2	3	4	5	6	7	8
	9	10	11	12	13	14	15
	16	17	18	19	20	21	22
	23	24	25	26	27	28	29
	30	1	2	3	4	5	6
J	7	8	9	10	11	12	13
	14	15	16	17	18	19	20
	21	22	23	24	25	26	27
	28	29	30	31	1	2	3
A	4	5	6	7	8	9	10
	11	12	13	14	15	16	17
	18	19	20	21	22	23	24
	25	26	27	28	29	30	31
S	1	2	3	4	5	6	7
	8	9	10	11	12	13	14
	15	16	17	18	19	20	21
	22	23	24	25	26	27	28
	29	30	1	2	3	4	5
O	6	7	8	9	10	11	12
	13	14	15	16	17	18	19
	20	21	22	23	24	25	26
	27	28	29	30	31	1	2
N	3	4	5	6	7	8	9
	10	11	12	13	14	15	16
	17	18	19	20	21	22	23
	24	25	26	27	28	29	30
D	1	2	3	4	5	6	7
	8	9	10	11	12	13	14
	15	16	17	18	19	20	21
	22	23	24	25	26	27	28
	29	30	31				

Calendars 10-12

Calendar #10

	Su	Mo	Tu	We	Th	Fr	Sa
			1	2	3	4	5
J	6	7	8	9	10	11	12
	13	14	15	16	17	18	19
	20	21	22	23	24	25	26
	27	28	29	30	31	1	2
F	3	4	5	6	7	8	9
	10	11	12	13	14	15	16
	17	18	19	20	21	22	23
	24	25	26	27	28	29	1
M	2	3	4	5	6	7	8
	9	10	11	12	13	14	15
	16	17	18	19	20	21	22
	23	24	25	26	27	28	29
	30	31	1	2	3	4	5
A	6	7	8	9	10	11	12
	13	14	15	16	17	18	19
	20	21	22	23	24	25	26
	27	28	29	30	1	2	3
M	4	5	6	7	8	9	10
	11	12	13	14	15	16	17
	18	19	20	21	22	23	24
	25	26	27	28	29	30	31
J	1	2	3	4	5	6	7
	8	9	10	11	12	13	14
	15	16	17	18	19	20	21
	22	23	24	25	26	27	28
	29	30	1	2	3	4	5
J	6	7	8	9	10	11	12
	13	14	15	16	17	18	19
	20	21	22	23	24	25	26
	27	28	29	30	31	1	2
A	3	4	5	6	7	8	9
	10	11	12	13	14	15	16
	17	18	19	20	21	22	23
	24	25	26	27	28	29	30
	31	1	2	3	4	5	6
S	7	8	9	10	11	12	13
	14	15	16	17	18	19	20
	21	22	23	24	25	26	27
	28	29	30	1	2	3	4
O	5	6	7	8	9	10	11
	12	13	14	15	16	17	18
	19	20	21	22	23	24	25
	26	27	28	29	30	31	1
N	2	3	4	5	6	7	8
	9	10	11	12	13	14	15
	16	17	18	19	20	21	22
	23	24	25	26	27	28	29
	30	1	2	3	4	5	6
D	7	8	9	10	11	12	13
	14	15	16	17	18	19	20
	21	22	23	24	25	26	27
	28	29	30	31			

Calendar #11

	Su	Mo	Tu	We	Th	Fr	Sa
				1	2	3	4
J	5	6	7	8	9	10	11
	12	13	14	15	16	17	18
	19	20	21	22	23	24	25
	26	27	28	29	30	31	1
F	2	3	4	5	6	7	8
	9	10	11	12	13	14	15
	16	17	18	19	20	21	22
	23	24	25	26	27	28	29
M	1	2	3	4	5	6	7
	8	9	10	11	12	13	14
	15	16	17	18	19	20	21
	22	23	24	25	26	27	28
	29	30	31	1	2	3	4
A	5	6	7	8	9	10	11
	12	13	14	15	16	17	18
	19	20	21	22	23	24	25
	26	27	28	29	30	1	2
M	3	4	5	6	7	8	9
	10	11	12	13	14	15	16
	17	18	19	20	21	22	23
	24	25	26	27	28	29	30
	31	1	2	3	4	5	6
J	7	8	9	10	11	12	13
	14	15	16	17	18	19	20
	21	22	23	24	25	26	27
	28	29	30	1	2	3	4
J	5	6	7	8	9	10	11
	12	13	14	15	16	17	18
	19	20	21	22	23	24	25
	26	27	28	29	30	31	1
A	2	3	4	5	6	7	8
	9	10	11	12	13	14	15
	16	17	18	19	20	21	22
	23	24	25	26	27	28	29
	30	31	1	2	3	4	5
S	6	7	8	9	10	11	12
	13	14	15	16	17	18	19
	20	21	22	23	24	25	26
	27	28	29	30	1	2	3
O	4	5	6	7	8	9	10
	11	12	13	14	15	16	17
	18	19	20	21	22	23	24
	25	26	27	28	29	30	31
N	1	2	3	4	5	6	7
	8	9	10	11	12	13	14
	15	16	17	18	19	20	21
	22	23	24	25	26	27	28
	29	30	1	2	3	4	5
D	6	7	8	9	10	11	12
	13	14	15	16	17	18	19
	20	21	22	23	24	25	26
	27	28	29	30	31		

Calendar #12

	Su	Mo	Tu	We	Th	Fr	Sa
					1	2	3
J	4	5	6	7	8	9	10
	11	12	13	14	15	16	17
	18	19	20	21	22	23	24
	25	26	27	28	29	30	31
F	1	2	3	4	5	6	7
	8	9	10	11	12	13	14
	15	16	17	18	19	20	21
	22	23	24	25	26	27	28
	29	1	2	3	4	5	6
M	7	8	9	10	11	12	13
	14	15	16	17	18	19	20
	21	22	23	24	25	26	27
	28	29	30	31	1	2	3
A	4	5	6	7	8	9	10
	11	12	13	14	15	16	17
	18	19	20	21	22	23	24
	25	26	27	28	29	30	1
M	2	3	4	5	6	7	8
	9	10	11	12	13	14	15
	16	17	18	19	20	21	22
	23	24	25	26	27	28	29
	30	31	1	2	3	4	5
J	6	7	8	9	10	11	12
	13	14	15	16	17	18	19
	20	21	22	23	24	25	26
	27	28	29	30	1	2	3
J	4	5	6	7	8	9	10
	11	12	13	14	15	16	17
	18	19	20	21	22	23	24
	25	26	27	28	29	30	31
A	1	2	3	4	5	6	7
	8	9	10	11	12	13	14
	15	16	17	18	19	20	21
	22	23	24	25	26	27	28
	29	30	31	1	2	3	4
S	5	6	7	8	9	10	11
	12	13	14	15	16	17	18
	19	20	21	22	23	24	25
	26	27	28	29	30	1	2
O	3	4	5	6	7	8	9
	10	11	12	13	14	15	16
	17	18	19	20	21	22	23
	24	25	26	27	28	29	30
	31	1	2	3	4	5	6
N	7	8	9	10	11	12	13
	14	15	16	17	18	19	20
	21	22	23	24	25	26	27
	28	29	30	1	2	3	4
D	5	6	7	8	9	10	11
	12	13	14	15	16	17	18
	19	20	21	22	23	24	25
	26	27	28	29	30	31	

Calendars 13-14

Calendar #13

	Su	Mo	Tu	We	Th	Fr	Sa
						1	2
J	3	4	5	6	7	8	9
	10	11	12	13	14	15	16
	17	18	19	20	21	22	23
	24	25	26	27	28	29	30
	31	1	2	3	4	5	6
	7	8	9	10	11	12	13
F	14	15	16	17	18	19	20
	21	22	23	24	25	26	27
	28	29	1	2	3	4	5
	6	7	8	9	10	11	12
M	13	14	15	16	17	18	19
	20	21	22	23	24	25	26
	27	28	29	30	31	1	2
	3	4	5	6	7	8	9
A	10	11	12	13	14	15	16
	17	18	19	20	21	22	23
	24	25	26	27	28	29	30
	1	2	3	4	5	6	7
	8	9	10	11	12	13	14
M	15	16	17	18	19	20	21
	22	23	24	25	26	27	28
	29	30	31	1	2	3	4
	5	6	7	8	9	10	11
J	12	13	14	15	16	17	18
	19	20	21	22	23	24	25
	26	27	28	29	30	1	2
	3	4	5	6	7	8	9
J	10	11	12	13	14	15	16
	17	18	19	20	21	22	23
	24	25	26	27	28	29	30
	31	1	2	3	4	5	6
	7	8	9	10	11	12	13
A	14	15	16	17	18	19	20
	21	22	23	24	25	26	27
	28	29	30	31	1	2	3
	4	5	6	7	8	9	10
S	11	12	13	14	15	16	17
	18	19	20	21	22	23	24
	25	26	27	28	29	30	1
	2	3	4	5	6	7	8
O	9	10	11	12	13	14	15
	16	17	18	19	20	21	22
	23	24	25	26	27	28	29
	30	31	1	2	3	4	5
	6	7	8	9	10	11	12
N	13	14	15	16	17	18	19
	20	21	22	23	24	25	26
	27	28	29	30	1	2	3
	4	5	6	7	8	9	10
D	11	12	13	14	15	16	17
	18	19	20	21	22	23	24
	25	26	27	28	29	30	31

Calendar #14

	Su	Mo	Tu	We	Th	Fr	Sa
							1
J	2	3	4	5	6	7	8
	9	10	11	12	13	14	15
	16	17	18	19	20	21	22
	23	24	25	26	27	28	29
	30	31	1	2	3	4	5
	6	7	8	9	10	11	12
F	13	14	15	16	17	18	19
	20	21	22	23	24	25	26
	27	28	29	1	2	3	4
	5	6	7	8	9	10	11
M	12	13	14	15	16	17	18
	19	20	21	22	23	24	25
	26	27	28	29	30	31	1
	2	3	4	5	6	7	8
A	9	10	11	12	13	14	15
	16	17	18	19	20	21	22
	23	24	25	26	27	28	29
	30	1	2	3	4	5	6
	7	8	9	10	11	12	13
M	14	15	16	17	18	19	20
	21	22	23	24	25	26	27
	28	29	30	31	1	2	3
	4	5	6	7	8	9	10
J	11	12	13	14	15	16	17
	18	19	20	21	22	23	24
	25	26	27	28	29	30	1
	2	3	4	5	6	7	8
J	9	10	11	12	13	14	15
	16	17	18	19	20	21	22
	23	24	25	26	27	28	29
	30	31	1	2	3	4	5
	6	7	8	9	10	11	12
A	13	14	15	16	17	18	19
	20	21	22	23	24	25	26
	27	28	29	30	31	1	2
	3	4	5	6	7	8	9
S	10	11	12	13	14	15	16
	17	18	19	20	21	22	23
	24	25	26	27	28	29	30
	1	2	3	4	5	6	7
	8	9	10	11	12	13	14
O	15	16	17	18	19	20	21
	22	23	24	25	26	27	28
	29	30	31	1	2	3	4
	5	6	7	8	9	10	11
N	12	13	14	15	16	17	18
	19	20	21	22	23	24	25
	26	27	28	29	30	1	2
	3	4	5	6	7	8	9
D	10	11	12	13	14	15	16
	17	18	19	20	21	22	23
	24	25	26	27	28	29	30
	31						

Julian Day Calendar

The ***Julian Day*** is the number of days since January 1, 4713 BCE. Numerous algorithms exist for converting between the Gregorian calendar and the Julian day number, but they may differ on dates prior to the adoption of the Gregorian calendar on October 15, 1582. These differences are due to use of the proleptic Julian calendar, the proleptic Gregorian calendar, or both (***proleptic*** means the use of a calendar for dates earlier than when the calendar was designed). Julian days start at noon; the list shown below uses the ***Modified Julian Day***, which starts at civil midnight.

Julian Day	Day of Week	Month	Day	Year
0	Monday	January	1	4713 BCE
2299161	Friday	October	15	1582
2300000	Thursday	January	31	1585
2305448	Saturday	January	1	1600
2341973	Friday	January	1	1700
2378497	Wednesday	January	1	1800
2400000	Tuesday	November	16	1858
2410000	Saturday	April	3	1886
2415021	Monday	January	1	1900
2418673	Saturday	January	1	1910
2420000	Wednesday	August	20	1913
2422325	Thursday	January	1	1920
2425978	Wednesday	January	1	1930
2429630	Monday	January	1	1940
2430000	Sunday	January	5	1941
2433283	Sunday	January	1	1950
2436935	Friday	January	1	1960
2440000	Thursday	May	23	1968
2440588	Thursday	January	1	1970
2444240	Tuesday	January	1	1980
2447893	Monday	January	1	1990
2450000	Monday	October	9	1995
2451545	Saturday	January	1	2000
2455198	Friday	January	1	2010
2458850	Wednesday	January	1	2020
2460000	Friday	February	24	2023
2462503	Tuesday	January	1	2030
2466155	Sunday	January	1	2040
2469808	Saturday	January	1	2050
2470000	Tuesday	July	12	2050
2473460	Thursday	January	1	2060
2477113	Wednesday	January	1	2070
2480000	Saturday	November	27	2077
2480765	Monday	January	1	2080
2484418	Sunday	January	1	2090
2488070	Friday	January	1	2100
2490000	Wednesday	April	15	2105
2500000	Sunday	August	31	2132
2600000	Friday	June	16	2406

Periodic Table (left half)

^{1}H Hydrogen	

^{3}Li Lithium	**^{4}Be** Beryllium
^{11}Na Sodium	**^{12}Mg** Magnesium

^{19}K Potassium	**^{20}Ca** Calcium	**^{21}Sc** Scandium	**^{22}Ti** Titanium	**^{23}V** Vanadium	**^{24}Cr** Chromium	**^{25}Mn** Manganese	**^{26}Fe** Iron	**^{27}Co** Cobalt
^{37}Rb Rubidium	**^{38}Sr** Strontium	**^{39}Y** Yttrium	**^{40}Zr** Zirconium	**^{41}Nb** Niobium	**^{42}Mo** Molybdenum	**^{43}Tc** Technetium	**^{44}Ru** Ruthenium	**^{45}Rh** Rhodium
^{55}Cs Cesium	**^{56}Ba** Barium	**^{57}La** Lanthanum	**^{72}Hf** Hafnium	**^{73}Ta** Tantalum	**^{74}W** Tungsten	**^{75}Re** Rhenium	**^{76}Os** Osmium	**^{77}Ir** Iridium
^{87}Fr Francium	**^{88}Ra** Radium	**^{89}Ac** Actinium	**^{104}Rf** Rutherfordium	**^{105}Db** Dubnium	**^{106}Sg** Seaborgium	**^{107}Bh** Bohrium	**^{108}Hs** Hassium	**^{109}Mt** Meitnerium

^{58}Ce Cerium	**^{59}Pr** Praseodymium	**^{60}Nd** Neodymium	**^{61}Pm** Promethium	**^{62}Sm** Samarium	**^{63}Eu** Europium	**^{64}Gd** Gadolinium
^{90}Th Thorium	**^{91}Pa** Protactinium	**^{92}U** Uranium	**^{93}Np** Neptunium	**^{94}Pu** Plutonium	**^{95}Am** Americium	**^{96}Cm** Curium

This is a standard periodic table of the elements, sorted by atomic number (number of protons in the nucleus). For example, H=1, He=2, Li=3, etc.. Exceptions are the Lanthanides (Ce...Lu) to be inserted after La, and the Actinides (Th...Lr) to be inserted after Ac. Atomic numbers, names, and masses appear on the following pages.

Periodic Table (right half)

										²He
										Helium

				⁵B	⁶C	⁷N	⁸O	⁹F	¹⁰Ne
				Boron	Carbon	Nitrogen	Oxygen	Fluorine	Neon
				¹³Al	¹⁴Si	¹⁵P	¹⁶S	¹⁷Cl	¹⁸Ar
				Aluminum	Silicon	Phosphorous	Sulfur	Chlorine	Argon
²⁸Ni	²⁹Cu	³⁰Zn	³¹Ga	³²Ge	³³As	³⁴Se	³⁵Br	³⁶Kr
Nickel	Copper	Zinc	Gallium	Germanium	Arsenic	Selenium	Bromine	Krypton
⁴⁶Pd	⁴⁷Ag	⁴⁸Cd	⁴⁹In	⁵⁰Sn	⁵¹Sb	⁵²Te	⁵³I	⁵⁴Xe
Palladium	Silver	Cadmium	Indium	Tin	Antimony	Tellurium	Iodine	Xenon
⁷⁸Pt	⁷⁹Au	⁸⁰Hg	⁸¹Tl	⁸²Pb	⁸³Bi	⁸⁴Po	⁸⁵At	⁸⁶Rn
Platinum	Gold	Mercury	Thallium	Lead	Bismuth	Polonium	Astatine	Radon
¹¹⁰Ds	¹¹¹Rg	¹¹²Cn	¹¹³Nh	¹¹⁴Fl	¹¹⁵Mc	¹¹⁶Lv	¹¹⁷Ts	¹¹⁸Og
Darmstadtium	Roentgenium	Copernicium	Nihonium	Flerovium	Moscovium	Livermorium	Tennessine	Oganesson

⁶⁵Tb	⁶⁶Dy	⁶⁷Ho	⁶⁸Er	⁶⁹Tm	⁷⁰Yb	⁷¹Lu
Terbium	Dysprosium	Holmium	Erbium	Thulium	Ytterbium	Lutetium
⁹⁷Bk	⁹⁸Cf	⁹⁹Es	¹⁰⁰Fm	¹⁰¹Md	¹⁰²No	¹⁰³Lr
Berkelium	Californium	Einsteinium	Fermium	Mendelevium	Nobelium	Lawrencium

Periodic Table (By Atomic Number)

1	H	Hydrogen	[1.00784; 1.00811]	41	Nb	Niobium	92.90637(1) *	81	Tl	Thallium	[204.382; 204.385]
2	He	Helium	4.002602(2)	42	Mo	Molybdenum	95.95(1)	82	Pb	Lead	207.2(1)
3	Li	Lithium	[6.938; 6.997]	43	Tc	Technetium	[98]	83	Bi	Bismuth	208.98040(1)
4	Be	Beryllium	9.0121831(5)	44	Ru	Ruthenium	101.07(2)	84	Po	Polonium	[209]
5	B	Boron	[10.806; 10.821]	45	Rh	Rhodium	102.90549(2) *	85	At	Astatine	[210]
6	C	Carbon	[12.0096; 12.0116]	46	Pd	Palladium	106.42(1)	86	Rn	Radon	[222]
7	N	Nitrogen	[14.00643; 14.00728]	47	Ag	Silver	107.8682(2)	87	Fr	Francium	[223]
8	O	Oxygen	[15.99903; 15.99977]	48	Cd	Cadmium	112.414(4)	88	Ra	Radium	[226]
9	F	Fluorine	18.998403163(6)	49	In	Indium	114.818(3)	89	Ac	Actinium	[227]
10	Ne	Neon	20.1797(6)	50	Sn	Tin	118.710(7)	90	Th	Thorium	232.0377(4)
11	Na	Sodium	22.98976928(2)	51	Sb	Antimony	121.760(1)	91	Pa	Protactinium	231.03588(1) *
12	Mg	Magnesium	[24.304; 24.307]	52	Te	Tellurium	127.60(3)	92	U	Uranium	238.02891(3)
13	Al	Aluminum	26.9815384(3) *	53	I	Iodine	126.90447(3)	93	Np	Neptunium	[237]
14	Si	Silicon	[28.084; 28.086]	54	Xe	Xenon	131.293(6)	94	Pu	Plutonium	[244]
15	P	Phosphorous	30.973761998(5)	55	Cs	Cesium	132.90545196(6)	95	Am	Americium	[243]
16	S	Sulfur	[32.059; 32.076]	56	Ba	Barium	137.327(7)	96	Cm	Curium	[247]
17	Cl	Chlorine	[35.446; 35.457]	57	La	Lanthanum	138.90547(7)	97	Bk	Berkelium	[247]
18	Ar	Argon	[39.792; 39.963] *	58	Ce	Cerium	140.116(1)	98	Cf	Californium	[251]
19	K	Potassium	39.0983(1)	59	Pr	Praseodymium	140.90766(1) *	99	Es	Einsteinium	[252]
20	Ca	Calcium	40.078(4)	60	Nd	Neodymium	144.242(3)	100	Fm	Fermium	[257]
21	Sc	Scandium	44.955908(5)	61	Pm	Promethium	[145]	101	Md	Mendelevium	[258]
22	Ti	Titanium	47.867(1)	62	Sm	Samarium	150.36(2)	102	No	Nobelium	[259]
23	V	Vanadium	50.9415(1)	63	Eu	Europium	151.964(1)	103	Lr	Lawrencium	[262]
24	Cr	Chromium	51.9961(6)	64	Gd	Gadolinium	157.25(3)	104	Rf	Rutherfordium	[265]
25	Mn	Manganese	54.938043(2) *	65	Tb	Terbium	158.925354(8) *	105	Db	Dubnium	[268]
26	Fe	Iron	55.845(2)	66	Dy	Dysprosium	162.500(1)	106	Sg	Seaborgium	[271]
27	Co	Cobalt	58.933194(3) *	67	Ho	Holmium	164.930328(7) *	107	Bh	Bohrium	[272]
28	Ni	Nickel	58.6934(4)	68	Er	Erbium	167.259(3)	108	Hs	Hassium	[270]
29	Cu	Copper	63.546(3)	69	Tm	Thulium	168.934218(6) *	109	Mt	Meitnerium	[276]
30	Zn	Zinc	65.38(2)	70	Yb	Ytterbium	173.045(10) *	110	Ds	Darmstadtium	[281]
31	Ga	Gallium	69.723(1)	71	Lu	Lutetium	174.9668(1)	111	Rg	Roentgenium	[280]
32	Ge	Germanium	72.630(8)	72	Hf	Hafnium	178.486(6) *	112	Cn	Copernicium	[285]
33	As	Arsenic	74.921595(6)	73	Ta	Tantalum	180.94788(2)	113	Nh	Nihonium	[284]
34	Se	Selenium	78.971(8)	74	W	Tungsten	183.84(1)	114	Fl	Flerovium	[289]
35	Br	Bromine	[79.901; 79.907]	75	Re	Rhenium	186.207(1)	115	Mc	Moscovium	[288]
36	Kr	Krypton	83.798(2)	76	Os	Osmium	190.23(3)	116	Lv	Livermorium	[293]
37	Rb	Rubidium	85.4678(3)	77	Ir	Iridium	192.217(2) *	117	Ts	Tennessine	[294]
38	Sr	Strontium	87.62(1)	78	Pt	Platinum	195.084(9)	118	Og	Oganesson	[294]
39	Y	Yttrium	88.90584(1) *	79	Au	Gold	196.966570(4) *				
40	Zr	Zirconium	91.224(2)	80	Hg	Mercury	200.592(3)				

Atomic masses are estimates based on IUPAC (International Union of Pure and Applied Chemistry) data as of May 2013, except elements marked with * indicate that the corresponding atomic masses have been updated more recently (Ytterbium in 2015, Haffnium in 2019, and the other 14 elements in 2017). Masses in square brackets such as [294] indicate the mass of the longest-lived isotope of the element (all isotopes are radioactive). Numbers in parentheses () indicate the uncertainty in the last digit of the mass. In cases where two numbers are shown, the element has two or more isotopes that are commonly known and mass numbers represent lower and upper bounds.

Periodic Table (By Element Name)

#	Sym	Name	Mass	#	Sym	Name	Mass	#	Sym	Name	Mass
89	Ac	Actinium	[227]	72	Hf	Hafnium	178.486(6) *	59	Pr	Praseodymium	140.90766(1) *
13	Al	Aluminum	26.9815384(3) *	108	Hs	Hassium	[270]	61	Pm	Promethium	[145]
95	Am	Americium	[243]	2	He	Helium	4.002602(2)	91	Pa	Protactinium	231.03588(1) *
51	Sb	Antimony	121.760(1)	67	Ho	Holmium	164.930328(7) *	88	Ra	Radium	[226]
18	Ar	Argon	[39.792; 39.963] *	1	H	Hydrogen	[1.00784; 1.00811]	86	Rn	Radon	[222]
33	As	Arsenic	74.921595(6)	49	In	Indium	114.818(3)	75	Re	Rhenium	186.207(1)
85	At	Astatine	[210]	53	I	Iodine	126.90447(3)	45	Rh	Rhodium	102.90549(2) *
56	Ba	Barium	137.327(7)	77	Ir	Iridium	192.217(2) *	111	Rg	Roentgenium	[280]
97	Bk	Berkelium	[247]	26	Fe	Iron	55.845(2)	37	Rb	Rubidium	85.4678(3)
4	Be	Beryllium	9.0121831(5)	36	Kr	Krypton	83.798(2)	44	Ru	Ruthenium	101.07(2)
83	Bi	Bismuth	208.98040(1)	57	La	Lanthanum	138.90547(7)	104	Rf	Rutherfordium	[265]
107	Bh	Bohrium	[272]	103	Lr	Lawrencium	[262]	62	Sm	Samarium	150.36(2)
5	B	Boron	[10.806; 10.821]	82	Pb	Lead	207.2(1)	21	Sc	Scandium	44.955908(5)
35	Br	Bromine	[79.901; 79.907]	3	Li	Lithium	[6.938; 6.997]	106	Sg	Seaborgium	[271]
48	Cd	Cadmium	112.414(4)	116	Lv	Livermorium	[293]	34	Se	Selenium	78.971(8)
20	Ca	Calcium	40.078(4)	71	Lu	Lutetium	174.9668(1)	14	Si	Silicon	[28.084; 28.086]
98	Cf	Californium	[251]	12	Mg	Magnesium	[24.304; 24.307]	47	Ag	Silver	107.8682(2)
6	C	Carbon	[12.0096; 12.0116]	25	Mn	Manganese	54.938043(2) *	11	Na	Sodium	22.98976928(2)
58	Ce	Cerium	140.116(1)	109	Mt	Meitnerium	[276]	38	Sr	Strontium	87.62(1)
55	Cs	Cesium	132.90545196(6)	101	Md	Mendelevium	[258]	16	S	Sulfur	[32.059; 32.076]
17	Cl	Chlorine	[35.446; 35.457]	80	Hg	Mercury	200.592(3)	73	Ta	Tantalum	180.94788(2)
24	Cr	Chromium	51.9961(6)	42	Mo	Molybdenum	95.95(1)	43	Tc	Technetium	[98]
27	Co	Cobalt	58.933194(3) *	115	Mc	Moscovium	[288]	52	Te	Tellurium	127.60(3)
112	Cn	Copernicium	[285]	60	Nd	Neodymium	144.242(3)	117	Ts	Tennessine	[294]
29	Cu	Copper	63.546(3)	10	Ne	Neon	20.1797(6)	65	Tb	Terbium	158.925354(8) *
96	Cm	Curium	[247]	93	Np	Neptunium	[237]	81	Tl	Thallium	[204.382; 204.385]
110	Ds	Darmstadtium	[281]	28	Ni	Nickel	58.6934(4)	90	Th	Thorium	232.0377(4)
105	Db	Dubnium	[268]	113	Nh	Nihonium	[284]	69	Tm	Thulium	168.934218(6) *
66	Dy	Dysprosium	162.500(1)	41	Nb	Niobium	92.90637(1) *	50	Sn	Tin	118.710(7)
99	Es	Einsteinium	[252]	7	N	Nitrogen	[14.00643; 14.00728]	22	Ti	Titanium	47.867(1)
68	Er	Erbium	167.259(3)	102	No	Nobelium	[259]	74	W	Tungsten	183.84(1)
63	Eu	Europium	151.964(1)	118	Og	Oganesson	[294]	92	U	Uranium	238.02891(3)
100	Fm	Fermium	[257]	76	Os	Osmium	190.23(3)	23	V	Vanadium	50.9415(1)
114	Fl	Flerovium	[289]	8	O	Oxygen	[15.99903; 15.99977]	54	Xe	Xenon	131.293(6)
9	F	Fluorine	18.998403163(6)	46	Pd	Palladium	106.42(1)	70	Yb	Ytterbium	173.045(10) *
87	Fr	Francium	[223]	15	P	Phosphorous	30.973761998(5)	39	Y	Yttrium	88.90584(1) *
64	Gd	Gadolinium	157.25(3)	78	Pt	Platinum	195.084(9)	30	Zn	Zinc	65.38(2)
31	Ga	Gallium	69.723(1)	94	Pu	Plutonium	[244]	40	Zr	Zirconium	91.224(2)
32	Ge	Germanium	72.630(8)	84	Po	Polonium	[209]				
79	Au	Gold	196.966570(4) *	19	K	Potassium	39.0983(1)				

Before they are formally named, new elements are given a working name based on their atomic number. New elements 113, 115, 117, and 118 had their working names replaced by provisional formal names in early 2016. Those provisional names were formally adopted in late 2016.

> 113:   Ununtrium   is now Nihonium
> 115:   Ununpentium is now Moscovium
> 117:   Ununseptium is now Tennessine
> 118:   Ununoctium   is now Oganesson

3: *Mathematics*

Mathematics is one of the major ways we understand the Universe: if you don't understand the math, you don't understand the problem. This section deals with numbers and the relationships between numbers. It covers accuracy vs. precision, base conversions, logarithms, squares and square roots (to 50 places), cubes and cube roots, factorials, factors of integers, common irrational numbers, and basic trigonometry. There is also a table of the first few prime numbers. In particular, there are tables of logarithms in different bases as well as tables of sines, cosines, and tangents. In many cases, the tables are not needed if a scientific pocket calculator is available; these tables are for when a calculator is not available (or not allowed, as on an exam).

For advanced computer science, there is one table of sines that lists the values in binary and hexadecimal as well as the more traditional decimal. Any assembly language programmers or numerical analysts will make direct use of this information.

Accuracy vs. Precision (Measurement)

Devices that measure some phenomenon are never perfect and almost never give the same result each time the measurement is performed. In a statistical sense, the ___accuracy___ of a set of samples (measurements) is determined by how close the average of those samples is to the correct answer, while ___precision___ is determined by how close the samples are to their own average (how reliably repeatable are the measurements). That is, accuracy is an error circle around the correct answer, and precision is an error circle around the samples. In general, you want both accuracy and precision (the error circles strongly overlap). If that is not possible, there are cases where accuracy is preferred over precision and other cases where precision is preferred over accuracy.

In taking samples from an accurate-but-not-very-precise instrument, increasing the number of samples tends to have the average of those samples converge on the correct answer. The sum of the measurement errors (the distance and direction between each sample and the correct answer) tends towards zero over time. The more samples, the better the average. With a precise instrument, any difference between the average of the samples and the correct answer may expose a systematic bias within that instrument.

These concepts are exemplified in example below of a shooting target. The left column shows accurate shots, as in both cases the *average* is very close to the center of the bull's eye, while the right column shows shots far away from the bull's eye. The top row shows high precision, as all shots are *clustered close together*, but the bottom row shows a wide dispersal pattern. Thus, the precise-but-not-accurate target in the upper-right indicates that the marksman is very skilled, but the weapon shows a systematic bias in its sighting apparatus.

	ACCURATE (CORRECT AVERAGE)	NOT ACCURATE (INCORRECT AVERAGE)
PRECISE (TIGHT CLUSTER)		
NOT PRECISE (WIDE CLUSTER)		

Accuracy vs. Precision (Numerical Analysis)

While the discussion on the previous page covers the most widely accepted interpretation of accuracy and precision, in the domain of acquiring measurements from some device, those terms mean something slightly different when talking about the numerical answers obtained from some purely computational process.

In ***numerical analysis***, accuracy refers to how close a computed answer is to the correct answer, and precision refers to the number of digits in the answer (usually either decimal digits or binary digits). Computationally, an answer with lots of digits may be no better than one with very few digits, and often leads people into a false confidence that it is the "more correct" of the two.

For example, an approximation to π that is 3.14 is a more accurate answer than 2.912633, even though the latter answer contains more digits of precision. In general you want both accuracy and precision, but as before sometimes an accurate answer is preferred over a precise answer, and sometimes vice versa.

In representing numbers with fractions on a computer, we talk about single precision, double precision, extended precision, etc. These formats differ in the number of binary digits (bits) available for storing the answers (precision), but say nothing about how "good" those answers may be (accuracy). Computers are finite machines. That means that there are limits on the precision of any numerical result obtains by a computational process. Exceeding those limits may still generate answers, but those answers will be meaningless.

For example, a spreadsheet formula such as =B10+1-B10 should always return 1 as its answer. However, if cell B10 contains a large enough number, the result will be zero. When this happens, this is an indication that the mathematical requirements of the problem have exceeded the precision of the computer. There are not enough digits available to represent <u>both</u> the very large number in cell B10 <u>and</u> the 1; the 1 gets rounded away during the addition, effectively reducing the formula to =B10-B10, which is zero. This is called ***catastrophic cancellation***. The spreadsheet will not indicate that anything is wrong; some results just got rounded off a little bit. In numerical analysis, the formula can be rewritten to keep the large values and the small values from generally interfering with one another. The spreadsheet formula in the example would be written as =B10-B10+1, which always returns 1 regardless of the contents of B10.

These and related topics are addressed later in this chapter (scientific notation, floating-point formats, rounding, interval arithmetic, universal numbers, etc.).

Scientific Notation in Math and on Computer

Very large and very small numbers need an efficient notation to express their values. For example, the numbers 123400000.0 and 0.00000001234 have the same four significant digits (1234), but the first number is very large and the second is very small. In both cases we need to know the significant digits, and where to place the decimal point relative to them. This is done by normalizing the number so that the decimal point is right after the first digit, and expressing the number of places left or right to shift the decimal point as a power of 10. Positive powers of 10 mean that the decimal point needs to be shifted to the right, and negative powers of 10 mean that the decimal point needs to be shifted to the left.

$$123400000.0 \qquad = 1.234 \times 10^8 \qquad \text{``1.234 times ten to the plus 8}^{TH}\text{ power''}$$
$$0.00000001234 \qquad = 1.234 \times 10^{-8} \qquad \text{``1.234 times ten to the minus 8}^{TH}\text{ power''}$$

In expressing these numbers on a computer, the "times ten to the power of" phrase is hard to write, because few computer systems (such as spreadsheets) allow either the $\times$ symbol or superscripts. To write these numbers on a computer, the letter **E** replaces the complicated phrase:

$$123400000.0 \qquad = 1.234 \times 10^8 \qquad \textbf{1.234E+8}$$
$$0.00000001234 \qquad = 1.234 \times 10^{-8} \qquad \textbf{1.234E-8}$$

Note that in math, a number such as 0.0000000123400 actually contains <u>six</u> significant digits, not four. Trailing zeroes explicitly written at the end of a fraction are significant, regardless of the fact that they do not change the value of the number. This number is written in scientific notation as 1.23400×10^{-8} or **1.23400E-8** but in the latter case care must be taken to format a number (in a spreadsheet or printed from a program) so that those trailing zeroes actually show up, as in many cases they will be automatically suppressed by the software.

Arithmetic with Scientific Notation

The basic arithmetic operations of add, subtract, multiply, and divide are often performed on numbers in scientific notation directly. As it turns out multiplication and division are less complicated than addition and subtraction.

Multiplication

Multiply the significant digits together, add the exponents, and normalize the result to put the decimal point after the first digit:

$$6.92 \times 10^5 \times 7.45 \times 10^3 = (6.92 \times 7.45) \times 10^{(5+3)} = 51.554 \times 10^8 = 5.1554 \times 10^9$$

Division

Divide the significant digits, subtract the exponents, and normalize the result to put the decimal point after the first digit:

$$6.92 \times 10^5 \div 7.45 \times 10^3 = (6.92 \div 7.45) \times 10^{(5-3)} = 0.928859\ldots \times 10^2 = 9.28859\ldots \times 10^1$$

Addition

Denormalize one number so it has the same exponent as the other, add the significant digits, and then normalize the result to put the decimal point after the first digit:

$$6.92 \times 10^5 + 7.45 \times 10^3 = 692 \times 10^3 + 7.45 \times 10^3 = 699.45 \times 10^3 = 6.9945 \times 10^5$$

Subtraction

Denormalize one number so it has the same exponent as the other, subtract the significant digits, and then normalize the result to put the decimal point after the first digit:

$$6.92 \times 10^5 - 7.45 \times 10^3 = 692 \times 10^3 - 7.45 \times 10^3 = 684.55 \times 10^3 = 6.8455 \times 10^5$$

In each case, the final number of significant digits might be more than what are required or recommended, so rounding the result to the correct precision would follow the normalization step.

Multiplier Prefixes

Normal use of prefixes like kilo- refer to human units such as grams or meters. In computing however, these prefixes are powers of 2 instead of powers of 10. As such the value of kilo- when describing the size of a file in bytes *is similar to but slightly different from* kilo- when describing distance in meters or mass in grams.

To eliminate the confusion, there are new prefixes for use with computer memory (kibi- to mean a factor of 1024 instead of kilo- to mean 1000), but these prefixes are not in common use. Most people still use kilobyte instead of kibibyte to indicate 1024 bytes.

Standard Prefix	Power of 10	Standard Value	Power of 1024	Power of 2	Computer Value	New Prefix
kilo-	10^3	1,000	1024^1	2^{10}	1,024	kibi-
mega-	10^6	1,000,000	1024^2	2^{20}	1,048,576	mebi-
giga-	10^9	1,000,000,000	1024^3	2^{30}	1,073,741,824	gibi-
tera-	10^{12}	1,000,000,000,000	1024^4	2^{40}	1,099,511,627,776	tebi-
peta-	10^{15}	1,000,000,000,000,000	1024^5	2^{50}	1,125,899,906,842,624	pebi-
exa-	10^{18}	1,000,000,000,000,000,000	1024^6	2^{60}	1,152,921,504,606,846,976	exbi-

Exponents and Logarithms

A number *a* raised to a power *N*, written as a^N, indicates the number *a* should be multiplied by itself *N* times. The power *N* is called the ***exponent***. For example, 5^3 is the same as $5 \times 5 \times 5 = 125$. Fractional exponents indicate roots: $5^{1/2}$ is the square root of 5, or 2.2360…, $5^{1/3}$ is the cube root of 5, or 1.7099…, and so on. These two forms may be combined: $5^{2/3}$ is the square of the cube root of 5, $(5^{1/3})^2$, or 2.9240…. Negative exponents indicate that the result is inverted: 5^{-3} is the same as $1/(5^3)$ or $1/125 = 0.008$.

The ***logarithm*** in some base *b* of a number *N* gives the power of *b* which would result in *N*. That is, the expression $log_b(N)$ really asks the simple question "what power of *b* gives me *N*?" Powers and logarithms are therefore inverses of one another. For example, $log_2(32) = 5$ because $2^5 = 32$ and vice versa.

Base *b* is usually 10 (common logs), the value $e = 2.7181828…$ (natural logs), or 2 (frequently used in computer science), but it can be any positive value. The term $log_e(N)$ is abbreviated as $ln(N)$, and e^N is abbreviated as $exp(N)$.

For the expression a^N both *a* and *N* may contain fractions, and in such cases logs and antilogs can help compute powers (the term ***antilog*** applied to some argument indicates raising the base used in computing the logarithm to the power of that argument). Thus, when neither *a* nor *N* are integers, the result is computed by $a^N = antilog(N \times log(a))$. For an example using the natural logs (that is, base *e*), this would be computed as $a^N = e^{(N \times ln(a))} = exp(N \times ln(a))$.

Graphs of N², N×log₂(N), N, log₂(N), logₑ(N), and log₁₀(N)

The time that a process runs on a computer is often describable by a polynomial based on the size of the problem. In general, as the problem size increases, the time to solve the problem also increases, but how fast that increase happens is determined by the efficiency of the algorithm.

For example, to look for a particular value in a list of unsorted items requires that every item in the list be examined up to the point that the desired item is found, or through the entire list if the item is not present. This is called a **_linear search_**, and the running time is directly proportional to the number of items in the list. The running time of linear search is described as $O(N)$, meaning that the polynomial is a line. The polynomial might be $3N+5$ or $6N-2$, but the constants don't matter as much as the fact the equation is dominated by N (the multiplier of N determines the slope of the line only; it is still a straight line).

If the list is sorted, the running time of a **_binary search_** will be proportional to the base 2 logarithm of N, described as $O(\log_2(N))$. The time to search grows as N grows, but not as fast as with linear. Binary search works by examining the middle item of the list, discarding the half of the list not containing the desired item, and continuing until either the item is found or the list is exhausted. The process is fast, but will not work unless the list is sorted.

Finally, the best-known common **_sorting algorithms_** run in time proportional to N times the base 2 logarithm of N, described as $O(N \times \log_2(N))$. Bad sorting algorithms run in $O(N^2)$ time. Sorting is expensive, but can be worth it if binary search is used on the result rather than linear search.

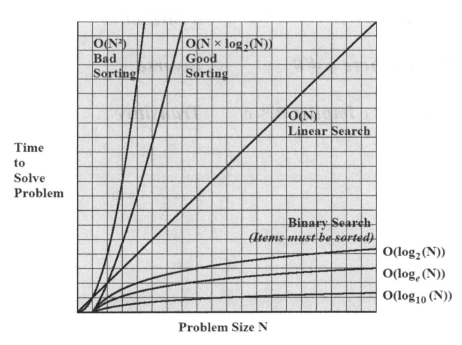

"Big-O" Running Times

Axioms of Arithmetic

$a + 0 = 0 + a = a$	*Identity*
$a \times 1 = 1 \times a = a$	*Identity*
$a \times 0 = 0 \times a = 0$	*Zero element*
$a + b = b + a$	*Commutative*
$a \times b = b \times a$	*Commutative*
$(a + b) + c = a + (b + c)$	*Associative*
$(a \times b) \times c = a \times (b \times c)$	*Associative*
$a \times (b + c) = a \times b \ + \ a \times c$	*Distributive*
$(b + c) \times a = b \times a \ + \ c \times a$	*Distributive*
$a \times \frac{1}{a} = 1$, where $a \neq 0$	*Inverse*
$a < b$ and $b < c$ implies $a < c$	*Transitive*

Powers and Logarithms

$a^0 = 1$ *for any a, including $0^0 = 1$*

$1^N = 1$ *for any N*

$0^N = 0$ *for any N > 0*

$a^N = a \times a^{N-1}$ *N is an integer > 0*

$a^N = antilog_b(N \times log_b(a))$ *N is a real number, a is positive, for any base b*

$a^b \times a^c = a^{(b+c)}$

$a^b \div a^c = a^{(b-c)}$

$a^{-b} = {}^1\!/_{a^b}$ *a^b can't be zero*

$a = log_b(N)$ *means* $b^a = N$ *for any base b and any N > 0*

$log_b(1) = 0$ *for any base b*

$log_b(b^N) = N$ *for any base b, b^N can't be zero*

$b^{log_b(N)} = N$ *for any base b, N can't be zero*

$log_b(M \times N) = log_b(M) + log_b(N)$ *for any base b*

$log_b(M^N) = N \times log_b(M)$ *for any base b*

$log_b(a) = \frac{log_x(a)}{log_x(b)}$ *for any base x*

Common Irrational Numbers

An irrational number is a number that is not a ratio of integers. Some irrational numbers are the solutions to polynomials; others are not. For example, the square root of two is the solution to the equation $x^2 - 2 = 0$. Similarly, the Golden Ratio ϕ is computed as $\frac{(1+\sqrt{5})}{2}$. However, there is no simple polynomial to compute π or e without use of infinite series or continued fractions. For example, one inefficient series to compute π (the Gregory-Leibniz series) is:

$$\pi = 4(\tfrac{1}{1} - \tfrac{1}{3} + \tfrac{1}{5} - \tfrac{1}{7} + \tfrac{1}{9} - \tfrac{1}{11} + \ldots)$$

Here is a table of common irrational numbers to 56 decimal places.

Constant	Value
Square root of 2	1.41421356237309504880168872420969807856967187537694807317... $\frac{99}{70}$ $\frac{140}{99}$ $\frac{239}{169}$ $\frac{577}{408}$ $\frac{1393}{985}$ $\frac{8119}{5741}$ $\frac{47321}{33461}$ $\frac{665857}{470832}$
Square root of 3	1.73205080756887729352744634150587236694280525381038062805... $\frac{97}{56}$ $\frac{265}{153}$ $\frac{1351}{780}$ $\frac{5042}{2911}$ $\frac{13775}{7953}$ $\frac{51409}{29681}$ $\frac{191861}{110771}$ $\frac{1694157}{978122}$
Square root of 5	2.23606797749978969640917366873127623544061835961152572427... $\frac{123}{55}$ $\frac{161}{72}$ $\frac{682}{305}$ $\frac{2889}{1292}$ $\frac{12238}{5473}$ $\frac{51841}{23184}$ $\frac{219602}{98209}$ $\frac{930249}{416020}$
SQRT(2)/2, sin(45°), cos(45°)	0.70710678118654752440084436210484903928483593768847403658... $\frac{70}{99}$ $\frac{169}{239}$ $\frac{985}{1393}$ $\frac{5741}{8119}$ $\frac{19601}{27720}$ $\frac{80782}{114243}$ $\frac{195025}{275807}$ $\frac{665857}{941664}$
SQRT(3)/2, sin(60°), cos(30°)	0.86602540378443864676372317075293618347140262690519031402... $\frac{84}{97}$ $\frac{181}{209}$ $\frac{989}{1142}$ $\frac{2521}{2911}$ $\frac{16296}{18817}$ $\frac{35113}{40545}$ $\frac{226974}{262087}$ $\frac{489061}{564719}$
SQRT(5)/2, $\phi - \tfrac{1}{2}$	1.11803398874989484820458683436563811772030917980576286213... $\frac{123}{110}$ $\frac{161}{144}$ $\frac{341}{305}$ $\frac{1866}{1669}$ $\frac{2889}{2584}$ $\frac{6119}{5473}$ $\frac{109801}{98209}$ $\frac{930249}{832040}$
$\frac{1}{\phi}$, $\phi - 1$	0.61803398874989484820458683436563811772030917980576286213... $\frac{21}{34}$ $\frac{55}{89}$ $\frac{233}{377}$ $\frac{610}{987}$ $\frac{2584}{4181}$ $\frac{10946}{17711}$ $\frac{75025}{121393}$ $\frac{514229}{832040}$
ϕ (Golden Ratio), (SQRT(5)+1)/2	1.61803398874989484820458683436563811772030917980576286213... $\frac{55}{34}$ $\frac{144}{89}$ $\frac{610}{377}$ $\frac{1597}{987}$ $\frac{6765}{4181}$ $\frac{28657}{17711}$ $\frac{196418}{121393}$ $\frac{1346269}{832040}$
ϕ^2, $\phi + 1$	2.61803398874989484820458683436563811772030917980576286213... $\frac{89}{34}$ $\frac{233}{89}$ $\frac{987}{377}$ $\frac{2584}{987}$ $\frac{10946}{4181}$ $\frac{46368}{17711}$ $\frac{317811}{121393}$ $\frac{2178309}{832040}$
e (Euler's Number)	2.71828182845904523536028747135266249775724709369995957496... $\frac{193}{71}$ $\frac{1071}{394}$ $\frac{2721}{1001}$ $\frac{15062}{5541}$ $\frac{23225}{8544}$ $\frac{49171}{18089}$ $\frac{419314}{154257}$ $\frac{1084483}{398959}$
π (Pi)	3.14159265358979323846264338327950288419716939937510582097... $\frac{22}{7}$ $\frac{333}{106}$ $\frac{355}{113}$ $\frac{52163}{16604}$ $\frac{75948}{24175}$ $\frac{103993}{33102}$ $\frac{833719}{265381}$ $\frac{3126535}{995207}$

Rational numbers <u>can</u> be used to approximate an irrational number to any desired degree of precision, but can never hit that value exactly. For example, the value of π can be approximated by $\frac{22}{7}$ (3.142857142857..., within 0.0013 of the correct value) or by $\frac{355}{113}$ (3.141592920353..., within 0.0000003 of the correct value), but neither is the exact value. Under each number in the table is a list of rational approximations, in order of increasing precision.

Rational Approximations to the Square Root of 2

The rational approximations (fractions) shown on the previous page are only a small sample of all possible such approximations. Only eight rational approximations were given for each number; those chosen were either commonly known fractions or made a significant improvement in precision over earlier values. Here is a table showing rational approximations to the square root of 2. For any fraction to be included in the list, it must be "better" than all fractions above it; the error is the absolute value of the difference between the approximation and the true value of the square root of 2 (the test number shown at the bottom of the table).

Numerator	Denominator	Approximation	Error
3	2	1.5000000000000000	0.0857864376269048
4	3	1.3333333333333333	0.0808802290397619
7	5	1.4000000000000000	0.0142135623730952
17	12	1.4166666666666667	0.0024531042935716
24	17	1.4117647058823530	0.0024488564907421
41	29	1.4137931034482758	0.0004204589248193
99	70	1.4142857142857144	0.0000721519126192
140	99	1.4141414141414141	0.0000721482316810
239	169	1.4142011834319526	0.0000123789411426
577	408	1.4142156862745099	0.0000021239014147
816	577	1.4142114384748700	0.0000021238982251
1393	985	1.4142131979695431	0.0000003644035520
3363	2378	1.4142136248948696	0.0000000625217744
4756	3363	1.4142134998513232	0.0000000625217720
8119	5741	1.4142135516460548	0.0000000107270404
19601	13860	1.4142135642135643	0.0000000018404691
47321	33461	1.4142135620573204	0.0000000003157747
66922	47321	1.4142135626888697	0.0000000003157745
114243	80782	1.4142135624272734	0.0000000000541782
275807	195025	1.4142135623637995	0.0000000000092957
390050	275807	1.4142135623823906	0.0000000000092955
665857	470832	1.4142135623746899	0.0000000000015947
Test Number		1.4142135623730951	

Computations with Rational Numbers

A rational number is a ***ratio*** of two integers, commonly expressed as the fraction A/B for some integers A and B. When A and B have a common factor (that is, the greatest common divisor, GCD, is greater than 1), the fraction should be reduced to its lowest form. For example, for the rational number $^{12}/_{15}$ the GCD(12,15) = 3, so the rational number can be reduced to $^{12 \div 3}/_{15 \div 3} = ^4/_5$.

Multiplication

When multiplying rational numbers, simply multiply the numerators together and multiply the denominators together. Reduce the result to its lowest form as needed.

Formula: $\qquad A/B \times C/D = {}^{AC}/_{BD}$

Example: $\qquad ^3/_4 \times ^6/_7 = {}^{18}/_{28}$, because GCD(18,28) = 2, $^{18 \div 2}/_{28 \div 2} = ^9/_{14}$

Division

Division of rational numbers, because one fraction is being divided by another, is the same as multiplying the first rational number by the *inverse* of the second. Reduce the result to its lowest form as needed.

Formula: $\qquad A/B \div C/D = A/B \times D/C = {}^{AD}/_{BC}$

Example: $\qquad ^1/_4 \div ^3/_8 = {}^1/_4 \times ^8/_3 = ^8/_{12}$, because GCD(8,12) = 4, $^{8 \div 4}/_{12 \div 4} = ^2/_3$

Addition and Subtraction

When adding or subtracting rational numbers, the denominators must be the same before the operation can take place. This requires modifying the rational numbers by multiplying each by an appropriate fraction, equal to 1 so as to not change the overall value, that results in the two rational numbers having the same denominator. Reduce the final result to its lowest form as needed.

Addition: $\qquad A/B + C/D = (A/B \times D/D) + (C/D \times B/B) = {}^{AD}/_{BD} + {}^{BC}/_{BD} = {}^{(AD + BC)}/_{BD}$

Subtraction: $\qquad A/B - C/D = (A/B \times D/D) - (C/D \times B/B) = {}^{AD}/_{BD} - {}^{BC}/_{BD} = {}^{(AD - BC)}/_{BD}$

Example: $\qquad ^3/_5 + ^2/_7 = (^3/_5 \times ^7/_7) + (^2/_7 \times ^5/_5) = {}^{21}/_{35} + {}^{10}/_{35} = {}^{(21 + 10)}/_{35} = {}^{31}/_{35}$

Computations with Complex Numbers

A ***complex number*** is a numeric value with a real part and an imaginary part. The imaginary part is denoted by i, which has the property that $i^2 = -1$. The real part is always written first, and then the imaginary part followed by an i (some systems, like Python, use j instead of i). Examples of complex numbers include (2+4i), (3-6i), (-4-7i), etc. A simple number like 12 can be written as (12+0i), but in such cases the imaginary part is usually omitted.

Addition and Subtraction

To add or subtract complex numbers, combine the real parts separately from the imaginary parts.

Addition:	(A+Bi) + (C+Di)	=	(A+C)+(B+D)i
Subtraction:	(A+Bi) – (C+Di)	=	(A–C)+(B–D)i

Example:	(3+4i) + (7+2i)	=	(3+7)+(4+2)i = (10+6i)

Multiplication

Multiplying complex numbers requires that four partial products be computed and the results added. This is equivalent to the "FOIL" (Firsts-Outers-Inners-Lasts) method for polynomials.

Formula:	(A+Bi) × (C+Di) =	(A×C) + (A×Di) + (Bi×C) + (Bi×Di) =
		AC + ADi + BCi + BDi^2 =
		(AC – BD) + (AD + BC)i

Example:	(3+4i) × (2+5i) =	(3×2) + (3×5i) + (4i×2) + (4i×5i) =
		6 + 15i + 8i + 20i^2 =
		(6-20) + (15+8)i = (-14+23i)

Division

Dividing one complex number by another requires that both be multiplied by some special value which turns the denominator into a real number with no complex part, but does not change the answer. This special value is the ***complex conjugate*** of the denominator. The complex conjugate of any number is that number with the sign of its imaginary part reversed.

Formula:	(A+Bi) ÷ (C+Di) =	[(A+Bi)×(C–Di)] ÷ [(C+Di)×(C–Di)] =
		[(A+Bi)×(C–Di)] ÷ [C²+D²]

Example:	(-14+23i) ÷ (3+4i) =	[(-14+23i)×(3–4i)] ÷ [(3+4i)×(3–4i)] =
		[(-14×3)+(-14×–4i)+(23i×3)+(23i×–4i)] ÷
		[(3×3)+(3×–4i)+(4i×3)+(4i×–4i)] =
		[-42 +56i + 69i – 92i^2] ÷ [9 – 12i + 12i – 16i^2] =
		[(-42+92) + (56+69)i] ÷ [9 + 16] =
		[50 + 125i] ÷ [25] = (2+5i)

Converting Between Base 10 and Another Base

The ***digits in any base*** N range from 0 to N-1. For example, in decimal (base 10) digits range from 0…9, and in binary (base 2) digits range from 0…1.

For ***bases greater than decimal*** (base 10), by tradition we use the capital Roman letters:
A=10, B=11, C=12, D=13, E=14, F=15, G=16, H=17, etc.
So, hexadecimal (base 16) uses digits 0…9 and A…F.

To convert a ***decimal integer to another base***, divide the integer by the desired base, save the remainder, and repeat the process on the quotient until it becomes zero. The remainders are the digits in the target base, generated from right-to-left.

To convert a ***decimal fraction to another base***, multiply the fraction by the desired base, save the whole part, and repeat the process on the fraction until it becomes zero (or until enough digits have been generated). The saved digits form the new fraction, left-to-right, in the target base.

To convert a ***number in another base to decimal***, multiply each digit in that base by the power of the base raised to the index of its position (the units place is always at index 0), and add the products together.

To convert ***binary to decimal***, write all the powers of 2 over their appropriate digits, and wherever there is a 1-bit add the corresponding power of 2 to the total (ignore any 0-bits).

Examples:

<u>Convert 97_{10} to base 3</u>
$97 \div 3 = 32$ R **1**
$32 \div 3 = 10$ R **2**
$10 \div 3 = 3$ R **1**
$3 \div 3 = 1$ R **0**
$1 \div 3 = 0$ R **1**
Result $= 10121_3$

<u>Convert 0.3125_{10} to base 2</u>
$.3125 \times 2$ $= \mathbf{0.625}$
$.625 \times 2$ $= \mathbf{1.25}$
$.25 \times 2$ $= \mathbf{0.5}$
$.5 \times 2$ $= \mathbf{1.0}$

Result $= .0101_2$

<u>Convert 102.37_8 to base 10</u>
$1\times8^2 + 0\times8^1 + 2\times8^0 + 3\times8^{-1} + 7\times8^{-2} =$
$1\times64 + 0\times8 + 2\times1 + 3\times\frac{1}{8} + 7\times\frac{1}{64} =$
$64 + 0 + 2 + \frac{3}{8} + \frac{7}{64} =$
$66\frac{31}{64} =$
Result $= 66.484375$

<u>Convert $2BE7_{16}$ to base 10</u>
$2\times16^3 + B\times16^2 + E\times16^1 + 7\times16^0 =$
$2\times4096 + 11\times256 + 14\times16 + 7\times1 =$
$8192 + 2816 + 224 + 7 =$
Result $= 11239_{10}$

<u>Convert 1101.01_2 to decimal</u>

2^3	2^2	2^1	2^0	2^{-1}	2^{-2}	(Powers of 2)
8	4	2	1	½	¼	(Powers of 2, computed)
1	1	0	1	0	1	(Digits of original number)
8 +	4 +		1 +		¼ =	$13\frac{1}{4} = 13.25$

Converting Between Base 2 and Base 2^N

To convert a number in ***base 2 to any base 2^N*** (base 4, base 8, base 16, etc.), group the bits in packets of N bits relative to the decimal point, and then convert each packet separately. If the left-most packet on the integer side of the decimal point contains fewer than N bits, pad it with 0 on the left. If the right-most packet on the fractional side of the decimal point contains fewer than N bits, pad it with 0 on the right. If the result of converting any packet is greater than 9, adjust the digit to use the appropriate capital Roman letter.

Examples: (Padding 0 bits are shown underlined)

Convert	**10101101110010.1001011₂**			**to base 16 (N=4)**		
Partition:	0010	1011	0111	0010	.	1001	0110
Compute:	2	11	7	2	.	9	6
Adjust:	2	B	7	2	.	9	6
Result:	2B72.96₁₆					

Convert 10101101110010.1001011_2 to base 16 (N=4)

Partition: $\underline{00}10$ 1011 0111 0010 . 1001 $011\underline{0}$

Compute: 2 11 7 2 . 9 6

Adjust: 2 B 7 2 . 9 6

Result: $2B72.96_{16}$

Convert 10101101110010.1001011_2 to base 8 (N=3)

Partition: $\underline{0}10$ 101 101 110 010 . 100 101 $1\underline{00}$

Compute: 2 5 5 6 2 . 4 5 4

Result: 25562.454_8

Convert 10101101110010.1001011_2 to base 4 (N=2)

Partition: 10 11 01 11 00 10 . 10 01 01 $1\underline{0}$

Compute: 2 3 1 3 0 2 . 2 1 1 2

Result: 231302.2112_4

To convert a number in ***base 2^N to base 2***, convert each digit of the original number separately into its own binary packet, but pad each packet out to N bits (pad with 0 on the left) as necessary. Extra leading and trailing 0 bits on the final result may be "de-padded" as required.

Examples: (Padding 0 bits are shown underlined)

Convert $2B72.96_{16}$ to base 2 (N=4)

Digits: 10 1011 111 10 . 1001 110

Pad to N: $\underline{00}10$ 1011 $\underline{0}111$ $\underline{00}10$. 1001 $\underline{0}110$

Result: $00101011011100 10.10010110$

De-Pad: 10101101110010.1001011

Convert 25562.454_8 to base 2 (N=3)

Digits: 10 101 101 110 10 . 100 101 100

Pad to N: $\underline{0}10$ 101 101 110 $\underline{0}10$. 100 101 100

Result: $010101101110010.100101100$

De-Pad: 10101101110010.1001011

Base Conversion Table (0 – 44)

Binary	Trinary	Quartic	Octal	Decimal	Hex
Base 2	Base 3	Base 4	Base 8	Base 10	Base 16
0	0	0	0	0	0
1	1	1	1	1	1
10	2	2	2	2	2
11	10	3	3	3	3
100	11	10	4	4	4
101	12	11	5	5	5
110	20	12	6	6	6
111	21	13	7	7	7
1000	22	20	10	8	8
1001	100	21	11	9	9
1010	101	22	12	10	A
1011	102	23	13	11	B
1100	110	30	14	12	C
1101	111	31	15	13	D
1110	112	32	16	14	E
1111	120	33	17	15	F
10000	121	100	20	16	10
10001	122	101	21	17	11
10010	200	102	22	18	12
10011	201	103	23	19	13
10100	202	110	24	20	14
10101	210	111	25	21	15
10110	211	112	26	22	16
10111	212	113	27	23	17
11000	220	120	30	24	18
11001	221	121	31	25	19
11010	222	122	32	26	1A
11011	1000	123	33	27	1B
11100	1001	130	34	28	1C
11101	1002	131	35	29	1D
11110	1010	132	36	30	1E
11111	1011	133	37	31	1F
100000	1012	200	40	32	20
100001	1020	201	41	33	21
100010	1021	202	42	34	22
100011	1022	203	43	35	23
100100	1100	210	44	36	24
100101	1101	211	45	37	25
100110	1102	212	46	38	26
100111	1110	213	47	39	27
101000	1111	220	50	40	28
101001	1112	221	51	41	29
101010	1120	222	52	42	2A
101011	1121	223	53	43	2B
101100	1122	230	54	44	2C

Base Conversion Table (45 – 89)

Binary Base 2	Trinary Base 3	Quartic Base 4	Octal Base 8	Decimal Base 10	Hex Base 16
101101	1200	231	55	45	2D
101110	1201	232	56	46	2E
101111	1202	233	57	47	2F
110000	1210	300	60	48	30
110001	1211	301	61	49	31
110010	1212	302	62	50	32
110011	1220	303	63	51	33
110100	1221	310	64	52	34
110101	1222	311	65	53	35
110110	2000	312	66	54	36
110111	2001	313	67	55	37
111000	2002	320	70	56	38
111001	2010	321	71	57	39
111010	2011	322	72	58	3A
111011	2012	323	73	59	3B
111100	2020	330	74	60	3C
111101	2021	331	75	61	3D
111110	2022	332	76	62	3E
111111	2100	333	77	63	3F
1000000	2101	1000	100	64	40
1000001	2102	1001	101	65	41
1000010	2110	1002	102	66	42
1000011	2111	1003	103	67	43
1000100	2112	1010	104	68	44
1000101	2120	1011	105	69	45
1000110	2121	1012	106	70	46
1000111	2122	1013	107	71	47
1001000	2200	1020	110	72	48
1001001	2201	1021	111	73	49
1001010	2202	1022	112	74	4A
1001011	2210	1023	113	75	4B
1001100	2211	1030	114	76	4C
1001101	2212	1031	115	77	4D
1001110	2220	1032	116	78	4E
1001111	2221	1033	117	79	4F
1010000	2222	1100	120	80	50
1010001	10000	1101	121	81	51
1010010	10001	1102	122	82	52
1010011	10002	1103	123	83	53
1010100	10010	1110	124	84	54
1010101	10011	1111	125	85	55
1010110	10012	1112	126	86	56
1010111	10020	1113	127	87	57
1011000	10021	1120	130	88	58
1011001	10022	1121	131	89	59

Table of Powers of Two ($2^{-10} - 2^{32}$)

N	2^N	2^N in Binary
-10	0.0009765625	0.0000000001
-9	0.001953125	0.0000000010
-8	0.00390625	0.0000000100
-7	0.0078125	0.0000001000
-6	0.015625	0.0000010000
-5	0.03125	0.0000100000
-4	0.0625	0.0001000000
-3	0.125	0.0010000000
-2	0.25	0.0100000000
-1	0.5	0.1000000000
0	1	1.0000000000
1	2	10.0000000000
2	4	100.0000000000
3	8	1000.0000000000
4	16	10000.0000000000
5	32	100000.0000000000
6	64	1000000.0000000000
7	128	10000000.0000000000
8	256	100000000.0000000000
9	512	1000000000.0000000000
10	1,024	10000000000.0000000000
11	2,048	100000000000.0000000000
12	4,096	1000000000000.0000000000
13	8,192	10000000000000.0000000000
14	16,384	100000000000000.0000000000
15	32,768	1000000000000000.0000000000
16	65,536	10000000000000000.0000000000
17	131,072	100000000000000000.0000000000
18	262,144	1000000000000000000.0000000000
19	524,288	10000000000000000000.0000000000
20	1,048,576	100000000000000000000.0000000000
21	2,097,152	1000000000000000000000.0000000000
22	4,194,304	10000000000000000000000.0000000000
23	8,388,608	100000000000000000000000.0000000000
24	16,777,216	1000000000000000000000000.0000000000
25	33,554,432	10000000000000000000000000.0000000000
26	67,108,864	100000000000000000000000000.0000000000
27	134,217,728	1000000000000000000000000000.0000000000
28	268,435,456	10000000000000000000000000000.0000000000
29	536,870,912	100000000000000000000000000000.0000000000
30	1,073,741,824	1000000000000000000000000000000.0000000000
31	2,147,483,648	10000000000000000000000000000000.0000000000
32	4,294,967,296	100000000000000000000000000000000.0000000000

Bits and Bytes

A ***bit*** is the smallest possible unit of information and may be either **0** or **1**, but no other values.

A ***byte*** is a packet of exactly 8 bits, treated as a single object.

The bits in a byte are independent from one another: any bit may be **0** or **1**.

A byte may hold any binary value from **00000000** through **11111111**.

There are $2^8 = 256$ unique values for a byte (for N bits, there are 2^N unique values).

An 8-bit byte may hold any hexadecimal number in the range **00**…**FF**.

An 8-bit byte holds exactly the same amount of information as ***two hexadecimal digits***.

Each 4-bit ***nybble*** in a byte represents exactly one hexadecimal digit.

Treated as ***unsigned numbers***, a byte may hold any decimal number in the range 0…255.

Treated as ***signed numbers***, a byte may hold any decimal number in the range -128…+127.

In signed representations, ***0 is considered to be positive***.

Computer memory is measured in bytes, kilobytes, megabytes, gigabytes, terabytes, petabytes, and exabytes (all powers of 1024; see the earlier table of multiplier prefixes and how the prefix "kilo-" is treated differently when referring to computer memory versus everything else):

1 kilobyte	= 1024 bytes (thousand+)	
1 megabyte	= 1024 kilobytes	= 1,048,576 bytes (million+)
1 gigabyte	= 1024 megabytes	= 1,073,741,824 bytes (billion+)
1 terabyte	= 1024 gigabytes	= 1,099,511,627,776 bytes (trillion+)
1 petabyte	= 1024 terabytes	= 1,125,899,906,842,624 bytes (quadrillion+)
1 exabyte	= 1024 petabytes	= 1,152,921,504,606,846,976 bytes (quintillion+)

Nearly all computers today use integers based on the 8-bit byte, and powers-of-two multiples of 8 bits (that is, 8 bits, 16 bits, 32 bits, and 64 bits). For example, a 64-bit computer can add two 64-bit numbers together in one step *directly in the hardware*. In contrast, a 32-bit computer can add two 64-bit numbers together as well, but to do so requires that it perform two 32-bit additions in its hardware, first on the lower 32 bits of the two numbers and then on the upper 32 bits. Thus, a 32-bit computer is slower than a 64-bit computer running at the same clock speed.

Converting Bytes from Decimal to Hexadecimal

To convert a number represented by a byte from decimal (0...255) into hexadecimal (**00**...**FF**) use the right-most digit of the decimal number as the column index and the other digits as the row index into the table below:

	Right-Most Decimal Digit									
	0	1	2	3	4	5	6	7	8	9
0	00	01	02	03	04	05	06	07	08	09
1	0A	0B	0C	0D	0E	0F	10	11	12	13
2	14	15	16	17	18	19	1A	1B	1C	1D
3	1E	1F	20	21	22	23	24	25	26	27
4	28	29	2A	2B	2C	2D	2E	2F	30	31
5	32	33	34	35	36	37	38	39	3A	3B
6	3C	3D	3E	3F	40	41	42	43	44	45
7	46	47	48	49	4A	4B	4C	4D	4E	4F
8	50	51	52	53	54	55	56	57	58	59
9	5A	5B	5C	5D	5E	5F	60	61	62	63
10	64	65	66	67	68	69	6A	6B	6C	6D
11	6E	6F	70	71	72	73	74	75	76	77
12	78	79	7A	7B	7C	7D	7E	7F	80	81
13	82	83	84	85	86	87	88	89	8A	8B
14	8C	8D	8E	8F	90	91	92	93	94	95
15	96	97	98	99	9A	9B	9C	9D	9E	9F
16	A0	A1	A2	A3	A4	A5	A6	A7	A8	A9
17	AA	AB	AC	AD	AE	AF	B0	B1	B2	B3
18	B4	B5	B6	B7	B8	B9	BA	BB	BC	BD
19	BE	BF	C0	C1	C2	C3	C4	C5	C6	C7
20	C8	C9	CA	CB	CC	CD	CE	CF	D0	D1
21	D2	D3	D4	D5	D6	D7	D8	D9	DA	DB
22	DC	DD	DE	DF	E0	E1	E2	E3	E4	E5
23	E6	E7	E8	E9	EA	EB	EC	ED	EE	EF
24	F0	F1	F2	F3	F4	F5	F6	F7	F8	F9
25	FA	FB	FC	FD	FE	FF				

(Left-Most Decimal Digit(s) labels the rows.)

For example, the hexadecimal value of decimal number 211 is found in row 21 and column 1, or **D3**, and the hexadecimal value of decimal number 93 is found in row 9 and column 3, or **5D**.

Note that the division method presented earlier to convert a decimal number into hexadecimal requires only a <u>single</u> division operation when the number will fit into a byte. For example:

$$211 \div 16 = 13 \text{ R } 3 = \textbf{D3}$$
$$93 \div 16 = 5 \text{ R } 13 = \textbf{5D}$$

Converting Bytes from Hexadecimal to Decimal

To convert a number represented by a byte from hexadecimal (**00**…**FF**) into decimal (0…255) use the right-most digit of the hexadecimal number as the column index and the left digit as the row index into the table below:

		Right-Most Hexadecimal Digit															
		0	**1**	**2**	**3**	**4**	**5**	**6**	**7**	**8**	**9**	**A**	**B**	**C**	**D**	**E**	**F**
	0	0	1	2	3	4	5	6	7	8	9	10	11	12	13	14	15
	1	16	17	18	19	20	21	22	23	24	25	26	27	28	29	30	31
	2	32	33	34	35	36	37	38	39	40	41	42	43	44	45	46	47
	3	48	49	50	51	52	53	54	55	56	57	58	59	60	61	62	63
	4	64	65	66	67	68	69	70	71	72	73	74	75	76	77	78	79
Left-Most Hexadecimal Digit	**5**	80	81	82	83	84	85	86	87	88	89	90	91	92	93	94	95
	6	96	97	98	99	100	101	102	103	104	105	106	107	108	109	110	111
	7	112	113	114	115	116	117	118	119	120	121	122	123	124	125	126	127
	8	128	129	130	131	132	133	134	135	136	137	138	139	140	141	142	143
	9	144	145	146	147	148	149	150	151	152	153	154	155	156	157	158	159
	A	160	161	162	163	164	165	166	167	168	169	170	171	172	173	174	175
	B	176	177	178	179	180	181	182	183	184	185	186	187	188	189	190	191
	C	192	193	194	195	196	197	198	199	200	201	202	203	204	205	206	207
	D	208	209	210	211	212	213	214	215	216	217	218	219	220	221	222	223
	E	224	225	226	227	228	229	230	231	232	233	234	235	236	237	238	239
	F	240	241	242	243	244	245	246	247	248	249	250	251	252	253	254	255

For example, the decimal value of hexadecimal **D3** is found in row D and column 3, or 211, and the decimal value of hexadecimal **5D** is found in row 5 and column D, or 93.

Note that this table is not necessary if you understand the base conversion process. For example:

$$\textbf{D3} = \textbf{D} \times 16^1 + \textbf{3} \times 16^0 = 13 \times 16 + 3 \times 1 = 208 + 3 = 211$$
$$\textbf{5D} = \textbf{5} \times 16^1 + \textbf{D} \times 16^0 = 5 \times 16 + 13 \times 1 = 80 + 13 = 93$$

Table of Logarithms (0.0 – 4.0)

N	Log₂(N)	Ln(N)	Log₃(N)	Log₈(N)	Log₁₀(N)	Log₁₆(N)
0.0	-∞	-∞	-∞	-∞	-∞	-∞
0.1	-3.32192809	-2.30258509	-2.09590327	-1.10730936	-1.00000000	-0.83048202
0.2	-2.32192809	-1.60943791	-1.46497352	-0.77397603	-0.69897000	-0.58048202
0.3	-1.73696559	-1.20397280	-1.09590327	-0.57898853	-0.52287875	-0.43424140
0.4	-1.32192809	-0.91629073	-0.83404377	-0.44064270	-0.39794001	-0.33048202
0.5	-1.00000000	-0.69314718	-0.63092975	-0.33333333	-0.30103000	-0.25000000
0.6	-0.73696559	-0.51082562	-0.46497352	-0.24565520	-0.22184875	-0.18424140
0.7	-0.51457317	-0.35667494	-0.32465953	-0.17152439	-0.15490196	-0.12864329
0.8	-0.32192809	-0.22314355	-0.20311401	-0.10730936	-0.09691001	-0.08048202
0.9	-0.15200309	-0.10536052	-0.09590327	-0.05066770	-0.04575749	-0.03800077
1.0	0.00000000	0.00000000	0.00000000	0.00000000	0.00000000	0.00000000
1.1	0.13750352	0.09531018	0.08675506	0.04583451	0.04139269	0.03437588
1.2	0.26303441	0.18232156	0.16595623	0.08767814	0.07918125	0.06575860
1.3	0.37851162	0.26236426	0.23881425	0.12617054	0.11394335	0.09462791
1.4	0.48542683	0.33647224	0.30627023	0.16180894	0.14612804	0.12135671
1.5	0.58496250	0.40546511	0.36907025	0.19498750	0.17609126	0.14624063
1.6	0.67807191	0.47000363	0.42781574	0.22602397	0.20411998	0.16951798
1.7	0.76553475	0.53062825	0.48299865	0.25517825	0.23044892	0.19138369
1.8	0.84799691	0.58778666	0.53502648	0.28266564	0.25527251	0.21199923
1.9	0.92599942	0.64185389	0.58424058	0.30866647	0.27875360	0.23149985
2.0	1.00000000	0.69314718	0.63092975	0.33333333	0.30103000	0.25000000
2.1	1.07038933	0.74193734	0.67534047	0.35679644	0.32221929	0.26759733
2.2	1.13750352	0.78845736	0.71768482	0.37916784	0.34242268	0.28437588
2.3	1.20163386	0.83290912	0.75814656	0.40054462	0.36172784	0.30040847
2.4	1.26303441	0.87546874	0.79688599	0.42101147	0.38021124	0.31575860
2.5	1.32192809	0.91629073	0.83404377	0.44064270	0.39794001	0.33048202
2.6	1.37851162	0.95551145	0.86974400	0.45950387	0.41497335	0.34462791
2.7	1.43295941	0.99325177	0.90409673	0.47765314	0.43136376	0.35823985
2.8	1.48542683	1.02961942	0.93719998	0.49514228	0.44715803	0.37135671
2.9	1.53605290	1.06471074	0.96914148	0.51201763	0.46239800	0.38401323
3.0	1.58496250	1.09861229	1.00000000	0.52832083	0.47712125	0.39624063
3.1	1.63226822	1.13140211	1.02984658	0.54408941	0.49136169	0.40806705
3.2	1.67807191	1.16315081	1.05874549	0.55935730	0.50514998	0.41951798
3.3	1.72246602	1.19392247	1.08675506	0.57415534	0.51851394	0.43061651
3.4	1.76553475	1.22377543	1.11392840	0.58851158	0.53147892	0.44138369
3.5	1.80735492	1.25276297	1.14031400	0.60245164	0.54406804	0.45183873
3.6	1.84799691	1.28093385	1.16595623	0.61599897	0.55630250	0.46199923
3.7	1.88752527	1.30833282	1.19089585	0.62917509	0.56820172	0.47188132
3.8	1.92599942	1.33500107	1.21517034	0.64199981	0.57978360	0.48149985
3.9	1.96347412	1.36097655	1.23881425	0.65449137	0.59106461	0.49086853
4.0	2.00000000	1.38629436	1.26185951	0.66666667	0.60205999	0.50000000

Table of Logarithms (4.0 – 8.0)

N	Log$_2$(N)	Ln(N)	Log$_3$(N)	Log$_8$(N)	Log$_{10}$(N)	Log$_{16}$(N)
4.0	2.00000000	1.38629436	1.26185951	0.66666667	0.60205999	0.50000000
4.1	2.03562391	1.41098697	1.28433569	0.67854130	0.61278386	0.50890598
4.2	2.07038933	1.43508453	1.30627023	0.69012978	0.62324929	0.51759733
4.3	2.10433666	1.45861502	1.32768861	0.70144555	0.63346846	0.52608416
4.4	2.13750352	1.48160454	1.34861457	0.71250117	0.64345268	0.53437588
4.5	2.16992500	1.50407740	1.36907025	0.72330833	0.65321251	0.54248125
4.6	2.20163386	1.52605630	1.38907631	0.73387795	0.66275783	0.55040847
4.7	2.23266076	1.54756251	1.40865210	0.74422025	0.67209786	0.55816519
4.8	2.26303441	1.56861592	1.42781574	0.75434480	0.68124124	0.56575860
4.9	2.29278175	1.58923521	1.44658422	0.76426058	0.69019608	0.57319544
5.0	2.32192809	1.60943791	1.46497352	0.77397603	0.69897000	0.58048202
5.1	2.35049725	1.62924054	1.48299865	0.78349908	0.70757018	0.58762431
5.2	2.37851162	1.64865863	1.50067375	0.79283721	0.71600334	0.59462791
5.3	2.40599236	1.66770682	1.51801217	0.80199745	0.72427587	0.60149809
5.4	2.43295941	1.68639895	1.53502648	0.81098647	0.73239376	0.60823985
5.5	2.45943162	1.70474809	1.55172859	0.81981054	0.74036269	0.61485790
5.6	2.48542683	1.72276660	1.56812974	0.82847561	0.74818803	0.62135671
5.7	2.51096192	1.74046617	1.58424058	0.83698731	0.75587486	0.62774048
5.8	2.53605290	1.75785792	1.60007123	0.84535097	0.76342799	0.63401323
5.9	2.56071495	1.77495235	1.61563126	0.85357165	0.77085201	0.64017874
6.0	2.58496250	1.79175947	1.63092975	0.86165417	0.77815125	0.64624063
6.1	2.60880924	1.80828877	1.64597537	0.86960308	0.78532984	0.65220231
6.2	2.63226822	1.82454929	1.66077634	0.87742274	0.79239169	0.65806705
6.3	2.65535183	1.84054963	1.67534047	0.88511728	0.79934055	0.66383796
6.4	2.67807191	1.85629799	1.68967525	0.89269064	0.80617997	0.66951798
6.5	2.70043972	1.87180218	1.70378777	0.90014657	0.81291336	0.67510993
6.6	2.72246602	1.88706965	1.71768482	0.90748867	0.81954394	0.68061651
6.7	2.74416110	1.90210753	1.73137288	0.91472037	0.82607480	0.68604027
6.8	2.76553475	1.91692261	1.74485816	0.92184492	0.83250891	0.69138369
6.9	2.78659636	1.93152141	1.75814656	0.92886545	0.83884909	0.69664909
7.0	2.80735492	1.94591015	1.77124375	0.93578497	0.84509804	0.70183873
7.1	2.82781902	1.96009478	1.78415516	0.94260634	0.85125835	0.70695476
7.2	2.84799691	1.97408103	1.79688599	0.94933230	0.85733250	0.71199923
7.3	2.86789646	1.98787435	1.80944121	0.95596549	0.86332286	0.71697412
7.4	2.88752527	2.00148000	1.82182561	0.96250842	0.86923172	0.72188132
7.5	2.90689060	2.01490302	1.83404377	0.96896353	0.87506126	0.72672265
7.6	2.92599942	2.02814825	1.84610009	0.97533314	0.88081359	0.73149985
7.7	2.94485845	2.04122033	1.85799881	0.98161948	0.88649073	0.73621461
7.8	2.96347412	2.05412373	1.86974400	0.98782471	0.89209460	0.74086853
7.9	2.98185265	2.06686276	1.88133956	0.99395088	0.89762709	0.74546316
8.0	3.00000000	2.07944154	1.89278926	1.00000000	0.90308999	0.75000000

Table of Logarithms (8.0 – 12.0)

N	Log₂(N)	Ln(N)	Log₃(N)	Log₈(N)	Log₁₀(N)	Log₁₆(N)
8.0	3.00000000	2.07944154	1.89278926	1.00000000	0.90308999	0.75000000
8.1	3.01792191	2.09186406	1.90409673	1.00597397	0.90848502	0.75448048
8.2	3.03562391	2.10413415	1.91526545	1.01187464	0.91381385	0.75890598
8.3	3.05311134	2.11625551	1.92629878	1.01770378	0.91907809	0.76327783
8.4	3.07038933	2.12823171	1.93719998	1.02346311	0.92427929	0.76759733
8.5	3.08746284	2.14006616	1.94797217	1.02915428	0.92941893	0.77186571
8.6	3.10433666	2.15176220	1.95861836	1.03477889	0.93449845	0.77608416
8.7	3.12101540	2.16332303	1.96914148	1.04033847	0.93951925	0.78025385
8.8	3.13750352	2.17475172	1.97954433	1.04583451	0.94448267	0.78437588
8.9	3.15380534	2.18605128	1.98982962	1.05126845	0.94939001	0.78845133
9.0	3.16992500	2.19722458	2.00000000	1.05664167	0.95424251	0.79248125
9.1	3.18586655	2.20827441	2.01005799	1.06195552	0.95904139	0.79646664
9.2	3.20163386	2.21920348	2.02000606	1.06721129	0.96378783	0.80040847
9.3	3.21723072	2.23001440	2.02984658	1.07241024	0.96848295	0.80430768
9.4	3.23266076	2.24070969	2.03958185	1.07755359	0.97312785	0.80816519
9.5	3.24792751	2.25129180	2.04921411	1.08264250	0.97772361	0.81198188
9.6	3.26303441	2.26176310	2.05874549	1.08767814	0.98227123	0.81575860
9.7	3.27798475	2.27212589	2.06817811	1.09266158	0.98677173	0.81949619
9.8	3.29278175	2.28238239	2.07751398	1.09759392	0.99122608	0.82319544
9.9	3.30742853	2.29253476	2.08675506	1.10247618	0.99563519	0.82685713
10.0	3.32192809	2.30258509	2.09590327	1.10730936	1.00000000	0.83048202
10.1	3.33628339	2.31253542	2.10496046	1.11209446	1.00432137	0.83407085
10.2	3.35049725	2.32238772	2.11392840	1.11683242	1.00860017	0.83762431
10.3	3.36457243	2.33214390	2.12280886	1.12152414	1.01283722	0.84114311
10.4	3.37851162	2.34180581	2.13160351	1.12617054	1.01703334	0.84462791
10.5	3.39231742	2.35137526	2.14031400	1.13077247	1.02118930	0.84807936
10.6	3.40599236	2.36085400	2.14894192	1.13533079	1.02530587	0.85149809
10.7	3.41953889	2.37024374	2.15748883	1.13984630	1.02938378	0.85488472
10.8	3.43295941	2.37954613	2.16595623	1.14431980	1.03342376	0.85823985
10.9	3.44625623	2.38876279	2.17434559	1.14875208	1.03742650	0.86156406
11.0	3.45943162	2.39789527	2.18265834	1.15314387	1.04139269	0.86485790
11.1	3.47248777	2.40694511	2.19089585	1.15749592	1.04532298	0.86812194
11.2	3.48542683	2.41591378	2.19905949	1.16180894	1.04921802	0.87135671
11.3	3.49825087	2.42480273	2.20715056	1.16608362	1.05307844	0.87456272
11.4	3.51096192	2.43361336	2.21517034	1.17032064	1.05690485	0.87774048
11.5	3.52356196	2.44234704	2.22312008	1.17452065	1.06069784	0.88089049
11.6	3.53605290	2.45100510	2.23100098	1.17868430	1.06445799	0.88401323
11.7	3.54843662	2.45958884	2.23881425	1.18281221	1.06818586	0.88710916
11.8	3.56071495	2.46809953	2.24656101	1.18690498	1.07188201	0.89017874
11.9	3.57288967	2.47653840	2.25424240	1.19096322	1.07554696	0.89322242
12.0	3.58496250	2.48490665	2.26185951	1.19498750	1.07918125	0.89624063

Table of Logarithms (12.0 – 16.0)

N	Log₂(N)	Ln(N)	Log₃(N)	Log₈(N)	Log₁₀(N)	Log₁₆(N)
12.0	3.58496250	2.48490665	2.26185951	1.19498750	1.07918125	0.89624063
12.1	3.59693514	2.49320545	2.26941340	1.19897838	1.08278537	0.89923379
12.2	3.60880924	2.50143595	2.27690513	1.20293641	1.08635983	0.90220231
12.3	3.62058641	2.50959926	2.28433569	1.20686214	1.08990511	0.90514660
12.4	3.63226822	2.51769647	2.29170609	1.21075607	1.09342169	0.90806705
12.5	3.64385619	2.52572864	2.29901729	1.21461873	1.09691001	0.91096405
12.6	3.65535183	2.53369681	2.30627023	1.21845061	1.10037055	0.91383796
12.7	3.66675659	2.54160199	2.31346583	1.22225220	1.10380372	0.91668915
12.8	3.67807191	2.54944517	2.32060500	1.22602397	1.10720997	0.91951798
12.9	3.68929916	2.55722731	2.32768861	1.22976639	1.11058971	0.92232479
13.0	3.70043972	2.56494936	2.33471752	1.23347991	1.11394335	0.92510993
13.1	3.71149491	2.57261223	2.34169257	1.23716497	1.11727130	0.92787373
13.2	3.72246602	2.58021683	2.34861457	1.24082201	1.12057393	0.93061651
13.3	3.73335434	2.58776404	2.35548433	1.24445145	1.12385164	0.93333859
13.4	3.74416110	2.59525471	2.36230264	1.24805370	1.12710480	0.93604027
13.5	3.75488750	2.60268969	2.36907025	1.25162917	1.13033377	0.93872188
13.6	3.76553475	2.61006979	2.37578791	1.25517825	1.13353891	0.94138369
13.7	3.77610399	2.61739583	2.38245636	1.25870133	1.13672057	0.94402600
13.8	3.78659636	2.62466859	2.38907631	1.26219879	1.13987909	0.94664909
13.9	3.79701298	2.63188884	2.39564846	1.26567099	1.14301480	0.94925324
14.0	3.80735492	2.63905733	2.40217350	1.26911831	1.14612804	0.95183873
14.1	3.81762326	2.64617480	2.40865210	1.27254109	1.14921911	0.95440581
14.2	3.82781902	2.65324196	2.41508491	1.27593967	1.15228834	0.95695476
14.3	3.83794324	2.66025954	2.42147258	1.27931441	1.15533604	0.95948581
14.4	3.84799691	2.66722821	2.42781574	1.28266564	1.15836249	0.96199923
14.5	3.85798100	2.67414865	2.43411500	1.28599367	1.16136800	0.96449525
14.6	3.86789646	2.68102153	2.44037096	1.28929882	1.16435286	0.96697412
14.7	3.87774425	2.68784749	2.44658422	1.29258142	1.16731733	0.96943606
14.8	3.88752527	2.69462718	2.45275536	1.29584176	1.17026172	0.97188132
14.9	3.89724043	2.70136121	2.45888494	1.29908014	1.17318627	0.97431011
15.0	3.90689060	2.70805020	2.46497352	1.30229687	1.17609126	0.97672265
15.1	3.91647664	2.71469474	2.47102164	1.30549221	1.17897695	0.97911916
15.2	3.92599942	2.72129543	2.47702985	1.30866647	1.18184359	0.98149985
15.3	3.93545975	2.72785283	2.48299865	1.31181992	1.18469143	0.98386494
15.4	3.94485845	2.73436751	2.48892857	1.31495282	1.18752072	0.98621461
15.5	3.95419631	2.74084002	2.49482010	1.31806544	1.19033170	0.98854908
15.6	3.96347412	2.74727091	2.50067375	1.32115804	1.19312460	0.99086853
15.7	3.97269265	2.75366071	2.50649000	1.32423088	1.19589965	0.99317316
15.8	3.98185265	2.76000994	2.51226931	1.32728422	1.19865709	0.99546316
15.9	3.99095486	2.76631911	2.51801217	1.33031829	1.20139712	0.99773872
16.0	4.00000000	2.77258872	2.52371901	1.33333333	1.20411998	1.00000000

Basic Trigonometry

The Unit Circle

In a circle of radius 1 (the unit circle), and a line at angle θ, the sine and cosine of the angle are defined as shown below:

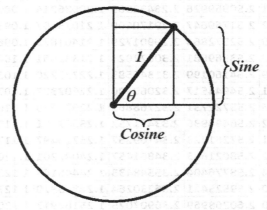

A *__sine wave__* shows the change in the value of the sine as the angle changes from 0° (0 radians) to 360° (2π radians). The following diagram shows a sine wave covering three full cycles:

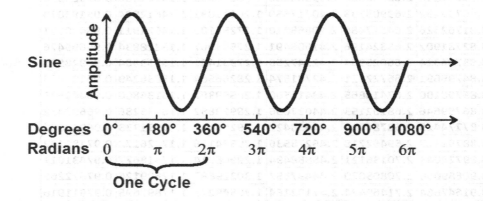

A cosine wave has the same shape as a sine wave, but is shifted out-of-phase by 90° ($\frac{\pi}{2}$ radians):

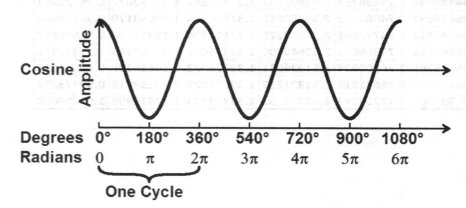

Basic Trigonometric Identities

$\sin^2 \theta + \cos^2 \theta = 1$

$\tan \theta = \sin \theta / \cos \theta$	$\sec \theta = 1 / \cos \theta$
$\cot \theta = \cos \theta / \sin \theta$	$\csc \theta = 1 / \sin \theta$

$\sin (\alpha + \beta) = \sin \alpha \cos \beta + \cos \alpha \sin \beta$	$\sin (\alpha - \beta) = \sin \alpha \cos \beta - \cos \alpha \sin \beta$
$\cos (\alpha + \beta) = \cos \alpha \cos \beta - \sin \alpha \sin \beta$	$\cos (\alpha - \beta) = \cos \alpha \cos \beta + \sin \alpha \sin \beta$

$\sin (^\pi/_2 - \theta) = +\cos \theta$	$\sin (\pi - \theta) = +\sin \theta$	$\sin (-\theta) = -\sin \theta$
$\cos (^\pi/_2 - \theta) = +\sin \theta$	$\cos (\pi - \theta) = -\cos \theta$	$\cos (-\theta) = +\cos \theta$
$\sin (^\pi/_2 + \theta) = +\cos \theta$	$\sin (\pi + \theta) = -\sin \theta$	$\sin (2\pi + \theta) = +\sin \theta$
$\cos (^\pi/_2 + \theta) = -\sin \theta$	$\cos (\pi + \theta) = -\cos \theta$	$\cos (2\pi + \theta) = +\cos \theta$

$$\sin x = \frac{x^1}{1!} - \frac{x^3}{3!} + \frac{x^5}{5!} - \frac{x^7}{7!} + \frac{x^9}{9!} - \frac{x^{11}}{11!} + \dots$$

$$\cos x = \frac{x^0}{0!} - \frac{x^2}{2!} + \frac{x^4}{4!} - \frac{x^6}{6!} + \frac{x^8}{8!} - \frac{x^{10}}{10!} + \dots$$

Sines Defined by Radicals

Degrees	Angle	Sine	Sine by Radicals (Excel Formula)
0°	0	0.000000000000000	0
3°	π/60	0.052335956242944	=((SQRT(6)+SQRT(2))*(SQRT(5)-1)-2*(SQRT(3)-1)*SQRT(5+SQRT(5)))/16
6°	π/30	0.104528463267653	=(SQRT(30-6*SQRT(5))-SQRT(5)-1)/8
9°	π/20	0.156434465040231	=(SQRT(10)+SQRT(2)-2*SQRT(5-SQRT(5)))/8
12°	π/15	0.207911690817759	=(SQRT(10+2*SQRT(5))-SQRT(15)+SQRT(3))/8
15°	π/12	0.258819045102521	=(SQRT(6)-SQRT(2))/4
18°	π/10	0.309016994374947	=(SQRT(5)-1)/4
21°	7π/60	0.358367949545300	=(2*(SQRT(3)+1)*SQRT(5-SQRT(5))-(SQRT(6)-SQRT(2))*(SQRT(5)+1))/16
24°	2π/15	0.406736643075800	=(SQRT(15)+SQRT(3)-SQRT(10-2*SQRT(5)))/8
27°	3π/20	0.453990499739547	=(2*SQRT(5+SQRT(5))-SQRT(10)+SQRT(2))/8
30°	π/6	0.500000000000000	=1/2
33°	11π/60	0.544639035015027	=((SQRT(6)+SQRT(2))*(SQRT(5)-1)+2*(SQRT(3)-1)*SQRT(5+SQRT(5)))/16
36°	π/5	0.587785252292473	=SQRT(10-2*SQRT(5))/4
39°	13π/60	0.629320391049837	=((SQRT(6)+SQRT(2))*(SQRT(5)+1)-2*(SQRT(3)-1)*SQRT(5-SQRT(5)))/16
42°	7π/30	0.669130606358858	=(SQRT(30+6*SQRT(5))-SQRT(5)+1)/8
45°	π/4	0.707106781186547	=SQRT(2)/2
48°	4π/15	0.743144825477394	=(SQRT(10+2*SQRT(5))+SQRT(15)-SQRT(3))/8
51°	17π/60	0.777145961456971	=(2*(SQRT(3)+1)*SQRT(5-SQRT(5))+(SQRT(6)-SQRT(2))*(SQRT(5)+1))/16
54°	3π/10	0.809016994374947	=(SQRT(5)+1)/4
57°	19π/60	0.838670567945424	=(2*(SQRT(3)+1)*SQRT(5+SQRT(5))-(SQRT(6)-SQRT(2))*(SQRT(5)-1))/16
60°	π/3	0.866025403784439	=SQRT(3)/2
63°	7π/20	0.891006524188368	=(2*SQRT(5+SQRT(5))+SQRT(10)-SQRT(2))/8
66°	11π/30	0.913545457642601	=(SQRT(30-6*SQRT(5))+SQRT(5)+1)/8
69°	23π/60	0.933580426497202	=((SQRT(6)+SQRT(2))*(SQRT(5)+1)+2*(SQRT(3)-1)*SQRT(5-SQRT(5)))/16
72°	2π/5	0.951056516295154	=SQRT(10+2*SQRT(5))/4
75°	5π/12	0.965925826289068	=(SQRT(6)+SQRT(2))/4
78°	13π/30	0.978147600733806	=(SQRT(30+6*SQRT(5))+SQRT(5)-1)/8
81°	9π/20	0.987688340595138	=(SQRT(10)+SQRT(2)+2*SQRT(5-SQRT(5)))/8
84°	7π/15	0.994521895368273	=(SQRT(15)+SQRT(3)+SQRT(10-2*SQRT(5)))/8
87°	29π/60	0.998629534754574	=(2*(SQRT(3)+1)*SQRT(5+SQRT(5))+(SQRT(6)-SQRT(2))*(SQRT(5)-1))/16
90°	π/2	1.000000000000000	1

Many people know a few special values for sine and cosine, such as $sin(0°) = cos(90°) = 0$, $sin(90°) = cos(0°) = 1$, $sin(30°) = cos(60°) = ½$, or even that $sin(60°) = cos(30°) = ½\sqrt{3}$ and $sin(45°) = cos(45°) = ½\sqrt{2}$. (See the table on the right-hand page.)

However, all sines and cosines of whole angles which are multiples of three have similar solutions, involving nothing more than integer constants and arithmetic, and radicals (square roots). The table presented here contains all angles between 0° and 90° which are multiples of 3°, and the sine of each angle expressed as an Excel spreadsheet formula. These results can be generated by using the formulae for adding and subtracting sines and cosines (from the previous page) on known values. For example, if sine and cosine are known for both 60° and for 45°, then $sin(15°) = sin(60°-45°) = sin(60°)×cos(45°) - cos(60°)×sin(45°) = (½\sqrt{3})(½\sqrt{2}) - (½)(½\sqrt{2}) = ¼\sqrt{6} - ¼\sqrt{2} = ¼(\sqrt{6}-\sqrt{2})$, which is the value in the table for $sin(15°)$.

Sines and Cosines of Common Angles

Degrees	Angle	Sine	Cosine	Sine	Cosine
0°	0	0	1	0.00000000000000	1.00000000000000
30°	π/6	½	½√3	0.50000000000000	0.86602540378444
45°	π/4	½√2	½√2	0.70710678118655	0.70710678118655
60°	π/3	½√3	½	0.86602540378444	0.50000000000000
90°	π/2	1	0	1.00000000000000	0.00000000000000
120°	2π/3	½√3	-½	0.86602540378444	-0.50000000000000
135°	3π/4	½√2	-½√2	0.70710678118655	-0.70710678118655
150°	5π/6	½	-½√3	0.50000000000000	-0.86602540378444
180°	π	0	-1	0.00000000000000	-1.00000000000000
210°	7π/6	-½	-½√3	-0.50000000000000	-0.86602540378444
225°	5π/4	-½√2	-½√2	-0.70710678118655	-0.70710678118655
240°	4π/3	-½√3	-½	-0.86602540378444	-0.50000000000000
270°	3π/2	-1	0	-1.00000000000000	0.00000000000000
300°	5π/3	-½√3	½	-0.86602540378444	0.50000000000000
315°	7π/4	-½√2	½√2	-0.70710678118655	0.70710678118655
330°	11π/6	-½	½√3	-0.50000000000000	0.86602540378444
360°	2π	0	1	0.00000000000000	1.00000000000000

This table shows both the sine and the cosine, in both radical form and decimal form, for common angles. The radical forms shown here are the values most often memorized by people studying trigonometry.

Sines, Cosines, Tangents 0°-45°

Degrees	Angle	Radians	Sine	Cosine	Tangent
0°	0	0.00000000000000	0.00000000000000	1.00000000000000	0.00000000000000
1°	π/180	0.01745329251994	0.01745240643728	0.99984769515639	0.01745506492822
2°	π/90	0.03490658503989	0.03489949670250	0.99939082701910	0.03492076949175
3°	π/60	0.05235987755983	0.05233595624294	0.99862953475457	0.05240777928304
4°	π/45	0.06981317007977	0.06975647374413	0.99756405025982	0.06992681194351
5°	π/36	0.08726646259972	0.08715574274766	0.99619469809175	0.08748866352592
6°	π/30	0.10471975511966	0.10452846326765	0.99452189536827	0.10510423526568
7°	7π/180	0.12217304763960	0.12186934340515	0.99254615164132	0.12278456090291
8°	2π/45	0.13962634015955	0.13917310096007	0.99026806874157	0.14054083470239
9°	π/20	0.15707963267949	0.15643446504023	0.98768834059514	0.15838444032454
10°	π/18	0.17453292519943	0.17364817766693	0.98480775301221	0.17632698070847
11°	11π/180	0.19198621771938	0.19080899537655	0.98162718344766	0.19438030913772
12°	π/15	0.20943951023932	0.20791169081776	0.97814760073381	0.21255656167002
13°	13π/180	0.22689280275926	0.22495105434387	0.97437006478524	0.23086819112556
14°	7π/90	0.24434609527921	0.24192189559967	0.97029572627600	0.24932800284318
15°	π/12	0.26179938779915	0.25881904510252	0.96592582628907	0.26794919243112
16°	4π/45	0.27925268031909	0.27563735581700	0.96126169593832	0.28674538575881
17°	17π/180	0.29670597283904	0.29237170472274	0.95630475596304	0.30573068145866
18°	π/10	0.31415926535898	0.30901699437495	0.95105651629515	0.32491969623291
19°	19π/180	0.33161255787892	0.32556815445716	0.94551857559932	0.34432761328967
20°	π/9	0.34906585039887	0.34202014332567	0.93969262078591	0.36397023426620
21°	7π/60	0.36651914291881	0.35836794954530	0.93358042649720	0.38386403503542
22°	11π/90	0.38397243543875	0.37460659341591	0.92718385456679	0.40402622583516
23°	23π/180	0.40142572795870	0.39073112848927	0.92050485345244	0.42447481620961
24°	2π/15	0.41887902047864	0.40673664307580	0.91354545764260	0.44522868530854
25°	5π/36	0.43633231299858	0.42261826174070	0.90630778703665	0.46630765815500
26°	13π/90	0.45378560551853	0.43837114678908	0.89879404629917	0.48773258856586
27°	3π/20	0.47123889803847	0.45399049973955	0.89100652418837	0.50952544949443
28°	7π/45	0.48869219055841	0.46947156278589	0.88294759285893	0.53170943166148
29°	29π/180	0.50614548307836	0.48480962024634	0.87461970713940	0.55430905145277
30°	π/6	0.52359877559830	0.50000000000000	0.86602540378444	0.57735026918963
31°	31π/180	0.54105206811824	0.51503807491005	0.85716730070211	0.60086061902756
32°	8π/45	0.55850536063819	0.52991926423321	0.84804809615643	0.62486935190933
33°	11π/60	0.57595865315813	0.54463903501503	0.83867056794542	0.64940759319751
34°	17π/90	0.59341194567807	0.55919290347075	0.82903757255504	0.67450851684243
35°	7π/36	0.61086523819802	0.57357643635105	0.81915204428899	0.70020753820971
36°	π/5	0.62831853071796	0.58778525229247	0.80901699437495	0.72654252800536
37°	37π/180	0.64577182323790	0.60181502315205	0.79863551004729	0.75355405010279
38°	19π/90	0.66322511575785	0.61566147532566	0.78801075360672	0.78128562650672
39°	13π/60	0.68067840827779	0.62932039104984	0.77714596145697	0.80978403319501
40°	2π/9	0.69813170079773	0.64278760968654	0.76604444311898	0.83909963117728
41°	41π/180	0.71558499331768	0.65605902899051	0.75470958022277	0.86928673781623
42°	7π/30	0.73303828583762	0.66913060635886	0.74314482547739	0.90040404429784
43°	43π/180	0.75049157835756	0.68199836006250	0.73135370161917	0.93251508613766
44°	11π/45	0.76794487087751	0.69465837045900	0.71933980033865	0.96568877480707
45°	π/4	0.78539816339745	0.70710678118655	0.70710678118655	1.00000000000000

Sines, Cosines, Tangents 45°-90°

Degrees	Angle	Radians	Sine	Cosine	Tangent
45°	π/4	0.78539816339745	0.70710678118655	0.70710678118655	1.00000000000000
46°	23π/90	0.80285145591739	0.71933980033865	0.69465837045900	1.03553031379057
47°	47π/180	0.82030474843734	0.73135370161917	0.68199836006250	1.07236871002468
48°	4π/15	0.83775804095728	0.74314482547739	0.66913060635886	1.11061251482919
49°	49π/180	0.85521133347722	0.75470958022277	0.65605902899051	1.15036840722101
50°	5π/18	0.87266462599717	0.76604444311898	0.64278760968654	1.19175359259421
51°	17π/60	0.89011791851711	0.77714596145697	0.62932039104984	1.23489715653505
52°	13π/45	0.90757121103705	0.78801075360672	0.61566147532566	1.27994163219308
53°	53π/180	0.92502450355700	0.79863551004729	0.60181502315205	1.32704482162041
54°	3π/10	0.94247779607694	0.80901699437495	0.58778525229247	1.37638192047117
55°	11π/36	0.95993108859688	0.81915204428899	0.57357643635105	1.42814800674211
56°	14π/45	0.97738438111683	0.82903757255504	0.55919290347075	1.48256096851274
57°	19π/60	0.99483767363677	0.83867056794542	0.54463903501503	1.53986496381458
58°	29π/90	1.01229096615671	0.84804809615643	0.52991926423321	1.60033452904105
59°	59π/180	1.02974425867665	0.85716730070211	0.51503807491005	1.66427948235052
60°	π/3	1.04719755119660	0.86602540378444	0.50000000000000	1.73205080756888
61°	61π/180	1.06465084371654	0.87461970713940	0.48480962024634	1.80404775527142
62°	31π/90	1.08210413623648	0.88294759285893	0.46947156278589	1.88072646534633
63°	7π/20	1.09955742875643	0.89100652418837	0.45399049973955	1.96261050550515
64°	16π/45	1.11701072127637	0.89879404629917	0.43837114678908	2.05030384157930
65°	13π/36	1.13446401379631	0.90630778703665	0.42261826174070	2.14450692050956
66°	11π/30	1.15191730631626	0.91354545764260	0.40673664307580	2.24603677390422
67°	67π/180	1.16937059883620	0.92050485345244	0.39073112848927	2.35585236582375
68°	17π/45	1.18682389135614	0.92718385456679	0.37460659341591	2.47508685341629
69°	23π/60	1.20427718387609	0.93358042649720	0.35836794954530	2.60508906469380
70°	7π/18	1.22173047639603	0.93969262078591	0.34202014332567	2.74747741945462
71°	71π/180	1.23918376891597	0.94551857559932	0.32556815445716	2.90421087767582
72°	2π/5	1.25663706143592	0.95105651629515	0.30901699437495	3.07768353717525
73°	73π/180	1.27409035395586	0.95630475596304	0.29237170472274	3.27085261848414
74°	37π/90	1.29154364647580	0.96126169593832	0.27563735581700	3.48741444384091
75°	5π/12	1.30899693899575	0.96592582628907	0.25881904510252	3.73205080756888
76°	19π/45	1.32645023151569	0.97029572627600	0.24192189559967	4.01078093353585
77°	77π/180	1.34390352403563	0.97437006478524	0.22495105434387	4.33147587428415
78°	13π/30	1.36135681655558	0.97814760073381	0.20791169081776	4.70463010947846
79°	79π/180	1.37881010907552	0.98162718344766	0.19080899537655	5.14455401597031
80°	4π/9	1.39626340159546	0.98480775301221	0.17364817766693	5.67128181961771
81°	9π/20	1.41371669411541	0.98768834059514	0.15643446504023	6.31375151467504
82°	41π/90	1.43116998663535	0.99026806874157	0.13917310096007	7.11536972238421
83°	83π/180	1.44862327915529	0.99254615164132	0.12186934340515	8.14434642797459
84°	7π/15	1.46607657167524	0.99452189536827	0.10452846326765	9.51436445422259
85°	17π/36	1.48352986419518	0.99619469809175	0.08715574274766	11.43005230276130
86°	43π/90	1.50098315671512	0.99756405025982	0.06975647374413	14.30066625671190
87°	29π/60	1.51843644923507	0.99862953475457	0.05233595624294	19.08113668772820
88°	22π/45	1.53588974175501	0.99939082701910	0.03489949670250	28.63625328291550
89°	89π/180	1.55334303427495	0.99984769515639	0.01745240643728	57.28996163075910
90°	π/2	1.57079632679490	1.00000000000000	0.00000000000000	+INFINITY

Sines, Cosines, Tangents 90°-135°

Degrees	Angle	Radians	Sine	Cosine	Tangent
90°	π/2	1.57079632679490	1.00000000000000	0.00000000000000	-INFINITY
91°	91π/180	1.58824961931484	0.99984769515639	-0.01745240643728	-57.28996163075950
92°	23π/45	1.60570291183478	0.99939082701910	-0.03489949670250	-28.63625328291580
93°	31π/60	1.62315620435473	0.99862953475457	-0.05233595624294	-19.08113668772820
94°	47π/90	1.64060949687467	0.99756405025982	-0.06975647374413	-14.30066625671190
95°	19π/36	1.65806278939461	0.99619469809175	-0.08715574274766	-11.43005230276130
96°	8π/15	1.67551608191456	0.99452189536827	-0.10452846326765	-9.51436445422260
97°	97π/180	1.69296937443450	0.99254615164132	-0.12186934340515	-8.14434642797460
98°	49π/90	1.71042266695444	0.99026806874157	-0.13917310096007	-7.11536972238422
99°	11π/20	1.72787595947439	0.98768834059514	-0.15643446504023	-6.31375151467504
100°	5π/9	1.74532925199433	0.98480775301221	-0.17364817766693	-5.67128181961771
101°	101π/180	1.76278254451427	0.98162718344766	-0.19080899537655	-5.14455401597031
102°	17π/30	1.78023583703422	0.97814760073381	-0.20791169081776	-4.70463010947846
103°	103π/180	1.79768912955416	0.97437006478524	-0.22495105434387	-4.33147587428416
104°	26π/45	1.81514242207410	0.97029572627600	-0.24192189559967	-4.01078093353585
105°	7π/12	1.83259571459405	0.96592582628907	-0.25881904510252	-3.73205080756888
106°	53π/90	1.85004900711399	0.96126169593832	-0.27563735581700	-3.48741444384091
107°	107π/180	1.86750229963393	0.95630475596304	-0.29237170472274	-3.27085261848414
108°	3π/5	1.88495559215388	0.95105651629515	-0.30901699437495	-3.07768353717525
109°	109π/180	1.90240888467382	0.94551857559932	-0.32556815445716	-2.90421087767583
110°	11π/18	1.91986217719376	0.93969262078591	-0.34202014332567	-2.74747741945462
111°	37π/60	1.93731546971371	0.93358042649720	-0.35836794954530	-2.60508906469380
112°	28π/45	1.95476876223365	0.92718385456679	-0.37460659341591	-2.47508685341630
113°	113π/180	1.97222205475359	0.92050485345244	-0.39073112848927	-2.35585236582375
114°	19π/30	1.98967534727354	0.91354545764260	-0.40673664307580	-2.24603677390422
115°	23π/36	2.00712863979348	0.90630778703665	-0.42261826174070	-2.14450692050956
116°	29π/45	2.02458193231342	0.89879404629917	-0.43837114678908	-2.05030384157930
117°	13π/20	2.04203522483337	0.89100652418837	-0.45399049973955	-1.96261050550515
118°	59π/90	2.05948851735331	0.88294759285893	-0.46947156278589	-1.88072646534633
119°	119π/180	2.07694180987325	0.87461970713940	-0.48480962024634	-1.80404775527142
120°	2π/3	2.09439510239320	0.86602540378444	-0.50000000000000	-1.73205080756888
121°	121π/180	2.11184839491314	0.85716730070211	-0.51503807491005	-1.66427948235052
122°	61π/90	2.12930168743308	0.84804809615643	-0.52991926423321	-1.60033452904105
123°	41π/60	2.14675497995303	0.83867056794542	-0.54463903501503	-1.53986496381458
124°	31π/45	2.16420827247297	0.82903757255504	-0.55919290347075	-1.48256096851274
125°	25π/36	2.18166156499291	0.81915204428899	-0.57357643635105	-1.42814800674212
126°	7π/10	2.19911485751286	0.80901699437495	-0.58778525229247	-1.37638192047117
127°	127π/180	2.21656815003280	0.79863551004729	-0.60181502315205	-1.32704482162041
128°	32π/45	2.23402144255274	0.78801075360672	-0.61566147532566	-1.27994163219308
129°	43π/60	2.25147473507268	0.77714596145697	-0.62932039104984	-1.23489715653505
130°	13π/18	2.26892802759263	0.76604444311898	-0.64278760968654	-1.19175359259421
131°	131π/180	2.28638132011257	0.75470958022277	-0.65605902899051	-1.15036840722101
132°	11π/15	2.30383461263251	0.74314482547739	-0.66913060635886	-1.11061251482919
133°	133π/180	2.32128790515246	0.73135370161917	-0.68199836006250	-1.07236871002468
134°	67π/90	2.33874119767240	0.71933980033865	-0.69465837045900	-1.03553031379057
135°	3π/4	2.35619449019234	0.70710678118655	-0.70710678118655	-1.00000000000000

Sines, Cosines, Tangents 135°-180°

Degrees	Angle	Radians	Sine	Cosine	Tangent
135°	3π/4	2.35619449019234	0.70710678118655	-0.70710678118655	-1.00000000000000
136°	34π/45	2.37364778271229	0.69465837045900	-0.71933980033865	-0.96568877480708
137°	137π/180	2.39110107523223	0.68199836006250	-0.73135370161917	-0.93251508613766
138°	23π/30	2.40855436775218	0.66913060635886	-0.74314482547739	-0.90040404429784
139°	139π/180	2.42600766027212	0.65605902899051	-0.75470958022277	-0.86928673781623
140°	7π/9	2.44346095279206	0.64278760968654	-0.76604444311898	-0.83909963117728
141°	47π/60	2.46091424531200	0.62932039104984	-0.77714596145697	-0.80978403319501
142°	71π/90	2.47836753783195	0.61566147532566	-0.78801075360672	-0.78128562650672
143°	143π/180	2.49582083035189	0.60181502315205	-0.79863551004729	-0.75355405010280
144°	4π/5	2.51327412287183	0.58778525229247	-0.80901699437495	-0.72654252800536
145°	29π/36	2.53072741539178	0.57357643635105	-0.81915204428899	-0.70020753820971
146°	73π/90	2.54818070791172	0.55919290347075	-0.82903757255504	-0.67450851684243
147°	49π/60	2.56563400043166	0.54463903501503	-0.83867056794542	-0.64940759319751
148°	37π/45	2.58308729295161	0.52991926423321	-0.84804809615643	-0.62486935190933
149°	149π/180	2.60054058547155	0.51503807491005	-0.85716730070211	-0.60086061902756
150°	5π/6	2.61799387799149	0.50000000000000	-0.86602540378444	-0.57735026918963
151°	151π/180	2.63544717051144	0.48480962024634	-0.87461970713940	-0.55430905145277
152°	38π/45	2.65290046303138	0.46947156278589	-0.88294759285893	-0.53170943166148
153°	17π/20	2.67035375555132	0.45399049973955	-0.89100652418837	-0.50952544949443
154°	77π/90	2.68780704807127	0.43837114678908	-0.89879404629917	-0.48773258856586
155°	31π/36	2.70526034059121	0.42261826174070	-0.90630778703665	-0.46630765815500
156°	13π/15	2.72271363311115	0.40673664307580	-0.91354545764260	-0.44522868530854
157°	157π/180	2.74016692563110	0.39073112848927	-0.92050485345244	-0.42447481620961
158°	79π/90	2.75762021815104	0.37460659341591	-0.92718385456679	-0.40402622583516
159°	53π/60	2.77507351067098	0.35836794954530	-0.93358042649720	-0.38386403503542
160°	8π/9	2.79252680319093	0.34202014332567	-0.93969262078591	-0.36397023426620
161°	161π/180	2.80998009571087	0.32556815445716	-0.94551857559932	-0.34432761328967
162°	9π/10	2.82743338823081	0.30901699437495	-0.95105651629515	-0.32491969623291
163°	163π/180	2.84488668075076	0.29237170472274	-0.95630475596304	-0.30573068145866
164°	41π/45	2.86233997327070	0.27563735581700	-0.96126169593832	-0.28674538575881
165°	11π/12	2.87979326579064	0.25881904510252	-0.96592582628907	-0.26794919243112
166°	83π/90	2.89724655831059	0.24192189559967	-0.97029572627600	-0.24932800284318
167°	167π/180	2.91469985083053	0.22495105434387	-0.97437006478524	-0.23086819112556
168°	14π/15	2.93215314335047	0.20791169081776	-0.97814760073381	-0.21255656167002
169°	169π/180	2.94960643587042	0.19080899537655	-0.98162718344766	-0.19438030913772
170°	17π/18	2.96705972839036	0.17364817766693	-0.98480775301221	-0.17632698070847
171°	19π/20	2.98451302091030	0.15643446504023	-0.98768834059514	-0.15838444032454
172°	43π/45	3.00196631343025	0.13917310096007	-0.99026806874157	-0.14054083470239
173°	173π/180	3.01941960595019	0.12186934340515	-0.99254615164132	-0.12278456090291
174°	29π/30	3.03687289847013	0.10452846326765	-0.99452189536827	-0.10510423526568
175°	35π/36	3.05432619099008	0.08715574274766	-0.99619469809175	-0.08748866352592
176°	44π/45	3.07177948351002	0.06975647374413	-0.99756405025982	-0.06992681194351
177°	59π/60	3.08923277602996	0.05233595624294	-0.99862953475457	-0.05240777928304
178°	89π/90	3.10668606854991	0.03489949670250	-0.99939082701910	-0.03492076949175
179°	179π/180	3.12413936106985	0.01745240643728	-0.99984769515639	-0.01745506492822
180°	π	3.14159265358979	0.00000000000000	-1.00000000000000	0.00000000000000

Sines, Cosines, Tangents 180°-225°

Degrees	Angle	Radians	Sine	Cosine	Tangent
180°	π	3.14159265358979	0.00000000000000	-1.00000000000000	0.00000000000000
181°	181π/180	3.15904594610974	-0.01745240643728	-0.99984769515639	0.01745506492822
182°	91π/90	3.17649923862968	-0.03489949670250	-0.99939082701910	0.03492076949175
183°	61π/60	3.19395253114962	-0.05233595624294	-0.99862953475457	0.05240777928304
184°	46π/45	3.21140582366957	-0.06975647374412	-0.99756405025982	0.06992681194351
185°	37π/36	3.22885911618951	-0.08715574274766	-0.99619469809175	0.08748866352592
186°	31π/30	3.24631240870945	-0.10452846326765	-0.99452189536827	0.10510423526568
187°	187π/180	3.26376570122940	-0.12186934340515	-0.99254615164132	0.12278456090291
188°	47π/45	3.28121899374934	-0.13917310096007	-0.99026806874157	0.14054083470239
189°	21π/20	3.29867228626928	-0.15643446504023	-0.98768834059514	0.15838444032454
190°	19π/18	3.31612557878923	-0.17364817766693	-0.98480775301221	0.17632698070847
191°	191π/180	3.33357887130917	-0.19080899537655	-0.98162718344766	0.19438030913772
192°	16π/15	3.35103216382911	-0.20791169081776	-0.97814760073381	0.21255656167002
193°	193π/180	3.36848545634906	-0.22495105434387	-0.97437006478524	0.23086819112556
194°	97π/90	3.38593874886900	-0.24192189559967	-0.97029572627600	0.24932800284318
195°	13π/12	3.40339204138894	-0.25881904510252	-0.96592582628907	0.26794919243112
196°	49π/45	3.42084533390889	-0.27563735581700	-0.96126169593832	0.28674538575881
197°	197π/180	3.43829862642883	-0.29237170472274	-0.95630475596304	0.30573068145866
198°	11π/10	3.45575191894877	-0.30901699437495	-0.95105651629515	0.32491969623291
199°	199π/180	3.47320521146872	-0.32556815445716	-0.94551857559932	0.34432761328967
200°	10π/9	3.49065850398866	-0.34202014332567	-0.93969262078591	0.36397023426620
201°	67π/60	3.50811179650860	-0.35836794954530	-0.93358042649720	0.38386403503542
202°	101π/90	3.52556508902855	-0.37460659341591	-0.92718385456679	0.40402622583516
203°	203π/180	3.54301838154849	-0.39073112848927	-0.92050485345244	0.42447481620960
204°	17π/15	3.56047167406843	-0.40673664307580	-0.91354545764260	0.44522868530854
205°	41π/36	3.57792496658838	-0.42261826174070	-0.90630778703665	0.46630765815500
206°	103π/90	3.59537825910832	-0.43837114678908	-0.89879404629917	0.48773258856586
207°	23π/20	3.61283155162826	-0.45399049973955	-0.89100652418837	0.50952544949443
208°	52π/45	3.63028484414821	-0.46947156278589	-0.88294759285893	0.53170943166148
209°	209π/180	3.64773813666815	-0.48480962024634	-0.87461970713940	0.55430905145277
210°	7π/6	3.66519142918809	-0.50000000000000	-0.86602540378444	0.57735026918963
211°	211π/180	3.68264472170804	-0.51503807491005	-0.85716730070211	0.60086061902756
212°	53π/45	3.70009801422798	-0.52991926423321	-0.84804809615643	0.62486935190933
213°	71π/60	3.71755130674792	-0.54463903501503	-0.83867056794542	0.64940759319751
214°	107π/90	3.73500459926787	-0.55919290347075	-0.82903757255504	0.67450851684243
215°	43π/36	3.75245789178781	-0.57357643635105	-0.81915204428899	0.70020753820971
216°	6π/5	3.76991118430775	-0.58778525229247	-0.80901699437495	0.72654252800536
217°	217π/180	3.78736447682769	-0.60181502315205	-0.79863551004729	0.75355405010279
218°	109π/90	3.80481776934764	-0.61566147532566	-0.78801075360672	0.78128562650672
219°	73π/60	3.82227106186758	-0.62932039104984	-0.77714596145697	0.80978403319501
220°	11π/9	3.83972435438753	-0.64278760968654	-0.76604444311898	0.83909963117728
221°	221π/180	3.85717764690747	-0.65605902899051	-0.75470958022277	0.86928673781623
222°	37π/30	3.87463093942741	-0.66913060635886	-0.74314482547739	0.90040404429784
223°	223π/180	3.89208423194735	-0.68199836006250	-0.73135370161917	0.93251508613766
224°	56π/45	3.90953752446730	-0.69465837045900	-0.71933980033865	0.96568877480707
225°	5π/4	3.92699081698724	-0.70710678118655	-0.70710678118655	1.00000000000000

Sines, Cosines, Tangents 225°-270°

Degrees	Angle	Radians	Sine	Cosine	Tangent
225°	5π/4	3.92699081698724	-0.70710678118655	-0.70710678118655	1.00000000000000
226°	113π/90	3.94444410950718	-0.71933980033865	-0.69465837045900	1.03553031379057
227°	227π/180	3.96189740202713	-0.73135370161917	-0.68199836006250	1.07236871002468
228°	19π/15	3.97935069454707	-0.74314482547739	-0.66913060635886	1.11061251482919
229°	229π/180	3.99680398706701	-0.75470958022277	-0.65605902899051	1.15036840722101
230°	23π/18	4.01425727958696	-0.76604444311898	-0.64278760968654	1.19175359259421
231°	77π/60	4.03171057210690	-0.77714596145697	-0.62932039104984	1.23489715653505
232°	58π/45	4.04916386462684	-0.78801075360672	-0.61566147532566	1.27994163219308
233°	233π/180	4.06661715714679	-0.79863551004729	-0.60181502315205	1.32704482162041
234°	13π/10	4.08407044966673	-0.80901699437495	-0.58778525229247	1.37638192047117
235°	47π/36	4.10152374218667	-0.81915204428899	-0.57357643635105	1.42814800674211
236°	59π/45	4.11897703470662	-0.82903757255504	-0.55919290347075	1.48256096851274
237°	79π/60	4.13643032722656	-0.83867056794542	-0.54463903501503	1.53986496381458
238°	119π/90	4.15388361974650	-0.84804809615643	-0.52991926423321	1.60033452904105
239°	239π/180	4.17133691226645	-0.85716730070211	-0.51503807491005	1.66427948235052
240°	4π/3	4.18879020478639	-0.86602540378444	-0.50000000000000	1.73205080756888
241°	241π/180	4.20624349730633	-0.87461970713940	-0.48480962024634	1.80404775527142
242°	121π/90	4.22369678982628	-0.88294759285893	-0.46947156278589	1.88072646534633
243°	27π/20	4.24115008234622	-0.89100652418837	-0.45399049973955	1.96261050550515
244°	61π/45	4.25860337486616	-0.89879404629917	-0.43837114678908	2.05030384157929
245°	49π/36	4.27605666738611	-0.90630778703665	-0.42261826174070	2.14450692050956
246°	41π/30	4.29350995990605	-0.91354545764260	-0.40673664307580	2.24603677390422
247°	247π/180	4.31096325242599	-0.92050485345244	-0.39073112848927	2.35585236582375
248°	62π/45	4.32841654494594	-0.92718385456679	-0.37460659341591	2.47508685341629
249°	83π/60	4.34586983746588	-0.93358042649720	-0.35836794954530	2.60508906469380
250°	25π/18	4.36332312998582	-0.93969262078591	-0.34202014332567	2.74747741945462
251°	251π/180	4.38077642250577	-0.94551857559932	-0.32556815445716	2.90421087767582
252°	7π/5	4.39822971502571	-0.95105651629515	-0.30901699437495	3.07768353717525
253°	253π/180	4.41568300754565	-0.95630475596304	-0.29237170472274	3.27085261848414
254°	127π/90	4.43313630006560	-0.96126169593832	-0.27563735581700	3.48741444384091
255°	17π/12	4.45058959258554	-0.96592582628907	-0.25881904510252	3.73205080756888
256°	64π/45	4.46804288510548	-0.97029572627600	-0.24192189559967	4.01078093353584
257°	257π/180	4.48549617762543	-0.97437006478524	-0.22495105434387	4.33147587428415
258°	43π/30	4.50294947014537	-0.97814760073381	-0.20791169081776	4.70463010947844
259°	259π/180	4.52040276266531	-0.98162718344766	-0.19080899537655	5.14455401597032
260°	13π/9	4.53785605518526	-0.98480775301221	-0.17364817766693	5.67128181961771
261°	29π/20	4.55530934770520	-0.98768834059514	-0.15643446504023	6.31375151467504
262°	131π/90	4.57276264022514	-0.99026806874157	-0.13917310096007	7.11536972238419
263°	263π/180	4.59021593274509	-0.99254615164132	-0.12186934340515	8.14434642797456
264°	22π/15	4.60766922526503	-0.99452189536827	-0.10452846326765	9.51436445422251
265°	53π/36	4.62512251778497	-0.99619469809175	-0.08715574274766	11.43005230276130
266°	133π/90	4.64257581030492	-0.99756405025982	-0.06975647374413	14.30066625671190
267°	89π/60	4.66002910282486	-0.99862953475457	-0.05233595624294	19.08113668772840
268°	67π/45	4.67748239534480	-0.99939082701910	-0.03489949670250	28.63625328291580
269°	269π/180	4.69493568786475	-0.99984769515639	-0.01745240643728	57.28996163075950
270°	3π/2	4.71238898038469	-1.00000000000000	0.00000000000000	+INFINITY

Sines, Cosines, Tangents 270°-315°

Degrees	Angle	Radians	Sine	Cosine	Tangent
270°	3π/2	4.71238898038469	-1.00000000000000	0.00000000000000	-INFINITY
271°	271π/180	4.72984227290463	-0.99984769515639	0.01745240643728	-57.28996163076070
272°	68π/45	4.74729556542458	-0.99939082701910	0.03489949670250	-28.63625328291610
273°	91π/60	4.76474885794452	-0.99862953475457	0.05233595624294	-19.08113668772850
274°	137π/90	4.78220215046446	-0.99756405025982	0.06975647374413	-14.30066625671190
275°	55π/36	4.79965544298441	-0.99619469809175	0.08715574274766	-11.43005230276140
276°	23π/15	4.81710873550435	-0.99452189536827	0.10452846326765	-9.51436445422255
277°	277π/180	4.83456202802429	-0.99254615164132	0.12186934340515	-8.14434642797458
278°	139π/90	4.85201532054424	-0.99026806874157	0.13917310096007	-7.11536972238421
279°	31π/20	4.86946861306418	-0.98768834059514	0.15643446504023	-6.31375151467505
280°	14π/9	4.88692190558412	-0.98480775301221	0.17364817766693	-5.67128181961772
281°	281π/180	4.90437519810407	-0.98162718344766	0.19080899537654	-5.14455401597033
282°	47π/30	4.92182849062401	-0.97814760073381	0.20791169081776	-4.70463010947845
283°	283π/180	4.93928178314395	-0.97437006478524	0.22495105434387	-4.33147587428416
284°	71π/45	4.95673507566390	-0.97029572627600	0.24192189559967	-4.01078093353585
285°	19π/12	4.97418836818384	-0.96592582628907	0.25881904510252	-3.73205080756888
286°	143π/90	4.99164166070378	-0.96126169593832	0.27563735581700	-3.48741444384092
287°	287π/180	5.00909495322373	-0.95630475596304	0.29237170472274	-3.27085261848414
288°	8π/5	5.02654824574367	-0.95105651629515	0.30901699437495	-3.07768353717526
289°	289π/180	5.04400153826361	-0.94551857559932	0.32556815445716	-2.90421087767583
290°	29π/18	5.06145483078356	-0.93969262078591	0.34202014332567	-2.74747741945462
291°	97π/60	5.07890812330350	-0.93358042649720	0.35836794954530	-2.60508906469380
292°	73π/45	5.09636141582344	-0.92718385456679	0.37460659341591	-2.47508685341630
293°	293π/180	5.11381470834339	-0.92050485345244	0.39073112848927	-2.35585236582375
294°	49π/30	5.13126800086333	-0.91354545764260	0.40673664307580	-2.24603677390422
295°	59π/36	5.14872129338327	-0.90630778703665	0.42261826174070	-2.14450692050956
296°	74π/45	5.16617458590322	-0.89879404629917	0.43837114678908	-2.05030384157930
297°	33π/20	5.18362787842316	-0.89100652418837	0.45399049973955	-1.96261050550515
298°	149π/90	5.20108117094310	-0.88294759285893	0.46947156278589	-1.88072646534633
299°	299π/180	5.21853446346305	-0.87461970713940	0.48480962024634	-1.80404775527142
300°	5π/3	5.23598775598299	-0.86602540378444	0.50000000000000	-1.73205080756888
301°	301π/180	5.25344104850293	-0.85716730070211	0.51503807491005	-1.66427948235052
302°	151π/90	5.27089434102288	-0.84804809615643	0.52991926423321	-1.60033452904105
303°	101π/60	5.28834763354282	-0.83867056794542	0.54463903501503	-1.53986496381458
304°	76π/45	5.30580092606276	-0.82903757255504	0.55919290347075	-1.48256096851274
305°	61π/36	5.32325421858271	-0.81915204428899	0.57357643635105	-1.42814800674211
306°	17π/10	5.34070751110265	-0.80901699437495	0.58778525229247	-1.37638192047117
307°	307π/180	5.35816080362259	-0.79863551004729	0.60181502315205	-1.32704482162041
308°	77π/45	5.37561409614253	-0.78801075360672	0.61566147532566	-1.27994163219308
309°	103π/60	5.39306738866248	-0.77714596145697	0.62932039104984	-1.23489715653505
310°	31π/18	5.41052068118242	-0.76604444311898	0.64278760968654	-1.19175359259421
311°	311π/180	5.42797397370236	-0.75470958022277	0.65605902899051	-1.15036840722101
312°	26π/15	5.44542726622231	-0.74314482547739	0.66913060635886	-1.11061251482919
313°	313π/180	5.46288055874225	-0.73135370161917	0.68199836006250	-1.07236871002468
314°	157π/90	5.48033385126219	-0.71933980033865	0.69465837045900	-1.03553031379057
315°	7π/4	5.49778714378214	-0.70710678118655	0.70710678118655	-1.00000000000000

Sines, Cosines, Tangents 315°-360°

Degrees	Angle	Radians	Sine	Cosine	Tangent
315°	7π/4	5.49778714378214	-0.70710678118655	0.70710678118655	-1.00000000000000
316°	79π/45	5.51524043630208	-0.69465837045900	0.71933980033865	-0.96568877480708
317°	317π/180	5.53269372882202	-0.68199836006250	0.73135370161917	-0.93251508613766
318°	53π/30	5.55014702134197	-0.66913060635886	0.74314482547739	-0.90040404429784
319°	319π/180	5.56760031386191	-0.65605902899051	0.75470958022277	-0.86928673781623
320°	16π/9	5.58505360638185	-0.64278760968654	0.76604444311898	-0.83909963117728
321°	107π/60	5.60250689890180	-0.62932039104984	0.77714596145697	-0.80978403319501
322°	161π/90	5.61996019142174	-0.61566147532566	0.78801075360672	-0.78128562650672
323°	323π/180	5.63741348394168	-0.60181502315205	0.79863551004729	-0.75355405010279
324°	9π/5	5.65486677646163	-0.58778525229247	0.80901699437495	-0.72654252800536
325°	65π/36	5.67232006898157	-0.57357643635105	0.81915204428899	-0.70020753820971
326°	163π/90	5.68977336150151	-0.55919290347075	0.82903757255504	-0.67450851684243
327°	109π/60	5.70722665402146	-0.54463903501503	0.83867056794542	-0.64940759319751
328°	82π/45	5.72467994654140	-0.52991926423321	0.84804809615643	-0.62486935190933
329°	329π/180	5.74213323906134	-0.51503807491005	0.85716730070211	-0.60086061902756
330°	11π/6	5.75958653158129	-0.50000000000000	0.86602540378444	-0.57735026918963
331°	331π/180	5.77703982410123	-0.48480962024634	0.87461970713940	-0.55430905145277
332°	83π/45	5.79449311662117	-0.46947156278589	0.88294759285893	-0.53170943166148
333°	37π/20	5.81194640914112	-0.45399049973955	0.89100652418837	-0.50952544949443
334°	167π/90	5.82939970166106	-0.43837114678908	0.89879404629917	-0.48773258856586
335°	67π/36	5.84685299418100	-0.42261826174070	0.90630778703665	-0.46630765815500
336°	28π/15	5.86430628670095	-0.40673664307580	0.91354545764260	-0.44522868530854
337°	337π/180	5.88175957922089	-0.39073112848927	0.92050485345244	-0.42447481620961
338°	169π/90	5.89921287174083	-0.37460659341591	0.92718385456679	-0.40402622583516
339°	113π/60	5.91666616426078	-0.35836794954530	0.93358042649720	-0.38386403503542
340°	17π/9	5.93411945678072	-0.34202014332567	0.93969262078591	-0.36397023426620
341°	341π/180	5.95157274930066	-0.32556815445716	0.94551857559932	-0.34432761328967
342°	19π/10	5.96902604182061	-0.30901699437495	0.95105651629515	-0.32491969623291
343°	343π/180	5.98647933434055	-0.29237170472274	0.95630475596304	-0.30573068145866
344°	86π/45	6.00393262686049	-0.27563735581700	0.96126169593832	-0.28674538575881
345°	23π/12	6.02138591938044	-0.25881904510252	0.96592582628907	-0.26794919243112
346°	173π/90	6.03883921190038	-0.24192189559967	0.97029572627600	-0.24932800284318
347°	347π/180	6.05629250442032	-0.22495105434387	0.97437006478524	-0.23086819112556
348°	29π/15	6.07374579694027	-0.20791169081776	0.97814760073381	-0.21255656167002
349°	349π/180	6.09119908946021	-0.19080899537655	0.98162718344766	-0.19438030913772
350°	35π/18	6.10865238198015	-0.17364817766693	0.98480775301221	-0.17632698070847
351°	39π/20	6.12610567450010	-0.15643446504023	0.98768834059514	-0.15838444032454
352°	88π/45	6.14355896702004	-0.13917310096007	0.99026806874157	-0.14054083470239
353°	353π/180	6.16101225953998	-0.12186934340515	0.99254615164132	-0.12278456090291
354°	59π/30	6.17846555205993	-0.10452846326765	0.99452189536827	-0.10510423526568
355°	71π/36	6.19591884457987	-0.08715574274766	0.99619469809175	-0.08748866352592
356°	89π/45	6.21337213709981	-0.06975647374413	0.99756405025982	-0.06992681194351
357°	119π/60	6.23082542961976	-0.05233595624294	0.99862953475457	-0.05240777928304
358°	179π/90	6.24827872213970	-0.03489949670250	0.99939082701910	-0.03492076949175
359°	359π/180	6.26573201465964	-0.01745240643728	0.99984769515639	-0.01745506492822
360°	2π	6.28318530717959	0.00000000000000	1.00000000000000	0.00000000000000

Sines 0°-45° in Decimal, Hexadecimal, and Binary

Angle	Radians	Sine	32-Bit Hexadecimal of Sine		9-Bit Binary of Sine	
			Round Down	Round Up	Round Down	Round Up
0°	0.00000000000000	0.00000000000000	0.00000000	0.00000000	0.000000000	0.000000000
1°	0.01745329251994	0.01745240643728	0.0477C2CA	0.0477C2CB	0.000001000	0.000001001
2°	0.03490658503989	0.03489949670250	0.08EF2C64	0.08EF2C65	0.000010001	0.000010010
3°	0.05235987755983	0.05233595624294	0.0D65E3A4	0.0D65E3A5	0.000011010	0.000011011
4°	0.06981317007977	0.06975647374413	0.11DB8F6D	0.11DB8F6E	0.000100011	0.000100100
5°	0.08726646259972	0.08715574274766	0.164FD6B8	0.164FD6B9	0.000101100	0.000101101
6°	0.10471975511966	0.10452846326765	0.1AC2609B	0.1AC2609C	0.000110101	0.000110110
7°	0.12217304763960	0.12186934340515	0.1F32D44C	0.1F32D44D	0.000111110	0.000111111
8°	0.13962634015955	0.13917310096007	0.23A0D92D	0.23A0D92E	0.001000111	0.001001000
9°	0.15707963267949	0.15643446504023	0.280C16CF	0.280C16D0	0.001010000	0.001010001
10°	0.17453292519943	0.17364817766693	0.2C7434FC	0.2C7434FD	0.001011000	0.001011001
11°	0.19198621771938	0.19080899537655	0.30D8DBBA	0.30D8DBBB	0.001100001	0.001100010
12°	0.20943951023932	0.20791169081776	0.3539B358	0.3539B359	0.001101010	0.001101011
13°	0.22689280275926	0.22495105434387	0.3996646D	0.3996646E	0.001110011	0.001110100
14°	0.24434609527921	0.24192189559967	0.3DEE97E5	0.3DEE97E6	0.001111011	0.001111100
15°	0.26179938779915	0.25881904510252	0.4241F706	0.4241F707	0.010000100	0.010000101
16°	0.27925268031909	0.27563735581700	0.46902B74	0.46902B75	0.010001101	0.010001110
17°	0.29670597283904	0.29237170472274	0.4AD8DF3E	0.4AD8DF3F	0.010010101	0.010010110
18°	0.31415926535898	0.30901699437495	0.4F1BBCDC	0.4F1BBCDD	0.010011110	0.010011111
19°	0.33161255787892	0.32556815445716	0.53586F40	0.53586F41	0.010100110	0.010100111
20°	0.34906585039887	0.34202014332567	0.578EA1D2	0.578EA1D3	0.010101111	0.010110000
21°	0.36651914291881	0.35836794954530	0.5BBE007F	0.5BBE0080	0.010110111	0.010111000
22°	0.38397243543875	0.37460659341591	0.5FE637BB	0.5FE637BC	0.010111111	0.011000000
23°	0.40142572795870	0.39073112848927	0.6406F48A	0.6406F48B	0.011001000	0.011001001
24°	0.41887902047864	0.40673664307580	0.681FE484	0.681FE485	0.011010000	0.011010001
25°	0.43633231299858	0.42261826174070	0.6C30B5DC	0.6C30B5DD	0.011011000	0.011011001
26°	0.45378560551853	0.43837114678908	0.7039176A	0.7039176B	0.011100000	0.011100001
27°	0.47123889803847	0.45399049973955	0.7438B8AD	0.7438B8AE	0.011101000	0.011101001
28°	0.48869219055841	0.46947156278589	0.782F49D0	0.782F49D1	0.011110000	0.011110001
29°	0.50614548307836	0.48480962024634	0.7C1C7BB7	0.7C1C7BB8	0.011111000	0.011111001
30°	0.52359877559830	0.50000000000000	0.80000000	0.80000000	0.100000000	0.100000000
31°	0.54105206811824	0.51503807491005	0.83D98907	0.83D98908	0.100000111	0.100001000
32°	0.55850536063819	0.52991926423321	0.87A8C9F5	0.87A8C9F6	0.100001111	0.100010000
33°	0.57595865315813	0.54463903501503	0.8B6D76BB	0.8B6D76BC	0.100010110	0.100010111
34°	0.59341194567807	0.55919290347075	0.8F274420	0.8F274421	0.100011110	0.100011111
35°	0.61086523819802	0.57357643635105	0.92D5E7C3	0.92D5E7C4	0.100100101	0.100100110
36°	0.62831853071796	0.58778525229247	0.96791823	0.96791824	0.100101100	0.100101101
37°	0.64577182323790	0.60181502315205	0.9A108CA2	0.9A108CA3	0.100110100	0.100110101
38°	0.66322511575785	0.61566147532566	0.9D9BFD8D	0.9D9BFD8E	0.100111011	0.100111100
39°	0.68067840827779	0.62932039104984	0.A11B2422	0.A11B2423	0.101000010	0.101000011
40°	0.69813170079773	0.64278760968654	0.A48DBA91	0.A48DBA92	0.101001001	0.101001010
41°	0.71558499331768	0.65605902899051	0.A7F37C09	0.A7F37C0A	0.101001111	0.101010000
42°	0.73303828583762	0.66913060635886	0.AB4C24B7	0.AB4C24B8	0.101010110	0.101010111
43°	0.75049157835756	0.68199836006250	0.AE9771CC	0.AE9771CD	0.101011101	0.101011110
44°	0.76794487087751	0.69465837045900	0.B1D52187	0.B1D52188	0.101100011	0.101100100
45°	0.78539816339745	0.70710678118655	0.B504F333	0.B504F334	0.101101010	0.101101011

Sines 45°-90° in Decimal, Hexadecimal, and Binary

Angle	Radians	Sine	32-Bit Hexadecimal of Sine		9-Bit Binary of Sine	
			Round Down	Round Up	Round Down	Round Up
45°	0.78539816339745	0.70710678118655	0.B504F333	0.B504F334	0.101101010	0.101101011
46°	0.80285145591739	0.71933980033865	0.B826A735	0.B826A736	0.101110000	0.101110001
47°	0.82030474843734	0.73135370161917	0.BB39FF06	0.BB39FF07	0.101110110	0.101110111
48°	0.83775804095728	0.74314482547739	0.BE3EBD41	0.BE3EBD42	0.101111100	0.101111101
49°	0.85521133347722	0.75470958022277	0.C134A5A5	0.C134A5A6	0.110000010	0.110000011
50°	0.87266462599717	0.76604444311898	0.C41B7D16	0.C41B7D17	0.110001000	0.110001001
51°	0.89011791851711	0.77714596145697	0.C6F309A8	0.C6F309A9	0.110001101	0.110001110
52°	0.90757121103705	0.78801075360672	0.C9BB129F	0.C9BB12A0	0.110010011	0.110010100
53°	0.92502450355700	0.79863551004729	0.CC736075	0.CC736076	0.110011000	0.110011001
54°	0.94247779607694	0.80901699437495	0.CF1BBCDC	0.CF1BBCDD	0.110011110	0.110011111
55°	0.95993108859688	0.81915204428899	0.D1B3F2C8	0.D1B3F2C9	0.110100011	0.110100100
56°	0.97738438111683	0.82903757255504	0.D43BCE6D	0.D43BCE6E	0.110101000	0.110101001
57°	0.99483767363677	0.83867056794542	0.D6B31D45	0.D6B31D46	0.110101101	0.110101110
58°	1.01229096615671	0.84804809615643	0.D919AE16	0.D919AE17	0.110110010	0.110110011
59°	1.02974425867665	0.85716730070211	0.DB6F50F3	0.DB6F50F4	0.110110110	0.110110111
60°	1.04719755119660	0.86602540378444	0.DDB3D742	0.DDB3D743	0.110111011	0.110111100
61°	1.06465084371654	0.87461970713940	0.DFE713BE	0.DFE713BF	0.110111111	0.111000000
62°	1.08210413623648	0.88294759285893	0.E208DA7B	0.E208DA7C	0.111000100	0.111000101
63°	1.09955742875643	0.89100652418837	0.E41900E9	0.E41900EA	0.111001000	0.111001001
64°	1.11701072127637	0.89879404629917	0.E6175DDA	0.E6175DDB	0.111001100	0.111001101
65°	1.13446401379631	0.90630778703665	0.E803C981	0.E803C982	0.111010000	0.111010001
66°	1.15191730631626	0.91354545764260	0.E9DE1D77	0.E9DE1D78	0.111010011	0.111010100
67°	1.16937059883620	0.92050485345244	0.EBA634C1	0.EBA634C2	0.111010111	0.111011000
68°	1.18682389135614	0.92718385456679	0.ED5BEBCC	0.ED5BEBCD	0.111011010	0.111011011
69°	1.20427718387609	0.93358042649720	0.EEFF2077	0.EEFF2078	0.111011101	0.111011110
70°	1.22173047639603	0.93969262078591	0.F08FB212	0.F08FB213	0.111100001	0.111100010
71°	1.23918376891597	0.94551857559932	0.F20D815F	0.F20D8160	0.111100100	0.111100101
72°	1.25663706143592	0.95105651629515	0.F378709A	0.F378709B	0.111100110	0.111100111
73°	1.27409035395586	0.95630475596304	0.F4D06373	0.F4D06374	0.111101001	0.111101010
74°	1.29154364647580	0.96126169593832	0.F6153F1A	0.F6153F1B	0.111101100	0.111101101
75°	1.30899693899575	0.96592582628907	0.F746EA3A	0.F746EA3B	0.111101110	0.111101111
76°	1.32645023151569	0.97029572627600	0.F8654CFB	0.F8654CFC	0.111110000	0.111110001
77°	1.34390352403563	0.97437006478524	0.F970510A	0.F970510B	0.111110010	0.111110011
78°	1.36135681655558	0.97814760073381	0.FA67E193	0.FA67E194	0.111110100	0.111110101
79°	1.37881010907552	0.98162718344766	0.FB4BEB49	0.FB4BEB4A	0.111110110	0.111110111
80°	1.39626340159546	0.98480775301221	0.FC1C5C64	0.FC1C5C65	0.111111000	0.111111001
81°	1.41371669411541	0.98768834059514	0.FCD924A1	0.FCD924A2	0.111111001	0.111111010
82°	1.43116998663535	0.99026806874157	0.FD823549	0.FD82354A	0.111111011	0.111111100
83°	1.44862327915529	0.99254615164132	0.FE17812D	0.FE17812E	0.111111100	0.111111101
84°	1.46607657167524	0.99452189536827	0.FE98FCA7	0.FE98FCA8	0.111111101	0.111111110
85°	1.48352986419518	0.99619469809175	0.FF069DA0	0.FF069DA1	0.111111110	0.111111111
86°	1.50098315671512	0.99756405025982	0.FF605B8B	0.FF605B8C	0.111111110	0.111111111
87°	1.51843644923507	0.99862953475457	0.FFA62F68	0.FFA62F69	0.111111111	1.000000000
88°	1.53588974175501	0.99939082701910	0.FFD813C5	0.FFD813C6	0.111111111	1.000000000
89°	1.55334303427495	0.99984769515639	0.FFF604BF	0.FFF604C0	0.111111111	1.000000000
90°	1.57079632679490	1.00000000000000	1.00000000	1.00000000	1.000000000	1.000000000

Table of Inverses, Squares & Roots, Cubes & Roots, Factors

N	1/N	N^2	Square Root of N	N^3	Cube Root of N	Factors of N
0	INFINITY	0	0.00000000000000	0	0.00000000000000	
1	1.00000000000000	1	1.00000000000000	1	1.00000000000000	1
2	0.50000000000000	4	1.41421356237310	8	1.25992104989487	2
3	0.33333333333333	9	1.73205080756888	27	1.44224957030741	3
4	0.25000000000000	16	2.00000000000000	64	1.58740105196820	2^2
5	0.20000000000000	25	2.23606797749979	125	1.70997594667670	5
6	0.16666666666667	36	2.44948974278318	216	1.81712059283214	2 3
7	0.14285714285714	49	2.64575131106459	343	1.91293118277239	7
8	0.12500000000000	64	2.82842712474619	512	2.00000000000000	2^3
9	0.11111111111111	81	3.00000000000000	729	2.08008382305190	3^2
10	0.10000000000000	100	3.16227766016838	1000	2.15443469003188	2 5
11	0.09090909090909	121	3.31662479035540	1331	2.22398009056932	11
12	0.08333333333333	144	3.46410161513775	1728	2.28942848510666	2^2 3
13	0.07692307692308	169	3.60555127546399	2197	2.35133468772076	13
14	0.07142857142857	196	3.74165738677394	2744	2.41014226417523	2 7
15	0.06666666666667	225	3.87298334620742	3375	2.46621207433047	3 5
16	0.06250000000000	256	4.00000000000000	4096	2.51984209978975	2^4
17	0.05882352941176	289	4.12310562561766	4913	2.57128159065824	17
18	0.05555555555556	324	4.24264068711928	5832	2.62074139420890	2 3^2
19	0.05263157894737	361	4.35889894354067	6859	2.66840164872194	19
20	0.05000000000000	400	4.47213595499958	8000	2.71441761659491	2^2 5
21	0.04761904761905	441	4.58257569495584	9261	2.75892417638112	3 7
22	0.04545454545455	484	4.69041575982343	10648	2.80203933065539	2 11
23	0.04347826086957	529	4.79583152331272	12167	2.84386697985157	23
24	0.04166666666667	576	4.89897948556636	13824	2.88449914061482	2^3 3
25	0.04000000000000	625	5.00000000000000	15625	2.92401773821287	5^2
26	0.03846153846154	676	5.09901951359278	17576	2.96249606840737	2 13
27	0.03703703703704	729	5.19615242270663	19683	3.00000000000000	3^3
28	0.03571428571429	784	5.29150262212918	21952	3.03658897187566	2^2 7
29	0.03448275862069	841	5.38516480713450	24389	3.07231682568585	29
30	0.03333333333333	900	5.47722557505166	27000	3.10723250595386	2 3 5
31	0.03225806451613	961	5.56776436283002	29791	3.14138065239139	31
32	0.03125000000000	1024	5.65685424949238	32768	3.17480210393640	2^5
33	0.03030303030303	1089	5.74456264653803	35937	3.20753432999583	3 11
34	0.02941176470588	1156	5.83095189484530	39304	3.23961180127748	2 17
35	0.02857142857143	1225	5.91607978309962	42875	3.27106631018859	5 7
36	0.02777777777778	1296	6.00000000000000	46656	3.30192724889463	2^2 3^2
37	0.02702702702703	1369	6.08276253029822	50653	3.33222185164595	37
38	0.02631578947368	1444	6.16441400296898	54872	3.36197540679896	2 19
39	0.02564102564103	1521	6.24499799839840	59319	3.39121144301417	3 13
40	0.02500000000000	1600	6.32455532033676	64000	3.41995189335339	2^3 5

Table of Factorials (0 – 40), Inverses, and Factors

N	N!	1/N!	Factors of N!
0	1.00000000000000E+000	1.00000000000000E+000	1
1	1.00000000000000E+000	1.00000000000000E+000	1
2	2.00000000000000E+000	5.00000000000000E-001	2
3	6.00000000000000E+000	1.66666666666667E-001	2 3
4	2.40000000000000E+001	4.16666666666667E-002	2^3 3
5	1.20000000000000E+002	8.33333333333333E-003	2^3 3 5
6	7.20000000000000E+002	1.38888888888889E-003	2^4 3^2 5
7	5.04000000000000E+003	1.98412698412698E-004	2^4 3^2 5 7
8	4.03200000000000E+004	2.48015873015873E-005	2^7 3^2 5 7
9	3.62880000000000E+005	2.75573192239859E-006	2^7 3^4 5 7
10	3.62880000000000E+006	2.75573192239859E-007	2^8 3^4 5^2 7
11	3.99168000000000E+007	2.50521083854417E-008	2^8 3^4 5^2 7 11
12	4.79001600000000E+008	2.08767569878681E-009	2^{10} 3^5 5^2 7 11
13	6.22702080000000E+009	1.60590438368216E-010	2^{10} 3^5 5^2 7 11 13
14	8.71782912000000E+010	1.14707455977297E-011	2^{11} 3^5 5^2 7^2 11 13
15	1.30767436800000E+012	7.64716373181982E-013	2^{11} 3^6 5^3 7^2 11 13
16	2.09227898880000E+013	4.77947733238738E-014	2^{15} 3^6 5^3 7^2 11 13
17	3.55687428096000E+014	2.81145725434552E-015	2^{15} 3^6 5^3 7^2 11 13 17
18	6.40237370572800E+015	1.56192069685862E-016	2^{16} 3^8 5^3 7^2 11 13 17
19	1.21645100408832E+017	8.22063524662433E-018	2^{16} 3^8 5^3 7^2 11 13 17 19
20	2.43290200817664E+018	4.11031762331216E-019	2^{18} 3^8 5^4 7^2 11 13 17 19
21	5.10909421717094E+019	1.95729410633913E-020	2^{18} 3^9 5^4 7^3 11 13 17 19
22	1.12400072777761E+021	8.89679139245057E-022	2^{19} 3^9 5^4 7^3 11^2 13 17 19
23	2.58520167388850E+022	3.86817017063068E-023	2^{19} 3^9 5^4 7^3 11^2 13 17 19 23
24	6.20448401733239E+023	1.61173757109612E-024	2^{22} 3^{10} 5^4 7^3 11^2 13 17 19 23
25	1.55112100433310E+025	6.44695028438447E-026	2^{22} 3^{10} 5^6 7^3 11^2 13 17 19 23
26	4.03291461126606E+026	2.47959626322480E-027	2^{23} 3^{10} 5^6 7^3 11^2 13^2 17 19 23
27	1.08888694504184E+028	9.18368986379555E-029	2^{23} 3^{13} 5^6 7^3 11^2 13^2 17 19 23
28	3.04888344611714E+029	3.27988923706984E-030	2^{25} 3^{13} 5^6 7^4 11^2 13^2 17 19 23
29	8.84176199373970E+030	1.13099628864477E-031	2^{25} 3^{13} 5^6 7^4 11^2 13^2 17 19 23 29
30	2.65252859812191E+032	3.76998762881590E-033	2^{26} 3^{14} 5^7 7^4 11^2 13^2 17 19 23 29
31	8.22283865417792E+033	1.21612504155352E-034	2^{26} 3^{14} 5^7 7^4 11^2 13^2 17 19 23 29 31
32	2.63130836933694E+035	3.80039075485474E-036	2^{31} 3^{14} 5^7 7^4 11^2 13^2 17 19 23 29 31
33	8.68331761881189E+036	1.15163356207720E-037	2^{31} 3^{15} 5^7 7^4 11^3 13^2 17 19 23 29 31
34	2.95232799039604E+038	3.38715753552116E-039	2^{32} 3^{15} 5^7 7^4 11^3 13^2 17^2 19 23 29 31
35	1.03331479663861E+040	9.67759295863189E-041	2^{32} 3^{15} 5^8 7^5 11^3 13^2 17^2 19 23 29 31
36	3.71993326789901E+041	2.68822026628664E-042	2^{34} 3^{17} 5^8 7^5 11^3 13^2 17^2 19 23 29 31
37	1.37637530912263E+043	7.26546017915307E-044	2^{34} 3^{17} 5^8 7^5 11^3 13^2 17^2 19 23 29 31 37
38	5.23022617466601E+044	1.91196320504028E-045	2^{35} 3^{17} 5^8 7^5 11^3 13^2 17^2 19^2 23 29 31 37
39	2.03978820811974E+046	4.90246975651354E-047	2^{35} 3^{18} 5^8 7^5 11^3 13^3 17^2 19^2 23 29 31 37
40	8.15915283247898E+047	1.22561743912839E-048	2^{38} 3^{18} 5^9 7^5 11^3 13^3 17^2 19^2 23 29 31 37

Table of Square Roots to 50 Places

N	Sqrt(N)	Rounding
0	0.00000000000000000000000000000000000000000000000000	Exact
1	1.00000000000000000000000000000000000000000000000000	Exact
2	1.41421356237309504880168872420969807856967187537694	Use High
3	1.73205080756887729352744634150587236694280525381038	Use Low
4	2.00000000000000000000000000000000000000000000000000	Exact
5	2.23606797749978969640917366873127623544061835961152	Use High
6	2.44948974278317809819728407470589139196594748065667	Use Low
7	2.64575131106459059050161575363926042571025918308245	Use Low
8	2.82842712474619009760337744841939615713934375075389	Use High
9	3.00000000000000000000000000000000000000000000000000	Exact
10	3.16227766016837933199889354443271853371955513932521	Use High
11	3.31662479035539984911493273667068668392708854558935	Use Low
12	3.46410161513775458705489268301174473388561050762076	Use Low
13	3.60555127546398929311922126747049594625129657384524	Use High
14	3.74165738677394138558374873231654930175601980777872	Use High
15	3.87298334620741688517926539978239961083292170529159	Use Low
16	4.00000000000000000000000000000000000000000000000000	Exact
17	4.12310562561766054982140985597407702514719922537362	Use Low
18	4.24264068711928514640506617262909423570901562613084	Use Low
19	4.35889894354067355223698198385961565913700392523244	Use Low
20	4.47213595499957939281834733746255247088123671922305	Use Low
21	4.58257569495584000658047193728008488984456576766797	Use Low
22	4.69041575982342955456563011354446628058822835341173	Use High
23	4.79583152331271954159743806416269391999670704190413	Use Low
24	4.89897948556635619639456814941178278393189496131334	Use Low
25	5.00000000000000000000000000000000000000000000000000	Exact
26	5.09901951359278483002822410902278198956377094609959	Use High
27	5.19615242270663188058233902451761710082841576143114	Use Low
28	5.29150262212918118100323150727852085142051836616490	Use Low
29	5.38516480713450403125071049154032955629512016164478	Use High
30	5.47722557505166113456969782800802133952744694997983	Use Low
31	5.56776436283002192211947129891854952047639337757041	Use Low
32	5.65685424949238019520675489683879231427868750150779	Use Low
33	5.74456264653802865985061146821892931822026445798279	Use Low
34	5.83095189484530047087415287754558307652139833488597	Use Low
35	5.91607978309961604256732829156161704841550123079434	Use Low
36	6.00000000000000000000000000000000000000000000000000	Exact
37	6.08276253029821968899968424520206706208497009478641	Use Low
38	6.16441400296897645025019238145424422523562402344457	Use Low
39	6.24499799839839820584689312093979446107295997799165	Use High
40	6.32455532033675866399778708886543706743911027865043	Use Low

All values shown are <u>truncated</u> after the 50TH decimal place. To get the *closest* value to the true square root, "Use Low" means to use the truncated number as-is (the 51ST digit is 4 or smaller and is rounded down), but "Use High" means to add one to the right-most digit (the 51ST digit is 5 or greater and needs to be rounded up).

Table of First 800 Primes

	0	40	80	120	160	200	240	280	320	360	400	440	480	520	560	600	640	680	720	760
0	2	179	419	661	947	1229	1523	1823	2131	2437	2749	3083	3433	3733	4073	4421	4759	5099	5449	5801
1	3	181	421	673	953	1231	1531	1831	2137	2441	2753	3089	3449	3739	4079	4423	4783	5101	5471	5807
2	5	191	431	677	967	1237	1543	1847	2141	2447	2767	3109	3457	3761	4091	4441	4787	5107	5477	5813
3	7	193	433	683	971	1249	1549	1861	2143	2459	2777	3119	3461	3767	4093	4447	4789	5113	5479	5821
4	11	197	439	691	977	1259	1553	1867	2153	2467	2789	3121	3463	3769	4099	4451	4793	5119	5483	5827
5	13	199	443	701	983	1277	1559	1871	2161	2473	2791	3137	3467	3779	4111	4457	4799	5147	5501	5839
6	17	211	449	709	991	1279	1567	1873	2179	2477	2797	3163	3469	3793	4127	4463	4801	5153	5503	5843
7	19	223	457	719	997	1283	1571	1877	2203	2503	2801	3167	3491	3797	4129	4481	4813	5167	5507	5849
8	23	227	461	727	1009	1289	1579	1879	2207	2521	2803	3169	3499	3803	4133	4483	4817	5171	5519	5851
9	29	229	463	733	1013	1291	1583	1889	2213	2531	2819	3181	3511	3821	4139	4493	4831	5179	5521	5857
10	31	233	467	739	1019	1297	1597	1901	2221	2539	2833	3187	3517	3823	4153	4507	4861	5189	5527	5861
11	37	239	479	743	1021	1301	1601	1907	2237	2543	2837	3191	3527	3833	4157	4513	4871	5197	5531	5867
12	41	241	487	751	1031	1303	1607	1913	2239	2549	2843	3203	3529	3847	4159	4517	4877	5209	5557	5869
13	43	251	491	757	1033	1307	1609	1931	2243	2551	2851	3209	3533	3851	4177	4519	4889	5227	5563	5879
14	47	257	499	761	1039	1319	1613	1933	2251	2557	2857	3217	3539	3853	4201	4523	4903	5231	5569	5881
15	53	263	503	769	1049	1321	1619	1949	2267	2579	2861	3221	3541	3863	4211	4547	4909	5233	5573	5897
16	59	269	509	773	1051	1327	1621	1951	2269	2591	2879	3229	3547	3877	4217	4549	4919	5237	5581	5903
17	61	271	521	787	1061	1361	1627	1973	2273	2593	2887	3251	3557	3881	4219	4561	4931	5261	5591	5923
18	67	277	523	797	1063	1367	1637	1979	2281	2609	2897	3253	3559	3889	4229	4567	4933	5273	5623	5927
19	71	281	541	809	1069	1373	1657	1987	2287	2617	2903	3257	3571	3907	4231	4583	4937	5279	5639	5939
20	73	283	547	811	1087	1381	1663	1993	2293	2621	2909	3259	3581	3911	4241	4591	4943	5281	5641	5953
21	79	293	557	821	1091	1399	1667	1997	2297	2633	2917	3271	3583	3917	4243	4597	4951	5297	5647	5981
22	83	307	563	823	1093	1409	1669	1999	2309	2647	2927	3299	3593	3919	4253	4603	4957	5303	5651	5987
23	89	311	569	827	1097	1423	1693	2003	2311	2657	2939	3301	3607	3923	4259	4621	4967	5309	5653	6007
24	97	313	571	829	1103	1427	1697	2011	2333	2659	2953	3307	3613	3929	4261	4637	4969	5323	5657	6011
25	101	317	577	839	1109	1429	1699	2017	2339	2663	2957	3313	3617	3931	4271	4639	4973	5333	5659	6029
26	103	331	587	853	1117	1433	1709	2027	2341	2671	2963	3319	3623	3943	4273	4643	4987	5347	5669	6037
27	107	337	593	857	1123	1439	1721	2029	2347	2677	2969	3323	3631	3947	4283	4649	4993	5351	5683	6043
28	109	347	599	859	1129	1447	1723	2039	2351	2683	2971	3329	3637	3967	4289	4651	4999	5381	5689	6047
29	113	349	601	863	1151	1451	1733	2053	2357	2687	2999	3331	3643	3989	4297	4657	5003	5387	5693	6053
30	127	353	607	877	1153	1453	1741	2063	2371	2689	3001	3343	3659	4001	4327	4663	5009	5393	5701	6067
31	131	359	613	881	1163	1459	1747	2069	2377	2693	3011	3347	3671	4003	4337	4673	5011	5399	5711	6073
32	137	367	617	883	1171	1471	1753	2081	2381	2699	3019	3359	3673	4007	4339	4679	5021	5407	5717	6079
33	139	373	619	887	1181	1481	1759	2083	2383	2707	3023	3361	3677	4013	4349	4691	5023	5413	5737	6089
34	149	379	631	907	1187	1483	1777	2087	2389	2711	3037	3371	3691	4019	4357	4703	5039	5417	5741	6091
35	151	383	641	911	1193	1487	1783	2089	2393	2713	3041	3373	3697	4021	4363	4721	5051	5419	5743	6101
36	157	389	643	919	1201	1489	1787	2099	2399	2719	3049	3389	3701	4027	4373	4723	5059	5431	5749	6113
37	163	397	647	929	1213	1493	1789	2111	2411	2729	3061	3391	3709	4049	4391	4729	5077	5437	5779	6121
38	167	401	653	937	1217	1499	1801	2113	2417	2731	3067	3407	3719	4051	4397	4733	5081	5441	5783	6131
39	173	409	659	941	1223	1511	1811	2129	2423	2741	3079	3413	3727	4057	4409	4751	5087	5443	5791	6133

In this table 2 is considered the "zeroth" prime, and is shown in yellow, because it is the only even prime number. The numbers along the side and top determine the index of all the odd primes. For example, the 99TH odd prime (the 100TH prime overall) would be in column 80 and row 19, or 541. *__Mersenne primes__*, primes that are of the form 2^N-1, are shown in green (the next four Mersenne primes after this table are 8191, 131071, 524287, and $2^{31}-1=2147483647$).

Lagrange Interpolation

Lagrange interpolation is a way of *passing a smooth curve through a set of points*. For two points the result is always a straight line, for three points the result is a quadratic (a parabola), for four points the result is always a cubic, and so on. While the method can be extended to have a smooth curve pass through any arbitrary number of points, it is not generally practical to do so beyond four points (cubic).

The method applies to curves in *any number of dimensions*. We may not be able to easily visualize a curve in four, five, or more dimensions, but the math is consistent. One interpolation is performed for each dimension, generating one unique polynomial for each dimension. The order of those polynomials will be based on the number of points that the curve must pass through. The polynomials are **_parametric equations_** of an independent variable (generally called *t* for time), where evaluating all polynomials at *t* will generate the point along the curve at that instant in time.

For example, a curve through five points (P_0, P_1, P_2, P_3, and P_4) and in three dimensions (*x*, *y*, and *z*) will require that one interpolation be performed on all the *x* coordinates from the five points, a second interpolation be performed on all the *y* coordinates from the five points, and a third interpolation be performed on all the *z* coordinates from the five points, generating three parametric polynomials of order four. The a_x, b_x, a_y, b_y, etc. are just simple constants (numbers) obtained from the interpolations:

$$x(t) = a_x t^4 + b_x t^3 + c_x t^2 + d_x t + e_x$$
$$y(t) = a_y t^4 + b_y t^3 + c_y t^2 + d_y t + e_y$$
$$z(t) = a_z t^4 + b_z t^3 + c_z t^2 + d_z t + e_z$$

For N points P_0 through P_{N-1}, the Lagrange interpolation for those points is given as follows. The term t_i represents the time at which the curve should go through point P_i; t_j represents when the curve should go through point P_j. These numbers are defined ahead of time. Generally, $t_0=0$, $t_{N-1}=1$, and all other t_i and t_j are somewhere between 0 and 1, but this is not a hard rule.

$$P(t) = \sum_{i=0}^{N-1} \left[\left(\prod_{j=0}^{N-1, i \neq j} \frac{(t - t_j)}{(t_i - t_j)} \right) P_i \right]$$

For example, a quadratic function through three points (P_1, P_1, P_2, N=3) would be expressed as:

$$P(t) = \frac{(t - t_1)(t - t_2)}{(t_0 - t_1)(t_0 - t_2)} P_0 + \frac{(t - t_0)(t - t_2)}{(t_1 - t_0)(t_1 - t_2)} P_1 + \frac{(t - t_0)(t - t_1)}{(t_2 - t_0)(t_2 - t_1)} P_2$$

Lagrange Interpolation (Continued)

By determining N, plugging in some user-chosen time constants, and doing some algebra, Lagrange interpolation reduces to the following forms:

Linear Case (N=2, P_0 at t=0, P_1 at t=1):

$$P(t) = (P_1 - P_0)t + P_0$$

Quadratic Case (N=3, P_0 at t=0, P_1 at t=½, P_2 at t=1):

$$P(t) = (2P_0 - 4P_1 + 2P_2)t^2 + (-3P_0 + 4P_1 - P_2)t + P_0$$

Cubic Case (N=4, P_0 at t=⅓, P_1 at t=⅓, P_2 at t=⅔, P_3 at t=1):

$$P(t) = at^3 + bt^2 + ct + d, \text{ where:}$$

$$a = ½(-9P_0 + 27P_1 - 27P_2 + 9P_3)$$

$$b = ½(18P_0 - 45P_1 + 36P_2 - 9P_3)$$

$$c = ½(-11P_0 + 18P_1 - 9P_2 + 2P_3)$$

$$d = P_0$$

Example:

Pass a parabola (quadratic) through points in the plane P_0=**(1,2)** at t=0, P_1=**(6,5)** at t=½, and P_2=**(8,1)** at t=1. The coordinate values of the points are shown in boldface below:

$$P_x(t) = (2×\mathbf{1} - 4×\mathbf{6} + 2×\mathbf{8})t^2 + (-3×\mathbf{1} + 4×\mathbf{6} - \mathbf{8})t + \mathbf{1}$$
$$P_y(t) = (2×\mathbf{2} - 4×\mathbf{5} + 2×\mathbf{1})t^2 + (-3×\mathbf{2} + 4×\mathbf{5} - \mathbf{1})t + \mathbf{2}$$

Which reduces to:

$$P_x(t) = (2-24+16)t^2 + (-3+24-8)t + 1$$
$$P_y(t) = (4-20+2)t^2 + (-6+20-1)t + 2$$

And finally:

$$P_x(t) = -6t^2 + 13t + 1$$
$$P_y(t) = -14t^2 + 13t + 2$$

The $P_x(t)$ polynomial describes the motion of the x coordinate as t changes; the $P_y(t)$ polynomial describes the motion of the y coordinate as t changes. Together, as t changes a point along the curve in two dimensions is traced out.

Cubic Bézier Curve

A cubic ***Bézier curve*** is defined by four points, but the curve does not go through two of the four. The curve starts at P_0, approaches but does not go through P_1, approaches but does not go through P_2, and ends at P_3. P_1 and P_2 are ***control points***, and each "belongs" to one of the end points: P_1 belongs to P_0 and P_2 belongs to P_3. The two pairs form ***control lines*** $P_0 \ldots P_1$ and $P_2 \ldots P_3$. The curve is ***tangent*** to the control lines at the end points.

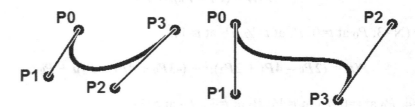

As with Lagrange interpolation, a Bézier curve may be in any number of dimensions, with one polynomial that describes the behavior of the curve in each dimension. The coefficients of the appropriate polynomials are determined as follows, where the curve goes through P_0 at $t=0$ and through P_3 at $t=1$:

$$P(t) = at^3 + bt^2 + ct + d, \text{ where:}$$

$$a = P_3 - 3P_2 + 3P_1 - P_0$$

$$b = 3P_2 - 6P_1 + 3P_0$$

$$c = 3P_1 - 3P_0$$

$$d = P_0$$

Two Bézier curves may be joined end-to-end seamlessly if the common end points and their respective control points are *all in a straight line*, as both curves will be tangent to the straight line at the same place (the common end points).

Quadratic Spline

A *quadratic spline* is also a Bézier curve (although the term "Bézier curve" is a generic term, it often refers to just the cubic version). Instead of two control points a quadratic spline has only one, shared between the two end points. The curve is again tangent to the control lines at each end point.

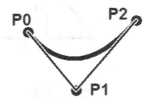

Note that the quadratic spline does <u>not</u> have the same shape as a cubic Bézier with its control points at the same position in space.

The coefficients of the appropriate polynomials are determined as follows, where the curve goes through P_0 at $t=0$ and through P_2 at $t=1$:

$$P(t) = at^2 + bt + c, \text{ where:}$$

$$a = P_2 - 2P_1 + P_0$$

$$b = 2P_1 - 2P_0$$

$$c = P_0$$

As with the cubic Bézier curve, quadratic splines (or any higher dimension Bézier curve) all share the property that the curves are tangent to the control lines at the end points. Because of this any such curves of this type may be joined together end-to-end seamlessly as long as the common end points and the corresponding control points are all in a straight line.

Note that Bézier curves and Quadratic splines may be drawn quickly on a graphics screen by use of *de Casteljau's Algorithm*. Cubic Bézier curves in particular can be used to synthesize circles and ellipses. See the Graphics, Image Processing, and Computational Geometry chapter for how to write programs in Python to do these tasks.

Plane Geometry

TRIANGLE

Area = ½bh

PARALLELOGRAM

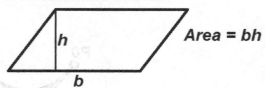

Area = bh

TRAPEZOID

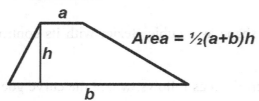

Area = ½(a+b)h

CIRCLE

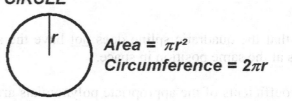

Area = πr^2
Circumference = $2\pi r$

CIRCLES, SECTORS, AND ARCS

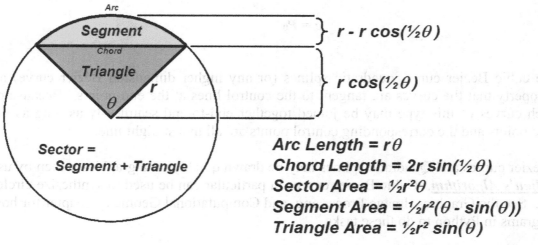

Sector =
Segment + Triangle

Arc Length = $r\theta$
Chord Length = $2r\sin(\frac{1}{2}\theta)$
Sector Area = $\frac{1}{2}r^2\theta$
Segment Area = $\frac{1}{2}r^2(\theta - \sin(\theta))$
Triangle Area = $\frac{1}{2}r^2\sin(\theta)$

Solid Geometry

SPHERE

Surface Area = $4\pi r^2$
Volume = $\frac{4}{3}\pi r^3$

CONE

Surface Area (base) = πr^2
Surface Area (wall) = $\pi r \sqrt{r^2 + h^2}$
Volume = $\frac{1}{3}\pi r^2 h$

CYLINDER

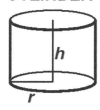

Surface Area (bases) = πr^2
Surface Area (wall) = $2\pi rh$
Volume = $\pi r^2 h$

Differentiation

$$f'(x) = \lim_{h \to 0} \frac{f(x+h) - f(x)}{h}$$

Function $f(x)$	Derivative $f'(x)$
$g(x) + h(x) + i(x) + \dots$	$g'(x) + h'(x) + i'(x) + \dots$
a	0
x	1
ax	a
ax^n	nax^{n-1}
e^x	e^x
a^x	$a^x \ln(a)$
$\ln(x)$	$\frac{1}{x}$
$\log_a(x)$	$\frac{1}{x} \log_a(e)$
$\sin(x)$	$\cos(x)$
$\cos(x)$	$-\sin(x)$
$\tan(x)$	$\sec^2(x)$
$\cot(x)$	$-\csc^2(x)$
$\sec(x)$	$\sec(x)\tan(x)$
$\csc(x)$	$-\csc(x)\cot(x)$
$\arcsin(x)$	$\frac{1}{\sqrt{(1-x^2)}}$
$\arccos(x)$	$\frac{-1}{\sqrt{(1-x^2)}}$
$\arctan(x)$	$\frac{1}{(1+x^2)}$
$\text{arccsc}(x)$	$\frac{-1}{|x|\sqrt{(x^2-1)}}$
$\text{arcsec}(x)$	$\frac{1}{|x|\sqrt{(x^2-1)}}$
$\text{arccot}(x)$	$\frac{-1}{(1+x^2)}$

a is a constant

Product Rule	$(f(x)\,g(x))' = f'(x)\,g(x) + f(x)\,g'(x)$
Quotient Rule	$(f(x)/g(x))' = [f'(x)\,g(x) - g'(x)\,f(x)]/(g(x))^2$
Quotient Rule (variation)	$(1/g(x))' = [-g'(x)]/(g(x))^2$
Chain Rule	$(f(g(x)))' = f'(g(x))\,g'(x)$

Integration

Where **F(x)** is the antiderivative of **f(x)** (that is, **F′ (x) = f(x)**), and **f(x)** is continuous on the closed interval **[a, b]**, then:

$$\int_a^b f(x)dx = F(b) - F(a)$$

Also:

$$\int \left(f(x) \pm g(x)\right) dx = \int f(x)\, dx \pm \int g(x)\, dx$$

Function	Indefinite Integral	Function	Indefinite Integrals
$\int a\, dx$	$ax + C$	$\int a\, f(x)\, dx$	$a \int f(x)\, dx$
$\int x^a\, dx$	$\dfrac{x^{a+1}}{a+1} + C$	$\int \dfrac{dx}{x}$	$ln\lvert x \rvert + C$
$\int e^{ax}\, dx$	$\dfrac{1}{a}e^{ax} + C$	$\int a^x dx$	$\dfrac{a^x}{ln(a)} + C$
$\int \dfrac{dx}{ax+b}$	$\dfrac{1}{a}ln\lvert ax+b \rvert + C$	$\int \dfrac{dx}{(x+a)^2}$	$\dfrac{-1}{x+a} + C$
$\int \dfrac{1}{1+x^2}dx$	$tan^{-1} x + C$	$\int \dfrac{dx}{a^2+x^2}$	$\dfrac{1}{a}tan^{-1}\dfrac{x}{a} + C$
$\int (x+a)^n dx$	$\dfrac{(x+a)^{n+1}}{n+1} + C, n \neq -1$	$\int \dfrac{x}{a^2+x^2}dx$	$\tfrac{1}{2}ln\lvert a^2+x^2 \rvert + C$
$\int \sqrt{x-a}\, dx$	$\tfrac{2}{3}(x-a)^{3/2} + C$	$\int \dfrac{dx}{\sqrt{x \pm a}}$	$2\sqrt{x \pm a} + C$
$\int \dfrac{dx}{\sqrt{a-x}}$	$-2\sqrt{a-x} + C$	$\int \dfrac{x}{\sqrt{x \pm a}}dx$	$\tfrac{2}{3}(x \mp 2a)\sqrt{x \pm a} + C$
$\int \sin ax\, dx$	$-\dfrac{1}{a}\cos ax + C$	$\int \cos ax\, dx$	$\dfrac{1}{a}\sin ax + C$
$\int \tan ax\, dx$	$-\dfrac{1}{a}ln\lvert \cos ax \rvert + C$	$\int \cot ax\, dx$	$\dfrac{1}{a}ln\lvert \sin ax \rvert + C$
$\int \sec ax\, dx$	$\dfrac{1}{a}ln\lvert \sec ax + \tan ax \rvert + C$	$\int \csc ax\, dx$	$\pm\dfrac{1}{a}ln\lvert \csc ax \mp \cot ax \rvert + C$
$\int \sec^2 ax\, dx$	$\dfrac{1}{a}\tan ax + C$	$\int \csc^2 ax\, dx$	$-\dfrac{1}{a}\cot ax + C$
$\int \dfrac{dx}{\sqrt{a^2-x^2}}$	$sin^{-1}\left(\dfrac{x}{a}\right) + C$	$\int \dfrac{dx}{\sqrt{x^2 \pm a^2}}$	$ln\left\lvert x + \sqrt{x^2 \pm a^2} \right\rvert + C$
$\int \dfrac{dx}{a^2+x^2}$	$\dfrac{1}{a}tan^{-1}\dfrac{x}{a} + C$	$\int \dfrac{dx}{x\sqrt{x^2-a^2}}$	$\dfrac{1}{a}sec^{-1}\left(\dfrac{x}{a}\right) + C$

Integration

4: *Numerical Representations*

This section is concerned with the practical aspects of storing and working with numbers on a computer. Computers are finite machines, but math is infinite in scope. This means that, from the outset, computers can only deal with a small subset of mathematics, and even then only with approximations to true mathematical values. The biggest dirty secret of computer science is that most of the interesting numbers in the Universe cannot be represented on a computer, either because those numbers are too large or too small to fit, or require far more precision than what is available.

In all cases, a particular computer has N bits to represent a number. Those N bits can be used to encode integers, floating-point numbers with fractions, or other exotic formats. In general, however, the limitation on the number of bits available puts serious constraints on numerical precision, and often the number of significant figures is in direct conflict with dynamic range. For example, integer representations contain all possible values in the range between the minimum and maximum possible values, but that range is fairly small. In contrast, floating-point representations have a much wider range of values than the equivalent-length integer representations can store, but not all possible values in that range are representable.

Integers

Computers always treat numbers as ***packets of bits*** with a fixed size. Call that size N (usually N=8, N=16, N=32, or N=64, depending on the design).

For any number of bits N, there are 2^N unique binary patterns, from $0000...0$ through $1111...1$.

Half of $2^N = 2^{N-1}$.

Treated as ***unsigned integers***, decimal values range from $0...2^N-1$.

In counting upwards from 0, the last possible pattern is 2^N-1. One more up-count wraps the value around to 0 again. This is called an ***unsigned overflow***.

Counting downwards from 2^N-1, the last possible pattern is 0. One more down-count wraps the value around to 2^N-1 again. This is called an ***unsigned underflow***.

If counting down from 0 gives 2^N-1, then in a ***signed*** sense 2^N-1 also can be interpreted as -1.

For ***signed numbers***, half of the 2^N patterns (that is, 2^{N-1} patterns) are considered to be negative. The other half include zero and the positives.

In the most common interpretation used today for binary ***signed numbers***, called Two's Complement, decimal values range from $-2^{N-1}...+2^{N-1}-1$.

In Two's Complement signed interpretations, ***zero is considered to be positive***.

In Two's Complement signed interpretations, there is ***one more negative than positive***.

In binary, the smallest (-2^{N-1}) and largest ($+2^{N-1}-1$) signed integer values are adjacent patterns.

In signed integers, counting up from the largest positive value gives the smallest negative. This is called a ***signed overflow***.

Counting down from the smallest negative value gives the largest positive. This is called a ***signed underflow***.

N	2^N	0	Unsigned Range 2^N-1	Signed Range -2^{N-1}	$+2^{N-1}-1$
8	256	0	255	-128	+127
16	65,536	0	65,535	-32,768	+32,767
32	4,294,967,296	0	4,294,967,295	-2,147,483,648	+2,147,483,647
64	18,446,744,073,709,551,616	0	18,446,744,073,709,551,615	-9,223,372,036,854,775,808	+9,223,372,036,854,775,807

Number Wheel for Signed and Unsigned Bytes

The following diagram shows two sections of a number wheel for 8-bit bytes. The binary numbers in the outer ring correspond to unsigned values, while the signed equivalents are in the inside ring. Starting at 0 and counting up, an unsigned overflow occurs when the value passes 255 back to 0. Starting at 255 and counting down, an unsigned underflow occurs when the value passes 0 back to 255. Crossing that boundary in either direction indicates an unsigned error. However, crossing the signed overflow / underflow boundary occurs at the other side of the wheel between +127 and -128, indicating a signed error.

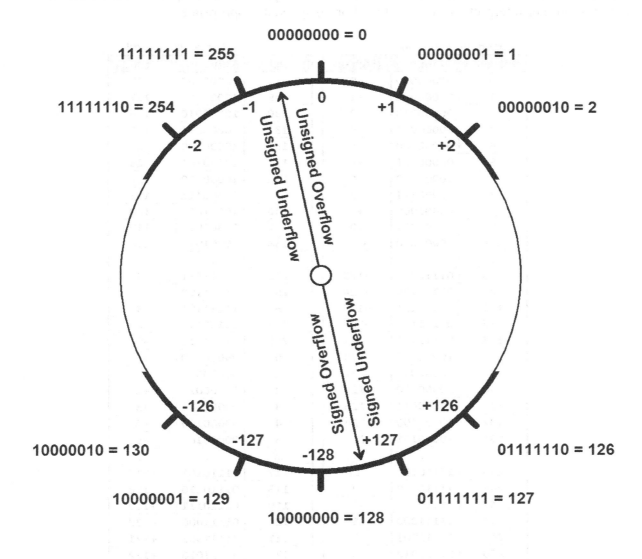

Unsigned and Two's Complement Signed Bytes

For a standard 8-bit byte there are 2^8=256 binary patterns, from 00000000 through 11111111. Patterns 00000000 through 01111111 are treated the same way in both interpretations, corresponding to decimal numbers 0 through 127. Patterns 10000000 through 11111111 are treated differently, however: as unsigned values 128 through 255, or as signed values -128 through -1. The left-most bit of signed integers is called the ***sign bit***, which is 0 for positives (and zero) and 1 for negatives. The techniques to add signed and unsigned binary integers is identical: one set of hardware can do both jobs. The computer simply adds bits, and the programmer interprets results as signed or unsigned as appropriate.

	Sorted by Unsigned			Sorted by Signed	
Unsigned	Binary	(Signed)	(Unsigned)	Binary	Signed
0	00000000	+0	128	10000000	-128
1	00000001	+1	129	10000001	-127
2	00000010	+2	130	10000010	-126
3	00000011	+3	131	10000011	-125
4	00000100	+4	132	10000100	-124
5	00000101	+5	133	10000101	-123
6	00000110	+6	134	10000110	-122
7	00000111	+7	135	10000111	-121
8	00001000	+8	136	10001000	-120
9	00001001	+9	137	10001001	-119
10	00001010	+10	138	10001010	-118
...	...	...	...	...	...
123	01111011	+123	251	11111011	-5
124	01111100	+124	252	11111100	-4
125	01111101	+125	253	11111101	-3
126	01111110	+126	254	11111110	-2
127	01111111	+127	255	11111111	-1
128	10000000	-128	0	00000000	+0
129	10000001	-127	1	00000001	+1
130	10000010	-126	2	00000010	+2
131	10000011	-125	3	00000011	+3
132	10000100	-124	4	00000100	+4
133	10000101	-123	5	00000101	+5
...	...	...	...	...	...
245	11110101	-11	117	01110101	+117
246	11110110	-10	118	01110110	+118
247	11110111	-9	119	01110111	+119
248	11111000	-8	120	01111000	+120
249	11111001	-7	121	01111001	+121
250	11111010	-6	122	01111010	+122
251	11111011	-5	123	01111011	+123
252	11111100	-4	124	01111100	+124
253	11111101	-3	125	01111101	+125
254	11111110	-2	126	01111110	+126
255	11111111	-1	127	01111111	+127

Relationships Between Various Signed Representations

There are three main ways to interpret binary patterns as signed integers: Sign & Magnitude, One's Complement, and Two's Complement. All have been used in real computer hardware, but all modern computers use Two's Complement. In all three cases the sign bit is the left-most bit, where 0 indicates positive and 1 indicates negative.

Both Sign & Magnitude and One's Complement have an equal number of positives and negatives, but allow for both +0 and -0 as distinct values.

Two's Complement has only one 0, but to compensate it has one more negative than there are positives (it is always a pattern where the sign bit is 1 and the rest of the bits are 0).

To negate a Sign & Magnitude integer, complement only the sign bit.

To negate a One's Complement integer, complement all bits.

To negate a Two's Complement integer, complement all bits and add 1. Discard any carry out of the left-most bit (this allows the act of negating zero to still remain zero, but has the bad side effect that the most negative number is its own negation).

	Sign & Magnitude	One's Complement	Two's Complement	
			100000...000000	-MAX-1
-MAX	111111...111111	100000...000000	100000...000001	-MAX
-MAX+1	111111...111110	100000...000001	100000...000010	-MAX+1
-MAX+2	111111...111101	100000...000010	100000...000011	-MAX+2
-MAX-3	111111...111100	100000...000011	100000...000100	-MAX-3
...	...	...	...	...
...	...	...	...	...
...	...	...	...	...
-4	100000...000100	111111...111011	111111...111100	-4
-3	100000...000011	111111...111100	111111...111101	-3
-2	100000...000010	111111...111101	111111...111110	-2
-1	100000...000001	111111...111110	111111...111111	-1
-0	100000...000000	111111...111111	Does Not Exist	-0
+0	000000...000000	000000...000000	000000...000000	+0
+1	000000...000001	000000...000001	000000...000001	+1
+2	000000...000010	000000...000010	000000...000010	+2
+3	000000...000011	000000...000011	000000...000011	+3
+4	000000...000100	000000...000100	000000...000100	+4
...	...	...	...	...
...	...	...	...	...
...	...	...	...	...
+MAX-3	011111...111100	011111...111100	011111...111100	+MAX-3
+MAX-2	011111...111101	011111...111101	011111...111101	+MAX-2
+MAX-1	011111...111110	011111...111110	011111...111110	+MAX-1
+MAX	011111...111111	011111...111111	011111...111111	+MAX

Binary Addition

Binary addition is simpler than decimal addition. When adding two binary numbers together, you start at the right and add each corresponding pair of bits, plus a possible carry from the next lowest digit, generating a sum bit and a carry bit that goes to the next higher digit. At most, there will be only three bits being added together. All possible combinations are shown in the following table:

A	B	C	Carry	Sum
0	0	0	0	0
0	0	1	0	1
0	1	0	0	1
0	1	1	1	0
1	0	0	0	1
1	0	1	1	0
1	1	0	1	0
1	1	1	1	1

Example:

	1	0	0	0	1	1	0	0		Carries
	1	0	0	0	1	1	1	0		Operand #1
+	1	0	1	0	1	1	0	0		Operand #2
	1	0	0	1	1	1	0	1	0	Sum

Mathematically, we are adding two 8-bit numbers together and getting a 9-bit result, equivalent to the problem in decimal of adding 142+172=314. The number of bits present in each of the three values does not matter. If instead we consider that two 8-bit bytes are being added together using <u>strict</u> 8-bit arithmetic, the results are very different. The interpretation also depends on whether the addition is performed using signed or unsigned arithmetic.

When the two bytes are considered as unsigned integers, all 8 bits represent magnitude values, and the 9TH (leftmost) bit of the sum indicates an ***unsigned overflow***. That is, the result of adding the two 8-bit numbers won't fit in 8 bits. If the 9TH bit was 0, everything would be OK, but because it is 1 we know there is a problem.

When the two bytes are considered as signed integers, the 9TH bit is <u>ignored</u> and the leftmost bit of each 8 bit byte is treated as its ***sign bit***. In the example, both of the operands are negative (their sign bits are 1), but the result is positive (the sign bit is 0). We have added two negative numbers together and obtained a positive result. This is a ***signed underflow*** (adding two positives together and getting a negative result would be a signed overflow).

For any binary addition using a strictly <u>fixed</u> number of bits, results may have a signed overflow/underflow, an unsigned overflow/underflow, both (as in the example), or neither. It is the responsibility of the programmer to write programs that check for these conditions and take appropriate actions when they occur.

Binary Subtraction

Here is a problem in binary subtraction. In each case, a bit from Operand #2 is subtracted from Operand #1, but in doing so it is possible and necessary to generate "borrows" just as we do in decimal.

	0	0	1	1	0	0	1	0	Operand #1
-	0	0	0	0	0	1	1	0	Operand #2
	0	0	1	0	1	1	0	0	Difference (Computed Directly)

While it is possible to create hardware for performing binary subtraction directly, computers today compute a subtraction by addition of complements. That is, instead of computing A – B, they compute A + (–B) instead. The creation of –B is done by forming the two's complement of B, which is to invert all the bits of B and add 1. Here is Operand #2 again, along with its one's complement (all bits inverted) and its two's complement (the one's complement plus 1).

0	0	0	0	0	1	1	0	Operand #2
1	1	1	1	1	0	0	1	Operand #2 One's Complement
1	1	1	1	1	0	1	0	Operand #2 Two's Complement

If this is easy to do in hardware (and it is), then computers can re-use the adder hardware instead of having specialized subtraction hardware. Here is the same problem, showing Operand #1 being added to the two's complement of Operand #2. The carry out of the leftmost bit is generally ignored for signed arithmetic, giving the same answer as when the subtraction is computed directly.

1	1	1	1	0	0	1	0		Carries
	0	0	1	1	0	0	1	0	Operand #1
+	1	1	1	1	1	0	1	0	Operand #2 Two's Complement
1	0	0	1	0	1	1	0	0	Sum

Closure Plots for Two's Complement Integer Arithmetic

The images on the following pages show the realm of valid and invalid computations for arithmetic using two's complement integers. A closure plot shows all possible computations for a given number of bits, which ones give correct results, which give overflows, which give underflows, and which lead to illegal results (such as division by zero). In each case the number along the x axis comes first and the number along the y axis comes second (that is, X + Y, X – Y, X × Y, and X ÷ Y). The grids shown are for 6-bit arithmetic (unsigned range 0…63 and signed range -32…+31), but the labels are such that it is possible to generalize to any number of bits. What may be surprising for each plot is the number of computations that lead to errors of some form; in some cases the number of invalid computations is vastly greater than those that are valid.

Closure Plots for Two's Complement Integer Addition

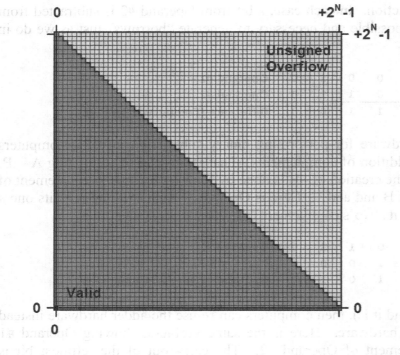

UNSIGNED ADDITION
X + Y

Only slightly more than one-half of all possible computations have a valid result. The rest of the computations would generate a result requiring more bits than are available, thus flagging an overflow condition.

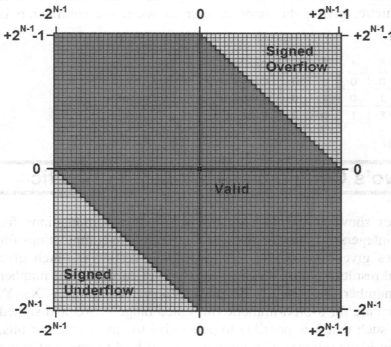

SIGNED ADDITION
X + Y

In a signed representation, only about a quarter of the possible computations are invalid. These include adding two positives and getting a negative result (overflow), or adding two negatives and getting a positive result (underflow).

When adding any positive to any negative, the result is always *between* the two, and thus is always legal. The result is closer to zero than is the operand which is furthest from zero.

Closure Plots for Two's Complement Integer Subtraction

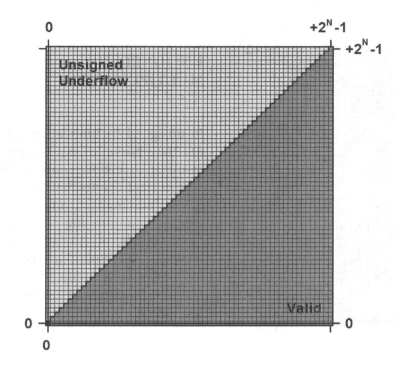

UNSIGNED SUBTRACTION
X – Y

The closure plots for subtraction are reflections of those for addition, and have the same number of valid and invalid results. In the unsigned case, underflow is generated when subtracting a large number from a small number; the true mathematical result would be negative, but negative numbers are not supported by unsigned arithmetic.

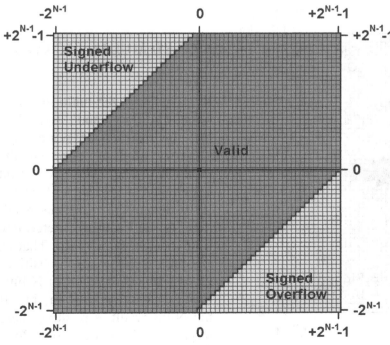

SIGNED SUBTRACTION
X – Y

In a signed representation, underflow is generated when subtracting a positive from a negative (which should be further negative) and getting a positive result. Overflow is generated when subtracting a negative from a positive (which should be positive) and getting a negative result.

Closure Plots for Two's Complement Integer Multiplication

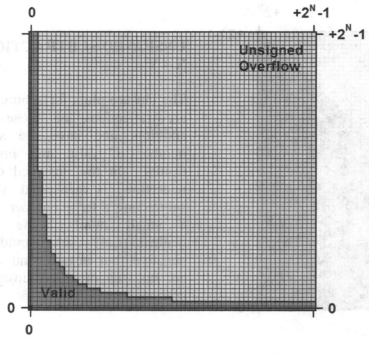

UNSIGNED MULTIPLICATION X × Y

In unsigned multiplication, <u>most</u> of the possible computations result in overflow; only a few give correct results that fit in the given number of bits. [In general, multiplying N digits times N digits (in any base) results in a result that requires 2N digits to guarantee there is enough space to hold all possible products.]

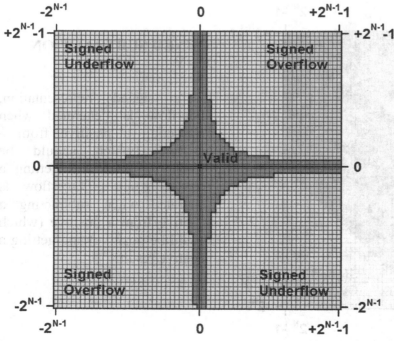

SIGNED MULTIPLICATION X × Y

In signed integer multiplication, both overflow and underflow indicate that there are not enough bits available to represent the product. Multiplying two N-bit operands and looking *only* at the low-order N bits of the result may not be enough to determine if an error has occurred. That is, if multiplying two positives gives a negative result in N bits, then overflow is certain, but if the N-bit result is positive there might still have been overflow. To avoid this problem, most computers explicitly compute a full 2N-bit product.

Closure Plots for Two's Complement Integer Division

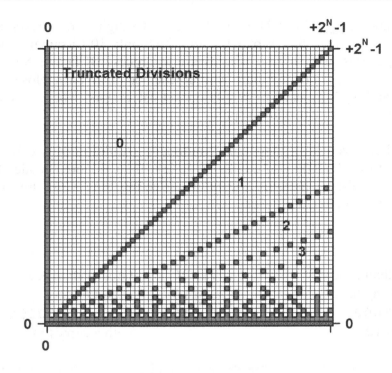

UNSIGNED DIVISION
X ÷ Y

In unsigned division, the bottom row of computations are all divisions by zero, which would generate errors. All filled cells are valid divisions from computations where the numerator is an even multiple of the denominator. All empty cells are cases where the division would have a non-zero fraction that must be discarded to give an integer result.

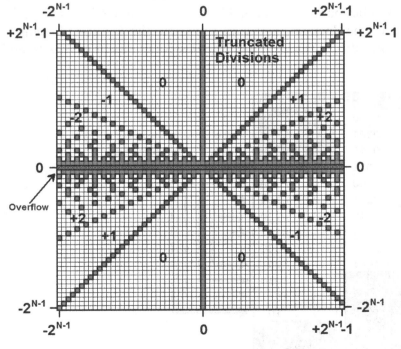

SIGNED DIVISION
X ÷ Y

In signed division, the middle row are all divisions by zero. All empty cells are cases where the mathematical result would have a non-zero fraction, except for the case of $-2^{N-1} \div -1$, which would give an overflow because in two's complement $+2^{N-1}$ is not represented.

BCD and XS3 Representations

In ***Binary Coded Decimal*** (BCD) and ***Excess-3*** (XS3), individual decimal digits are represented by 4-bit nybbles. However, 4 bits are enough for 16 patterns, of which only 10 (decimal digits 0…9) are used, leaving 6 illegal patterns in each case. Hardware to process BCD and XS3 is slightly slower than pure binary hardware, but numbers are represented in a form closer to traditional decimal. Hence, BCD and XS3 are used in simple pocket calculators, where ease of data entry and display is more important than calculation speed.

BCD digits correspond to the unsigned values of their binary numbers. Addition of two BCD digits may get a binary result greater than 9 (falling in the illegal zone). If so, 6 more is added to the result, thus jumping over the six illegal patterns and both correcting the BCD sum and generating carry information to the next higher BCD digit.

```
  5      0101                                    7      0111
 +3   +  0011                                   +5   +  0101
  8     01000    Not greater than 9, so...      12     01100    Greater than 9, so...
                 ...don't add anything.               +00110    ...add 6 more
        01000    Result is 8 (1000),                   10010    Result is 2 (0010),
                 with no carry (0).                            with a carry (1).
```

In XS3 the binary values are shifted by +3. This complicates addition, because when adding two digits, each too big by 3, the result will be too high by 6, and 3 must be subtracted to correct for this. However, the 9's complement of the decimal digit corresponds to the 1's complement of the binary number, thus simplifying negation. For example, the 9's complement of 3 is 6, and the corresponding 1's complement of 0110 is 1001.

4-Bit Binary		BCD	Binary	XS3	Binary	
0	0000	0	0000	Illegal		XS3 9's Complement =
1	0001	1	0001			Binary 1's Complement
2	0010	2	0010			
3	0011	3	0011	0	0011	
4	0100	4	0100	1	0100	
5	0101	5	0101	2	0101	
6	0110	6	0110	3	0110	
7	0111	7	0111	4	0111	
8	1000	8	1000	5	1000	
9	1001	9	1001	6	1001	
10	1010	Illegal		7	1010	
11	1011			8	1011	
12	1100			9	1100	
13	1101			Illegal		
14	1110					
15	1111					

Gray Code

Gray Code, or *Reflected Binary Code* (Frank Gray, 1947) is a binary code where each pair of successive numbers differ by at most one bit (that is, their *Hamming Distance* is exactly 1). For N bits, the 2^N binary patterns are rearranged (permuted) so that each pattern differs by only one bit from the pattern that comes before and the pattern that comes after (each of the 2^N patterns is used exactly once). The Gray code for any number can be formed by taking the exclusive-OR of each adjacent pair of bits within the binary representation of that number (as needed, leading zeroes may be assumed to exist at the left side of the binary number). The table below shows all patterns for numbers 0 through 31 (five bits). Gray codes are useful in many places, including optical angle encoders for robot wheels.

N	Binary	Gray
0	00000	00000
1	00001	00001
2	00010	00011
3	00011	00010
4	00100	00110
5	00101	00111
6	00110	00101
7	00111	00100
8	01000	01100
9	01001	01101
10	01010	01111
11	01011	01110
12	01100	01010
13	01101	01011
14	01110	01001
15	01111	01000
16	10000	11000
17	10001	11001
18	10010	11011
19	10011	11010
20	10100	11110
21	10101	11111
22	10110	11101
23	10111	11100
24	11000	10100
25	11001	10101
26	11010	10111
27	11011	10110
28	11100	10010
29	11101	10011
30	11110	10001
31	11111	10000

Floating-Point

Floating-point numbers commonly use the ***IEEE 754*** specification document. This specification defines such numbers as having three fields: a ***sign bit*** field, a ***biased exponent*** field, and a ***mantissa*** (or ***significand***) field. The number of bits in the biased exponent field determines the dynamic range of the numbers, while the number of bits in the mantissa determines the precision (significant figures).

Exponents may be positive or negative, but have a ***bias value*** added to them to make the number stored in the biased exponent field always positive. This simplifies hardware for comparing relative magnitudes of two floating-point numbers. For any number of bits B in the biased exponent field, the ***bias*** is computed as:

$$\text{Bias} = 2^{B-1}-1$$

IEEE 754 defines several formats for floating-point numbers, based on the total number of bits used to store them. These include ***single precision*** (shown below), ***double precision***, and ***extended precision***. With minor exceptions for extended precision, all formats follow the same design, which can be applied to an arbitrary number of bits for things such as ***quarter precision*** and ***half precision***, as shown in the table. All normalized, non-zero binary values start with $1.\text{xxxxx}...$, allowing that leading 1-bit to be suppressed for efficient storage. In extended precision only, the leading 1-bit is <u>not</u> suppressed, and is explicitly stored in the result.

Sign   Biased Exponent   Mantissa (Significand)

		Bits in each Field				Dynamic Range (Normalized)	Significant Figures
	Bits	Sign	Exponent	Mantissa	Bias		
Quarter Precision	8	1	3	4	3	±0.25...±15.5	1.5
Half Precision	16	1	5	10	15	±0.0000610352...±65504	3.3
Single Precision	32	1	8	23	127	$\pm 1.1755 \times 10^{-38}...\pm 3.4028 \times 10^{+38}$	7.2
Double Precision	64	1	11	52	1023	$\pm 2.2251 \times 10^{-308}...\pm 1.7977 \times 10^{+308}$	16.0
Extended Precision	80	1	15	64	16383	$\pm 3.362 \times 10^{-4932}...\pm 1.1897 \times 10^{+4932}$	19.3

Example of Converting a Decimal Number to Single Precision

1. Start with arbitrary Decimal Number: +17.1875
2. Convert to Pure Binary: +10001.0011
3. Write in Binary Scientific Notation: $+1.00010011 \times 2^4$
4. Extract Fraction from Binary Scientific: .00010011 (Suppress leading 1-bit)
5. Pad Fraction to 23 Bits: **00010011000000000000000**
6. Add Bias (127) to Exponent: 127 + 4 = 131
7. Convert Biased Exponent to 8-Bit Binary: 131 = **10000011**
8. Process Sign Information: + means sign bit = **0**
9. Assemble and store final number (exponent field is underlined):
<u>0**10000011**00010011000000000000000</u>

Table of Generalized Floating-Point Values

Regardless of the number of bits in the biased exponent or in the mantissa, values follow the same guidelines for how they are to be constructed. In each of the examples below, the ellipsis (…) indicates that all bits in between have the same value, up to the width of the corresponding field. If the field is shorter than what is shown, common bits may be eliminated down to the unique values for that field. For example, the biased exponent for 5.0 is `1000...0001`, which would be `10001` for a 5-bit exponent field, `10000001` for an 8-bit exponent field, `10000000001` for an 11-bit exponent field, and so on.

In all IEEE 754 floating-point representations, except for extended precision, the mantissa suppresses the leading 1-bit in non-zero ***normalized*** numbers to get one more bit of precision out of the format than can be explicitly stored. The format also supports ***denormals*** (values close to zero that observe special rules), ***infinity*** (which absorbs computations, such as $1 + \infty = \infty$), and ***Not-A-Numbers***, or ***NaN***, used to indicate undefined values (such as $0/0$, ∞/∞, $0\times\infty$, $\infty-\infty$, etc.). ***Quiet NaN*** propagate through computations giving an erroneous result that must be handled at the end, while ***Signaling NaN*** errors must be handled at the time they are generated, and can contain an arbitrarily-chosen identifying number to indicate the specific type of error.

	Sign Bit	Biased Exponent	Mantissa (Significand)	Notes
Quiet NaN	0	1111...1111	1xxxxxxxxxxx...xxxxxxxx	Some x may be 1
Signaling NaN	0	1111...1111	0xxxxxxxxxxx...xxxxxxxx	Some x must be 1
Infinity	0	1111...1111	000000000000...00000000	
Largest Normalized	0	1111...1110	111111111111...11111111	$1.11111...\times2^{BIAS}$
10.0	0	1000...0010	010000000000...00000000	$1.01000\times2^3 = 1010 = 10.0$
9.0	0	1000...0010	001000000000...00000000	$1.00100\times2^3 = 1001 = 9.0$
8.0	0	1000...0010	000000000000...00000000	$1.00000\times2^3 = 1000 = 8.0$
7.0	0	1000...0001	110000000000...00000000	$1.11000\times2^2 = 111 = 7$
6.0	0	1000...0001	100000000000...00000000	$1.10000\times2^2 = 110 = 6$
5.0	0	1000...0001	010000000000...00000000	$1.01000\times2^2 = 101 = 5$
4.0	0	1000...0001	000000000000...00000000	$1.00000\times2^2 = 100 = 4$
3.0	0	1000...0000	100000000000...00000000	$1.10000\times2^1 = 11 = 3$
2.0	0	1000...0000	000000000000...00000000	$1.00000\times2^1 = 10 = 2$
1.0	0	0111...1111	000000000000...00000000	$1.00000\times2^0 = 1 = 1$
0.75	0	0111...1110	100000000000...00000000	$1.10000\times2^{-1} = 0.11 = 0.75$
0.5	0	0111...1110	000000000000...00000000	$1.00000\times2^{-1} = 0.1 = 0.5$
0.25	0	0111...1101	000000000000...00000000	$1.00000\times2^{-2} = 0.01 = 0.25$
0.1	0	0111...1011	100110011001...10011001	Last Bits may be Rounded
Smallest Normalized	0	0000...0001	000000000000...00000000	$1.000000...00000\times2^{-BIAS+1}$
Largest Denormal	0	0000...0000	111111111111...11111111	$0.111111...11111\times2^{-BIAS+1}$
Smallest Denormal	0	0000...0000	000000000000...00000001	$0.000000...00001\times2^{-BIAS+1}$
Zero	0	0000...0000	000000000000...00000000	All Bits Zero

All Positive Quarter-Precision Values (High End)

It is instructive to examine one simple floating-point format in detail. On this and the next page are all possible positive quarter-precision floating-point values and their binary, binary scientific notation, and decimal interpretations. (Negative values are the same but with the sign bit set to 1.) This page contains the high-end values. Quiet NaN values are shown in orange, Signaling NaN values in yellow, and infinity in magenta. All other values on this page are normalized. Notice that adding 1 to the largest normalized value (15.5) *as if it was an integer* gives infinity.

BINARY	SCIENTIFIC	VALUE	BINARY	SCIENTIFIC	VALUE
0-111-1111	Quiet NaN	Code 7	0-101-1111	$+1.1111 \times 2^2$	7.75
0-111-1110	Quiet NaN	Code 6	0-101-1110	$+1.1110 \times 2^2$	7.50
0-111-1101	Quiet NaN	Code 5	0-101-1101	$+1.1101 \times 2^2$	7.25
0-111-1100	Quiet NaN	Code 4	0-101-1100	$+1.1100 \times 2^2$	7.00
0-111-1011	Quiet NaN	Code 3	0-101-1011	$+1.1011 \times 2^2$	6.75
0-111-1010	Quiet NaN	Code 2	0-101-1010	$+1.1010 \times 2^2$	6.50
0-111-1001	Quiet NaN	Code 1	0-101-1001	$+1.1001 \times 2^2$	6.25
0-111-1000	Quiet NaN	Code 0	0-101-1000	$+1.1000 \times 2^2$	6.00
0-111-0111	Signaling NaN	Code 7	0-101-0111	$+1.0111 \times 2^2$	5.75
0-111-0110	Signaling NaN	Code 6	0-101-0110	$+1.0110 \times 2^2$	5.50
0-111-0101	Signaling NaN	Code 5	0-101-0101	$+1.0101 \times 2^2$	5.25
0-111-0100	Signaling NaN	Code 4	0-101-0100	$+1.0100 \times 2^2$	5.00
0-111-0011	Signaling NaN	Code 3	0-101-0011	$+1.0011 \times 2^2$	4.75
0-111-0010	Signaling NaN	Code 2	0-101-0010	$+1.0010 \times 2^2$	4.50
0-111-0001	Signaling NaN	Code 1	0-101-0001	$+1.0001 \times 2^2$	4.25
0-111-0000	+INFINITY		0-101-0000	$+1.0000 \times 2^2$	4.00
0-110-1111	$+1.1111 \times 2^3$	15.5	0-100-1111	$+1.1111 \times 2^1$	3.875
0-110-1110	$+1.1110 \times 2^3$	15.0	0-100-1110	$+1.1110 \times 2^1$	3.750
0-110-1101	$+1.1101 \times 2^3$	14.5	0-100-1101	$+1.1101 \times 2^1$	3.625
0-110-1100	$+1.1100 \times 2^3$	14.0	0-100-1100	$+1.1100 \times 2^1$	3.500
0-110-1011	$+1.1011 \times 2^3$	13.5	0-100-1011	$+1.1011 \times 2^1$	3.375
0-110-1010	$+1.1010 \times 2^3$	13.0	0-100-1010	$+1.1010 \times 2^1$	3.250
0-110-1001	$+1.1001 \times 2^3$	12.5	0-100-1001	$+1.1001 \times 2^1$	3.125
0-110-1000	$+1.1000 \times 2^3$	12.0	0-100-1000	$+1.1000 \times 2^1$	3.000
0-110-0111	$+1.0111 \times 2^3$	11.5	0-100-0111	$+1.0111 \times 2^1$	2.875
0-110-0110	$+1.0110 \times 2^3$	11.0	0-100-0110	$+1.0110 \times 2^1$	2.750
0-110-0101	$+1.0101 \times 2^3$	10.5	0-100-0101	$+1.0101 \times 2^1$	2.625
0-110-0100	$+1.0100 \times 2^3$	10.0	0-100-0100	$+1.0100 \times 2^1$	2.500
0-110-0011	$+1.0011 \times 2^3$	9.5	0-100-0011	$+1.0011 \times 2^1$	2.375
0-110-0010	$+1.0010 \times 2^3$	9.0	0-100-0010	$+1.0010 \times 2^1$	2.250
0-110-0001	$+1.0001 \times 2^3$	8.5	0-100-0001	$+1.0001 \times 2^1$	2.125
0-110-0000	$+1.0000 \times 2^3$	8.0	0-100-0000	$+1.0000 \times 2^1$	2.000

All Positive Quarter-Precision Values (Low End)

This page continues the table, from where the previous page left off, down to zero. Values that are denormalized are shown in green, zero is in magenta, and all other values are normalized. In some sense, zero is the smallest of the denormals. The difference between adjacent pairs of normalized numbers increases towards infinity and decreases towards zero (the largest two such numbers differ by 0.5, while the smallest two differ by only 0.015625). This is entirely characteristic of all floating-point formats. All larger formats can be generalized from this one.

BINARY	SCIENTIFIC	VALUE	BINARY	SCIENTIFIC	VALUE
0-011-1111	$+1.1111 \times 2^{0}$	1.9375	0-001-1111	$+1.1111 \times 2^{-2}$	0.484375
0-011-1110	$+1.1110 \times 2^{0}$	1.8750	0-001-1110	$+1.1110 \times 2^{-2}$	0.468750
0-011-1101	$+1.1101 \times 2^{0}$	1.8125	0-001-1101	$+1.1101 \times 2^{-2}$	0.453125
0-011-1100	$+1.1100 \times 2^{0}$	1.7500	0-001-1100	$+1.1100 \times 2^{-2}$	0.437500
0-011-1011	$+1.1011 \times 2^{0}$	1.6875	0-001-1011	$+1.1011 \times 2^{-2}$	0.421875
0-011-1010	$+1.1010 \times 2^{0}$	1.6250	0-001-1010	$+1.1010 \times 2^{-2}$	0.406250
0-011-1001	$+1.1001 \times 2^{0}$	1.5625	0-001-1001	$+1.1001 \times 2^{-2}$	0.390625
0-011-1000	$+1.1000 \times 2^{0}$	1.5000	0-001-1000	$+1.1000 \times 2^{-2}$	0.375000
0-011-0111	$+1.0111 \times 2^{0}$	1.4375	0-001-0111	$+1.0111 \times 2^{-2}$	0.359375
0-011-0110	$+1.0110 \times 2^{0}$	1.3750	0-001-0110	$+1.0110 \times 2^{-2}$	0.343750
0-011-0101	$+1.0101 \times 2^{0}$	1.3125	0-001-0101	$+1.0101 \times 2^{-2}$	0.328125
0-011-0100	$+1.0100 \times 2^{0}$	1.2500	0-001-0100	$+1.0100 \times 2^{-2}$	0.312500
0-011-0011	$+1.0011 \times 2^{0}$	1.1875	0-001-0011	$+1.0011 \times 2^{-2}$	0.296875
0-011-0010	$+1.0010 \times 2^{0}$	1.1250	0-001-0010	$+1.0010 \times 2^{-2}$	0.281250
0-011-0001	$+1.0001 \times 2^{0}$	1.0625	0-001-0001	$+1.0001 \times 2^{-2}$	0.265625
0-011-0000	$+1.0000 \times 2^{0}$	1.0000	0-001-0000	$+1.0000 \times 2^{-2}$	0.250000
0-010-1111	$+1.1111 \times 2^{-1}$	0.96875	0-000-1111	$+0.1111 \times 2^{-2}$	0.234375
0-010-1110	$+1.1110 \times 2^{-1}$	0.93750	0-000-1110	$+0.1110 \times 2^{-2}$	0.218750
0-010-1101	$+1.1101 \times 2^{-1}$	0.90625	0-000-1101	$+0.1101 \times 2^{-2}$	0.203125
0-010-1100	$+1.1100 \times 2^{-1}$	0.87500	0-000-1100	$+0.1100 \times 2^{-2}$	0.187500
0-010-1011	$+1.1011 \times 2^{-1}$	0.84375	0-000-1011	$+0.1011 \times 2^{-2}$	0.171875
0-010-1010	$+1.1010 \times 2^{-1}$	0.81250	0-000-1010	$+0.1010 \times 2^{-2}$	0.156250
0-010-1001	$+1.1001 \times 2^{-1}$	0.78125	0-000-1001	$+0.1001 \times 2^{-2}$	0.140625
0-010-1000	$+1.1000 \times 2^{-1}$	0.75000	0-000-1000	$+0.1000 \times 2^{-2}$	0.125000
0-010-0111	$+1.0111 \times 2^{-1}$	0.71875	0-000-0111	$+0.0111 \times 2^{-2}$	0.109375
0-010-0110	$+1.0110 \times 2^{-1}$	0.68750	0-000-0110	$+0.0110 \times 2^{-2}$	0.093750
0-010-0101	$+1.0101 \times 2^{-1}$	0.65625	0-000-0101	$+0.0101 \times 2^{-2}$	0.078125
0-010-0100	$+1.0100 \times 2^{-1}$	0.62500	0-000-0100	$+0.0100 \times 2^{-2}$	0.062500
0-010-0011	$+1.0011 \times 2^{-1}$	0.59375	0-000-0011	$+0.0011 \times 2^{-2}$	0.046875
0-010-0010	$+1.0010 \times 2^{-1}$	0.56250	0-000-0010	$+0.0010 \times 2^{-2}$	0.031250
0-010-0001	$+1.0001 \times 2^{-1}$	0.53125	0-000-0001	$+0.0001 \times 2^{-2}$	0.015625
0-010-0000	$+1.0000 \times 2^{-1}$	0.50000	0-000-0000	$+0.0000 \times 2^{-2}$	+ZERO

Rounding Methods

Rounding reduces the significant digits in a number. It often means *round to integer*, which is a special case of *round to a specified precision*. For example, 24.61247 can be rounded to the integer 25, to four decimal places as 24.6125, and to one significant digit as 20, and the binary number 10010.1001 can be rounded to the integer 10011, to two places as 10010.10, and to three places as 10010.101. Rules apply relative to the digit being rounded, regardless of whether this is exactly at the decimal point, to the left, or to the right. There are many methods for rounding currently in use (without loss of generality, all methods shown here round to integers):

Round Down / Floor:

The ***floor*** function means "pick the largest integer less than or equal to the argument" and is written as $\lfloor x \rfloor$. This is equivalent to rounding down. For example, $\lfloor 65 \rfloor = 65$ (already an integer), and so are both $\lfloor 65.1 \rfloor = 65$ and $\lfloor 65.9 \rfloor = 65$. When the argument is negative, however, $\lfloor -65 \rfloor = -65$ (still an integer), but both $\lfloor -65.1 \rfloor = -66$ and $\lfloor -65.9 \rfloor = -66$.

Round Up / Ceiling:

The ***ceiling*** function means "pick the smallest integer greater than or equal to the argument" and is written as $\lceil x \rceil$. This is equivalent to rounding up. For example, $\lceil 65 \rceil = 65$ (already an integer), and but both $\lceil 65.1 \rceil = 66$ and $\lceil 65.9 \rceil = 66$. When the argument is negative, however, $\lceil -65 \rceil = -65$ (still an integer), and so are both $\lceil -65.1 \rceil = -65$ and $\lceil -65.9 \rceil = -65$.

Round Towards Zero / Truncate:

The ***truncate*** function means "throw away any fraction" which on any argument with a non-zero fraction gives a result that is closer to zero (integers are unchanged). For example, Truncate(65.1) = Truncate(65.9) = 65, and Truncate(-65.1) = Truncate(-65.9) = -65. Many programming languages have either a `trunc` function or an `int` function built-in which performs truncation.

Round Away from Zero:

This means "for any argument with a non-zero fraction, pick the next integer further away from zero" (integers are unchanged). For example, RoundAway(65.1) = RoundAway(65.9) = 66, and RoundAway(-65.1) = RoundAway(-65.9) = -66.

Round to Nearest (½ is a special case):

This means "pick the closest integer." For example, Round(65.1) = 65, Round(65.9) = 66, Round(-65.1) = -65, Round(-65.9) = -66. This method requires special attention when the fraction is exactly one-half, however. Any of the above approaches can be used (round half up, down, away from zero, or towards zero), but may also include round half towards the nearest even integer or round half towards the nearest odd integer. The `round` function in many programming languages is either Round Half Away From Zero or Round Half to Nearest Even (also called ***Banker's Rounding***); programmers must know which one the language supports.

Table of Rounding Examples

This table shows all the rounding methods described on the previous page, and all round to integers. Cases for round to nearest when the fraction is exactly one-half are shown in gray.

N	Round Down	Round Up	Round Towards Zero	Round Away From Zero	Round to Nearest, but Round Half...					
					Up	Down	Away From Zero	Towards Zero	To Even	To Odd
	Floor	Ceiling	Truncate	Zero						
4.75	4	5	4	5	5	5	5	5	5	5
4.50	4	5	4	5	5	4	5	4	4	5
4.25	4	5	4	5	4	4	4	4	4	4
4.00	4	4	4	4	4	4	4	4	4	4
3.75	3	4	3	4	4	4	4	4	4	4
3.50	3	4	3	4	4	3	4	3	4	3
3.25	3	4	3	4	3	3	3	3	3	3
3.00	3	3	3	3	3	3	3	3	3	3
2.75	2	3	2	3	3	3	3	3	3	3
2.50	2	3	2	3	3	2	3	2	2	3
2.25	2	3	2	3	2	2	2	2	2	2
2.00	2	2	2	2	2	2	2	2	2	2
1.75	1	2	1	2	2	2	2	2	2	2
1.50	1	2	1	2	2	1	2	1	2	1
1.25	1	2	1	2	1	1	1	1	1	1
1.00	1	1	1	1	1	1	1	1	1	1
0.75	0	1	0	1	1	1	1	1	1	1
0.50	0	1	0	1	1	0	1	0	0	1
0.25	0	1	0	1	0	0	0	0	0	0
0.00	0	0	0	0	0	0	0	0	0	0
-0.25	-1	0	0	-1	0	0	0	0	0	0
-0.50	-1	0	0	-1	0	-1	-1	0	0	-1
-0.75	-1	0	0	-1	-1	-1	-1	-1	-1	-1
-1.00	-1	-1	-1	-1	-1	-1	-1	-1	-1	-1
-1.25	-2	-1	-1	-2	-1	-1	-1	-1	-1	-1
-1.50	-2	-1	-1	-2	-1	-2	-2	-1	-2	-1
-1.75	-2	-1	-1	-2	-2	-2	-2	-2	-2	-2
-2.00	-2	-2	-2	-2	-2	-2	-2	-2	-2	-2
-2.25	-3	-2	-2	-3	-2	-2	-2	-2	-2	-2
-2.50	-3	-2	-2	-3	-2	-3	-3	-2	-2	-3
-2.75	-3	-2	-2	-3	-3	-3	-3	-3	-3	-3
-3.00	-3	-3	-3	-3	-3	-3	-3	-3	-3	-3
-3.25	-4	-3	-3	-4	-3	-3	-3	-3	-3	-3
-3.50	-4	-3	-3	-4	-3	-4	-4	-3	-4	-3
-3.75	-4	-3	-3	-4	-4	-4	-4	-4	-4	-4
-4.00	-4	-4	-4	-4	-4	-4	-4	-4	-4	-4
-4.25	-5	-4	-4	-5	-4	-4	-4	-4	-4	-4
-4.50	-5	-4	-4	-5	-4	-5	-5	-4	-4	-5
-4.75	-5	-4	-4	-5	-5	-5	-5	-5	-5	-5

Interval Arithmetic

An ***interval*** is defined as a range containing low bound and a high bound, within which the true value of a number is guaranteed to lie. For example, the number **a** is written as the interval [a,ā], where the true value is: a ≤ **a** ≤ ā. If a = ā then **a** is ***exact***, but if a < ā then the true value of **a** may be anywhere within that interval.

In practical floating-point systems, irrational numbers and numbers with very long fractions cannot contain all possible digits, so intervals form a practical way to constrain calculations. For example, π is approximately 3.14159265358979…, but the following intervals are all acceptable representations of π: [3.14, 3.15], [3.1415, 3.1416], [3.141592, 3.141593]. The only difference between these intervals is the tightness of the bounds.

The number 2 is the interval [2, 2] (exact under all floating-point systems).

Arithmetic on Intervals:

In each case, if rounding is required then the results of computing the low bounds are rounded down (towards –infinity) and the results of computing the high bounds are rounded up (towards +infinity).

[a,ā] + [b,б] = [a + b, ā + б]

[a,ā] – [b,б] = [a – б, ā – b]

[a,ā] × [b,б] = [min(ab, aб, āb, āб), max(ab, aб, āb, āб)]

[a,ā] ÷ [b,б] = [a,ā] × [1/б, 1/b], so long as 0 is not in [b,б] (divide by zero)

In the case of addition, for example, the interval [a + b, ā + б] is computed so that a + b is rounded down and ā + б is rounded up.

Example:

π = 3.1415926…, so we might use the interval [3.14, 3.15]
e = 2.7182818…, so we might use the interval [2.71, 2.72]
π + e = [3.14 + 2.71, 3.15 + 2.72] = [5.85, 5.87] (interval size = 0.02)

Using tighter intervals gives a better answer:
π = 3.1415926…, so we might use the interval [3.1415, 3.1416]
e = 2.7182818…, so we might use the interval [2.7182, 2.7183]
π + e = [3.1415 + 2.7182, 3.1416 + 2.7183] = [5.8597, 5.8599] (interval size = 0.0002)

In both cases the "true" answer of 5.8598744… lies between the low and high bounds of the resulting interval. Interval arithmetic provides a way of determining if the result of a calculation is reliable enough to be trusted (small interval) or not (large interval).

Universal Numbers (UNUM)

While interval arithmetic is one approach to the automatic handling of error bounds in computations, an argument can be made that it generates bounds that are unnecessarily coarse (that is, giving an answer where the size of the interval is larger than it should be). This is the case made by John L. Gustafson in his book "The End of Error – UNUM Computing" (CRC Press, 2015). In his book, he advocates for an extension to the IEEE floating-point format so that the sizes (in bits) of both the exponent field and the mantissa field are allowed to vary. Doing so allows for an extremely efficient use of the bits, reducing both the number of NaN patterns and problems with round-off errors, and tightly controlling the error bounds. Varying the number of bits in a number also may lead to power savings in battery-powered mobile devices if smaller numbers are required more frequently than larger ones. Here is Dr. Gustafson's proposal for the ***Universal Number*** (or ***UNUM***) format. Refer to his book for more details.

Sign	Exponent	Fraction (Mantissa)	UBIT	Exp Size	Frac Size
s	e	f	u	es-1	fs-1
	← es bits →	← fs bits →			

In this format, the sign, exponent, and fraction (mantissa) fields have the same interpretations as in IEEE 754, but the length of the exponent field is controlled by the new ***exponent size*** field, and the length of the mantissa is controlled by the new ***fraction size*** field. The sizes of those new fields must be defined up front, but are usually very small, and the numbers they contain are *one less* than their true values in order to use the bits most efficiently. The new 1-bit ***ubit*** field will be described later. The three fields together form the ***utag***, stored along with every number.

Suppose, for example, the size of the exponent size field is defined as 4 bits and the size of the fraction size field is defined as 7 bits (he calls this a "{4,7} environment"). The unsigned range of values for four bits is between 0 and $2^4-1 = 15$, but because the value stored is one less than desired these same four bits can represent any value between 1 and 16. Similarly, the unsigned range of values for seven bits is between 0 and $2^7-1 = 127$, but because the value stored is one less than desired these same seven bits can represent any value between 1 and 128. This means that the exponent field may be between 1 and 16 bits in length, and the fraction (mantissa) field may be between 1 and 128 bits in length. Thus, a floating-point number part may be as small as 3 bits (1-bit sign, 1-bit exponent, 1-bit fraction) or as large as 145 bits (1-bit sign, 16-bit exponent, 128-bit fraction). This easily subsumes the quarter, half, single, double, and quadruple precision IEEE formats. With the additional fixed overhead of 12 bits for this particular utag definition (one bit for the ubit, 4 bits for the exponent size field, and 7 bits for the fraction size field) UNUMs for the {4,7} environment may thus range between 15 and 157 bits in length.

The ***ubit***, or ***uncertainty bit***, is 0 when the value of the floating-point number is exact, but when it is 1 the value is in an open interval between two representable values. In this case the floating-point number is considered to have an additional fraction bit, and its true value is somewhere between one extreme where that fraction bit is 0 and the other extreme where the fraction bit is 1. This subsumes interval arithmetic, insuring that the intervals are as small as possible (that is, the interval is no larger than one ***unit in the last place***, or 1 ***ULP***).

Universal Numbers (UNUM)

5: *Truth Tables and Gates*

This section deals with the basic operations behind any Boolean (two-valued) logic system, as well as how to use the digital functional elements (gates) that implement those operations. Gates are an abstract layer between the mathematics of computing and the electronic devices that perform those computations. A design based on gates is largely independent of the actual hardware used to construct that design. As technology improves over time (and it should), the mathematics of the design remain unchanged.

The circuits shown start with simple connections of two to four gates, then quickly go to more and more complicated designs. As the complexity increases, previous designs are incorporated as black boxes into the new designs. This increase in abstraction is typical of computer architectures. For example, a simple memory circuit called a flip-flop requires two gates, but a more complicated one requires six. That more complicated flip-flop is then treated as a basic building block to construct counters and shift registers, which are then themselves used to construct even more intricate designs such as pseudo-random number generators or serial adder/subtractors. These highly complex designs are rarely shown at the basic gate level.

Truth Tables

One Input

A	NOT
0	1
1	0

Two Inputs

A	B	AND	NAND	OR	NOR	XOR	XNOR
0	0	0	1	0	1	0	1
0	1	0	1	1	0	1	0
1	0	0	1	1	0	1	0
1	1	1	0	1	0	0	1

Three Inputs

A	B	C	AND	NAND	OR	NOR
0	0	0	0	1	0	1
0	0	1	0	1	1	0
0	1	0	0	1	1	0
0	1	1	0	1	1	0
1	0	0	0	1	1	0
1	0	1	0	1	1	0
1	1	0	0	1	1	0
1	1	1	1	0	1	0

General Rules

NOT: The output is 1 if the input is 0; the output is 0 if the input is 1.
       (NOT only ever has one input.)

AND: The output is 1 if **all** inputs are 1; the output is 0 if **any** input is 0.
NAND: The output is 0 if **all** inputs are 1, the output is 1 if **any** input is 0.

OR: The output is 1 if **any** input is 1; the output is 0 if **all** inputs are 0.
NOR: The output is 0 if **any** input is 1, the output is 1 if **all** inputs are 0.

XOR: The output is 1 if inputs **differ**, the output is 0 if inputs are the **same**.
XNOR: The output is 0 if inputs **differ**, the output is 1 if inputs are the **same**.
       (XOR and XNOR generally apply only to two inputs.)

DeMorgan's Theorems

DeMorgan's Theorems can be used to translate expressions using AND into expressions using OR, and vice versa. With only AND and NOT, or with only OR and NOT, any logical expression can be formed. This is particularly important in computer design, where devices of one particular type may be needed, but only devices of another type are available.

A NAND B = (NOT A) OR (NOT B)
= NOT (A AND B)

A AND B = NOT ((NOT A) OR (NOT B))
= NOT (A NAND B)

A NOR B = (NOT A) AND (NOT B)
= NOT (A OR B)

A OR B = NOT ((NOT A) AND (NOT B))
= NOT (A NOR B)

Simple Primitive Gates

GATE SYMBOL	FUNCTION	NOTES
AND	The output is 1 if **all** inputs are 1; the output is 0 if **any** input is 0.	These four gates, in practice, may have any arbitrary number of input lines (but always at least two). Most commonly, actual physical gate devices will have only two or three input lines, but occasionally it is necessary to have gates with 4, 8, or even more inputs. The function description applies equally in all cases.
NAND	The output is 0 if **all** inputs are 1; the output is 1 if **any** input is 0.	
OR	The output is 1 if **any** input is 1; the output is 0 if **all** inputs are 0.	
NOR	The output is 0 if **any** input is 1; the output is 1 if **all** inputs are 0.	
XOR	The output is 1 if the inputs are **different**; the output is 0 if the inputs are the **same**.	XOR gates almost always have only two inputs. There is an XNOR gate, but it is rarely used in practice.
NOT	The output is 1 if the input is 0; the output is 0 if the input is 1. The output is **not** what the input is.	NOT gates always have exactly one input.

Half-Adders

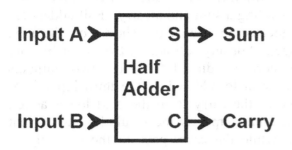

A half-adder can add two bits, generating a sum and a carry (binary numbers 0+0=00, 0+1=1+0=01, and 1+1=10, representing decimal numbers 0, 1, and 2). Half-adders *cannot* add together three bits, which is necessary to create a general purpose binary adder.

The circuits shown below all implement the functions of a half-adder.

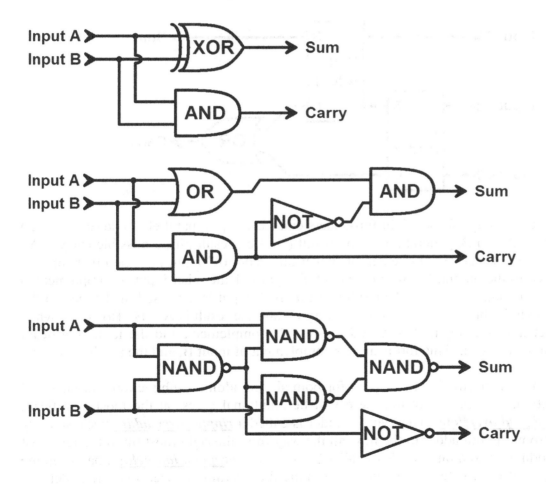

Full-Adders

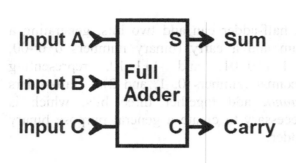

A full-adder can add three bits, also generating a sum and a carry. Full-adders are connected in chains (as shown on the next page). For any full-adder, two input bits are the corresponding bits of the two numbers you wish to add, while the third input is to receive the carry from the next lower adder. The sum output is the result for the current bit, while the carry goes to the next higher adder. The circuit below shows how to construct a full-adder from half-adders.

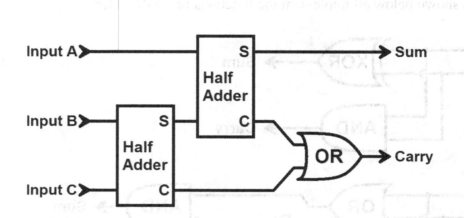

The circuit on the next page shows eight full-adders connected up in parallel to add (or subtract) two 8-bit numbers, A and B, generating a 9-bit result (an 8-bit result plus a possible carry). An XOR-gate acts like a selective complementor: when one "control" input is 0 the other input is passed unchanged to the output, but when the control input is 1 the other input is complemented on its way to the output. When the Add/Subtract line is 0, input B is passed unchanged to the adder, the least significant adder gets a 0 on its carry in, and the result is A + B. However, when the Add/Subtract line is 1, input B is turned into its 1's complement, and the least significant adder gets a 1 on its carry in. This forms the 2's complement of input B, and the result is A − B.

Note that the same adder circuit can be used for both signed addition/subtraction and unsigned addition/subtraction. In real hardware, there will be additional gates on the most significant adder to detect ***signed overflow***. This type of adder is called a ***ripple carry adder*** because carry bits can ripple from one full adder to the next all the way from the right most bit to the left most (for example, adding +1 to a number that is all 1 bits). These ***propagation delays***, based on the cumulative delays of each gate in the chain, determine the maximum speed that the adder can generate a valid output. In contrast, a ***carry lookahead adder*** (not shown here) adds a lot more circuitry to the basic adder in order to speed up the overall process by anticipating when carries will be generated, and thus reduce propagation delays.

8-Bit Parallel Adder-Subtractor

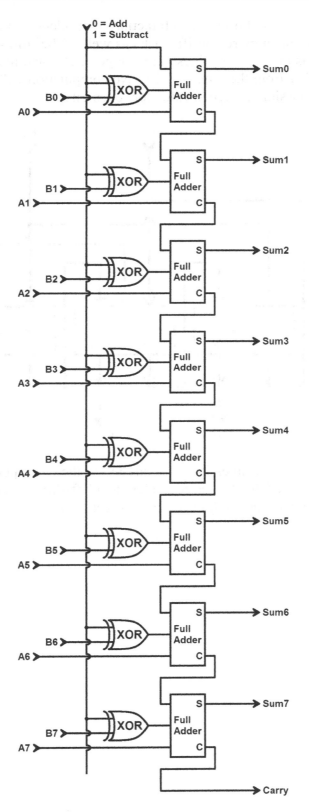

Multiply By 5

Rather than general purpose addition and subtraction, half-adder and full-adder circuits can be hooked together to form much more specific tasks as well.. The following circuit, for example, takes in a 4-bit number as input, with values in the range 0…15, and multiplies that number by 5, resulting in a 7-bit number from the range 0…75. No computation will give a result between 76 and 127 (the maximum possible unsigned value for seven bits).

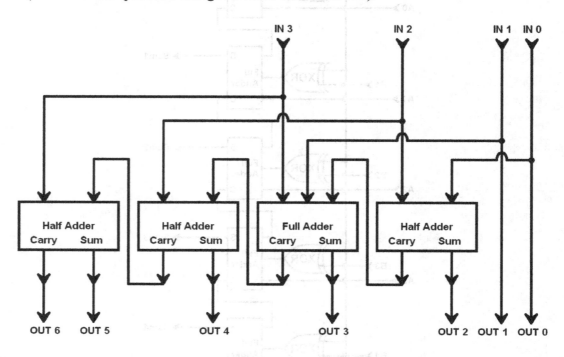

Notice that every input bit contributes its value directly to the corresponding output bit, but also to the bit two positions to the left. This is equivalent to a left-shift of two bits, multiplying the bit times 4. In essence, the adders are adding $N + N{\times}4$ to get $N{\times}5$.

2:1 Multiplexer

All **_multiplexers_** select one input from a group of inputs, and pass that input's value directly to the output. All other inputs are ignored.

This particular circuit selects <u>one of two</u> inputs to pass to the output. The A0 line controls which data input is selected. When that data input is 0 the output is 0, and when that data input is 1 the output is 1.

When A0=0, the lower AND-gate is cut off, and the upper AND-gate is active, so DATA 0 IN is passed to DATA OUT.

When A0=1, the upper AND-gate is cut off, and the lower AND-gate is active, so DATA 1 IN is passed to DATA OUT.

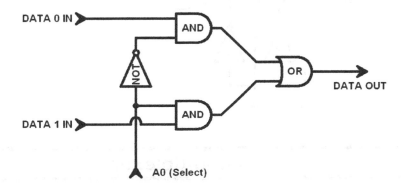

4:1 Multiplexer

This circuit selects one of four inputs to pass to the output. Two inputs in each AND-gate listen to control inputs A1 and A0, directly or via NOT-gates. One AND-gate will have both inputs from A1 and A0 equal to 1, and only that AND-gate will pass its DATA IN value to OUTPUT.

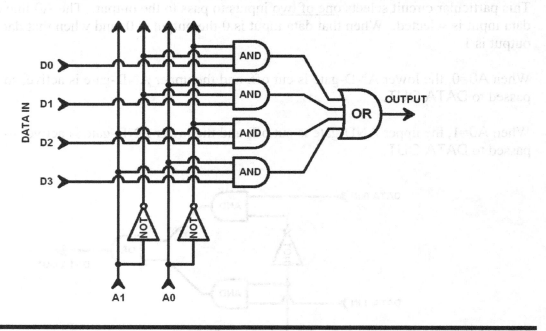

1:4 Demultiplexer

A ***demultiplexer*** passes one input to only one out of a number of outputs. The DATA IN line goes to all AND-gates, only one of which has both of its other inputs from A1 and A0 equal to 1. The input value will go to only that AND-gate's output. All other AND-gates will output 0.

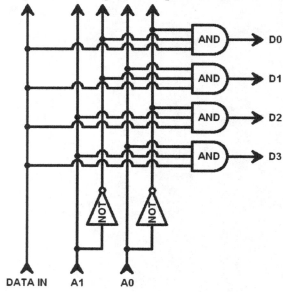

3-Stage Barrel Shifter

A **_barrel shifter_** uses 2:1 multiplexers (MUX) in combination in order to shift a long binary number by an arbitrary amount (equivalent to multiplication or division by a power of two). The following barrel shifter is designed for an 8-bit number, which can be shifted by any amount between 0 and 7 bits. The left-most bank of MUX circuits shift the number by either 0 or 4 places, the middle bank shifts the result by 0 or another 2 places, and the right-most bank by either 0 or 1 place.

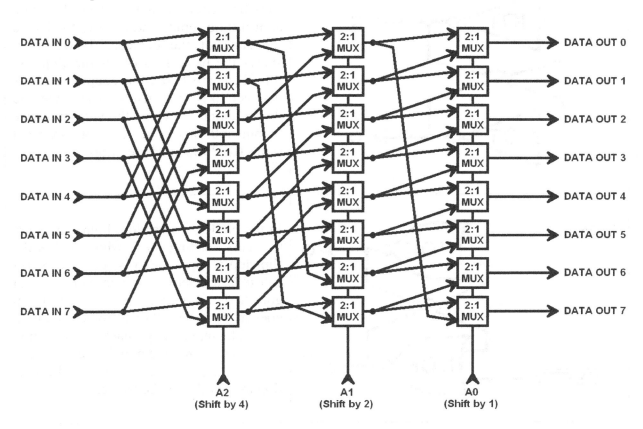

This circuit generalizes to any number of bits. For N control inputs, there will be 2^N data bits to be shifted, which can be shifted by any amount between 0 and 2^N-1 places. In terms of hardware costs, there will be $N \times 2^N$ multiplexers required, each with two AND-gates, an OR-gate, and a NOT-gate.

N	2^N						
Control Inputs	Data Bits	Max Shift	Needed MUX	AND Gates	OR Gates	NOT Gates	Total Gates
1	2	1	2	4	2	2	8
2	4	3	8	16	8	8	32
3	8	7	24	48	24	24	96
4	16	15	64	128	64	64	256
5	32	31	160	320	160	160	640
6	64	63	384	768	384	384	1536

Simple Set-Reset Flip-Flops

A ***flip-flop*** (or ***bistable multivibrator***) is a device that can remember one bit of information. The following circuits show several approaches; all with inputs are called ***set-reset flip-flops*** because one input sets the remembered value to 1, and the other input resets it to 0.

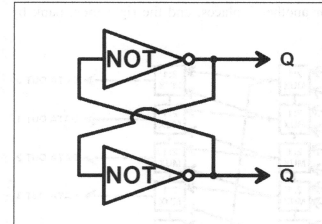

This first circuit is not a practical design, as it has no inputs and no way to change the state of the device. However, it shows the basic idea of all flip-flops, in that there are two cross-coupled devices that act like NOT gates, where the top device outputs a 1 and the bottom device outputs a 0, or *vice versa*. Both are legal states (the "flip" and the "flop").

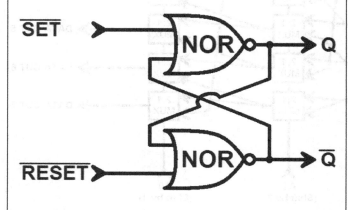

In the NOR-gate version, both inputs are normally "resting" at 0, which makes the flip-flop act like the cross-coupled NOT-gates shown above. If one NOR's input goes to 1, its output is forced to 0, the 0 goes to the other NOR to force its output to 1. The input can go back to the resting state, as the circuit is now locked. Setting the other input briefly to 1 sets the flip-flop in the other locked state.

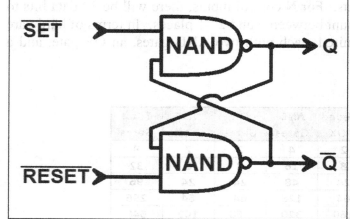

In the NAND-gate version, both inputs are normally "resting" at 1, which again makes the flip-flop act like the cross-coupled NOT-gates. If one NAND's input goes to 0, its output is forced to 1, the 1 goes to the other NAND to force its output to 0. The input can go back to the resting state, as the circuit is now locked. Setting the other input briefly to 0 sets the flip-flop in the other locked state.

D-Flip-Flop

The D (or Data) flip-flop is one of the most important components of a computer. There are other types of flip-flops as well, including **_J-K flip-flops_** and **_Toggle flip-flops_**, but the **_D-flip-flop_** can be used in place of those others in most applications.

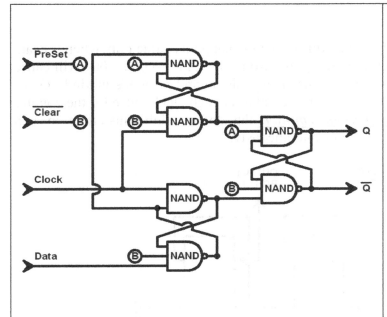

A D-flip-flop is constructed by connecting three NAND-based set-reset flip-flops together, as shown. When the Clock input is 0, the flip-flop remembers the last value (0 or 1) that it was told, and that value appears on output Q (its complement appears on output Q̄). The Data input is ignored while the Clock is 0.

As Clock goes to 1, the current value on Data is *latched* in to the flip-flop – any subsequent changes to Data are ignored until Clock goes back to 0 and then to 1 again. The D-flip-flop is thus said to be *edge-triggered*. It grabs the Data value as Clock goes from 0 to 1, but at no other time.

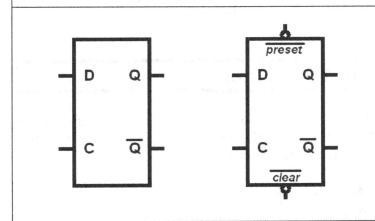

The D-flip-flop is then drawn as a "black box" instead of as its component gates. By adding control lines to various of the internal NAND-gates, the flip-flop can be forced to act as a simple set-reset flip-flop. Those inputs, shown as preset and clear (with bars over them), are normally resting at 1, and activate only when brought to 0, overriding anything else going on with the flip-flop until they return to the resting state of 1.

Asynchronous Binary Counter (3 Bits Shown)

Connecting the $\overline{Q}$ output back to the D input on a D-flip-flop forces it to act as a ***Toggle flip-flop***, which reverses its value every clock pulse. Connecting several of these together as shown creates a simple unsigned binary counter. It takes two clock pulses for any flip-flop to set and then reset; the flip-flop on its left then requires four pulses to set and reset, the one to its left requires eight, and so on.

This is called an ***asynchronous counter*** as each flip-flop will change its value only when it hears the signal to do so from its neighbor to the right – going from 111…111 to 000…000 will cause a ripple across the counter as each flip-flop hears its change signal and responds in kind. Gates are not instantaneously fast, so there will be a short interval after each clock pulse for the counter to settle to its final value. There are ***synchronous counters*** that do not exhibit this effect; in such counters all flip-flops that need to change do so simultaneously.

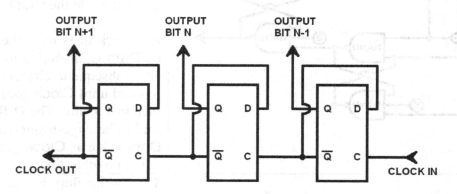

Divide by 10 Counter

A simple 4-bit asynchronous binary counter can be turned in to a BCD (binary coded decimal) counter with the addition of a single NAND-gate. When the counter reaches 10 (binary 1010), the NAND-gate quickly resets all flip-flops in the counter back to 0.

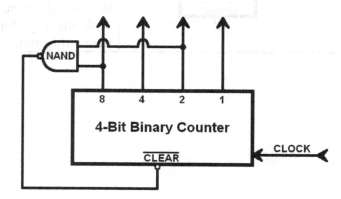

Shift Registers

A ***shift register*** connects the Q output of one flip-flop directly to the D input of the next. All Clock lines are tied together, so a clock pulse activates all flip-flops simultaneously. Values in the shift register march across the flip-flops from the input to the final output in perfect lock step, either to the left or to the right depending on the type of shift register. Remember that a shift-left is equivalent to a multiplication by 2, and a shift-right is equivalent to division by 2.

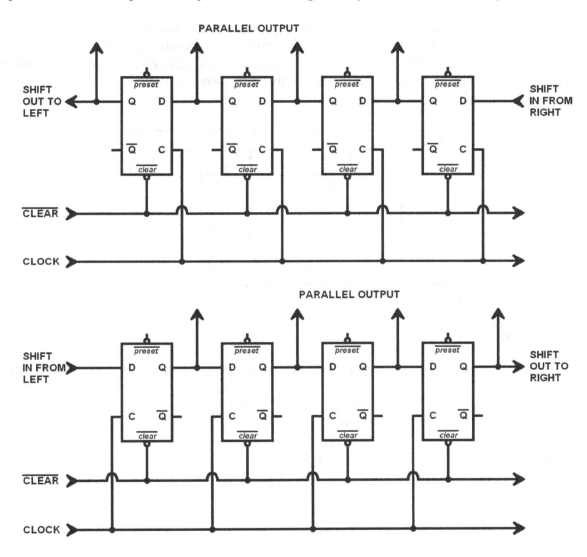

Walking Ring Counter

A ***walking ring counter*** (also known as a ***twisted ring counter*** or ***Möbius ring counter***) steps through a repeating pattern much in the way of a traditional binary counter, but generates a different sequence. No sequence covers all of the possible binary values for a particular counter (except in the case of a 2-bit counter). Such counters are configured as simple shift registers where the complement of the last output is fed back to the input.

In the following 3-bit walking ring, an initial value of 000 is followed by 100, 110, 111, 011, 001, and then back to 000. However, if the value 010 is ever loaded into the counter, it cycles from 010 to 101 to 010 to 101 forever. All walking ring counters of more than two bits have multiple loops, so care must be taken to ensure that the correct initial value is loaded in to the counter (or is regularly reloaded into the counter).

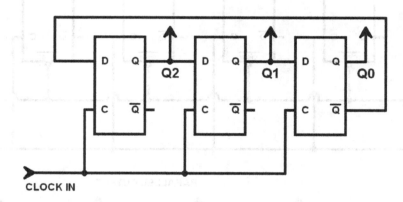

Count patterns:

        2 Bits: Loop #1:   00, 10, 11, 01, 00 (see also Two-Phase Non-Overlapping Clock)

        3 Bits: Loop #1:   000, 100, 110, 111, 011, 001, 000
               Loop #2:   010, 101, 010

        4 Bits: Loop #1:   0000, 1000, 1100, 1110, 1111, 0111, 0011, 0001, 0000
               Loop #2:   0100, 1010, 1101, 0110, 1011, 0101, 0010, 1001, 0100

Linear Feedback Shift Register (LFSR)

One mechanism for generating pseudo-random numbers very quickly in hardware is a ***linear feedback shift register***, or LFSR. A sequence of D-flip-flops is connected as a traditional shift register, but where the input is derived through a series of XOR-gates connected to two or more flip-flop outputs. Each clock pulse generates a new number.

Not all connection patterns are optimal; for N flip-flops some connection patterns force the register to go through 2^N-1 binary patterns before repeating (the maximum possible), while others have much shorter sequences. The optimal placement of the connections is determined by a binary polynomial function based on the length of the register (called the ***feedback polynomial***). The following LFSR has 6 bits and an optimal connection pattern, so it will go through $2^6-1 = 63$ distinct patterns before repeating.

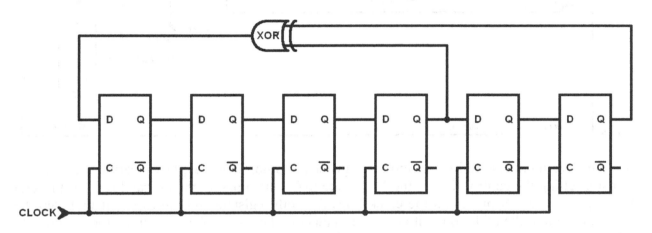

All LFSR circuits must take care to prevent 0 from ever appearing in the shift register – the value 000…000 is always followed by 000…000 (remember that 0 XOR 0 is still 0).

LFSR numbers aren't random enough for many purposes. To build a better source of pseudo-random numbers, a ***shrinking generator*** (Coppersmith, Krawczyk, Mansour, 1993) uses two LFSRs with different feedback polynomials (even different lengths) running in parallel. Both are clocked at the same time. If the *first* LFSR outputs a 0 both registers are clocked again, and this continues until the first LFSR outputs a 1; only then does the output of the *second* LFSR get treated as a data bit in the output sequence.

An even better approach is the ***alternating step generator*** (Günther, 1987), which uses three LFSRs with different feedback polynomials. The first LFSR is always clocked; its output determines which of the other two LFSRs gets clocked. The output is the exclusive OR of the output bits of those other two LFSRs, thus producing output bits at consistent, regular intervals (unlike the shrinking generator).

These are all simple enough to build in screamingly fast hardware. They are pseudo-random in that they will generate the same sequences of numbers when started at the same values. The distribution of bits may appear statistically random, but the overall sequences are repeatable.

Serial Adder

In contrast to the earlier parallel adder, a serial adder uses much simpler hardware to do the same thing, but trades off circuit complexity for time. Regardless of the lengths of the two registers needed to hold the numbers (the accumulator and the operand register), only one full adder, one XOR-gate for subtraction, and one D-flip-flop for the carry bit are needed.

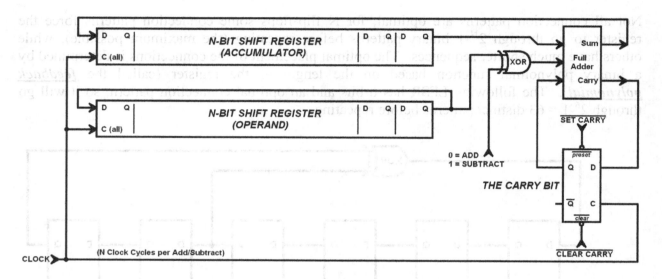

Once the two numbers are loaded into the registers, addition is initiated by clearing the carry bit to 0 and setting the control line on the XOR-gate to 0, which passes the operand register through unchanged. Then, N pulses on the clock lines for both registers and the carry bit will step the numbers through the adder one bit at a time, replacing the value of the accumulator with its old value plus the operand register. The value of the operand register is recycled back into place.

For subtraction, the control line on the XOR-gate is set to 1 to complement the value of the operand register as it clocks through the adder. The carry bit is also initially set to 1 (which will add 1 more to the total) to properly generate the 2's complement of the operand register. Again, N pulses on the clock lines will perform the subtract.

While the hardware is simple, the downside of this approach is that it is very slow. Running time is proportional to the number of bits being added or subtracted.

Two-Phase Non-Overlapping Clock

A 2-bit walking ring counter goes through states 00, 10, 11, 01, and back to 00. Only one loop exists, and every possible bit combination is represented. By adding AND-gates to the flip-flops to detect the 10 and 01 states, a ***two-phase clock generator*** is created. These are used when circuit actions cannot happen at or near the same instant in time: first do *this*, then do *that*. Many microprocessor chips either require a two-phase clock or generate their own internally.

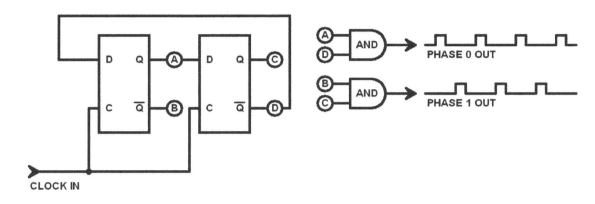

16-Phase Sequencer

A combination of a two-phase clock generator, a 4-bit asynchronous binary counter, and a 1:16 demultiplexer results in a sequencing circuit that can control up to 16 time-dependent actions. On phase 1 the clock generator advances the counter while the data line to the demultiplexer is 0 (turning off all 16 outputs), and once the counter settles to its final value the selected output is activated on phase 0. No two output lines are activated at adjacent times; there is always a brief interval between any pair of outputs where none of the outputs are activated. This gives all downstream circuits a chance to settle their values before the next action comes in.

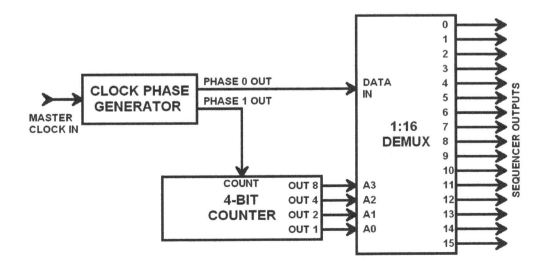

Two-Phase Non-Overlapping Clock

A John walking blue counter goes through states 00, 10, 11, 01, and back to 00. One-one loop exists and every possibly bit combination is represented. By adding AND gates to the flip-flops to detect the 10 and 01 states, a *two-phase clock* can be formed. These are used when circuit actions that must happen in or near the same instant happen first to do that. Many microprocessor chips either require a two-phase clock or generate their own internally.

16-Phase Sequencer

A combination of a two-phase clock generator, a 4-bit synchronous binary counter, and a 1-to-16 demultiplexer results in a sequencing circuit that can count up to 16 time-separated actions. In phase 1 the clock generator advances the counter while the data runs to the demultiplexer is 0 (coming off all outputs), and once the counter settles to its final value the selected output is activated in phase 2. Between any two adjacent lines are activated at different times, there is always a brief interval between any pair of outputs where all the outputs are not active. This gives all downstream circuits a chance to settle their values before the next action comes in.

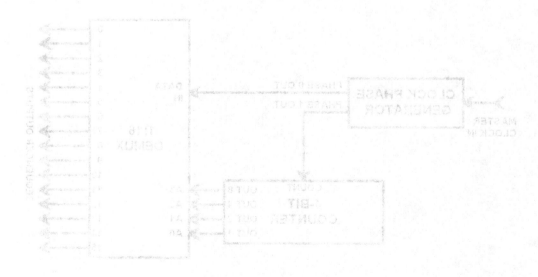

6: *Electronics*

Here are some basic electronics concepts (Ohm's Law, component types, resistor color codes, capacitor codes), along with circuit diagrams for actual devices that can be constructed to implement some basic digital logic gates. These include simple switches, electromechanical relays, diode logic, and discrete transistor logic. At the end of the chapter, there is a section on how to use the popular 7400-series (TTL) and 4000-series (CMOS) chips to build actual working hardware.

All have been used in actual, practical computing devices. Some are modern, but many are archaic technologies by today's standards. All those shown here are simple enough, however, that someone skilled with a soldering iron can build and test working demonstrations.

Ohm's Law

Ohm's Law is the relationship between voltage in Volts (V), current in Amps (I), and resistance in Ohms (R), and also power in Watts (P).

$$I = V / R \qquad V = I \times R \qquad R = V / I$$

For resistive loads only:

$$P = I \times V \qquad P = I^2 \times R \qquad P = V^2 / R$$

Electronic Device Types

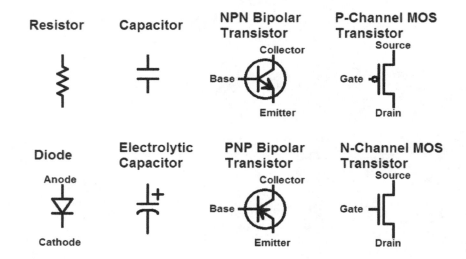

Resistors restrict the flow of current in an electronic device. Diodes generally pass current in one direction, but not the other. Capacitors store and discharge electrons; electrolytic capacitors have a polarity that must be observed to avoid damage. Bipolar transistors act as current switches, where a small change in current at the base causes a large change in current between emitter and collector. MOS transistors act as voltage switches, where a small change in voltage at the gate causes a large change in voltage drop across source and drain.

Resistor Color Codes

For a 4-band resistor, use the following table. In a 5-band resistor, the first three bands are significant digits, the fourth band is the multiplier, and the fifth band is the tolerance. Commercial 4-band resistor values are shown at the right (the tolerance band is not shown).

Color		Band 1	Band 2	Multiplier Band 3	Tolerance Band 4
Black		0	0	×1	-
Brown		1	1	×10	±1%
Red		2	2	×100	±2%
Orange		3	3	×1,000	±3%
Yellow		4	4	×10,000	±4%
Green		5	5	×100,000	±0.50%
Blue		6	6	×1,000,000	±0.25%
Violet		7	7	×10,000,000	±0.10%
Gray		8	8	×100,000,000	±0.05%
White		9	9	-	-
Gold		-	-	×0.1	±5%
Silver		-	-	×0.01	±10%
None		-	-	-	±20%

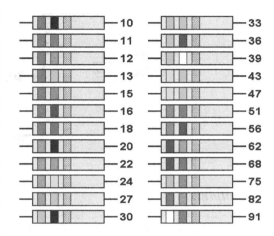

For example, a resistor with the color bands yellow-violet-red-gold is $4 - 7 - \times100 - \pm5\%$, or 4700 Ohms (also known as 4.7K), plus-or-minus 5 percent. Similarly, a resistor marked with color bands brown-black-yellow is $1 - 0 - \times10,000$, or 100,000 Ohms (also known as 100K).

Capacitor Codes

Large capacitors may have their capacitance values printed on the side in easy-to-read letters (particularly electrolytic capacitors). Many ceramic capacitors, however, are too small for this, and must indicate their value in *picofarads* (pF) by a numeric code such as 102 or 473. In these codes, the first two digits are significant, and the third is the power-of-ten multiplier. For example, a capacitor marked as "473" is $47\times10^3 = 47000$ picofarads, or 0.047 *microfarads* (µF). Here is a sample table of common values:

Code	Meaning	pF	µF	Code	Meaning	pF	µF	Code	Meaning	pF	µF
102	10×100	1000	0.0010	103	10×1000	10000	0.010	104	10×10000	100000	0.10
122	12×100	1200	0.0012	123	12×1000	12000	0.012	124	12×10000	120000	0.12
152	15×100	1500	0.0015	153	15×1000	15000	0.015	154	15×10000	150000	0.15
182	18×100	1800	0.0018	183	18×1000	18000	0.018	184	18×10000	180000	0.18
222	22×100	2200	0.0022	223	22×1000	22000	0.022	224	22×10000	220000	0.22
272	27×100	2700	0.0027	273	27×1000	27000	0.027	274	27×10000	270000	0.27
332	33×100	3300	0.0033	333	33×1000	33000	0.033	334	33×10000	330000	0.33
392	39×100	3900	0.0039	393	39×1000	39000	0.039	394	39×10000	390000	0.39
472	47×100	4700	0.0047	473	47×1000	47000	0.047	474	47×10000	470000	0.47
562	56×100	5600	0.0056	563	56×1000	56000	0.056	564	56×10000	560000	0.56
682	68×100	6800	0.0068	683	68×1000	68000	0.068	684	68×10000	680000	0.68
822	82×100	8200	0.0082	823	82×1000	82000	0.082	824	82×10000	820000	0.82

Resistor Networks

The following two circuits are essentially identical. Two resistors are connected in series with a power source, and the voltage is being measured across the bottom of the two resistors. In the left, the power source (a battery) is drawn explicitly, and in the right all voltages, in or out, are measured with respect to the common ground.

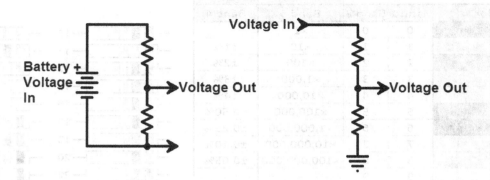

Example:

If the battery is 10 volts, the top resistor is 50 Ohms, and the bottom resistor is 150 Ohms, then the current flowing through the resistors is the source voltage divided by the total resistance, or $10_{volts} / 200_{Ohms} = 0.05_{amps}$, or 50 milliamps (also written as 50ma).

The voltage measured across the bottom resistor is then $0.05_{amps} \times 150_{Ohms} = 7.5_{volts}$. As the bottom resistor is ¾ of the total resistance, it drops ¾ of the input voltage. Resistor networks can perform ***analog division*** of input voltages.

Simple Switched Logic Circuits

The simplest demonstration of circuits that perform logic functions requires nothing more complicated than a battery (shown at the left), a small light bulb (shown at the right), a couple of switches, and some wire. These are manual circuits that require human action to open or close the switches.

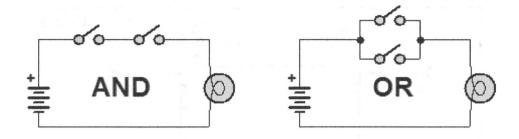

Relay Circuits

Relays extend the notions above to include automatic actions, without the need for human intervention. A **_relay_** is a coil of wire that acts like a magnet when current flows through the coil. When the coil is not energized, the associated switch is in its up, or relaxed state. When the coil turns into a magnet, the switch armature is pulled down, relaying the closed circuit from top to bottom. De-energizing the coil causes the switch to pop up to the relaxed position (it is spring loaded). Relays *may have more than one set of switches* connected by the same armature: all switches are popped up or all switches are pulled down at the same time.

The following circuit is a relay implementation of a NOT-gate. The output has a positive voltage (logic 1) as long as the coil is off (logic 0), but as soon as the coil is energized (logic 1) the output switch opens (logic 0).

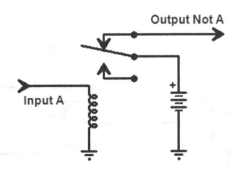

Relay Circuits (Continued)

These four circuits each require two relays. They implement the four basic logic functions AND, OR, NAND, and NOR just by how the switches are wired. All switches are shown with the circuit inputs at logic 0 (all relays un-energized). Relays with multiple sets of independent switches can perform more than one of these functions at the same time.

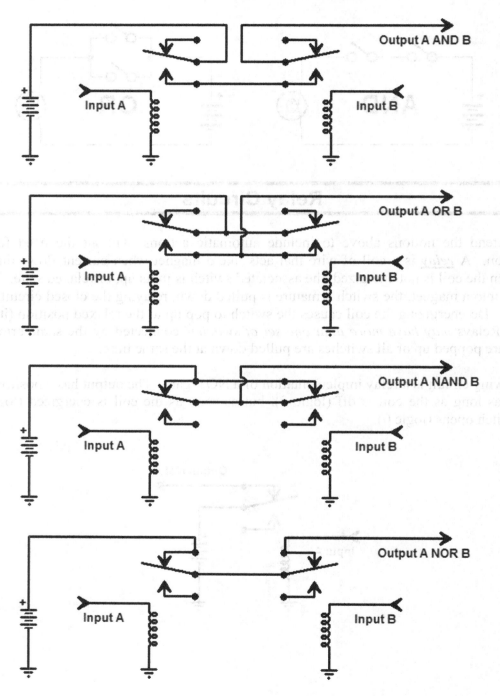

Diode Circuits

Diode circuits were among the very first implementations of logic devices for computers. They have the advantages over relays of being very small, very fast, and non-mechanical (no moving parts to wear out). A diode conducts electricity in only one direction, but not in the other.

This first circuit is a diode AND-gate. When the inputs are all at logic 1 (+ voltage), none of the diodes conduct and the output is dragged to logic 1 through the pull-up resistor. When any input or any combination of inputs are at logic 0 (ground), the corresponding diodes conduct and the output is dragged to logic 0 as well.

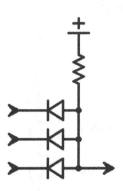

This second circuit is a diode OR-gate. When all inputs are at logic 0 (ground), none of the diodes conduct and the output is dragged to logic 0 through the pull-down resistor. When any input or any combination of inputs are at logic 1 (+ voltage), the corresponding diodes conduct and the output is dragged to logic 1.

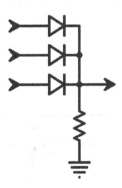

In practice, diodes have a conducting voltage drop of about 0.6 volts, meaning that the AND-gate can never output a true logic 0 (0 volts, or ground) and the OR-gate can never output a true logic 1 (+ voltage). If multiple circuits are connected together, each stage exhibits the 0.6 volt error, and these errors will accumulate to the point that the overall circuit will not work. To compensate, the diode AND-gate and OR-gate circuits often formed the front end to a transistor-based inverter-amplifier, which not only corrected for the voltage drop but also added a NOT function, turning them into NAND and NOR gates, respectively. One of the first types of integrated circuits used this so-called ***diode-transistor-logic*** (DTL).

Transistor Circuits

These circuits are examples of ***resistor-transistor-logic*** (RTL). Transistors of this type (NPN) conduct (between collector and emitter) when their inputs (the base) go positive – the resistors on the inputs, usually between 1K and 4.7K, are to limit the base current to avoid damaging the transistors.

This first circuit is an RTL NAND-gate. As long as one or both of the inputs are at logic 0 (ground), at least one transistor is not conducting, and the output is dragged to logic 1 (the + voltage) through the pull-up resistor. Only when both inputs are at logic 1 do both transistors conduct, dragging the output down to logic 0.

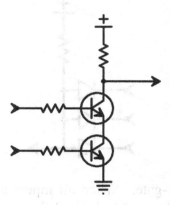

This second circuit is an RTL NOR-gate. When all inputs are at logic 0 (ground), none of the transistors are conducting, and the output is dragged to logic 1 (the + voltage) through the pull-up resistor. When any input is at logic 1 the corresponding transistor conducts, dragging the output down to logic 0.

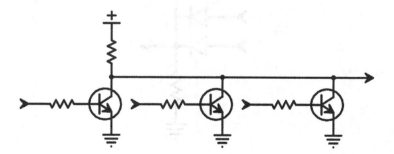

One of the very first types of ***integrated circuits*** used RTL logic. In practice, transistors are not perfect switches, so the output voltages are going to be only "close" to V+ or ground. Care must be taken to avoid having these effects accumulate over many circuit stages.

Designs using primarily transistors and few resistors are called ***transistor-transistor-logic*** (TTL). A series of integrated circuits that used TTL, called the 7400-series, was very popular from the late 1960s onwards (although less frequent today, TTL is still in use). This series of chips will be covered a few pages from now.

CMOS Transistor Circuits

Most modern integrated circuits use ***complementary metal oxide semiconductor*** (CMOS) transistors. CMOS transistors come in two type: P-channel and N-channel. A P-channel transistor (drawn with a circle on its gate connection) conducts current between source and drain when its gate is grounded but not when the gate is at a positive voltage. An N-channel transistor (drawn with no circle on the gate connection) conducts when the gate is positive, but not when the gate is at ground. CMOS transistors are used in the 4000-series chips, described later.

This first circuit implements a CMOS NOT-gate. When the input is at logic 0 (ground) the P-channel (top) transistor conducts but the N-channel (bottom) does not, thus dragging the output to logic 1 (+ voltage). When the input is at logic 1 (+ voltage) the N-channel transistor conducts but the P-channel does not, dragging the output to logic 0 (ground). When either transistor is cut off, there is a nearly-infinite resistance between + voltage and ground, so in both output 0 and output 1 states there is nearly no current being drawn by the circuit. Only when the circuit is switching from 0 to 1 or 1 to 0 do both transistors conduct partially. The more switching that happens per unit time, the more current is drawn (that is, the faster the computer, the more power it uses).

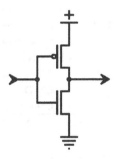

In a CMOS NAND-gate, when either or both inputs are at logic 0 (ground) the corresponding P-channel transistors conduct, dragging the output to logic 1 (+ voltage), and the corresponding N-channel transistors are cut off. Only when both inputs are at logic 1 are both P-channel transistors cut off and both N-channel transistors conducting, dragging the output to logic 0.

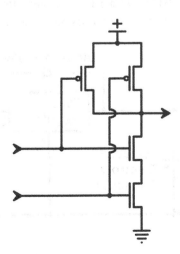

7400-Series TTL and 4000-Series CMOS Integrated Circuits

Many computers from the 1960s onwards used small integrated circuit chips that implemented gate circuits using ***TTL*** (***Transistor-Transistor Logic***). The most popular series of such chips all had part numbers that start with 74. The first chip in this series is the 7400 quad two-input NAND (a 14-pin chip containing four NAND gates, each with two inputs), so the entire line of chips is referred to as the ***7400-series***. A similar but not identical series of CMOS parts are from the ***4000-series***. Hundreds of parts in these series have been created, some with just a few gates (***small scale integration***) and some with many (medium and large scale integration), and several improvements to the technology have also occurred over the years. Today, many circuits use much larger chips, such as CPU chips, instead of small-scale integration, but these smaller chips are still used as "glue logic" to interface between devices.

Logic Series	Delay per Gate (ns)	mW per Gate	Supply Voltage	Notes
7400	10	10	4.75-5.25	Original Series, released in 1966
74L00	33	1	4.75-5.25	1971, Obsolete, replaced by 74LS00
74H00	6	22	4.75-5.25	1971, Replaced by 74S00
74S00	3	19-20	4.75-5.25	Schottky diodes for faster operation
74LS00	9-10	2	4.75-5.25	Low-power Schottky
74AS00	1.7	8	4.75-5.25	Advanced Schottky
74ALS00	4	1.2	4.75-5.25	Low-power 74AS00
74F00	3.4	4-6	4.75-5.25	Fairchild Specific, 1978
74C00	50	*	4-15	CMOS variant
74HC00	9-12	*	2-6	CMOS, Similar to 74LS00
74HCT00	9-12	*	4.75-5.25	CMOS, compatible with 7400

* = Much lower power (~0.001 mW) but is dependent on speed

The diagrams on the following pages show a very small number of representative chips from the 7400 TTL series and the 4000 CMOS series, which often have either 14 or 16 metal pins, one-tenth of an inch apart, in two rows three-tenths of an inch apart, numbered as shown (the dot and the notch identify pin 1). Parts can be obtained from on-line sources, generally from the 74LS00 family or later. To experiment with these devices, a 5-volt power supply is needed, a breadboard socket, some wire, switches, and LEDs. Here is a power supply schematic, using a 7805 three-terminal voltage regulator, which will suffice for experiments:

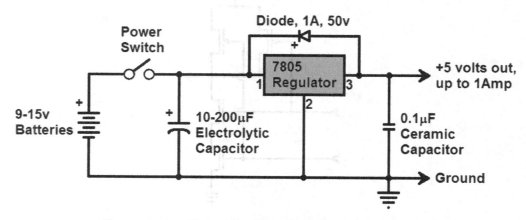

7400-Series TTL Integrated Circuits

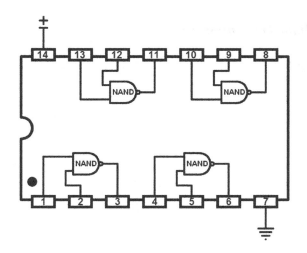

Quad Two-Input NAND

7400
7403 Open Collector.

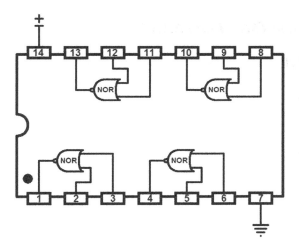

Quad Two-Input NOR

7402

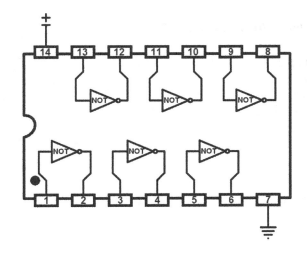

Hex Inverter

7404
7405 Open Collector.
7406 Open Collector (30v, 40ma).
7414 Schmitt Trigger.
7416 Open Collector (15v, 40ma).

7400-Series TTL Integrated Circuits

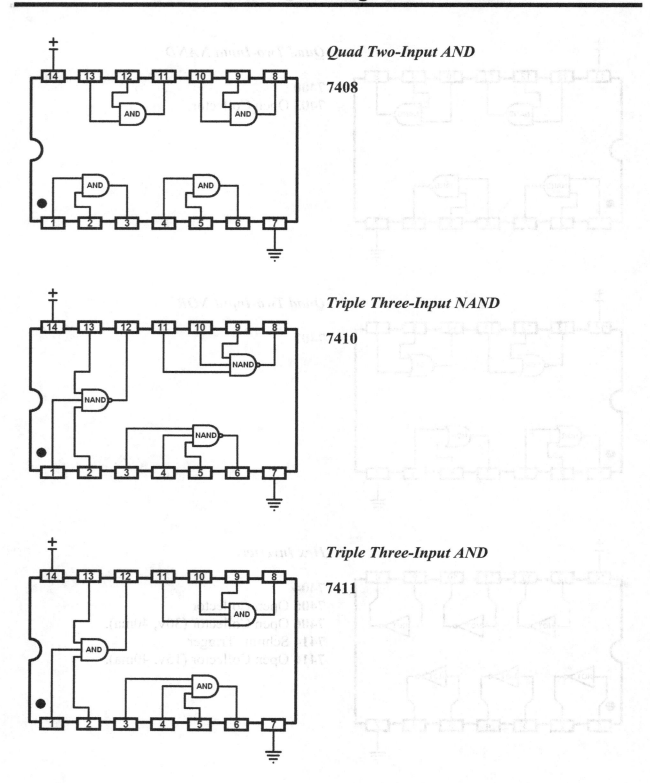

Quad Two-Input AND

7408

Triple Three-Input NAND

7410

Triple Three-Input AND

7411

7400-Series TTL Integrated Circuits

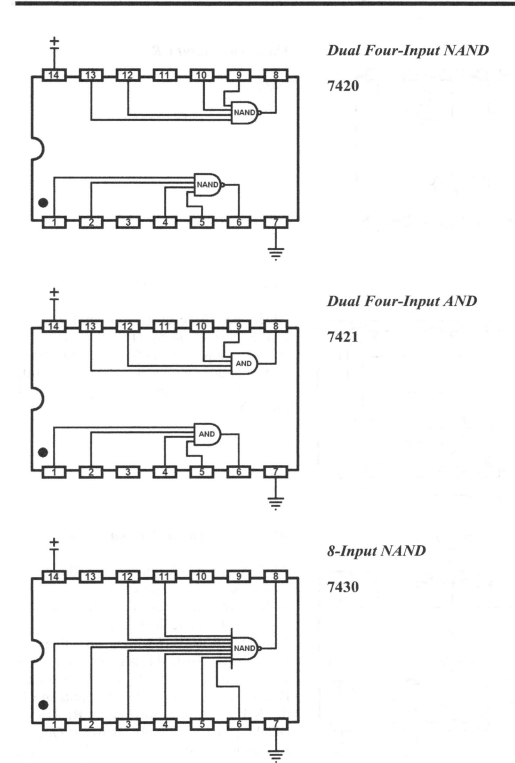

Dual Four-Input NAND

7420

Dual Four-Input AND

7421

8-Input NAND

7430

7400-Series TTL Integrated Circuits

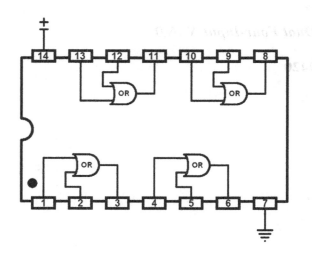

Quad Two-Input OR

7432

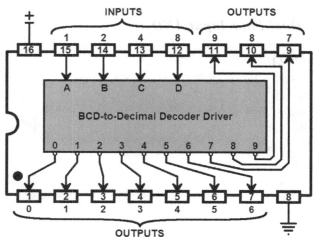

BCD to Decimal Decoder/Driver

7445 Open Collector (30v, 80ma).
74145 Open Collector (15v, 80ma).
Valid inputs are 0000 through 1001; corresponding output is pulled low (to 0). No output activated when input is 1010 through 1111.

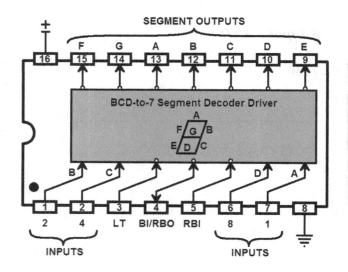

BCD to 7 Segment Decoder/Driver

7447 Open Collector (30v, 40ma) for Common-Anode displays.
7448 Internal resistor pull-ups for Common-Cathode displays.
74247 Same as 7447 with 6 and 9 flags.
LT = Lamp Test: All segments on when LT=0. RBI = Ripple Blanking Input: Blanks when RBI=0 and all inputs are 0. Set RBI=0 on left-most digit. BI/RBO = Blanking Input / Ripple Blanking Output: Blanks when BI=0, outputs RBO=0 when display is blanked. Connect RBO to RBI of digit to right (except rightmost digit).

7400-Series TTL Integrated Circuits

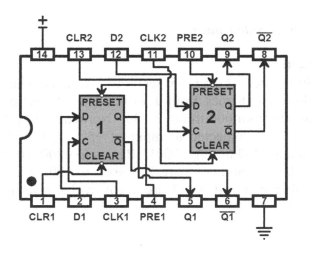

Dual D Flip-Flop

7474
Each independent flip-flop is an edge-triggered D-type, which copies input D to output Q when clock C rises from 0 to 1. Clear=0 forces Q=0; Preset=0 forces Q=1. $\overline{Q}$=1 when Q=0, and vice versa (except both=1 when Clear=Preset=0, which is unstable).

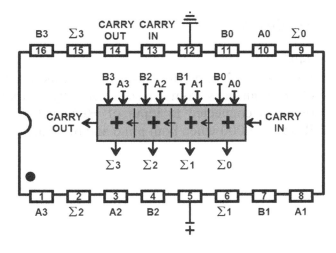

4-Bit Adder

7483
Four full-adders with internal carries. Adds $B_3B_2B_1B_0 + A_3A_2A_1A_0 + C_{IN}$, giving $C_{OUT}\Sigma_3\Sigma_2\Sigma_1\Sigma_0$. To add more bits, connect C_{OUT} to C_{IN} of the next chip to the left.

NOTE: Most data sheets label the bits as 4321 instead of 3210. The labels are changed here to more closely reflect the numeric interpretations of the bits.

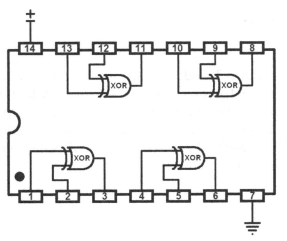

Quad Two-Input XOR

7486

7400-Series TTL Integrated Circuits

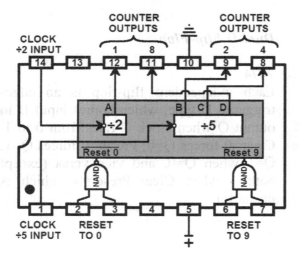

÷10 Decade Counter

7490

Split into ÷2 and ÷5 sections. Counts when clock input goes from 1 to 0. The ÷5 section counts from 000 through 100. Normally, output of ÷2 is connected to input of ÷5 to get BCD output 0000 through 1001. Resets to 0000 when both pin 2 and pin 3 are 1. Resets to 1001 when both pin 6 and pin 7 are 1 (overrides reset to 0000).

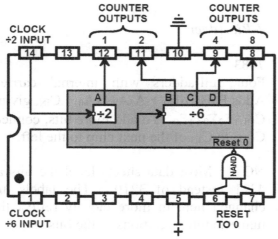

÷12 Counter

7492

Split into ÷2 and ÷6 sections. Counts when clock input goes from 1 to 0. Normally, output of ÷2 is connected to input of ÷6 to get ÷12. Resets to 0000 when both pin 6 and pin 7 are 1.

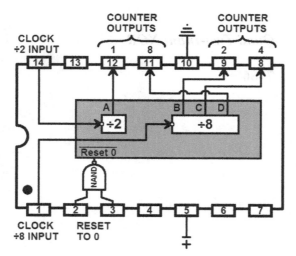

÷16 Counter

7493

Split into ÷2 and ÷8 sections. Counts when clock input goes from 1 to 0. The ÷8 section counts from 000 through 100. Normally, output of ÷2 is connected to input of ÷8 to get output 0000 through 1111. Resets to 0000 when both pin 2 and pin 3 are 1.

7400-Series TTL Integrated Circuits

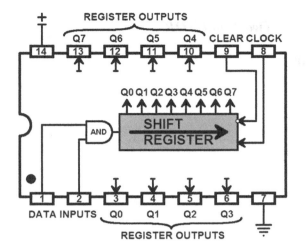

8-Bit Parallel Out, Serial Shift Register

74164
On clock transition from 0 to 1, shifts all data by one bit and makes Q0 whatever was the AND of the two data input lines (hold one data input at 1 to make the other a single input). All bits=0 when CLEAR=0.

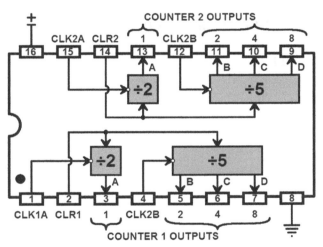

Dual ÷10 Decade Counter

74390
Chip contains two BCD counters, each divided into a ÷2 and a ÷5 section with a common clear (CLR). Counts when clock input CLK goes from 1 to 0. Connect pins 12 and 13 together, and connect pins 3 and 4 together, to get true BCD counting 0000 through 1001. Resets to 0000 with CLR=1.

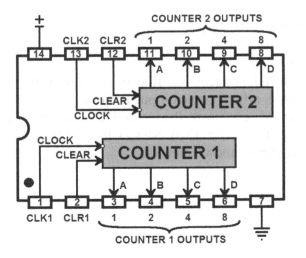

Dual ÷16 Counter

74393
Chip contains two 4-bit binary counters. Counts when clock input CLK goes from 1 to 0. True binary counting 0000 through 1111. Resets to 0000 when CLR=1.

4000-Series CMOS Integrated Circuits

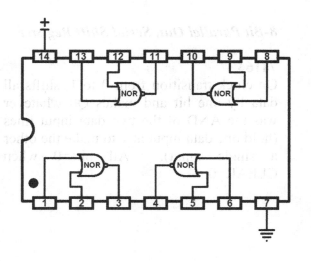

Quad Two-Input NOR

4001

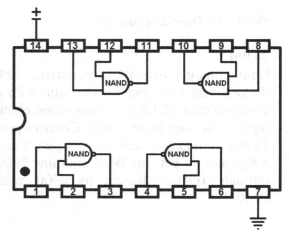

Quad Two-Input NAND

4011

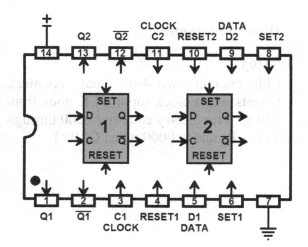

Dual D Flip-Flop

4013
Each independent flip-flop is an edge-triggered D-type, which copies input D to output Q when clock C rises from 0 to 1 and SET=RESET=0. RESET=1 forces Q=0; SET=1 forces Q=1. $\overline{Q}$=1 when Q=0, and vice versa.

4000-Series CMOS Integrated Circuits

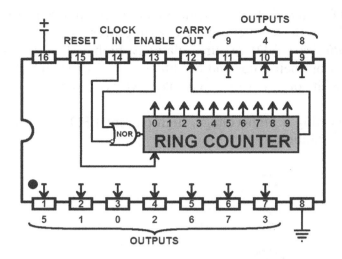

Divide by 10 Ring Counter

4017

When ENABLE=RESET=0, 0-to-1 transitions on $CLOCK_{IN}$ steps counter through states 0-9, then repeats (selected state output=1, all other outputs=0). Counting is paused when ENABLE=1. Counter is forced into state 0 when RESET=1. $CARRY_{OUT}=1$ for states 0-4 and $CARRY_{OUT}=0$ for states 5-9 (to be connected to $CLOCK_{IN}$ of another 4017).

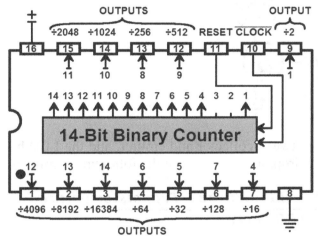

14-Stage binary Ripple Counter

4020

Contains 14-bit binary counter for dividing input clock by powers of 2 between ÷2 and ÷16384, but ÷4 and ÷8 outputs are not available. When RESET=0, 1-to-0 transitions on CLOCK advance counter. Counter is forced to 0 when RESET=1.

Hex Inverter

4049

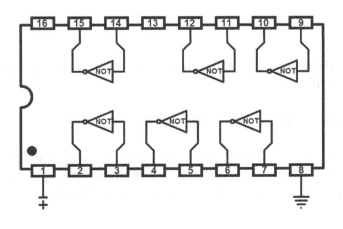

LED Output Circuits

Logic levels are often at +5 volts (for older DTL and TTL logic devices), or at +3.3 or even +1.0 volts for modern devices. The lower the voltage, the smaller are the overall power requirements for the device. However, ***light emitting diodes*** (LED) require relatively high voltages and currents, both of which are largely dependent on their color and brightness. Red LEDs usually take around 2.2 volts at 30 milliamps, while white or blue LEDs may take 5 volts or more.

This results in an interface problem in connecting a high-voltage, high-current LED to a low-voltage, low current logic circuit. Here is one solution:

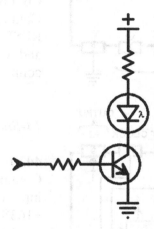

The NPN transistor may drop around 0.6 volts between collector and emitter, and the LED has a voltage drop itself. To compute the value of the dropping resistor, use the following formula:

$$Resistor = \frac{Power\ supply\ voltage - LED\ voltage - Transistor\ voltage}{LED\ current}$$

The input resistor on the base of the transistor is usually 1K to 4.7K ohms, and does not affect the calculations for the dropping resistor.

Example:

A red LED drops 2.2 volts at 30 milliamps. The transistor drops 0.6 voltage across collector and emitter. The power supply is 5 volts.

Dropping Resistor $_{Ohms}$ = $(5 - 2.2 - 0.6)_{volts}$ / $(0.030)_{amps}$ = 2.2_{volts} / 0.03_{amps} = 73.3_{Ohms}

The closest stock resistors available are 68 Ohms and 75 Ohms. The 68 Ohm resistor would increase the LED current slightly, and the 75 Ohm resistor would decrease the LED current slightly. Either is acceptable as long as the maximum current ratings of the LED are not exceeded.

LED Output Circuits (Continued)

The process for interfacing an LED to 7400-series logic gates is in many ways simpler than with discrete components. Some people simply hook the output of a logic gate to an LED, but most logic gates cannot provide quite enough current to drive the LED adequately. Instead, an open-collector output device such as one NOT-gate from a 7406 can usually sink enough current to drive an LED (two or more such gates can be wired in parallel to sink even more current). The input to the NOT-gate interfaces with the rest of the logic circuitry; when the input line is at logic 1 the LED turns on, and when the input is at logic 0 the LED is off. Use the calculations on the previous page to compute the correct value for the dropping resistor (the output transistor of the 7406 drops about 0.7 volts).

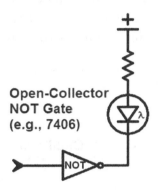

Open-Collector
NOT Gate
(e.g., 7406)

Hardware Input

Getting information into a circuit is as important as getting information out of it. A simple resistor-switch combination can do the job, with a caveat. In the circuit below, the resistor is usually between 1K and 2.2K Ohms. When the switch is open, the output line is pulled high to the supply voltage by the resistor, outputting a logic 1. When the switch is closed, the output line is pulled to ground, outputting a logic 0. The resistor prevents a short-circuit between the power supply and ground. The caveat is that when the switch closes (and to a lesser extent when the switch is opened), the metal pieces of the switch tend to *bounce*, causing multiple changes in the output state, from 1 to 0 to 1 to 0, etc., until the switch settles.

Clock Generation

For circuits that involve counters or flip-flops, including microprocessor chips, a source of pulses is necessary, called a ***clock generator***. In these circuits, also called ***oscillators*** or ***astable multivibrators***, one or more output lines go from 0 to 1 to 0 to 1 continuously (generally at a high rate of speed). The transitions from 0 to 1 and from 1 to 0 are what drive the actions of the rest of the circuitry.

Modern computers use a ***crystal oscillator*** to generate the pulses. These devices use a piece of quartz crystal, cut precisely to vibrate at a specific frequency when voltage is applied (+5v), plus a small amount of additional electronics to clean up and interface the result with other circuitry. These devices come in modules that fit into the same sockets as a 14-pin integrated circuit (some modules are smaller), but only have 4 connecting pins (two for power, one output, and one with no connection). Output frequencies range from 1 MHz to many tens or hundreds of MHz.

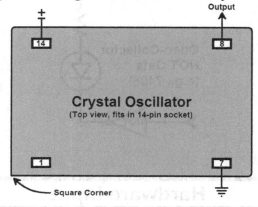

Experimenters can build their own oscillators out of discrete components. In the circuit below, the two R_L load resistors are usually around 1K Ohms; these are for output interfacing only and do not control the timing. Output 2 is always the inverse of Output 1 (when one outputs 0 the other outputs 1, and vice versa). Timing is controlled by the two numbered RC pairs; if the two pairs are identical the ***duty cycle*** will be 50% (same amount of time outputting 0 as outputting 1), but they need not be the same. The time-per-cycle in seconds will be $ln(2) \times (R_1 \times C_1 + R_2 \times C_2)$, resistors measured in megohms and capacitors measured in microfarads ($ln(2) = 0.69314...$). For example, if $R_1 = R_2 = 1M\Omega$ and $C_1 = C_2 = 0.1\mu F$, then one cycle would be $0.69314 \times (1M\Omega \times 0.1\mu F + 1M\Omega \times 0.1\mu F) = 0.69314 \times (0.1 + 0.1) = 0.1386$ seconds long, or 7.2 Hz with a 50% duty cycle.

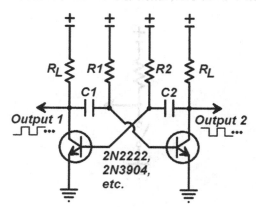

Clock Generation: the 555 Timer

One of the most popular integrated circuit chips ever designed is the 555 timer, originally developed by Signetics in 1971 and now manufactured by many other companies. Many billions of these 8-pin chips have been made.

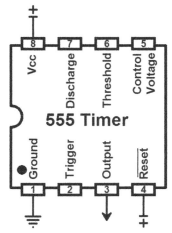

To generate clock pulses, only a small handful of passive components are needed. A typical circuit design is shown below. The diode is optional: if present the capacitor C charges through R_1 and discharges through R_2 (allowing nearly a 50% duty cycle, depending on R_1 and R_2), but if the diode is omitted then C charges through <u>both</u> R_1 and R_2 and discharges through R_2 alone (not a 50% duty cycle, but fewer components). R_1 can be made a variable resistor to control the output frequency (or a combination of a variable resistor and a fixed resistor to make certain R_1 never goes to zero). For long-period (slow) clocks, C may be a large electrolytic capacitor.

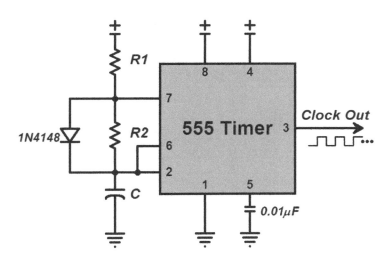

<u>Without</u> the diode, the output on pin 3 is high for $T_{high} = ln(2) \times C \times (R_1 + R_2)$ seconds, and the output is low for $T_{low} = ln(2) \times C \times R_2$ seconds. (Remember that $ln(2) = 0.69314....$) The total time-per-cycle is thus $T_{high} + T_{low} = ln(2) \times C \times (R_1 + 2R_2)$ seconds per cycle, and the output frequency, $1/(T_{high} + T_{low})$ cycles per second, is:

$$Frequency\ (Hz) = \frac{1}{ln(2) \times C \times (R_1 + 2R_2)}$$

<u>With</u> the diode, the high time will be $T_{high} = ln((2 \times V_{cc} - 3 \times V_{diode}) / (V_{cc} - 3 \times V_{diode})) \times C \times R_1$ seconds. For typical values, V_{cc}=5 volts and V_{diode}=0.7 volts, this will be approximately $1.002 \times C \times R_1$ seconds. The low time will be unchanged: $T_{low} = ln(2) \times C \times R_2$ seconds. As before, the output frequency is $1/(T_{high} + T_{low})$ cycles per second.

Clock Generation: the 555 Timer

One of the most popular integrated circuit chips ever designed is the 555 timer, originally developed by Signetics in 1971 and now manufactured by many other companies. Many billions of these 8-pin chips have been made.

To generate clock pulses only a small handful of passive (no IC) components are needed. A typical circuit design is shown below. The diode is optional; if present the capacitor C charges through R1 and discharges through R2 following nearly a 50% duty cycle. Depending on R1 and R2, both the diode is omitted than C charges through both R1 and R2 and discharges through R2 (not a 50% duty cycle, but never components). R2 can be made a variable resistor to control the output frequency. With a combination of a variable resistor and a fixed resistor to make certain R2 never goes to zero. For long periods slow clocks it may be a large electrolytic capacitor.

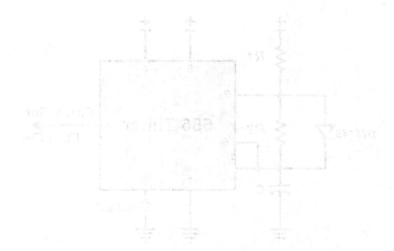

Without the diode the output on pin 3 is high for $t_{high} = ln(2)(C)(R1+R2)$ seconds and the output is low for $t_{low} = ln(2)(C)(R2)$ seconds. (Remember that $ln(2) = 0.693147...$). The total time per cycle is thus $t_{total} = t_{high} + t_{low} = ln(2)(C)(R1+2R2)$ seconds per cycle, and the output frequency, in cycles per second, is:

$$\text{Frequency (Hz)} = \frac{1}{ln(2) \times C \times (R1 + 2R2)}$$

With the diode, the high time will be $t_{high} = ln(2)(C)(\frac{V_{cc}-2V_{diode}}{V_{cc}-V_{diode}})(R1)$ seconds. For typical values $V_{cc}=5$ volts and $V_{diode}=0.7$ volts, this will be approximately $ln(2)(C)(R1)$ seconds. The low time will be unchanged: $t_{low} = ln(2)(C)(R2)$ seconds. As before, the output frequency is 1/($t_{high} + t_{low}$) cycles per second.

7: *Software Interfaces*

This section covers the interfaces and commands for a number of software programs. Many of the tools are command-line driven (MS-DOS, UNIX, emacs, FTP), while a few cover some of the tricks of dealing with graphical interfaces (particularly the Apple Macintosh™ and Microsoft Windows™). In most cases, command-line driven interfaces require that the user remember arcane and difficult commands; these tables will help in those situations where the commands have not yet been memorized.

MS-DOS Internal Commands

CD / CHDIR	Change the active default subdirectory

```
CD                    CD ..                 CD \
CD A:                 CD A:\                CD FROG
CD A:FROG             CD A:\FROG            CD \FROG
```

CLS	Clear Screen

```
CLS
```

COPY	Copy a file or files to a new name, disk or subdirectory

```
COPY FRED.DAT SAM.TXT      COPY FRED.DAT
COPY FRED.* A:\            COPY A:*.*
COPY *.* A:
COPY A:*.* B:
```

DEL / ERASE	Delete a file or files

```
DEL FRED.DAT              DEL *.DAT
DEL *.*                   DEL A:\*.*
DEL C:\TEMP\*.*
```

DIR	Get a directory listing (**/W** = wide display, **/P** = pause every screen full)

```
DIR                      DIR /W /P
DIR A:                   DIR A:*.*
DIR C:\*.DAT             DIR C:\TEMP\FRED.*
```

MD / MKDIR	Make a new subdirectory

```
MD GLOP                  MD FROG\GLOP
MD A:GLOP                MD A:FROG\GLOP
MD A:\GLOP               MD A:\FROG\GLOP
```

RD / RMDIR	Remove an existing subdirectory (must be empty)

```
RD GLOP                  RD FROG\GLOP
RD A:GLOP                RD A:FROG\GLOP
RD A:\GLOP               RD A:\FROG\GLOP
```

REN / RENAME	Rename a file

```
REN FRED.DAT SAM.TXT
REN FRED.* SAM.*
REN A:\FRED.TXT SAM.TXT
```

TYPE	Type out the contents of a text file to the screen

```
TYPE FROG.TXT            TYPE A:FROG.TXT
TYPE A:\FROG.TXT         TYPE A:\TEMP\FROG.TXT
```

MS-DOS External Commands

ATTRIB Find or change the attributes of files (**R**ead, **A**rchive, **S**ystem, **H**idden)
`ATTRIB`
`ATTRIB A:`
`ATTRIB GLOP.DAT`
`ATTRIB A:GLOP.DAT`
`ATTRIB +R +A +S +H GLOP.DAT`
`ATTRIB -R -A -S -H GLOP.DAT`

CHKDSK Check the disk to see how much space is left
`CHKDSK`
`CHKDSK A:`

COMP Compare two files to see if they are identical
`COMP GLOP.DAT SAM.TXT`
`COMP A:GLOP.DAT SAM.TXT`

DEFRAG Defragment a disk
`DEFRAG`

DISKCOMP Compare two diskettes to see if they are identical
`DISKCOMP A: B:`

DISKCOPY Make an identical copy of one diskette onto another
`DISKCOPY A: B:`

FORMAT Prepare a disk to receive data (**/U** = unconditional, **/S** = bootable system)
`FORMAT A:`
`FORMAT A: /U`
`FORMAT A: /S`

SORT Create sorted copy of a text file (**/R** = reverse sort, **/+n** = first character)
`SORT <INFILE.DAT >OUTFILE.DAT`
`SORT /R <INFILE.DAT >OUTFILE.DAT`
`SORT /+9 <INFILE.DAT >OUTFILE.DAT`

UNIX Commands

Account Commands

`du`	Show disk usage	`du -k ~	sort -n	more`
`logout`	Log out of the UNIX account	`logout`
`passwd`	Change your password	`passwd`
`quota`	Show remaining disk space available	`quota`

Directory Management

`cd`	Change current directory	`cd glop    cd ~    cd ..`
`mkdir`	Make a subdirectory	`mkdir glop`
`pwd`	Print the working directory path	`pwd`
`rmdir`	Remove a directory	`rmdir glop`

File Management

`cat`	Concatenate files together or list a file	`cat frog.txt`
`chmod`	Change permissions on a file or files	`chmod 644 frog.txt`
`cp`	Copy a file or files	`cp frog.txt toad.txt`
`ls`	List names of files	`ls -al`
`more`	List a text file one screen-full at a time	`more frog.txt`
`mv`	Move a file to another directory or name	`mv frog.txt toad.txt`
`rm`	Remove a file or files	`rm frog.txt`

Printing

`lpq`	Ask about the status of a print queue	`lpq -Psaturn`
`lpr`	Send a text file to a print queue	`lpr -Psaturn frog.txt`
`lprm`	Remove a job from a print queue	`lprm -Psaturn 121`

Miscellaneous

`clear`	Clear the screen	`clear`
`emacs`	Start the emacs text editor	`emacs index.html`
`fg`	Reactivate a foreground process	`fg`
`man`	Access pages in the help manual	`man command`
Ctrl z	Suspend current process, create new process (return to previous process with **fg**)	
Ctrl c	Abort current command, get next command prompt	

UNIX chmod Command

Symbolic Form (u=user, g=group, o=others, a=ugo, r=read, w=write, x=execute)
```
chmod ugo±rwx filename
chmod a±rwx filename
chmod ugo=rwx filename
chmod a=rwx filename
```

Symbolic Examples (the ? indicates "unknown" or "no change")
```
chmod a+rx public_html              (sets to r?xr?xr?x)
chmod ugo+rx public_html            (sets to r?xr?xr?x)
chmod a+r,u+w,go-w index.html       (sets to rw?r-?r-?)
```

Absolute Form (each of the three n is an octal digit from the Codes table below)
```
chmod nnn filename
```

Absolute Examples
```
chmod 755 public_html               (sets to rwxr-xr-x)
chmod 644 index.html                (sets to rw-r--r--)
chmod 600 private.txt               (sets to rw-------)
```

UNIX Permission Codes (each n)
```
---     0
--x     1
-w-     2
-wx     3
r--     4
r-x     5
rw-     6
rwx     7
```

emacs Commands

Remember that Ctrl is <u>held down</u> while the following key is struck, but Esc is <u>struck and released</u> before striking the next key. Some emacs literature refers to the Esc character as the "meta" key, which can be either Esc or Alt depending on the system.

Ctrl**x**Ctrl**c**	Exit emacs. If necessary it will prompt for saving the file under the current name.
Ctrl**x**Ctrl**w**	Write the data to a file (possibly under a new name) without exiting emacs.
Ctrl**x**Ctrl**s**	Save the file under the current name.
Ctrl**g**	Abort the current command (may require several Ctrl**g** to clear everything up).
Ctrl**l**	Repaint the screen and scroll the text so the cursor is near the screen center.
Ctrl**x u**	Undo last change.
Ctrl**h t**	Take the emacs tutorial (recommended for new emacs users).
Ctrl**f**	Go forwards one character (same as →).
Ctrl**b**	Go backwards one character (same as ←).
Ctrl**n**	Go down to next line (same as ↓).
Ctrl**p**	Go up to previous line (same as ↑).
Ctrl**a**	Go to the beginning of the line.
Ctrl**e**	Go to the end of the line.
Ctrl**v**	Go down one page of text
Esc **v**	Go up one page of text.
Esc **a**	Go to beginning of sentence.
Esc **e**	Go to end of sentence.
Esc **f**	Go forwards one word.
Esc **b**	Go backwards one word.
Esc **<**	Go to beginning of file.
Esc **>**	Go to end of file.
Ctrl**d**	Delete the character under the cursor.
Ctrl**k**	Delete (kill) from cursor to end of line (if line is blank, delete whole line).
Ctrl**s**	Search forward
Ctrl**r**	Search reverse
Ctrl**z**	Suspend emacs, go back to command line (use UNIX **fg** command to return).

ftp Commands

open   Open a connection to a remote site.
             open *ftp.remotesite.com*
             Remote site will issue a username and password challenge.
             Enter `anonymous` for username, and your email address for password.
             Password will not echo (not show up on screen) as you type it in.

dir, ls   Get a listing of files in current remote directory (`dir` is preferred).
             dir
             ls -al

cd   Change current directory.
             cd *pub*   (Change into `pub` directory, `pub` must be visible to `dir`)
             cd *images*   (Change into `images` directory, `images` must be visible)
             cd ..   (Change into parent directory, up one level)

pwd   Print working directory (ask ftp to show the current remote directory path).
             pwd

binary   All subsequent file transfers (`get` and `put`) will make no changes to file.
             binary

ascii   All subsequent file transfers will change end-of-line terminators to adjust carriage
             return and line feed characters for receiving system. Use for text files only.
             ascii

get   Fetch a file from current directory on remote system into current directory on
             local system (the directory from which ftp was started).
             get *remotefile.gif*   (File must be in current remote directory.)

put   Put a file from current directory on local system into current directory on remote
             system. User must have write permission; not often true for anonymous logins.
             put *index.html*   (File must be in current local directory.)

mget, mput Same as `get` and `put`, but allow multiple files to be moved by using wildcards.
             mget **.gif*   (Get all `.gif` files from current remote directory)

close   Close the currently open session. The ftp program remains running.
             close

quit   Terminate the ftp program and return to UNIX command prompt.
             quit

Mac vs. Windows Shortcuts

OS Commands	Windows	Mac (⌘ = Command)
Capture screen to Clipboard	`PrtScr`	⌘ `Ctrl` `⇧ Shift` 3
Capture screen to File	*none*	⌘ `⇧ Shift` 3
		(Saves .*PNG File to desktop)*

Many commands are specific to some particular program. However, over the years a common set of shortcut commands has evolved, and most programs (especially text editors, word processors, and spreadsheets) observe some subset of these. Do not be surprised, however, if a program has no shortcut for one of the commands shown below, uses a different shortcut for a command, or uses a shortcut for a different command altogether.

File Commands	Windows	Mac (⌘ = Command)
Create a New File	`Ctrl` N	⌘ N
Open a File	`Ctrl` O	⌘ O
Save a File	`Ctrl` S	⌘ S
Save a File with a new name	*none*	⌘ `⇧ Shift` S
Print a File	`Ctrl` P	⌘ P
Exit a Program	`Alt` X or `Alt` `F4`	⌘ Q

Editing Commands	Windows	Mac (⌘ = Command)
Select All	`Ctrl` A	⌘ A
Cut	`Ctrl` X	⌘ X
Copy	`Ctrl` C	⌘ C
Paste	`Ctrl` V	⌘ V
Undo	`Ctrl` Z	⌘ Z
Redo	`Ctrl` `⇧ Shift` Z	⌘ `⇧ Shift` Z
Find	`Ctrl` F	⌘ F
Find Again	`F3`	⌘ G
Replace	`Ctrl` R	Option-⌘ F

Miscellaneous Commands	Windows	Mac (⌘ = Command)
Help	`F1`	*none*

Paths to Folders on Macintosh and Windows

The underlined path names are to be filled in with the account name for the user currently logged in to the computer. I log in as user "Bill" so for me the blank would be filled in with `Bill`.

Active Desktop folder:
Win 10:   `C:\Users\____\Documents\Desktop`
Win 7,8:   `C:\Users\____\Desktop`
Win VISTA: `C:\Users\____\Desktop`
Win XP: `C:\Documents and Settings\____\Desktop`
Mac OS/X: `/Users/____/Desktop`

My Documents folder:
Win 8,10:   `C:\Users\____\Documents`
Win 7:   `C:\Users\____\My Documents`
Win VISTA: `C:\Users\____\Documents`
Win XP: `C:\Documents and Settings\____\My Documents`
Mac OS/X: `/Users/____/Documents`

SendTo menu:
Win 7,8,10:   `C:\Users\____\AppData\Roaming\Microsoft\Windows\SendTo`
Win VISTA: `C:\Users\____\AppData\Roaming\Microsoft\Windows\SendTo`
Win XP: `C:\Documents and Settings\____\SendTo`   (normally hidden)

Accessories programs folder:
Win (all):   `C:\Windows\System32`
Mac OS/X: `/Applications`   and   `/Applications/Utilities`

Microsoft Word's `Normal.dotm` or `Normal.dot` style sheet file:
Win 7,8,10   `C:\Users\____\AppData\Roaming\Microsoft\Templates`
Win VISTA   `C:\Users\____\AppData\Roaming\Microsoft\Templates`

Win XP: `C:\Documents and Settings\____\Application Data\`
                          `Microsoft\Templates`

Mac OS/X: `/Users/____/Library/Application Support/`
                          `Microsoft/Office/User Templates`

8: *Color Models*

Color is an important part of dealing with modern computers. This section covers the most common models for color in use on a computer, and contains several tables showing the colors available for use in HTML Web pages.

Printers and artists use a reflective or ***subtractive color model***. Printers have tanks of cyan, magenta, and yellow ink, with a special tank for black ink (CMYK), while artists use red, yellow, and blue as their primary colors (RYB). The visible color is what is not absorbed by the pigment. Each of these are workable color models, but are not what are used in computer displays.

The color model used in computers today is an ***additive color model***, where the primary colors of transmitted light are red, green, and blue (RGB). Colors on a computer monitor or TV are formed by mixing red, green, and blue in various amounts.

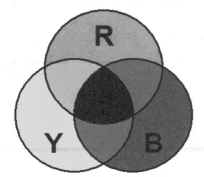
Paint, Crayons, etc.

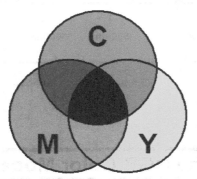
Ink Jet & Laser Printers

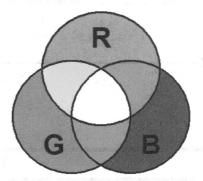
TVs, Monitors, HTML, etc.

It should be noted that there are many other color models in existence, several of which much more closely the human visual response than does RGB (such as CIE, HSL, HSV, HIS, etc.). Unfortunately, a color in one such model may have no counterpart in another. RGB is not a particularly good model, as it turns out, but is largely adequate for our use.

The Color Spectrum

The following diagram shows the color response of the human visual system. The retina contains cone cells which respond more-or-less strongly to different frequencies of light. One set of cells responds strongly to red (long wavelengths), one to green (medium wavelength), and one to blue (short wavelengths), shown by the long bars at the top of the following image.

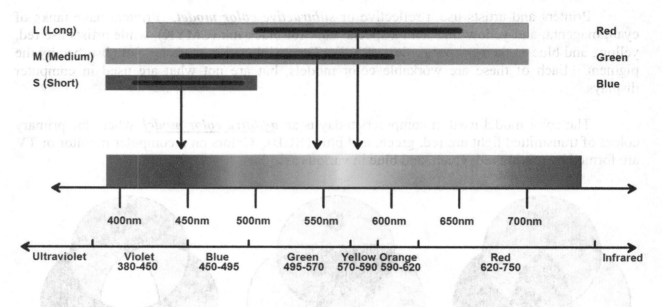

The RGB Color Model

The most common RGB format used in computing is called 24-bit color, where there is one byte (8 bits) for each of the three primaries. Each primary is then a number between 0 (off) and 255 (full power), which in hexadecimal is the range **00**...**FF**. This gives $256 \times 256 \times 256 = 16,777,216$ unique colors.

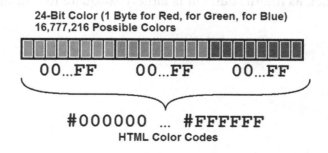

The **.PNG** graphics format supports up to 48-bit color (with 16 bits, or 2 bytes, per primary), but most modern equipment cannot display this many colors. In this format each color primary is a number between 0 (off) and 65535 (full power), or in hexadecimal **0000**...**FFFF**.

Building RGB Colors

Colors in the 24-bit RGB model are constructed by selecting a value between 0 and 255 (between **00** and **FF** in hexadecimal) for each of the three primary colors, red, green, and blue. The eight most basic colors are shown below. All primaries turned off (**00**) gives black, while all three primaries at full power (**FF**) gives white. Yes, red plus green equals yellow.

	Decimal			Hex			Web Design	
	R	G	B	R	G	B	HTML	Short
Black	0	0	0	00	00	00	#000000	#000
Blue	0	0	255	00	00	FF	#0000FF	#00F
Green	0	255	0	00	FF	00	#00FF00	#0F0
Cyan	0	255	255	00	FF	FF	#00FFFF	#0FF
Red	255	0	0	FF	00	00	#FF0000	#F00
Magenta	255	0	255	FF	00	FF	#FF00FF	#F0F
Yellow	255	255	0	FF	FF	00	#FFFF00	#FF0
White	255	255	255	FF	FF	FF	#FFFFFF	#FFF

Note that in HTML, the named color Green refers to a dark green (**#008000**), while the primary green shown here (**#00FF00**) is called Lime in HTML. Also, Magenta and Fuchsia are synonyms (both **#FF00FF**), as are Cyan and Aqua (both **#00FFFF**).

Also, Short Hex can be used in CSS (Cascading Style Sheets) when all three primaries are formed from repeated digits. Thus, **#FF00FF** has the Short Hex value **#F0F**, and **#AA11EE** has the Short Hex **#A1E**, but the color **#F302AA** has <u>no</u> Short Hex equivalent. Short Hex cannot be used in pure HTML, only in CSS and SVG applications.

Shades of gray/grey are formed when all three primaries have *exactly the same value*. This means that **#000000** is a *very* dark gray (Black), **#FFFFFF** is a *very* light gray (White), and **#808080** is a mid-range gray (Gray or Grey). HTML defines the names DarkGray and DarkGrey as **#A9A9A9**, and both LightGray and LightGrey as **#D3D3D3**.

Interpreting RGB Colors in 3D

RGB colors can be interpreted as points in a cube, where the three axes are the primary colors red, green, and blue. In the diagrams below, the red axis points up, the green axis points to the right, and the blue axis points away from the viewing position. (There is nothing special about this arrangement; the red axis could point to the right and green could point up, for example.)

In each diagram, the position of the described color is at the top of the vertical spike, with its red, green, and blue coordinates shown appropriately on the axes.

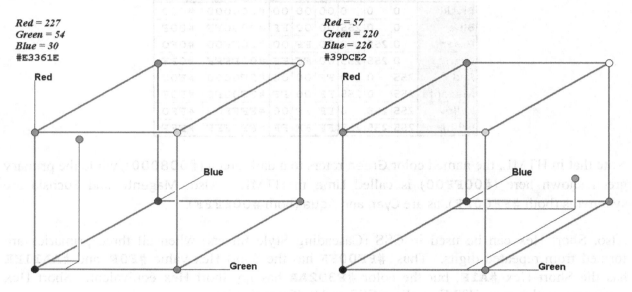

Red = 227
Green = 54
Blue = 30
#E3361E

Red = 57
Green = 220
Blue = 226
#39DCE2

To interpret a color without converting its hexadecimal values back into decimal, just look at the three primary values and ask if, relatively speaking, they are low, medium, or high values. For example, the left color **#E3361E** has red=**E3**, green=**36**, and blue=**1E**. The dominant digit for the red is **E**, which is very high on a scale of **0**...**F**. However, the dominant digit for the green is **3** and the dominant digit for the blue is **1**, which are both very low. High red, low green, and low blue means this color is very reddish. Similarly, the **#39DCE2** has low red (**3**) but high green (**D**) and high blue (**E**), which is a cyan color.

The 216 Browser Safe Colors

The browser safe colors are a set of 216 colors distributed evenly throughout the color space of 16,777,216 possible colors. A browser on an older computer with limited color capability will use one of these 216 whenever an arbitrary color from a Web page is encountered. The color shown may not be exactly the color desired, but it will be close.

All browser safe colors are constructed strictly from the following set of primary color values:

Hexadecimal	#00	#33	#66	#99	#CC	#FF
Decimal	0	51	102	153	204	255

Combinations of these six unique values give the 216 browser safe colors (6×6×6 = 216). Thus, **#33CC00** is browser safe, but **#33AA00** and **#34A2F3** are not.

The following color cube (showing only the front face, BLUE is hidden) shows the layout of the browser safe colors. Any arbitrary 24-bit color will fall into one of the 216 cubes, and the color of that cube will be what is shown on-screen.

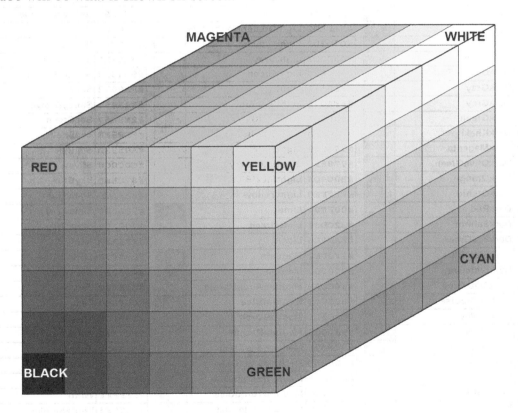

The ~~147~~ 148 Browser Defined Colors (Sorted By Name)

#F0F8FF	AliceBlue		#F8F8FF	GhostWhite		#FFDEAD	NavajoWhite
#FAEBD7	AntiqueWhite		#FFD700	Gold		#000080	Navy
#00FFFF	Aqua		#DAA520	GoldenRod		#FDF5E6	OldLace
#7FFFD4	Aquamarine		#808080	Gray		#808000	Olive
#F0FFFF	Azure		#808080	Grey		#6B8E23	OliveDrab
#F5F5DC	Beige		#008000	Green		#FFA500	Orange
#FFE4C4	Bisque		#ADFF2F	GreenYellow		#FF4500	OrangeRed
#000000	Black		#F0FFF0	Honeydew		#DA70D6	Orchid
#FFEBCD	BlanchedAlmond		#FF69B4	HotPink		#EEE8AA	PaleGoldenRod
#0000FF	Blue		#CD5C5C	IndianRed		#98FB98	PaleGreen
#8A2BE2	BlueViolet		#4B0082	Indigo		#AFEEEE	PaleTurquoise
#A52A2A	Brown		#FFFFF0	Ivory		#DB7093	PaleVioletRed
#DEB887	Burlywood		#F0E68C	Khaki		#FFEFD5	PapayaWhip
#5F9EA0	CadetBlue		#E6E6FA	Lavender		#FFDAB9	PeachPuff
#7FFF00	Chartreuse		#FFF0F5	LavenderBlush		#CD853F	Peru
#D2691E	Chocolate		#7CFC00	LawnGreen		#FFC0CB	Pink
#FF7F50	Coral		#FFFACD	LemonChiffon		#DDA0DD	Plum
#6495ED	CornflowerBlue		#ADD8E6	LightBlue		#B0E0E6	PowderBlue
#FFF8DC	Cornsilk		#F08080	LightCoral		#800080	Purple
#DC143C	Crimson		#E0FFFF	LightCyan		#663399	RebeccaPurple *
#00FFFF	Cyan		#FAFAD2	LightGoldenRodYellow		#FF0000	Red
#00008B	DarkBlue		#D3D3D3	LightGray		#BC8F8F	RosyBrown
#008B8B	DarkCyan		#D3D3D3	LightGrey		#4169E1	RoyalBlue
#B8860B	DarkGoldenRod		#90EE90	LightGreen		#8B4513	SaddleBrown
#A9A9A9	DarkGray		#FFB6C1	LightPink		#FA8072	Salmon
#A9A9A9	DarkGrey		#FFA07A	LightSalmon		#F4A460	SandyBrown
#006400	DarkGreen		#20B2AA	LightSeaGreen		#2E8B57	SeaGreen
#BDB76B	DarkKhaki		#87CEFA	LightSkyBlue		#FFF5EE	SeaShell
#8B008B	DarkMagenta		#778899	LightSlateGray		#A0522D	Sienna
#556B2F	DarkOliveGreen		#778899	LightSlateGrey		#C0C0C0	Silver
#FF8C00	DarkOrange		#B0C4DE	LightSteelBlue		#87CEEB	SkyBlue
#9932CC	DarkOrchid		#FFFFE0	LightYellow		#6A5ACD	SlateBlue
#8B0000	DarkRed		#00FF00	Lime		#708090	SlateGray
#E9967A	DarkSalmon		#32CD32	LimeGreen		#708090	SlateGrey
#8FBC8F	DarkSeaGreen		#FAF0E6	Linen		#FFFAFA	Snow
#483D8B	DarkSlateBlue		#FF00FF	Magenta		#00FF7F	SpringGreen
#2F4F4F	DarkSlateGray		#800000	Maroon		#4682B4	SteelBlue
#2F4F4F	DarkSlateGrey		#66CDAA	MediumAquaMarine		#D2B48C	Tan
#00CED1	DarkTurquoise		#0000CD	MediumBlue		#008080	Teal
#9400D3	DarkViolet		#BA55D3	MediumOrchid		#D8BFD8	Thistle
#FF1493	DeepPink		#9370DB	MediumPurple		#FF6347	Tomato
#00BFFF	DeepSkyBlue		#3CB371	MediumSeaGreen		#40E0D0	Turquoise
#696969	DimGray		#7B68EE	MediumSlateBlue		#EE82EE	Violet
#696969	DimGrey		#00FA9A	MediumSpringGreen		#F5DEB3	Wheat
#1E90FF	DodgerBlue		#48D1CC	MediumTurquoise		#FFFFFF	White
#B22222	FireBrick		#C71585	MediumVioletRed		#F5F5F5	WhiteSmoke
#FFFAF0	FloralWhite		#191970	MidnightBlue		#FFFF00	Yellow
#228B22	ForestGreen		#F5FFFA	MintCream		#9ACD32	YellowGreen
#FF00FF	Fuchsia		#FFE4E1	MistyRose			
#DCDCDC	Gainsboro		#FFE4B5	Moccasin			

* Added in 2014 in memory of Rebecca Meyer,
daughter of Web consultant Eric A. Meyer.

The ~~147~~ 148 Browser Defined Colors (Sorted By Number)

#000000	Black		#808000	Olive		#EEE8AA	PaleGoldenRod	
#000080	Navy		#808080	Gray		#F08080	LightCoral	
#00008B	DarkBlue		#808080	Grey		#F0E68C	Khaki	
#0000CD	MediumBlue		#87CEEB	SkyBlue		#F0F8FF	AliceBlue	
#0000FF	Blue		#87CEFA	LightSkyBlue		#F0FFF0	Honeydew	
#006400	DarkGreen		#8A2BE2	BlueViolet		#F0FFFF	Azure	
#008000	Green		#8B0000	DarkRed		#F4A460	SandyBrown	
#008080	Teal		#8B008B	DarkMagenta		#F5DEB3	Wheat	
#008B8B	DarkCyan		#8B4513	SaddleBrown		#F5F5DC	Beige	
#00BFFF	DeepSkyBlue		#8FBC8F	DarkSeaGreen		#F5F5F5	WhiteSmoke	
#00CED1	DarkTurquoise		#90EE90	LightGreen		#F5FFFA	MintCream	
#00FA9A	MediumSpringGreen		#9370DB	MediumPurple		#F8F8FF	GhostWhite	
#00FF00	Lime		#9400D3	DarkViolet		#FA8072	Salmon	
#00FF7F	SpringGreen		#98FB98	PaleGreen		#FAEBD7	AntiqueWhite	
#00FFFF	Aqua		#9932CC	DarkOrchid		#FAF0E6	Linen	
#00FFFF	Cyan		#9ACD32	YellowGreen		#FAFAD2	LightGoldenRodYellow	
#191970	MidnightBlue		#A0522D	Sienna		#FDF5E6	OldLace	
#1E90FF	DodgerBlue		#A52A2A	Brown		#FF0000	Red	
#20B2AA	LightSeaGreen		#A9A9A9	DarkGray		#FF00FF	Fuchsia	
#228B22	ForestGreen		#A9A9A9	DarkGrey		#FF00FF	Magenta	
#2E8B57	SeaGreen		#ADD8E6	LightBlue		#FF1493	DeepPink	
#2F4F4F	DarkSlateGray		#ADFF2F	GreenYellow		#FF4500	OrangeRed	
#2F4F4F	DarkSlateGrey		#AFEEEE	PaleTurquoise		#FF6347	Tomato	
#32CD32	LimeGreen		#B0C4DE	LightSteelBlue		#FF69B4	HotPink	
#3CB371	MediumSeaGreen		#B0E0E6	PowderBlue		#FF7F50	Coral	
#40E0D0	Turquoise		#B22222	FireBrick		#FF8C00	DarkOrange	
#4169E1	RoyalBlue		#B8860B	DarkGoldenRod		#FFA07A	LightSalmon	
#4682B4	SteelBlue		#BA55D3	MediumOrchid		#FFA500	Orange	
#483D8B	DarkSlateBlue		#BC8F8F	RosyBrown		#FFB6C1	LightPink	
#48D1CC	MediumTurquoise		#BDB76B	DarkKhaki		#FFC0CB	Pink	
#4B0082	Indigo		#C0C0C0	Silver		#FFD700	Gold	
#556B2F	DarkOliveGreen		#C71585	MediumVioletRed		#FFDAB9	PeachPuff	
#5F9EA0	CadetBlue		#CD5C5C	IndianRed		#FFDEAD	NavajoWhite	
#6495ED	CornflowerBlue		#CD853F	Peru		#FFE4B5	Moccasin	
#663399	RebeccaPurple		#D2691E	Chocolate		#FFE4C4	Bisque	
#66CDAA	MediumAquaMarine		#D2B48C	Tan		#FFE4E1	MistyRose	
#696969	DimGray		#D3D3D3	LightGray		#FFEBCD	BlanchedAlmond	
#696969	DimGrey		#D3D3D3	LightGrey		#FFEFD5	PapayaWhip	
#6A5ACD	SlateBlue		#D8BFD8	Thistle		#FFF0F5	LavenderBlush	
#6B8E23	OliveDrab		#DA70D6	Orchid		#FFF5EE	SeaShell	
#708090	SlateGray		#DAA520	GoldenRod		#FFF8DC	Cornsilk	
#708090	SlateGrey		#DB7093	PaleVioletRed		#FFFACD	LemonChiffon	
#778899	LightSlateGray		#DC143C	Crimson		#FFFAF0	FloralWhite	
#778899	LightSlateGrey		#DCDCDC	Gainsboro		#FFFAFA	Snow	
#7B68EE	MediumSlateBlue		#DDA0DD	Plum		#FFFF00	Yellow	
#7CFC00	LawnGreen		#DEB887	Burlywood		#FFFFE0	LightYellow	
#7FFF00	Chartreuse		#E0FFFF	LightCyan		#FFFFF0	Ivory	
#7FFFD4	Aquamarine		#E6E6FA	Lavender		#FFFFFF	White	
#800000	Maroon		#E9967A	DarkSalmon				
#800080	Purple		#EE82EE	Violet				

The CMY Color Model

In contrast to RGB, which is an <u>additive</u> model based on transmitted light, ***CMY*** (***cyan-magenta-yellow***) is a <u>subtractive</u> model based on reflected light. While values in the RGB color space are generally integers in the range [0 … 255], values in the CMY color space are real numbers in the range [0.0 … 1.0]. Red and cyan are photographic inverses, as are green and magenta, and also blue and yellow.

To convert RGB to CMY:

```
C = 1.0 - (R / 255.0)
M = 1.0 - (G / 255.0)
Y = 1.0 - (B / 255.0)
```

To convert CMY to RGB:

```
R = ⌊(1.0 - C) * 255.0⌋
G = ⌊(1.0 - M) * 255.0⌋
B = ⌊(1.0 - Y) * 255.0⌋
```

Note that the floor function $\lfloor x \rfloor$ returns the largest integer less than or equal to argument *x*. For positive numbers, this function is equivalent to the `int` or `trunc` functions available in most computer languages, such as Python:

```
R = int((1.0 - C) * 255.0)
G = int((1.0 - M) * 255.0)
B = int((1.0 - Y) * 255.0)
```

NOTE: Newer computer display systems may have other limits for R, G, and B than the traditional one-byte range [0 … 255]. For example, using two bytes instead of one gives a legal range of [0 … 65535] (as seen in `.PNG` files with 48-bit color). If you find this to be the case, replace all instances of 255.0 in the conversions with 65535.0 instead.

The CMYK Color Model

Most computer inkjet and laser printers use a variation of CMY called **_CMYK_** (**_cyan-magenta-yellow-black_**). While it is possible to blend cyan, magenta, and yellow to make black, doing so is an expensive way of printing text, and any misalignment in the print heads would tend to give color halos around the edges of characters. It is much more cost effective to have a separate black ink tank or toner cartridge. However, this does complicate the conversion from and to the RGB model. The conversions below are written in the Python programming language.

To convert RGB to CMYK:

```
R2 = R / 255.0
G2 = G / 255.0
B2 = B / 255.0
K  = 1.0 - max(R2,G2,B2)
if (K >= 1.0):
    C = 0.0
    M = 0.0
    Y = 0.0
else:
    C  = (1.0 - R2 - K) / (1.0 - K)
    M  = (1.0 - G2 - K) / (1.0 - K)
    Y  = (1.0 - B2 - K) / (1.0 - K)
```

To convert CMYK to CMY (use the CMY to RGB conversion to go the rest of the way):

```
C = (C * (1.0 - K) + K)
M = (M * (1.0 - K) + K)
Y = (Y * (1.0 - K) + K)
```

To convert CMY to CMYK:

```
K = min(C, M, Y)

if (K >= 1):
    C = 0
    M = 0
    Y = 0
else:
    C = (C - K) / (1.0 - K)
    M = (M - K) / (1.0 - K)
    Y = (Y - K) / (1.0 - K)
```

The CMYK Color Model

9: *Character Sets*

Computers have to be able to display results on-screen. The most common mechanism is through text characters. The earliest computers had limited character sets, often with fixed-size characters (such as grids of 5×7 pixels or 8×8 pixels or some other small size). The characters so formed were readable, but inflexible – they always looked the same.

Eventually this was addressed by allowing grids (bitmaps) of essentially arbitrary size within which to draw characters, requiring people were to buy bitmap images for each font in each desired size. For example, Times Roman 12 point had one set of bitmaps, but Times Roman 10 point was another set, as were Times Roman 12 point Bold, Times Roman 12 point Italic, Courier 12 point, Helvetica 12 point, etc. Each set of bitmaps took up memory, and printing was limited only to the fonts on hand.

More modern computers use character sets with outlines based on mathematical curves. These characters can be scaled to any size just by multiplying all the coefficients of their curves by the appropriate scale factor. If the Times Roman typeface is installed, then any Times Roman font at any point size is automatically available. The operating system of the computer becomes responsible for rendering the pictures of the characters to display on-screen, as bitmaps, from the mathematical curves scaled to the desired size.

Traditionally, character sets were English-centric, using the Roman alphabet alone. Some of the earliest computers supported upper-case letters only, as the machines were primarily designed for numerical calculations, but not large amounts of expository text. Later machines supported both upper and lower case letters in ASCII (the American Standard Code for Information Interchange). ASCII is a 7-bit code (0…127), now usually stored in an 8-bit byte but taking up only 128 of the 256 available patterns. The earliest IBM-PC used the other 128 characters for box outlines, math symbols, and a few letters with diacritical marks, but these patterns are no longer considered standard.

Today, with computers used to handle text from all languages around the world, there are literally tens of thousands of characters that must be represented in binary. The Unicode Consortium maintains the standard used worldwide, defining ***code points*** that map a particular character from some language onto a fixed number. However, the first 128 code points are designed to be identical to ASCII, specifically for backwards compatibility. Storing these numbers as a list of bytes can be done in a number of ways, including UTF-8 and UTF-16. The UTF-8 format is shown in the later chapter on coding.

The tables in this chapter cover the IBM-PC character set, standard ASCII, dot patterns for those characters, and a number of the most common character sets used by computers today. The final table contains a small subset of the characters (entities) that translate a code point (or an entity name) onto an actual character that shows up on screen in a Web page.

Typeface Table: Traditional 7-Bit ASCII (0...63)

CONTROL CHARACTERS (NON-PRINTING)			SPECIALS		
CODE	BINARY	INTERPRETATION	CODE	BINARY	SYMBOL
0	0000000	NUL (Null)	32	0100000	
1	0000001	SOH (Start of Header)	33	0100001	!
2	0000010	STX (Start of Text)	34	0100010	"
3	0000011	ETX (End of Text)	35	0100011	#
4	0000100	EOT (End of Transmission)	36	0100100	$
5	0000101	ENQ (Enquiry)	37	0100101	%
6	0000110	ACK (Acknowledgement)	38	0100110	&
7	0000111	BEL (Bell)	39	0100111	'
8	0001000	BS (Backspace), ← Bksp	40	0101000	(
9	0001001	HT (Horizontal Tab), Tab	41	0101001	)
10	0001010	LF (Line Feed)	42	0101010	*
11	0001011	VT (Vertical Tab)	43	0101011	+
12	0001100	FF (Form Feed)	44	0101100	,
13	0001101	CR (Carriage Return), Enter ←	45	0101101	-
14	0001110	SO (Shift Out)	46	0101110	.
15	0001111	SI (Shift In)	47	0101111	/
16	0010000	DLE (Data Link Escape)	48	0110000	0
17	0010001	DC1 (Device Control 1, or XON)	49	0110001	1
18	0010010	DC2 (Device Control 2)	50	0110010	2
19	0010011	DC3 (Device Control 3, or XOFF)	51	0110011	3
20	0010100	DC4 (Device Control 4)	52	0110100	4
21	0010101	NAK (Negative Acknowledgement)	53	0110101	5
22	0010110	SYN (Synchronous Idle)	54	0110110	6
23	0010111	ETB (End of Transmission Block)	55	0110111	7
24	0011000	CAN (Cancel)	56	0111000	8
25	0011001	EM (End of Medium)	57	0111001	9
26	0011010	SUB (Substitute)	58	0111010	:
27	0011011	ESC (Escape), Esc	59	0111011	;
28	0011100	FS (File Separator)	60	0111100	<
29	0011101	GS (Group Separator)	61	0111101	=
30	0011110	RS (Record Separator)	62	0111110	>
31	0011111	US (Unit Separator)	63	0111111	?

Typeface Table: Traditional 7-Bit ASCII (64...127)

UPPER CASE				LOWER CASE		
CODE	BINARY	SYMBOL		CODE	BINARY	SYMBOL
64	1000000	@		96	1100000	`
65	1000001	A		97	1100001	a
66	1000010	B		98	1100010	b
67	1000011	C		99	1100011	c
68	1000100	D		100	1100100	d
69	1000101	E		101	1100101	e
70	1000110	F		102	1100110	f
71	1000111	G		103	1100111	g
72	1001000	H		104	1101000	h
73	1001001	I		105	1101001	i
74	1001010	J		106	1101010	j
75	1001011	K		107	1101011	k
76	1001100	L		108	1101100	l
77	1001101	M		109	1101101	m
78	1001110	N		110	1101110	n
79	1001111	O		111	1101111	o
80	1010000	P		112	1110000	p
81	1010001	Q		113	1110001	q
82	1010010	R		114	1110010	r
83	1010011	S		115	1110011	s
84	1010100	T		116	1110100	t
85	1010101	U		117	1110101	u
86	1010110	V		118	1110110	v
87	1010111	W		119	1110111	w
88	1011000	X		120	1111000	x
89	1011001	Y		121	1111001	y
90	1011010	Z		122	1111010	z
91	1011011	[		123	1111011	{
92	1011100	\		124	1111100		
93	1011101	]		125	1111101	}
94	1011110	^		126	1111110	~
95	1011111	_		127	1111111	DELETE

NOTES:

Control characters explicitly brought out to the keyboard are shown as ⟨← Bksp⟩, ⟨Tab⇆⟩, ⟨Enter ←⟩, ⟨Esc⟩. Only a few other control characters saw common use.

The ⟨Enter ←⟩ key on PCs enters both a CR and an LF character into a text file (e.g., Windows Notepad), while old-style Macs used just CR, and UNIX systems use just LF to terminate lines of text. FTP programs using ASCII mode are allowed to change line terminators when copying files from one type of computer to another.

Only the second bit from the left differs between an upper-case letter (bit=0) and its lower-case equivalent (bit=1).

Only the left-most bit differs between an upper-case letter (bit=1) and its control equivalent (bit=0). Control characters were entered from Teletype keyboards by holding down ⟨Ctrl⟩ and hitting the appropriate letter. ⟨Ctrl⟩H is the same as ⟨← Bksp⟩, for example.

DEL or DELETE (code 127) is non-printing, and was used on paper tape punches to obliterate a mistyped character by backing up and punching out all 7 holes. Computers reading in the tape would ignore those codes.

Typeface Table: PC Character Set (Text Mode)

#		#		#		#		#		#		#		#	
0		32		64	@	96	`	128	Ç	160	á	192	└	224	α
1	☺	33	!	65	A	97	a	129	ü	161	í	193	┴	225	β
2	☻	34	"	66	B	98	b	130	é	162	ó	194	┬	226	Γ
3	♥	35	#	67	C	99	c	131	â	163	ú	195	├	227	π
4	♦	36	$	68	D	100	d	132	ä	164	ñ	196	─	228	Σ
5	♣	37	%	69	E	101	e	133	à	165	Ñ	197	┼	229	σ
6	♠	38	&	70	F	102	f	134	å	166	ª	198	╞	230	µ
7	•	39	'	71	G	103	g	135	ç	167	º	199	╟	231	τ
8	◘	40	(	72	H	104	h	136	ê	168	¿	200	╚	232	Φ
9	○	41	)	73	I	105	i	137	ë	169	⌐	201	╔	233	Θ
10	◙	42	*	74	J	106	j	138	è	170	¬	202	╩	234	Ω
11	♂	43	+	75	K	107	k	139	ï	171	½	203	╦	235	δ
12	♀	44	,	76	L	108	l	140	î	172	¼	204	╠	236	∞
13	♪	45	-	77	M	109	m	141	ì	173	¡	205	═	237	φ
14	♫	46	.	78	N	110	n	142	Ä	174	«	206	╬	238	ε
15	☼	47	/	79	O	111	o	143	Å	175	»	207	╧	239	∩
16	►	48	0	80	P	112	p	144	É	176	░	208	╨	240	≡
17	◄	49	1	81	Q	113	q	145	æ	177	▒	209	╤	241	±
18	↕	50	2	82	R	114	r	146	Æ	178	▓	210	╥	242	≥
19	‼	51	3	83	S	115	s	147	ô	179	│	211	╙	243	≤
20	¶	52	4	84	T	116	t	148	ö	180	┤	212	╘	244	⌠
21	§	53	5	85	U	117	u	149	ò	181	╡	213	╒	245	⌡
22	▬	54	6	86	V	118	v	150	û	182	╢	214	╓	246	÷
23	↨	55	7	87	W	119	w	151	ù	183	╖	215	╫	247	≈
24	↑	56	8	88	X	120	x	152	ÿ	184	╕	216	╪	248	°
25	↓	57	9	89	Y	121	y	153	Ö	185	╣	217	┘	249	∙
26	→	58	:	90	Z	122	z	154	Ü	186	║	218	┌	250	·
27	←	59	;	91	[	123	{	155	¢	187	╗	219	█	251	√
28	∟	60	<	92	\	124			156	£	188	╝	220	▄	252	ⁿ
29	↔	61	=	93	]	125	}	157	¥	189	╜	221	▌	253	²
30	▲	62	>	94	^	126	~	158	₧	190	╛	222	▐	254	■
31	▼	63	?	95	_	127	⌂	159	ƒ	191	┐	223	▀	255	

PC Character Set (8×8 Matrix)

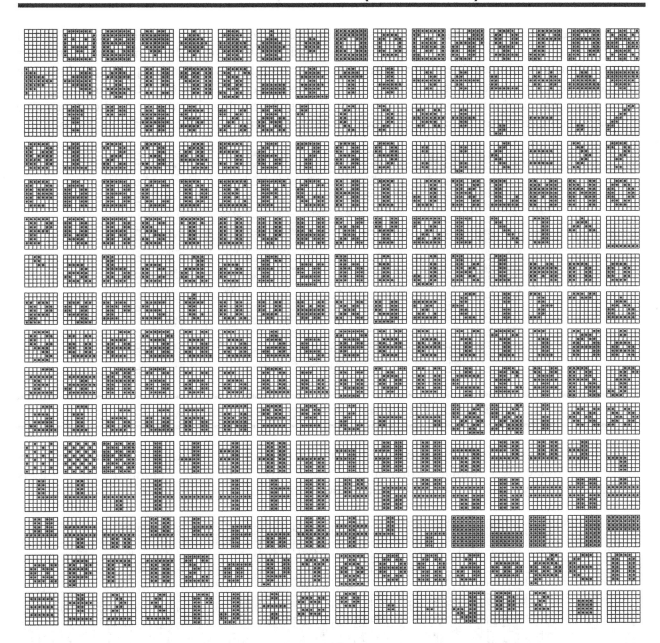

The PC character set presented here and on the previous page uses a simple 8×8 pixel grid. Letters within the grid are constructed so that inter-character and inter-line space is automatically built-in: there are one or two blank columns of pixels at the right of each letter, and one blank row below (which also provides space for descenders). This means that the grids can be painted on screen adjacent to one another, both horizontally and vertically, and the letters will have enough space between them to be readable. In contrast, there are a number of characters such as the box-drawing lines and corners which extend to the edges of each grid, allowing single-line and double-line boxes to be drawn with continuous edges (no gaps).

ASCII Character Set (4×6 Matrix)

Even smaller character sets than 8×8 are sometimes required. Here is a complete table of ASCII (7-bit) characters using a 3×5 character definition inside a 4×6 grid. Many of the characters are readable, but a number of them (particularly the lower-case letters and some special symbols) are difficult to interpret, except perhaps in context. If the 3×5 rule is violated, letters such as g, j, p, and q could use the bottom row of pixels to hold their descenders, but doing so allows possible collisions between those characters and the characters directly below them on the next line.

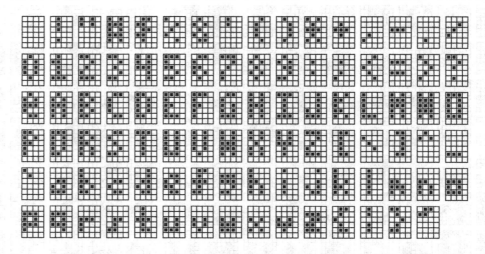

ASCII Character Set (6×8 Matrix)

A more common, and much more readable, character set uses a 5×7 character definition in a 6×8 matrix. Character sets similar to that shown below have been used in point-of-sale terminals (using 5×7 displays) and in the Tandy Model 100 Portable (a proto-laptop from the early 1980s).

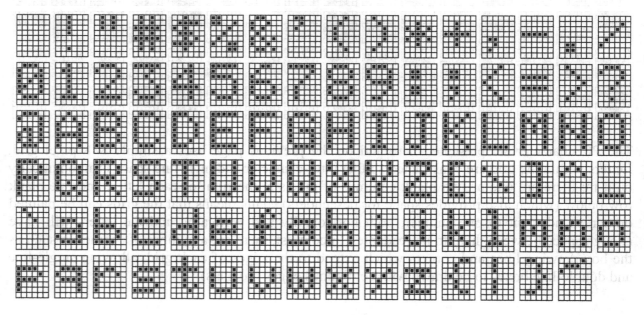

7-Segment Displays

Seven segment displays were designed for calculators, which at minimum need the digits 0…9 and the minus sign. Many letters and symbols from the ASCII set also can be formed, but not <u>all</u> letters, not even by combining the upper case and lower case sets. Some non-ASCII symbols can be made, such as the degree (°) and the equivalence (≡) symbols. Variations include omitting the top flag on the 6 and the bottom flag on the 9, and including a flag on the 7. Overlaps are inevitable, such as between 0/O, 1/I, 2/Z, and 5/S, (and also between the b and the flagless 6).

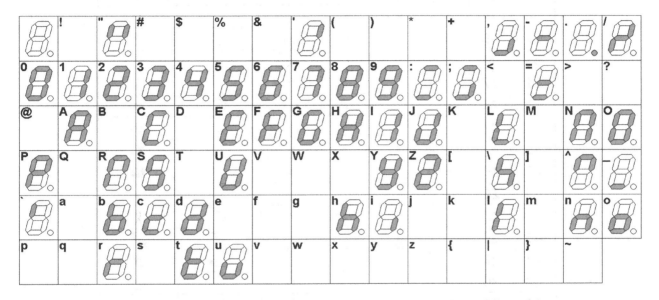

Character Anti-Aliasing

Screens in modern computer systems are large enough to display nicely shaped characters. Defining characters as exclusively black pixels on a white background (monochrome) can result in harsh edges. In the "A" shown below left, the outer sloping edges look like a jagged staircase, thus forming an ***alias*** for the intended smooth edge. By allowing pixels to be different shades of gray or different colors, edges are blurred so that at a distance they appear much smoother to the eye. This process is called ***anti-aliasing***. The letters below right have been anti-aliased.

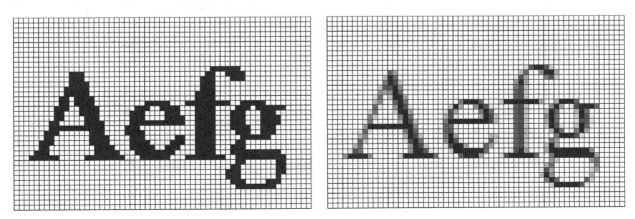

Standard Typefaces: Characters 32-63

Code	Hex	Arial	Courier	Times	Symbol	Wingdings	Webdings
32	20						
33	21	!	!	!	!		
34	22	"	"	"	∀		
35	23	#	#	#	#		
36	24	$	$	$	∃		
37	25	%	%	%	%		
38	26	&	&	&	&		
39	27	'	'	'	∋		
40	28	(	(	(	(		
41	29	)	)	)	)		
42	2A	*	*	*	*		
43	2B	+	+	+	+		
44	2C	,	,	,	,		
45	2D	-	–	-	−		
46	2E	.	.	.	.		
47	2F	/	/	/	/		
48	30	0	0	0	0		
49	31	1	1	1	1		
50	32	2	2	2	2		
51	33	3	3	3	3		
52	34	4	4	4	4		
53	35	5	5	5	5		
54	36	6	6	6	6		
55	37	7	7	7	7		
56	38	8	8	8	8		
57	39	9	9	9	9		
58	3A	:	:	:	:		
59	3B	;	;	;	;		
60	3C	<	<	<	<		
61	3D	=	=	=	=		
62	3E	>	>	>	>		
63	3F	?	?	?	?		

Standard Typefaces: Characters 64-95

Code	Hex	Arial	Courier	Times	Symbol	Wingdings	Webdings
64	40	@	@	@	≅		
65	41	A	A	A	A		
66	42	B	B	B	B		
67	43	C	C	C	X		
68	44	D	D	D	Δ		
69	45	E	E	E	E		
70	46	F	F	F	Φ		
71	47	G	G	G	Γ		
72	48	H	H	H	H		
73	49	I	I	I	I		
74	4A	J	J	J	ϑ		
75	4B	K	K	K	K		
76	4C	L	L	L	Λ		
77	4D	M	M	M	M		
78	4E	N	N	N	N		
79	4F	O	O	O	O		
80	50	P	P	P	Π		
81	51	Q	Q	Q	Θ		
82	52	R	R	R	P		
83	53	S	S	S	Σ		
84	54	T	T	T	T		
85	55	U	U	U	Y		
86	56	V	V	V	ς		
87	57	W	W	W	Ω		
88	58	X	X	X	Ξ		
89	59	Y	Y	Y	Ψ		
90	5A	Z	Z	Z	Z		
91	5B	[	[	[	[		
92	5C	\	\	\	∴		
93	5D	]	]	]	]		
94	5E	^	^	^	⊥		
95	5F	_	_	_	_		

Standard Typefaces: Characters 96-127

Code	Hex	Arial	Courier	Times	Symbol	Wingdings	Webdings
96	60	`	`	`	‾	♊	▱
97	61	a	a	a	α	♋	✔
98	62	b	b	b	β	♌	⚲
99	63	c	c	c	χ	♍	▢
100	64	d	d	d	δ	♎	♥
101	65	e	e	e	ε	♏	⬛
102	66	f	f	f	φ	♐	🚌
103	67	g	g	g	γ	♑	■
104	68	h	h	h	η	♒	⛽
105	69	i	i	i	ι	♓	ⓘ
106	6A	j	j	j	φ	er	✈
107	6B	k	k	k	κ	&	⚜
108	6C	l	l	l	λ	●	✦
109	6D	m	m	m	μ	○	♟
110	6E	n	n	n	ν	■	●
111	6F	o	o	o	ο	□	⛴
112	70	p	p	p	π	▣	🚑
113	71	q	q	q	θ	❑	( )
114	72	r	r	r	ρ	❒	✕
115	73	s	s	s	σ	◆	?
116	74	t	t	t	τ	◆	📰
117	75	u	u	u	υ	◆	🚉
118	76	v	v	v	ϖ	❖	🚐
119	77	w	w	w	ω	◆	¡
120	78	x	x	x	ξ	⊠	⊘
121	79	y	y	y	ψ	☒	⊖
122	7A	z	z	z	ζ	⌘	⊗
123	7B	{	{	{	{	✿	✹
124	7C	|	|	|	|	✾	|
125	7D	}	}	}	}	"	✹
126	7E	~	~	~	~	"	⟋
127	7F	▯	▯	▯	▯	▯	▯

Standard Typefaces: Characters 128-159

Code	Hex	Arial	Courier	Times	Symbol	Wingdings	Webdings
128	80	€	€	€	□	⓪	👤
129	81				□	①	👤
130	82	‚	‚	‚	□	②	👤
131	83	ƒ	ƒ	ƒ	□	③	👤
132	84	„	„	„	□	④	🖐
133	85	…	…	…	□	⑤	👽
134	86	†	†	†	□	⑥	🏋
135	87	‡	‡	‡	□	⑦	⛷
136	88	ˆ	ˆ	ˆ	□	⑧	🏂
137	89	‰	‰	‰	□	⑨	🏄
138	8A	Š	Š	Š	□	⑩	🏊
139	8B	‹	‹	‹	□	❶	🏃
140	8C	Œ	Œ	Œ	□	❶	🏍
141	8D				□	❷	🚲
142	8E	Ž	Ž	Ž	□	❸	🚗
143	8F				□	❹	⊞
144	90				□	❺	🛢
145	91	'	`	'	□	❻	💰
146	92	'	'	'	□	❼	💳
147	93	"	\\	"	□	❽	▤
148	94	"	//	"	□	❾	👪
149	95	•	•	•	□	❿	🗡
150	96	–	–	–	□	ೞ	👄
151	97	—	—	—	□	ೞ	🗣
152	98	˜		˜	□	ೞ	★
153	99	™	™	™	□	ೞ	📧
154	9A	š	š	š	□	ೞ	📩
155	9B	›	›	›	□	ೞ	📄
156	9C	œ	œ	œ	□	ೞ	📑
157	9D				□	ೞ	📄
158	9E	ž	ž	ž	□	·	📃
159	9F	Ÿ	ÿ	Ÿ	□	•	🖼

Standard Typefaces: Characters 160-191

Code	Hex	Arial	Courier	Times	Symbol	Wingdings	Webdings
160	A0				□	·	
161	A1	¡	¡	¡	ϒ	○	
162	A2	¢	¢	¢	′	◯	
163	A3	£	£	£	≤	◉	
164	A4	¤	¤	¤	/	⊙	
165	A5	¥	¥	¥	∞	◎	
166	A6	¦	¦	¦	ƒ	○	
167	A7	§	§	§	♣	■	
168	A8	¨	¨	¨	♦	□	
169	A9	©	©	©	♥	▲	
170	AA	ª	ª	ª	♠	✦	
171	AB	«	«	«	↔	★	
172	AC	¬	¬	¬	←	✳	
173	AD	-	—	-	↑	✺	
174	AE	®	®	®	→	✸	
175	AF	‾	‾	‾	↓	❀	
176	B0	°	°	°	°	⊕	
177	B1	±	±	±	±	✛	
178	B2	²	²	²	″	✦	
179	B3	³	³	³	≥	⌗	
180	B4	´	´	´	×	◈	
181	B5	µ	µ	µ	∝	✪	
182	B6	¶	¶	¶	∂	☆	
183	B7	·	·	·	•	🕐	
184	B8	¸	¸	¸	÷	🕑	
185	B9	¹	¹	¹	≠	🕒	
186	BA	º	º	º	≡	🕓	
187	BB	»	»	»	≈	🕔	
188	BC	¼	¼	¼	…	🕕	
189	BD	½	½	½	|	🕖	
190	BE	¾	¾	¾	—	🕗	
191	BF	¿	¿	¿	↵	🕘	

Standard Typefaces: Characters 192-223

Code	Hex	Arial	Courier	Times	Symbol	Wingdings	Webdings
192	C0	À	À	À	ℵ	⌚	▤
193	C1	Á	Á	Á	ℑ	⌚	✎
194	C2	Â	Â	Â	ℜ	⌚	⌨
195	C3	Ã	Ã	Ã	℘	↩	⚲
196	C4	Ä	Ä	Ä	⊗	↪	🎮
197	C5	Å	Å	Å	⊕	⇦	(
198	C6	Æ	Æ	Æ	∅	⇨	℧
199	C7	Ç	Ç	Ç	∩	⇧	🖥
200	C8	È	È	È	∪	⇩	📱
201	C9	É	É	É	⊃	⬅	☎
202	CA	Ê	Ê	Ê	⊇	➦	🖥
203	CB	Ë	Ë	Ë	⊄	✻	▯
204	CC	Ì	Ì	Ì	⊂	✠	▬
205	CD	Í	Í	Í	⊆	✄	▣
206	CE	Î	Î	Î	∈	✂	🖨
207	CF	Ï	Ï	Ï	∉	✁	🔒
208	D0	Ð	Ð	Ð	∠	✃	🔓
209	D1	Ñ	Ñ	Ñ	∇	✀	⚷
210	D2	Ò	Ò	Ò	®	✄	⬇
211	D3	Ó	Ó	Ó	©	✆	⬆
212	D4	Ô	Ô	Ô	™	✇	⬮
213	D5	Õ	õ	Õ	∏	⌫	○
214	D6	Ö	Ö	Ö	√	⌦	☇
215	D7	×	×	×	·	◄	☁
216	D8	Ø	Ø	Ø	¬	➢	🌧
217	D9	Ù	Ù	Ù	∧	▲	☁
218	DA	Ú	Ú	Ú	∨	▼	🌧
219	DB	Û	Û	Û	⇔	☚	☁
220	DC	Ü	Ü	Ü	⇐	☛	☔
221	DD	Ý	Ý	Ý	⇑	☟	☂
222	DE	Þ	Þ	Þ	⇒	☝	🐾
223	DF	ß	ß	ß	⇓	←	≋

Standard Typefaces: Characters 224-255

Code	Hex	Arial	Courier	Times	Symbol	Wingdings	Webdings
224	E0	à	à	à	◊	→	☾
225	E1	á	á	á	⟨	↑	🌡
226	E2	â	â	â	®	↓	👑
227	E3	ã	ã	ã	©	↖	✈
228	E4	ä	ä	ä	™	↗	🍽
229	E5	å	å	å	Σ	↙	🍸
230	E6	æ	æ	æ	(	↘	🔔
231	E7	ç	ç	ç	|	←	🏧
232	E8	è	è	è	\	→	Ⓟ
233	E9	é	é	é	⌈	↑	♿
234	EA	ê	ê	ê	|	↓	△
235	EB	ë	ë	ë	⌊	↖	🐞
236	EC	ì	ì	ì	⌠	↗	🐗
237	ED	í	í	í	{	↙	💥
238	EE	î	î	î	|	↘	💥
239	EF	ï	ï	ï	|	⇐	≥
240	F0	ð	ð	ð	□	⇒	∈
241	F1	ñ	ñ	ñ	)	⇑	✈
242	F2	ò	ò	ò	⌡	⇓	🐦
243	F3	ó	ó	ó	⌈	⇔	🖋
244	F4	ô	ô	ô	|	⇕	🐛
245	F5	õ	õ	õ	⌡	⬉	🐈
246	F6	ö	ö	ö	)	⬈	🐕
247	F7	÷	÷	÷	|	⬋	🔧
248	F8	ø	ø	ø	)	⬊	🔨
249	F9	ù	ù	ù	⌉	▫	🗡
250	FA	ú	ú	ú	|	▫	🗡
251	FB	û	û	û	⌋	✗	🗺
252	FC	ü	ü	ü	)	✓	🌐
253	FD	ý	ý	ý	}	☒	🌐
254	FE	þ	þ	þ	)	☑	🌍
255	FF	ÿ	ÿ	ÿ	□	🪟	🕊

HTML Entities

Control Entities

Code	Name	is
"	"	"
&	&	&
<	<	<
>	>	>

Assorted Random Entities

Code	Name	is	Code	Name	is	Code	Name	is
Ĳ	Ĳ	IJ	ƒ	ƒ	ƒ			
ĳ	ĳ	ij	θ	θ	θ			
Œ	Œ	Œ	π	π	π			
œ	œ	œ	φ	φ	φ			

HTML5 Entities (Subset)

Code	Name	is
…	…	…
‰	‰	‰
⁄	⁄	/
€	€	€
℞	℞	℞
™	™	™
Å	Å	Å
ℵ	ℵ	ℵ
ℶ	ℶ	ℶ
ℷ	ℷ	ℷ
ℸ	ℸ	ℸ
⅓	⅓	⅓
⅔	⅔	⅔
⅕	⅕	⅕
⅖	⅖	⅖
⅗	⅗	⅗
⅘	⅘	⅘
⅙	⅙	⅙
⅚	⅚	⅚
⅛	⅛	⅛
⅜	⅜	⅜
⅝	⅝	⅝
⅞	⅞	⅞
∀	∀	∀
∃	∃	∃
∄	∄	∄
∈	∈	∈
∏	∏	∏
∑	∑	Σ
∓	∓	∓
√	√	√
∞	∞	∞
∫	∫	∫
∴	∴	∴
≠	≠	≠
≡	≡	≡
≤	≤	≤
≥	≥	≥
☎	☎	☎

ISO-8859-1 Latin-1 Entities

Code	Name	is	Code	Name	is	Code	Name	is
			À	À	À	à	à	à
¡	¡	¡	Á	Á	Á	á	á	á
¢	¢	¢	Â	Â	Â	â	â	â
£	£	£	Ã	Ã	Ã	ã	ã	ã
¤	¤	¤	Ä	Ä	Ä	ä	ä	ä
¥	¥	¥	Å	Å	Å	å	å	å
¦	¦	¦	Æ	Æ	Æ	æ	æ	æ
§	§	§	Ç	Ç	Ç	ç	ç	ç
¨	¨	¨	È	È	È	è	è	è
©	©	©	É	É	É	é	é	é
ª	ª	ª	Ê	Ê	Ê	ê	ê	ê
«	«	«	Ë	Ë	Ë	ë	ë	ë
¬	¬	¬	Ì	Ì	Ì	ì	ì	ì
­	­	-	Í	Í	Í	í	í	í
®	®	®	Î	Î	Î	î	î	î
¯	¯	¯	Ï	Ï	Ï	ï	ï	ï
°	°	°	Ð	Ð	Ð	ð	ð	ð
±	±	±	Ñ	Ñ	Ñ	ñ	ñ	ñ
²	²	²	Ò	Ò	Ò	ò	ò	ò
³	³	³	Ó	Ó	Ó	ó	ó	ó
´	´	´	Ô	Ô	Ô	ô	ô	ô
µ	µ	µ	Õ	Õ	Õ	õ	õ	õ
¶	¶	¶	Ö	Ö	Ö	ö	ö	ö
·	·	·	×	×	×	÷	÷	÷
¸	¸	¸	Ø	Ø	Ø	ø	ø	ø
¹	¹	¹	Ù	Ù	Ù	ù	ù	ù
º	º	º	Ú	Ú	Ú	ú	ú	ú
»	»	»	Û	Û	Û	û	û	û
¼	¼	¼	Ü	Ü	Ü	ü	ü	ü
½	½	½	Ý	Ý	Ý	ý	ý	ý
¾	¾	¾	Þ	Þ	Þ	þ	þ	þ
¿	¿	¿	ß	ß	ß	ÿ	ÿ	ÿ

HTML Entities

10: *The Internet and Web Design*

This section is devoted to networking concepts (types of networks, network addressing schemes, etc.), as well as the tools needed to design and construct Web pages. Web design can be divided into three major areas: basic HTML, Cascading Style Sheets (CSS), and Scalable Vector Graphics (SVG) files. The CSS is very basic, and does not cover CSS 2 or CSS 3. Similarly, JavaScript has its own chapter and is not covered in this section (although linking JavaScript programs into a Web page is shown).

Types of Networks

Point-to-Point: Direct connection between each pair of computers, network stays running when one fails. For N computers, each computer requires N–1 ports, and there are $^{N\times(N-1)}\!/_2 = O(N^2)$ connections.

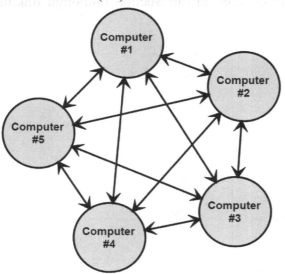

Star: Simple satellite computers, each with one port, network stays running when any fails. Central computer is very fast and expensive; network fails if it fails. For N computers, central computer needs N ports.

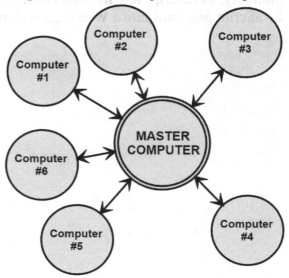

Token-Ring: Each computer requires only two ports (one in, one out), passes ***token*** around ring to determine who gets to talk. Network fails if any link is broken.

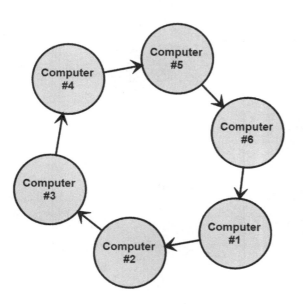

Ethernet: All computers connected to each other directly via simple devices (***hub***), each hears everyone's traffic. Slows down as traffic increases. Requires ***routers*** or ***switches*** to isolate sections of network.

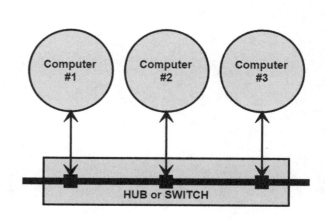

Home Networking

The following diagram shows a typical home network with several computers. A single-user system would omit everything but one computer connected directly to the cable modem. In this case the **_router_** at the center isolates all the computers from the Internet behind a single **_IP address_**. The router contains a **_switch_** that prevents one local computer from seeing the traffic of any other, but the two computers connected to the **_hub_** can see each other's traffic (hubs are very simple devices, rare today). All local wireless devices to connect to the network through the router; in general the router cannot be bypassed (no point-to-point connections). Most wireless (Wi-Fi) follows a communications standard developed by IEEE called the **_802.11_** document.

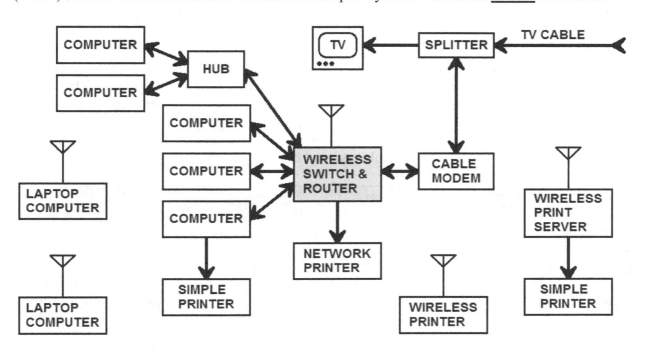

Wireless Networking

The common 802.11 wireless specifications are shown in the table below:

IEEE Standard	Maximum Data Rate	Release Date	Data Streams	Range (meters)	Note
802.11	2 Mb/s	1997	1	100 m	Original specification, obsolete today
802.11a	54 Mb/s	1999	1	120 m	NOT interoperable with either b or g
802.11b	10 Mb/s	1999	1	140 m	Compatible with 802.11g at slower speed
802.11g	54 Mb/s	2003	1	140 m	Compatible with 802.11b at slower speed
802.11n	>100 Mb/s	2009	4	250 m	Multiple radio links, up to 150 Mb/s
802.11ac	>400 Mb/s	2013	8	35 m	Multiple radio links, up to 1.3 Gb/s
802.11ad	7 Gb/s	2012	1	3.3 m	High data rate but short range
802.11ax	>10 Gb/s	2020	4 (up to 8)	Unknown	IEEE official acceptance expected late 2020
802.11ay	20-40 Gb/s	2020	4	300-500 m	To be released in 2020

IP Addresses

All Internet devices have an ***IP address***.

Internet ***domain names*** (such as `cs.umass.edu`) are mapped into IP addresses by the DNS (***Domain Name System***). If a local DNS does not know the mapping from domain name to IP address, it has other DNS ***name servers*** to ask. Once a domain name is resolved into an IP address (if it is found), DNS servers along the path remember that mapping in their local ***caches***. Mappings from domain name to IP address have a ***time-to-live*** (***TTL***), after which they are flushed from the cache, and must be searched for again. Changing the IP address for a particular domain name means that it will take time before all DNS caches have been updated with the new value.

IPv4 (Internet Protocol version 4) has been in use since the early 1980s. An IPv4 address is 32 bits, giving 2^{32}=4,294,967,296 unique addresses, denoted as four bytes separated by periods (such as `128.119.34.102`, for example). Some addresses have special meanings and are not available for general use. Originally, IPv4 used ***classful addressing***, where each byte in a class A, B, or C address described either part of the <u>network</u> name or part of the <u>host</u> (machine) name within the network. Class D was for multicast, and class E was reserved for other uses.

	IPv4 Format (X indicates part of Network ID, Y indicates part of Host ID)	Number of Unique		Address Range	
		Network IDs	Host IDs	Start	End
Class A	0XXXXXXX.YYYYYYYY.YYYYYYYY.YYYYYYYY	128	16,777,216	0.0.0.0	127.255.255.255
Class B	10XXXXXX.XXXXXXXX.YYYYYYYY.YYYYYYYY	16,384	65,536	128.0.0.0	191.255.255.255
Class C	110XXXXX.XXXXXXXX.XXXXXXXX.YYYYYYYY	2,097,152	256	192.0.0.0	223.255.255.255
Class D	1110????.????????.????????.????????	-	-	224.0.0.0	239.255.255.255
Class E	1111????.????????.????????.????????	-	-	240.0.0.0	255.255.255.255

A few very large sites, such as countries or large corporations, might use class A, medium-to-large companies might use class B, and individuals or small companies might use class C. A network site needing more than 256 hosts would need to either use two or more distinct class C networks, or use a class B network (potentially wasting most of the host ID numbers).

Classless Inter-Domain Routing (CIDR), allowed the boundary between network ID and host ID to float, instead of being on fixed boundaries, allowing much more fine-tuned control of the number of networks and number of machines on each network (example: `128.119.34.102/8` puts the boundary between network ID and host ID eight bits in from the left). CIDR is still in use today. Even with CIDR, IPv4 addresses were exhausted in early 2011.

IPv6, was developed as a replacement for IPv4 in the 1990s and was deployed in 2006, but is still slow to adopt. An IPv6 address is 128 bits, divided into eight 16-bit words, separated by periods. This gives $2^{128} \approx 3.4 \times 10^{38}$ unique addresses, far more than IPv4. The decimal value of each word can range from 0 to 65535. An example of an IPv6 address is `6192.178.46.1097.2342.923.647.1191` (in decimal).

Reserved IPv4 Addresses

The following table shows a list of reserved IP addresses for IPv4, and is subject to change over time as reserved addresses become allocated and as IPv4 is slowly replaced by IPv6.

CLASS	SPECIAL IP ADDRESSES	START	END	COUNT	MEANING
A	0.0.0.0/8	0.0.0.0	0.255.255.255	16,777,216	"This" Network
	10.0.0.0/8	10.0.0.0	10.255.255.255	16,777,216	Private-Use Networks
	127.0.0.0/8	127.0.0.0	127.255.255.255	16,777,216	Loopback
B	128.0.0.0/16	128.0.0.0	128.0.255.255	65,536	Reserved but Subject to Reallocation
	169.254.0.0/16	169.254.0.0	169.254.255.255	65,536	Link Local
	172.16.0.0/12	172.16.0.0	172.31.255.255	1,048,576	Private-Use Networks
C	192.0.0.0/24	192.0.0.0	192.0.0.255	256	Reserved but Subject to Reallocation
	192.0.2.0/24	192.0.2.0	192.0.2.255	256	Test Net
	192.88.99.0/24	192.88.99.0	192.88.99.255	256	6to4 Relay Anycast
	192.168.0.0/16	192.168.0.0	192.168.255.255	65,536	Private-Use Networks
	198.18.0.0/15	198.18.0.0	198.19.255.255	131,072	Network Interconnect Device Benchmark Testing
	223.255.255.0/24	223.255.255.0	223.255.255.255	256	Reserved but Subject to Reallocation
D	224.0.0.0/4	224.0.0.0	239.255.255.255	268,435,456	Multicast
E	240.0.0.0/4	240.0.0.0	255.255.255.255	268,435,456	Reserved for Future Use
				588,579,840	TOTAL SPECIAL ADDRESSES

As an example, my network printer is at 192.168.1.106 and my home solar panel controller is at 192.168.1.100, both ***private use*** network addresses. A machine on the inside of the local network can see both devices, but no machine outside the local network (that is, on the Internet in general) can access either one.

Uniform Resource Locator (URL) format

```
http://www.xyz.com/~fred/taxes/2015/tax_return.html
```

| PROTOCOL | HOST ADDRESS | USERNAME | FOLDER PATH | RESOURCE |

A ***Uniform Resource Locator*** (***URL***) is the name and path to a particular file, on some server, that is desired by a user. As its name implies, it is a uniform way to locate resources on the Web.

The ***protocol*** is one of many allowable; if omitted most assume **http://** as the default protocol, although the secure (encrypted) **https://** protocol is becoming more and more common. Other allowable protocols include `telnet://`, `ftp://`, and `gopher://` (obsolete). The protocol is the particular set of rules used for communicating information over the Internet.

Normally ***host addresses*** (the same as domain names) are the names of particular computers, and are mapped into IP addresses by ***DNS***, the ***Domain Name System***. DNS uses a series of servers to resolve names into IP addresses, including the current computer running the browser; if one machine does not know, it has a list of other machines it can ask. If no machine knows the IP address the browser returns a "server not found" message. In any DNS server, DNS mappings have a ***time to live*** setting (***TTL***), measured in time intervals from seconds to months, after which they expire and must be refreshed by a new DNS search. This is to adapt to machines changing their IP addresses, or to correct for wrong or malicious DNS mappings (called ***cache poisoning***). Note that a user is allowed to enter an IP address directly, if known, instead of a host address (such as `http://128.119.34.46`). Multiple host names may map onto the same IP address.

Usernames are denoted by a ***tilde*** (**~**), and might not be present in a URL. These indicate the private account of a particular person on the host.

The ***folder path*** may contain many folders and subfolders, or none. Folders along a path are separated by forward slashes (**/**).

The ***resource*** is the name of the actual file being fetched from the server. It may be any kind of file (**.htm**, **.html**, **.gif**, **.jpg**, **.png**, **.txt**, **.css**, etc.), but if omitted the resource file **index.html** or **index.htm** is assumed by default (**.htm** files are allowed today because of pre-1995 Microsoft Windows only permitting three-character file extensions). If the resource does not exist on the server, the browser returns a ***404 error***.

Top-Level Domains on the Internet

Traditional TLD	Interpretation
.com	Commercial
.edu	Education
.gov	United States Government
.int	International Organizations (Restricted)
.mil	United States Military
.net	Network Infrastructures
.org	Organizations
Newer TLD	**Interpretation**
.aero	Air Transport Industry
.arpa	Address and Routing Parameter Area (Restricted)
.asia	Asia-Pacific Region
.biz	Business
.cat	Catalan Language and Culture
.coop	Cooperatives
.info	Informational Sites (Unrestricted)
.jobs	Employment
.mobi	Mobile Devices
.museum	Museums
.name	Individuals, Families
.post	Postal Services
.pro	Professions
.tel	Telephone / Internet Connections
.travel	Travel Agents and Tourism
.xxx	Porn Sites (approved June 2010)

Top Level Country Codes on the Internet (by Country Name)

.af	Afghanistan
.ax	Åland
.al	Albania
.dz	Algeria
.as	American Samoa
.ad	Andorra
.ao	Angola
.ai	Anguilla
.aq	Antarctica
.ag	Antigua, Barbuda
.ar	Argentina
.am	Armenia
.aw	Aruba
.ac	Ascension Island
.au	Australia
.at	Austria
.az	Azerbaijan
.bs	Bahamas
.bh	Bahrain
.bd	Bangladesh
.bb	Barbados
.eus	Basque Country
.by	Belarus
.be	Belgium
.bz	Belize
.bj	Benin
.bm	Bermuda
.bt	Bhutan
.bo	Bolivia
.bq	Bonaire (reserved, not yet in use)
.ba	Bosnia, Herzegovina
.bw	Botswana
.bv	Bouvet Island
.br	Brazil
.io	British Indian Ocean Territory

.vg	British Virgin Islands
.bzh	Brittany (approved 2014)
.bn	Brunei
.bg	Bulgaria .бг (2016)
.bf	Burkina Faso
.bi	Burundi
.kh	Cambodia / Khmer / Kâmpŭchea
.cm	Cameroon
.ca	Canada
.cv	Cape Verde
.ky	Cayman Islands
.cf	Central African Republic
.td	Chad / Tchad
.cl	Chile
.cx	Christmas Island
.cc	Cocos / Keeling Islands
.co	Colombia
.km	Comoros
.ck	Cook Islands
.cr	Costa Rica
.ci	Côte d'Ivoire
.hr	Croatia / Hrvatska
.cu	Cuba
.cw	Curaçao
.cy	Cyprus
.cz	Czech Republic
.cs	Czechoslovakia (removed)
.kp	Democratic People's Rep. Korea
.cd	Democratic Rep. of the Congo
.dk	Denmark
.dj	Djibouti
.dm	Dominica
.do	Dominican Republic
.dd	East Germany (never used)
.tl	East Timor

Top Level Country Codes on the Internet (by Country Name)

.tp	East Timor (removed 2015, see .tl)	.ht	Haiti
.ec	Ecuador	.hm	Heard Island, McDonald Islands
.eg	Egypt مصر .	.hn	Honduras
.sv	El Salvador	.hk	Hong Kong
.gq	Equatorial Guinea	.hu	Hungary
.er	Eritrea (inactive)	.is	Iceland
.ee	Estonia	.in	India भारत.
.et	Ethiopia	.id	Indonesia
.eu	European Union	.ir	Iran
.fk	Falkland Islands	.iq	Iraq
.fo	Faroe Islands	.ie	Ireland
.fm	Federated States of Micronesia	.im	Isle of Man
.fj	Fiji	.il	Israel
.fi	Finland	.it	Italy
.fr	France	.jm	Jamaica
.gf	French Guiana	.jp	Japan
.pf	French Polynesia	.je	Jersey
.tf	French Southern & Antarctic Lands	.jo	Jordan
.ga	Gabon	.kz	Kazakhstan
.gm	Gambia	.ke	Kenya
.ge	Georgia	.ki	Kiribati
.de	Germany / Deutschland	.krd	Kurdistan (introduced 2014)
.gh	Ghana	.kw	Kuwait
.gi	Gibraltar	.kg	Kyrgyzstan
.gb	Great Britain (deprecated)	.la	Laos
.gr	Greece	.lv	Latvia
.gl	Greenland	.lb	Lebanon
.gd	Grenada	.ls	Lesotho
.gp	Guadeloupe	.lr	Liberia
.gu	Guam	.ly	Libya
.gt	Guatemala	.li	Liechtenstein
.gg	Guernsey	.lt	Lithuania
.gn	Guinea	.lu	Luxembourg
.gw	Guinea-Bissau	.mo	Macau
.gy	Guyana	.mk	Macedonia

Top Level Country Codes on the Internet (by Country Name)

Code	Country	Code	Country
.mg	Madagascar	.pk	Pakistan
.mw	Malawi	.pw	Palau
.my	Malaysia	.pa	Panama
.mv	Maldives	.pg	Papua New Guinea
.ml	Mali	.py	Paraguay
.mt	Malta	.cn	People's Republic of China .中国
.mh	Marshall Islands	.pe	Peru
.mq	Martinique	.ph	Phillipines
.mr	Mauritania	.pn	Pitcairn Islands
.mu	Mauritius	.pl	Poland
.yt	Mayotte	.pt	Portugal
.mx	Mexico	.pr	Puerto Rico
.md	Moldova	.qa	Qatar
.mc	Monaco	.kr	Republic of Korea
.mn	Mongolia	.cg	Republic of the Congo
.me	Montenegro	.re	Réunion
.ms	Montserrat	.ro	Romania
.ma	Morocco	.ru	Russia .рф (2010)
.mz	Mozambique	.rw	Rwanda
.mm	Myanmar	.gs	S. Georgia, S. Sandwich Islands
.na	Namibia	.sh	Saint Helena
.nr	Nauru	.kn	Saint Kitts, Nevis
.np	Nepal	.lc	Saint Lucia
.nl	Netherlands	.mf	Saint Martin (not in use)
.an	Netherlands Antilles (see .bq)	.vc	Saint Vincent, the Grenadines
.nc	New Caledonia	.pm	Saint-Pierre, Miquelon
.nz	New Zealand	.ws	Samoa / Western Samoa
.ni	Nicaragua	.sm	San Marino
.ne	Niger	.st	São Tomé, Principe
.ng	Nigeria	.sa	Saudi Arabia .السعودية
.nu	Niue	.sn	Senegal
.nf	Norfolk Island	.rs	Serbia .срб (2011)
.mp	Northern Mariana Islands	.sc	Seychelles
.no	Norway	.sl	Sierra Leone
.om	Oman	.sg	Singapore

Top Level Country Codes on the Internet (by Country Name)

`.sx`	Sint Maarten	`.us`	United States of America
`.sk`	Slovakia	`.vi`	United States Virgin islands
`.si`	Slovenia	`.uy`	Uruguay
`.sb`	Solomon Islands	`.uz`	Uzbekistan
`.so`	Somalia	`.vu`	Vanuatu
`.za`	South Africa	`.va`	Vatican City
`.ss`	South Sudan (approved 2019)	`.ve`	Venezuela
`.su`	Soviet Union (deprecated, see `.ru`)	`.vn`	Vietnam
`.es`	Spain	`.wf`	Wallis and Futuna
`.lk`	Sri Lanka	`.eh`	Western Sahara (not yet in use)
`.ps`	State of Palestine	`.ye`	Yemen
`.sd`	Sudan	`.yu`	Yugoslavia (removed 2010)
`.sr`	Suriname	`.zr`	Zaire (removed 2001, see `.cd`)
`.sj`	Svalbard, Jan Mayen Islands (not in use)	`.zm`	Zambia
`.sz`	Swaziland/Eswatini	`.zw`	Zimbabwe
`.se`	Sweden		
`.ch`	Switzerland		
`.sy`	Syria		
`.tw`	Taiwan, Republic of China `.台湾`		
`.tj`	Tajikistan		
`.tz`	Tanzania		
`.th`	Thailand		
`.tg`	Togo		
`.tk`	Tokelau		
`.to`	Tonga		
`.tt`	Trinidad, Tobago		
`.tn`	Tunisia		
`.tr`	Turkey		
`.tm`	Turkmenistan		
`.tc`	Turks and Caicos Islands		
`.tv`	Tuvalu		
`.ug`	Uganda		
`.ua`	Ukraine `.укр` (2013)		
`.ae`	United Arab Emirates `امارات.`		
`.uk`	United Kingdom		

Top Level Country Codes on the Internet (by Domain)

Code	Country	Code	Country
.ac	Ascension Island	.bw	Botswana
.ad	Andorra	.by	Belarus
.ae	United Arab Emirates امارات.	.bz	Belize
.af	Afghanistan	.bzh	Brittany (approved 2014)
.ag	Antigua, Barbuda	.ca	Canada
.ai	Anguilla	.cc	Cocos / Keeling Islands
.al	Albania	.cd	Democratic Rep. of the Congo
.am	Armenia	.cf	Central African Republic
.an	Netherlands Antilles (see .bq)	.cg	Republic of the Congo
.ao	Angola	.ch	Switzerland
.aq	Antarctica	.ci	Côte d'Ivoire
.ar	Argentina	.ck	Cook Islands
.as	American Samoa	.cl	Chile
.at	Austria	.cm	Cameroon
.au	Australia	.cn	People's Republic of China .中国
.aw	Aruba	.co	Colombia
.ax	Åland	.cr	Costa Rica
.az	Azerbaijan	.cs	Czechoslovakia (removed)
.ba	Bosnia, Herzegovina	.cu	Cuba
.bb	Barbados	.cv	Cape Verde
.bd	Bangladesh	.cw	Curaçao
.be	Belgium	.cx	Christmas Island
.bf	Burkina Faso	.cy	Cyprus
.bg	Bulgaria .бг (2016)	.cz	Czech Republic
.bh	Bahrain	.dd	East Germany (never used)
.bi	Burundi	.de	Germany / Deutschland
.bj	Benin	.dj	Djibouti
.bm	Bermuda	.dk	Denmark
.bn	Brunei	.dm	Dominica
.bo	Bolivia	.do	Dominican Republic
.bq	Bonaire (reserved, not yet in use)	.dz	Algeria
.br	Brazil	.ec	Ecuador
.bs	Bahamas	.ee	Estonia
.bt	Bhutan	.eg	Egypt مصر.
.bv	Bouvet Island	.eh	Western Sahara (not yet in use)

Top Level Country Codes on the Internet (by Domain)

.er	Eritrea (inactive)		.hu	Hungary
.es	Spain		.id	Indonesia
.et	Ethiopia		.ie	Ireland
.eu	European Union		.il	Israel
.eus	Basque Country		.im	Isle of Man
.fi	Finland		.in	India . भारत
.fj	Fiji		.io	British Indian Ocean Territory
.fk	Falkland Islands		.iq	Iraq
.fm	Federated States of Micronesia		.ir	Iran
.fo	Faroe Islands		.is	Iceland
.fr	France		.it	Italy
.ga	Gabon		.je	Jersey
.gb	Great Britain (deprecated)		.jm	Jamaica
.gd	Grenada		.jo	Jordan
.ge	Georgia		.jp	Japan
.gf	French Guiana		.ke	Kenya
.gg	Guernsey		.kg	Kyrgyzstan
.gh	Ghana		.kh	Cambodia / Khmer / Kâmpŭchea
.gi	Gibraltar		.ki	Kiribati
.gl	Greenland		.km	Comoros
.gm	Gambia		.kn	Saint Kitts, Nevis
.gn	Guinea		.kp	Democratic People's Rep. Korea
.gp	Guadeloupe		.kr	Republic of Korea
.gq	Equatorial Guinea		.krd	Kurdistan (introduced 2014)
.gr	Greece		.kw	Kuwait
.gs	S. Georgia, S. Sandwich Islands		.ky	Cayman Islands
.gt	Guatemala		.kz	Kazakhstan
.gu	Guam		.la	Laos
.gw	Guinea-Bissau		.lb	Lebanon
.gy	Guyana		.lc	Saint Lucia
.hk	Hong Kong		.li	Liechtenstein
.hm	Heard Island, McDonald Islands		.lk	Sri Lanka
.hn	Honduras		.lr	Liberia
.hr	Croatia / Hrvatska		.ls	Lesotho
.ht	Haiti		.lt	Lithuania

Top Level Country Codes on the Internet (by Domain)

Code	Country	Code	Country
.lu	Luxembourg	.nr	Nauru
.lv	Latvia	.nu	Niue
.ly	Libya	.nz	New Zealand
.ma	Morocco	.om	Oman
.mc	Monaco	.pa	Panama
.md	Moldova	.pe	Peru
.me	Montenegro	.pf	French Polynesia
.mf	Saint Martin (not in use)	.pg	Papua New Guinea
.mg	Madagascar	.ph	Phillipines
.mh	Marshall Islands	.pk	Pakistan
.mk	Macedonia	.pl	Poland
.ml	Mali	.pm	Saint-Pierre, Miquelon
.mm	Myanmar	.pn	Pitcairn Islands
.mn	Mongolia	.pr	Puerto Rico
.mo	Macau	.ps	State of Palestine
.mp	Northern Mariana Islands	.pt	Portugal
.mq	Martinique	.pw	Palau
.mr	Mauritania	.py	Paraguay
.ms	Montserrat	.qa	Qatar
.mt	Malta	.re	Réunion
.mu	Mauritius	.ro	Romania
.mv	Maldives	.rs	Serbia .срб (2011)
.mw	Malawi	.ru	Russia .рф (2010)
.mx	Mexico	.rw	Rwanda
.my	Malaysia	.sa	Saudi Arabia . السعودية
.mz	Mozambique	.sb	Solomon Islands
.na	Namibia	.sc	Seychelles
.nc	New Caledonia	.sd	Sudan
.ne	Niger	.se	Sweden
.nf	Norfolk Island	.sg	Singapore
.ng	Nigeria	.sh	Saint Helena
.ni	Nicaragua	.si	Slovenia
.nl	Netherlands	.sj	Svalbard, Jan Mayen Islands (not in use)
.no	Norway	.sk	Slovakia
.np	Nepal	.sl	Sierra Leone

Top Level Country Codes on the Internet (by Domain)

.sm	San Marino	.vc	Saint Vincent, the Grenadines
.sn	Senegal	.ve	Venezuela
.so	Somalia	.vg	British Virgin Islands
.sr	Suriname	.vi	United States Virgin islands
.ss	South Sudan (approved 2019)	.vn	Vietnam
.st	São Tomé, Principe	.vu	Vanuatu
.su	Soviet Union (deprecated, see .ru)	.wf	Wallis and Futuna
.sv	El Salvador	.ws	Samoa / Western Samoa
.sx	Sint Maarten	.ye	Yemen
.sy	Syria	.yt	Mayotte
.sz	Swaziland/Eswatini	.yu	Yugoslavia (removed 2010)
.tc	Turks and Caicos Islands	.za	South Africa
.td	Chad / Tchad	.zm	Zambia
.tf	French Southern & Antarctic Lands	.zr	Zaire (removed 2001, see .cd)
.tg	Togo	.zw	Zimbabwe
.th	Thailand		
.tj	Tajikistan		
.tk	Tokelau		
.tl	East Timor		
.tm	Turkmenistan		
.tn	Tunisia		
.to	Tonga		
.tp	East Timor (removed 2015, see .tl)		
.tr	Turkey		
.tt	Trinidad, Tobago		
.tv	Tuvalu		
.tw	Taiwan, Republic of China .台湾		
.tz	Tanzania		
.ua	Ukraine .укр (2013)		
.ug	Uganda		
.uk	United Kingdom		
.us	United States of America		
.uy	Uruguay		
.uz	Uzbekistan		
.va	Vatican City		

HTML Basic Page

The simplest possible HTML Web page (other than a `.txt` file) is shown below. It has a title that appears at the top of the browser window, and a space for the page content. Every other setting (font, background color, etc.) uses its default value. Web pages will work without the `<!DOCTYPE html>` directive, but including it is highly recommended. Items enclosed in angle brackets are called **_tags_**, and most surround text and are of the form `<TAG>...</TAG>`. Some tags have an opening tag but <u>not</u> a closing tag. Tags may be in upper case or lower case; standards committees recommend **_lower case_**, but this book uses upper case for clarity. Opening tags may also contain **_attributes_** of the form `NAME="value"` (the quotes are required).

```
<!DOCTYPE html>

<HTML>
    <HEAD>
        <TITLE>Web page title goes here</TITLE>
    </HEAD>

    <BODY>
        Contents of Web page go here
        Contents of Web page go here
    </BODY>
</HTML>
```

The next most simple form of HTML Web page is to include color information in the `<BODY>` tag, or to specify the name of a graphic image file to be "cookie cutter" stamped across the background of the browser windows behind any page content. All five of these attributes are **_deprecated_**, and while they still work their use is discouraged in favor of CSS style sheets.

```
<!DOCTYPE html>

<HTML>
    <HEAD>
        <TITLE>Web page title goes here</TITLE>
    </HEAD>

    <BODY BACKGROUND="URL of image"         May appear simply as <BODY>.
          BGCOLOR="color"                   All five <BODY> attributes are
          TEXT="color"                      optional and can occur in any order.
          LINK="color"                      Also, all five have been deprecated
          VLINK="color">                    in favor of style sheets.

        Contents of Web page go here
        Contents of Web page go here
    </BODY>
</HTML>
```

HTML Page with CSS

This version includes references to **_Cascading Style Sheet_** (**_CSS_**) styles, either stored in an external file or written into the HTML Web page itself. The <LINK> and <STYLE> sections are optional. The <LINK> loads an external file containing CSS information available to all Web pages (that is, any Web page that links to the same file has the same style formats). Any items in the local <STYLE> block override definitions from that linked external file for the current document only.

```
<!DOCTYPE html>

<HTML>
    <HEAD>
        <TITLE>Web page title goes here</TITLE>

        <LINK REL="stylesheet" TYPE="text/css" HREF="file.css">

        <STYLE TYPE="text/css">
            Cascading Style Sheet statements go here
            Cascading Style Sheet statements go here
        </STYLE>
    </HEAD>

    <BODY>
        Contents of Web page go here
        Contents of Web page go here
    </BODY>
</HTML>
```

It is also possible to override styles on a tag-by-tag basis by placing a STYLE="..." attribute within individual tags (not shown here).

HTML Page with JavaScript

The <SCRIPT> sections are optional. The first <SCRIPT> tag loads an external file of JavaScript program code available to all Web pages (that is, any HTML page that links to the same external JavaScript file has access to all of its functions). The second <SCRIPT> tag contains local JavaScript program code available only to the current document. The third <SCRIPT> tag contains program code to be run immediately after it is encountered by the browser, and usually calls functions defined in the earlier sections. The closing </SCRIPT> tag is required in all cases.

```
<!DOCTYPE html>

<HTML>
    <HEAD>
        <TITLE>Web page title goes here</TITLE>

        <SCRIPT TYPE="text/javascript" SRC="file.js"></SCRIPT>

        <SCRIPT TYPE="text/javascript">
            <!--
            JavaScript program statements go here
            JavaScript program statements go here
            //-->
        </SCRIPT>
    </HEAD>

    <BODY>
        Contents of Web page go here
        Contents of Web page go here

        <SCRIPT TYPE="text/javascript">
            <!--
            JavaScript program statements go here
            JavaScript program statements go here
            //-->
        </SCRIPT>

        Contents of Web page go here
        Contents of Web page go here
    </BODY>
</HTML>
```

HTML Page with CSS and JavaScript

This version contains both CSS and JavaScript, both stored in external files and defined locally. Nearly all Web pages today use CSS, and those that also use JavaScript will have the general form outlined here.

```
<!DOCTYPE html>

<HTML>
    <HEAD>
        <TITLE>Web page title goes here</TITLE>

        <LINK REL="stylesheet" TYPE="text/css" HREF="file.css">

        <STYLE TYPE="text/css">
            Cascading Style Sheet statements go here
            Cascading Style Sheet statements go here
        </STYLE>

        <SCRIPT TYPE="text/javascript" SRC="file.js"></SCRIPT>

        <SCRIPT TYPE="text/javascript">
            <!--
            JavaScript program statements go here
            JavaScript program statements go here
            //-->
        </SCRIPT>
    </HEAD>

    <BODY>
        Contents of Web page go here
        Contents of Web page go here

        <SCRIPT TYPE="text/javascript">
            <!--
            JavaScript program statements go here
            JavaScript program statements go here
            //-->
        </SCRIPT>

        Contents of Web page go here
        Contents of Web page go here
    </BODY>
</HTML>
```

HTML CSS Basics: The Cascade

Every tag has a list of ***default attributes***. Those attributes may be overridden by definitions stored in an external `.css` file. The defaults <u>and</u> the external `.css` file may be overridden by the local `<STYLE>` block in the current HTML document. Everything (the defaults, the `.css` file, and the local `<STYLE>` block) may be overridden by `STYLE="..."` attributes placed within individual tags. This process of what gets control of the format of a tag is what defines the ***cascade***.

Styles from Style Sheet (in `<HEAD>` section)

```
<LINK REL="stylesheet"
      TYPE="text/css"
      HREF="filename">
```

Styles from Style Sheet Example

```
<LINK REL="stylesheet"
      TYPE="text/css"
      HREF="MySheet.css">
```

The external `.css` style sheet file is a simple text file containing a group of definitions of how tag attributes should be modified. These are all of the general form:

```
selector,selector,selector {property:value ; property:value}
```

where `selector` is the name of a tag like `BODY` or `H1` or `P`, `property` is the name of a style associated with the tag, and `value` is the new setting for that property. Blanks and line breaks can be used to space out definitions to make them easy to read. Semicolons separate different `property:value` pairs (the last definition in the list is allowed to either include or omit the trailing semicolon). Note that any syntax errors (generally using the wrong symbols) will cause the entire style definition to be ignored. Omitting the `}` or using the wrong symbol in place of it will cause the current style definition to absorb the one that follows it.

Embedded Styles (in `<HEAD>` section)

```
<STYLE TYPE="text/css">
    selector,
    selector,
    selector  {
            property:value ;
            property:value ;
            property:value
          }
</STYLE>
```

Embedded Styles Example

```
<STYLE TYPE="text/css">
    H1,H2 {color:red ;
            text-align:center}
    HR {width:50%}
    P {text-align:justify ;
       font-family:'Arial' ;
       font-size:16pt ;
       color:blue}
</STYLE>
```

Within the `<STYLE>...</STYLE>` tag pair, style definitions follow the exactly same format as in external `.css` files. Any style definitions made here override any selectors with the same names stored in an external `.css` file.

HTML CSS Basics: The Cascade (Continued)

Inline Styles (in individual tags)

```
<tag STYLE="property:value">
    or
<tag STYLE="property:value ; property:value ; property:value">
```

Individual tags can override *everything* defined earlier for that tag only (the defaults, the `.css` file, etc.) by including a `STYLE="property:value"` attribute definition.

Inline Style Example

```
<H1 STYLE="color:red">
```

Example of the Cascade

The `MySheet.css` file contains the following text to define all `H1` headings to be `blue` (among other style definitions for other tags):

```
H1 {color:blue}
```

Any `<H1>...</H1>` tag in the HTML document that uses `MySheet.css` will be `blue` instead of `black` (the default), *unless that style is overridden*. The HTML document is then:

```
<!DOCTYPE html>

<HTML>
    <HEAD>
        <LINK REL="stylesheet"
              TYPE="text/css"
              HREF="MySheet.css">

        <STYLE TYPE="text/css">
            H1 {color:red}
        </STYLE>
    </HEAD>

    <BODY>
        <H1>Heading text</H1>
        ...
        <H1 STYLE="color:green">
            Heading text
        </H1>
    </BODY>
</HTML>
```

The `MySheet.css` file defines all `H1` headings to be `blue` for <u>any document</u> that links to it.

This <u>local</u> style definition overrides `MySheet.css` and makes all `H1` headings in <u>this document</u> `red`.

Text shows in `red` in the browser.

This use of the `STYLE` attribute overrides everything to make <u>this one</u> `H1` heading appear in `green`.

HTML Basic Formatting Tags

Comments

```
<!-- Comment may appear anywhere, all text is ignored -->
```

Text Markup Tags (in-line, do not affect line flow)   Example

`<B>`*text to make boldface*`</B>`	**Frog**
`<I>`*text to make italic*`</I>`	*Frog*
`<TT>`*text to make typewriter font*`</TT>`	`Frog`
`<SUP>`*text to make superscript*`</SUP>`	X^{Frog}
`<SUB>`*text to make subscript*`</SUB>`	X_{Frog}
`<DEL>`*text to delete (strikethrough)*`</DEL>`	~~Frog~~
`<INS>`*text to insert (underline)*`</INS>`	<u>Frog</u>
`<SPAN>`*no changes to text except with CSS*`</SPAN>`	Frog
`<PRE>`*preformatted text with spacing and line breaks preserved*`</PRE>`	

Note: to use several markup tags on the same piece of text, treat each tag pair as a unique set of parentheses, and <u>balance</u> them. If not properly balanced, some browsers can get confused and give oddly formatted text. For example, to make text both bold and italic:

`<B><I>`...`</I></B>`	Good, italic entirely inside bold
`<I><B>`...`</B></I>`	Good, bold entirely inside italic
`<B><I>`...`</B></I>`	Bad, italic not stopped before bold stopped
`<I><B>`...`</I></B>`	Bad, bold not stopped before italic stopped

Headings and Line Breaks (affect line flow)

` `	*or* ` `	Break line at current point
`<HR>`	*or* `<HR />`	Draw horizontal rule
`<P>`*Paragraph of text*`</P>`		Define a paragraph of text
`<H1>`*Heading text*`</H1>`		Heading size #1 (largest)
`<H2>`*Heading text*`</H2>`		Heading size #2
`<H3>`*Heading text*`</H3>`		Heading size #3
`<H4>`*Heading text*`</H4>`		Heading size #4
`<H5>`*Heading text*`</H5>`		Heading size #5
`<H6>`*Heading text*`</H6>`		Heading size #6 (smallest)
`<DIV>`*no changes to enclosed text except with CSS*`</DIV>`		

Most of these tags put blank space above and below the enclosed text. Many browsers allow the `</P>` closing paragraph tag to be omitted, but this is considered poor practice.

HTML Deprecated BODY Attributes

Deprecated BODY Attributes

```
<BODY BACKGROUND="URL of image"
      BGCOLOR="value"
      TEXT="value"
      LINK="value"
      VLINK="value">
```

The *value* in all these cases is an HTML color name or six-digit hexadecimal color code such as #45F2C1.

Use Instead

```
<STYLE TYPE="text/css">
    BODY {background-image:url("URL of image") ;
          background-color:value ;
          color:value}
    A:link {color:value}
    A:visited {color:value}
    A:hover {color:value}
    A:active {color:value}
</STYLE>
```

The *value* in all these cases is an HTML color name, a six-digit hexadecimal color code, or a CSS short-hex color code. Note: hover and active are in CSS only, and are not present in raw HTML.

```
<BODY>
```

BODY tag is now very simple.

If present, ***pseudoclasses*** A:link (link color before link is clicked), A:visited (link color after its page has been visited), A:hover (link color with the mouse floating over it), and A:active (link color that is clicked but not released), *must appear in this order*.

HTML Deprecated Tags

Deprecated Simple Tags | Use Instead / See Also

```
<S>strikethrough</S>
```
Use `<DEL>...</DEL>`
```
<STRIKE>strikethrough</STRIKE>
```
Use `<DEL>...</DEL>`
```
<U>underline</U>
```
Use `<INS>...</INS>`
```
<XMP>preformatted text</XMP>
```
Use `<PRE>...</PRE>` and entities
```
<CENTER>text to center</CENTER>
```
CSS style `text-align:center`

```
<FONT FACE="typeface name"
      COLOR="color"
      SIZE="font size 1...7">
    affected text
</FONT>
```
CSS style `font-family`
CSS style `color`
CSS style `font-size`

HTML Link Tags

Every link uses the "anchor" tag, requiring both something to click on and where to go when the link is clicked (using a "hypertext reference", or `HREF` attribute). The general format is:

`<A HREF="`*`link`***`">`***`Clickable item`***`</A>`**

There are several basic types of links, as outlined below.

Link to an External Resource

Resource may be either a `.html` or `.htm` Web page, a `.gif`, `.jpg`, or a `.png` image, or some other kind of external file. File may be local, requiring only its name, or remote, requiring a full `http://` address. The clickable item may be text, an image, or a combination of the two. The optional `TARGET="_blank"` attribute loads the linked resource into a new browser window.

`<A HREF="`*`URL of resource`***`">`***`Clickable item`***`</A>`**

`<A HREF="`*`URL of resource`***`" TARGET="_blank">`***`Clickable item`***`</A>`**

Resource names may <u>not</u> contain blanks: filenames that contain blanks must have every blank character replaced by the hexadecimal code **`%20`** (the blank character is at position 32 in the ASCII character table; decimal 32 is hex 20). The resource file `My Little Pony.jpg` must be referenced by the opening anchor tag `<A HREF="My%20Little%20Pony.jpg">`.

Link to an Email Address

When clicked, the link opens the current email program on the client computer.

`<A HREF="mailto:`*`email address`***`">`***`Clickable item`***`</A>`**

Link to a point inside Current Page

The *name* must be the same in all places; one to define the target, and the others to jump to that target. Jump points may be either above or below the target.

`<A HREF="#`*`name`***`">`***`Clickable item above target`***`</A>`**

...

`<A NAME="`*`name`***`">`***`Target point`***`</A>`**

...

`<A HREF="#`*`name`***`">`***`Clickable item below target`***`</A>`**

HTML Image Tags

Embedded Bitmap Images (SRC is the only required attribute)

All bitmapped images (`.gif`, `.jpg`, `.png`, etc.) can be embedded into a Web page with the `<IMG>` tag. The `SRC` attribute is required. While the `ALT` attribute is also listed as required it can be omitted without failure of the tag. Setting either `WIDTH` or `HEIGHT` but not both automatically sets the other attribute appropriately; set both to change the aspect ratio of the image. The `USEMAP` attribute is used only in client-side image maps, covered later.

```
<IMG SRC="URL of image resource"
     WIDTH="Width of image in pixels"
     HEIGHT="Height of image in pixels"
     ALT="Alternate text when image cannot be shown"
     TITLE="Title text for mouse flyover"
     USEMAP="#map name">
```

Embedded .SVG Image

Scalable Vector Graphics (`.svg`) files often cannot be shown in a browser using the `<IMG>` tag. They must be placed into an internal frame `<IFRAME>` instead. The `WIDTH` and `HEIGHT` of the frame must be included and must match the size of the graphic or unwanted scroll bars will appear. Set `FRAMEBORDER` to "no" to blend the graphic seamlessly into the referring document.

```
<IFRAME SRC="URL of .svg file"
        WIDTH="pixels"
        HEIGHT="pixels"
        FRAMEBORDER="NO"></IFRAME>
```

SVG is new enough that not all browsers support it well. Some browsers may do so through the `<IMG>` tag as described above, or use the `<EMBED>` tag instead of `<IFRAME>`, but `<IFRAME>` is increasing in support and is the recommended approach when `<IMG>` is unavailable.

```
<EMBED SRC="URL of .svg file">
```

Favorite Icons (favicons) in Title Bar (not supported by all browsers)

Favorite icons customize the browser's title bar and/or browser tabs with a small image, using a single `LINK` tag located in the `<HEAD>...</HEAD>` section. Traditionally, these are 16×16 pixel, 16-color `.ico` files, but both `.gif` and `.png` file types and 32×32 images are now allowed (the `SIZES` and `TYPE` attributes may be optional in some browsers):

```
<LINK REL="icon" HREF="URL of image resource"
      SIZES="pixelsxpixels"
      TYPE="image/file type of image resource">
```

HTML Unordered List Tags

Use the ***unordered list*** <UL>...</UL> to create bulleted lists, where the order of the items in the list does not matter. Bullet symbols can be discs (solid circles), squares, or open circles. By default, the disc is the first bullet to be used. Unordered lists inside of unordered lists rotate through the three bullet symbol types, but the symbol type can be overridden or omitted. The </LI> closing list item tag can be omitted in many browsers, but this is bad practice and should be avoided.

Basic Structure

```
<UL>
    <LI>List item</LI>
    <LI>List item</LI>
    ...
    <LI>List item</LI>
</UL>
```

TYPE Attributes (Deprecated, not supported in HTML 5)

```
<UL TYPE="disc">                                ●
<UL TYPE="square">                              ■
<UL TYPE="circle">                              ○
```

list-style-type Styles

```
<UL STYLE="list-style-type:disc">               ●
<UL STYLE="list-style-type:square">             ■
<UL STYLE="list-style-type:circle">             ○
<UL STYLE="list-style-type:none">
```

HTML Ordered List Tags

Use the ***ordered list*** `<OL>...</OL>` to create lists where the order of the items in the list is important. By default, items are numbered in decimal (1,2,3,4,…), and ordered lists inside of ordered lists also use decimal numbers. The symbol can be overridden or omitted. The `</LI>` closing list item tag can be omitted in many browsers, but this is bad practice and should be avoided.

Basic Structure

```
<OL>
    <LI>List item</LI>
    <LI>List item</LI>
    ...
    <LI>List item</LI>
</OL>
```

Attributes

`<OL REVERSED>`	List appears in reverse order (New in HTML 5)
`<OL START="number">`	List starts counting at given number (default=1)

TYPE Attributes (Deprecated, not supported in HTML 5)

`<OL TYPE="1">`	Numbers (default)	1,2,3,4,…
`<OL TYPE="A">`	Upper case Letters	A,B,C,D,…
`<OL TYPE="a">`	Lower case Letters	a,b,c,d,…
`<OL TYPE="I">`	Upper case Roman	I,II,III,IV,…
`<OL TYPE="i">`	Lower case Roman	i,ii,iii,iv,…

`list-style-type` Styles

`<OL STYLE="list-style-type:decimal">`	1,2,3,4,…
`<OL STYLE="list-style-type:decimal-leading-zero">`	01,02,03,04,…
`<OL STYLE="list-style-type:upper-alpha">`	A,B,C,D,…
`<OL STYLE="list-style-type:lower-alpha">`	a,b,c,d,,…
`<OL STYLE="list-style-type:upper-roman">`	I,II,III,IV,…
`<OL STYLE="list-style-type:lower-roman">`	i,ii,iii,iv,…
`<OL STYLE="list-style-type:none">`	

HTML Table Tags

Tables <TABLE>...</TABLE> are made up of *rows* <TR>...</TR>, while rows are made up of *data cells* <TD>...</TD> or *header cells* <TH>...</TH>. Data cells and header cells may be merged with adjacent cells by <TD COLSPAN="*number*">, <TD ROWSPAN="*number*">, <TH COLSPAN="*number*">, and <TH ROWSPAN="*number*">.

Basic Structure

<TABLE>	Start of table
<TR>	Start of row 1
<TD>...**</TD>**	First column of row 1
<TD>...**</TD>**	Second column of row 1
...	
<TD>...**</TD>**	Last column of row 1
</TR>	End of row 1
<TR>	Start of row 2
<TD>...**</TD>**	First column of row 2
<TD>...**</TD>**	Second column of row 2
...	
<TD>...**</TD>**	Last column of row 2
</TR>	End of row 2
...	
<TR>	Start of last row
<TD>...**</TD>**	First column of last row
<TD>...**</TD>**	Second column of last row
...	
<TD>...**</TD>**	Last column of last row
</TR>	End of last row
</TABLE>	End of table

Use **<TH>**...**</TH>** instead of **<TD>**...**</TD>** for bold, centered table headers.

The table structure as shown will <u>not</u> display borders (lines) around the cells. Use either <TABLE BORDER> (deprecated) or <TABLE STYLE="border:1px"> (preferred) to show the table as a proper table.

HTML Table Tags (Continued)

Table Attributes

`<TD COLSPAN="`*`number`*`">`	Merge *number* cells horizontally
`<TD ROWSPAN="`*`number`*`">`	Merge *number* cells vertically

Attributes in <TABLE> (Deprecated, not supported in HTML 5)

`<TABLE BORDER="`*`number`*`">`	Width of table border in pixels
`<TABLE BORDER>`	Same as `BORDER="1"`
`<TABLE BGCOLOR="`*`value`*`">`	Background color of table
`<TABLE WIDTH="`*`number`*`">`	Width in pixels or % of table

Attributes in <TR>, <TD>, and <TH> (Deprecated, not supported in HTML 5)

`WIDTH="`*`number`*`"`	Width in pixels or % (`TD` and `TH`)
`BGCOLOR="`*`value`*`"`	Background color of row, cell, or header cell
`ALIGN="`*`value`*`"`	Horizontal: `left`, `right`, `center`, `justify`
`VALIGN="`*`value`*`"`	Vertical: `top`, `middle`, `bottom`, `baseline`

Styles. Can be used in <TABLE>, <TR>, <TD>, and <TH> tags, except where noted.

`STYLE="border:`*`1`*`px solid `*`value`*`"`	Specify border color, width.
`STYLE="background-color:`*`value`*`"`	Specify background color.
`STYLE="text-align:`*`value`*`"`	Horiz.: `left`, `right`, `center`, `justify`
`STYLE="vertical-align:`*`value`*`"`	Vert.: `top`, `middle`, `bottom`, `baseline`
`STYLE="color:`*`value`*`"`	Text color.
`STYLE="width:`*`value`*`"`	Size in pixels or %.
`STYLE="height:`*`value`*`"`	Size in pixels or %.
`STYLE="margin-left:`*`value`*`"`	Size in pixels, %, or `auto` (`TABLE` only).
`STYLE="margin-right:`*`value`*`"`	Size in pixels, %, or `auto` (`TABLE` only).

Styles or attributes such as `color`, `text-align`, and `background-color` are *hierarchical*: assigning a value at the `TABLE` level affects all rows and all cells of the table, which can be overridden for a particular row by assigning a similar value at the `TR` level, and that overridden for an individual cell by assigning a value at the `TH` or `TD` level.

The most common style definitions will go into the `<STYLE>...</STYLE>` block or an external `.css` file, such as: `TABLE, TH, TD {border:1px solid black}` to establish a minimum border around all tables and every cell within them. Set both the left and right margins to `auto`, as in `TABLE {margin-left:auto ; margin-right:auto}` to center tables on the screen.

HTML Client Side Image Maps

A ***client side image map*** is a way of having different regions in a single image link to different URLs. Regions may be circular, rectangular, or arbitrary polygons. Clicking on any of these regions jumps to the associated link. There are rules for what to do if regions overlap and what happens when the background not cover by any region is clicked.

Rectangles are defined by the x and y coordinates of the upper left corner and the lower right corner (four numbers). Circles are defined by the x and y coordinates of the center and the circle's radius (three numbers). Polygons are defined by an x and y coordinate for every vertex point in the polygon (the number of vertices coordinate pairs). Some browsers require that the "loop be closed" by making the last point a repeat of the first, but that is largely unnecessary today. A map may contain any number of rectangles, circles, and polygons, as required by the geometry of the shapes in the image that need links.

Raster images (`.jpg`, `.gif`, `.png`) are defined with coordinate <0,0> in the upper left corner, and all x and y values in the `COORDS` attributes are expressed in terms of pixels relative to that corner.

The earliest definitions are treated with the <u>highest</u> priority; this is particularly important in areas that overlap. The default shape (if present) must be the <u>last</u> area in the list.

The `<MAP>` and its associated `<IMG>` can be <u>anywhere</u> in the body of the HTML document; they need not be close to each other. However, the map <u>names must match</u>. An HTML document may contain multiple images and multiple maps; the map names allow each image to find its map. Here is the general format:

```
<IMG SRC="URL of image resource" USEMAP="#map name">


<MAP NAME="map name">

    <AREA SHAPE="rect" COORDS="x1,y1,x2,y2" HREF="URL">

    <AREA SHAPE="circle" COORDS="x,y,radius" HREF="URL">

    <AREA SHAPE="poly" COORDS="x1,y1,x2,y2,…,xn,yn"
                                            HREF="URL">

    <AREA SHAPE="default" HREF="Default URL">
</MAP>
```

HTML Client Side Image Maps (Example)

In this example, the image is a 320×240 pixel graphic stored in a file called `MyPicture.gif` and stored in the same directory folder as the referring HTML document. The upper left pixel is at location <0,0> and the lower right pixel is at location <319,239>. This image contains three clickable regions: a rectangle, a circle that partially overlaps the rectangle, and a triangle (these regions probably do not appear in the actual image). All vertices are indicated by red dots, and all are on 10-pixel boundaries (a 10-pixel grid is shown for reference; the grid is likely <u>not</u> part of the actual image either). Clicking in the rectangle links to `www.rectangle.com`, clicking in the circle links to `www.circle.com`, clicking in the triangle links to `www.triangle.com`, and clicking anywhere else in the image links to `www.other.com`. The circle must come before the rectangle because of the overlap, and the default must come last, but the triangle (polygon) overlaps nothing and can go anywhere before the default.

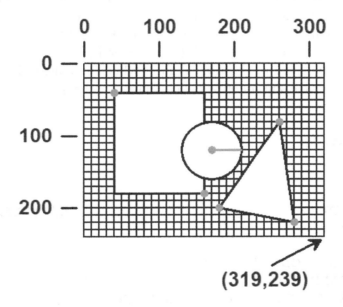

(319,239)

```
<IMG SRC="MyPicture.gif" USEMAP="#MyMap">

<MAP NAME="MyMap">
    <AREA SHAPE="circle"
         COORDS="170,120,40"
         HREF="http://www.circle.com/">
    <AREA SHAPE="rect"
         COORDS="40,40,160,180"
         HREF="http://www.rectangle.com/">
    <AREA SHAPE="poly"
         COORDS="180,200,280,220,260,80"
         HREF="http://www.triangle.com/">
    <AREA SHAPE="default"
         HREF="http://www.other.com/">
</MAP>
```

HTML Frame Tags

**Frames** are a way of dividing a browser window into sub-windows, each containing a unique Web page. This means that one window must have a mechanism for controlling the others, deciding when and what to load into the other windows, etc.

**Frames are **deprecated** and are unsupported in HTML 5**. Also, many Web sites forbade the use of frames with their content, so frames are falling out of favor. They are presented here for completeness.

Master Document

The master document controls all the frames and is the main page to be loaded into the browser. In this example the master is split into two columns, each its own frame. The left frame is 200 pixels wide, and the right frame takes up the remainder of the browser window. The first document `left.html` loads into the first (left) frame, and the second document `right.html` loads into the second (right) frame, both by default when the master document is loaded. The `NAME` attribute of the `FRAME` tag identifies each frame for the `TARGET` of a `<A HREF="...">` link.

```
<!DOCTYPE html>

<HTML>
    <HEAD>
        <TITLE>Web page title goes here</TITLE>
    </HEAD>

    <FRAMESET COLS="200,*">
        <FRAME SRC="left.html"  NAME="MyLeftDoc">
        <FRAME SRC="right.html" NAME="MyRightDoc">
    </FRAMESET>

    <NOFRAMES>
        Text to show if browser cannot support frames
    </NOFRAMES>
</HTML>
```

Browsers ignore tags that they do not recognize. If a browser does support frames, it will know how to properly handle the `<FRAMESET>`...`</FRAMESET>` tag, and it will know to ignore the contents of the `<NOFRAMES>`...`</NOFRAMES>` tag. If a browser does not support frames, however, then the `<FRAMESET>`, `<FRAME>`, and the `<NOFRAMES>` tags will not be recognized, will thus be ignored, and the contents of the `<NOFRAMES>`...`</NOFRAMES>` tag will appear on screen.

HTML Frame Tags (Continued)

Left Frame Document *left.html*

Links here in the <u>left</u> frame document use their TARGET attribute to load the linked item into the <u>right</u> frame, identified by the target name. The left frame stays on-screen. The contents of the right frame are replaced by the appropriate Web page each time a link in the left frame is clicked.

```
<!DOCTYPE html>

<HTML>
    <HEAD>
        <TITLE>Web page title goes here</TITLE>
    </HEAD>

    <BODY>
        <A HREF="http://…" TARGET="MyRightDoc">
            Click to load Web resource #1 into right frame
        </A>

        <A HREF="http://…" TARGET="MyRightDoc">
            Click to load Web resource #2 into right frame
        </A>

        <A HREF="http://…" TARGET="MyRightDoc">
            Click to load Web resource #3 into right frame
        </A>
    </BODY>
</HTML>
```

FRAMESET Options

`<FRAMESET COLS="200,*">`	Left frame 200 pixels, right frame varies
`<FRAMESET COLS="25%,75%">`	Left frame 25% of screen width, right 75%
`<FRAMESET ROWS="200,*">`	Top frame 200 pixels, bottom frame varies
`<FRAMESET ROWS="25%,75%">`	Top frame 25% of screen, bottom 75%

HTML Form Tags

Object names identify the input control to the remote CGI program, and should all be unique, *except* for radio buttons that belong to the same group. Each group of related radio buttons will have a name unique to that group, and all buttons within that group will share the name.

```
<FORM METHOD="POST"   NAME="object name"
                      ACTION="URL of remote CGI program">

    <INPUT TYPE="reset" VALUE="text for reset button">
    <INPUT TYPE="submit" VALUE="text for submit button">
    <INPUT TYPE="image" SRC="image file for submit button">

    <INPUT TYPE="text"           -or-        TYPE="password"
        NAME="object name"
        SIZE="number"
        VALUE="default text preset in edit box"
        MAXLENGTH="number">

    <INPUT TYPE="button"         -or-        TYPE="hidden"
        NAME="object name"
        VALUE="text for button caption"
        ONCLICK="JavaScript function">

    <INPUT TYPE="checkbox"
        NAME="object name"
        CHECKED>                             The CHECKED is optional

    <INPUT TYPE="radio"
        NAME="object name for whole group of buttons"
        VALUE="unique text for this button"
        CHECKED>                             The CHECKED is optional

    <SELECT NAME="object name">
        <OPTION>first text item in drop-down list
        <OPTION>second text item in drop-down list
        ...
        <OPTION>last text item in drop-down list
    </SELECT>

    <TEXTAREA
        NAME="object name"
        COLS="number"
        ROWS="number">
        default text goes here, may span several rows
    </TEXTAREA>
</FORM>
```

HTML Form Tags with JavaScript

Forms can be used to submit information to a remote site through the URL of a remote CGI program script (as shown on the previous page), but they are also useful entirely in the local context of an HTML page. This often involves linking a button on a form to a JavaScript function, which can then *reach back* into the form to extract other information from its objects.

In the following example, there is a form named `MyForm` that contains two text edit boxes and a button to click that says Compute the Square. When the user clicks the button, its `ONCLICK` attribute calls the JavaScript `Square` function, which shows in the second text box the square of any number typed into the first text box.

The `Square` function *reaches back* into the `document`, finds the `MyForm` form, finds the object named `MyInput` within the form, and grabs its `value` (a string). The string is converted to an integer with `parseInt` and assigned to local variable `N`. The value of variable `N` is squared and assigned to local variable `Answer`. The function then *reaches back* into the `document` again, finds the `MyForm` form again, finds the object named `MyAnswer` within the form, and assigns its `value` the result in `Answer` converted to a string. The form and other variable names are shown in different colors to indicate where they are defined and used.

```
<!DOCTYPE html>

<HTML>
  <HEAD>
    <TITLE>Factorial with Forms</TITLE>

    <SCRIPT TYPE="text/javascript">
      <!--
          function Square () {
              var N = parseInt(document.MyForm.MyInput.value) ;
              var Answer = N * N ;
              document.MyForm.MyAnswer.value = String(Answer) ;
          }
      //-->
    </SCRIPT>
  </HEAD>

  <BODY>
    <FORM NAME="MyForm">
      <INPUT TYPE="text" NAME="MyInput">Input Number<BR>
      <INPUT TYPE="text" NAME="MyAnswer">Number Squared<BR>
      <INPUT TYPE="button" VALUE="Compute the Square"
                        ONCLICK="Square();">
    </FORM>
  </BODY>
</HTML>
```

CSS and HTML Colors

Color Specifications

Colors in pure HTML are either ***color names*** or 6-digit ***hexadecimal codes*** (prefixed with the # symbol). CSS allows those, but also permits 3-digit ***short hex*** codes, and two ways to use an `rgb` function: arguments can be either 0....255 byte values or percentages, but not a mix. Short hex can be used in CSS only when all three values in hexadecimal have the first digit the same as the second (for example, `#CC4411` is `#C41` in short hex, but `#C27796` has no short hex).

Colors and Color Mixing	Example (using white)	
Color Name	`white`	(HTML,CSS)
Hexadecimal (6 digit)	`#FFFFFF`	(HTML,CSS)
Short Hex (3 digit)	`#FFF`	(CSS only)
RGB Decimal (0...255)	`rgb(255,255,255)`	(CSS only)
RGB Percent (0%...100%)	`rgb(100%,100%,100%)`	(CSS only)

Browser-Safe Color Values

A browser safe color picks all three (R, G, B) values from this list. If any value is <u>not</u> from this list, the color is <u>not</u> browser safe. There are exactly 6×6×6 = 216 browser safe colors.

Hex	Short Hex	Percent	Decimal
00	0	0%	0
33	3	20%	51
66	6	40%	102
99	9	60%	153
CC	C	80%	205
FF	F	100%	255

Color Names

See the color models chapter for all named HTML colors, as well as a deeper discussion of browser safe colors. The colors shown here are a subset of the named colors, and are guaranteed to work on all browsers. Where possible, the short hex version is also shown.

Name	Hex (Not Browser Safe)	Name	Hex (Browser Safe)	Short Hex
`silver`	`#C0C0C0`	`black`	`#000000`	`#000`
`navy`	`#000080`	`blue`	`#0000FF`	`#00F`
`green`	`#008000`	`lime`	`#00FF00`	`#0F0`
`teal`	`#008080`	`aqua`	`#00FFFF`	`#0FF`
`maroon`	`#800000`	`red`	`#FF0000`	`#F00`
`purple`	`#800080`	`fuchsia`	`#FF00FF`	`#F0F`
`olive`	`#808000`	`yellow`	`#FFFF00`	`#FF0`
`gray`	`#808080`	`white`	`#FFFFFF`	`#FFF`

CSS Styles: Lengths

Most objects in an HTML Web page are automatically resized as the browser window is resized by the user. However, certain items need to be measured in absolute units, particularly in CSS.

Length Units		Examples
`%`	Percent	`100%`
`px`	Pixels	`500px`
`cm`	Centimeters	`1cm`
`in`	Inches	`2in`
`mm`	Millimeters	`25mm`
`pc`	Picas (`1pc = 0.1667in` = ⅙ inch)	`3pc`
`pt`	Points (`72pt = 1in`)	`12pt`
`em`	Ems	`1em`

(For a 16-point font: `1em=16pt`, for a 12-point font: `1em=12pt`, etc.)

As an example, the `<HR>` tag draws a line across the browser window, with a small gap on each end. Setting the width of the line to 50% of the browser window, no matter how the browser window is resized, can be done using the raw HTML `<HR WIDTH="50%">` (deprecated, not supported in HTML 5) or the CSS `<HR STYLE="width:50%">` forms. To set the width of the line to exactly two inches would use `<HR STYLE="width:2in">`.

CSS Styles: Body and Links

Background Properties	**Possible Values**
`background-color`	`transparent`|*color value*
`background-image`	`none`|`url("`*file name*`")`
`background-repeat`	`repeat`|`repeat-x`|`repeat-y`|`no-repeat`
`background-attachment`	`scroll`|`fixed` (`fixed` used when `no-repeat` is on)
`background-position`	*percentage*|*percentage1 percentage2*| *length*|*length1 length2*|`left top`| `left center`|`left bottom`|`right top`| `right center`|`right bottom`|`center top`| `center center`|`center bottom`

Link Pseudoclass for <A> tag (when present, items must appear in this order)

`A:link`	`{color:`*value*`}`	Replaces `LINK` attribute of `BODY`
`A:visited`	`{color:`*value*`}`	Replaces `VLINK` attribute of `BODY`, not supported 100%
`A:hover`	`{color:`*value*`}`	Color when mouse floats over link, no HTML equivalent
`A:active`	`{color:`*value*`}`	Color when mouse clicks link, no HTML equivalent

Old Approach (HTML Only)   New Approach (CSS)

```
<!DOCTYPE html>

<HTML>
  <HEAD>
    <TITLE>title</TITLE>
    ...
  </HEAD>

<BODY
  BACKGROUND="dog.gif"
  BGCOLOR="green"
  TEXT="black"
  LINK="blue"
  VLINK="magenta">
     page content
     goes here
  </BODY>
</HTML>
```

```
<!DOCTYPE html>

<HTML>
  <HEAD>
    <TITLE>title</TITLE>
    ...
    <STYLE TYPE="text/css">
       BODY {
          background—image:
                url("dog.gif") ;
          background-color:green ;
          color:black}
       A:link    {color:blue}
       A:visited {color:magenta}
       A:hover   {color:value}
       A:active  {color:value}
    </STYLE>
  </HEAD>

  <BODY>
       page content goes here
  </BODY>
</HTML>
```

CSS Styles: Text and Fonts

Text Properties	Possible Values
color	*color value*
text-align	left | right | center | justify
text-decoration	none | underline | overline | line-through | blink
text-indent	*length* | *percentage*
text-transform	capitalize | uppercase | lowercase | none
text-shadow	none | *color value* | *length*
letter-spacing	normal | *length*
word-spacing	normal | *length* | *percentage*
vertical-align	baseline | sub | super | top | text-top | middle | bottom | text-bottom | *length* | *percentage*

Font Properties	Possible Values
font-family	*font name* | cursive | fantasy | monospace | sans-serif | serif
font-size	xx-small | x-small | small | medium | large | x-large | xx-large | larger | smaller | *length* | *percentage*
font-style	normal | italic | oblique
font-variant	normal | small-caps
font-weight	normal | bold | lighter | bolder | 100 | 200 | 300 | 400 | 500 | 600 | 700 | 800 | 900
font-stretch	normal | ultra-condensed | extra-condensed | condensed | semi-condensed | semi-expanded | expanded | extra-expanded | ultra-expanded
font-size-adjust	none | *number*
line-height	normal | *number* | *length* | *percentage*

Example for P (if no Times use Times New Roman, if neither then use any serif typeface)

```
<STYLE TYPE="text/css">
    P {font-family:Times, 'Times New Roman', serif ;
       font-size:12pt ;
       text-align:justify ;
       text-indent:0.5in ;
       color:red}
</STYLE>
```

CSS Styles: Custom Classes

A *class* in CSS is a mechanism for extending HTML. There are two main ways of doing so: (1) adding new capabilities to an existing tag, and (2) creating generic capabilities that can be applied to any tag.

Adding a Class to an Existing Tag

The general format is to define in the <STYLE>...</STYLE> block or in an external .css file a set of *property*: *value* definitions for an <u>existing tag</u> with a <u>new class name</u>:

```
<STYLE TYPE="text/css">
    tag.newclass {property:value ; property:value}
</STYLE>
```

Then to use the new class and all of its properties in a tag:

```
<tag CLASS="newclass">
```

For example, paragraph tags <P> have default settings: paragraphs are in the Times New Roman typeface, have a normal font size, are black, are left justified, etc. To change a single paragraph to red and 24 points <u>without classes</u> we would have to write:

```
<P STYLE="color:red ; font-size:24pt">
```

and do that in every paragraph tag that needed the change. Unfortunately, putting those definitions in the <STYLE>...</STYLE> block as P {color:red ; font-size:24pt} would change *every* paragraph throughout the HTML document, not just those few we are interested in changing. The better solution is to extend the paragraph tag by creating a class that includes these same definitions:

```
<STYLE TYPE="text/css">
    P.bigred {color:red ; font-size:24pt}
</STYLE>
```

Paragraphs normally do not have a bigred definition, but now they do. Setting a single paragraph to red and 24 points is done by adding the newly created class name to the tag wherever it is needed:

```
<P CLASS="bigred">
```

If these special paragraphs need any other changes (such as making them fully justified or indented, for example), only the properties of the bigred class definition need to be changed. This is much simpler, smaller, and easier to maintain than doing it the hard way, but it only applies to paragraphs, not to headings or any other tag. Making the same changes to other tags requires that they, too, have their own private and unique class with those same definitions.

CSS Styles: Custom Classes (Continued)

A generic approach also uses classes, but these classes defined in such a way that they are not attached to any particular tag. Instead, they are ***anonymous classes*** that can be attached as needed to the appropriate tags.

Creating an Anonymous Class

The general format is to define in the <STYLE>...</STYLE> block or an external .css file a set of *property:value* definitions for <u>no specific tag</u> but with a <u>new class name</u> (notice that there is no tag name, and the class name starts with a dot):

```
<STYLE TYPE="text/css">
     .newclass {property:value ; property:value}
</STYLE>
```

For example, desired font characteristics might be to have text both green and underlined. To do this in a single paragraph <u>without classes</u> we would have to type:

```
<P STYLE="color:green ; text-decoration:underline">
```

and in a single large heading:

```
<H1 STYLE="color:green ; text-decoration:underline">
```

These are identical except for the tag name. The better solution is to create an anonymous class containing those definitions and then apply the class to <u>whatever tag requires it</u>. Here is the class definition:

```
<STYLE TYPE="text/css">
     .specialfont {color:green ; text-decoration:underline}
</STYLE>
```

Applying that class to a paragraph, a large heading, a small heading, etc., to make each one green and underlined, results in very short tags:

```
<P CLASS="specialfont">
<H1 CLASS="specialfont">
<H6 CLASS="specialfont">
```

When they are well-engineered, anonymous classes can make the HTML document significantly easier to write, modify, debug, and read than if the document was written without classes.

CSS Styles: SPAN

Up to this point CSS is used to modify the definition of a particular tag, and thus all the text that that tag type can affect throughout the document. For example, creating a style definition for P, H1, etc., affects *every instance* of a paragraph or large header, unless overridden as part of the cascade, and *affects all the text* inside the paragraph or header. This approach does not, however, allow for the style modification of an arbitrary <u>section</u> of anonymous text.

Solving that problem is what the <SPAN> tag is for (as well as <DIV>). The <SPAN> tag has <u>no natural effect by itself</u> on the text that it surrounds, but is used in combination with style definitions. For example, the following two HTML phrases have *absolutely identical effects*:

```
...text text text text text text...
...text text <SPAN>text text</SPAN> text text...
```

That is, <SPAN>...</SPAN> by itself doesn't do anything. However, the <SPAN> tag can specify styles that override anything currently in effect, such as the color, typeface, decoration, or point size of the paragraph or header within which the text is enclosed. The general form is:

```
...text text <SPAN STYLE="...">text text</SPAN> text text...
```

To change just the specified text to green and underlined instead of the current settings cannot be done by modifying the global style of any other tag, but is simple here:

```
...text text <SPAN STYLE="color:green ;
         text-decoration:underline">text text</SPAN> text text...
```

It is obvious that the HTML code will get very complicated if there are a lot of formatting changes to make in a lot of places. However, creating an anonymous class can simplify the process, defined as follows:

```
<STYLE TYPE="text/css">
    .specialfont {color:green ; text-decoration:underline}
</STYLE>
```

Then, for every section of text in the document that needs to be green and underlined, regardless of where that text is located, the code becomes:

```
...text text <SPAN CLASS="specialfont">text text</SPAN> text text...
```

Note that the <FONT> tag <u>would</u> work for changing the colors in a section of text, but not for other effects such as underlining. However, <FONT> has been deprecated (for many reasons) so its use is no longer recommended.

CSS Styles: DIV

The <DIV> tag is very similar to the <SPAN> tag, in that it does not change the natural appearance of any of the enclosed text. However, the <DIV>...</DIV>, indicating a ***division***, also generates a visual line-break similar to that of <P>...</P> and <H1>...</H1>. That is, it breaks the current line and generates blank space above and below the division.

As with <SPAN>, the <DIV> tag can be used with local style definitions or with classes to change the appearance of the enclosed text. For example, to make the enclosed text both green and underlined, with blank space above and below, the following code would work:

```
<DIV STYLE="color:green ; text-decoration:underline">
    text text
    text text
    text text
</DIV>
```

However, using the specialfont anonymous class defined earlier, the division could also be written as:

```
<DIV CLASS="specialfont">
    text text
    text text
    text text
</DIV>
```

One very useful application for a division is to generate a page break <u>after</u> a block of text when printing the Web page:

```
<DIV STYLE="page-break-after:always">
    text text
    text text
    text text
</DIV>
```

Note that <DIV> and <SPAN> are often used (even overused) in combination with each other. Divisions can contain other divisions, spans can contain spans, and divisions can contain spans. Each one represents a local change in the style of the current text.

SVG (Scalable Vector Graphics) File Format

Scalable Vector Graphics (*SVG*) files are text files that contain the <u>descriptions of pictures</u>, rather than two-dimensional bitmaps (arrays of pixels). Since every object in an SVG file is described numerically in terms of its position and size, the image can be scaled up or down in size by multiplying the coordinates and sizes of every object by a simple scale factor (a single number). A browser will then render the scaled image perfectly on screen at the new size without *aliasing*, a common problem when scaling bitmapped images.

See the earlier section on embedding images to see how to reference an SVG file from within an HTML Web page.

Follow the template here exactly, except for putting the desired image width and height numbers in the appropriate slots and for putting in your own comments. <u>Case matters</u>: unlike HTML, tag names are *required to be in lower case*. The CDATA section is to protect literal character data (code) that might be misinterpreted if the SVG file is embedded directly into a Web page.

```
<?xml version="1.0" encoding="UTF-8" standalone="no"?>

<!-- HTML-like comments can go pretty much anywhere -->

<svg
    xmlns:svg="http://www.w3.org/2000/svg"
    xmlns="http://www.w3.org/2000/svg"
    version="1.1"
    x="0px"
    y="0px"
    width="_____px"
    height="_____px"
    >

    <style type="text/css">
        <![CDATA[

            Style and class definitions go here, such as:
            line {stroke-linecap:round}
            .mytext {font-family:'Courier New' ; font-weight:bold}

        ]]>
    </style>

            Object definitions go here (rectangles, circles, ellipses, lines, polylines, polygons,
            text, etc.).

</svg>
```

SVG (Scalable Vector Graphics) File Format

Tags in SVG are either *<tag ...*/> (singleton tags, where the trailing slash is <u>required</u> in all such cases) or *<tag ...>text</tag>* (tags that enclose text). Tag names are in lower case.

Tag Layout for most SVG Objects, `class` and `style` are optional

```
<tag class="classname"
     attribute="value" attribute="value"
     attribute="value" attribute="value"
     style="property:value ; property:value"/>
```
or
```
<tag class="classname"
     attribute="value" attribute="value"
     attribute="value" attribute="value"
     style="property:value ; property:value">
     enclosed text
</tag>
```

Common Presentation Attributes

`fill="`*color*`"`	Interior color (any CSS color specification or `none`)
`fill-opacity="`*number*`"`	Interior transparency (0.0=transparent, 1.0=opaque)
`stroke="`*color*`"`	Outline color (any CSS color specification or `none`)
`stroke-width="`*number*`"`	Outline width (default=pixels)
`stroke-linecap="`*option*`"`	Ends of lines (`butt`, `round`, `square`)
`stroke-linejoin="`*option*`"`	Joins of lines end-to-end (`miter`, `round`, `bevel`)
`font-family="`*font name*`"`	Same as CSS (`monospace`, `serif`, etc., or name list)
`font-size="`*number*`"`	Same as CSS (`small`, `medium`, `large`, or a point size)
`font-weight="`*option*`"`	Same as CSS (`normal`, `bold`, etc.)
`font-style="`*option*`"`	Same as CSS (`normal`, `italic`, etc.)

Common Style Options (in the `style="`...`"` attribute)

`fill:`*color*`;`	Interior color (any CSS color specification or `none`)
`fill-opacity:`*number*`;`	Interior transparency (0.0=transparent, 1.0=opaque)
`stroke:`*color*`;`	Outline color (any CSS color specification or `none`)
`stroke-width:`*number*`;`	Outline width (default=pixels)
`stroke-linecap:`*option*`;`	Ends of lines (`butt`, `round`, `square`)
`stroke-linejoin:`*option*`;`	Joins of lines end-to-end (`miter`, `round`, `bevel`)
`font-family:`*font name*`;`	Same as CSS (`monospace`, `serif`, etc., or name list)
`font-size:`*number*`;`	Same as CSS (`small`, `medium`, `large`, or a point size)
`font-weight:`*option*`;`	Same as CSS (`normal`, `bold`, etc.)
`font-style:`*option*`;`	Same as CSS (`normal`, `italic`, etc.)

SVG File Format (Scalable Vector Graphics)

SVG Drawing Objects	Description of Attributes

`<rect`   **Rectangle object**

`class=``"classname"`	Optional reference to class definitions
`x=``"number"`	X coordinate of upper left corner
`y=``"number"`	Y coordinate of upper left corner
`width=``"number"`	Width of rectangle in pixels
`height=``"number"`	Height of rectangle in pixels
`rx=``"number"`	X-radius of rounded corners (optional)
`ry=``"number"`	Y-radius of rounded corners (optional)
`fill=``"color"`	Interior color or `none`
`stroke=``"color"`	Outline color or `none`
`stroke-width=``"number"`	Outline thickness (Default=1)
`style=``"styles list"`	Style-based options
`/>`	End of Rectangle Object

`<circle`   **Circle object**

`class=``"classname"`	Optional reference to class definitions
`cx=``"number"`	X coordinate of center point
`cy=``"number"`	Y coordinate of center point
`r=``"number"`	Circle radius
`fill=``"color"`	Interior color or `none`
`stroke=``"color"`	Outline color or `none`
`stroke-width=``"number"`	Outline thickness (Default=1)
`style=``"styles list"`	Style-based options
`/>`	End of Circle Object

`<ellipse`   **Ellipse object**

`class=``"classname"`	Optional reference to class definitions
`cx=``"number"`	X coordinate of center point
`cy=``"number"`	Y coordinate of center point
`rx=``"number"`	X radius
`ry=``"number"`	Y radius
`fill=``"color"`	Interior color or `none`
`stroke=``"color"`	Outline color or `none`
`stroke-width=``"number"`	Outline thickness (Default=1)
`style=``"styles list"`	Style-based options
`/>`	End of Ellipse Object

SVG File Format (Continued)

SVG Drawing Objects	**Description of Attributes**

```
<line
    class="classname"
    x1="number"
    y1="number"
    x2="number"
    y2="number"
    stroke="color"
    stroke-width="number"
    stroke-linecap="option"
    style="styles list"
/>
```

Line object
Optional reference to class definitions
X coordinate of first point
Y coordinate of first point
X coordinate of second point
Y coordinate of second point
Line color
Outline thickness (Default=1)
Ends of lines (butt, round, square)
Style-based options
End of Line Object

```
<polyline
    class="classname"
    points="list of points"
    stroke="color"
    stroke-width="number"
    stroke-linejoin="option"
    style="styles list"
/>
```

Multipoint line
Optional reference to class definitions
Coordinates of points: "2,3 9,4 5,8"
Line color
Outline thickness (Default=1)
Joins of lines end-to-end (miter, round, bevel)
Style-based options
End of Polyline Object

```
<polygon
    class="classname"
    points="list of points"
    fill="color"
    stroke="color"
    stroke-width="number"
    stroke-linejoin="option"
    style="styles list"
/>
```

Multipoint enclosed object
Optional reference to class definitions
Coordinates of points: "2,3 9,4 5,8"
Interior color or none
Outline color or none
Outline thickness (Default=1)
Joins of lines end-to-end (miter, round, bevel)
Style-based options
End of Polygon Object

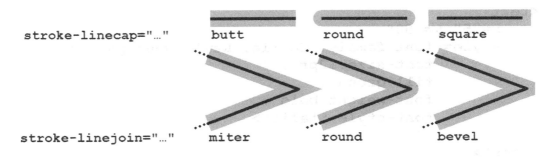

stroke-linecap="…"   butt   round   square

stroke-linejoin="…"   miter   round   bevel

SVG File Format (Continued)

SVG Text Object

SVG Text Object	Description of Attributes
`<text`	**Start of the opening tag**
`class="``classname`**`"`**	Optional reference to class definitions
`x="``number`**`"`**	X coordinate on screen of left edge of text
`y="``number`**`"`**	Y coordinate on screen of bottom edge of text
`font-family="``name`**`"`**	Same as CSS (`monospace`, `serif`, etc., or name list)
`font-size="``number`**`"`**	Same as CSS (`small`, `medium`, `large`, or a point size)
`font-weight="``option`**`"`**	Same as CSS (`normal`, `bold`, etc.)
`font-style="``option`**`"`**	Same as CSS (`normal`, `italic`, etc.)
`fill="``color`**`"`**	Text interior color (use `none` for outlined text)
`stroke="``color`**`"`**	Text outline color (not often used)
`style="``styles list`**`"`**	List of text style options
`>`	**End of the opening tag**
`text to draw`	The actual text to paint into the graphic
`</text>`	**Closing tag**

SVG Text Example Using Just Presentation Attributes

```
<text
    x="5" y="50"
    font-family="'Courier New', monospace"
    font-size="12pt"
    fill="green"
    font-weight="bold"
    font-style="italic">
    William T. Verts
</text>
```

SVG Text Example Using Mostly Styles

```
<text
    x="5" y="50"
    style="font-family:'Courier New', monospace ;
        font-size:12pt ;
        fill:green ;
        font-weight:bold ;
        font-style:italic">
    William T. Verts
</text>
```

SVG Classes

Classes work the same way for SVG files as in CSS. A class can be associated with a <u>specific tag</u>, such as `line.myclass {stroke-linecap:round}`, and invoked on a case-by-case basis with that tag type as `<line class="myclass" …/>`. <u>Anonymous classes</u> such as `.mystroke {stroke-width:1 ; stroke:red}` are invoked where appropriate, as in `<line class="mystroke" …/>` or `<circle class="mystroke" …/>`.

For example, to place the word "Sunday" at location <80,80> on the screen, in 18-point bold Times New Roman, without classes, would require the following code. The same code would be written for Monday, for Tuesday, for Wednesday, etc., just with different x and y coordinates:

```
<text x="80" y="80"
      fill="black"
      font-family="'Times New Roman', serif"
      font-size="18pt"
      font-weight="bold">Sunday</text>
```

Manually specifying every required format in the individual text tags themselves makes the SVG code take up a lot of space. Instead, an anonymous class (called `.headers` here) is created to hold all of the necessary style information:

```
<style type="text/css">
    <![CDATA[
        polygon {stroke-linejoin:miter}
        .headers {fill:black;
                  font-family:'Times New Roman', serif;
                  font-size:18pt;
                  font-weight:bold;}
    ]]>
</style>
```

Each text string that uses those styles can now be expressed very simply by using the class name instead of writing out all the formats individually. Every string below is bold 18-point Times New Roman:

```
<text x="80"  y="80" class="headers">Sunday</text>
<text x="200" y="80" class="headers">Monday</text>
<text x="320" y="80" class="headers">Tuesday</text>
<text x="440" y="80" class="headers">Wednesday</text>
<text x="560" y="80" class="headers">Thursday</text>
<text x="680" y="80" class="headers">Friday</text>
<text x="800" y="80" class="headers">Saturday</text>
```

SVG Classes

11: **Productivity Tools**

This section deals with traditional software productivity tools. In particular, some basic features, tricks, and tips of Microsoft Office™ tools are covered, including how to overprint characters in Microsoft Word™ and a list of the most common functions of the Microsoft Excel™ spreadsheet. The differences between the older Lotus 1-2-3™ spreadsheet and Microsoft Excel are also covered.

Overprinting Strings in Word

To *overprint* two strings of characters, follow the steps below:

1.   Insert a ***field code***:

    Windows: Click `Ctrl` `F9`
    Mac: Click ⌘ `F9`

    This enters the string **{   }** into the document. Clicking anywhere in that string highlights it in gray.

2.   Type the following string into the curly braces, but make sure that there are no spaces *except* for exactly one space between the **Q** and the **** characters:

    {EQ \o(_,_)}

3.   Replace the first underline with one character or string of characters to overprint, the second underline with the other string of characters to overprint.

4.   Right-click the object and select Toggle Field Codes to make the two strings of characters overprint.

Example #1:

Make one character the lower case **x**, the other character the single quote **'**:

{EQ \o(x,')}

The result is **x̍**   (an **x** with a quote on top).

Example #2:

Make one character the lower case **a**, the other character the combining macron (the overbar):

{EQ \o(a,‾)}

The result is **ā**   (an **a** with an overbar). On the Mac, the combining macron character is inserted by Option-Shift-Comma.

Line Breaks in Excel

To put a line break in the middle of a text cell in Excel, first enter the entire line as one long formula. Edit the line by double-clicking the formula, place the cursor where the line break needs to be, then:

Windows: Click `Alt` `Enter ↵`
Mac: Click `Ctrl` Option `Enter ↵` or ⌘ Option `Enter ↵`

Lotus 1-2-3 vs. Excel

Category	Lotus 1-2-3	Microsoft Excel

Formulae	Entered string can start with digits, plus, minus, parentheses, the @ sign (for functions), or any symbol that makes the string look like a formula. Examples:
	`(A1+1)` or `+A1+1` or `1+A1`
		Entered string always starts with an equal sign. Examples:
		`=A1+1`
		`=(A1+1)`
		`=1+A1`

Numbers	Entered string can start with a digit, plus, or minus, but only contains symbols that make the string look like a number. Example: `123.4` or `-12.1E+10`	Same as Lotus 1-2-3. Example: `123.4` or `-12.1E+10` (However, see definition of text, below.)

Text	Entered string can start with a letter, or may start with quote (`'`), double quote (`"`), or up-carat (`^`) to encode left, right, or center justification, respectively. Special symbols do not appear on screen. Example: `"FROG` (right justified)	Not a formula or number. If the entered string starts with a letter, does not start with an equal sign, or contains characters that are not part of a number, then it is text. Formatting is separate. Examples:
		`FROG`
		`123 Main Street`

Cell References	One or more letters followed by one or more digits. To make a column absolute place a $ before the letters. To make a row absolute place a $ before the digits.	Same as Lotus 1-2-3. Examples: Relative: `C4` (Rel. column, rel. row) Mixed: `$C4` (Abs. column, rel. row) Mixed: `C$4` (Rel. column, abs. row) Absolute: `$C$4` (Abs. column, abs. row)
Ranges in Function Arguments	Cell references in a range are separated by <u>two dots</u>. Example: `A1..C9`	Cell references in a range are separated by a <u>colon</u>. Example: `A1:C9`

Functions	Always starts with an at-sign (@), followed by the function name, and a list of arguments in parentheses. No parentheses if no arguments. Examples:
	`@DATE(2013,7,3)`
	`@SUM(A1..C9)`
	`@AVG(A1,12,X1+1,A1..C9)`
	`@NOW`
	`@PI`
		The function name followed by a list of arguments in parentheses. All functions have parentheses, even those with no arguments (parentheses are empty). Examples:
		`DATE(2013,7,3)`
		`SUM(A1:C9)`
		`AVERAGE(A1,12,X1+1,A1:C9)`
		`NOW()`
		`PI()`

Logical Operators AND, OR, and NOT	<u>Operators</u> are inside expressions, always surrounded by hash-marks.
	`(Q1) #AND# (Q2)`
	`(Q1) #OR# (Q2)`
	`#NOT# (Q1)`
		Not used as operators, but as <u>functions</u> with logical arguments:
		`AND(Q1,Q2)`
		`OR(Q1,Q2)`
		`NOT(Q1)`

Excel Functions (Basic)

Math Functions with flexible argument lists, such as (A1,B7:C15,16,Z99*7)

SUM (...)	Returns sum of arguments
PRODUCT (...)	Returns product of arguments
MIN (...)	Returns minimum value of arguments
MAX (...)	Returns maximum value of arguments
STDEV (...)	Returns standard deviation of arguments
VAR (...)	Returns variance of arguments
COUNT (...)	Returns count of numeric arguments
COUNTA (...)	Returns count of non-empty arguments
AVERAGE (...)	Returns average of arguments. Same as SUM (...) / COUNT (...).

Math Functions (and Inverse Functions) with exactly one numeric argument
(Arguments to trigonometric functions are all expressed in radians, not degrees)

ABS (*number*)		Returns absolute value of argument
SQRT (*number*)		Returns square root of argument
INT (*number*)		Returns integer portion of argument, rounded down
LOG10 (*number*)		Returns common logarithm of argument
LN (*number*)	(inverse of **EXP**)	Returns natural logarithm of argument
EXP (*number*)	(inverse of **LN**)	Returns e (2.71828...) raised to power of argument
SIN (*number*)	**ASIN** (*number*)	Returns trigonometric sine/arcsine of argument
COS (*number*)	**ACOS** (*number*)	Returns trigonometric cosine/arccosine of argument
TAN (*number*)	**ATAN** (*number*)	Returns trigonometric tangent/arctan of argument
SINH (*number*)	**ASINH** (*number*)	Returns hyperbolic sine/arcsine of argument
COSH (*number*)	**ACOSH** (*number*)	Returns hyperbolic cosine/arccosine of argument
TANH (*number*)	**ATANH** (*number*)	Returns hyperbolic tangent/arctangent of argument
DEGREES (*number*)		Returns argument converted from radians to degrees
RADIANS (*number*)		Returns argument converted from degrees to radians

Date & Time Functions

NOW ()	Returns serial date/time number from system clock
DATE (*year,month,day*)	Returns serial date integer (days from 1/1/1900)
TIME (*hour,minute,second*)	Returns serial time fraction (portion since midnight)
YEAR (*serial date number*)	Returns year portion of serial date/time number
MONTH (*serial date number*)	Returns month portion of serial date/time number
DAY (*serial date number*)	Returns day portion of serial date/time number
HOUR (*serial date number*)	Returns hour portion of serial date/time number
MINUTE (*serial date number*)	Returns minute portion of serial date/time number
SECOND (*serial date number*)	Returns second portion of serial date/time number

Excel Functions (String and Text)

CHAR (*number* **)**

Returns the character corresponding to the position of *number* within the current font: CHAR (169) returns the copyright © symbol.

CONCATENATE (*string, string, ...* **)**

Join strings end-to-end. Same as the & operator. Both CONCATENATE ("dog", "house") and "dog" & "house" return "doghouse".

LEN (*string* **)**

Returns length of *string* (number of characters). LEN ("doghouse") returns 8.

REPT (*string, number* **)**

Repeat the *string* the specified *number* of times. REPT ("X", 5) returns "XXXXX".

FIND (*string, string* **)**
SEARCH (*string, string* **)**

Find position of first string within second string. FIND ("h", "doghouse") returns 4. Returns an error if first string is not found within second. FIND is case sensitive, SEARCH is not.

LEFT (*string, number* **)**

Returns left *number* characters from *string*. LEFT ("doghouse", 3) returns "dog".

RIGHT (*string, number* **)**

Returns right *number* characters from *string*. RIGHT ("doghouse", 3) returns "use".

MID (*string, number, number* **)**

Returns characters from *string*, first *number* is starting position, second *number* is count. MID ("doghouse", 3, 4) returns "ghou".

LOWER (*string* **)**

Returns *string* in all lower-case characters. LOWER ("DogHouse") returns "doghouse".

UPPER (*string* **)**

Returns *string* in all upper-case characters. UPPER ("DogHouse") returns "DOGHOUSE".

Excel Functions (IF and Counting)

IF(*question*,*Tvalue*,*Fvalue***)**   Returns second argument if question is true, returns third argument if question is false. Examples:
```
=IF(A1>0,25,35)
=IF(B1+5<=SQRT(Z6),"FROG","TOAD")
```

COUNTIF(*range*,*criteria***)**   Searches *range* for all values matching *criteria*, returns <u>count</u> of those that match. Exact numeric match criteria use a number alone; exact string match criteria and comparison criteria need quotes around the expression. Examples:
```
=COUNTIF(A1:A10,0)          (number)
=COUNTIF(A1:A10,"A+")       (string)
=COUNTIF(A1:A10,">90")      (comparison)
```

SUMIF(*range*,*criteria***)**   Searches *range* for all values matching *criteria*, returns <u>sum</u> of those that match, otherwise same as COUNTIF. Examples:
```
=SUMIF(A1:A10,0)
=SUMIF(A1:A10,">90")
```

SUMIF(*range1*,*criteria*,*range2***)**   Searches *range1* for all values matching *criteria*, for those that match returns <u>sum</u> of corresponding items from *range2*. Example:
```
=SUMIF(A1:A10,">90",B1:B10)
```

Excel Functions (Look-Up)

VLOOKUP(*value,range,column***)**

Searches column 1 of table (*range*) for *value*, when the first row is found where *value* ≥ column 1, returns the value of the cell from *column* number of that row. Table must be <u>sorted in ascending order</u> on column 1.

Example: Look up the value of cell `A1` in the table `B10:C15` (sorted in ascending order on the data in column 1, which is `B`), and when the correct row is found return the value in column 2, which is `C`:
`=VLOOKUP(A1,B10:C15,2)`
Usually, the range is absolute so the formula can be copied down a whole column of values to look up:
`=VLOOKUP(A1,$B$10:$C$15,2)`

VLOOKUP(*value,range,column,***FALSE)**

Searches column 1 of table (*range*) for *value* as before, except that when first row is found where *value* <u>exactly equals</u> the value in column 1, returns cell from *column* number of that row. Table does not have to be sorted.

Excel Functions (Math Functions with no Arguments)

PI()

Returns 3.14159265358979323… to the best possible value for double-precision floating-point arithmetic.

RAND()

Returns a random number ≥0 and <1, which changes whenever the spreadsheet is changed or is re-evaluated (i.e., hitting the F9 key in Windows).

NOW()

Returns current date and time from the system clock, where whole part is the number of days since the start of the 20TH Century (January 1, 1900 is day number 1), and the fraction is the portion of the day since midnight. January 1, 2020 is day 43831, and 6:00pm is 0.75 (three-quarters of the way through the day). The fraction 0.99999… is just before midnight of the following day.

Excel Functions (Math Functions that Round)

TRUNC (*number* **)** Rounds towards zero to nearest integer. TRUNC (3.6) returns 3, and TRUNC (-3.6) returns -3.

INT (*number* **)** Rounds down (towards minus infinity) to nearest integer. INT (3.6) returns 3, INT (-3.6) returns -4. Same as FLOOR (*number*, 1). Same as TRUNC (*number*) for positive values.

ROUND (*number*, *digits* **)** Rounds to nearest, for given number of decimal places (0 to get integers). Rounds one-half of least significant digit away from zero. ROUND (3.5, 0) returns 4, ROUND (PI (), 3) returns 3.142 (π rounded to three decimal places).

FLOOR (*number*, *significance* **)** Rounds down (towards minus infinity) to nearest multiple of *significance* (usually 1 to round to an integer, but can be 0.1, 0.001, etc.).

CEILING (*number*, *significance* **)** Rounds up (towards positive infinity) to nearest multiple of *significance* (usually 1 to round to an integer, but can be 0.1, 0.001, etc.).

Excel Functions (Financial)

PMT (*rate*, *periods*, *present val* **)** Returns amount of payment needed for a loan of present val, paid back at rate interest for periods payments. Interest rate must be compatible with payback periods; if interest rate is annual but payback is monthly, interest rate must be divided by 12.

Example (6% annually, paid back monthly over 30 years, for a $100000 loan):
      =PMT (0.06/12, 30*12, 100000)
This returns -599.55 as its result (amount owed per month). However,
      =PMT (0.06/12, 30*12, -100000)
returns +599.55 as the result (amount of the payment per month). Use whichever form generates the value with the desired sign.

Excel Functions (Complex Arithmetic)

Complex numbers are stored in Excel (2007 and later) as strings. Thus, to enter the complex number $5+3i$ into a cell you type the string `5+3i` in as the formula. Almost all functions that handle complex numbers start with **IM** (imaginary) as part of the function name.

Complex Conversion Functions

COMPLEX(*real,imaginary***)** — Create a complex number from a real part and an imaginary part. For example, COMPLEX(5,3) or COMPLEX(A1,B1), where A1=5 and B1=3, both create the complex number $5+3i$ (as string 5+3i).

IMREAL(*complex***)** — Returns the real component of a complex number. For example, IMREAL("5+3i") returns the number 5 (not a string).

IMAGINARY(*complex***)** — Returns the imaginary component of a complex number. For example, IMAGINARY("5+3i") returns the number 3 (not a string).

Complex Math Functions with flexible complex argument lists

IMSUM(...**)** — Returns sum of complex arguments

IMPRODUCT(...**)** — Returns product of complex arguments

Complex Math Functions with exactly two complex arguments

IMSUB(*complex,complex***)** — Returns first complex argument minus second

IMDIV(*complex,complex***)** — Returns first complex argument divided by second

Complex Math Functions with exactly one complex argument

IMABS(*complex***)** — Returns numeric modulus ("length") of argument

IMSQRT(*complex***)** — Returns complex square root of argument

IMLOG2(*complex***)** — Returns complex logarithm base 2 of argument

IMLOG10(*complex***)** — Returns complex logarithm base 10 of argument

IMLN(*complex***)** — Returns complex natural logarithm of argument

IMEXP(*complex***)** — Returns e (2.71828…) raised to power of argument

IMSIN(*complex***)** — Returns complex trigonometric sine of argument

IMCOS(*complex***)** — Returns complex trigonometric cosine of argument

Miscellaneous Complex Math Functions

IMPOWER(*complex,number***)** — Returns first complex argument raised to power of second numeric argument.

12: *General Programming Concepts*

Humans write programs in a computer language with a specific syntax, which are then converted by other programs into a form understandable by the computer. The instructions that we write may be very general and high level, or they may be very close to the architecture of the processor itself.

Programs in a high-level language like Pascal or C are translated into the raw binary instructions understandable by the gates of the processor by a program called a ***compiler***. Low-level assembly language programs are direct 1:1 representations of the native instructions of a particular processor chip (such as the MOS 6502) and are translated into the equivalent raw binary by a program called an ***assembler***. Once the raw binary has been obtained, it is directly runnable by the computer, and the source text of the program written by the programmer is not needed for the program to run. The binary for one type of processor will not be executable by another type of processor.

lower level
Programs written in a language like BASIC are interpreted: a source statement is examined by a translator called an ***interpreter***, and if it is correct it is executed immediately. The next statement is examined and executed, then the next, and so on. If the first statement is re-encountered, as in a loop, it must be re-examined and re-executed. Interpreted languages require the presence of the translator to operate, and run much slower than compiled programs, but they tend to be highly interactive and are easily modifiable. An interpreter written to run on one type of computer generally will not run on another, although interpreters can be written to run on different machines that interpret the same source language (for example, a BASIC interpreter written to run on a PC won't run on a Mac, but a separate interpreter can be written to run on a Mac that interprets the same version of BASIC).

Mid-level
Somewhere in the middle are programming languages like Java. Java programs are compiled, but they get compiled to ***byte codes*** for a ***virtual machine*** (one that does not exist in actual hardware). The Java Virtual Machines (JVM) that run the byte codes are interpreters written for specific hardware platforms or specific operating systems. Once written correctly, any JVM should interpret (run) the byte codes from a Java program in exactly the same way. (Although due to differences in how each JVM is implemented, this rarely happens in practice.)

Most Python interpreters are programs written in C. That is, someone wrote a C program that knows how to interpret Python programs. The C program is compiled only for a particular type of computer, but it interprets Python programs as fast as is possible for that computer. Another approach is Jython, which is a Python interpreter written in Java. This has the advantage that the Java program only had to be compiled once, and its byte codes will be interpreted by any underlying JVM, but has the disadvantage that Python programs are now slow due to being doubly-interpreted, once by the Python interpreter and once by the JVM that runs the interpreter itself. *one language can be written to interp another*

This section covers basic programming concepts, and illustrates a few of the differences between the 6502, x86, and ARM assembly languages, JavaScript, Python, and Pascal.

Flowcharting

1, 2.3

The flow of control of a computer program falls into three major categories: sequences, selections, and iterations (subroutine calls will be covered on the next page). These concepts are shown below in flowchart form. Each rectangular box represents a single action to be taken by the computer, such as getting an input value from the user, printing a result, or assigning the result of a computation to a variable. Each diamond box represents a question asked by the computer, with one of two possible paths to follow based on the outcome of the question. Flow of control strictly follows the direction indicated by the arrows.

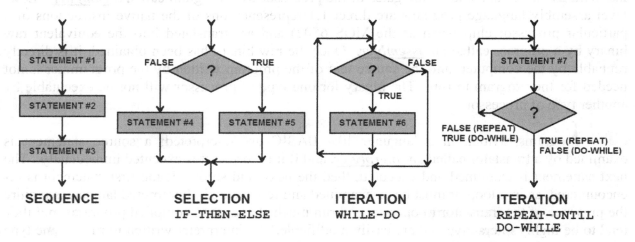

SEQUENCE   SELECTION   ITERATION   ITERATION
IF-THEN-ELSE   WHILE-DO   REPEAT-UNTIL
DO-WHILE

1. A ***sequence*** establishes the order in which a group of actions is to be taken. The actions cannot be performed in any other order than what is indicated by the flow arrows. *order*

2. A ***selection*** gives the computer the choice of two possible actions based on the answer to a yes-or-no question. In most computer languages this structure is called an ***if-statement***. If both action statements are present this is called more specifically an IF-THEN-ELSE (IF the question is true THEN execute one statement ELSE execute the other statement). One or the other of the action statements could be omitted. If an action statement is omitted it is most commonly the one on the false branch; this variant is called an IF-THEN.

3. An ***iteration*** is a way for the computer to execute the same statements over and over, as many times as necessary. This is also called a ***loop***. The most common structure is called a ***while-loop*** in many languages: WHILE the question is true DO the statement. The loop-test comes first, and only if true does the statement get executed (meaning that if the test was initially false the statement will never be performed at all). One variation has the statement come first and the loop-test at the <u>bottom</u> of the loop (after the statement has been executed at least once). This is called a ***repeat-until*** loop in Pascal: REPEAT the statement UNTIL the question becomes true. In JavaScript it has a slightly different structure called a ***do-while***: DO the statement WHILE the question is true. Python only supports the while-loop, but not the repeat-until or the do-while.

Any statement block can be replaced by any of the four structures, to as deep a level as necessary.

Flow of Control

Nearly all languages have a mechanism for code re-use called a ***subroutine***, ***procedure***, or ***function***. In the following diagram, the same code needs to be executed in two different places in the main program. Rather than write the code twice, the code is written *once* as a subroutine and is *called* from the places it is needed. Relative to explicitly including the code twice, this approach saves time, code space, and generally makes a program easier to debug. Subroutines remember where they were called from, so when their actions are complete they return back to the next instruction after the call. A subroutine that calls itself is ***recursive***.

2nd
two are
subsets of
subroutine

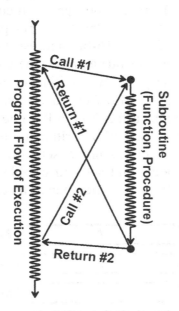

A subroutine that returns a value back to where it was called is a ***function***. A subroutine that does not return a value is a ***procedure***. Some languages make a syntactic distinction between the two (Pascal explicitly has both procedures and functions), while other languages do not (in Python all subroutines are functions; some functions return a value and some don't).

Values are communicated into a subroutine through ***parameters***. A parameter in the interface to a function is called a ***formal parameter***: it has a name (and possibly a data type), and that name is used only within the body of the subroutine. A subroutine is then called with ***actual parameters***, which are the values and variables to be acted upon by the subroutine. Those values get "plugged in" to the formal parameters. Variables used as actual parameters may or may not have the same names as the formal parameters that they go into.

There are many mechanisms for passing parameters. The two most common are ***call-by-reference*** (the <u>address</u> of a variable is passed in; supported by Pascal) and ***call-by-value*** (the <u>value</u> of a variable or expression is passed in; supported by both Pascal and Python). Changes to the value of a formal parameter in call-by-reference are seen back in the calling environment, but any changes to the value of a formal parameter in call-by-value are local to the subroutine only.

MOS 6502 Reference (Registers)

The MOS Technology, Inc. 6502 is an 8-bit CPU chip from the 1970s. It ran in the Apple][™, the Kim-1™, the Rockwell AIM-65™, and a number of other small platforms. While it sees limited use today, it is simple enough to understand completely. It also provides a good baseline for understanding more modern processors, particularly **_Reduced Instruction Set Computers_** (**_RISC_**) such as the ARM (used in many cell phones).

The 6502 has one 8-bit accumulator (A), two 8-bit index registers (X, Y), an 8-bit stack pointer (S), an 8-bit program status byte (P), and a 16-bit program counter (PC) which can address 64K bytes of memory divided into 256 pages of 256 bytes per page. Any byte in memory can be referenced in absolute mode using a 2-byte (16-bit) address, but bytes in page 0 can be addressed in zero-page mode using only a 1-byte (8-bit) address (the upper byte of the address is assumed to be zero). The stack is fixed to page 1. S is initialized under program control to **FF**; push instructions store into the byte in page 1 at offset S and then S is decremented; pop instructions reverse the process. Many instructions affect bits in P, to be tested by branch instructions: N is set if a result is negative, V is set in case of an arithmetic overflow, Z is set if a result equals zero, and C operates as the carry bit. Programmers set D to make adds and subtracts operate in BCD mode instead of in binary mode, and set I to disable interrupt requests (B is set by an interrupt if generated by a break instruction rather than as an external event).

A	8-Bit Accumulator
X	8-Bit Index Register
Y	8-Bit Index Register
0 0 0 0 0 0 0 1 S	8-Bit Stack Pointer (Page 1)
N V B D I Z C	8-Bit Program Status
PC	16-Bit Program Counter

Instructions occupy one, two, or three successive bytes of memory. The first byte is always the **_op code_**, which tells the processor what action to perform and how many more bytes follow the op code byte, if any. One additional byte can be treated either as an 8-bit constant value, an address in page 0, or as a relative offset; two additional bytes form an absolute address to anywhere in memory. Many instructions also add the contents of either the X or Y index registers to an address, allowing the processor to step through memory one byte at a time.

For example, if the op code is **E8** (hexadecimal), the processor knows that the action to perform is to add one to index register X; no additional bytes are necessary to complete the instruction. If the op code is **65**, the processor knows that the action is to add a value to accumulator A, where the value is in page 0 at the address specified by the next byte after the op code. If the op code is **7D**, the action is to add to accumulator A the byte at the address formed by the next two bytes after the op code plus the contents of index register X.

MOS 6502 Reference (Memory Layout)

Rather than remember what **E8**, **65**, and **7D** mean, people use ***mnemonics*** such as **INX** and **ADC**, plus other text, to represent these instructions. A translator called an ***assembler*** must figure out from the ***source code*** text what op code and what addressing mode is required for each instruction. For example, the mnemonic **INX** (increment X) is translated into the single byte **E8**, the phrase **ADC 03** (add with carry zero-page) is translated into the two byte instruction **65 03**, but **ADC #03** (add with carry immediate) is translated into the two byte instruction **69 03** (notice the different op code), and **ADC 1234,X** (add with carry absolute indexed by X) is translated into the three byte instruction **7D 34 12** (addresses on the 6502 are stored in memory least-significant byte first, called ***little endian***).

Page 0 is used for variables, and page 1 is used for the stack; most user programs start at the beginning of page 2 (address **0200**) and proceed upwards through low ***random access memory*** (***RAM***). At the high end of memory three addresses (six bytes) have special uses as ***interrupt vectors***, and as such those addresses have to be in ***read-only memory*** (***ROM***):

NMI   (**FFFA**, **FFFB**): where to jump in case of a ***non-maskable interrupt***.
RESET (**FFFC**, **FFFD**): where to jump in case of a power-on or ***reset*** condition.
IRQ   (**FFFE**, **FFFF**): where to jump in case of an external ***interrupt request*** or a **BRK** (break) instruction that could be masked or blocked by the I status bit.

In the middle were addresses used for communicating with the outside world (***I/O ports***), or perhaps no memory was present at those addresses at all.

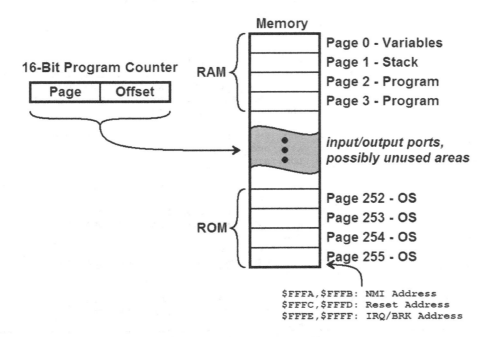

MOS 6502 Reference (Addressing Modes)

The initial chip described here supports 56 unique instructions, and 13 unique ***addressing modes*** (revisions to the chip added more instructions). The table shows the addressing modes, the instructions that use each mode, how many bytes are needed by each instruction, and how many clock cycles the processor takes to execute each instruction. The original 6502 ran at a 1 MHz clock speed, so an instruction requiring two cycles to execute would complete in $^2/_{1,000,000}$ of a second. ***Implied addressing*** means that the op code contains all the information necessary to execute the instruction, and so is a one-byte instruction. ***Accumulator addressing*** involves only the A register; these are one-byte instructions as well. ***Immediate addressing*** uses the byte after the op code as a constant data value. ***Relative addressing*** (used only by the conditional branches) uses the byte after the op code as a signed integer [-128…+127], sign-extended to 16 bits, to add to PC if a test condition is true. ***Zero-page addressing*** uses the byte after the op code as an address in page 0; that address may be first modified by adding an index register to it (***zero-page indexed by X or by Y***). ***Absolute addressing*** uses the <u>two</u> bytes after the op code as a 16-bit address; that address may, too, be modified by adding an index register to it (***absolute indexed by X or by Y***). Indirect means that the address in an instruction is to a pair of bytes in memory that contain the <u>actual</u> address to use. ***Absolute indirect*** (used only by **JMP**) has a two byte address following the op code pointing to a place in memory containing the final two-byte target address. Both indexed indirect modes use page 0: ***preindexed by X*** first adds X to the zero-page address to find the address in page 0 of the final address; ***postindexed by Y*** looks at the two-byte contents stored at the zero-page address and adds Y to that to form the final address.

Addressing Mode	Bytes	Cycles	Instructions that use this Mode
Implied	1	2	CLC, CLD, CLI, CLV, DEX, DEY, INX, INY, NOP, SEC, SED, SEI, TAX, TAY, TSX, TXA, TXS, TYA
		3	PHA, PHP
		4	PLA, PLP
		6	RTI, RTS
		7	BRK
Accumulator	1	2	ASL, LSR, ROL, ROR
Immediate	2	2	ADC, AND, CMP, CPX, CPY, EOR, LDA, LDX, LDY, ORA, SBC
Relative	2	2**	BCC, BCS, BEQ, BMI, BNE, BPL, BVC, BVS
Zero-Page	2	3	ADC, AND, BIT, CMP, CPX, CPY, EOR, LDA, LDX, LDY, ORA, SBC, STA, STX, STY
		5	ASL, DEC, INC, LSR, ROL, ROR
Zero-Page, indexed by X	2	4	ADC, AND, CMP, EOR, LDA, LDY, ORA, SBC, STA, STY
		6	ASL, DEC, INC, LSR, ROL, ROR
Zero-Page, indexed by Y	2	4	LDX, STX
Absolute	3	3	JMP
		4	ADC, AND, BIT, CMP, CPX, CPY, EOR, LDA, LDX, LDY, ORA, SBC, STA, STX, STY
		6	ASL, DEC, INC, JSR, LSR, ROL, ROR
Absolute, indexed by X	3	4*	ADC, AND, CMP, EOR, LDA, LDY, ORA, SBC
		5	STA
		7	ASL, DEC, INC, LSR, ROL, ROR
Absolute, indexed by Y	3	4*	ADC, AND, CMP, EOR, LDA, LDX, ORA, SBC
		5	STA
Absolute Indirect	3	5	JMP
Zero-Page Indirect, preindexed by X	2	6	ADC, AND, CMP, EOR, LDA, ORA, SBC, STA
Zero-Page Indirect, postindexed by Y	2	5*	ADC, AND, CMP, EOR, LDA, ORA, SBC
		6	STA

* = add 1 cycle if page boundary is crossed

** = add 1 cycle if branch is taken to same page,
add 2 cycles if branch is taken to different page

MOS 6502 Reference (Instruction Op Codes)

	OP	Meaning	Interpretation	Affected Flags	Imp	Acc	Imm	Rel	ZP	ZP,X	ZP,Y	Abs	Abs,X	Abs,Y	(Abs)	(ZP,X)	(ZP),Y
1	ADC	Add with Carry	$A \leftarrow A + M + C$	NVZC			69		65	75		6D	7D	79		61	71
2	AND	Logical AND	$A \leftarrow A$ AND M	NZ			29		25	35		2D	3D	39		21	31
3	ASL	Arithmetic Shift Left	$C \leftarrow M_7M_6M_5M_4M_3M_2M_1M_0 \leftarrow 0$	NZC		0A			06	16		0E	1E				
4	BCC	Branch if Carry Clear	If $C = 0$ then $PC \leftarrow PC+2+offset$					90									
5	BCS	Branch if Carry Set	If $C = 1$ then $PC \leftarrow PC+2+offset$					B0									
6	BEQ	Branch if Equal	If $Z = 1$ then $PC \leftarrow PC+2+offset$					F0									
7	BIT	Bit Test	$Z \leftarrow (A$ AND $M)=0, N \leftarrow M_7, V \leftarrow M_6$	NZV					24			2C					
8	BMI	Branch if Minus	If $N = 1$ then $PC \leftarrow PC+2+offset$					30									
9	BNE	Branch if Not Equal	If $Z = 0$ then $PC \leftarrow PC+2+offset$					D0									
10	BPL	Branch if Plus	If $N = 0$ then $PC \leftarrow PC+2+offset$					10									
11	BRK	Break (Interrupt)	Push $PC+2_{16}$, Push P, $PC \leftarrow (\$FFFE_{16})$	I	00												
12	BVC	Branch if Overflow Clear	If $V = 0$ then $PC \leftarrow PC+2+offset$					50									
13	BVS	Branch if Overflow Set	If $V = 1$ then $PC \leftarrow PC+2+offset$					70									
14	CLC	Clear Carry	$C \leftarrow 0$	C	18												
15	CLD	Clear Decimal Mode	$D \leftarrow 0$	D	D8												
16	CLI	Clear Interrupt Disable	$I \leftarrow 0$	I	58												
17	CLV	Clear Overflow	$V \leftarrow 0$	V	B8												
18	CMP	Compare Accumulator	$A - M$	NZC			C9		C5	D5		CD	DD	D9		C1	D1
19	CPX	Compare with X	$X - M$	NZC			E0		E4			EC					
20	CPY	Compare with Y	$Y - M$	NZC			C0		C4			CC					
21	DEC	Decrement	$M \leftarrow M - 1$	NZ					C6	D6		CE	DE				
22	DEX	Decrement X	$X \leftarrow X - 1$	NZ	CA												
23	DEY	Decrement Y	$Y \leftarrow Y - 1$	NZ	88												
24	EOR	Exclusive OR	$A \leftarrow A$ EOR M	NZ			49		45	55		4D	5D	59		41	51
25	INC	Increment	$M \leftarrow M + 1$	NZ					E6	F6		EE	FE				
26	INX	Increment X	$X \leftarrow X + 1$	NZ	E8												
27	INY	Increment Y	$Y \leftarrow Y + 1$	NZ	C8												
28	JMP	Jump	$PC \leftarrow M_{16}$									4C			6C		
29	JSR	Jump to Subroutine	Push $PC+2_{16}$; $PC \leftarrow M_{16}$									20					
30	LDA	Load Accumulator	$A \leftarrow M$	NZ			A9		A5	B5		AD	BD	B9		A1	B1
31	LDX	Load X	$X \leftarrow M$	NZ			A2		A6		B6	AE		BE			
32	LDY	Load Y	$Y \leftarrow M$	NZ			A0		A4	B4		AC	BC				
33	LSR	Logical Shift Right	$0 \rightarrow M_7M_6M_5M_4M_3M_2M_1M_0 \rightarrow C$	NZC		4A			46	56		4E	5E				
34	NOP	No Operation	–		EA												
35	ORA	Inclusive OR	$A \leftarrow A$ OR M	NZ			09		05	15		0D	1D	19		01	11
36	PHA	Push Accumulator	Push A		48												
37	PHP	Push Processor Status	Push P		08												
38	PLA	Pull Accumulator	Pop A		68												
39	PLP	Pull Processor Status	Pop P	All	28												
40	ROL	Rotate Left	$C \leftarrow M_7M_6M_5M_4M_3M_2M_1M_0 \leftarrow C$	NZC		2A			26	36		2E	3E				
41	ROR	Rotate Right	$C \rightarrow M_7M_6M_5M_4M_3M_2M_1M_0 \rightarrow C$	NZC		6A			66	76		6E	7E				
42	RTI	Return from Interrupt	Pop P; Pop PC_{16}	All	40												
43	RTS	Return from Subroutine	Pop PC_{16}; $PC \leftarrow PC+1$		60												
44	SBC	Subtract with Carry	$A \leftarrow A - M -$ NOT(C)	NVZC			E9		E5	F5		ED	FD	F9		E1	F1
45	SEC	Set Carry	$C \leftarrow 1$	C	38												
46	SED	Set Decimal	$D \leftarrow 1$	D	F8												
47	SEI	Set Interrupt Disable	$I \leftarrow 1$	I	78												
48	STA	Store Accumulator	$M \leftarrow A$						85	95		8D	9D	99		81	91
49	STX	Store X	$M \leftarrow X$						86		96	8E					
50	STY	Store Y	$M \leftarrow Y$						84	94		8C					
51	TAX	Transfer A to X	$X \leftarrow A$	NZ	AA												
52	TAY	Transfer A to Y	$Y \leftarrow A$	NZ	A8												
53	TSX	Transfer S to X	$X \leftarrow S$	NZ	BA												
54	TXA	Transfer X to A	$A \leftarrow X$	NZ	8A												
55	TXS	Transfer X to S	$S \leftarrow X$	NZ	9A												
56	TYA	Transfer Y to A	$A \leftarrow Y$	NZ	98												

Intel x86 Reference (Registers)

Intel developed a series of processors that have been used in computers since the 1970s, starting with an 8-bit chip called the 8080. Later, the more powerful 8086 chip, and its variant the 8088 chip used in the 1981 IBM PC™, were developed, and all "PCs" since then used the 8086 and its descendants. Subsequent chips include the 286, 386, 486, Pentium and its derivatives, all collectively known as the *x86 series*. The 8088, 8086, and 286 are all 16-bit chips, the 386, 486, and Pentium are 32-bit chips, and the x86-64 from AMD then adopted by Intel is a 64-bit chip. All designs have multiple variations with different capabilities.

The baseline chips have eight 16-bit integer *registers* in the processor: **AX**, **BX**, **CX**, **DX**, **BP**, **SP**, **SI**, and **DI**. Registers **AX**, **BX**, **CX**, and **DX** are divided into a low byte and a high byte, accessible to programs as **AH**, **AL**, **BH**, **BL**, etc. The 32-bit versions of the chips extend all registers to 32 bits, but retain backwards compatibility with the earlier 16-bit chips: **EAX** refers to a 32-bit register, **AX** refers to the low 16 bits of **EAX**, and **AH** and **AL** still refer to the high and low bytes of **AX**, respectively. The 64-bit chips extend all eight registers to 64 bits, also maintaining backwards compatibility with earlier chips: **RAX** is 64 bits, with **EAX** forming its lower 32 bits. Eight new registers **R8** through **R15** are also available. This is illustrated below:

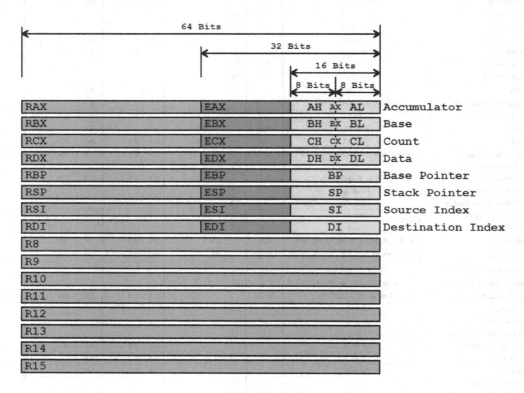

The 64-bit chips can also reference the low-order 32-bit, 16-bit, and 8-bit chunks of *all* registers, (not shown). Baseline chips have an additional eight 80-bit extended precision floating-point registers **ST0** though **ST7**, in a separate *coprocessor* chip for the 8088 though 386 but integrated into the main processor from the 486 onwards. Later chips include eight 64-bit MMX registers, sixteen 128-bit XMM registers, and sixteen 256-bit YMM registers for parallel computations.

Intel x86 Reference (Registers)

The 8088 and 8086 can address 1 megabyte of memory: this requires 20 bits to uniquely specify individual bytes. These are 16-bit chips, and a 16-bit address can only address 64 kilobytes of memory. To make a 16-bit chip work with 20-bit addresses, the work-around was to use **_segment registers_**. A segment register is a 16-bit register shifted left by four bits; that is, the value in a segment register represents the leftmost 16 bits of a 20-bit address and where the rightmost 4 bits are zero. Thus, a segment register formed the starting 20-bit address of a 64K block (segment) of memory, and the desired offset within that segment was added to the segment register to get the final 20-bit address. The original processors have four segment registers: **CS** (Code Segment), **DS** (Data Segment), **SS** (Stack Segment), and **ES** (Extra Segment). Instructions are loaded from memory relative to **CS**, data relative to **DS**, and the stack relative to **SS**. **ES** can be used for any addressing purpose as needed. The simplest (.**COM**) programs on the PC had **CS**, **DS**, and **SS** pointing to the same place, so the entire program, code, data, and stack, had to fit in no more than 64K of memory. Later (.**EXE**) programs could change segment registers to move segments around, resulting in programs of arbitrary size at a corresponding increase in complexity. Later 32-bit and 64-bit chips preserve segment registers for backwards compatibility with earlier programs, but they are no longer needed for new programs since addresses may be a full 32 or 64 bits in length (although no system has 2^{64} bytes of memory).

Registers **AX**, **BX**, **CX**, and **DX**, their 8-bit subsections, and their 32-bit and 64-bit counterparts, are considered **_general purpose registers_** in that addition, subtraction, and bit-wise logical operations such as exclusive-or, and operations that involve moving one register's contents to another, can be performed between any two registers of the same size. For example, **BX** can be added to **AX**, or **BL** can be exclusive-ORed to **CH**, or **EDX** can be moved to **EBX**, in any order or combination. These are **_symmetric instructions_**.

However, **AX** (and without loss of generality, **EAX** and **RAX**) is considered the **_accumulator_**, where most arithmetic operations occur. **BX** is often used as the **_base_** starting address to an array of memory locations. **CX** is used for **_counting_**, and there are specialized instructions to subtract one from **CX** then jump to another place in memory if the result is (or is not) equal to zero. **AX** is always used for multiplication, and the double-length product always goes into both **DX** (the **_data_** register) and **AX**. Not all registers can be used in the same ways. These are **_asymmetric instructions_**.

The other registers are even more specialized. **SP** is the offset of the top of the stack (relative to **SS**), and **BP** is used by subroutines to identify where their parameters are located on the stack. **SI** and **DI** are used to move large blocks for data from one location in memory to another: load up **SI** with the start of the source address, **DI** with the start of the destination address, **CX** with the number of bytes to move, then all the bytes can be moved from source to destination in a single instruction. These complicated, specialized, and rarely used instructions are what make the x86 series a **_Complex Instruction Set Computer_**, or **_CISC_**.

Intel x86 Reference (Registers and Addressing Modes)

The x86 is a **_two-address machine_**: a computation such as addition specifies the destination register, which is <u>also</u> the first source register, and a separate source of <u>the same size</u>. These are instructions of the form `op-code dest,src` where the **_op-code_** is a **_mnemonic_** that indicates what the instruction does (move, add, etc.), `dest` is the destination (a register or memory location), and `src` is the source (a register, memory location, or constant). Here are examples:

Format	**Meaning**
MOV `register,constant`	`register = constant`
MOV `register,address`	`register = RAM[address]`
MOV `register1,register2`	`register1 = register2`
MOV `register1,[register2]`	`register1 = RAM[register2]`
MOV `address,constant`	`RAM[address] = constant`
MOV `address,register`	`RAM[address] = register`
ADD `register,constant`	`register = register + constant`
ADD `register,address`	`register = register + RAM[address]`
ADD `register1,register2`	`register1 = register1 + register2`

For an example, the contents of memory variables `Frog` and `Toad` and the constant 5 will be added together, with the result stored in memory variable `Newt`. In a high-level language, a programmer would write the statement: `Newt = Frog + Toad + 5`. The assembler would figure out where the three variables are actually located in memory and how big they are, and would provide the addresses and sizes of these variables when necessary. The addition will be 8, 16, 32, or 64 bits at a time, depending on which registers are used. The following examples all do the same thing, but in different ways and with different registers:

8-Bit	16-Bit	32-Bit	64-Bit
MOV AL,Frog	MOV AX,Frog	MOV EAX,Frog	MOV RAX,Frog
ADD AL,Toad	ADD AX,Toad	ADD EAX,Toad	ADD RAX,Toad
ADD AL,5	ADD AX,5	ADD EAX,5	ADD RAX,5
MOV Newt,AL	MOV Newt,AX	MOV Newt,EAX	MOV Newt,RAX

8-Bit	16-Bit	32-Bit	64-Bit
MOV AL,Frog	MOV AX,Frog	MOV EAX,Frog	MOV RAX,Frog
MOV BL,Toad	MOV BX,Toad	MOV EBX,Toad	MOV RBX,Toad
ADD AL,BL	ADD AX,BX	ADD EAX,EBX	ADD RAX,RBX
ADD AL,5	ADD AX,5	ADD EAX,5	ADD RAX,5
MOV Newt,AL	MOV Newt,AX	MOV Newt,EAX	MOV Newt,RAX

The expression `ADD AX,BX` adds the contents of register `BX` to whatever is in register `AX` (that is, `AX = AX + BX`), and `ADD EAX,EBX` means add `EBX` to `EAX`. This works because `AX` and `BX` are the same size (both 16 bits), as are `EAX` and `EBX` (both 32 bits). However, the instruction `ADD EAX,BX` is *illegal*, because `EAX` is 32 bits but `BX` is only 16 bits. Similarly, the instruction `ADD Newt,Toad` is *illegal* because adding one memory location to another is not supported.

Intel x86 Reference (Symmetric Instructions)

An operation such as ADD also affects the status bits in the ***program status word*** (***PSW***). Some of the PSW bits are not used, but of those that are the most important are CF (carry flag), ZF (zero flag) SF (sign flag), and OF (overflow flag). These flags are set to 1 or cleared to 0 depending on the result of a computation. For example, when adding two numbers together, ZF is set if the result is zero and is cleared otherwise. Similarly, SF is set if the result is negative and cleared if the result is greater than or equal to zero. CF is set if there is a carry out of the most significant bit of the result (that is, an unsigned overflow), and OF is set if there is a signed overflow (adding two positives and getting a negative result, or vice versa). These status flags are used to make decisions about how to proceed in the program. Not all instructions affect all bits in the PSW, and some instructions affect none. Note that CMP and TEST do not change any data registers; they make a computation strictly for the purpose of affecting the status bits, but then discard the result of that computation.

Instruction		Meaning	Affected Flags	Description
ADC	*dest,src*	dest = dest+src+CF	SF,ZF,OF,CF	Add with carry
ADD	*dest,src*	dest = dest+src	SF,ZF,OF,CF	Add
SBB	*dest,src*	dest = dest-src-CF	SF,ZF,OF,CF	Subtract with borrow
SUB	*dest,src*	dest = dest-src	SF,ZF,OF,CF	Subtract
CMP	*dest,src*	dest - src	SF,ZF,OF,CF	Compare
AND	*dest,src*	dest = dest AND src	SF,ZF	Bitwise AND
OR	*dest,src*	dest = dest OR src	SF,ZF	Bitwise OR
XOR	*dest,src*	dest = dest XOR src	SF,ZF	Bitwise XOR
TEST	*dest,src*	dest AND src	SF,ZF	Bitwise AND
NOT	*dest*	dest = NOT dest		Bitwise NOT
DEC	*dest*	dest = dest - 1	SF,ZF,OF	Decrement
INC	*dest*	dest = dest + 1	SF,ZF,OF	Increment
NEG	*dest*	dest = -dest	SF,ZF,OF,CF	Negate (2's comp)
CLC		CF = 0	CF	Clear Carry
CMC		CF = NOT CF	CF	Complement Carry
STC		CF = 1	CF	Set Carry
MOV	*dest,src*	dest = src		Move data
XCHG	*dest,src*	Swap dest with src		Exchange

These instructions primarily deal with simple arithmetic and data movement and are fairly symmetric in their use of registers. Most other instructions are not so general: they often require specific registers in order to work, so program code has to be written to make those registers available when needed.

Intel x86 Reference (Multiply and Divide)

For multiplication, there are two different instructions: MUL (unsigned multiplication) and IMUL (signed multiplication), and they always use the same special registers in their operation. When multiplying two N-digit integers together in any base, the result contains up to 2N digits. So, when multiplying two 8-bit integers the result will be 16 bits, when multiplying two 16-bit integers the result will be 32 bits, and so on. For the x86 architecture, this means that the result of multiplying two registers together will require two single-length registers to hold the double-length product.

However, the A register (AL, AX, or EAX) is always one source of the multiplication, and both registers A and D (AX, DX, EAX, EDX) are used to receive the product, depending on the size of the numbers being multiplied. The other source is either a memory variable or another register (later extensions to the instruction set also allow the second source to be a constant, as well as other forms not shown here). If the source (*src*) is 8 bits, the multiplication is AL × *src*, with the 16-bit result going to AX (that is, the high byte of the product to AH and the low byte to AL). If the source is 16 bits, the multiplication is AX × *src*, with the high 16 bits of the result going to DX and the low 16 bits to AX. If the source is 32 bits, the multiplication is EAX × *src*, with the high 32 bits going to EDX and the low 32 bits to EAX. The general format is:

MUL	*src*	*(No need to specify the destination register)*
IMUL	*src*	*(No need to specify the destination register)*

For example:

IMUL BL	AX = AL × BL	8-bit operands, 16-bit product
IMUL CH	AX = AL × CH	8-bit operands, 16-bit product
IMUL BX	DX:AX = AX × BX	16-bit operands, 32-bit product
IMUL CX	DX:AX = AX × CX	16-bit operands, 32-bit product
IMUL EBX	EDX:EAX = EAX × EBX	32-bit operands, 64-bit product
IMUL ECX	EDX:EAX = EAX × ECX	32-bit operands, 64-bit product

Division is the inverse of the process of multiplication, as expected, with instructions DIV (unsigned division) and IDIV (signed division). In these cases, a 2N-bit dividend is divided by an N-bit divisor, giving an N-bit quotient and an N-bit remainder. As before, the A and D registers have special uses:

IDIV BL	AL = AX ÷ BL	8-bit quotient AL, remainder AH
IDIV CH	AL = AX ÷ CH	8-bit quotient AL, remainder AH
IDIV BX	AX = DX:AX ÷ BX	16-bit quotient AX, remainder DX
IDIV CX	AX = DX:AX ÷ CX	16-bit quotient AX, remainder DX
IDIV EBX	EAX = EDX:EAX ÷ EBX	32-bit quotient EAX, remainder EDX
IDIV ECX	EAX = EDX:EAX ÷ ECX	32-bit quotient EAX, remainder EDX

Intel x86 Reference (Sign Extension)

For divisions where the dividend is the same size as the divisor, it is important that the register containing the required upper half of the now double-wide dividend be the correct value. That is, to perform the signed division AL ÷ BL, it is necessary that AH be initialized to either hexadecimal 00 if AL is positive or FF if AL is negative. Similarly, when dividing AX by BX, it is necessary that DX be initialized to 0000 if AX is positive and FFFF if AX is negative, and when dividing EAX by EBX it is necessary that EDX be initialized to 00000000 if EAX is positive and FFFFFFFF if EAX is negative. To accomplish this, there are special instructions that perform ***sign-extension*** of the appropriate registers, by copying the sign (leftmost) bit of the lower register throughout the upper register it makes the two-register dividend the same sign as the one-register dividend:

CBW	Extend sign bit of AL into AH	Convert Byte to Word
CWD	Extend sign bit of AX into DX	Convert Word to Double Word
CDQ	Extend sign bit of EAX into EDX	Convert Double Word to Quad Word
CDQE	Extend sign bit of EAX into RAX	Convert Double Word to Quad Word
CQO	Extend sign bit of RAX into RDX	Convert Quad Word to Oct Word

For example, if memory variables Frog and Toad were both 16 bit signed integers, and the task was to perform a signed divide of Frog by Toad, the sequence of instructions would be either:

MOV	**AX,Frog**	Move memory variable Frog into AX
CWD		Sign extend AX into DX
MOV	**BX,Toad**	Move memory variable Toad into BX
IDIV	**BX**	AX = DX:AX ÷ BX, quotient to AX, remainder to DX

or

MOV	**AX,Frog**	Move memory variable Frog into AX
CWD		Sign extend AX into DX
IDIV	**Toad**	AX = DX:AX ÷ Toad, quotient to AX, remainder to DX

Intel x86 Reference (Transfers of Control)

Programs will not just start at the first instruction and run in a straight-line simple sequence until they hit the last instruction. At some point in the execution, control needs to be transferred to some other place in the code, either before the current point (as in a while-loop or repeat-loop), or after the current point (as in an if-then or if-then-else statement). These transfers of control are called **_jumps_**, and are either **_conditional jumps_** or **_unconditional jumps_**.

An unconditional jump (JMP) simply changes the point in the code at which execution occurs. A conditional jump tests one or more of the bits in the PSW, and takes the jump if the PSW bits match the desired condition, but simply executes the next instruction in sequence without taking the jump if the PSW bits do not match. For example, JZ takes the jump if ZF (the zero flag) is set to 1, indicating that the last instruction to affect ZF had a zero result. It does not take the jump if ZF is 0 (indicating that the last instruction to affect ZF was not zero). Here is a table of the most common, as well as a few of the more uncommon, conditional jumps:

	Op-Code	Jump if...		Op-Code	Jump if...	
SIMPLE FLAGS	JC	Carry	CF=1	JNC	Not Carry	CF=0
	JO	Overflow	OF=1	JNO	Not Overflow	OF=0
	JS	Signed (Negative)	SF=1	JNS	Not Signed (Negative)	SF=0
	JZ	Zero	ZF=1	JNZ	Non-Zero	ZF=0
EQUALITY	JE	Equal	ZF=1	JNE	Not Equal	ZF=0
UNSIGNED	JA	Above	CF=0 and ZF=0	JBE	Below or Equal	CF=1 or ZF=1
	JB	Below	CF=1	JAE	Above or Equal	CF=0
	JNA	Not Above	CF=1 or ZF=1	JNBE	Not Below or Equal	CF=0 and ZF=0
	JNAE	Not Above or Equal	CF=1	JNB	Not Below	CF=0
SIGNED	JG	Greater Than	ZF=0 and SF=OF	JLE	Less Than or Equal	ZF=1 or SF≠OF
	JL	Less Than	SF≠OF	JGE	Greater Than or Equal	SF=OF
	JNG	Not Greater Than	ZF=1 or SF≠OF	JNLE	Not Less Than or Equal	ZF=0 and SF=OF
	JNL	Not Less Than	SF=OF	JNGE	Not Greater Than or Equal	SF≠OF
UNUSUAL	JCXZ	CX is Zero	CX=0	JECXZ	ECX is Zero	ECX=0
UNUSUAL	LOOP	Decrement CX/ECX, Then Jump if CX/ECX ≠ 0				
	LOOPZ	Decrement CX/ECX, Then Jump if CX/ECX ≠ 0 and ZF=1				
	LOOPNZ	Decrement CX/ECX, Then Jump if CX/ECX ≠ 0 and ZF=0				

Subroutines are set-aside sections of code that are used many times by different places in the program. They correspond to procedures or functions in high-level languages. A subroutine has a labeled entry point at the start of its code, and a return at the bottom. To **_call_** a subroutine the CALL instruction pushes the address of the next instruction on the stack, and then jumps to the entry point. At the end of the subroutine, the RET instruction pops the return address off the stack and jumps to it, picking up execution at the next instruction after the CALL. Parameters are passed into and out of a subroutine through the registers or on the stack. A variation of the RET instruction is RET *n*, where *n* more bytes are popped off the stack after the return address is popped; this is to discard any call-by-value parameters.

Intel x86 Reference (Stack)

The **_stack_** is a reserved region of memory for holding information temporarily, and the top of the stack is known through the SP register. The stack starts at the high address of this region and grows downwards. To put a register onto the stack requires a **_push_**, such as `PUSH AX`, and to extract a register from the stack requires a **_pop_**, such as `POP AX`.

16-Bit		32-Bit		64-Bit		NOTE
PUSH AX	POP AX	PUSH EAX	POP EAX	PUSH RAX	POP RAX	
PUSH BX	POP BX	PUSH EBX	POP EBX	PUSH RBX	POP RBX	
PUSH CX	POP CX	PUSH ECX	POP ECX	PUSH RCX	POP RCX	
PUSH DX	POP DX	PUSH EDX	POP EDX	PUSH RDX	POP RDX	
PUSH SP	POP SP	PUSH ESP	POP ESP	PUSH RSP	POP RSP	Push current value of SP
PUSH BP	POP BP	PUSH EBP	POP EBP	PUSH RBP	POP RBP	
–	–	–	–	PUSH R8	POP R8	New Registers: R8…R15
PUSH SI	POP SI	PUSH ESI	POP ESI	PUSH RSI	POP RSI	
PUSH DI	POP DI	PUSH EDI	POP EDI	PUSH RDI	POP RDI	
PUSHF	POPF	PUSHFD	POPFD	PUSHFQ	POPFQ	Program Status Flags
PUSH *num*	–	PUSH *num*	–	PUSH *num*	–	Starting with 80188/80186

When calling a subroutine, most registers contain values that must be preserved in the calling code, but the subroutine must use those same registers for its own purposes. Subroutines receive **_parameters_** through the stack, use the stack for **_local variables_**, and are responsible for saving and restoring all registers on the stack appropriately. The following 32-bit code calls a subroutine that is passed a four-byte parameter on the stack, which is discarded on return. The first three instructions in the subroutine set up a **_stack frame_**: the parameter is in the stack only 8 bytes above the address in EBP (with the return address and the saved EBP in between), and the local variable is 4 bytes below EBP, regardless of what happens to ESP later:

```
...                          MySub  PUSH EBP              Save base register,
MOV   EAX,Param1                    MOV  EBP,ESP          build a stack frame,
PUSH  EAX                           SUB  ESP,4            allocate 1 local var.
CALL  MySub                         PUSH EAX              Save all general
...                                 PUSH EBX              purpose registers.
MOV   EAX,Param2                    PUSH ECX
PUSH  EAX                           PUSH EDX
Call  MySub                         MOV  EAX,[EBP+8]      Get parameter,
...                                 MOV  [EBP-4],EAX      store in local var.
...                                 ...                  Do useful work here.
MOV   EAX,Param3                    POP  EDX              Restore all general
PUSH  EAX                           POP  ECX             purpose registers.
Call  MySub                         POP  EBX
...                                 POP  EAX
MOV   EAX,Param4                    MOV  ESP,EBP          Deallocate local var.
PUSH  EAX                           POP  EBP             Restore base register.
Call  MySub                         RET  4               RET, ditch parameter.
```

Intel x86 Reference (Instruction Lengths)

Instructions on the x86 are variable in length from between 1 and 15 bytes. Simple instructions such as PUSH AX (50) or CLC (F8, clear carry) take up only a single byte. Instructions that operate on registers only, such as MOV BX,AX or SUB AX,BX take two bytes (one byte for the op-code and one to specify the registers). Instructions that load registers with 16-bit constants take three bytes, such as MOV AX,*constant* (one byte for the op-code and two bytes for the constant in little endian format). Instructions that reference 16-bit addresses take four bytes (two bytes for the op-code and registers and two bytes for the address in little endian format), such as ADD AX,*variable*. Other instructions take more bytes. Note that MOV AX,0 takes three bytes, but XOR AX,AX has the *same effect* and only takes two. Also, CMP AX,0 (three bytes) and OR AX,AX (two bytes) affect ZF in the *same way*. These are ways to reduce code size.

In the diagram below is the method for figuring out instructions for register-to-register operations (not involving memory). The first byte is the op-code, and the second shows the addressing mode. For simple register-to-register operations the first two bits of the addressing mode byte are both 1 (for operations involving memory these bits will have different values). The remaining six bits of the addressing mode byte determine the two registers that will be involved. The op-code distinguishes 8-bit operations from 16-bit from 32-bit. In 8-bit and 16-bit operations, Reg1 is the destination register and Reg2 is the source register, but in order to accommodate 32-bit operations these had to be reversed.

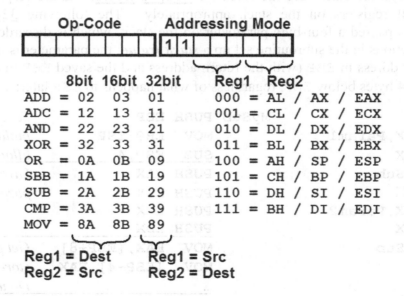

	8bit	16bit	32bit		Reg1	Reg2					
ADD =	02	03	01	000 =	AL	/	AX	/	EAX
ADC =	12	13	11	001 =	CL	/	CX	/	ECX
AND =	22	23	21	010 =	DL	/	DX	/	EDX
XOR =	32	33	31	011 =	BL	/	BX	/	EBX
OR =	0A	0B	09	100 =	AH	/	SP	/	ESP
SBB =	1A	1B	19	101 =	CH	/	BP	/	EBP
SUB =	2A	2B	29	110 =	DH	/	SI	/	ESI
CMP =	3A	3B	39	111 =	BH	/	DI	/	EDI
MOV =	8A	8B	89						

Reg1 = Dest   Reg1 = Src
Reg2 = Src   Reg2 = Dest

For example, ADD BL,AH (add AH to BL) is an 8-bit addition, so the op-code will be 02 hexadecimal. The addressing mode byte will then be 11-011-100, or DC in hexadecimal, making the complete 8-bit instruction 02 DC. Similarly, ADD EAX,EBX (add EBX to EAX) will be 01 for the op-code, with the addressing mode 11-011-000 or D8, making the complete 32-bit addition instruction 01 D8. Just this simple diagram describes 1728 distinct instructions (9 instruction types × 3 register sizes × 8 sources × 8 destinations). All of the other thousands of x86 instructions are encoded in similar fashions.

Intel x86 Reference (Summary)

The instructions covered in this section are enough for people to gain some insight into the x86 architecture, along with an understanding of some of its limitations. The requirement to maintain utter backwards compatibility with earlier chip models, even if those earlier designs contained poor decisions (or decisions that made sense at the time but quickly became indefensible), has constrained the later designs Also, as the processors advance from one model to another, more instructions are added as capabilities are expanded. There is an extensive set of instructions in the x86 architecture that have <u>not</u> been covered here, including:

Shift and Rotate Instructions

Bits in the registers may be shifted to the left or to the right (SHL, SHR), or rotated (ROL, ROR), and rotates may also go through CF (RCL, RCR). In a rotate, the bits that would "fall off the end" wrap around to the other end of the register. In a shift, those bits are lost. In a right-shift, the left most bit may also be sign extended (SAR). In some chips, the amount of a shift or rotate is always one bit at a time, or may be controlled by the count value in CL. In more modern chips, the amount of a shift or rotate may be an arbitrary constant.

String Copy Instructions

One of the more bizarre abilities of the x86 is the ability to copy a large array of bytes from one section of memory to another in a single instruction. The MOVSB (move string byte) instruction copies one byte from the address where SI points to where DI points, then increments both SI and DI. It requires a special instruction ***prefix*** called REP, which repeats an instruction and decrements CX until CX equals zero. The setup requires that SI contain the starting address of the block being copied, DI contain the starting address of the destination block, and CX contain the number of bytes to copy. The single instruction REP MOVSB then copies the entire block.

x87 Coprocessor Instructions

When the 8088 chip was first designed, there was not enough space on the chip to include hardware for floating-point arithmetic. Those functions were performed by the 8087 coprocessor chip, a slave chip plugged in next to the 8088. This was continued through the 286 and 386 line, until the 486 and Pentium were able to include the x87 hardware on the same chip. There are an extensive list of coprocessor instructions available, supporting single precision, double precision, and extended precision arithmetic. (All internal calculations are performed in extended precision.) Capabilities include floating-point add, subtract, multiply, and divide, along with square root, exponential, logarithm, and many other mathematical operations.

Software Interrupts

Software interrupts are "subroutine calls" where the subroutine addresses are not known to the calling program, but are instead stored in ***interrupt vectors*** known only to the operating system. MS-DOS used them for such things as plotting pixels or getting keyboard characters.

ARM Reference (Registers)

The ARM™ (once Advanced RISC Machines, and before that Acorn RISC Machines) series of chips are among the most widely used chips in existence. They are in millions of small devices: cell phones, game machines, embedded processors, and in a wide variety of other applications. The term **_RISC_** means **_Reduced Instruction Set Computer_**: unlike the x86 line with its wide range of complicated (and in some cases rarely used) CISC instructions, RISC machines use a very small number of very simple but extremely fast instructions. This reduces the size and power consumption of the chips relative to CISC machines, making them ideal for portable, battery powered devices. (Older x86 chips executed their CISC instructions directly in hardware, but as successive revisions got more and more complicated the recent x86 chips translate CISC instructions on-the-fly into a series of RISC instructions and then execute those.)

The 32-bit ARM 7 architecture will be discussed here, as it is one of the most common chips in existence. (The newer ARM 8 series is 64 bits.) The ARM 7 contains sixteen 32-bit integer registers, named **R0** through **R15**. All registers are general purpose *except* **R15** (the **_program counter_** that tells where the next instruction to be executed is located in memory, known as PC), **R14** (the **_link register_** used by subroutines, known as LR), and **R13** (the **_stack pointer_**, known as SP). While not enforced by hardware, **R12** is also typically reserved as well (the **_instruction pointer_**, also used by subroutines and known as IP), leaving **R0** through **R11** free for computations.

The ARM is a **_three-address machine_**: a computation such as addition specifies the destination register, a source register, and a second source (which may be a register or a constant, either of which may be shifted or rotated left or right by some number of bits). Here are some examples:

Assembly language	Meaning
ADD R0,R1,R2	R0 = R1 + R2
ADD R0,R1,R0	R0 = R1 + R0
ADD R0,R0,R0	R0 = R0 + R0
ADD R0,R0,#1	R0 = R0 + 1
ADD R0,R1,R2,LSL #3	R0 = R1 + (R2 * 8)

Every instruction is exactly 32 bits in size (4 bytes), and is **_word aligned_**, meaning that the right most two bits of every instruction address are 00. Again, this simplifies program flow, as it is completely predictable where an instruction starts (unlike the x86 where instructions are between 1 and 15 bytes long).

ARM Reference (Condition Codes)

As with the x86 architecture, the ARM has status flags Z, N, C, and O that indicate if the result of a computation was zero, negative, generated a carry (unsigned overflow) or generated a signed overflow, respectively. A more complex test example is to compare two numbers, then look at the exclusive-or of N and V: if 1 the first number was less than (`LT`) the second, but if 0 the first number was greater than or equal (`GE`) to the second. Unlike the x86, however, testing the flags can happen on *every* instruction, not just jump instructions. This is called ***conditional execution***. Many instructions have the option to set the flags as a result of the computation or not set the flags, as needed by the program. These capabilities greatly simplify and streamline program flow over other processors.

Code	Flags Tested	Execute Instruction If...
EQ	Z=1	Last result was zero
NE	Z=0	Last result was non-zero
CS *or* HS	C=1	Last result set the carry, unsigned higher or same
CC *or* LO	C=0	Last result cleared the carry, unsigned lower
MI	N=1	Last result was negative
PL	N=0	Last result was positive or zero
VS	V=1	Last result had an overflow
VC	V=0	Last result did not have overflow
HI	((not C) orr Z)=0	Last result was unsigned higher
LS	((not C) orr Z)=1	Last result was unsigned lower or same
GE	(N eor V)=0	Last result was signed greater than or equal
LT	(N eor V)=1	Last result was signed less than
GT	(Z orr (N eor V))=0	Last result was signed greater than
LE	(Z orr (N eor V))=1	Last result was signed less than or equal

Instructions need not test anything: the default condition "test" always returns true, so instructions can execute without looking at *any* of the flag bits. All of the following examples add 1 to register R0, but some set the flags afterwards and some don't, and some perform the addition only if the Z status flag is 1:

ADD	R0,R0,#1	Always add 1 to register R0.
ADDS	R0,R0,#1	Always add 1 to register R0 and set the flags based on the result.
ADDEQ	R0,R0,#1	If the last operation was zero (Z=1) then add 1 to register R0.
ADDEQS	R0,R0,#1	If the last operation was zero (Z=1) then add 1 to register R0 and set the flags based on the result.

ARM Reference (Instruction Types)

The first group of instructions are based primarily on simple integer arithmetic. These include add $x+y$, subtract $x-y$, reverse subtract $y-x$, with (ADC, SBC, RSC) and without (ADD, SUB, RSB) involving the carry bit, along with bitwise logical operations AND, ORR (inclusive-OR), EOR (exclusive-OR), and a variety of comparison tests that set the flags but do not save the result of the computation (TST, TEQ, CMP, CMN). These instructions mostly follow the three-address format, with a destination register Rd, a source register R1, and a second source R2 which may be either a register or constant. The instruction list is sorted in order of numeric op-code order; see the diagram on the next page.

Instruction	Meaning	Affected Flags	Description
AND *Rd,R1,R2*	Rd = R1 AND R2	N,Z,C	Bitwise AND
EOR *Rd,R1,R2*	Rd = R1 XOR R2	N,Z,C	Bitwise exclusive OR
SUB *Rd,R1,R2*	Rd = R1 - R2	N,Z,V,C	Subtract
RSB *Rd,R1,R2*	Rd = R2 - R1	N,Z,V,C	Reverse Subtract
ADD *Rd,R1,R2*	Rd = R1 + R2	N,Z,V,C	Add
ADC *Rd,R1,R2*	Rd = R1 + R2 + C	N,Z,V,C	Add with Carry
SBC *Rd,R1,R2*	Rd = R1 - R2 + C - 1	N,Z,V,C	Subtract with Carry
RSC *Rd,R1,R2*	Rd = R2 - R1 + C - 1	N,Z,V,C	Reverse Sub. w/Carry
TST *Rd,R1,R2*	R1 AND R2	N,Z,C	Bit Test
TEQ *Rd,R1,R2*	R1 XOR R2	N,Z,C	Test Equal
CMP *R1,R2*	R1 - R2	N,Z,V,C	Compare
CMN *R1,R2*	R1 + R2	N,Z,V,C	Compare negative
ORR *Rd,R1,R2*	Rd = R1 OR R2	N,Z,C	Inclusive OR
MOV *Rd,R2*	Rd = R2	N,Z,C	Move
BIC *Rd,R1,R2*	Rd = R1 AND NOT R2	N,Z,C	Bit Clear
MVN *Rd,R2*	Rd = NOT R2	N,Z,C	Move Negative

All of these instructions may be conditionally executed, and most have the option of setting or not setting the condition codes as a result of the computation (it would not make much sense for the comparisons to not set the condition codes, as setting the codes is their express purpose).

Multiplication on the ARM is a special instruction type, and comes in two forms: a simple multiplication, and a ***multiply and accumulate*** that is particularly useful in the types of computations used in graphics or ***digital signal processing***. In both cases the result is only 32 bits (no double precision). Register Rd cannot be the same as R1 in early versions of the chip. Both support conditional execution, and both optionally can set the condition codes.

Instruction	Meaning	Affected Flags	Description
MUL *Rd,R1,R2*	Rd = R1 × R2	N,Z	Multiply
MLA *Rd,R1,R2,R3*	Rd = R1 × R2 + R3	N,Z	Multiply Accumulate

Integer division is <u>not</u> available at all on the ARM 7.

ARM Reference (Arithmetic Format)

Here is the layout for all instructions that perform simple integer arithmetic. These instructions are identified by the 00 towards the left side of the 32 bits. The condition codes test the various status flags, and only allow the instruction to execute if the condition is satisfied. The op-code determines the action of the instruction. If the S bit is 1 the result of the instruction will set the status flags appropriately, but if S is 0 the status flags remain unaffected. The Operand 1 register and the Destination register each specify one of the sixteen registers.

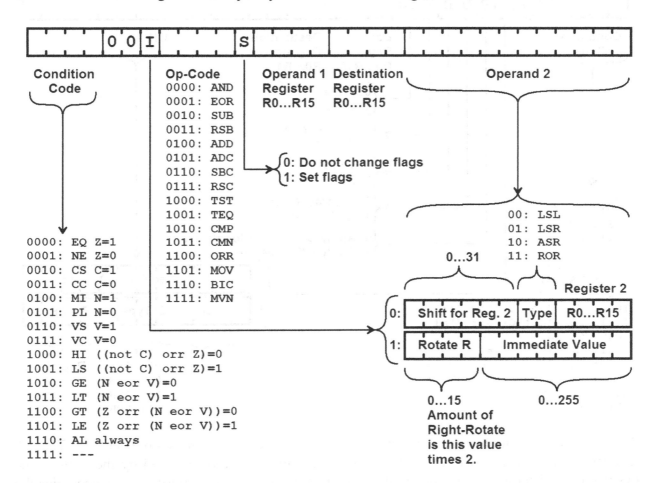

Operand 2 is much more complicated, and how it works is dependent on the I (immediate) bit. If I is 0, then the 12-bit Operand 2 field contains a register, how the contents of that register should be shifted or rotated, and by how much. The shift can be a simple shift left (LSL), simple shift right (LSR), arithmetic (sign extended) shift right (ASR), or rotate right (ROR). A setting of "no shift" would be LSL by 0 places. Not shown is that the amount that operand register 2 can be shifted can also be determined by a *fourth* register coded into the Operand 2 field. However, if the I bit is 1, the ***immediate value*** (constant) in the right most 8 bits is rotated right by 0, 2, 4, 6, 8, …, 30 places, generating a wide variety of both large and small constants. The instruction ADCEQS R0,R0,#1 thus means "If Z=1 then add-with-carry register R0 and the constant 1, put the result back in R0, and set the status flags as a result of the addition".

ARM Reference (Loads and Stores)

Unlike the x86 architecture, where nearly every arithmetic instruction can fetch an operand from memory, the ARM has only two main instructions that directly reference memory: load (LDR) and store (STR). (There are a very few other instruction that reference memory as well.) Here is the general format of this type of instruction:

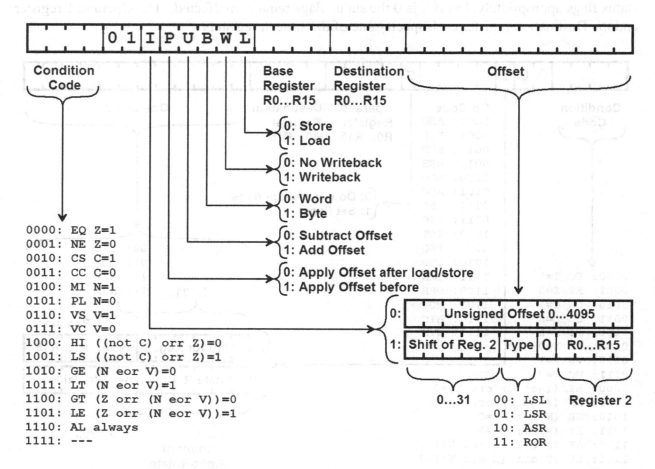

As usual, the condition code determines whether to execute the instruction at all. The 01 identifies this as a memory reference instruction, load or store determined by the L bit. The destination register is where a load will put the item fetched from memory, and also contains the item that will go to memory in a store instruction. The memory address is computed by adding or subtracting (determined by the U bit) an offset to the value in a specified base register (often the program counter R15 or the stack pointer R13). That offset can be a simple integer in the range 0...4095, or it can be the contents of a third register shifted in some manner; this is determined by the I bit. The W bit determines if the new address is written back into the base register, and the P bit controls whether that write back happens before or after the load/store. Referencing a 32-bit word or an 8-bit byte is determined by the B bit. While this is complicated, the assembler figures how to set all the bits for a simple load like LDR R0, Frog or a simple store like STR R3, Toad. More complex examples are shown on the next page.

ARM Reference (Array References and the Stack)

If register R8 contains the address in memory to the start of an array of words, for example, then fetching the first 4-byte word of the array into register R0 is accomplished by LDR R0, [R8], getting the second word by LDR R0, [R8,#4], the third by LDR R0, [R8,#8], and so on. Referencing memory before the array is also allowed by LDR R0, [R8,#-4], using negative offsets. In this example, R8 contains the ***base address*** of the array, and items in memory are referenced at offsets relative to ***base register*** R8. The value in R8 does not change.

To use the ***stack***, the stack pointer is in R13 (often abbreviated as the synonym SP to emphasize the stack nature of the instructions that use it). Stacks grow downwards from high memory to low memory, so a push of a 32-bit word decreases SP by 4 before the store and a pop increases SP by 4 after the load. The stack pointer register is used as a memory reference in much the same way as above, with one exception. For example, LDR R0, [R13] gets the top word from the stack (also written as LDR R0, [SP]) but as it stands *the stack pointer does not change*. That makes the stack unusable as a stack.

This is where write back comes in. To push register R0 onto the stack, the instruction is written as STR R0, [SP,#-4]!, which means the memory address to use is R13 minus 4 (four bytes below the current value of the stack pointer), the ! indicates that that final address is written back into R13, thus moving the stack pointer to the new top of the stack, and finally the contents of R0 are stored at that new location. The write back of R13 happens <u>before</u> the store. To pop the stack, all of the address handling operates in reverse. The instruction LDR R0, [SP],#4 means load R0 from memory at the address in R13, but only after the instruction is complete add 4 to R13, thus popping the top off the stack. The write back of R13 happens <u>after</u> the load.

When pushing a number of registers on the stack, it is important to remember the ***last-in-first-out*** nature of stacks: pop registers off of the stack in the reverse of the order that they were pushed:

```
STR R0,[SP,#-4]!        Push R0
STR R1,[SP,#-4]!        Push R1
STR R2,[SP,#-4]!        Push R2
...
LDR R2,[SP],#4          Pop R2
LDR R1,[SP],#4          Pop R1
LDR R0,[SP],#4          Pop R0
```

The stack pointer can be used to allocate ***local variables*** as well: SUB SP,SP,#4 drops the stack pointer by four bytes, allocating one 32-bit value on the stack. Adding that 4 back to SP discards the local variable. Allocating two variables is done by SUB SP,SP,#8, three variables by SUB SP,SP,#12, and so on (four bytes per variable).

ARM Reference (Jumps and Subroutines)

There are two main instructions on the ARM for jumping to a different location in the program, called **branch** (B) and **branch and link** (BL). The format of this instruction type is shown below:

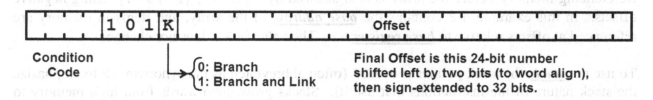

Condition Code

0: Branch
1: Branch and Link

Final Offset is this 24-bit number shifted left by two bits (to word align), then sign-extended to 32 bits.

As usual, the condition code determines whether to execute the instruction at all. The 101 identifies this as a branch instruction. The K bit (from li<u>nk</u>) determines if this is a simple branch, or a branch-and-link. The final offset is the 24-bit number from the instruction, shifted left by two bits because all data and instruction addresses are 32-bit word aligned, and the left most bit is sign-extended to fill out the 32 bits. This forms a signed offset with a very wide range.

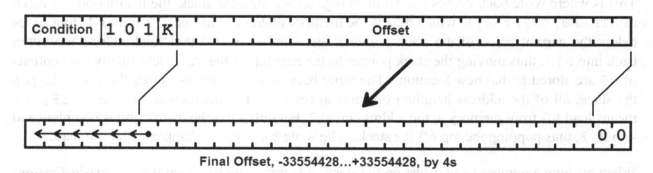

Final Offset, -33554428...+33554428, by 4s

A branch (B) instruction is a simple jump relative to the program counter in R15 (also known as PC), which by the time the instruction executes will be 8 bytes beyond the start of the branch instruction itself. The offset is added to that number to find the target of the jump. Thus, the target can be as much as 33 million bytes before or after the current point in the program.

A branch-and-link (BL) instruction operates in exactly the same manner as a branch, except that the address of the instruction after the BL is copied into R14 (the link register, LR) by the hardware. This becomes a **subroutine call**, where the return address is in LR. To return to the instruction after the call, the last instruction in the subroutine merely moves the link register into the program counter: MOV PC, LR (the same as MOV R15, R14).

As with any ARM instruction, the condition codes control whether or not the instruction is actually executed. For example, B Target always branches (jumps) to the target address, but BEQ Target only takes the branch if Z=1. Similarly, subroutine calls may also take advantage of conditional execution.

ARM Reference (Subroutines)

Combining stack operations with the `BL` instruction sets up everything needed to call subroutines with parameters on the stack, have those subroutines preserve their own registers on the stack, and return gracefully. Here is the simplest possible subroutine. It does not preserve any of the registers, including the return address, and thus cannot itself call any other subroutines.

Main Program	Subroutine	
...	MySub	
BL MySub	...	*Do useful work here*
...	MOV PC,LR	

Here is a version that *does* preserve registers that it changes, including R14 (LR), so it is **_transparent_** to the calling routine, and can call other subroutines without losing track of its own return address. Note that the last two subroutine instructions can be replaced with one by popping the stack directly into the program counter: `LDR PC,[SP],#4`

Main Program	Subroutine		
...	MySub	STR LR,[SP,#-4]!	*Push LR on stack*
BL MySub		STR R0,[SP,#-4]!	*Push R0 on stack*
...		STR R1,[SP,#-4]!	*Push R1 on stack*
BL MySub		...	*Do useful work here*
...		LDR R1,[SP],#4	*Pop R1 from stack*
BL MySub		LDR R0,[SP],#4	*Pop R0 from stack*
...		LDR LR,[SP],#4	*Pop LR from stack*
		MOV PC,LR	*Return from sub.*

Calling a subroutine with parameters pushed on the stack is complicated, as the subroutine must now reach into the stack for the values of its parameters or local variables. Register R12 (IP) is used to build a **_stack frame_** so that the parameters and variables have a stable reference point.

Main Program	Subroutine		
LDR R0,Param1	MySub	STR LR,[SP,#-4]!	*Push LR on stack*
STR R0,[SP,#-4]!		STR IP,[SP,#-4]!	*Push IP on stack*
LDR R0,Param2		MOV IP,SP	*Build a stack frame,*
STR R0,[SP,#-4]!		SUB SP,SP,#4	*Allocate a local var.*
BL MySub		STR R0,[SP,#-4]!	*Push R0 on stack*
LDR R0,[SP],#4		*Param1 is always at IP+12*	
STR R0,Param2		*Param2 is always at IP+8*	
LDR R0,[SP],#4		*Local variable is always at IP-4*	
STR R0,Param1		LDR R0,[SP],#4	*Pop R0 from stack*
		MOV SP,IP	*Discard local var.*
		LDR IP,[SP],#4	*Pop IP from stack*
		LDR PC,[SP],#4	*Pop and return*

ARM Reference (Floating-Point)

The ARM 7 also includes a floating-point unit, which *does* include division. There are eight floating-point registers, F0 through F7. Floating-point numbers observe the IEEE 754 specification, and may be single, double, or extended precision, and results may be rounded in several different ways (to nearest, towards zero, towards $+\infty$, or towards $-\infty$). Floating-point instructions follow the same basic format as the integer instructions, with a destination (indicated by Fd below) and a source (indicated by F1 below), that may be any of the eight registers. The second source (F2 below) may be any of the eight registers as well, or one of a small number of special constants: 0.0, 1.0, 2.0, 3.0, 4.0, 5.0, 0.5, or 10.0. Some combinations of registers are not allowed, such as multiplying a register by itself and putting the result back into the same register. Floating-point instructions are subject to the same rules for conditional execution as the integer instructions. The floating-point unit has its own status register, where problems such as division by zero, operations on NaN or infinity, or overflow are reported. Here are a list of the basic floating-point instructions (others include sine, cosine, exponential, log, etc.):

Instruction	Meaning	Description
ADF Fd,F1,F2	Fd = F1 + F2	Add
SUF Fd,F1,F2	Fd = F1 - F2	Subtract
RSF Fd,F1,F2	Fd = F2 - F1	Reverse Subtract
MUF Fd,F1,F2	Fd = F1 × F2	Multiply
DVS Fd,F1,F2	Fd = F1 ÷ F2	Divide
RDF Fd,F1,F2	Fd = F2 ÷ F1	Reverse Divide
POW Fd,F1,F2	Fd = F1 ^ F2	Power
RPW Fd,F1,F2	Fd = F2 ^ F1	Reverse Power
ABS Fd,F1	Fd = Abs(F1)	Absolute Value
SQT Fd,F1	Fd = Sqrt(F1)	Square Root
CMF Fd,F1,F2	F1 - F2	Compare
FLT Fd,R1	Fd = Float(R1)	Make Float from integer
FIX Rd,F1	Rd = Int(F1)	Make Integer from float
LDF Rd,var	Rd = RAM[var]	Load float from memory
STF Rd,var	RAM[var] = Rd	Store float into memory

For example, the high-level language program statement X = A * B + C - 1 is translated into ARM floating-point as:

Single Precision		Double Precision	
LDFS	F0,A	LDFD	F0,A
LDFS	F1,B	LDFD	F1,B
MUFS	F0,F0,F1	MUFD	F0,F0,F1
LDFS	F1,C	LDFD	F1,C
ADFS	F0,F0,F1	ADFD	F0,F0,F1
SUFS	F0,F0,#1	SUFD	F0,F0,#1
STFS	F0,X	STFD	F0,X

ARM Reference (Summary)

The summaries given here of the ARM architecture and of the earlier x86 and 6502 architectures are nowhere close to being complete. The intent was to present enough detail to describe the vast differences between various machine architectures, and to give interested people enough of a background to appreciate some of the design decisions between them. A deeper understanding would take a full reference manual dedicated to each architecture.

In the case of the ARM, the simplicity of the RISC architecture belies its sophistication. Every instruction is the same length, there are only a few different instruction types and even fewer of those can access memory, and any operation can use any of the registers. Contrast that with the x86 CISC architecture, where instructions are variable in length, there are an enormous number of different instruction types and addressing modes, and many of those instructions can access memory directly. There are also extraordinarily complex x86 instructions that are rarely used.

What has not been discussed about the ARM architecture includes the following items, for which an interested programmer must seek out the language and operations manuals for the specific ARM chip in use:

Instructions

There are a few complicated instructions on the ARM, including those that can load multiple registers from or store multiple registers into a block of memory. Others not covered here include operations on the status register, swapping a register with a location in memory, etc.

Interrupts

Interrupts, both hardware and software, are vital parts of any machine architecture. They allow for interfacing the processor with external devices, and also allow programmers to simplify the design of complex programs such as operating systems.

Supervisor Modes

What has been described here is a subset of the programmer's model of the ARM 7 architecture. However, the chip actually has registers that only become available when interrupts occur; those registers get "swapped in" for certain of the main registers when high-level supervisory code (think operating systems) gets activated. There are several levels of this available.

Advanced Processor Types

Finally, this summary cannot conclude without noting that the chip described here has been in use since the mid-1990s, and has in large part been superseded by newer designs, including 64-bit variants.

JavaScript Quick Reference

Language Characteristics

Layout: Free-format. Indentation does <u>not</u> matter. Statements may appear anywhere on a line, multiple statements may appear on the same line if separated by semicolons (semicolons may be omitted when the end-of-line unambiguously ends a statement, but doing so is not recommended), and statements may be broken across lines (when unambiguous).

Case: Matters. Most language keywords and function names are in lower case. Variable names must agree on case. For example, names `X1` and `x1` refer to different variables.

Typing: Dynamic. The type of a variable depends on the type of the expression assigned to it, and may change as the program runs. For example, `X = 5` (numeric type) may be followed immediately by `X = "frog"` (string type).

Blocks: Denoted by `{...}`. Blocks of related statements (inside a `while`-loop or an `if` statement) are surrounded by curly braces. The `{...}` may be on the same line, or separated by many lines of code.

Comments: Denoted by `//` and extends to the end-of-line. Anything after `//` on a line is ignored. Also, any text surrounded by `/*` up through `*/` (may span lines).

Strings: Denoted by `'text'` (single quotes) or by `"text"` (double quotes).

Relations:

Equality:	`==`		Inequality:	`!=`
Less-Than:	`<`		Greater-Than-Or-Equal:	`>=`
Greater-Than:	`>`		Less-Than-Or-Equal:	`<=`

Assignment: `name = expression ;`   Variable *name* is visible everywhere.
`var name = expression ;`   Variable *name* is only visible within the function where the statement appears.

Output: `writeln ("string")`   Write string into current document.
`writeln (expression)`   Write value into current document.

Conversion: `parseFloat("string")`   Converts string argument into equivalent number. `X = parseFloat("12.34")` returns the number 12.34 in variable `X`.
`String(number)`   Converts numeric argument into equivalent string. `S = String(12.34)` returns the string `"12.34"` in variable `S`.

Python Quick Reference (Continued)

Data Types

All values are strings, plain integers, arbitrary-precision long integers (Python 2 only), double-precision floating-point numbers, or complex numbers. Types are determined at run-time as expressions are evaluated. Python also supports lists, tuples, sets, and dictionaries.

Arithmetic Structures

Operators +, −, *, /, and % represent addition, subtraction, multiplication, division, and modulus respectively, and observe normal order-of-operation rules. Python 2 and Python 3 differ in the interpretation of the / operator (see also the // operator). The statement X = Y + 3 * Z is evaluated identically to the parenthesized version X = (Y + (3 * Z)). Shortcut operators exist for assignment statements where the assigned variable is *also* part of the computed expression. The statement X = X + 7 may be written as X += 7 instead. Lists are **_mutable_** sequences of items defined by square brackets, such as X = [3, 4.6, "frog"]. Tuples are **_immutable_** lists defined by parentheses, such as X = (3, 4.6, "frog").

Language Structures

Parentheses around conditions are optional but recommended. Conditions use the relational operators from the previous page. Indentation is critical. Colons are required at the end of if, elif, else, while, for, try, except, finally, and def statements. To ask if variable X *contains* the value 0, the condition is (X == 0). In contrast, the statement X = 0 (one equal sign, no parentheses) *assigns* 0 to the variable X. In an if statement, elif and else are optional (there may be multiple elif statements). Use try to protect code that might crash, except code runs only when crash occurs, finally code runs whether crash occurs or not.

```
if (condition):                try:                      try:
    #statement                     #statement                #statement
    #statement                     #statement                #statement
elif (condition):              finally:                  except:
    #statement                     #statement                #statement
    #statement                     #statement                #statement
else:
    #statement:
    #statement


while (condition):             for variable in sequence:
    #statement                     #statement
    #statement                     #statement


def nameoffunction (parameter,parameter,…,parameter=default):
    #statement
    #statement
    return expression      # expression is optional
```

Pascal Quick Reference

Language Characteristics

Layout: Free-format. Indentation does <u>not</u> matter. Statements may appear anywhere on a line, multiple statements may appear on the same line. All statements are separated by semicolons, and statements may be broken across lines.

Case: Does <u>not</u> matter. Keywords and variable names need not agree or be consistent on case. For example, names X1 and x1 refer to the same variable, as do keywords Begin, begin, and BEGIN.

Typing: Static. The type of a variable is defined at compile-time and may not change throughout the program. For example, the definition var X : Integer ; means that X := 5 ; is legal while X := 'frog' ; is always illegal.

Blocks: Denoted by Begin...End. Blocks of related statements (inside a program, function, procedure, while-loop, or an if statement) are surrounded by special keywords Begin and End. The Begin...End may be on the same line, or separated by many lines of code. The Begin...End pair may be omitted if the block contains only a single statement, or is inside a repeat-loop.

Comments: Denoted by (*...*) or {...}. Anything in between either set is ignored. Comments may span many lines.

Strings: Denoted by 'text' (single quotes only). To put a quote character inside a string, stutter it. For example the word "don't" would be coded as 'don''t', and '''' encodes a one-character string containing a single quote.

Relations:
Equality:	=	Inequality:	<>
Less-Than:	<	Greater-Than-Or-Equal:	>=
Greater-Than:	>	Less-Than-Or-Equal:	<=

Assignment: *name* := *expression* ;   Variable *name* is visible in scope where it is defined. Note the assignment operator is **:=** and not simply = as it is in other languages.

Input: Readln(*name*) ;   Enter a value of correct type into variable.

Output:
Write ('*string*') ;   Write *string* into current document.
Write (*expression*) ;   Write value into current document.
Writeln ('*string*') ;   Write *string* followed by new line.
Writeln (*expression*) ;   Write value followed by new line.

Pascal Quick Reference (Continued)

Data Types

All values are strings, integers, characters, Booleans (`true` or `false`), or floating-point numbers. Different implementations of Pascal may allow more varieties of data types. Types are determined at compile-time and may not be changed as the program runs. Pascal also supports pointers and records, which are beyond the scope of this document at the current time.

Arithmetic Structures

Operators `+`, `-`, `*`, and `/` represent addition, subtraction, multiplication, and division, respectively, and observe normal order-of-operation rules. The `DIV` operator performs division on integers only, and `MOD` computes the remainder of an integer division. The assignment statement `X := Y + 3 * Z ;` is evaluated identically to `X := (Y + (3 * Z)) ;`. There are no shortcut operators: the statement `X := X + 7 ;` can only be written this way.

Language Structures

Parentheses around simple conditions are <u>not</u> required but <u>are</u> allowed. Conditions use the relational operators from the previous page. To ask if variable `X` <u>*contains*</u> the value `0`, the condition would be `(X = 0)`, for example. In contrast, the statement `X := 0` <u>*assigns*</u> `0` to the variable `X`. Note that there is <u>no</u> semicolon before the `Else` keyword. In an `If` statement the `Else` block is optional.

```
If condition Then              While condition Do
    Begin                          Begin
    (*statements*)                 (*statements*)
    (*statements*)                 (*statements*)
    End                            End ;
Else
    Begin                      Repeat
    (*statements*)                 (*statements*)
    (*statements*)                 (*statements*)
    End ;                      Until (condition) ;


Function nameoffunction (parameter,parameter,…) : type ;
    var name : type ;          (* name visible locally *)
Begin
    (*statements*)
End ;


Procedure nameofprocedure (parameter,parameter,…) ;
    var name : type ;          (* name visible locally *)
Begin
    (*statements*)
End ;
```

Compilation: Internal Representation RPN

A programmer writes a statement such as **X = (A + B) − (C + D)** in a text editor, following the syntax rules of some programming language. This means to take the contents of memory at locations indicated by variable names **A**, **B**, **C**, and **D**, add and subtract them appropriately, then store the result in memory at the location indicated by variable **X**. Whether the result in **X** is an integer, a float, a string, or something else depends on the data types of all the variables.

A compiler would first translate or ***parse*** the expression into a ***parenthesis-free notation*** such as ***RPN*** (***reverse Polish notation***, also known as ***Polish postfix***, first described in 1924 by mathematician Jan Łukasiewicz, 1878-1956). In RPN, values are *pushed onto or popped off of a stack*. Most mathematical operations pop the top two items off the stack, perform the operation, and push the result back onto the stack. The statement above would be translated into RPN as:

PUSH A	(*A is on the stack, depth=1*)
PUSH B	(*A and B are on the stack, depth=2*)
ADD	(*A+B is on the stack, depth=1*)
PUSH C	(*A+B and C are on the stack, depth=2*)
PUSH D	(*A+B and C and D are on the stack, depth=3*)
ADD	(*A+B and C+D are on the stack, depth=2*)
SUBTRACT	(*the final result is on the stack, depth=1*)
POP X	(*X holds the result, the stack is now empty*)

No parentheses are ever needed, and most expressions require only a handful of slots on the stack (the example only requires three slots). Many calculators by Hewlett-Packard used RPN from the 1970s through the 2010s with a four-slot stack.

Compilation: Internal Representation Binary Tree

Another way of representing an expression, also without parentheses, is to use a ***binary tree***, as shown below. The square nodes (***leaf nodes***) represent values or variables, while the circular nodes (***internal nodes***) represent the mathematical operations to be performed on the two items that are connected to it below. This tree shows the example expression above:

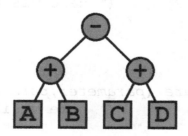

Compilation: First Optimizations

<u>O*ptimization*</u> can happen once programmer's statements have been translated into RPN or into an equivalent binary tree. The sequence **PUSH** x **| PUSH** x **| SUBTRACT** (representing the expression $x - x$, for any common value x) can be replaced by just **PUSH 0**. The sequence **PUSH 0 | ADD** can be eliminated entirely. The total number of rules determines the level of optimization that can be performed. Here is a <u>very incomplete</u> list of possible transformations:

PUSH x **| PUSH** x **| SUBTRACT** →	**PUSH 0**
PUSH 0 | MULTIPLY →	**PUSH 0**
PUSH 0 | ADD →	*nothing*
PUSH 0 | SUBTRACT →	*nothing*
PUSH 1 | MULTIPLY →	*nothing*
PUSH 1 | DIVIDE →	*nothing*

A programmer might then write a statement such as **Q = R + (S - S) * T**, which if converted blindly to RPN would result in:

PUSH R	(*R* is on the stack, depth=1)
PUSH S	(*R* and *S* are on the stack, depth=2)
PUSH S	(*R* and *S* and *S* are on the stack, depth=3)
SUBTRACT	(*R* and *0* are on the stack, depth=2)
PUSH T	(*R* and *0* and *T* are on the stack, depth=3)
MULTIPLY	(*R* and *0* are on the stack, depth=2)
ADD	(*R* is on the stack, depth=1)
POP Q	(*Q* holds the result, the stack is now empty)

By applying appropriate replacement rules to look for specific patterns, the expression can be reduced to the much simpler form:

PUSH R	(*R* is on the stack, depth=1)
POP Q	(*Q* holds the result, the stack is now empty)

Here is the sequence of optimizations for the expression in tree form:

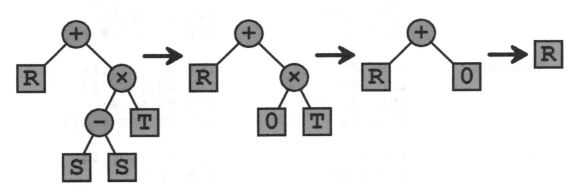

Compilation: RPN into Code

From an optimized binary tree or RPN, a compiler mechanically generates an internally coded form of assembly language for the particular architecture of the target processor. Each RPN command generated from the statement **X = (A + B) − (C + D)** is converted into a small number of equivalent assembly language instructions (we are assuming that all variables are integers). Note the great difference between the basic 8088 architecture (16-bit registers **AX**, **BX**, **CX**, and **DX**) and the ARM architecture (32-bit registers **R0** through **R15**); this is why a program written for one type of chip won't run on another type. Without loss of generality, the 16-bit 8088 code can be turned into 32-bit code by replacing register **AX** with **EAX** and **BX** with **EBX**, and into 64-bit code by replacing **AX** with **RAX** and **BX** with **RBX**. These instructions will run on the appropriate processor when converted into binary, but it is not very efficient code. A compiler might stop here, which is fine for a program to be written quickly and run once, but not for a program that needs to be as fast as possible and is expected to be run many times.

RPN	8088 Assembly	ARM Assembly
PUSH A	MOV AX,A PUSH AX	LDR R0,A STR R0,[SP,#-4]!
PUSH B	MOV AX,B PUSH AX	LDR R0,B STR R0,[SP,#-4]!

ADD	POP BX
	POP AX
	ADD AX,BX
	PUSH AX
		LDR R1,[SP],#4
		LDR R0,[SP],#4
		ADD R0,R0,R1
		STR R0,[SP,#-4]!

PUSH C	MOV AX,C PUSH AX	LDR R0,C STR R0,[SP,#-4]!
PUSH D	MOV AX,D PUSH AX	LDR R0,D STR R0,[SP,#-4]!

ADD	POP BX
	POP AX
	ADD AX,BX
	PUSH AX
		LDR R1,[SP],#4
		LDR R0,[SP],#4
		ADD R0,R0,R1
		STR R0,[SP,#-4]!

SUBTRACT	POP BX
	POP AX
	SUB AX,BX
	PUSH AX
		LDR R1,[SP],#4
		LDR R0,[SP],#4
		SUB R0,R0,R1
		STR R0,[SP,#-4]!

POP X	POP AX MOV X,AX	LDR R0,[SP],#4 STR R0,X

Compilation: Peephole Optimization

Once internal assembly language instructions have been generated, a second optimization step called ***peephole optimization*** can take place. This process looks across groups of instructions (through a small peephole), often adjacent instructions, to look for longer patterns that can be replaced by shorter patterns. The complexity and depth of the rule base largely determines how much optimization can take place. A small set of rules may include "if you see a push of one register followed immediately by a pop into another register, replace those two instructions by one instruction that simply moves the first register into the second." Another rule is "if you load a register from memory and then immediately move that register into another register, replace those two instructions with one instruction that loads the correct register from memory directly." A third is "if you see a push of a register followed some time later by a pop of the same register, and that register isn't used or modified in between, then eliminate the push and the pop." Finally, "if you load a register from memory, and then add that same register to another, replace those two instructions with one that adds from memory to the destination register directly."

Those four simple rules alone result in the following optimization for the 8088 code. In our example, the original code was 22 instructions, but through that very small number of rules the code can be mechanically reduced to only 9 instructions. Not only does the result take less memory, it also runs faster as well.

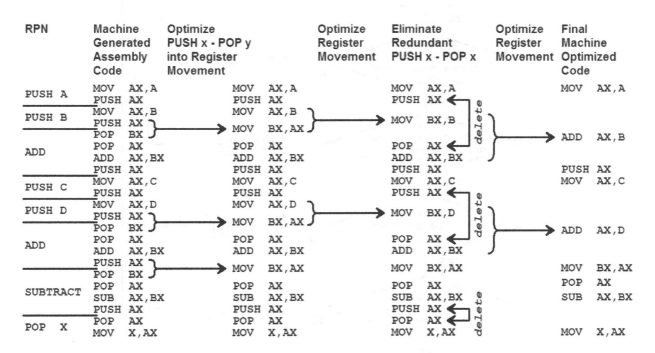

It should be noted that hand-written assembly code can reduce this to only six 8088 instructions instead of nine (**MOV AX,A | ADD AX,B | MOV BX,C | ADD BX,D | SUB AX,BX | MOV X,AX**). Early optimizers were often no better than hand-written code, but today's have significantly better code analysis and have *many* more replacement rules than are shown here. Few people write assembly code directly any more, as compilers have gotten so good.

How to Write a Program: The Process

Writing a program, singly or in a group, is an intensely interactive process, as exemplified by the flowchart below. Much of a programmer's time is spent in a text editor, be it a standalone text editor such as Windows Notepad, Mac Text Edit, emacs, or some other package, or as part of an **_IDE_** (**_Integrated Development Environment_**). It is not uncommon to follow *any* of the backwards pointing arrows at any time in the process, due to syntax errors, run time errors (bugs), or realizations that the entire approach needs to be discarded and rewritten from scratch.

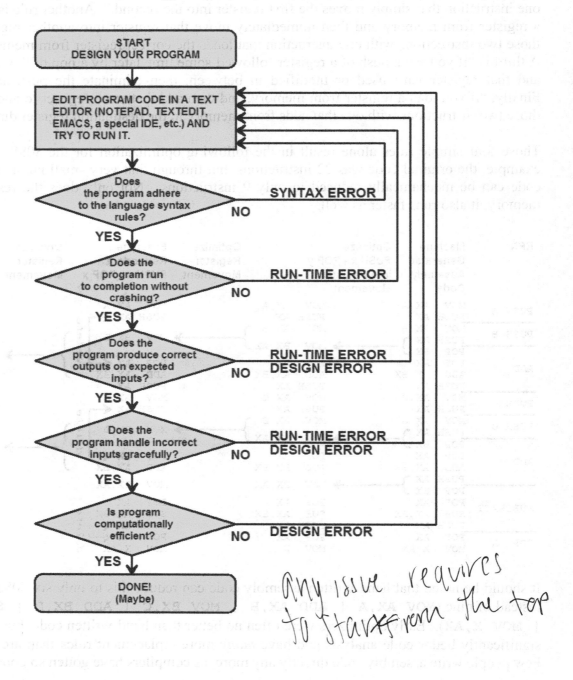

Any issue requires to start from the top

Assignment Statements

All languages have some form of assignment statement, `variable = expression`, where a value is computed and stored in memory at a location associated with a named, typed variable. For example, the following expressions all compute a new value from variables **A**, **B**, **C**, and **D**, and assign that value to variable **X**, replacing any value that **X** may have contained previously:

JavaScript:	**X = (A + B) − (C + D) ;**
Python:	**X = (A + B) − (C + D)**
Pascal:	**X := (A + B) − (C + D) ;**

Think of `variable = expression` as "the variable <u>is assigned</u> the value of the expression" or "the variable <u>becomes</u> the value of the expression" or "the variable <u>receives</u> the value of the expression."

A special case to consider is when the affected variable also appears as part of the expression. One of the more common variants is to add 1 to an integer variable, as used in counting loops. In each case shown below, the old numerical value of **X** has 1 added to it, and the resulting new value is then assigned back to **X**, replacing the old value with the new value:

	Canonical Version	**Alternative Versions**
JavaScript:	**X = X + 1 ;**	**X += 1 ; X++ ;**
Python:	**X = X + 1**	**X += 1**
Pascal:	**X := X + 1 ;**	

Note that languages such as Python permit the expression **X + 1** to stand by itself as a program statement, and the new value is computed correctly, but that *value is then discarded*. Variable **X** is <u>not</u> changed! In order to have **X** change it *must* appear on the left side of an assignment statement. *NO X+1: Instead, X = X + 1*

When **X** is a numeric variable, the order of the operands does not matter: **X = X + 1** is the same as **X = 1 + X** and variable **X** ends up with the same final value in both cases.

For string variables in any language that supports them, as well as lists and tuples in Python, the addition operator **+** means ***concatenation*** (glue together end-to-end) instead of addition. The order of operands matters a lot: the string expression **"DOG" + "HOUSE"** is **"DOGHOUSE"**, but the string expression **"HOUSE" + "DOG"** is **"HOUSEDOG"**. Similarly, in Python the list expression **[3,8,2] + [4,9,1]** is **[3,8,2,4,9,1]**, but the list expression **[4,9,1] + [3,8,2]** is **[4,9,1,3,8,2]** (this is true for tuples as well).

If string variable **S** contains the value **"FROG"**, then **S = S + "*"** would end up with **S** equal to **"FROG*"**, but **S = "*" + S** would end up with **S** equal to **"*FROG"** instead. Similarly, if list variable **L** contains the value **[3,8,2]**, then **L = L + [4]** ends up with **L** equal to **[3,8,2,4]**, but **L = [4] + L** ends up with **L** equal to **[4,3,8,2]** instead.

Multiple Conditions #1

In many programs, there are a number of statements to be executed, but only if certain criteria are met. Action #1 is performed if Condition #1 is true, Action #2 is performed if Condition #2 is true, and so on. The following flowchart is one way to accomplish this. If performing Action #1 changes how Condition #2 or Condition #3 asks their questions, and if performing Action #2 changes how Condition #3 asks its question, then this is the appropriate approach to take. If all the conditions and associated actions are mutually exclusive (that is, Condition #1 and Action #1 are irrelevant to Condition #2 and Action #2, and both are irrelevant to Condition #3 and Action #3), then the conditions and their actions can appear in any order.

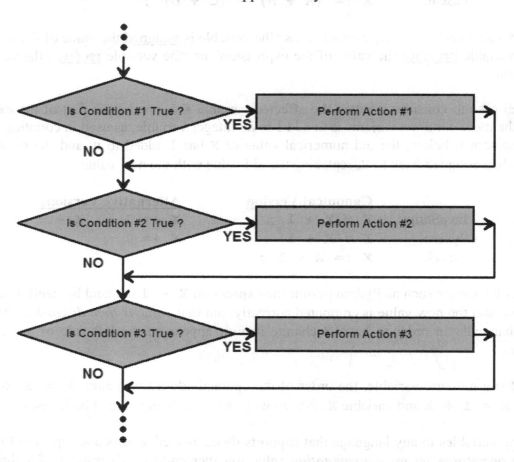

Often, however, the conditions are related in some way and each individual action does *not* interfere with any future conditions or actions. For example, a program might have a single variable that indicates which of the many code blocks to execute. The variable would have the value 1 if Action #1 is to be executed, the value 2 if Action #2 is to be executed, and the value 3 if Action #3 is to be executed, and so on, and none of the actions change the value of the test variable. In this case, the approach shown here is generally <u>not</u> appropriate, because even if the variable was 1, and Action #1 was performed, the variable will *still be tested* to see if it is 2 and then 3, and both tests will be false. While this approach still works, it is very inefficient (the problem will be addressed in the next flowchart).

Multiple Conditions #1

JavaScript

```javascript
if (condition1) {
    // Statement Action #1
    }

if (condition2) {
    // Statement Action #2
    }

if (condition3) {
    // Statement Action #3
    }
```

Python

```python
if (condition1):
    # Statement Action #1
if (condition2):
    # Statement Action #2
if (condition3):
    # Statement Action #3
```

Pascal

```pascal
If (condition1) Then
    Begin
        (* Statement Action #1 *) ;
    End ;

If (condition2) Then
    Begin
        (* Statement Action #2 *) ;
    End ;

If (condition3) Then
    Begin
        (* Statement Action #3 *) ;
    End ;
```

Multiple Conditions #2

In the case where all conditions are related, and no actions interfere with those conditions, then the following structure is more efficient than the previous version. As soon as the matching condition is found, no other conditions are tested. All languages permit a network of nested if statements, as shown on the next page.

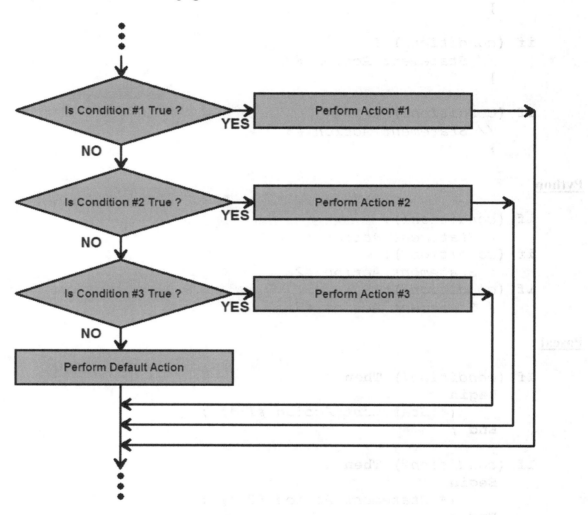

In the even more specialized case of all conditions comparing a single variable to different values, and choosing an action based on those values, Pascal has a special language structure not found in Python (JavaScript has a similar structure called a switch statement):

```
Case variable Of
value1 : Begin (* Statement Action #1 *) End ;
value2 : Begin (* Statement Action #2 *) End ;
value3 : Begin (* Statement Action #3 *) End ;
Else     Begin (* Default Action *) End ;
End ;
```

Multiple Conditions #2

JavaScript

```javascript
if (condition1) {
    // Action #1
} else if (condition2) {
    // Action #2
} else if (condition3) {
    // Action #3
} else {
    // Default Action
}
```

Python

```python
if (condition1):
    # Action #1
else:
    if (condition2):
        # Action #2
    else:
        if (condition3):
            # Action #3
        else:
            # Default Action
```

```python
if (condition1):
    # Action #1
elif (condition2):
    # Action #2
elif (condition3):
    # Action #3
else:
    # Default Action
```

Pascal

```pascal
If (condition1) Then
    Begin
        (* Statement Action #1 *) ;
    End
Else
    If (condition2) Then
        Begin
            (* Statement Action #2 *) ;
        End
    Else
        If (condition3) Then
            Begin
                (* Statement Action #3 *) ;
            End
        Else
            Begin
                (* Default Action *) ;
            End ;
```

Single Counter Loop

A counter loop is how a program executes a series of statements (the payload) multiple times. There are many variations, but the simplest and most common is shown in flowchart form below. It requires a variable (such as `Counter`) that will take on successive values from the first legal to the last legal value in steps of some increment. The name of the counter variable is arbitrary, and could be `Counter`, `MyCounter`, `I`, `J`, `Frog`, `Index`, or whatever the programmer requires. In many cases the starting value is 0 and the increment is 1, but this is not required.

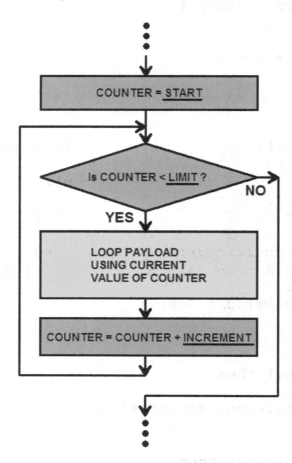

For each legal value of the counter variable, the payload code is run. For example, if the starting value is 0, the limit is 10, and the increment is 1, then the payload code will be run for the counter equal to 0, run again for the counter equal to 1, run again for the counter equal to 2, and so on up to and including the case where the counter is equal to 9. The payload is run 10 times, for the counter taking on successive values 0, 1, 2, 3, 4, 5, 6, 7, 8, and 9.

If the starting value is greater than or equal to the limit then the loop payload will not be run at all. In some circumstances the test to exit the loop may be performed with <= instead of <, in which case the example would run 11 times from the sequence 0, 1, 2, 3, 4, 5, 6, 7, 8, 9, and 10.

Single Counter Loop

Here are typical examples of counter loops. In each case the loop payload is code that uses the counter variable to distinguish one run of the payload from the next. Counting down is similar to counting up, but requires some minor modifications:

JavaScript

```
// Count up from 0 to 9          // Count down from 9 to 0
Counter = 0 ;                    Counter = 9 ;
while (Counter < 10) {           while (Counter >= 0) {
    // Loop Payload                  // Loop Payload
    Counter = Counter + 1 ;          Counter = Counter - 1 ;
    }                                }
```

Python

```
# Count up from 0 to 9           # Count down from 9 to 0
Counter = 0                      Counter = 9
while (Counter < 10):            while (Counter >= 0):
    # Loop Payload                   # Loop Payload
    Counter = Counter + 1            Counter = Counter - 1


# Count up from 0 to 9           # Count down from 9 to 0
Counter = 0                      Counter = 9
while (Counter <= 9):            while (Counter > -1):
    # Loop Payload                   # Loop Payload
    Counter = Counter + 1            Counter = Counter - 1
```

Pascal

```
(* Count up from 0 to 9 *)       (* Count down from 9 to 0 *)
Counter := 0 ;                   Counter := 9 ;
While (Counter < 10) Do          While (Counter >= 0) Do
    Begin                            Begin
        (* Loop Payload *)               (* Loop Payload *)
        Counter := Counter+1;            Counter := Counter-1;
    End ;                            End ;
```

Almost all counter loops use integers instead of floats. Tests for equality on floats are subject to round-off errors from which integers are immune.

Double Counter Loop

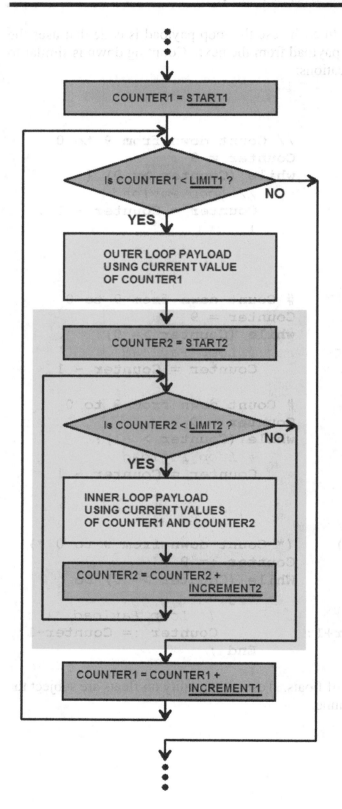

A double counter loop is simply one single counter loop embedded inside a second single counter loop. Each loop needs its own unique counter variable, and its own starting value, limit value, and increment. In the example here, each set of values is identified by a number: `Counter1`, `Start1`, `Limit1`, and `Increment1` for the outer loop, but `Counter2`, `Start2`, `Limit2`, and `Increment2` for the inner loop. (Variable names are arbitrary.)

The "outer loop payload" is code that is dependent only on the value of `Counter1`, just as in a single counter loop. The shaded area contains the inner loop, and while it is technically *part of* the outer loop payload, it is set off here in a different color to indicate that it is a self-contained block.

The "inner loop payload" has access to both `Counter1` and `Counter2`.

The outer loop runs its payload `Limit1` times. For each time through the outer loop, the inner loop runs `Limit2` times, so the inner loop payload runs a total of `Limit1` × `Limit2` times.

Double Counter Loop

JavaScript

```javascript
// Count up from 0 to 9
Counter1 = 0 ;
while (Counter1 < 10) {
    // Outer Loop Payload
    // Count up from 0 to 9
    Counter2 = 0 ;
    while (Counter2 < 10) {
        // Inner Loop Payload
        Counter2 += 1 ;
    }
    Counter1 += 1 ;
}
```

```javascript
// Count up from 1 to 10
Counter1 = 1 ;
while (Counter1 <= 10) {
    // Outer Loop Payload
    // Count up from 1 to 10
    Counter2 = 1 ;
    while (Counter2 <= 10) {
        // Inner Loop Payload
        Counter2 += 1 ;
    }
    Counter1 += 1 ;
}
```

Python

```python
# Count up from 0 to 9
Counter1 = 0
while (Counter1 < 10):
    # Outer Loop Payload
    # Count up from 0 to 9
    Counter2 = 0 ;
    while (Counter2 < 10):
        # Inner Loop Payload
        Counter2 += 1
    Counter1 += 1
```

```python
# Count up from 1 to 10
Counter1 = 1
while (Counter1 < 11):
    # Outer Loop Payload
    # Count up from 1 to 10
    Counter2 = 1 ;
    while (Counter2 < 11):
        # Inner Loop Payload
        Counter2 += 1
    Counter1 += 1
```

Pascal

```pascal
(* Count up from 0 to 9 *)
Counter1 := 0 ;
While (Counter1 < 10) Do
    Begin
        (* Outer Loop Payload *)
        (* Count up from 0 to 9 *)
        Counter2 := 0 ;
        While (Counter2 < 10) Do
            Begin
                (* Inner Loop Payload *)
                Counter2 := Counter2 + 1 ;
            End ;
        Counter1 := Counter1 + 1 ;
    End ;
```

Interactive Loop #1

Many computer programs have to stop processing briefly to ask for input from the user. However, there are never any guarantees that the user will always enter something in the expected range of legal values. Solving this problem requires that the user enter a value, then the code checks it to see it is in the proper range, and if not asks the user again. This process must repeat until the user eventually behaves themselves and enters a legal value.

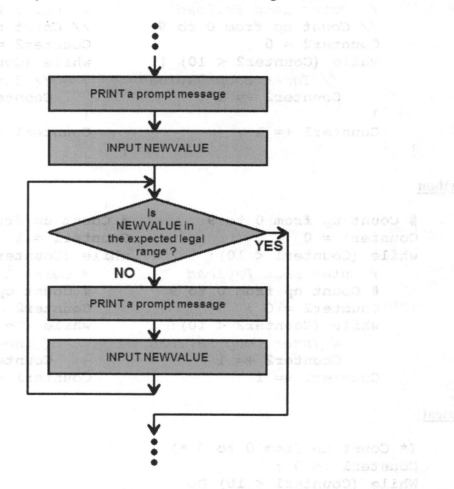

Depending on the language, the **PRINT** and the **INPUT** statements may be part of the same command, and so those block pairs will be joined into one statement. This is true in both JavaScript and Python, but are two explicit statements in Pascal.

In all the code examples on the next page, it is assumed that `LowLimit` and `HighLimit` are variables that have already been defined and given a value. Alternatively, constant values (numbers) can be used in their place. It is also assumed that values to be entered are integers, hence the use of `ParseInt` in JavaScript and `int` in Python, but replacing those function calls with `ParseFloat` (JavaScript) and `float` (Python) will allow for floating-point values to be entered instead. In Pascal, defining `NewValue` as either `integer` or `real` is all that is necessary.

Interactive Loop #1

JavaScript

```javascript
NewValue = parseInt(window.prompt("Enter a value")) ;
while (NewValue < LowLimit) or (NewValue > HighLimit) {
    NewValue = parseInt(window.prompt("Enter a value")) ;
}
```

Python 2

```python
NewValue = input("Enter a value: ")
while (NewValue < LowLimit) or (NewValue > HighLimit):
    NewValue = input("Enter a value: ")
```

Python 3

```python
NewValue = int(input("Enter a value: "))
while (NewValue < LowLimit) or (NewValue > HighLimit):
    NewValue = int(input("Enter a value: "))
```

Pascal

```pascal
Write ('Enter a value: ') ;
Readln (NewValue) ;
While (NewValue < LowLimit) Or (NewValue > HighLimit) Do
    Begin
        Write ('Enter a value: ') ;
        Readln (NewValue) ;
    End ;
```

Interactive Loop #2

In a lot of cases, it is impractical to have two separate but identical blocks of code to prompt the users for input and have them enter their responses. To get around the problem and only have one copy of the input code, simply initialize the input variable to an <u>illegal</u> value before entering the loop. Since it by definition is *not* legal, the test will *immediately* fail and execute the body of the loop, which is to get an input from the user.

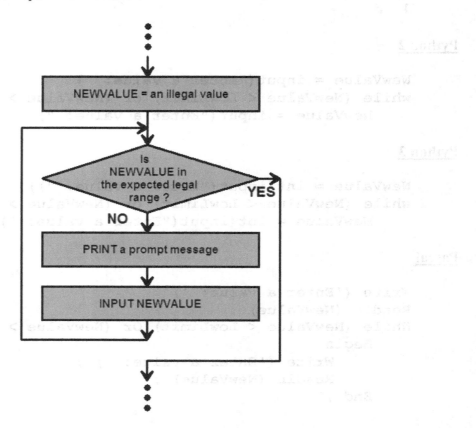

If the code is designed to allow users to enter values between 1 and 10 inclusive, for example, then the low limit is 1 and the high limit is 10, and variable `NewValue` can be initialized to anything outside that range such as 0, -1, 1000, etc. Care must be taken to pick an initial value that is outside the range of legal values.

As before, all the code examples on the next page assume that `LowLimit` and `HighLimit` are integer variables that have already been defined and given a value, or are constant values (numbers). In the Python 3 example, the `try-except` block is to prevent the user from entering a value that is not an integer at all. If they enter an arbitrary string or a float as the result of the `input` function, trying to convert it to an integer with the `int` function will normally *crash the program* at that point. By putting the problematic statement inside the `try` block, any error of that type will then jump to the code in the `except` block, which allows the program to recover gracefully. This can also be done in Python 2, as well as JavaScript and newer versions of Pascal (with different syntax; JavaScript calls it a `try-catch`).

Interactive Loop #2

JavaScript

```
NewValue = LowLimit - 1 ;
while (NewValue < LowLimit) or (NewValue > HighLimit) {
    NewValue = parseInt(window.prompt("Enter a value")) ;
}
```

Python 2

```
NewValue = LowLimit - 1
while (NewValue < LowLimit) or (NewValue > HighLimit):
    NewValue = input("Enter a value: ")
```

Python 3

```
NewValue = LowLimit - 1
while (NewValue < LowLimit) or (NewValue > HighLimit):
    NewValue = int(input("Enter a value: "))
```

Python 3 with Error Correction

```
NewValue = LowLimit - 1
while (NewValue < LowLimit) or (NewValue > HighLimit):
    try:
        NewValue = int(input("Enter a value: "))
    except:
        NewValue = LowLimit - 1
```

Pascal

```
NewValue := LowLimit - 1 ;
While (NewValue < LowLimit) Or (NewValue > HighLimit) Do
    Begin
        Write ('Enter a value: ') ;
        Readln (NewValue) ;
    End ;
```

Interactive Loop #3

Some languages support a loop type where the exit test is performed at the *bottom* of the loop instead of at the top. In those languages the following structure is appropriate for interactive code:

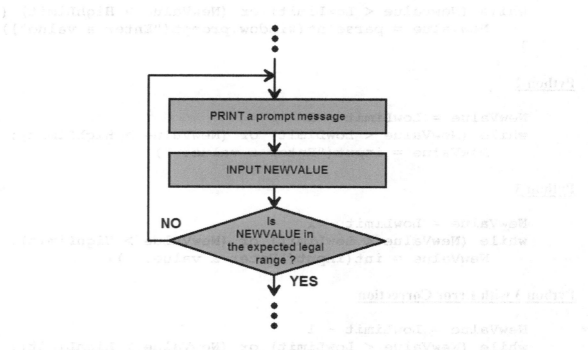

In this case the user is forced to enter a value *before* the first test to see if it is valid. If the value is not valid the loop goes back to the input statements and asks for a new value, and this process repeats until the value is indeed valid. When the value is finally legal the loop exits.

Interactive Loop #3

This type of loop is available in JavaScript but not in Python. Pascal does have a matching structure, but notice that its exit condition is the *opposite* of that in JavaScript. A JavaScript loop performs the loop body <u>while the condition **is** true</u>, but the Pascal loop performs the loop body <u>until the condition **becomes** true</u>.

JavaScript

```
do {
    NewValue = parseInt(window.prompt("Enter a value")) ;
} while (NewValue < LowLimit) or (NewValue > HighLimit) ;
```

Python

There is no direct equivalent to this structure in Python, but it can be simulated with an extra bool (true-false) variable and a while-loop. In this version variable More is set to True at the beginning of the loop to force the while-loop to execute the loop body at least once. The true or false result of the test at the end of the loop is assigned to More, which will be discovered by the while-loop in the very next step.

```
More = True
while (More):
    NewValue = int(input("Enter a value: "))
    More = (NewValue < LowLimit) or (NewValue > HighLimit)
```

or with error checking:

```
More = True
while (More):
    try:
        NewValue = int(input("Enter a value: "))
    except:
        NewValue = LowLimit - 1
    More = (NewValue < LowLimit) or (NewValue > HighLimit)
```

Pascal

```
Repeat
    Write ('Enter a value: ') ;
    Readln (NewValue) ;
Until (NewValue >= LowLimit) and (NewValue <= HighLimit) ;
```

Building Strings and Lists #1

Building up a string or list incrementally requires both a counter loop and the notion of adding a new item to an already existing string or list. The following two flowcharts show the process of building a variable called `Result`, on the left building a string of 10 **X** characters ("XXXXXXXXXX"), and on the right building a list containing the integers 0 through 9 ([0,1,2,3,4,5,6,7,8,9]). While both of these *particular* values can be created by brute force (that is, `Result = "XXXXXXXXXX"` or `Result = [0,1,2,3,4,5,6,7,8,9]`), creating strings or lists containing hundreds or thousands of items (or an unknown number of items specified by the user when the program is running) is not practical without a counter loop to control the number of items that are concatenated to the result. In each example below, change the loop exit test to something like `Is Counter < 10000 ?` to make this clear.

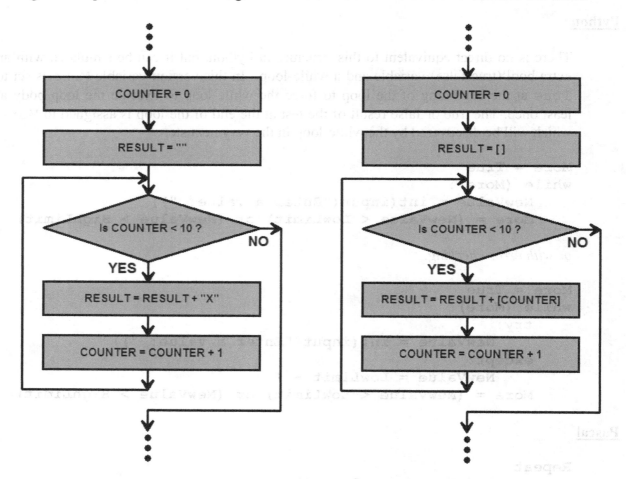

The `Result` variable is initialized to an empty string or an empty list, and the counter loop concatenates a new item onto the end of `Result` the correct number of times (here, ten times).

Building Strings and Lists #1

JavaScript (Strings only, no Lists)

```
Counter = 0 ;
Result = "" ;                  // Initialize to empty string
while (Counter < 10) {
    Result = Result + "X" ;
    Counter = Counter + 1 ;
}
```

Python

```
Counter = 0
Result = ""                    # Initialize to empty string
while (Counter < 10):
    Result = Result + "X"
    Counter = Counter + 1
```

```
Counter = 0
Result = []                    # Initialize to empty list
while (Counter < 10):
    Result = Result + [Counter]
    Counter = Counter + 1
```

Pascal (Strings only on later versions, no Lists)

```
Counter := 0 ;
Result := '' ;                 (* Initialize to empty string *)
While (Counter < 10) Do
    Begin
        Result := Result + 'X' ;
        Counter := Counter + 1 ;
    End ;
```

Notice that in each example, the new items appended to the end of `Result` must be of the same data type as `Result`. If `Result` is a string, then the new item *must also* be a string (surrounded by quotes). If `Result` is a list, then the new item *must also* be a list (surrounded by square brackets). In the Python list example, omitting the square brackets will cause the program to <u>fail</u> because `Result` and `Counter` are <u>different data types</u> (string and integer, respectively). `Counter` *must* be enclosed in square brackets to create a list of one item that can be concatenated with the list in `Result`:

```
Result = Result + Counter      # This fails
Result = Result + [Counter]    # This is correct
```

Building Strings and Lists #2

While a counter loop is always an effective way to construct a list or a string, it is often simpler to forgo the counter entirely and use the length of the string or the length of the list directly as the mechanism for controlling the loop. The left flowchart below shows the process for building a string of 10 **X** characters ("XXXXXXXXXX") and the right flowchart shows how to build a list containing ten copies of some variable **X** (which could itself be a string or a number or some other data type).

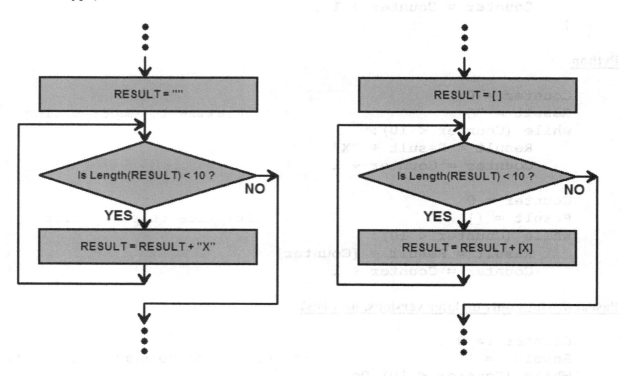

Note that in both cases the variable Result could be initialized to some value other than an empty string or an empty list. For example, in the string version on the left, if the first statement was Result = "Frog", the code will pad Result out to ten characters "FrogXXXXXX", appending six more "X" characters to the right side of Result. Similarly, if the loop payload statement was Result = "X" + Result the code would create the string "XXXXXXFrog" (appending the six "X" characters to the left side instead of to the right).

Note also that the appended character could be a blank (" ") instead of "X" in order to left-justify (Result = Result + " ") or right-justify (Result = " " + Result) a string into a fixed number of characters. Variable Result is not altered in either case if its initial value already contained 10 or more characters.

Building Strings and Lists #2

JavaScript (Strings only, no Lists)

```
Result = "" ;                   // Initialize to empty string
while (Result.length < 10) {
    Result = Result + "X" ;
}
```

Python

```
Result = ""                     # Initialize to empty string
while (len(Result) < 10):
    Result = Result + "X"


Result = []                     # Initialize to empty list
while (len(Result) < 10):
    Result = Result + [X]


Result = input("Enter a short string: ")
while (len(Result) < 10):
    Result = Result + " "       # Left-justify the string


Result = input("Enter a short string: ")
while (len(Result) < 10):
    Result = " " + Result       # Right-justify the string
```

Pascal (Strings only on later versions, no Lists)

```
Result := '' ;                  (* Initialize to empty string *)
While (Length(Result) < 10) Do
    Begin
        Result := Result + 'X' ;
    End ;
```

Stepping Around a Circle

A common task in computational geometry applications is to step through increasing angles (in radians) around the circumference of a circle by taking some fixed number of steps. There are several obvious and not-so-obvious ways to accomplish this, but some of the simplest methods can suffer from round-off errors that in the worst case cause the code to take the wrong number of steps, and in the best case generate angles that are slightly off from what they should be. These problems occur in the following two flowcharts. In both cases the *number of steps* to take around the circle is defined by integer variable Segments, which has a value of 3 or greater, and the *change in angle* between steps is computed in variable Step as 2π/Segments.

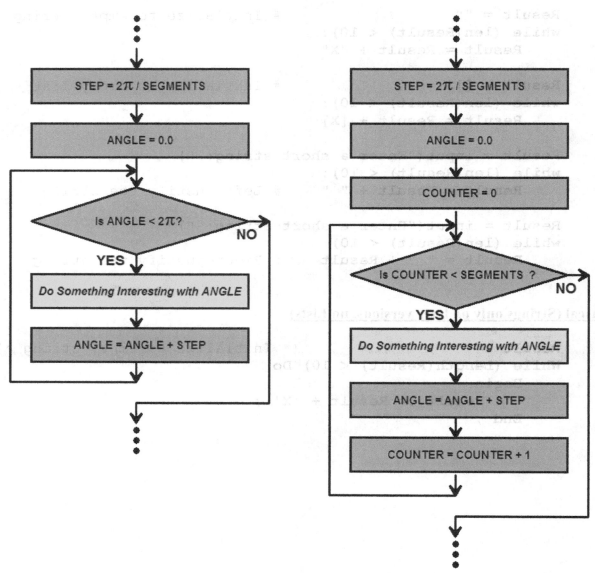

The version on the left is both simple and *mathematically* correct, but is wrong *computationally* because of round-off error in Step. This error accumulates in Angle such that its expected stopping value might not hit 2π exactly, but may be slightly too small, giving one extra step.

Stepping Around a Circle (Preferred)

The second version on the previous page avoids the problem of the first version by taking *exactly* Segments steps through use of a counter-loop, but as before the error in Angle accumulates over time.

Rather than generate a value for Angle from its previous value, however, the version on this page computes Angle directly from multiplying together the values of Step and Counter. While round-off errors are still present in Angle (due to the unavoidable round-off error in Step), it does *not accumulate* over time.

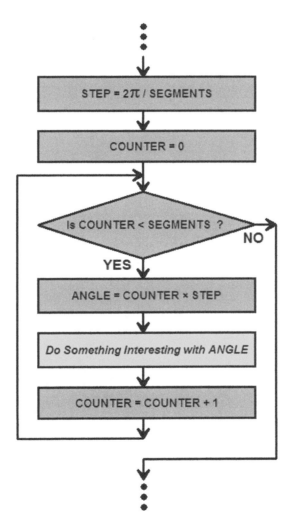

The "do something interesting" block often uses Angle to compute the *<x,y>* coordinates of the corresponding point on the circumference of the circle. If the circle's radius is known, then the coordinates are computed as follows:

```
X = Radius × Cosine(Angle)
Y = Radius × Sine(Angle)
```

Stepping Around a Circle (Preferred)

The second version on the previous page avoids the problem of the first version by taking every segment's steps through use of a counter-loop, but as before the error in x is the accumulates over time.

Rather than generate a value for ANGLE from its previous value, the version on this page computes ANGLE directly from multiplying together the values of COUNTER and STEPSIZE. While round-off errors are still present in ANGLE (if either value is not exactly representable in binary), it does not accumulate over time.

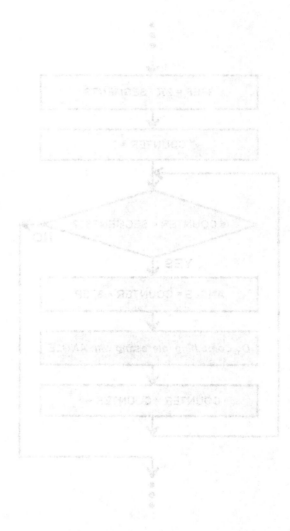

The do something interesting block often uses ANGLE to compute the x-y coordinates of the corresponding point on the circumference of the circle with radius RADIUS, in which case then the coordinates are computed as follows:

$$X = Radius \times Cosine(Angle)$$
$$Y = Radius \times Sine(Angle)$$

13: *JavaScript Reference Manual*

JavaScript (not to be confused with Java) is the scripting language built in to most Web browsers today. No complete coverage is possible, of course, but it is hoped that enough background has been presented here to allow users to branch out and create their own code for their own unique requirements.

JavaScript has an interesting relationship with HTML, particularly with HTML forms. There are several ideas that need examination:

1:    JavaScript can be used in Web pages where HTML code needs to be dynamically generated when the page is loaded (generating a table of 1000 square roots in a Web page, for example, can be accomplished in a very few lines of JavaScript). No HTML forms are needed in this case.

2:    In Web pages that <u>do</u> use the <FORM>...</FORM> tag, the form data can be "submitted" to a remote server for processing there (such as when something is ordered on-line). No JavaScript is needed in this case. This was covered in the chapter on Web design.

3:    At the intersection, however, is the case where an HTML form describes and controls bits of geometry on-screen (including text boxes, buttons, check-boxes, and radio-buttons, as well as HTML objects such as images), and JavaScript is the "glue" that couples an action such as a button-click with a response (updating a computation in a text box, changing an image reference, etc.). Web pages designed this way are highly interactive, and many Web games use this technique. That is, the game is played in the browser directly, and does not require a live Internet connection.

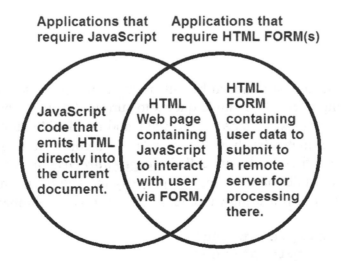

JavaScript Simple Data Types

Unlike many languages, JavaScript has a very limited number of distinct data types. This has both advantages and disadvantages for the programmer.

Numbers

Unlike languages that make a distinction between integers and floats (like Python and Pascal), <u>all</u> numbers in JavaScript are represented internally in the 64-bit double-precision floating-point format. Numbers may be written with or without a decimal point, with or without digits to the right of the decimal point, and with or without an e or E followed by an (positive or negative) exponent. Here are some examples:

```
1234
1234.5678
1.234e8      same as    123400000
1.234e+8     same as    123400000
1.234E+8     same as    123400000
1.234e-8     same as    0.00000001234
1.234E-8     same as    0.00000001234
```

Booleans

Booleans are values that can result from conditional expressions such as X < Y. Depending on the values of X and Y, the result of the expression is either true (X is less than Y) or false (X is not less than Y). There are only two Boolean constants, and they must be typed in lower case:

```
true
false
```

Strings

Strings are lists of characters surrounded by either single quotes or double quotes. The quotes are not part of the string itself. Use single quotes to surround a string that must contain double quotes (such as `'type="text/javascript"'`), and use double quotes to surround a string that must contain single quotes (such as `"don't"`). Use codes starting with the backslash to embed special characters; these codes are called ***escape characters*** and are shown in the table on the next page. String variables have a length property that returns the number of characters in the string. For example, if X is a string variable, X.length is the number of characters in X.

```
"This is a simple string"
'This is a simple string'
"This string 'likes' single quotes"
"C:\\Users\\Bill\\Desktop\\"    (Backslashes entered as escape characters
                                  to specify Windows path names)
```

JavaScript Escape Characters

All escape characters start with a backslash. To get a literal backslash, type two in a row. Many escape characters are for non-printing characters such as new lines, and a few have HTML entity equivalents. As Web browsers, and by extension JavaScript, must deal with many languages, support for Unicode is available, but the Unicode character must be entered by its two-digit or four-digit hexadecimal value.

Escape	Unicode	Meaning	HTML Entity	
\"	\u0022	Double Quote (")	"	"
\'	\u0027	Single Quote (')		'
\\	\u005C	Backslash (\)		\
	\u00A0	Non-Breaking Space		
\b	\u0008	ASCII Backspace		
\f	\u000C	ASCII Formfeed		
\n	\u000A	ASCII Linefeed (new line)		
\r	\u000D	ASCII Carriage Return		
\t	\u0009	ASCII Tab		
\v	\u000B	ASCII Vertical Tab		
\xdd	\u00dd	ASCII Character (dd is two hex digits)		
\udddd	\udddd	Unicode Character (dddd is four hex digits)		

JavaScript Structure

JavaScript is ***free-form***. Statements may be written one per line, spread across many lines, or many statements per line (unlike Python, which is written strictly one statement per line). Semicolons are used to separate statements. If a statement naturally ends at a line break the semicolon is optional, but using them is always the preferred style, and they are required when writing multiple statements per line. For example, the following structures are all equivalent:

No Semicolons
(Not Recommended)
```
X = 5
Y = 6
Z = X + Y
```

Semicolons
(Preferred)
```
X = 5 ;
Y = 6 ;
Z = X + Y ;
```

Multiple Statements per Line,
One Statement Split Across Lines
```
X = 5 ; Y = 6 ; Z =
X + Y ;
```

Curly braces are used to group statements together in a block, such as in an `if` or `while` (the semicolon is optional before the closing brace):

```
if (A < B) { X = 5 ; Y = 6 ; Z = X + Y }
```

JavaScript uses ***dynamic typing***. This means that a variable can be assigned an integer one time, and assigned a string some time later. Variables are ***case sensitive*** (variable X and variable x are different). It is not recommended practice to use two variable names that differ only by case.

JavaScript Comments

There are two ways to specify comments in JavaScript. The first is to put two slashes in a row; the rest of the line after the `//` is then ignored. The other form is to bracket the text, even across multiple lines, by `/*` and `*/` symbols.

JavaScript Assignments

Essentially all languages support assignment of value to variable, and JavaScript is no exception:

```
variable = expression ;
```

The expression is first evaluated, and then the variable receives its value. The equal sign is thought of as "is assigned" or "gets the value of"; the variable gets the value of the expression. The expression is thus allowed to reference the <u>old</u> value of the variable before it takes on its <u>new</u> value. Here are some examples (notice the semicolons and the dynamic typing):

```
X = 5 ;           // Variable X gets number 5
X = "Frog" ;      // Variable X gets string "Frog" (5 is gone)
X = 6 ;           // Variable X gets number 6 ("Frog" is gone)
X = X + 1 ;       // Variable X gets number 7
```

Multiple variables are allowed to receive the same value at (essentially) the same time:

```
X = Y = Z = 5 ;       // Z = 5, then Y = Z, then X = Y
```

Statements of the form `variable = variable operator value` may be condensed into a more efficient form whenever the variable on the left side of the equal sign is <u>the same</u> as the variable on the right. The following statements are equivalent (all math operators supported):

```
X = X + 1 ;     is the same as    X += 1 ;
X = X - 1 ;     is the same as    X -= 1 ;
X = X * 2 ;     is the same as    X *= 2 ;
X = X / Y ;     is the same as    X /= Y ;
```

There are even more efficient shortcuts, but care must be taken in their use. To increment (add 1 to) a variable use `++` and to decrement (subtract 1 from) a variable use `--` instead:

```
X++ ;      // Postfix increment: Use X, increment X after
X-- ;      // Postfix decrement: Use X, decrement X after
++X ;      // Prefix  increment: Increment X, use X after
--X ;      // Prefix  decrement: Decrement X, use X after
```

The difference is in <u>when</u> the increment or decrement takes place: the expression `Y = X++ ;` is the same as `{ Y = X ; X = X + 1 }`, but the nearly identical expression `Y = ++X ;` is the same as `{ X = X + 1 ; Y = X }`, which has a very different result.

JavaScript Array Type

An array is a list of values of any data type surrounded by square brackets and separated by commas. The first item is at position 0, the second is at position 1, etc. Usually, literal array constants are assigned to variables for later use:

```
var Names = ["Fred", "Sam", "Mary"] ;
var Years = [1969, 1492, 1066, 2001] ;
```

In these examples, `Names[0]` contains the string `"Fred"`, `Names[1]` contains the string `"Sam"`, and `Names[2]` contains the string `"Mary"`. Similarly, `Years[0]` contains the number `1969`, `Years[1]` contains the number `1492`, and so on. Array references may be on either the left or the right side of an assignment statement:

```
X = Names[0] ;        // X gets "Fred", Names[0] is unchanged
Names[0] = "Bob" ;  // "Fred" replaced by "Bob" in Names[0]
```

The size of an array may be obtained from its `length` property. For the arrays given above, `Names.length` is the value 3, and `Years.length` is the value 4.

JavaScript Object Type

An object is a list of ***key-value*** pairs surrounded by curly braces, where each key-value pair is a key, a colon, and a value, and each key-value pair is separated from the next by a comma:

```
var Frog = {Name:"Kermit", Color:"Green", Age:30}
```

To access a property of the variable `Frog`, append a dot and the name of the property. `Frog.Name` contains the string `"Kermit"`, `Frog.Color` contains the string `"Green"`, and `Frog.Age` contains the number `30`.

To erase a property of an object, delete it:

```
delete Frog.Name ;
```

To ask if an object contains a property use the `in` operator (the property name must be quoted):

```
if ("Name" in Frog) { … }
```

As with arrays, object properties may be on either side of an assignment statement. If the property doesn't currently exist when a value is assigned to it, the property is created:

```
X = Frog.Name ;       // X gets "Kermit"
Frog.Name = "Bob" ; // "Kermit" replaced by "Bob"
```

JavaScript Operator Precedence

LEVEL	OPERATOR	MEANING	EXAMPLE	EXPLANATION OR USAGE
HIGH	()	Grouping	X = (2 * (3 + 4)) ;	Parentheses override order of operations
	.	Member Access	X = Frog.Name ;	Object element (Name field of Frog object)
	[]	Computed Member Access	X = MyArray[5] ;	Array element (first one at MyArray[0])
	new ƒ (…)	new (with argument list)	X = new Date(A,B) ;	Returns a new object
	ƒ (…)	Function Call	X = MyFunction(Y) ;	Calls MyFunction, X gets return value
	new	new (without argument list)	X = new Date ;	Same as: X = new Date() ;
	++	Postfix Increment	X = Y++ ;	{ X = Y ; Y = Y + 1 }
	--	Postfix Decrement	X = Y-- ;	{ X = Y ; Y = Y - 1 }
	!	Logical NOT	X = !Y ;	!true=false, !false=true
	~	Bitwise NOT	X = ~Y ;	~0001 = 1110 (one's complement)
	+	Unary Plus	X = +Y ;	Does not change value
	-	Unary Negation	X = -Y ;	Negates (changes sign)
	++	Prefix Increment	X = ++Y ;	{ Y = Y + 1 ; X = Y }
	--	Prefix Decrement	X = --Y ;	{ Y = Y - 1 ; X = Y }
	typeof	typeof	S = typeof(X) ;	"number", "string", "boolean", "object", "function", "undefined"
	void	void	void expr ;	Evaluate expression, return undefined.
	delete	delete	delete Frog.Name ;	Removes property from object.
	*	Multiplication	X = Y * Z ;	2 * 5 = 10
	/	Division	X = Y / Z ;	5 / 2 = 2.5
	%	Remainder	X = Y % Z ;	5 % 2 = 1
	+	Addition	X = Y + Z ;	2 + 5 = 7
	-	Subtraction	X = Y - Z ;	2 - 5 = -3
	<<	Bitwise Left Shift	X = Y << Z ;	0100 << 1 = 1000
	>>	Bitwise Right Shift	X = Y >> Z ;	0100 >> 1 = 0010
	>>>	Bitwise Unsigned Right Shift	X = Y >>> Z ;	1001… >>> 1 = 01001… (sign=0)
	<	Less Than	X < Y	All conditionals return either true or
	<=	Less Than Or Equal to	X <= Y	false. Typically used in if or while
	>	Greater Than	X > Y	statements:
	>=	Greater Than Or Equal to	X >= Y	if (X < Y) { … }
	in	in	X in Y	while (X < Y) { … }
	instanceof	instanceof	X instanceof Y	if ("Name" in Frog) { … }
	==	Equality	X == Y	Tests for equality compare across types:
	!=	Inequality	X != Y	(5==5) and (5=="5") are both true.
	===	Strict Equality	X === Y	Strict equality requires identical types:
	!==	Strict Inequality	X !== Y	(5===5) is true, (5==="5") is false.
	&	Bitwise AND	X = Y & Z ;	1101 & 0011 = 0001
	^	Bitwise XOR	X = Y ^ Z ;	1101 ^ 0011 = 1110
	|	Bitwise OR	X = Y | Z ;	1101 | 0011 = 1111
	&&	Logical AND	X = Y && Z ;	Only true if both arguments true
	||	Logical OR	X = Y || Z ;	Only false if both arguments false
	□ ? □ : □	Conditional	X = Y < Z ? M : N ;	if (Y < Z) {X=M} else {X=N}
	=	Assignment	X = Y ;	X = Y ;
	+=	Addition Assignment	X += Y ;	X = X + Y ;
	-=	Subtraction Assignment	X -= Y ;	X = X - Y ;
	*=	Multiplication Assignment	X *= Y ;	X = X * Y ;
	/=	Division Assignment	X /= Y ;	X = X / Y ;
	%=	Modulo Assignment	X %= Y ;	X = X % Y ;
	<<=	Bitwise Left Shift Assign.	X <<= Y ;	X = X << Y ;
	>>=	Bitwise Right Shift Assign.	X >>= Y ;	X = X >> Y ;
	>>>=	Unsigned Right Shift Assign.	X >>>= Y ;	X = X >>> Y ;
	&=	Bitwise AND Assignment	X &= Y ;	X = X & Y ;
	^=	Bitwise XOR Assignment	X ^= Y ;	X = X ^ Y ;
	|=	Bitwise OR Assignment	X |= Y ;	X = X | Y;
	yield	yield	These operators involve "iterators", special functions that allow for	
	yield*	yield*	efficient stepping through an object or collection.	
	...	Spread		
LOW	,	Comma / Sequence	expr, expr, expr	Most often used in for-loops

JavaScript Dialogs

There are a number of mechanisms available for getting information into and out of a JavaScript program while it is running. These are all in the form of dialog boxes that pop up when activated and disappear when closed. The dialogs belong to the `window` object, which is specified as part of the call to the dialog function (it may be omitted, but its use is generally preferred).

Alert

Use the `alert` dialog to inform the user of something. The function has one argument, which is a string or an object that can be turned into a string, and has the form(s):

```
alert(message) ;              // window omitted
window.alert(message) ;       // preferred version
```

For example:

```
window.alert("Hello") ;
window.alert("The answer is " + 5) ;
```

Confirm

Use the `confirm` dialog to get from the user a yes-or-no answer. The function has one string argument, and has the form:

```
variable = window.confirm(message) ;
```

For example:

```
X = window.confirm("Are you OK?") ;
```

The result will be `true` if the user clicks OK, and `false` if the user clicks Cancel.

Prompt

Use the `prompt` dialog to get a text string from the user. The function has two string arguments (the question being asked and the default answer), and has the form:

```
variable = window.prompt(message, default) ;
```

For example:

```
X = window.prompt("Where do you live?", "USA") ;
```

The default string is `"USA"`, but the user can type in something else instead. The result will be the entered string if the user clicks OK, and `null` if the user clicks Cancel.

JavaScript Program Structures

Functions

```
function name (parameter, parameter, …, parameter) {
    variable = expression ;      // Global variable
    var variable = expression ;  // Local variable
    // statement
    return
}

function name (parameter, parameter, …, parameter) {
    variable = expression ;      // Global variable
    var variable = expression ;  // Local variable
    // statement
    return expression
}
```

Example:

```
function MyFunction (X,Y) {
    var Result = Math.sqrt(X*X + Y*Y) ;
    return Result
}
```

Conditional Execution

```
if (expression) {                   if (expression) {
    // statement 1                      // statement 1
}                                   } else if (expression) {
                                        // statement 2
                                    } else {
                                        // statement 3
                                    }

switch(expression) {
    case x:
        // statement 1
        break ;
    case y:
        // statement 2
        break ;
    default:
        // statement 3
}
```

JavaScript Program Structures (Continued)

Loops

```
while (expression) {
    // statement
}
```

Expression is tested before any statements get executed. If `true`, statements are executed and expression is tested again. Loops until expression becomes `false`. If initially `false`, the statements will not be executed at all.

```
do {
    // statement
} while (expression) ;
```

Statements are executed before expression is tested. If expression is `true`, statements are executed again. Loops until expression becomes `false`. If initially `false`, the statements will still be executed once. (Similar to the `Repeat-Until` loop of Pascal, with the exit condition reversed.)

```
for (init ; test ; update) {
    // statement
}
```

Typically, the `init` statement initializes the loop control variable, the `test` returns `true` while the loop should proceed, and the `update` changes the loop control variable.

Example:

```
for (I=0 ; I<10 ; I++) { ____ }
```

Exceptions (Error Handling)

```
try {
    // statement
}
catch (argument) {
    // statement
}
finally {
    // statement
}
```

The `try` block contains statements that may or may not generate an error (such as an undefined variable or function call that uses the wrong name). If an error occurs, the `catch` code block will handle it. The `argument` is the name of an object variable that will contain the text of the error. The `catch` block will <u>not</u> be executed if no error occurred. Regardless of whether or not there was an error, the `finally` code block will always execute. Both the `catch` and `finally` blocks are optional, but at least one must be present.

Example:

```
try { X = Q + 1 ; }     // variable Q was never defined
catch (MyBad) { window.alert (MyBad.message) ; }
finally { window.alert ("All done") ; }
```

JavaScript Global Functions

`Infinity`	Numeric infinity	`X = Infinity ;`
`NaN`	Not-a-Number	`X = NaN ;`
`undefined`	Undefine a variable	`X = undefined ;`
`null`	Absence of an object value	`X = null ;`

`decodeURI()` — Convert special hex codes back except `#$&+,/:;=?@`.
```
decodeURI("%41%26") = "A%26"
```

`decodeURIComponent()` — Convert <u>all</u> special hex codes back into uncoded version.
```
decodeURIComponent("%41%26") = "A&"
```

`encodeURI()` — Replace special characters such as blanks in URL with `%` and two-digit hex codes so that a browser can handle it:
```
encodeURI("/X Y.html") = "/X%20Y.html"
```

`encodeURIComponent()` — Replace <u>all</u> specials including `#$&+,/:;=?@` in a URL:
```
encodeURIComponent("http://www.x.com/")
= "http%3A%2F%2Fwww.x.com%2F"
```

`eval($S$)` — Evaluate string S and return its numeric value
```
eval("4+5") = 9
```

`isFinite($X$)` — Is X a number?
```
isFinite(3) = true
isFinite(NaN) = false
isFinite(Infinity) = false
```

`isNaN($X$)` — Is X a NaN?
```
isNaN(3) = false
isNaN(NaN) = true
isNaN(Infinity) = false
```

`Number($X$)` — Convert X into a number object (see functions next page).
```
Number("3.4") = 3.4
```

`parseFloat($S$)` — Parse string S into a float.
```
parseFloat("3.4") = 3.4
```

`parseInt($S$)` — Parse string S into an integer.
```
parseInt("3.4") = 3
```

`String($X$)` — Convert value X into a string.
```
String(4+5) = "9"
```

JavaScript Number Functions

Number.EPSILON
Smallest possible representable difference in numbers
`2.220446049250313E-16`, 2^{-52}

Number.MAX_SAFE_INTEGER
Largest representable integer in continuous group
`9007199254740991`, $+2^{53}-1$

Number.MAX_VALUE
Largest representable number
`1.7976931348623157e+308`

Number.MIN_SAFE_INTEGER
Smallest representable integer in continuous group
`-9007199254740991`, $-(2^{53}-1)$

Number.MIN_VALUE
Smallest representable number `5e-324`

Number.NaN
Not-A_Number `NaN`

Number.NEGATIVE_INFINITY
Negative Infinity `-Infinity`

Number.POSITIVE_INFINITY
Positive Infinity `+Infinity`

Number.isFinite(*X***)**
Is X a number?
```
Number.isFinite(3) = true
Number.isFinite(NaN) = false
Number.isFinite(Infinity) = false
```

Number.isNaN(*X***)**
Is X a NaN?
```
Number.isNaN(3) = false
Number.isNaN(NaN) = true
Number.isNaN(Infinity) = false
```

Number.isSafeInteger(*X***)**
Is X a safe integer (between `MIN_SAFE_INTEGER` and `MAX_SAFE_INTEGER`)?
```
Number.isSafeInteger(3) = true
Number.isSafeInteger(3.4) = false
```

Number.parseFloat(*S***)**
Parse string S into a float.
```
Number.parseFloat("3.4") = 3.4
```

Number.parseInt(*S***)**
Parse string S into an integer.
```
Number.parseInt("3.4") = 3
```

JavaScript Math Functions

`Math.E`	Euler's Constant.	`2.718281828459045`
`Math.LN2`	Natural log of 2.	`0.6931471805599453`
`Math.LN10`	Natural log of 10.	`2.302585092994046`
`Math.LOG10E`	Common log of *e*.	`0.4342944819032518`
`Math.PI`	Pi (π).	`3.141592653589793`
`Math.SQRT1_2`	Square root of ½.	`0.7071067811865476`
`Math.SQRT2`	Square root of 2.	`1.4142135623730951`
`Math.abs(`*X*`)`	Absolute value (positive).	`Math.abs(-4) = 4`
`Math.acos(`*X*`)`	Arc cosine (in radians) of X.	`Math.acos(0) = 1.57...` ($\pi/2$)
`Math.asin(`*X*`)`	Arc sine (in radians) of X.	`Math.asin(1) = 1.57...` ($\pi/2$)
`Math.atan(`*X*`)`	Arc tangent (in radians) of X.	`Math.atan(1) = 0.78...` ($\pi/4$)
`Math.atan2(`*Y*`,`*X*`)`	Arc tangent (in radians) of Y/X.	`Math.atan(1,1) = 0.78...`
`Math.ceil(`*X*`)`	Smallest whole number $\geq$ X.	`Math.ceil(7.1) = 8.0`
`Math.cos(`*X*`)`	Cosine of X (in radians).	`Math.cos(0) = 1.0`
`Math.exp(`*X*`)`	e^X (where e=2.71828…).	`Math.exp(1) = 2.71828...`
`Math.floor(`*X*`)`	Largest whole number $\leq$ X.	`Math.floor(7.9) = 7.0`
`Math.log(`*X*`)`	Natural log (base *e*) of X.	`Math.log(Math.E) = 1.0`
`Math.max(`*X1*`,`*X2*`,…,`*Xn*`)`	Maximum of list.	`Math.max(3,7,2,5) = 7`
`Math.min(`*X1*`,`*X2*`,…,`*Xn*`)`	Minimum of list.	`Math.min(3,7,2,5) = 2`
`Math.pow(`*X*`,`*Y*`)`	X^Y power.	`Math.pow(4.0,2.0) = 16.0`
`Math.random()`	Random number ≥ 0, <1.	`Math.random()`

JavaScript Math Functions (Continued)

`Math.round(`*X*`)`	Closest integer to X
	(Round half up)
		`Math.round(3.4) = 3`
		`Math.round(3.5) = 4`
		`Math.round(3.6) = 4`

`Math.sine(`*X*`)`	Sine of X (in radians).	`Math.sin(Math.PI/2) = 1`
`Math.sqrt(`*X*`)`	Square root of X (X $\geq$ 0)	`Math.sqrt(16) = 4`
`Math.tan(`*X*`)`	Tangent of X (in radians).	`Math.tan(Math.PI/4) = 1`

JavaScript Date Functions

A date is an ***object*** that must be explicitly created with `new` (and often assigned to a variable). A date object's methods allow extraction of its various components. The first form creates a date using the current date and time from the system clock:

```
D = new Date()
```

The second form creates a user-defined date. The *year* and *month* parameters are required; all others are optional and if omitted use their default values (*day* = 1, *hours* = *minutes* = *seconds* = *milliseconds* = 0). The *month* parameter ranges from 0 (January) up through 11 (December).

```
D = new Date(year,month,day,hours,minutes,seconds,milliseconds)
```

Here are the date methods that allow extraction of the individual pieces of a date:

`getDate()`	Day of month, 1…31 (depending on month).
`getDay()`	Day of Week (0=Sunday, 1=Monday, …, 6=Saturday).
`getMonth()`	Month of Year (0=January, 1=February, …, 11=December).
`getYear()`	Year minus 1900; two-digit year for 20TH Century (deprecated).
`getFullYear()`	Four-digit Year (preferred instead of `getYear()`).
`getHours()`	Hours since midnight of current day (military time), 0…23.
`getMinutes()`	Minutes since start of current hour, 0…59.
`getSeconds()`	Seconds since start of current minute, 0…59.
`getMilliseconds()`	Milliseconds since start of current second (0…999).

Usage of these methods is to express the name of the date variable, a dot, and then the method name. For example, the following statement extracts the year component from a date stored in variable D (as defined above) and assigns that value to variable `MyYear`:

```
MyYear = D.getFullYear() ;
```

JavaScript to HTML Linking

JavaScript code may be placed into an HTML document inside a `<SCRIPT>`...`</SCRIPT>` tag pair, which may be either in the `<HEAD>`...`</HEAD>` section (usually functions go there) or in the `<BODY>`...`</BODY>` section (usually computations and calls to functions go there). The opening tag can be in any of three forms, although the first one is deprecated and its use is no longer recommended:

```
<SCRIPT LANGUAGE="JavaScript">      ...    </SCRIPT> (deprecated)
<SCRIPT TYPE="text/javascript">     ...    </SCRIPT> (preferred)
<SCRIPT>                            ...    </SCRIPT> (allowed)
```

The only language currently supported is JavaScript, so it is not strictly necessary to specify the language, but including the `TYPE="text/javascript"` attribute allows for the possibility that other languages may be available at some point in the future.

JavaScript code may also be placed into an external file with a `.js` file extension and linked from within a Web page:

```
<SCRIPT TYPE="text/javascript" SRC="file.js"></SCRIPT>
```

JavaScript normally ignores any text inside an `<NOSCRIPT>`...`</NOSCRIPT>` tag pair. However, some Web browsers cannot interpret JavaScript, or a user may have disabled JavaScript on their browser. In such cases any HTML that is present inside a `<NOSCRIPT>`...`</NOSCRIPT>` tag pair is then activated. JavaScript code is often embedded directly inside an HTML Web page, but in browsers where JavaScript isn't supported, any JavaScript code would appear as text in the Web page unless steps were taken to block it. A combination of HTML comments (`<!--` ... `-->`) and JavaScript comments (`//`) are used to hide code in this situation. Proper Web design then results in the following general approach:

```
<SCRIPT TYPE="text/javascript">
    <!--
        JavaScript code goes here
    //-->
</SCRIPT>

<NOSCRIPT>
    HTML goes here to show when JavaScript is disabled
</NOSCRIPT>
```

If JavaScript is supported, it ignores the `<!--` opening HTML comment, and its own `//` hides the `-->` HTML closing comment, allowing the code to run. If JavaScript is not supported, the `<SCRIPT>` and `</SCRIPT>` tags are ignored by the browser, the HTML comment hides all of the JavaScript code, and the `<NOSCRIPT>`...`</NOSCRIPT>` shows alternate information.

JavaScript and HTML

JavaScript can emit code directly into the current HTML document as the Web page is being rendered. Doing so requires the `document` object, and the `writeln` function. Any strings written into the document must contain properly configured HTML. Here is a simple example:

```
<!DOCTYPE html>

<HTML>
    <HEAD>
        <TITLE>Simple JavaScript Linking</TITLE>
    </HEAD>

    <BODY>
        <SCRIPT TYPE="text/javascript">
            <!--
                document.writeln ("<H1>Hello!</H1>") ;
                document.writeln ("<P>Here is some text</P>") ;
            //-->
        </SCRIPT>
    </BODY>
</HTML>
```

This is not a good use of JavaScript. However, the full power of JavaScript gives something that is extremely difficult to pull off otherwise. The following code writes the square roots of the first 1000 integers into the current document. Generating a million lines requires only changing the loop limit. The "`<BR>`" in the `writeln` makes each square root appear on a separate line.

```
<!DOCTYPE html>

<HTML>
    <HEAD>
        <TITLE>Simple JavaScript Linking</TITLE>
    </HEAD>

    <BODY>
        <SCRIPT TYPE="text/javascript">
            <!--
                for (I=0 ; I<1000 ; I++) {
                    X = Math.sqrt(I) ;
                    document.writeln(X, "<BR>") ;
                }
            //-->
        </SCRIPT>
    </BODY>
</HTML>
```

JavaScript Events

Events in JavaScript are when something happens caused by the user (such as a mouse click or key press) or by the browser (loading a page). They can be associated with most (but not all) HTML *elements* such as <IMG> or <INPUT> (buttons, text boxes, etc.), or even elements not generally associated with events such as <P> or <H1>. The general form of an event trigger embedded in an HTML tag is: <*element onEvent*="*handler*">, where element is the HTML tag name, onEvent is the name of a particular type of event (from the list below), and handler is most often the name of a JavaScript function to call when the event is triggered. An input button that calls MyFunction when clicked with the mouse would be written as:

```
<INPUT TYPE="button" onclick="MyFunction() ;">
```

Mouse Events

onclick	Left-click element.
oncontextmenu	Right-click element.
ondblclick	Double-click element.
onmousedown	Press any mouse button while on element.
onmouseenter	Mouse enters element.
onmouseleave	Mouse exits element.
onmousemove	Move moves over element.
onmouseover	Move moves over element or any child elements.
onmouseout	Mouse exits element or any child elements.
onmouseup	Release mouse button.

Keyboard Events (most often used on <INPUT TYPE="text"> boxes).

onkeydown	When <u>any</u> key is pressed, even Alt, Ctrl, etc.
onkeypress	When an <u>enterable</u> key is pressed.
onkeyup	When <u>any</u> key is released.

Frame Events

onerror	Triggered when an error loading an <IMG> image occurs.
onload	Triggered when an object is loaded (often used on <BODY> to indicate when page finishes loading).

Form Events

onchange	Triggered when an object changes, such as a radio button, checkbox, text input area (when user clicks outside of field), etc.
onsubmit	Triggered when user hits a "submit" button. Often used to validate form entries before sending form contents to a remote script.

JavaScript Events (Example)

This Web page uses three `.gif` images to simulate a 3D push-button. The default view is flat, without 3D (the crosshatching is not part of the image, and does not appear on screen). When the mouse rolls over the image the `onmouseover` event triggers JavaScript function `Show` to reach back into the form `MyForm` to change the image source (`src`) associated with the name `MyButton` to the view of an unclicked 3D button. When the image is clicked, `onmousedown` calls `Click` to change the view to the button pushed-in, and also perform some action. When the mouse is released, `onmouseup` calls `Show` again, and when the mouse moves out of the image `onmouseout` calls `Hide` to change the button back to the default.

```
<!DOCTYPE html>

<HTML>
    <HEAD>
        <TITLE>Button Rollover Test</TITLE>

        <SCRIPT TYPE="text/javascript">
            <!--
                function Show () {
                    document.MyForm.MyButton.src="Normal.gif" ;
                }

                function Hide () {
                    document.MyForm.MyButton.src="Default.gif" ;
                }

                function Click () {
                    document.MyForm.MyButton.src="Clicked.gif" ;
                    // Perform some action here
                }
            //-->
        </SCRIPT>
    </HEAD>

    <BODY BGCOLOR="#C0C0C0">
        <FORM NAME="MyForm">
            <IMG SRC="Default.gif" NAME="MyButton"
                onmouseover="Show();"     onmouseout="Hide();"
                onmousedown="Click();"    onmouseup="Show();">
        </FORM>
    </BODY>
</HTML>
```

14: *JavaScript Code Examples*

Here are some basic (and not so basic) examples of Web pages containing program code written in JavaScript. Anyone with a Web browser can write programs that do things. JavaScript is not the best environment for writing code, as programs tend not to tell you much when they crash, but it is how a lot of the Web works these days.

The examples here are of two major forms: Web pages that generate HTML code dynamically through JavaScript, and Web pages that interact with the user through JavaScript.

JavaScript List of Square Roots

Generate on-screen an unordered list of numbers from 1 to 100 and their square roots. The function definition is in the <HEAD> section, but the call to the function is in the <BODY> section. In the function the `document.writeln` statements write HTML code on-the-fly into the current Web page as it is being rendered by the browser.

```
<!DOCTYPE html>

<HTML>
  <HEAD>
    <TITLE>List of Square Roots</TITLE>

    <SCRIPT TYPE="text/javascript">
      <!--

      function SquareRoots () {
        document.writeln ("<UL>") ;
        I = 1 ;
        while (I <= 100) {
          document.writeln("<LI>Sqrt(", I, ") is ",
                                    Math.sqrt(I), "</LI>") ;
          I = I + 1 ;
        }
        document.writeln ("</UL>") ;
      }

      //-->
    </SCRIPT>
  </HEAD>

  <BODY>
    <SCRIPT TYPE="text/javascript">
      <!--
        SquareRoots () ;
      //-->
    </SCRIPT>
  </BODY>
</HTML>
```

JavaScript Bad Monster Movies

In this script, the JavaScript code is embedded directly into the `<BODY>` of the Web page, and again emits code into the current document as it runs. It emits 100 titles for bad monster movies, such as "Attack of the Slime people", directly into the Web page as it is being rendered. To do this, two arrays (`Verbs` and `Nouns`) must be defined and populated with values. In each pass of the main loop, one noun and one verb is chosen at random from the arrays, a movie title string is constructed, and the string is written into the current document as an entry in an unordered list.

```
<!DOCTYPE html>

<HTML>
  <HEAD>
    <TITLE>JavaScript Monster Movies</TITLE>
  </HEAD>

  <BODY>
    <SCRIPT TYPE="text/javascript">
    <!--

    var Verbs = ["Attack", "Escape", "Return", "Revenge"]
    var Nouns = ["Mole", "Zombie", "Moon", "Slime", "Monkey"]

    document.writeln ("<UL>") ;
    X = 1 ;
    while (X <= 100) {
      Verb = Verbs[Math.floor(Math.random() * Verbs.length)] ;
      Noun = Nouns[Math.floor(Math.random() * Nouns.length)] ;
      document.writeln ("<LI>") ;
      document.writeln (Verb + " of the " + Noun + " people");
      document.writeln ("</LI>") ;
      X = X + 1 ;
    }

    document.writeln ("</UL>") ;

    //-->
    </SCRIPT>

  </BODY>
</HTML>
```

JavaScript Factorial without Forms

Here is a script that like those shown earlier emits code into the current document. This time the function computes the factorial of an integer N (the product of all integers from 1 through N) passed into the function through its parameter list. The function only computes the desired value; the code that writes it into the document is in the <BODY> of the Web page.

```
<!DOCTYPE html>

<HTML>
  <HEAD>
    <TITLE>JavaScript Factorial without Forms</TITLE>

    <SCRIPT TYPE="text/javascript">
     <!--

     function Factorial (N) {
       var I = 1 ;
       var F = 1 ;
       while (I <= N) {
         F = F * I ;
         I = I + 1 ;
         }
       return (F) ;
     }

     //-->
    </SCRIPT>
  </HEAD>

  <BODY>
    <SCRIPT TYPE="text/javascript">
     <!--

     I = 1 ;
     while (I <= 171) {
       document.writeln ("I = ", I, " Factorial = ",
                         Factorial(I), "<BR>") ;
       I = I + 1 ;
     }

     //-->
    </SCRIPT>
  </BODY>
</HTML>
```

JavaScript Factorial with Forms

This version also computes factorials, but does so through a Web form. The form displays two edit boxes, one for the input number and one for the result. It also has a button, which when clicked calls function `Interactive`; that function communicates with both the form and the `Factorial` function. The user enters a number, clicks the button, and the answer is displayed. The colors make it easy to spot the form name and variable definitions, as well as their use.

```html
<!DOCTYPE html>

<HTML>
  <HEAD>
    <TITLE>JavaScript Factorial with Forms</TITLE>

    <SCRIPT TYPE="text/javascript">
      <!--

      function Factorial (N) {
        var I = 1 ;
        var F = 1 ;
        while (I <= N) {
          F = F * I ;
          I = I + 1
          }
        return (F) ;
      }

      function Interactive () {
        var N = parseFloat(document.MyForm.MyInput.value) ;
        document.MyForm.MyAnswer.value = String(Factorial(N)) ;
      }

      //-->
    </SCRIPT>
  </HEAD>

  <BODY>
    <FORM NAME="MyForm">
        <INPUT TYPE="text" NAME="MyInput"><BR>
        <INPUT TYPE="text" NAME="MyAnswer"><BR>
        <INPUT TYPE="button"
               VALUE="Factorial"
               onClick="Interactive();">
    </FORM>
  </BODY>
</HTML>
```

JavaScript Button Rollovers

The anchor tag <A> contains two attributes to call the ShowImage function when the user moves the mouse over the link and when the user moves the mouse away from the link. Each call tells ShowImage which of two graphics files (Clicked.png and Normal.png, both of which must be in the same folder as the Web page itself) is to be attached to the <IMG> in the link. This allows the graphic to change when the user moves in and out of the link area. The ShowImage function works by building up a string either as:

```
        document.MyButton1.src = "Normal.png"
```

or as:

```
        document.MyButton1.src = "Clicked.png"
```

and then executing (evaluating) that string as a command.

```html
<!DOCTYPE html>

<HTML>
  <HEAD>
    <TITLE>Button Rollover</TITLE>

    <SCRIPT TYPE="text/javascript">
      <!--

      function ShowImage (ItemName, ImageName) {
        eval ('document.'+ItemName+'.src = "'+ImageName+'"') ;
      }

      //-->
    </SCRIPT>
  </HEAD>

<BODY>
  <A HREF="http://www.cnn.com/"
    onMouseOver="ShowImage('MyButton1', 'Clicked.png') ;"
    onMouseOut="ShowImage('MyButton1', 'Normal.png') ;">
      <IMG SRC="Normal.png"
           NAME="MyButton1"
           STYLE="border-style:none">
  </A>

</BODY>
</HTML>
```

JavaScript Camera Watcher

This script has a function that every few seconds fetches an image file from a server somewhere and assigns it to an on-screen <IMG>. If the server updates the image on a regular basis, this Web page will monitor those changes. The <IMG> has no SRC attribute by default, but the Refresh function takes care of that with the document.MyImage.src statement. The URL has a new random number appended to it for every refresh; this is to ensure that the URL is different each time it loads, fooling the browser into fetching a new copy instead of using the stale version in the cache. The blank should be filled in with the address of an image that updates regularly; addresses that have worked in the past are shown at the bottom of the page (although there is no guarantee that they will update frequently, nor is there any guarantee that they will even continue to work at all).

```html
<!DOCTYPE html>

<HTML>
  <HEAD>
    <TITLE>JavaScript Camera Watcher</TITLE>

    <SCRIPT TYPE="text/javascript">
      <!--

      var RefreshInterval = 10 ;        // Seconds
      var MyURL = '_____' ;

      function Refresh () {
        document.MyImage.src = MyURL + "?" + Math.random() ;
        setTimeout ("Refresh()", RefreshInterval * 1000) ;
      }

      window.onload = Refresh ;

      //-->
    </SCRIPT>
  </HEAD>

  <BODY>
    <IMG NAME="MyImage" WIDTH="960">
  </BODY>
</HTML>
```

Try:
```
'http://www.wyoroad.info/highway/webcameras/I80Summit/I80Summit.jpg'
'http://birice.vaisala.com/photos/02864822_0699DE56_cam1.jpg'
'https://webcam.oregonstate.edu/cam/mu/live/live.jpg'
```

JavaScript Submitting Forms with Validation

Submitting forms to a remote server often involves validation of the values entered by the user. This can be done on the server side, but performing those checks on the client side via JavaScript will result in fewer network interactions. Here is a sample Web page for a final exam in some on-line course. The student must fill in their ID number, their name, their answers of course, and they must sign the exam to indicate that they didn't cheat (in this case by clicking a check box).

The form contains an `onsubmit` event, which when triggered calls the `Validate` function in the script block of the heading section. That function returns `True` only if the student filled in their ID and name, signed the form, and has verified that they wish to submit their answers for grading. If any required item is missing they will get an error dialog explaining the problem and the function returns `False` (also if they decide not to submit the exam at this time).

```html
<!DOCTYPE html>

<HTML>
  <HEAD>
    <TITLE>FINAL EXAM</TITLE>

    <SCRIPT TYPE="text/javascript">
      <!--

        function Validate() {

          if (document.FinalExam.ID_Number.value == "")
            { window.alert("Missing ID Number") ;
              return false }

          if (document.FinalExam.Real_Name.value == "")
            { window.alert("Missing Name") ;
              return false }

          if (!document.FinalExam.Signature.checked)
            { window.alert("Please sign the exam.") ;
              return false }

          if (!window.confirm("Submit this exam?"))
            { return false }

          return true ;
        }

      //-->
    </SCRIPT>
  </HEAD>
```

JavaScript Submitting Forms with Validation (Continued)

This page shows the body of the Web page, containing the form with the exam questions. The ACTION must reference the Web address of a remote script somewhere that will receive and grade the exam. The form is only submitted to that script if Validate returns True, but not if it returns False for any reason. The form name and its variables are shown in different colors, so that you can match them with where they are used in the Validate function on the previous page.

```
...

<BODY>
  <FORM NAME="FinalExam" METHOD="POST"
        ACTION="https://.../Exam_Grader.cgi"
        ONSUBMIT="return Validate()">

    <INPUT TYPE="text" NAME="ID_Number">ID Number<BR>
    <INPUT TYPE="text" NAME="Real_Name">Student Name<BR>
    <INPUT TYPE="submit" VALUE="Submit Exam"><BR>

    <BR><HR><BR>

    <H1>FINAL EXAM</H1>

    <H2>Question #1</H2>
    What is the Answer?<BR>
    <INPUT TYPE="text" NAME="Answer1"><BR>

    <H2>Question #2</H2>
    What is the Answer?<BR>
    <INPUT TYPE="text" NAME="Answer2"><BR>

    <BR><HR><BR>

    Check box to sign Exam:
    <INPUT TYPE="checkbox" NAME="Signature">
  </FORM>
</BODY>
</HTML>
```

This is in many ways a much simpler approach to data validation than sending form data to a central server and getting back a response, then doing it over and over again if there are any problems.

15: *Python Reference Manual*

Here is a basic reference guide to Python. Most functions will run under any version of Python. However, where differences between Python 2 and Python 3 are significant, those differences will be outlined in red.

This guide covers most of the basic data types, built-in functions, and some of the functions available in a handful of the standard libraries. A brief introduction to ***object-oriented programming*** (***OOP***) is covered, and several examples in future chapters depend on OOP. No complete coverage is possible, of course, but it is hoped that enough background has been presented here to allow users to branch out and create their own code for their own unique requirements.

Python Environment

Python is an ***interpreter***, which means that the Python development environment must be present at all times in order to run a Python program (no standalone `.EXE` files). There are several development environments available, including IDLE from `www.python.org`. Most such environments divide the Python experience into two sections: the interactive section and the programming section.

In the <u>interactive section</u>, statements may be entered for immediate execution at the >>> ***command prompt***. Whenever the >>> is seen, code or expressions may be typed in, functions may be defined, libraries loaded, and variables explored. In the following examples, the user types in the material in boldface at the command prompt, and Python types out the answers:

```
>>> 1+2
3
>>> "Dog" + "house"
'Doghouse'
>>> 1.0/3.0
0.3333333333333333
>>> import math
>>> math.sqrt(2)
1.4142135623730951
>>> X = 5 * 8
>>> X
40
>>> X + 1
41
>>> X
40
>>> X = X + 1
>>> X
41
```

In the <u>programming section</u>, which may be a separate window on the screen or a separate panel in the current window, programmers write code to be executed by Python, but that code is <u>not</u> executed immediately. Instead, when all the code has been written it is saved to a `.py` file, and then execution begins at the first line of the file.

If there are any ***syntax errors*** in the file, the Python interpreter will stop at the offending line and describe the error before execution can take place at all. If the program has no syntax errors but encounters a ***run time error*** when it is executing, the program will crash and the offending line will be highlighted. In some cases, the actual error will be <u>earlier</u> in the program from where it is indicated, and the error line simply highlights the point at which Python determines that it cannot continue. It is on the programmer to trace the execution back to where the error actually occurred. In both cases it will be necessary for the programmer to correct the text of the program, save it again, and attempt to execute it once more. This may happen many times.

Python Variable Names and Printing

Variables are ***memory locations*** where values are stored. Variables have a name given by the programmer, a <u>value</u> established by the program statements that use them, and a <u>data type</u>, which in Python is established by the data type of the value assigned to the variables. Python uses ***dynamic typing***, where the type of a variable (integer, float, string, etc.) can change as the program runs. (Contrast this with ***static typing***, where the data type is fixed by the programmer at design time and never changes throughout the lifetime of the program.)

Variable names in Python start with either a letter or the underscore, and may contain any number of letters, digits, or underscores. The underscore is often used to take the place of a blank, which cannot be in a variable name. Names are ***case sensitive***: variable FROG is different from variable Frog or variable frog. Differences in capitalization are common causes of run time errors. It is considered *bad programming practice* to have two distinct variables that differ only in the case of letters, but there are a very few occasions where it is useful.

Legal Variable Names	Illegal Variable Names	
X23	23X	(Does not start with letter or _)
Frog	Frog$	(Illegal character)
Total_Count	Q2.3	(Illegal character)
_X_	My Total	(Cannot contain blank)

Variable names should reflect the quantity that the variables contain. For example, a variable designed to hold the count of the number of dogs in a city should be named something like Count_Of_Dogs or Dog_Count or Total_Dogs, but not something like X or Q (unintuitive names) or Total_Cats (misleading name).

The length of a variable name is arbitrary. Generally, names that are too short do not convey their meaning well (what does Q or Z7 mean?), but names that are too long become unwieldy and difficult to manage by the programmer: My_Total_of_all_Dogs_in_the_City is probably too long. This is a judgement call, but 5-12 characters is often a good compromise.

Note that *asking* for the value of a variable by typing its name at the >>> prompt is <u>different</u> from having the program *print* the value of the variable. Both have the value appear in the interactive section (also called the ***console***), but the difference is dependent on whether the programmer is in control or the program is in control. The print statement is used by programs to cause output to appear on the console. The print statement has a slightly different syntax in Python 2 versus Python 3:

```
print expression,expression,expression,…,expression    # Python 2
print (expression,expression,expression,…,expression)  # Python 3
```

Python Basic Layout

Unlike many languages, Python is <u>not</u> free-form, but instead programs are written one statement per line of text. There are a few exceptions to this rule, but it is a good first assumption.

Comments

Comments start with the # symbol and go to the end of the current line. All text after the # is ignored. Use comments liberally throughout a program to document how it operates.

Indentation

Indentation is critically important, as there are no required braces or semicolons to denote blocks or the ends of statements. *White space matters.* Statements that belong to the same block must have the same indentation level:

Legal Indentation

```
if (expression):
    statement 1
    statement 2
    statement 3
else:
    if (expression):
        statement 4
        statement 5
        statement 6
    else:
        statement 7
        statement 8
        statement 9
```

Illegal Indentation

```
if (expression):
    statement 1
      statement 2
    statement 3
else:
    if (expression):
        statement 4
      statement 5
        statement 6
    else:
        statement 7
      statement 8
        statement 9
```

In the legal indentation example, each `if` and its corresponding `else` are at the same level because they form parts of the same structure. Statements 1, 2, and 3 all have the same indentation level in their block, as do statements 4, 5, and 6 and statements 7, 8, and 9 in their respective blocks. Each block *may* have a different indentation from other blocks, but as a matter of clarity this is not recommended. The number of spaces is arbitrary, and can be as low as 1 space per indentation level, but many Python programs use 4 spaces per level as shown here.

In the illegal indentation example, the first `if` and its corresponding `else` are <u>not</u> lined up, nor are the statements within any of the three blocks. Any Python interpreter will flag these as errors and not permit the program to start running. Only the second `if`-`else` is lined up properly.

Python Basic Layout (Continued)

Line Joins #1 (Optional)

Lines of code which follow any line that naturally ends in a **_colon_** (`if, elif, else, for, while, try, except, finally, def,` etc.) are indented relative to that first line. However, when there is only a <u>single</u> following indented line that line *may* be placed on the end of the same line as the one with the colon:

<u>**Legal**</u>

```
if (expression):
    statement 1
else:
    statement 2
```

<u>**Equivalent, Also Legal**</u>

```
if (expression): statement 1
else: statement 2
```

However, if there are multiple indented lines after the colon, they <u>must all</u> remain indented on separate lines. You <u>may not</u> bring the first of those indented lines up to the same line as the one with the colon.

<u>**Legal**</u>

```
if (expression):
    statement 1
    statement 2
    statement 3
```

<u>**Illegal**</u>

```
if (expression): statement 1
    statement 2
    statement 3
```

Line Joins #2 (Optional)

Several successive statements *may* be joined onto the same line if they are separated by **_semicolons_**. This is not common practice, but it is legal, and comes in handy occasionally, particularly when that new line can be placed after a colon, as in the following example:

<u>**Legal**</u>

```
if (expression):
    statement 1
    statement 2
```

<u>**Equivalent, Also Legal**</u>

```
if (expression): statement 1 ; statement 2
```

Line Splits

Statements *may* span multiple lines. To do so, each line to be continued must end with a \ as the <u>last</u> character of the line. Indentation does not matter on any line after the first one in the group. However, **_parameter lists_** for functions *may span multiple lines without the trailing* \ as it is clear from context when more items are needed. All parameter lists in this book that span multiple lines use the \ continuation character even though it is not technically required.

Python Assignment Statements

All assignment statements in Python are of the form:

$$variable = expression$$

A variable on the left side of the equal sign is assigned the value of the expression on the right side of the equation. The equal sign can be interpreted as "gets the value" or "is assigned" or "receives." For example, the expression X = 5 is interpreted as "variable X gets the value 5" where the old value of X is lost, to be replaced by 5. That is, the previous value of X is irrelevant; it is now 5. → *can be replaced as coding goes on*

However, the assignment statement X = X + 1 is interpreted as "the <u>new</u> value of X gets the <u>old</u> value of X plus one." In this case the previous value of X is used in the expression, and only after the value of the expression has been completely computed will X be updated to its new value. For example, if X was 5 before the statement X = X + 1 is executed, it will be 6 afterwards.

It is legal, but rarely useful, to write a statement in Python that consists of just the expression, such as X + 1 by itself on a line. The expression <u>will</u> be evaluated, but because it is not assigned to a variable, that expression is *simply discarded*. Some types of expressions may have **<u>side effects</u>** which would make this kind of statement useful (particularly those that contain function calls), but in general writing an expression by itself is bad programming practice.

Python Multiple Assignment

Python also allows multiple assignments in the same statement. The general form of this is:

```
variable1, variable2 = expression1, expression2
```

For example, the statement $X, Y = 4, 5$ assigns 4 to X and assigns 5 to Y. This can be written as $X = 4$ on one line followed on the next line by $Y = 5$, so it may be initially unclear where this is useful.

Consider as an example, however, the act of swapping the contents of two variables X and Y (useful when sorting). That is, if X is 4 and Y is 5 before the swap, X will be 5 and Y will be 4 after the swap. <u>Without</u> multiple assignment a third variable such as Temp is needed to hold one value while the other is being moved:

```
Temp = X
X = Y
Y = Temp
```

<u>With</u> multiple assignment the swap can be done in one statement without a temporary variable. <u>All</u> the expressions are evaluated before <u>any</u> of the assignments occur:

```
X, Y = Y, X
```

Given that variables X and Y contain two numbers, where it is desired that X contain the <u>smallest</u> of the pair and Y contain the <u>largest</u> (thus sorting them in ascending order), a multiple assignment statement can be combined on the same line as an `if` statement as follows:

```
if (X > Y): X, Y = Y, X
```

This single line replaces what would be four lines of code without multiple assignment. The swap happens only if X is larger than Y.

Python Functions

Functions provide a way of writing code once and using it in many places with different values passed in through the ***parameter list***. Passing parameters to a function is based strictly on their positions. The first ***actual parameter*** in the ***function call*** plugs into the first ***formal parameter*** of the function, the second actual parameter plugs into the second formal parameter, and so on. The names of the parameters are largely irrelevant; only their positions matter.

In the following example, the definition (def) of Function_1 contains three formal parameters P, D, and Q, which can be thought of as sockets into which values are plugged in from outside. When the function is called, the value of Q in the calling routine plugs into formal parameter P, the value 5 plugs into formal parameter D, and the result of computing 3*W plugs into formal parameter Q. Note that variable Q in the calling routine has no relationship to formal parameter Q in the function; they *might* be related in some way, or they may be completely different variables with different data types and only coincidentally have the same name.

The function can have its own ***local variables***, which may or may not have the same names as variables in other functions. Those variables vanish when the function exits. Changes to parameters and local variables are <u>allowed and expected</u>, but those <u>changes are not seen</u> by the calling routine (with few exceptions).

A true function returns some value as its result, and in this case that result is assigned to the variable X in the calling routine. The value returned can have any name local to the function (it does not have to be called Result, but instead could be called Answer, Z, Frog, or anything at all). A return statement usually appears at the end of a function; if missing one is assumed to be there (but with no return value). A return may also appear within the function body.

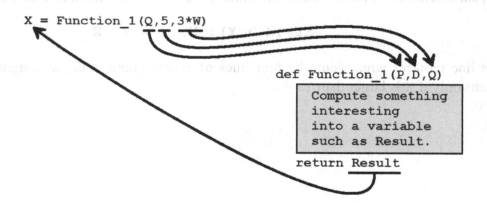

When a function is called, memory for all the local variables, incuding the formal parameters, are automatically allocated by Python in a new local environment (on a ***stack***), the function is executed, and upon exit all the allocated variables are discarded. In a ***recursive function***, the line that calls the function is inside the function itself. All the rules are the same, except that new memory for local variables is allocated each time the function is called by itself, and that memory is discarded when the function exits back to the previous environment.

Python Functions (Continued)

Functions need not return a value at all, particularly if they have ***side effects*** such as printing information to the console, writing information to a file, or changing a global variable. In these cases, the return stands by itself, and when it executes, control is passed back to the calling routine at the statement after the function call. The examples on this page do not return values.

When `Function_2` is called, actual parameter B plugs into formal parameter A, actual parameter C plugs into formal parameter B, and the value of 2*A plugs into formal parameter C (the =7 will be explained in the next section). Variables A, B, and C in the calling routine and variables A, B, and C in the function are not necessarily related; only their positions matter.

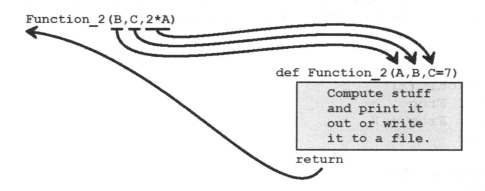

The third parameter C=7 defines formal parameter C as having a ***default value***, meaning that the function call can *omit the third actual parameter* and the function will still run correctly. In the following function call, actual parameter B plugs into formal parameter A and actual parameter C plugs into formal parameter B as before, but the call omits the third parameter. The function will automatically use 7 as the value of formal parameter C. In the previous example, the value of 2*A *overrides the default* and is used instead of the 7.

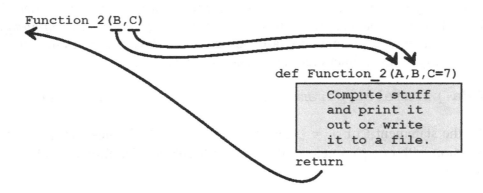

A function which normally returns a value (but also has side effects) can be used as shown in these examples without assigning the return value to a variable. The return value will simply be discarded in that case. The converse is not true, however: assigning the result of `Function_2` to a variable returns the special Python value `none`.

Python Global Variables

Normally, variables in a function are created when the function is activated and are discarded when the function returns. However, variables may be shared *without* going through the parameter list or the `return` statement by declaring them as ***global*** variables. Any function that declares a variable as `global` can see the value of that variable as if it was written on a blackboard, and can change it, and the variable is <u>not</u> discarded when the function exits. In the example below, variable `Frog` is defined outside of the two functions, and both declare it as global. Calling either function will use the current value of `Frog` and will update that value in a way that the other can see immediately whenever it is called. Both these functions therefore have ***side effects***. Global variables must be used with caution, as the side effects of calling one function may have unintended consequences when calling another function. There are some circumstances where global variables are necessary, but in general they are to be avoided.

```
Frog = 0                          # Initialization

def Function1 (X):
    global Frog
    Frog = Frog + X
    return

def Function2 (X):
    global Frog
    Frog = Frog * X
    return
```

Python Lambda Expressions

Functions normally start with a `def` statement, contain many program statements, and end with a `return` (and may contain other `return` statements as well). However, there is a simpler way of defining functions that can be entirely expressed in <u>one line</u>, called a ***lambda expression***. Lambda expressions may be assigned to variables, and then those variables may then be used as if they were properly defined functions. The basic syntax is:

> **lambda** *parameter,parameter : expression using parameters*

For example, the statement `Cube = lambda X : X*X*X` defines variable `Cube` to be the lambda expression with one parameter `X` that returns `X` cubed. The function call `Cube(3)` then returns the value 27.

Variables may be assigned different lambda expressions at different times, so the action of calling a function by its name will perform different computations depending upon which lambda expression is currently assigned to it.

Python Functions as Parameters

Functions may be parameters to other functions. This allows a receiving function to be told through its parameter list what actual function needs to be called. In the following example, function `MyFunction` is passed through the parameter list a number in `X` and a function in `FN`. It then returns the value from calling function `FN` with `X` as its argument, *whatever function FN happens to be*. The `print` statements call `MyFunction` twice, first where `X` will be the number 5 and `FN` will be the `Square` function, and second where `X` will be the number 3 and `FN` will be the `Cube` function. The values printed will be 25 and 27, respectively.

```
def MyFunction(X,FN):
    return FN(X)

def Square(Q):
    return Q*Q

def Cube(Q):
    return Q*Q*Q

print (MyFunction(5,Square))
print (MyFunction(3,Cube))
```

This is where lambda expressions become extremely useful. Rather than explicitly define the `Square` and `Cube` functions, the second parameter to `MyFunction` can be an anonymous lambda expression, as in the following code (with the same results as above):

```
def MyFunction(X,FN):
    return FN(X)

print (MyFunction(5,lambda Q : Q*Q))
print (MyFunction(3,lambda Q : Q*Q*Q))
```

Alternatively, the `Square` and `Cube` functions could be defined as named lambda expressions:

```
Square = lambda Q : Q*Q
Cube   = lambda Q : Q*Q*Q

print (MyFunction(5,Square))
print (MyFunction(3,Cube))
```

Python Simple Data Types

bool　　Short for Boolean, named after mathematician George Boole. Logical result of comparisons, but compatible with `int` data type. Two values only: `True` (synonym for integer 1) and `False` (synonym for integer 0). Conditions for `if`-statements and `while`-loops permit any non-zero value to be considered true.

```
X = True                    # X is now True, old value gone.
X = (Y < Z)                 # X=True if Y<Z, False otherwise.
X = X + (Y < Z)             # X=X+1 if Y<Z, otherwise X=X+0

if (X < Y):                 # Performs following statements
                            # only if the condition is True.

while (X < Y):              # Performs following statements
                            # as long as X stays less than Y.
```

int, long　　In **Python 2** there is a distinction between `int` and `long`, where `int` represents integers that fit into the native register size of the underlying processor chip and can be manipulated at the native speed of the processor <u>hardware</u>, but any computations that exceed the limits of `int` are automatically changed into <u>software</u> `long` integers, at a corresponding penalty in processing speed. Computations on `long` values are <u>much slower</u> than on `int` values, but may contain any number of digits. A `long` constant is denoted by an `L` as a suffix, which can be used as a constructor, even for values that would normally fit into an `int`. The `int` type is typically either 32 bits or 64 bits in length:

　　　　32 bit range: –2147483647…+2147483647
　　　　64 bit range: –9223372036854775807…+9223372036854775807

```
X = 5                       # X is now 5, old value gone
X = X + 1                   # X is now 6
X = 5L                      # X is now a long 5, not an int 5
X = 381293781238123932923944892384  # X is a long
```

int　　In **Python 3**, there is only the `int` type; the `long` type has been subsumed into `int`. If a computation exceeds the native register size of the processor, arbitrary-precision software integers are automatically and seamlessly used (again, at a penalty in processing speed).

```
X = 5                       # X is now 5, old value gone
X = X + 1                   # X is now 6
X = 381293781238123932923944892384  # X is still an int
```

Python Simple Data Types (Continued)

float   Native double-precision floating-point (number with fractions). Range is from $\pm10^{-308}...\pm10^{+308}$, with 15-16 significant digits. Constructor requires a decimal point or E for scientific notation. Subject to round-off errors in certain computations. In computations involving both `float` and `int` (or `long` in Python 2), any `int` (or `long`) values are often automatically converted to `float`, but converting a `float` back to an `int` (or `long`) requires use of a conversion function.

```
X = 5.0          # X is now a float 5.0
X = 5E3          # X is now a float 5000.0
X = 5.1E-3       # X is now a float 0.0051
```

complex   Pair of `float` values representing a number on the complex plane. The letter `j` is used to indicate the imaginary component (instead of `i` as used in math) and is part of the constructor. Arithmetic works as expected, but complex values can only be compared for equality (not less than or greater than).

```
X = 5+4j         # X is now a complex (5.0+4.0j)
X = 5.0+4.0j     # X is now a complex (5.0+4.0j)
```

Python Structured Data Types

list   Mutable sequence of any type, including other lists. Constructor uses square brackets [and]. May be empty. Indexed, using square brackets, from 0 up through length-1, or from -1 down to –length of list. Use `range` function to generate long sequences easily.

```
X = []                 # X is empty list
X = [4, 6, 2, 1]       # X is list of four integers
X = [9, "a", [1, 3]]   # X is list of int, string, list
X = [2, 4] + ["a"]     # X is list = [2, 4, "a"]
X = [2, 4] * 3         # X is list = [2, 4, 2, 4, 2, 4]
X = range(5)           # X is list = [0, 1, 2, 3, 4]
Y = X[0]               # Y is first item in X
Y = X[1]               # Y is second item in X
Y = X[-1]              # Y is last item in X
Y = X[len(X)-1]        # Y is last item in X
X[2] = 9               # Change third element of X to 9
```

tuple   Immutable sequence of any type, including other tuples. Constructor uses parentheses (and), but care must be taken to avoid confusion and conflicts with other uses for parentheses. May be empty. Indexed, using square brackets, from 0 up through length-1, or from -1 down to –length of tuple.

```
X = ()                 # X is empty tuple
X = (3,)               # X is tuple of one integer
X = (4, 6, 2, 1)       # X is tuple of four integers
X = (9, "a", [1, 3])   # X is tuple of int, string, list
X = (2, 4) * 3         # X is tuple = (2, 4, 2, 4, 2, 4)
Y = X[0]               # Y is first item of tuple
Y = X[-1]              # Y is last item of tuple
X[2] = 9               # ILLEGAL, TUPLES ARE IMMUTABLE
```

string   Immutable sequence of characters only. Constructors use matched pairs of single quotes ', double quotes ", or triple-single ''', or triple-double """ quotes. Triple-quoted strings are allowed to span multiple lines. Indexed, using square brackets, from 0 up through length-1, or from -1 down to –length of string.

```
X = ""                 # X is empty string
X = "frog"             # X is 4-characters string
X = 'I said "Hello"'   # X is 14-characters including "
X = "Dog" + "House"    # X is "DogHouse"
X = "AB" * 5           # X is "ABABABABAB"
Y = X[0]               # Y is first character of X
Y = X[-1]              # Y is last character of X
Y = X[len(X)-1]        # Y is last character of X
X[2] = "9"             # ILLEGAL, STRINGS ARE IMMUTABLE
```

Python Structured Data Types (Continued)

bytearray Python 2.6 and later only. Mutable sequence of byte values 0...255. Used to create streams of bytes for writing to a binary file. Argument is a list of integers.

```
X = bytearray([5,255,9]) # X is bytes 5, 255, 9
X[1] = 37                 # X is bytes 5, 37, 9
```

bytes Python 3 and later only. Immutable sequence of byte values 0...255. Used to create streams of bytes for writing to a binary file. Argument is a list of integers. (Earlier versions of Python may have a bytes function with different behavior.)

```
X = bytes([5,255,9])      # X is bytes 5, 255, 9
X[1] = 37                 # ILLEGAL, BYTES ARE IMMUTABLE
```

dict Dictionary: hash table of ***key-value pairs***. Constructor uses curly braces { and }. May be empty. A dictionary entry is a key, a colon, and a value, such as 5:"A" (5 is the key, and "A" is the value associated with that key). Keys are simple or immutable types (not lists). Values may be any type, including other dictionaries.

```
D = {}                # D is an empty dictionary
D = {5:"A", 9:"Q"}    # D contains D[5]="A" and D[9]="Q"
D[9] = 23             # D contains D[5]="A" and D[9]=23
D["cat"] = 12         # D also contains D["cat"]=12
Y = D[5]              # Y is "A"
Y = D["cat"]          # Y is 12
Y = D.keys()          # Y is list [5, "cat", 9]
Y = D.values()        # Y is list ["A", 12, 23]
Y = 9 in D            # Y is True (9 is one of the keys)
Y = 42 in D           # Y is False (no key matches 42)
len(D)                # Returns number of items in D
del D[5]              # Removes D[5] from dictionary
D.update(D2)          # Merges dictionary D2 into D
```

Python Structured Data Types (Continued)

set   <u>Unordered mutable collection</u> of distinct **_keys_**. Like a dictionary, except that there are only keys, no values. Constructor uses curly braces { and }, or the set function. (Note that S = {} creates an empty dictionary, not an empty set.)

```
S = set()               # S is an empty set
S = set([3,4,9])        # S contains 3,4,9
S = {3,4,9}             # S contains 3,4,9
T = S | {4,5}           # T contains 3,4,5,9 (union)
T = S & {4,5}           # T contains 4 (intersection)
T = S - {4,5}           # T contains 3,9 (difference)
T = S ^ {4,5}           # T contains 3,5,9 (symmetric dif)
Y = 3 in S              # Y is True  (set membership)
Y = 7 in S              # Y is False (set membership)
Y = S == {3,4,9}        # Y is True  (set equality test)
Y = S != {3,4,9}        # Y is False (set inequality test)
Y = S <= {3,4,9}        # Y is True  (improper subset)
Y = S <  {3,4,9}        # Y is False (proper subset)
Y = S >= {3,4,9}        # Y is True  (improper superset)
Y = S >  {3,4,9}        # Y is False (proper superset)
S.add(12)               # S contains 3,4,9,12
S.discard(4)            # S contains 3,9,12
S.discard(15)           # S contains 3,9,12 (no change)
S.clear()               # S is now an empty set
```

frozenset <u>Immutable set</u>. Same as set, except that set contents cannot be changed after creation (that is, add, discard, clear, or any other methods that would change the underlying structure of the set do not exist).

```
S = frozenset()         # S is an empty frozenset
S = frozenset([3,4,9])  # S contains 3,4,9
S.add(12)               # ILLEGAL, FROZENSETS ARE
                        # IMMUTABLE
```

Whenever a float is involved, answer is a float

Python Arithmetic

In general, arithmetic in Python follows the normal rules of mathematics, but there are some special considerations with respect to data types. In particular, a `bool` is effectively an `int`, arithmetic involving both `int` and `float` values generally have `float` results, and operations with `int` or `float` and `complex` generally have `complex` results, but there are exceptions such as division of integers (`int` result in **Python 2** but `float` result in **Python 3**).

Addition

```
int   + int   → int       8 + 6     → 14
int   + float → float     8 + 6.0   → 14.0
float + int   → float     8.0 + 6   → 14.0
float + float → float     8.0 + 6.0 → 14.0
```

Subtraction

```
int   - int   → int       8 - 6     → 2
int   - float → float     8 - 6.0   → 2.0
float - int   → float     8.0 - 6   → 2.0
float - float → float     8.0 - 6.0 → 2.0
```

Multiplication

```
int   * int   → int       8 * 6     → 48
int   * float → float     8 * 6.0   → 48.0
float * int   → float     8.0 * 6   → 48.0
float * float → float     8.0 * 6.0 → 48.0
```

Division

```
int   / int   → int       8 / 6     → 1         (Python 2)
int   / int   → float     8 / 6     → 1.333333... (Python 3)
int   / float → float     8 / 6.0   → 1.333333...
float / int   → float     8.0 / 6   → 1.333333...
float / float → float     8.0 / 6.0 → 1.333333...
```

Floor Division (Rounded Towards -∞)

```
int   // int   → int       8 // 6    → 1,   8 // -6   → -2
int   // float → float     8 // 6.0  → 1.0, 8 // -6.0 → -2.0
float // int   → float     8.0 // 6  → 1.0, 8.0 //-6  → -2.0
float // float → float     8.0 // 6.0→ 1.0, 8.0 //-6.0→ -2.0
```

Modulus (Remainder)

```
int   % int   → int       8 % 6     → 2
int   % float → float     8 % 6.0   → 2.0
float % int   → float     8.0 % 6   → 2.0
float % float → float     8.0 % 6.0 → 2.0
```

Python Operator Precedence

Arithmetic in Python (and most computer language) follow the normal precedence rules: exponentiation before multiplication and division before addition and subtraction (and expressions with several operators in a row of the same precedence level are evaluated left-to-right). However, there are a lot more operators available than just add, subtract, multiply, divide, and power. Here is a table showing all Python operators, their precedence level, their interpretation, and an example or explanation where appropriate.

LEVEL	OPERATOR	MEANING	EXAMPLE	VALUE	EXPLANATION or NOTES
1	**	Power	X = 2**5	32	2.0**5 = 32.0
2	~	Bitwise One's Complement	X = ~1	-2	~0001 = 1110
	+	Unary Plus	X = +5	5	
	-	Unary Minus	X = -5	-5	
3	*	Multiply	X = 10 * 3	30	
	/	Divide	X = 10 / 3	3.333…	int 3 in Python 2
	%	Modulo (Remainder)	X = 10 % 3	1	
	//	Floor Division	X = 10 // 3	3	10.0 // 3 = 3.0
4	+	Addition	X = 2+5	7	
	-	Subtraction	X = 2-5	-3	
5	>>	Bitwise Right Shift	X = 4 >> 1	2	0100 >> 1 = 0010
	<<	Bitwise Left Shift	X = 4 << 1	8	0100 << 1 = 1000
6	&	Bitwise AND	X = 13 & 3	1	1101 & 0011 = 0001
7	^	Bitwise XOR	X = 13 ^ 3	14	1101 ^ 0011 = 1110
	|	Bitwise OR	X = 13 | 3	15	1101 | 0011 = 1111
8	<=	Less than or Equal to	X <= Y	True or False	
	<	Less than	X < Y	True or False	
	>	Greater than	X > Y	True or False	
	>=	Greater than or Equal to	X >= Y	True or False	
9	!=	Not Equal	X != Y	True or False	
	==	Equality	X == Y	True or False	
10	=	Assignment	X = 2	2	
	**=	Power Assignment	X **= 2		X = X ** 2
	+=	Addition Assignment	X += 2		X = X + 2
	-=	Subtraction Assignment	X -= 2		X = X - 2
	*=	Multiplication Assignment	X *= 2		X = X * 2
	/=	Division Assignment	X /= 2		X = X / 2
	%=	Modulo Assignment	X %= 2		X = X % 2
	//=	Floor Division Assignment	X //= 2		X = X // 2
11	is	Identity	X is Y	True or False	
	is not	Identity	X is not Y	True or False	
12	in	Membership	X in range(5)	True or False	
	not in	Membership	X not in range(5)	True or False	
13	not	Logical Not	not (X == Y)	True or False	
	or	Logical OR	X or Y	True or False	
	and	Logical AND	X and Y	True or False	

Python Program Structures

Functions

```
def Name (parameterlist):          def Name (parameterlist):
    # statement                        # statement
    # statement                        # statement
    return                             return expression
```

Conditional Execution (several variations)

```
if (expression):                   if (expression):
    # statement                        # statement
    # statement                        # statement
elif (expression):
    # statement
    # statement                    if (expression):
elif (expression):                     # statement
    # statement                        # statement
    # statement                    else:
else:                                  # statement
    # statement                        # statement
    # statement
```

Loops

```
while (expression):                for variable in sequence:
    # statement                        # statement
    # statement                        # statement
else:                              else:              Optional, used only
    # statement                        # statement    with break in loop
```

Exceptions (Error Handling)

```
try:                               try:
    # statement                        # statement
    # statement                        # statement
except:                            finally:
    # statement                        # statement
    # statement                        # statement
```

Special Control Statements

pass	Do nothing (often a placeholder for future code or for busy-wait loops).
break	Immediately exit smallest enclosing `for` or `while` loop.
continue	Immediately continue with next pass through current loop.

Python Formatting Values as Strings

To format a value as a string with a particular number of digits and decimal places, use either the `"%_._f" % X` (float) or the `"%_d" % N` (int) expressions, with actual numbers in the blanks to indicate the desired precision. Some blanks are optional. An `int` value may be used with `float` formats. Other, non-formatting characters, are included in the resulting string as-is. This is most often used in conjunction with a `print` statement. Examples shown below:

`"%s" % X`	X is any type with a string representation, returns that string.
`"%f" % X`	X is `float`, returns string with 6 digits to right of decimal (default).
`"%9f" % X`	X is `float`, returns 9 digit string, 6 to right of decimal, blanks pad on left.
`"%09f" % X`	X is `float`, returns 9 digit string, 6 to right of decimal, zeroes pad on left.
`"%.2f" % X`	X is `float`, returns string with 2 digits to right of decimal.
`"%9.2f" % X`	X is `float`, returns 9 digit string, 2 to right of decimal, blanks pad on left.
`"%09.2f" % X`	X is `float`, returns 9 digit string, 2 to right of decimal, zeroes pad on left.
`"%d" % N`	X is `int`, returns string with minimal number of digits.
`"%9d" % N`	X is `int`, returns 9 digit string, blanks pad to left.
`"%09d" % N`	X is `int`, returns 9 digit string, zeroes pad to left.
`"%x" % N`	X must be `int`, returns lower case hexadecimal.
`"%X" % N`	X must be `int`, returns upper case hexadecimal.

To format multiple values into the same formatting string, the values must be in a <u>tuple</u>. In the following example, the value of N uses the `%d` format and the value of X uses the `%f` format:

```
print ("The answers are %d and %f" % (N,X))
```

Python Escape Characters

Escape characters are non-printing characters which may need to be part of a string. To specify an escape character, the `\` (backslash) is used as a *prefix* to a special letter code, an up to three-digit octal (base 8) number, or an `x` and a two-digit hexadecimal number. The use of the backslash as the prefix requires that it escape itself to get the backslash as a literal character.

Escape	Meaning
`\"`	Double Quote (")
`\'`	Single Quote (')
`\\`	Backslash (\)
`\a`	ASCII Bell (BEL)
`\b`	ASCII Backspace (BS)
`\f`	ASCII Formfeed (FF)
`\n`	ASCII Linefeed (LF)
`\r`	ASCII Carriage Return (CR)
`\t`	ASCII Horizontal Tab (TAB)
`\v`	ASCII Vertical Tab (VT)
`\ooo`	ASCII Character (<u>ooo</u> is one to three digit octal number)
`\xhh`	ASCII Character (<u>hh</u> is two digit hex number)

Python List Comprehensions, Structure Creation

Lists may be constructed in any of a number of ways, but one of the most elegant is the ***list comprehension***. A list comprehension consists of the square bracket constructor, but inside the brackets is an expression, a `for`-loop, and optionally an `if`-statement. The `for`-loop variable is often, but not required to be, part of the expression. As the `for`-loop runs, the expression is evaluated for every value of the `for`-loop variable and each time a new item is added to the result list (unless there is also an `if`-statement). If an `if`-statement <u>is</u> present, it tests each value of the `for`-loop variable to determine whether or not the expression needs to be evaluated at all. List comprehensions may be nested as well.

For these examples, remember that `range(N)` returns a list of integers from 0 to N−1, the `%` operator computes the remainder from a division, and ASCII characters `"0"..."9"` have numeric values between 48 and 57.

List Comprehension	Result
`[0 for X in range(5)]`	`[0,0,0,0,0]`
`[X for X in range(5)]`	`[0,1,2,3,4]`
`[X+1 for X in range(5)]`	`[1,2,3,4,5]`
`[X*X for X in range(5)]`	`[0,1,4,9,16]`
`[X*X for X in range(10) if X % 2 == 0]`	`[0,4,16,36,64]`
`[X*Y for X in range(4) for Y in range(4)]`	`[0,0,0,0,0,1,2,3,` `0,2,4,6,0,3,6,9]`
`[chr(X) for X in range(48,58)]`	`['0','1','2','3','4',` `'5','6','7','8','9']`

Any <u>list</u>, <u>tuple</u>, or <u>string</u> multiplied by an integer will create a repeated copy of that value, so the list comprehension `[0 for X in range(5)]` can be simplified as `[0]*5` or as `5*[0]`.

Expression	Result
`[0]*5`	`[0,0,0,0,0]`
`["X"]*10`	`["X","X","X","X","X","X","X","X","X","X"]`
`[4,"Frog",6.7]*3`	`[4,"Frog",6.7,4,"Frog",6.7,4,"Frog",6.7]`
`"Frog"*3`	`"FrogFrogFrog"`
`(3,7,2)*3`	`(3,7,2,3,7,2,3,7,2)`

Items can be added/appended to a list `X` by addition. If `X` is `[1,7,2]` then `X = X + [4]` gives `[1,7,2,4]`, but `X = [4] + X` gives `[4,1,7,2]` (the order matters). Adding an item to the end of a list may also use the `append` method. For example, `X.append(4)` has the same result as `X = X + [4]`.

Python List, Tuple, and String Slicing

Regardless of whether they are mutable or immutable, lists, tuples, and strings share many characteristics, including how they are indexed, and how to extract "slices" from them.

For any list L the first item (which can be of any type) is at L[0], the second at L[1], the third at L[2], up to the last item at L[len(L)-1]. Conversely, the last item is *also* at L[-1], the next to last at L[-2], down to the first item at L[-len(L)]. This is also true for any tuple T (the first item, of any type, is at T[0] and the last is at T[len(T)-1] or at T[-1]), or any string S (the first character is at S[0] and the last character is at S[len(S)-1] or at S[-1]).

A *slice* of a list, tuple, or string is a <u>new</u> list, tuple, or string containing a subsection of the original structure. The subsection is indicated by numbers in the subscript brackets separated by a *colon*. In all of the following examples assume that list L = [4,9,3,1,5,7,4], that tuple T = (4,9,3,1,5,7,4), and string S = "doghouse". There are four cases to consider.

L[M:N] or T[M:N] or S[M:N]

Start at position M and extract everything up through *but not including* position N. Using the values above, L[3:6] is [1,5,7], T[3:6] is (1,5,7), and S[3:6] is "hou". This is used to extract the middle of an existing structure.

L[M:] or T[M:] or S[M:]

Start at position M and extract everything up through the end of the structure. Using the same values above, L[3:] is [1,5,7,4], T[3:] is (1,5,7,4), and S[3:] is "house". This is used to extract the end of an existing structure.

L[:N] or T[:N] or S[:N]

Start at position 0 and extract everything up through *but not including* position N. Using the same values above, L[:3] is [4,9,3], T[:3] is (4,9,3), and S[:3] is "dog". This is used to extract the beginning of an existing structure.

L[:] or T[:] or S[:]

Start at position 0 and extract everything up through the end of the structure (that is, make a new copy of the entire thing). For lists, however, this performs a *shallow copy* of the top level of the list; no copies are made of any sublists, but only the pointers to those sublists are copied. For example, if L = [1,2,[3,4],5] and then M = L[:], any change to L[2] will also be seen in M[2]. To make a completely independent copy of L, use M = copy.deepcopy(L).

Note that the [X:] and [:X] forms extract the left section and the right section of a structure based on position X <u>without gaps or overlaps</u>. For the values above, S[:3] is "dog" and S[3:] is "house", so S[:3] + S[3:] is just S.

Python List Special Cases

Lists have properties that can trip up the unwary programmer. Here are a few of the most common cases to consider.

Shared Structures

An existing list L points to its structure that contains the individual values in the list. Assigning that list to another variable X does not copy the structure, but instead makes X point to the same structure as L. This is in order to save memory, as lists can become quite large. Changing an element of one changes the other (it's the same structure):

```
>>> L = [4,9,3,1,5,7,4]      # Assign a new list to L
>>> X = L                    # X now points at L's structure
>>> X[2] = "Frog"            # Changing an element of X…
>>> L                        #
[4,9,'Frog',1,5,7,4]         # …changes L as well.
```

Lists as parameters to functions

As described earlier, parameters passed to a function are discarded on function exit, and any changes to those variables are not seen by the calling routine. For lists, this statement is both true <u>and</u> false. It is true that any changes to the list parameter itself will not be seen by the calling routine: it will still be a list after the function exits, and it will contain the same number of elements as when it was called. However, the function *may change the elements of the list and those changes will be seen by the calling routine*. Those changes affect the <u>structure</u> that the list points to, not the fact that it was a list in the first place.

```
def MyFunction (L):
    L[2] = "Frog"         # This change will be seen outside
    return
```

Cloning Lists

To create a completely new copy of an existing list, including new copies of all sublists, use the deepcopy function from the copy library.

```
>>> import copy
>>> L = [4,9,[3,7,2],1,5,7,4]        # Assign a new list to L
>>> X = copy.deepcopy(L)             # Make a deep copy of L
>>> X[2][1] = "Frog"                 # Change X
>>> L                                # L still unchanged
[4,9,[3,7,2],1,5,7,4]
>>> X                                # X changed
[4,9,[3,'Frog',2],1,5,7,4]
```

Python Importing Functions

One of Python's strengths is the extensive set of ***external function libraries*** available in every implementation of the language. These libraries contain math functions (`math`), string functions (`string`), functions for handling times and dates (`time`), random number functions (`random`), etc. There are also a number of ***standard functions*** always available as part of the native language definition. When a function from an external library is needed, that library must be included into the current program with the `import` statement. However, there are several ways that `import` can be used, each with advantages and disadvantages. In the following examples, five functions, all from the `math` library, need to be used: `sqrt` (square root), `sin` (sine), `cos` (cosine), `exp` (e^x), and `log` (natural log, or ln).

Example #1 – Complete Failure

When <u>no import</u> statement is used, <u>all five</u> of the function calls will fail. None of the functions are defined. If all five statements are in a row, the program will crash upon discovery of the first failure. Even though all five *are* defined in the `math` library, none are known to the current program without importing the `math` library in some way (unless the programmer defines their own versions of these functions in the current program, which is allowed).

```
print (sqrt(2.0))          # Fails (Program crashes here)
print (sin(0.0))           # Fails
print (cos(0.0))           # Fails
print (exp(1.0))           # Fails
print (log(1.0))           # Fails
```

Example #2 – Preferred Approach

The simplest solution is to simply `import` the `math` library at the start of the program. Calling any function from that library requires that the library name be appended to the front of the function name with a period. The expression `math.sqrt` says to use the `sqrt` function specifically from the `math` library. Similarly, `math.sin` uses the `sin` function from `math`. However, even though `cos`, `exp`, and `log` *are* in `math`, and `math` *was* imported, leaving out the library name leaves them undefined. They all need the `math.` prefix in order to work.

```
import math
print (math.sqrt(2.0))     # Succeeds
print (math.sin(0.0))      # Succeeds
print (cos(0.0))           # Fails (Program crashes here)
print (exp(1.0))           # Fails
print (log(1.0))           # Fails
```

This is one of the preferred solutions, as the library containing the desired function is carefully identified every time the function is called. Any local function with the same name as a library function will <u>not</u> interfere with the library function.

Python Importing Functions (Continued)

Example #3

In this case, only those few functions from a library known to be needed in a program are actually imported. The `sqrt` and `sin` functions are imported by name, and by doing so the source library does not need to be specified when these function are called. Those functions not identified in the `import` statement are not defined unless the programmer defines their own versions; in such cases it is difficult to tell just by looking if a function is locally defined or is imported by name from a library. That is, suppose the programmer writes their own `cos` function; there is *no longer any syntactic difference* in how the `sin` from `math` and the new local `cos` functions are called. You can't tell by looking where the functions came from.

```
from math import sqrt,sin
print (sqrt(2.0))          # Succeeds
print (sin(0.0))           # Succeeds
print (cos(0.0))           # Fails (Program crashes here)
print (exp(1.0))           # Fails
print (log(1.0))           # Fails
```

Example #4

The most open approach is to basically import *everything* from a library by name. Every defined function in the library is then imported and can be called without specifying its library name. Sometimes this is acceptable, but it *often leads to name collisions* with local functions.

```
from math import *
print (sqrt(2.0))          # Succeeds
print (sin(0.0))           # Succeeds
print (cos(0.0))           # Succeeds
print (exp(1.0))           # Succeeds
print (log(1.0))           # Succeeds
```

Python Creating Local Libraries

Programmers do not need to rely solely on libraries created by other people. They can put commonly used functions in their own separate `.py` files and `import` those files into programs that need them. Note that most Python interpreters translate new or changed `.py` libraries into `.pyc` files; doing so speeds up the `import` statement whenever that library is needed. Technically, programmers could distribute `.pyc` files instead of their original source code in order to protect their intellectual property, but Python interpreters are updated frequently enough that `.pyc` files become out of date quickly.

Python Standard Functions

abs(N) Absolute value. N may be any numeric type (int, long, float, or complex). Except for complex arguments, result is the positive magnitude of the number. For complex arguments, result is the distance between 0+0j and N.

abs(7)	**= 7**	**abs(7.4)**	**= 7.4**
abs(-7)	**= 7**	**abs(-7.4)**	**= 7.4**
abs(3+4j)	**= 5.0**		

chr(N) Character. N must be an integer in the range 0…255, and corresponds to the code for the desired ASCII character. Function returns a single-character string. Used to generate special characters not normally on a keyboard. See also ord.

chr(65)	**= "A"**	**chr(169)**	**= "©"**

eval(S) Evaluate a string. S is a string containing a valid Python expression. Function returns result and type from evaluating the expression.

eval("1.0/8.0")= 0.125	**eval("1+2")**	**= 3**

float(N)
float(S) Convert to floating-point. N can be any numeric type (int, long, or float) except complex). S is a string that looks like a valid decimal number. Result is the equivalent floating-point number.

float(5)	**= 5.0**	**float(5.0)**	**= 5.0**
float("5")	**= 5.0**		

hex(N) Convert to hexadecimal string. N must be an int or a long, only. Result is a string of the equivalent hexadecimal (base 16) representation of N, prefaced by the string **"0x"**. **Python 2:** When N is a long, result will have an "L" suffix.

hex(91)	**= "0x5b"**	**hex(91L)**	**= "0x5bL"**

input(S) Get input from the user. Prints S on the console without a new-line, then waits for the user to enter a string and hit [Enter↵]. **Python 2:** the string entered is converted to an int or float depending on what the user typed in. **Python 3:** the result is always a string. The result is nearly always assigned to a variable.

MyInput = input("Enter something: ")

int(N)
int(S) Convert to integer. N can be any numeric type (int, long, float) except complex. S is a string that looks like an integer (but not a float). Result is the equivalent integer. When N is a float, the result is <u>truncated</u> (the fraction is discarded, rounding the number towards zero as it is converted into an int). Result is 0 if N is omitted. **Python 2:** The result is of type int if N falls in the range defined for an int; otherwise a long is returned.

int(5)	**= 5**	**int(7.9)**	**= 7**
int("5")	**= 5**	**int()**	**= 0**
int(5.0E20)	= 500000000000000000000	(Python 3)	
int(5.0E20)	= 500000000000000000000L	(Python 2)	

Python Standard Functions (Continued)

isinstance(*O*,*T*) Tests object O to see if it is of type T. Returns `True` or `False`. T may be the name of a type, or a tuple containing several types. Good for asking if a number is an `int`, `float`, `long`, or `complex`.

```
isinstance(3,int)                      = True
isinstance(3.4,int)                    = False
isinstance(3.4,float)                  = True
isinstance(3.4,(int,float))            = True
isinstance(3+4j,(int,float,complex))   = True
```

len(*L*) Length. L may be a list, tuple, string, range, set, or dictionary. Returns number of items in L.

```
len([4,2,7,8]) = 4       len([])        = 0
len((4,2,7,8)) = 4       len(())        = 0
len("cat")     = 3       len("")        = 0
len(range(10)) = 10      len(range(0))  = 0
len({4:"cat"}) = 1       len({})        = 0
```

list(*L*) Create a list. L may be a list, tuple, or string. Returns a new list containing the items from L as individual list entries. Warning: does NOT do a deep copy of lists (copies only top level of list; if source list is shared between two variables, a change to a sublist of the source will also change that entry in the copy).

```
list([3,8,4])  = [3,8,4]
list((3,8,4))  = [3,8,4]
list("cat")    = ["c","a","t"]
```

long(*N*) Convert to `long`. **Python 2 only. Subsumed into `int` in Python 3.** N can be any numeric type (`int`, `long`, or `float`) except `complex`.

long(*S*) S is a string that looks like a valid integer or long integer. Result is the equivalent long integer. When N is a `float`, the result is truncated (rounded towards zero). Result is `0L` if N is omitted.

```
long(5)        = 5L      long(5L)       = 5L
long(5.9)      = 5L      long("5")      = 5L
```

max(*N*,*N*,...,*N*) Maximum. N may be any numeric type except `complex`, and may also be a string, list, or tuple. Result is the largest argument. Numbers are compared by numeric value; strings are compared alphabetically. Lists have higher values than numbers, and strings have higher values than both.

```
max(4,7,2)       = 7            max(4,7.6,2)   = 7.6
max("frog","bat","dog","toad","cat")   = "toad"
```

min(*N*,*N*,...,*N*) Minimum. Same as **max**, except that result is the smallest argument.

```
min(4,7,2)       = 2            min(4,1.6,2)   = 1.6
min("frog","bat","dog","toad","cat")   = "bat"
```

Python Standard Functions (Continued)

oct(*N*) Convert to octal string. N must be an `int` or a `long`, only. Result is a string containing the octal (base 8) representation of N, prefaced by "0" (Python2) or "0o" (Python 3). **Python 2:** Result has an "L" suffix when N is a `long`.

```
oct(91)        = "0133"    (Python 2)
oct(91)        = "0o133"   (Python 3)
```

open(*S1,S2*) Open a file for reading or writing. S1 is the name of the file to open. S2 is the mode, and is generally either "r" for reading, "w" for writing, or "a" for appending. Binary (non-text) files also have "b" appended to the mode string. Returns a file handle to be used in reading from, writing to, or closing the file. Opened files <u>must</u> be closed when no longer needed.

```
Outfile = open("Hello.txt","w")
Outfile.write("Hello, World!\n")
Outfile.close()
```

ord(*S*) Ordinal. S must be a single character (a string of length 1). Returns the numeric value for that character. See also `chr`.

```
ord("A")       = 65              ord("0")        = 48
```

pow(*N1,N2*) Raise to a power. N1 and N2 must be `int` or `float`. Returns $N1^{N2}$ as a `float` if either are `float`, `int` if both are `int` and $N2 \geq 0$. Same as N1**N2.

range(*N*) Range of integers. N must be `int`. Returns a list or range class of integers from 0 up through N−1. That is, it returns a list containing N integers starting at 0. Often used to control `for`-loops. An empty list [] is returned if $N \leq 0$.

```
range(10)      = [0,1,2,3,4,5,6,7,8,9]
range(3)       = [0,1,2]
range(0)       = []
```

range(*N1,N2*) Range of integers. Both N1 and N2 must be `int`. Returns a list or range class of integers from N1 up through but <u>not</u> including N2. Either or both may be negative. N1 must be strictly less than N2 or an empty list [] will be returned.

```
range(1,10)    = [1,2,3,4,5,6,7,8,9]
range(-1,2)    = [-1,0,1]
range(10,1)    = []
```

range(*N1,N2,N3*) Range of integers. N1, N2, and N3 must be `int`. Returns a list or range class of integers from N1 through N2, but <u>not</u> including N2, in steps of N3. Any may be negative, but N3 must create a valid sequence between N1 and N2 or an empty list [] will be returned.

```
range(1,10,3)  = [1,4,7]
range(10,1,-1) = [10,9,8,7,6,5,4,3,2]
range(1,10,-1) = []
```

Python Standard Functions (Continued)

raw_input(*S*) **Python 2 only. For Python 3 see the `input` function.** Get a string from the user. Prints *S* on the console without a new-line, then waits for the user to enter a string and hit [Enter←]. Whatever the user entered (up through but not including the new-line character) is returned as the value of the function. The result is nearly always assigned to a variable.

```
MyInput = raw_input("Enter a string: ")
```

round(*N*) Round to a whole number. *N* may be any numeric type (int, long, float) except complex. **Python 2:** Result is a <u>float</u> ending in .0 (zero fraction). For fractions of 0.5, the result is <u>rounded away from zero</u>. **Python 3:** Result is an int. For fractions of 0.5, the result is <u>rounded to the nearest even</u>.

<u>Python 2</u>			<u>Python 3</u>		
round(5.1)	=	5.0	round(5.1)	=	5
round(5.9)	=	6.0	round(5.9)	=	6
round(-5.1)	=	-5.0	round(-5.1)	=	-5
round(-5.5)	=	-6.0	round(-5.5)	=	-6
round(3.5)	=	4.0	round(3.5)	=	4 ←
round(4.5)	=	5.0	round(4.5)	=	4 ←
round(5.5)	=	6.0	round(5.5)	=	6 ←
round(6.5)	=	7.0	round(6.5)	=	6 ←
round(5L)	=	5.0	round(-5.9)	=	-6

round(*N1*,*N2*) Returns *N1* rounded to *N2* digits. *N1* and *N2* may be any numeric type (int, long, float) except complex. Result is a <u>float</u>, even if the fraction is zero.

```
round(123.4567,2)   = 123.46
round(123.4567,0)   = 123.0
```

str(*O*) Convert to a string. Object *O* can be any data type. Returns a string of characters that have the same appearance as what would be seen if the object was printed.

```
str(5)          = "5"        str(5.0)       = "5.0"
str(5+4j)       = "(5+4j)"   str("cat")     = "cat"
str([4,2,1])    = "[4,2,1]"
```

sum(*L*) Add up elements from a list or tuple. *L* can be an explicit list or tuple, or may be the result of a range, but the contents of *L* must be numeric (any numeric type).

```
sum([4,1,3])    = 8          sum((4,1,3))   = 8
sum(range(100))= 4950
```

tuple(*L*) Create a tuple. *L* may be a list, tuple, or string. Returns a new tuple containing the items from *L* as individual tuple entries.

```
tuple([3,8,4]) = (3,8,4)
tuple((3,8,4)) = (3,8,4)
tuple("cat")   = ("c","a","t")
```

Python String Methods

Strings have built-in functions that are always available. It is not necessary to import any library to use to these functions. In the examples below, string variable X contains the 8-character string "dog Food", and none of the functions change the value of X.

`X.capitalize()`	`X.capitalize()`	returns `"Dog food"`
`X.lower()`	`X.lower()`	returns `"dog food"`
`X.swapcase()`	`X.swapcase()`	returns `"DOG fOOD"`
`X.upper()`	`X.upper()`	returns `"DOG FOOD"`

`X.find(S)`	Searches from the left, returns index of S in X, –1 if not found.
`X.rfind(S)`	Searches from the right, returns index of S in X, –1 if not found.

	`X.find("o")`	returns 1 (index of the o in dog)
	`X.rfind("o")`	returns 6 (index of the second o in Food)
	`X.find("z")`	returns –1 (not found)

`X.lstrip(S)`	Strips all copies of S from left end of X.
`X.rstrip(S)`	Strips all copies of S from right end of X.
`X.strip(S)`	Strips all copies of S from both ends of X.

	`X.lstrip("d")`	returns `"og Food"`
	`X.rstrip("d")`	returns `"dog Foo"`
	`X.strip("d")`	returns `"og Foo"`

`X.zfill(N)`	Zero-fills X on left to N characters.
	`X.zfill(12)` returns `"0000dog Food"`

`X.expandtabs(N)`	Expands all tab characters (`\t`) to tab stop of N, default of N=8.

Python String Functions (`import string`)

`string.ascii_letters`	Same as `ascii_lowercase + ascii_uppercase`
`string.ascii_lowercase`	`"abcdefghijklmnopqrstuvwxyz"`
`string.ascii_uppercase`	`"ABCDEFGHIJKLMNOPQRSTUVWXYZ"`
`string.digits`	`"0123456789"`
`string.hexdigits`	`"0123456789abcdefABCDEF"`
`string.octdigits`	`"01234567"`
`string.printable`	All printable characters (digits, letters, punctuation, space)
`string.punctuation`	`"!\"#$%&'()*+,-./:;<=>?@[\\]^_`{|}~"`
`string.whitespace`	All whitespace (blanks, tabs, newlines, etc.)

Python Math Functions (`import math`)

`math.ceil(`*X*`)`	Smallest whole number $\geq$ X.	`math.ceil(7.1) = 8.0`
`math.floor(`*X*`)`	Largest whole number $\leq$ X.	`math.floor(7.9) = 7.0`
`math.exp(`*X*`)`	e^x (where e=2.71828…).	`math.exp(1) = 2.71828…`
`math.log(`*X*`)`	Natural log (base e) of X.	`math.log(math.e) = 1.0`
`math.log10(`*X*`)`	Common log (base 10) of X.	`math.log10(100) = 2.0`
`math.pow(`*X,Y*`)`	X^Y, returns float.	`math.pow(2,8) = 256.0`
`math.sqrt(`*X*`)`	Square root of X, returns float.	`math.sqrt(16) = 4.0`
`math.acos(`*X*`)`	Arc cosine (in radians) of X.	`math.acos(0) = 1.57…` ($\pi/2$)
`math.asin(`*X*`)`	Arc sine (in radians) of X.	`math.asin(1) = 1.57…` ($\pi/2$)
`math.atan(`*X*`)`	Arc tangent (in radians) of X.	`math.atan(1) = 0.78…` ($\pi/4$)
`math.atan2(`*Y,X*`)`	Arc tangent (in radians) of Y/X.	`math.atan2(1,1) = 0.78…`
`math.cos(`*X*`)`	Cosine of X (in radians).	`math.cos(0) = 1.0`
`math.hypot(`*X,Y*`)`	Hypotenuse $\sqrt{X^2+Y^2}$.	`math.hypot(3,4) = 5.0`
`math.sin(`*X*`)`	Sine of X (in radians).	`math.sin(math.pi/2) = 1.0`
`math.tan(`*X*`)`	Tangent of X (in radians).	`math.tan(math.pi/4) = 1.0`
`math.degrees(`*X*`)`	Convert X in radians to degrees.	`math.degrees(`π`) = 180.0`
`math.radians(`*X*`)`	Convert X in degrees to radians.	`math.radians(180) = `π
`math.cosh(`*X*`)`	Hyperbolic cosine of X.	`math.cosh(0) = 1.0`
`math.sinh(`*X*`)`	Hyperbolic sine of X.	`math.sinh(0) = 0.0`
`math.tanh(`*X*`)`	Hyperbolic tangent of X.	`math.tanh(0) = 0.0`
`math.pi`	π (to accuracy of machine)	`3.141592653589793…`
`math.e`	Euler's e (to accuracy of machine)	`2.718281828459045…`

Python Time Functions (`import time`)

`time.clock()` — Returns 0.0 on first call. Returns the number of seconds since the first call on all subsequent calls. Use this to compute the execution time of a module of code. **DEPRECATED** in Python 3.3, removed in Python 3.8. Use `time.perf_counter` instead.

`time.time()` — Returns the number of seconds and fractions of seconds since midnight, January 1, 1970 (start of the current epoch), but valid only up through sometime in the year 2038. Returns a float.

`time.sleep(`N`)` — Pauses program for N seconds. N can be a float.

`time.localtime(`T`)`
`time.localtime()`

T is a time instant, such as returned from `time.time()`. If omitted, T is assumed to be the current value of `time.time()`. Returns a tuple (**Python 2**) or a structure (**Python 3**) containing nine numbers: year, month, day, hour, minute, second, day of week, day of year, daylight savings time. The day of week runs from 0=Monday to 6=Sunday. Can be converted into a list or tuple with the `list` or `tuple` type conversion functions. For example, on Sunday, June 14, 2015, at 8:58:10pm, with daylight savings time in effect, the expression:

```
list(time.localtime(time.time()))
```
returns:
```
[2015, 6, 14, 20, 58, 10, 6, 165, 1]
```

`time.asctime(`T`)`
`time.asctime()`

T is a time tuple or time structure, such as returned from `time.localtime(...)`. If omitted, T is assumed to be the current value of `time.localtime()`. Returns a formatted string of the time and date. For example, using the tuple above, the expression:

```
time.asctime((2015,6,14,20,58,10,6,165,1))
```
returns:
```
"Sun Jun 14 20:58:10 2015"
```

`time.perf_counter()`

Python 3 only. Returns a number of fractional seconds from a performance counter. The value from the first call is undefined; only the amount of elapsed time between successive calls is meaningful. Surround code to be measured with calls to `time.perf_counter()` and save the difference to determine how long the code takes to execute, in seconds.

Python Random Functions (`import random`)

`random.seed(`*N*`)` Initialize random number generator using N. N can be any simple object (number, string, etc.). Not required for using random numbers, but can be used to restart the random number sequence at the same point each time.

`random.randrange(`*N*`)`

Returns a random integer from 0 up through N $-$ 1 (effectively picking an integer from `range(N)`, but without actually building a range). N must be positive, and should be an integer but may be a float if it is a whole number. Each call will return a different value from the range. For example, to return a random integer between 1 and 6, use the expression: `random.randrange(6)+1` (the random number will be between 0 and 5, inclusive, and the +1 shifts the range to 1 through 6).

`random.randrange(`*N1,N2,N3*`)`

Returns a random number greater than or equal to N1, less than N2, and with a step of N3 (a step of 1 is used if N3 is omitted). N1, N2, and N3 should all be integers, but may be floats if all three are whole numbers. They may be negative to generate appropriate sequences. For example, to return a random integer between 1 and 6, inclusive, use the expression: `random.randrange(1,7)`, but to pick a integer from only the values 1, 3, and 5, use the expression `random.randrange(1,6,2)`.

`random.randint(`*N1,N2*`)`

Return a random integer between N1 and N2, <u>inclusive</u>. N1 and N2 should both be integers, but may be floats if both are whole numbers. For example, to return a random integer between 1 and 6, inclusive, use the expression `random.randint(1,6)`.

`random.random()`

Return a random float greater than or equal to 0.0, but less than 1.0. The result may be scaled to an appropriate range of values. For example, to return a random integer between 1 and 6, inclusive, use the expression: `int(random.random()*6+1)`.

`random.choice(`*L*`)`

Pick an item at random from L (L may be a list, a tuple, or a string). For example, to pick a random integer between 1 and 6, inclusive, use the expression `random.choice([1,2,3,4,5,6])`. Here are some other examples:

```
random.choice([1.5, 9.6, 5.3])
random.choice(["dog", "cat", "bat"])
random.choice("frog")
```

Python CGI Functions (`import cgi`)

Web pages that submit form data to a server activate a script (program) on the server to process those form data. The script can be in any of a number of languages, including Python. Here is a simple Python script to receive the form data, build a Web page from the form data, and return the resulting page back to the browser.

The key to this program is the ***common gateway interface*** (`cgi`) module. Once imported, it can use the `cgi.FieldStorage()` function to ask for the form data which accompany the request that activated the script. Those form data come back in a <u>class</u> similar to a dictionary of key-value pairs, each key entry the name of the object on the Web page (check box, radio button, text box, etc.) and the corresponding value the information entered by the user. This script simply echoes the data back as a list to the browser. (Note that the first line of the script is required by UNIX servers to know where on the disk the Python interpreter is located.) Also, all `print` statements in this example use Python 2 as that is still common on Web servers; to change to Python 3 surround each argument with parentheses.

```
#!/usr/bin/python

import cgi

MyForm = cgi.FieldStorage()

print "Content-type: text/html\n"
print ""
print "<HTML>"
print "    <HEAD>"
print "        <TITLE>Received Data</TITLE>"
print "    </HEAD>"
print ""
print '    <BODY BGCOLOR="Yellow">'
print "        <H1>Welcome!</H1>"
print "        <OL>"

for Key in MyForm.keys():
    Value = MyForm[Key].value
    print "            <LI>", Key, " = ", Value, "</LI>"

print "        </OL>"
print "    </BODY>"
print "</HTML>"
```

Python Mail Functions (`import smtplib`)

Here is a simple Python 3 script that sends a text message to one recipient. Most of the script involves setting up a bunch of strings so that the email is properly formatted; the actual email is sent by the last half of the code. The imported module is the ***simple mail transport protocol library*** (`smtplib`). To send an email, a variable that opens a server link is necessary (the `smtplib.SMTP("localhost")` call), but because `localhost` is not secure it may need to be replaced by the address of an actual email server. The call to `sendmail` does the actual sending. The `To` address is a <u>list</u>; this list can hold as many email addresses as necessary and all will receive the message. Regardless of whether or not the email was sent successfully, the link to the mail server needs to be closed with `quit()`. Finally, we get a report of whether or not the process was successful. WARNING: As you can imagine, this script is ripe for abuse by unethical people. While it has legitimate uses, it can also be used to spam a billion people. DO NOT DO THIS. You can get into serious legal trouble, and I will report any occurrences of misuse that I find. Use your powers only for good.

```python
#!/usr/bin/python

import smtplib

From = "Fred Q. Smith <fqsmith@yyyyyyyyyyy.com>"
To = "xyz@xxxxxxxx.com"
Subject = "Hello there"
Text = """Here is a long message that
spans many lines and represents
the contents of the mail message."""

Message = "From: "    + From    + "\r\n" + \
          "To: "      + To      + "\r\n" + \
          "Subject: " + Subject + "\r\n" + \
          Text

try:
    Server = smtplib.SMTP("localhost")

    try:
        Code = Server.sendmail(From, [To], Message)
    finally:
        Server.quit()

    if Code: Status = "Error in sending mail"
    else:    Status = "Mail sent correctly"
except Exception as E:
    Status = "Server Fail: " + str(E)

print (Status)
```

Python File Handling

Working with external files in Python is fairly straightforward. Programs need to be able to <u>read</u> information in from files, to be able to <u>write</u> new material out to files, and to <u>append</u> information to the end of existing files. Files may be either readable ***text files*** or ***binary files***. Each opened file requires the use of a unique ***file handle***; a variable through which the program can "talk" to the file. The file handle is in some sense the interface between the extremely fast program that requires or creates the data and the very slow external storage mechanism, often a hard disk.

For example, when bytes are written to a file those bytes do not go immediately to the hard disk, but instead go to an internal ***buffer***: a block of fast internal memory. Only whenever the buffer gets full or when the file is closed is the buffer flushed to the disk. Files <u>must be closed</u> when processing is complete. The basic program flow is to create a file handle to an external file (open), write new material to the file handle (write), then close the file handle (close). For reading from a file the process is similar: create a file handle to an existing external file (open), read material from the file (read or readlines), then close the file handle (close). The Python open statement both creates a handle and controls how the file is to be used:

$$NewHandle = \textbf{open}(Filename, Mode)$$

Variable *NewHandle* is the newly created file handle, *Filename* is a string that describes the name and location of the external file, and Mode is one of the string options from the following table. From here on out the file is controlled exclusively through NewHandle.

	Reading (r), Writing (w), or Appending (a)		Reading and Writing (r+, w+), or Reading and Appending (a+)	
	Text Mode	Binary Mode	Text Mode	Binary Mode
READING: File must exist, pointer starts at beginning of file.	**r**	**rb**	**r+**	**rb+**
WRITING: Overwrites existing file, creates file if it does not exist.	**w**	**wb**	**w+**	**wb+**
APPENDING: Appends to existing file, pointer starts at end of file, creates file if it does not exist.	**a**	**ab**	**a+**	**ab+**

For example, to create and open a text file called MyData.txt for writing, a programmer would write something like the following statement:

```
NewHandle = open("MyData.txt", "w")
```

After that, new strings are written to the text file with several statements of the form NewHandle.write("*new stuff*") and the file is closed with Newhandle.close() after all new material has been created. Material may not be written to a file after it is closed.

Python File Handling (Continued)

Line Breaks

Line breaks (new lines) must be explicitly included in text files (but not binary files) by adding a \n code at the end of each line written out. The following code writes only <u>one</u> line to a file:

```
NewHandle = open("MyData.txt", "w")
NewHandle.write("Line #1")
NewHandle.write("Line #2")
NewHandle.write("Line #3")
NewHandle.close()
```

The contents of `MyData.txt` are on one line all run together:

```
Line #1Line #2Line #3
```

However, the following code includes the \n new lines and has the expected output:

```
NewHandle = open("MyData.txt", "w")
NewHandle.write("Line #1\n")
NewHandle.write("Line #2\n")
NewHandle.write("Line #3\n")
NewHandle.close()
```

The contents of `MyData.txt` are now on multiple lines as expected:

```
Line #1
Line #2
Line #3
```

Seek and Ye Shall Find

The `seek` command sets the current pointer for (re)reading or (re)writing information in a file. The first parameter is an integer offset (number of bytes) into the file. The optional second parameter is 0 (absolute file position, the default), 1 (relative to current position), or 2 (relative to file's end). The line `NewHandle.seek(0)` places the pointer at the beginning of the file, even if the information from the beginning of the file has already been read in or written out.

File Naming Conventions

On PCs folders on paths are separated by backslashes (\), but the Mac uses regular slashes (/). Backslash is the Python *escape character*; to use a literal backslash they must be duplicated.

```
Filename = "C:\\users\\verts\\Desktop\\Test.txt"    # PC
Filename = "/users/verts/Desktop/Test.txt"          # Mac
```

Python Reading from Text Files

When reading from a text file, there are basically two approaches: read in the entire file as one large string, or read in the file as a list of strings, one line per string. In both cases, the line-breaks will be included as part of the result. In the open statement, the second parameter "r" is to specify that a text file is to be read in.

Here is the version that reads in the entire file as one string. After the file is opened, its entire contents are assigned to variable X, returned as the result of the function.

```
def ReadFileAsOneString (Filename):
    Infile = open(Filename, "r")
    X = Infile.read()
    Infile.close()
    return X
```

Here is a version that reads in the file as a list of strings. The first entry in the list will contain the first line of the file (including the line break), the second entry of the list will contain the second line of the file, and so on. The length of the returned list will be the number of lines in the imported file.

```
def ReadFileAsListOfStrings (Filename):
    Infile = open(Filename, "r")
    X = Infile.readlines()
    Infile.close()
    return X
```

This version is the same as above, with the exception that the line breaks at the end of each line are stripped off. The return statement uses a ***list comprehension*** to scan through the entire list one string at a time, strip off the line break ("\n") at the end of each string (using the rstrip function), and build a new list from the results; that new list is returned from the function.

```
def ReadFileAsListOfStrings (Filename):
    Infile = open(Filename, "r")
    X = Infile.readlines()
    Infile.close()
    return [C.rstrip("\n") for C in X]
```

Python Writing to Text Files

Writing text to an external file in Python is fairly straightforward. The file needs to be opened, text is written to the file, and then the file is closed. In the `open` statement, the second parameter `"w"` is to specify that a ***text file*** is to be written out. In each of the `write` statements there is an explicit \n at the end of each line. Without those \n (***new line***) characters, the text in the file would all appear on one continuous line. For text mode files on Windows a new line (\n) emits <u>both</u> a carriage return and a line feed character, while on a Mac a new line emits only a line feed character.

```python
def WriteATextFile(Filename):
    MyFile    = open(Filename,"w")
    MyFile.write ("Now is the time\n")
    MyFile.write ("for all good men\n")
    MyFile.write ("to come to the aid\n")
    MyFile.write ("of their party!\n")
    MyFile.close()
    return
```

Python Writing to Binary Files

Writing binary data to an external file is also straightforward. In the code below, parameter `MyList` is a list of integers in the range 0…255 (byte values) to be written to the file specified by `Filename`. In Python 2 the bytes are written out as a list of (one-byte) characters, while in Python 3 there is a new function `bytes` which will convert the list into a list of packed bytes suitable for writing. The code is currently configured for Python 3, but can be changed to Python 2 just by moving the comment symbol. In the `open` statement, `"wb"` specifies that a ***binary file*** is to be written out.

```python
def WriteABinaryFile(Filename, MyList):
    MyFile    = open(Filename,"wb")
    MyFile.write(bytes(MyList))                      # Python 3
#   for Item in MyList: MyFile.write(chr(Item))      # Python 2
    MyFile.close()
    return
```

Python Object Oriented Programming

Object Oriented Programming (***OOP***) is a technique to bundle a set of ***methods*** (functions) and the specific data upon which those methods operate into a single package where the data can only be used by the correct tools. This ***encapsulates*** the data and methods into a ***class***; where ***instantiating*** the class creates an ***object*** and calls its ***constructor*** method called __init__ (notice the double underscores). The constructor initializes its own data (or calls a method which initializes its data); each variable defined locally within the class has `self.` as its prefix. All methods also always have `self` as their first parameter, even though `self` is never explicitly included in a call to that method.

In the template below, *TName* is the name of the class and can be anything the programmer desires, although it is traditional to start class names with `T` to indicate "type". The __init__ constructor is passed any initial data that the object will need, and those values are stored in local variables that belong to the object (`self.variable`). Any method can access those variables; a *variable* by itself belongs to the method alone, but `self.variable` belongs to the entire object. Any method that calls another method must also prefix its name with `self.` as well.

```
class TName(object):

    def __init__ (self, NewVar1, NewVar2, NewVar3):
        self.Var1 = NewVar1
        self.Var2 = NewVar2
        self.Var3 = NewVar3
        # any other initialization code goes here.
        return

    def Method1 (self, Var4, Var5):
        # some kind of processing goes here involving Var4,
        # Var5, self.Var1, self.Var2, and self.Var3
        return

    def Method2 (self, Var6, Var7):
        # some kind of processing goes here involving Var6,
        # Var7, self.Var1, self.Var2, and self.Var3
        return
```

The class is instantiated by calling the class name as if it was a function, assigning the result to an object variable as in `X = TName (Value1, Value2, Value3)`, and then using `X` to access the object's methods as in `X.Method1 (Value4, Value5)`, for example.

Explicitly "deallocating" objects is unnecessary, as Python has a built-in ***garbage collector*** that will dispose of structures after they are no longer needed. More advanced OOP concepts include ***inheritance*** (one class extending the capabilities of another) and ***polymorphism*** (where a method call from one of a series of related classes determines which actual method must be called).

Python Object Oriented Programming (Example)

This simple class, called `TCircle`, encapsulates information about circles. The constructor calls the `setRadius` method to initialize the `self.Radius` variable to a non-negative value. All other methods get some computed information about a circle with that radius: the radius itself, the computed area (πr^2) of the circle, and the circumference ($2\pi r$) of the circle. The radius can be changed by explicitly calling the `setRadius` method.

```python
import math

class TCircle(object):

    def __init__ (self, NewRadius):
        self.setRadius(NewRadius)
        return

    def setRadius (self, NewRadius):
        if NewRadius < 0.0: NewRadius = 0.0
        self.Radius = NewRadius
        return

    def getRadius (self):
        return self.Radius

    def getArea (self):
        return math.pi * self.Radius * self.Radius

    def getCircumference (self):
        return math.pi * self.Radius * 2.0
```

Here is a sample interactive use of the `TCircle` class:

```
>>> X = TCircle(5.0)          # Instantiate new object
>>> X.getRadius()             # Call getRadius method
5.0
>>> X.getArea()               # Call getArea method
78.53981633974483
>>> X.getCircumference()      # Call getCircumference method
31.41592653589793
>>> X.setRadius(10)           # Change radius from 5.0 to 10
>>> X.getRadius()             # Call getRadius method
10
>>> X.getArea()               # Call getArea method
314.1592653589793
>>> X.getCircumference()      # Call getCircumference method
62.83185307179586
```

Python Object Oriented Programming (Example)

16: *Python Code Examples*

Here are some basic (and not so basic) functions written in Python. Most will run under any version of Python, however differences between Python 2 and Python 3 are called out when appropriate. There are simple helper routines that extend the capabilities of the Python language, as well as much more complicated routines that support the evaluation of polynomials and the creation of HTML files (including an object-oriented approach).

Python Basic Helper Functions

This first group of functions are simple helper functions that either are not part of Python or are in a module that might not be available. Simple functions that consist of nothing but a `def` and a `return` may be written on one line as shown here, or as a lambda expression.

Return closest integer to argument `N`. `N` may be any simple numeric type (integer or float, or long integer in Python 2). The `round` function rounds `N` to the nearest whole number (be careful: some implementations round half to nearest even, while others round half away from zero). The `int` function converts the result to an integer. This routine is particularly handy in graphics programs that are trying to paint the nearest pixel to a computed point. Note that in Python 2 the `round` function returns a `float`, while in Python 3 `round` returns an `int`. In all further examples in this book, whenever you see the construction `int(round(...))` you can substitute a call to the `INT` function as defined here if you are using Python 2, but just the `round` function if you are using Python 3. However, there will be no problems if you use either `INT(...)` or `int(round(...))` in Python 3; the results will be the same in all cases.

```
def INT (N): return int(round(N))
```

Similarly, Python 2 the `ceil` (ceiling) and `floor` functions in the `math` module do the appropriate rounding but return `float` results; their counterparts in Python 3 return `int` results instead. To guarantee `int` results in Python 2 or to simplify the calls, use the following functions (it never hurts to `int` a number that is already an integer):

```
def CEILING (N): return int(math.ceil(N))
```

```
def FLOOR (N): return int(math.floor(N))
```

This function simulates the `IF` function in a spreadsheet. Either the value of `N1` is returned or the value of `N2` is returned; which one is returned depends on Boolean parameter `B`. `N1` and `N2` can be of any data type, not just numbers.

```
def IF (B,N1,N2):
    if (B): return N1
    else:    return N2
```

Function `Odd` returns `True` if its argument is an odd number and returns `False` if the argument is even. Function `Even` has the opposite behavior.

```
def Odd (N): return ((N % 2) == 1)
```

```
def Even (N): return ((N % 2) == 0)
```

Python Basic Helper Functions (Continued)

Here are two methods for computing the greatest common divisor of two numbers. The first implements the classical algorithm in a traditional program style, while the second exploits the multiple-assignment technique of Python. Remember that GCD(12,15) = 3, for example.

```
def GCD (A,B):
    while (B > 0):
        Temp = B
        B    = A % B
        A    = Temp
    return A

def GCD (A,B):
    while (B > 0): A, B = B, A % B
    return A
```

This first function computes the least common multiple of two numbers. It requires the presence of the GCD function (above). Remember that LCM(12,15) = 60, for example. The second function returns the LCM of a list of integers: LCMofList([12,15,25]) = 300.

```
def LCM (A,B): return A * B // GCD(A,B)

def LCMofList (L):                    # L is a list of integers
    N = L[0]
    for I in L[1:]: N = LCM(I,N)
    return N
```

These two functions convert between degrees and radians. Remember that 2π radians = 360°. There are equivalent functions in the math module.

```
def Radians(D): return D / 180.0 * math.pi

def Degrees(R): return R * 180.0 / math.pi
```

These two functions convert between the Fahrenheit and Celsius temperature scales. Remember that 0°C = 32°F, 100°C = 212°F, and -40°C = -40°F.

```
def Fahrenheit(C): return (C * 1.8) + 32.0

def Celsius(F): return (F - 32.0) / 1.8
```

Python Logs and Powers

These routines all compute a type of logarithm. The `math.log` function computes the natural logarithm (base *e*). In this group, `Log` computes the common logarithm (base 10), `Lg` computes the logarithm base 2, and `NLg` computes $N \times \log_2(N)$.

```python
def Log (N): return math.log(N) / math.log(10)

def Lg (N):  return math.log(N) / math.log(2)

def NLg (N): return N * math.log(N) / math.log(2)
```

Python provides a square root function `sqrt` in the `math` module; these routines simplify the computation of squares, cubes, square roots, and cube roots. All return a float as their results.

```python
def Sqrt (N): return math.sqrt(N)

def Square (N): return float(N) * float(N)

def Cube (N): return float(N) * float(N) * float(N)

def CubeRt(N): return math.exp(math.log(N)/3)
```

The expression 2^N can be computed as `math.exp(N*math.log(2))`, but this routine returns an exact integer result instead of a float subject to round-off error. There are even more efficient ways to compute this value than what is shown here.

```python
def TwoToPower(N):
    Result = 1
    for I in range(1,N+1): Result = Result * 2
    return Result
```

Python Strings and Factorials

Convert a byte value into two hexadecimal characters. `HexByte(255)` returns FF, for example. Parameter N must be in the range 0...255; any value outside that range will crash the program.

```
def HexByte (N):
    Alphabet = "0123456789ABCDEF"
    return Alphabet[N // 16] + Alphabet[N % 16]
```

These routines return a string corresponding to argument N (which may be of any type, but is typically an integer or float). The `strN` function pads the result on the left with spaces until the result is at least `Width` characters in length; `str0` pads the result on the left with zeroes (two versions are shown). For example, `str0(23,4)` results in the 4-character string `"0023"`. The `Width` parameter is optional, and if left out will use the default value of 5. For example, `str0(23)` results in the 5-character string `"00023"`.

```
def strN (N,Width=5):
    S = str(N)
    while (len(S) < Width): S = " " + S
    return S

def str0 (N,Width=5):                            # Version 1
    S = str(N)
    while (len(S) < Width): S = "0" + S
    return S

def str0 (N,Width=5):                            # Version 2
    return str(N).zfill(Width)
```

Here are two ways of computing factorials (remember that 0! = 1, 1! = 1, 2! = 2, 3! = 6, 4! = 24, etc.). The first method is fast, but requires an explicit loop. The second requires fewer lines but is _**recursive**_, where the "loop" is built-in to the recursive calls.

```
def Factorial (N):
    F = 1
    for I in range(1,N+1): F = F * I
    return F

def Factorial2 (N):
    if (N <= 1): return 1
    return N * Factorial2(N-1)
```

Python Sorting (Simple but Slow)

It has been said that 70% or more of what any computer does during its operational lifetime is either searching for something in a list or sorting the list in order (which often makes searching go that much faster). The sorting algorithms presented on this page that sort a Python list L of numbers (or strings) in-place all have the benefit of being short and easy to program, but that is about all they have going for them. <u>All</u> run in $O(N^2)$ time in the worst case; ***Bubble Sort*** is $O(N^2)$ in the best and average cases as well: for any list of length N it will *always* make exactly $^{N×(N-1)}/_2$ comparisons (which is $\frac{1}{2}N^2 - \frac{1}{2}N$ comparisons, dominated by the N^2 term) regardless of whether or not the list was sorted to begin with. Both ***Exchange Sort*** and ***Insertion Sort*** will run in $O(N)$ time if the list was initially sorted, but quickly degenerate to close to $O(N^2)$ time for nearly any other initial ordering. Insertion Sort *is* slightly better than Exchange Sort on average, and it generalizes to the much better Shell's Sort shown on the next page.

```python
def BubbleSort (L):
    for I in range(len(L)-1):
        for J in range(I+1,len(L)):
            if L[I] > L[J]:
                Temp = L[I]
                L[I]  = L[J]
                L[J]  = Temp
    return


def ExchangeSort (L):
    More  = True
    N     = len(L)
    while More:
        More = False
        N = N - 1
        for I in range(N):
            if L[I] > L[I+1]:
                Temp    = L[I]
                L[I]    = L[I+1]
                L[I+1]  = Temp
                More    = True
    return


def InsertionSort (L):
    for I in range(1,len(L)):
        J = I
        Test = L[J]
        while (J > 0) and (Test < L[J-1]):
            L[J]    = L[J-1]
            J = J - 1
        L[J] = Test
    return
```

Python Sorting (Advanced)

Shellsort (Donald Shell, 1959) uses Insertion Sort on widely separated groups of items to get them roughly near where they should go, then successively narrows the group size until the last step is identical to the basic Insertion Sort. The faster *Quicksort* (Tony Hoare, 1959) is a recursive technique that runs on average in O(N log N) time, but can degenerate to O(N^2) in rare cases. Shellsort is preferred when the overhead of recursion is not desirable.

```python
def Shellsort (L):
    N = len(L)
    M = N // 2
    while (M > 0):
        for J in range(M,N):
            T = L[J]
            I = J - M
            while (I >= 0) and (L[I] > T):
                L[I+M] = L[I]
                I = I - M
            if (I+M != J): L[I+M] = T
        M = M // 2
    return

def Quicksort (L):

    def LocalSort (Low, High):
        if (Low >= High): return
        L2      = Low
        H2      = High
        Pivot   = L[(L2+H2) // 2]
        while (L2 <= H2):
            while L[L2] < Pivot: L2 = L2 + 1
            while L[H2] > Pivot: H2 = H2 - 1
            if L2 <= H2:
                Temp = L[L2]
                L[L2] = L[H2]
                L[H2] = Temp
                L2 = L2 + 1
                H2 = H2 - 1
        if Low <  H2: LocalSort(Low,H2)
        if L2 < High: LocalSort(L2,High)
        return

    LocalSort (0, len(L)-1)
    return
```

NOTE: *Timsort* (Tim Peters, 2002), used by the Python sort method, **L.sort()**, runs in O(N) best-case time and O(N log N) worst-case, but takes <u>thousands</u> of lines of code to implement!

Python Polynomials

Python lists are a natural way to represent ___polynomials___: the polynomial $2x^3 + 5x^2 - 4x + 3$ can be represented by the list `[3,-4,5,2]` where the coefficient for a particular exponent of x is in the list at the index position which matches the exponent. That is, the coefficient for the x^3 term is in the list at position 3. In order to make Python polynomials useful, individual functions for addition, subtraction, etc., must be written. Surprisingly, functions for calculus differentiation and integration are far simpler than those for multiplication and division.

As the math operations proceed, it is possible that a result is obtained where the high-order coefficients are 0, and it is also possible that a particular coefficient is computed as a float with no fraction instead of as an integer. The `polyNormalize` function addresses these issues, as well as making sure that a polynomial always has at least one constant term, even if that term is 0 (returning `[0]` instead of an empty list `[]`). This function is called at the end of every math function. For example, `polyNormalize([1,4,3.0,2,0,0,0,0])` returns `[1,4,3,2]`.

```
def polyNormalize (P):
    Q = [0] * max(len(P),1)
    for I in range(len(P)):
        if (abs(P[I] - float(int(P[I]))) < 1.0E-14):
            Q[I] = int(P[I])
        else:
            Q[I] = P[I]
    while (len(Q) > 1) and (Q[-1] == 0): del Q[-1]
    return Q
```

The `polyScale` function multiplies a polynomial P0 by a constant C, and returns the normalized result. For example, `polyScale([1,4,3,2], 2)` returns `[2,8,6,4]`, and `polyScale([1,4,3,2], 0)` returns `[0]`. This is used in polynomial division.

```
def polyScale (P0,C=1):
    return polyNormalize([P * C for P in P0])
```

The `polyShift` function, also used in division, multiplies a polynomial by x^{PLACES}, which is the same as adding `Places` entries of `0` to the beginning of the list.

```
def polyShift (P0, Places=0):
    return [0] * Places + P0
```

Python Polynomials (Continued)

The `polyStr` function takes in a list that represents a polynomial and returns a string that closely matches how we write polynomials in math. This includes suppressing terms with zero coefficients, suppressing coefficients or exponents that are equal to 1, separating terms with blanks, etc.

```python
def polyStr (P):
    S = ""
    for Exponent in range(len(P)-1,-1,-1):
        Coefficient = P[Exponent]
        if (Coefficient != 0):
            if (Coefficient < 0):
                if (S != ""):
                    S = S + " - "
                else:
                    S = S + "-"
            else:
                if (S != ""):
                    S = S + " + "
            if (Exponent == 0) or (abs(Coefficient) != 1):
                S = S + str(abs(Coefficient))
            if (Exponent >= 1):
                S = S + "X"
            if (Exponent >  1):
                S = S + "^" + str(Exponent)
    if S == "": S = "0"
    return S
```

Here are some examples:

`polyStr([1,4,3,2])`	returns	`"2X^3 + 3X^2 + 4X + 1"`
`polyStr([1,4,0,2])`	returns	`"2X^3 + 4X + 1"`
`polyStr([1,4,-3,-2])`	returns	`"-2X^3 - 3X^2 + 4X + 1"`
`polyStr([1,1,1,1])`	returns	`"X^3 + X^2 + X + 1"`
`polyStr([0,1,1,1])`	returns	`"X^3 + X^2 + X"`

Python Polynomials (Continued)

Here are the basic math routines for polynomials. In the case of add, subtract, and multiply, the size of the result can be estimated and that list can be initialized to all zeroes. In the case of `polyAdd`, the general expectation is that two polynomials will be added together, but the function allows for the possibility of adding together three. In `polySubtract`, the returned result is P0 - P1.

```
def polyAdd (P0,P1,P2=[]):
    P = [0] * max(1,len(P0),len(P1),len(P2))
    for I in range(len(P0)): P[I] = P[I] + P0[I]
    for I in range(len(P1)): P[I] = P[I] + P1[I]
    for I in range(len(P2)): P[I] = P[I] + P2[I]
    return polyNormalize(P)

def polySubtract (P0,P1):
    P = [0] * max(1,len(P0),len(P1))
    for I in range(len(P0)): P[I] = P[I] + P0[I]
    for I in range(len(P1)): P[I] = P[I] - P1[I]
    return polyNormalize(P)
```

For `polyMultiply`, every term from P0 is multiplied by every term in P1, and the resulting partial product is added to the result at the position indicated by the sum of their exponents.

```
def polyMultiply (P0,P1):
    P = [0] * max(1,len(P0)+len(P1))
    for I in range(len(P0)):
        for J in range(len(P1)):
            P[I+J] = P[I+J] + P0[I] * P1[J]
    return polyNormalize(P)
```

Division is very complicated and intricate, and uses many of Python's more sophisticated list-based techniques. Unlike other functions, `polyDivide` returns a list of <u>two</u> results, the quotient and the remainder of dividing P0 by P1, instead of just a single polynomial value. It also uses several functions defined earlier (`polySubtract`, `polyShift`, `polyScale`). This function does <u>not</u> check for division by zero (that is, division by [0]).

```
def polyDivide (P0,P1):
    Quotient = []
    Remainder= polyNormalize(P0)
    while (Remainder != [0]) and (len(Remainder) >= len(P1)):
        T = float(Remainder[-1]) / float(P1[-1])
        Quotient = [T] + Quotient
        Remainder = polySubtract(Remainder,                          \
            polyScale(polyShift(P1, len(Remainder)-len(P1)), T))
    return [polyNormalize(Quotient),polyNormalize(Remainder)]
```

Python Polynomials (Continued)

Here are the functions for differentiating and integrating polynomials. Notice how simple they are, in contrast to the polynomial division function. Integration allows for an optional constant C to be added in.

```
def polyDifferentiate (P):
    Q = [0] * max(1,len(P)-1)
    for I in range(1,len(P)): Q[I-1] = I * P[I]
    return polyNormalize(Q)

def polyIntegrate (P,C=0):
    Q = [0] * (len(P)+1)
    Q[0] = C
    for I in range(len(P)): Q[I+1] = float(P[I]) / float(I+1)
    return polyNormalize(Q)
```

Here are some examples:

`polyDifferentiate([1,4,3,2])`	returns	`[4,6,6]`

That is, $\frac{d}{dx}(2x^3+3x^2+4x+1) = 6x^2 + 6x + 4$

`polyIntegrate([4,6,6])`	returns	`[0,4,3,2]`
`polyIntegrate([4,6,6], 1)`	returns	`[1,4,3,2]`

This last function evaluates a polynomial P0 at a particular value for X:

```
def polyEvaluate (P0, X=0):
    Result = 0
    Power = 1
    for P in P0:
        Result = Result + P * Power
        Power = Power * X
    return Result
```

Python Writing HTML Files (version 1)

Python programs can be used to write out files. In this case, the program writes out HTML Web page code. The Web page will contain a table with 1000 rows, each row of the table containing a number (in the range 0 to 999) and its square root. Creating by hand a table with 1000 (or some other number) of rows would be very difficult, but for a program it is a trivial exercise. To change the number of rows, only the `for`-loop needs to be changed, and the program run again. However, the function is not general, and the opening HTML prolog and closing epilog have to be included in every similar function that creates a Web file.

```python
import math

def WriteHTML(Filename):
    MyFile = open(Filename, "w")
    MyFile.write ("<!DOCTYPE html>\n")
    MyFile.write ("<HTML>\n")
    MyFile.write ("    <HEAD>\n")
    MyFile.write ("        <TITLE>My Spiffy Web Page</TITLE>\n")
    MyFile.write ("    </HEAD>\n")
    MyFile.write ("    <BODY>\n")
    MyFile.write ("        <H1>Welcome!</H1>\n")
    MyFile.write ("        <TABLE BORDER>\n")

    for I in range(1000):
        MyFile.write ("        <TR>\n")
        MyFile.write ("          <TD>" + str(I) + "</TD>\n")
        MyFile.write ("          <TD>"+str(math.sqrt(I))+"</TD>\n")
        MyFile.write ("        </TR>\n")

    MyFile.write ("        </TABLE>\n")
    MyFile.write ("    </BODY>\n")
    MyFile.write ("</HTML>\n")
    MyFile.close()
    return
```

Python Writing HTML Files (version 2)

This version does the same task as on the previous page. Notice that the file handle `MyFile` is now a global variable, shared with the `Write` function. By using `Write`, there is no possibility of forgetting the `\n` new line character at the end of each line in the text file, and its presence simplifies the rest of the code. However, this version is not general either, and the use of global variables is generally discouraged.

```python
import math

def Write (S):
    global MyFile
    MyFile.write (S + "\n")
    return

def WriteHTML(Filename):
    global MyFile
    MyFile = open(Filename, "w")
    Write ("<!DOCTYPE html>")
    Write ("<HTML>")
    Write ("    <HEAD>")
    Write ("        <TITLE>My Spiffy Web Page</TITLE>")
    Write ("    </HEAD>")
    Write ("    <BODY>")
    Write ("        <H1>Welcome!</H1>")
    Write ("        <TABLE BORDER>")

    for I in range(1000):
        Write ("            <TR>")
        Write ("                <TD>" + str(I) + "</TD>")
        Write ("                <TD>" + str(math.sqrt(I)) + "</TD>")
        Write ("            </TR>")

    Write ("        </TABLE>")
    Write ("    </BODY>")
    Write ("</HTML>")
    MyFile.close()
    return
```

Python Writing HTML Files (version 3) Object-Oriented

One this page is a general object-oriented approach to creating a Web page file. The ***class*** THTML has a ***constructor*** (__init__, note the double-underscores), along with one ***method*** function Close to close down the file and another Write that always remembers to append a new line to the end of any string being written to the file.

The class is ***instantiated*** by assigning a new variable to the result of calling "function" THTML with the desired output file name, the Web page title, and the background color. That new variable is an ***object*** that now has access to all methods in the class, such as Write and Close. Creating an object automatically calls its constructor, which defines the variables local to the class and in this case writes out the HTML prolog to the file. To complete the task, call Close to write out the HTML epilog and close the file.

The nice thing about this approach is that multiple Web pages can be created simultaneously, as each instantiation of the class creates a file handle local to each object.

```python
class THTML(object):

    def __init__ (self, NewFilename, NewTitle, NewColor):
        self.Handle = open(NewFilename, "w")
        self.Filename = NewFilename
        self.Title = NewTitle
        self.Color = NewColor
        self.Write ("<!DOCTYPE html>")
        self.Write ("<HTML>")
        self.Write ("    <HEAD>")
        self.Write ("        <TITLE>" + self.Title + "</TITLE>")
        self.Write ("    </HEAD>")
        self.Write ('')
        self.Write ('    <BODY BGCOLOR="' + self.Color + '">')
        return

    def Close (self):
        self.Write ("    </BODY>")
        self.Write ("</HTML>")
        self.Handle.close()
        return

    def Write (self,S):
        self.Handle.write(S + "\n")
        return
```

Python Writing HTML Files (version 3 Example)

Once the code on the previous page has been written and debugged, it can be used to simplify the creation of Web pages. Here is a sample function that uses the THTML class defined on the previous page to do the same task as in version 1 and version 2 of writing out a Web page containing a table of square roots. X is the new object variable, created when the class was instantiated with the call to THTML. Any call to X.Write adds a new line of text to the output file. Care must be taken that any text written to the file observe the correct syntax for HTML. The call to X.Close writes the final HTML to the file and closes it.

```python
import math

def WriteHTML(Filename):
    X = THTML(Filename,"My Spiffy Web Page","cyan")
    X.Write ("          <H1>Welcome!</H1>")
    X.Write ("          <TABLE BORDER>")
    for I in range(1000):
        X.Write ("          <TR>")
        X.Write ("              <TD>" + str(I) + "</TD>")
        X.Write ("              <TD>" + str(math.sqrt(I)) + "</TD>")
        X.Write ("          </TR>")
    X.Write ("          </TABLE>")
    X.Close()
    return
```

Python Writing HTML Files (version 3 Example)

17: *Graphics, Image Processing, and Computational Geometry*

This section covers some of the basic concepts behind computer graphics. There is other relevant material scattered through this book (particularly in the previous chapter on Python code), but here is where we discuss the differences between raster and vector systems, as well as the various graphics file types that you are likely to encounter. A practical example of drawing a 3D sculptured button for use with Web pages and JavaScript is described.

This section also covers topics in image processing and computational geometry. The functions are presented here include filtering an image (to improve the focus, blur or emboss it, etc.), reducing the colors in an image, flipping or mirroring or rotating an image, dithering an image, computing information about triangles and circles, blending curves, linear algebra routines for graphics, code for generating graphics canvases and bitmap files, 3D/4D/5D transformations, etc.

Code examples are shown in Python or a Python-like pseudocode due to the simplicity of the language. Most code examples can be translated into other languages as needed with little difficulty. All functions written in Python depend only on functions that have been previously defined. Most examples are version agnostic and can be implemented in either Python 2 or Python 3. Where the difference *does* matter, functions will be clearly labeled in red as needing Python 2 or Python 3.

Raster vs. Vector

A ***cathode ray tube*** (CRT) is a ***vacuum tube*** with one (monochrome) or three (color) electron guns emitting a stream of electrons (cathode rays) towards a phosphor-coated glass faceplate, energizing the phosphor and making it glow with a brightness in proportion to the energy of the beam. In monochrome, all phosphor emits the same color (usually green, orange, or white). In the case of color, each electron beam is tuned to strike phosphors of one color only, either red, green, or blue. After being energized, the phosphor energies decrease and the glow diminishes over time. CRT displays are largely obsolete today.

Graphics comes in two major styles, ***raster*** and ***vector***.

Raster means to sweep a horizontal line across the face of the CRT, painting light and dark areas by adjusting the electron beam energy. After each line is complete it paints the next line in a slightly different vertical position, position, ultimately painting every area on the face plate. When the whole image is complete, it has to start over and paint it again before the light emitted from the phosphors fades.

Raster hardware for CRTs is either ***interlaced*** (painting every other line in one field, then going back and painting every other line in the other field) or ***progressive*** (displaying all lines from top to bottom, then going back to the top to do it all over again). Interlaced scanning was used in TV because the early electronics were not fast enough to paint the image progressively without it flickering, but later CRT computer monitors were fast enough to support progressive scans.

Standard analog television in the USA was raster, interlaced, and updated images 29.97 frames per second (reduced from 30 frames per second to accommodate the upgrade from B&W to color TV). Analog TV was phased out in the USA in 2009 in favor of HDTV.

Vector on CRTs means to sweep a graphics line directly from where the line needs to start to where the line needs to end, regardless of where those end points are located on the screen. A graphics image is built up from only the lines that need to be drawn. The image must be continuously re-drawn many times per second to keep it bright on the screen. Vector images have sharp continuous lines, but will eventually start to flicker if there are so many lines to draw that the phosphors dim before the lines can be repainted.

Raster computer images are rectangular arrays of ***pixels***. Each pixel takes up space in memory. The amount of memory available per pixel determines the number of unique colors that it can display. Pixels are square or rectangular, so angled lines exhibit a staircase effect called ***aliasing***, not a problem with vector systems. Pixels today are most often square. Graphics data stored in `.SVG` files are in vector format, but are rendered as pixels on raster devices.

Computer graphics hardware scans through every pixel in memory, reading out its value and displaying the corresponding color on screen many times per second. Modern ***liquid crystal displays*** (LCD) and ***light emitting diode*** (LED) flat-panel displays have enough electronics at each pixel on the screen that flicker is largely eliminated.

Pixels and Palettes

Nearly all computer graphics systems today are raster based. A graphics image is a rectangular array of pixel values held in computer memory.

There are two methods for identifying the coordinates of any pixel: ***corner-based*** and ***center-based***. In center-based, each unique column (x) and row (y) indicates the <u>center</u> of the identified pixel. In corner-based, each unique column (x) and row (y) indicates the <u>corner</u> between pixels. Both have their advantages and disadvantages for drawing images. See the sections later in this chapter on drawing boxes and rectangles for how to work with each of these two models when programming practical graphical applications.

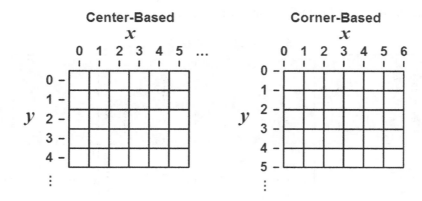

In both cases, the coordinate system is ***upside-down*** from normal Cartesian coordinates, with (0,0) at the upper-left corner. This is due to how pixels are laid out linearly in memory.

Graphics systems capable of full 24-bit color or 48-bit color have ***enough memory for each pixel*** to completely specify its color, independently of all other pixels. For 24-bit color this requires three bytes per pixel, one byte each for red, green, and blue, allowing 256 levels for each primary and 16,777,216 total unique colors. For 48-bit color this requires six bytes per pixel, two bytes each for red, green, and blue, allowing 65,536 levels for each primary and approximately 281 trillion unique colors. A 1024×768 image using 24-bit color thus requires 2,359,296 bytes of storage.

Graphics systems without that much memory use a ***palette*** or ***color look-up table*** (CLUT). A system using a palette is called ***indexed color***. Each entry in the palette table has full color resolution, but the table is ***limited in size to the total number of colors*** available (most often a power-of-2 between 2 and 256). A 256-color system for example has 256 full-color definitions in the palette, but it only takes 8 bits to determine which color from the table to use. Similarly, the palette for a 16-color system contains 16 full-color definitions, but it only takes 4 bits to determine which color to use. Finally, a monochrome system has a table containing only two full-color definitions (often black and white, but may be other values), and it takes a single bit to determine which palette entry to use. This technique reduces the memory needed to display images containing few unique colors, without compromising the color quality of each pixel.

Graphics File Formats

Here is a table describing several different graphics file types. Some support full 24-bit color (or even 48-bit color), others require a palette. Some are **_uncompressed_**, others use **_lossy_** or **_lossless compression_**. Some support one or more colors to be treated as transparent (letting a background show through), and some support simple animations.

Lossy compression means that the pixel values from the image in memory may be changed in order to reduce the corresponding file size; if done correctly the user will not notice. Lossless compression means that no pixel value from the image is changed in order to be stored in the file. Lossy compression is good for photographs of natural scenes, but terrible for images with sharp edges (cartoons, text, and line-art). Lossless compression is good for images with sharp edges, but may result in a too-large file for photographs.

	Bits per Pixel	Maximum Supported Colors	Indexed Color (Palette)	Suitable for...				Supports...					Notes
				Photographs	Cartoons	Text/Line Art	Web use	Compression	Animation	Transparency	Interlaced Display	MS Paint	
.BMP	1	2	Yes	Half-Tones	Excellent	Excellent	No	None	No	No	No	All Versions	There is a rarely-used lossless compression variant called .RLE (Run-Length Encoding).
	4	16		Poor									
	8	256		Marginal									
	24	16,777,216	No	Excellent									
.GIF (1987, 1989)	1	2	Yes	Half-Tones	Excellent	Excellent	Yes	Lossless	Yes	Yes	Yes (Vertical, 4 passes)	≥ Windows ME	One color in the palette may be defined as "transparent" indicating that it not be painted on screen. Patent issues in the 1990s on the LZW compression technique used by .GIF spawned development of the .PNG format, but all relevant patents have expired.
	2	4											
	3	8		Poor									
	4	16											
	5	32											
	6	64											
	7	128											
	8	256		Marginal									
.JPG (1992)	24	16,777,216	No	Excellent	Poor	Poor	Yes	Lossy	No	No	Yes (Rare Support)	≥ Windows 98	A user-selected "Quality" setting from 0...100 correlates image quality with file size (0 → worst image quality but smallest file, 100 → best image quality but biggest file, often around 70...90 for photographs).
.PNG (1996)	1	2	Yes	Half-Tones	Excellent	Excellent	Yes	Lossless	No	Yes	Yes (Adam7, 7 passes)	≥ Windows XP	Indexed formats allow one color to be defined as transparent, but non-indexed formats allow inclusion of an additional "Alpha Channel". 16-Bit format is Gray-scale only (requires 32 bits when also using an Alpha Channel). 48-Bit format requires 64 bits when also using an Alpha Channel.
	2	4		Poor									
	4	16											
	8	256		Marginal									
	16	65,536		Good									
	24	16,777,216	No	Excellent									
	48	281,474,976,710,656											

Interlaced Display of Graphic Images

Many graphic file types contain images stored in raster order: the data for line 4 comes after the data for line 3 and before the data for line 5. Reading out the data from the file one line at a time is called ***progressive display***. Both `.GIF` and `.PNG` support ***interlaced display*** in addition to progressive display. Lines of pixels (in the case of `.GIF`) or individual pixels (in the case of `.PNG`) are stored in their files so that widely separated areas of the image are painted first, then intermediate areas next, and closer and closer regions are painted until the entire image is complete. This was most important in the days of slow dial-up connections to the Internet.

Interlaced `.GIF` files require four passes over the image before it is complete, painting different lines of the image in each pass. Such an image first contains lines 0, 8, 16, … (pass 1), then lines 4, 12, 20, … (pass 2), then lines 2, 6, 10, … (pass 3), and finally lines 1, 3, 5, 7, … (pass 4).

Interlaced `.PNG` files use a two-dimensional technique (called ***Adam 7***) that requires seven passes over each 8×8 block of pixels. The numbers in the grid below indicate which pass each pixel belongs to.

In both cases, pixels not yet painted with their correct colors can be painted with temporary values from known pixels to give the illusion of a complete picture that becomes more detailed over time. For example, when painting pass 1 in a `.GIF` file, the data for line 0 can be copied to lines 1…7, line 8 can be copied to lines 9…15, and so on. Then, in pass 2, the data for line 4 are copied to lines 5…7, line 12 copied to lines 13…15, etc., replacing the earlier data. Similarly, in a `.PNG` file the value for the single pixel in pass 1 defines the color of the entire 8×8 block, the pixel for pass 2 replaces the rightmost 8×4 block (8 rows by 4 columns), the two pixels for pass 3 replace the lower left and lower right 4×4 blocks, and so on.

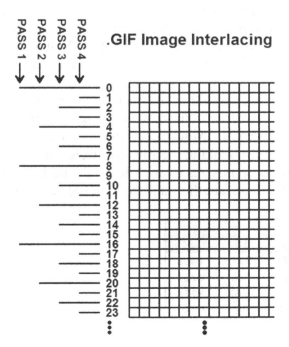

.GIF Image Interlacing

.PNG Image Interlacing

1	6	4	6	2	6	4	6
7	7	7	7	7	7	7	7
5	6	5	6	5	6	5	6
7	7	7	7	7	7	7	7
3	6	4	6	3	6	4	6
7	7	7	7	7	7	7	7
5	6	5	6	5	6	5	6
7	7	7	7	7	7	7	7

Icon Files

Microsoft introduced the .ICO file format with an early version of Windows as a way to graphically indicate a link to a file. It has undergone many revisions since then. In its basic configuration, an .ICO file has a small number of allowable sizes and allowable color depths: 16×16, 32×32, 48×48, or 64×64 pixels, with 2, 16, or 256 colors. Early Web browsers supported only the 16×16, 16-color icon as a "favorite" or ***favicon***, but now support other sizes.

Internally, each icon file contains <u>two</u> grids of data: an XOR-mask and an AND-mask, neither of which is compressed (they are much like a bitmap in that way). The XOR-mask contains the color information, and the AND-mask (which is always 1 bit per pixel) acts as a transparency mask. As an example, here is a 16×16, 16-color icon at actual size: ⊗. For that icon, here are the XOR-mask and the AND-mask, respectively:

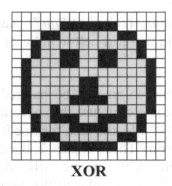
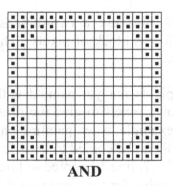

XOR AND

In the AND-mask, any pixel indicated by a square dot is treated as transparent, allowing a background image pixel to show through (thus creating the illusion of a non-square image). Any empty pixel in the AND-mask is opaque, forcing the corresponding pixel from the XOR-mask to appear in that spot. The only odd situation is if a pixel has a non-zero color in the XOR-mask but is <u>also</u> transparent in the AND-mask; in this case the icon pixel is XOR-ed with the background pixel it overlays. While allowed, it tends not to happen too often in practice.

For the standard icon configurations mention above file sizes are fixed. Just by examining the file size it is possible to determine the size and number of colors: by knowing that the icon file is 318 bytes in size we know it must be 16×16, 16-color. Modern revisions to the format permit 24-bit or 32-bit color, or even embedded .PNG files, making the file size irrelevant. A variation called an icon list can embed multiple icons of different sizes in one file, so the best selection can be made from the list for the current application. Here are the standard icon file sizes in bytes:

Pixels in Icon	Colors		
	2	16	256
16x16	198	318	1406
32x32	326	766	2238
48x48	838	1662	3774
64x64	1094	2686	5694

3D Sculptured Buttons

In a raster based system, it is often useful to be able to draw a picture of a button with a 3D look to it. Here is an annotated blow-up of such a button, in both un-clicked (popped out) and clicked (pushed in) views.

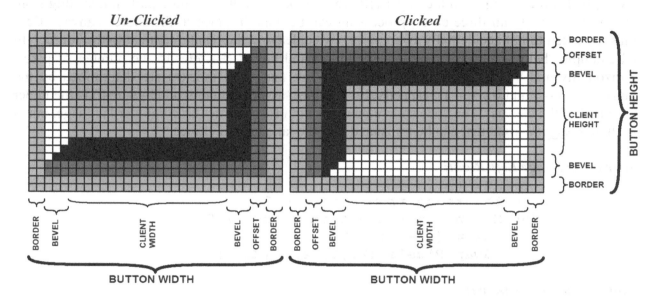

The underline{border} is the band around the outside of the button to isolate it from adjacent objects. May be omitted (set to 0 thickness).

The offset is a band on the lower-right when the button is popped-out, but is on the upper-left when the button has been clicked. This gives the illusion of movement when the button is pushed and released. The color of this band (shown dark here) is often the same color as the border. The offset is often no more than one or two pixels thick, and may be omitted entirely.

The bevel is what gives the button its 3D appearance. When the button is popped-out the top and left edges are light and the bottom and right edges are dark, giving the appearance of an object sticking out towards you with sunlight coming from above. When the button is pushed-in, the top and left edges are dark and the bottom and right edges are light, giving the appearance of an object recessed away from you. Bevels are usually no more than two or three pixels thick.

The client area is where you draw the material that should appear on the top of the button.

You need to create two unique designs for any button:
    Un-Clicked: top & left bevel light, bottom & right bevel dark, offset below and to right.
    Clicked: top & left bevel dark, bottom & right bevel light, offset above and to left.

In a Web page, use JavaScript to alternate between the images as the mouse rolls over (`onMouseOver`) or rolls away from (`onMouseOut`) the button.

Image Processing: Mirroring, Flipping, and Rotating 180°

In mirroring an image, all pixels in the left half of image are swapped with the corresponding pixels in the right half. Similarly, when flipping an image, all pixels in the upper half of the image are swapped with their counterparts in the lower half of the image. When rotating by 180°, pixels proceeding from the upper left are swapped with their counterparts proceeding from the lower right. In all three cases, processing can be done in-place in the source canvas. Care must be taken to not accidentally swap pixels twice, leaving the result identical to the source. In all examples below, it is assumed that width (W) and height (H) refer to the number of pixels horizontally and vertically in an image canvas, but that pixel indexes are determined by the ranges 0…W − 1 and 0…H − 1, respectively. It is also assumed that pixel (X=0,Y=0) is the upper left pixel of the canvas. The code shown below is not in any particular computer language, but is written in ***pseudo-code*** that can be translated into the language of choice.

Mirror the Image Left-Right:

```
for Y in the range from 0 to H - 1:
    for X1 in the range from 0 to W / 2:
        X2 = (W - 1) - X1
        Swap Pixels (X1,Y) and (X2,Y)
```

Flip the Image Up-Down:

```
for X in the range from 0 to W - 1:
    for Y1 in the range from 0 to H / 2:
        Y2 = (H - 1) - Y1
        Swap Pixels (X,Y1) and (X,Y2)
```

Rotate the Image 180°:

```
Pixels = W * H
X1 = 0
Y1 = 0
for I in the range from 1 to Pixels / 2:
    X2 = (W - 1) - X1
    Y2 = (H - 1) - Y1
    Swap Pixels (X1,Y1) and (X2,Y2)
    X1 = (X1 + 1) mod W            { Remainder of dividing by W }
    if X1 is 0: Y1 = Y1 + 1
```

In Mirror, the division W / 2 is assumed to be an integer division, where a computation such as 123 / 2 gives 61 (integer) and not 61.5 (floating-point). In cases where the image is an odd number of pixels wide, the pixel in the middle of the row being scanned is thus ignored rather than being swapped with itself. In Flip, the H / 2 division works the same way, ignoring the pixel in the middle rows of images that are an odd number of pixels high. Rotate is more complicated, requiring careful treatment of the interaction between rows and columns.

Image Processing: Rotation

Image Rotation requires a destination canvas in addition to the source canvas because the width (W) and height (H) of the source canvas cannot be guaranteed to be the same. Indeed, the width of the source is translated into the height of the destination, and the height of the source into the width of the destination. Coordinates have to be swapped correspondingly, as shown below:

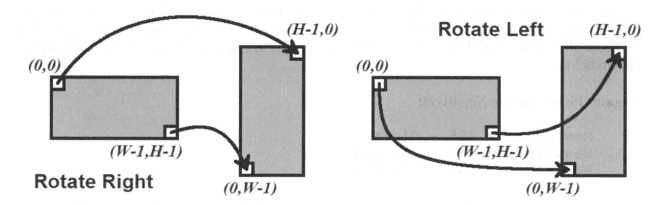

Rotate Right:

```
for Y in the range from 0 to H - 1:
    for X in the range from 0 to W - 1:
        Destination (H-1-Y,X) gets Source (X,Y)
```

Rotate Left:

```
for Y in the range from 0 to H - 1:
    for X in the range from 0 to W - 1:
        Destination (Y,W-1-X) gets Source (X,Y)
```

Image Processing: Enhancing Image Contrast

Enhancing the ***contrast*** of an image requires <u>two</u> passes over all pixels in the canvas. In pass #1, all the red components are totaled separately, as are all the green components and the blue components, then those totals are divided by the total number of pixels to get the average red, the average green, and the average blue values. In pass #2, the components of every pixel subtract off their respective averages, multiply those differences by a <u>scale factor</u>, the averages are added back, then the results are converted back to integers and clipped to the legal range of the color components (0…255 for 24-bit color or 0…65535 for 48-bit color). The scale factor is usually a small number such as 1.25 or 1.5 (scale factors less than 1.0 decrease the contrast).

```
NewRed   = int((OldRed   - AverageR) * Scale + AverageR)
NewGreen = int((OldGreen - AverageG) * Scale + AverageG)
NewBlue  = int((OldBlue  - AverageB) * Scale + AverageB)
```

Image Processing: Pixel Filters

Simple filtering can be done *in-place on the current canvas*. Every pixel in the canvas (or in a region) is transformed, but each is transformed independently from all other pixels. In general, the red components of a pixel are transformed separately from the green components and the blue components, but in a few cases one depends on the other. In these examples, 24-bit color is assumed: the red, green, and blue components are stored in single bytes where 0 means off, 128 is half-power, and 255 is on at full power. For a 48-bit color system that uses two bytes per primary, 65535 would be the full-power value and 32768 is the half-power value, and those numbers should be should be substituted for 255 and 128, respectively, in all the pseudo-code shown below.

Negate (Photographic Negative):

```
NewRed    = 255 - OldRed
NewGreen  = 255 - OldGreen
NewBlue   = 255 - OldBlue
```

Brighten by N (Darken if N is negative. Each component is explicitly clipped to 0…255)**:**

```
NewRed    = max(0, min(255, OldRed   + N))
NewGreen  = max(0, min(255, OldGreen + N))
NewBlue   = max(0, min(255, OldBlue  + N))
```

Rotate Primary Colors (**Temp** is needed if new and old values refer to the same pixel)**:**

```
Temp      = OldRed
NewRed    = OldGreen
NewGreen  = OldBlue
NewBlue   = Temp
```

Convert to Gray Scale:

```
Brightness= int((OldRed + OldGreen + OldBlue) / 3)
NewRed    = Brightness
NewGreen  = Brightness
NewBlue   = Brightness
```

Convert to Gray Scale tuned for Human Visual System:

```
Brightness= int(OldRed   * 0.299 +
               OldGreen * 0.587 +
               OldBlue  * 0.114)
NewRed    = Brightness
NewGreen  = Brightness
NewBlue   = Brightness
```

Image Processing: Pixel Filters (Continued)

Convert to Black & White (`Limit` determines how bright the pixel must be to turn it white):

```
Brightness= {Choose a brightness method from last page}
if Brightness > Limit then Value = 255 else Value = 0
NewRed    = Value
NewGreen  = Value
NewBlue   = Value
```

Convert to Black, White, and Gray (needs a high limit to determine when to go white and a low limit to determine when to go black; gray is anything in the middle):

```
Brightness= {Choose a brightness method from last page}
if Brightness > HighLimit then Value = 255 else
if Brightness < LowLimit  then Value = 0    else
                               Value = 128
NewRed    = Value
NewGreen  = Value
NewBlue   = Value
```

Convert to 8 Color RGB (`Limit` determines how bright each primary must be to change it):

```
if OldRed   > Limit then NewRed   = 255 else NewRed   = 0
if OldGreen > Limit then NewGreen = 255 else NewGreen = 0
if OldBlue  > Limit then NewBlue  = 255 else NewBlue  = 0
```

Note: Resulting colors are black, blue, green, cyan, red, magenta, yellow, and white.

Convert to 8 Color RGB Variation (pixel brightness determines when changes are made):

```
Limit     = {Choose a brightness method from last page}
if OldRed   > Limit then NewRed   = 255 else NewRed   = 0
if OldGreen > Limit then NewGreen = 255 else NewGreen = 0
if OldBlue  > Limit then NewBlue  = 255 else NewBlue  = 0
```

Convert to Sepia:

```
NewRed    = int(OldRed*0.393+OldGreen*0.769+OldBlue*0.189)
NewGreen  = int(OldRed*0.349+OldGreen*0.686+OldBlue*0.168)
NewBlue   = int(OldRed*0.272+OldGreen*0.534+OldBlue*0.131)
```

Note: The final results of the computations for each component may be out of range. If so, they must be clipped to 0…255 for 24-bit color or to 0…65535 for 48-bit color.

Image Processing: Neighborhood Filters

Neighborhood filtering *requires a destination canvas* in addition to the source canvas; these operations *cannot* be performed in-place on the source canvas. The destination canvas is exactly the same size as the source. The color values of each pixel in the new canvas will depend on the corresponding pixel in the source canvas, as well as the pixels in the immediate neighborhood of that source pixel. Neighbors that would be off the edge of the canvas are usually considered to be either black or the same color as the pixel being processed; this decision *will* affect the outcome of filtering, and must be considered carefully when implementing filtering algorithms.

Each RGB pixel has a red component, a green component, and a blue component. For 24-bit color each of these values range from 0 through 255 (one byte per component), and for 48-bit color each value ranges from 0 through 65535 (two bytes per component). Black is always (0,0,0): no red, green, or blue. White is (255,255,255) in 24-bit color and (65535,65535,65535) in 48-bit color: full-power red, full-power green, and full-power blue. For RGB images, the filtering process is performed independently on the red, the green, and the blue components.

The color components of each source pixel and its neighbors are multiplied by the appropriate weight from a filter matrix, those values are summed, the sum is divided by a scale factor, an offset is added, and the results are clipped to the appropriate range (0…255 or 0…65535, as required). This process determines the color of the corresponding pixel in the destination canvas. The diameter of the neighborhood is N, which is 0 in the simplest case (1×1) but is most often larger, sometimes significantly so (the larger the value of N, the slower the filtering process becomes). Care must be taken to avoid referencing non-existent pixels off the edge of the canvas. Here is the general equation, along with a few sample filters.

$$NewPixel_{(c,r)} = \left\{ \sum_{x=-N}^{+N} \sum_{y=-N}^{+N} \left(Weight_{(x,y)} \times OldPixel_{(c+x,r+y)} \right) \right\} \div Divisor + Offset$$

The following two filters are included for completeness, but in reality would not be used in practice in this form. Neither one looks at any pixels in the neighborhood of the pixel being transformed. "Unity" multiplies each pixel's red, green, and blue component by 1, divides by 1, and adds zero, which has no effect on the image. "Negate" multiplies each pixel's red, green, and blue component by -1, divides by 1, and adds the 100% value for the color system in use (255 when using 1 byte for each red, green, and blue component, 65535 when using 2 bytes). Instead, the much simpler in-place process for photographic negatives presented earlier would be used. There is no point in implementing either one of these filters.

Unity (1×1)
Divisor = 1
Offset = 0%

Negate (1×1)
Divisor = 1
Offset = 100%

Image Processing: Neighborhood Filters (Edge Detection)

Edge Detect (3x3) Inside
Divisor = 1
Offset = 0%

Edge Detect (3x3) Outside
Divisor = 1
Offset = 0%

Line Detect (3x3) 0 Degrees ===
Divisor = 1
Offset = 0%

Line Detect (3x3) 90 Degrees |||
Divisor = 1
Offset = 0%

Line Detect (3x3) 45 Degrees ///
Divisor = 1
Offset = 0%

Line Detect (3x3) 135 Degrees \\\
Divisor = 1
Offset = 0%

These edge and line detection filters tend to result in black images with enhanced edges in white; in practice the detection step is *often followed by a negation step* to get blackish lines on a white background, and/or a *color reduction to monochrome*. The edge detect filters detect edges in any orientation, while the line detect filters detect lines in their preferred orientation.

The difference between the "inside" edge detect and "outside" edge detect is largely irrelevant for photographs of natural scenes, but is significant when performing edge detection on cartoon-like black-and-white images. The image on the left below is the source image. The middle image shows the application of the "inside" edge filter (the line is on the black side of the edge, inside the black object), and the right image shows the application of the "outside" edge filter (the line is on the white side of the edge, outside of the black object).

Original **Inside Edges** **Outside Edges**

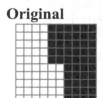 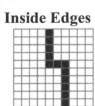 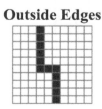

Care must be taken when handling pixels at the periphery of the original image to avoid additional edge artifacts from appearing.

Image Processing: Neighborhood Filters (Blurring)

Average of 4 (2x2)
Divisor = 4
Offset = 0%

0	0	0
0	1	1
0	1	1

Gaussian Blur 1 (3x3)
Divisor = 16
Offset = 0%

1	2	1
2	4	2
1	2	1

Blur Low (3x3)
Divisor = 9
Offset = 0%

1	1	1
1	1	1
1	1	1

Gaussian Blur 2 (5x5)
Divisor = 256
Offset = 0%

1	4	6	4	1
4	16	24	16	4
6	24	36	24	6
4	16	24	16	4
1	4	6	4	1

Blur Medium (5x5)
Divisor = 25
Offset = 0%

1	1	1	1	1
1	1	1	1	1
1	1	1	1	1
1	1	1	1	1
1	1	1	1	1

Gaussian Blur 3 (5x5)
Divisor = 273
Offset = 0%

1	4	7	4	1
4	16	26	16	4
7	26	41	26	7
4	16	26	16	4
1	4	7	4	1

Blur High (7x7)
Divisor = 49
Offset = 0%

1	1	1	1	1	1	1
1	1	1	1	1	1	1
1	1	1	1	1	1	1
1	1	1	1	1	1	1
1	1	1	1	1	1	1
1	1	1	1	1	1	1
1	1	1	1	1	1	1

Gaussian Blur 4 (7x7)
Divisor = 1064
Offset = 0%

0	0	0	5	0	0	0
0	5	18	32	18	5	0
0	18	64	100	64	18	0
5	32	100	100	100	32	5
0	18	64	100	64	18	0
0	5	18	32	18	5	0
0	0	0	5	0	0	0

Blurring averages a pixel with its neighborhood in some way. The Gaussian blurs on the right tend to be much "softer" than the rectangular blurs on the left for filters of the same size. Average of 4 can actually be performed in-place, without a new canvas, similar to dithering (discussed later).

Image Processing: Neighborhood Filters (Focus)

-1	0	-1
0	7	0
-1	0	-1

Focus 1 (3x3)
Divisor = 3
Offset = 0%

0	-1	0
-1	7	-1
0	-1	0

Detail (3x3)
Divisor = 3
Offset = 0%

-1	0	0	0	-1
0	0	0	0	0
0	0	7	0	0
0	0	0	0	0
-1	0	0	0	-1

Focus 2 (5x5)
Divisor = 3
Offset = 0%

0	0	0	-1	0	0	0
0	-1	0	0	0	-1	0
0	0	0	0	0	0	0
-1	0	0	11	0	0	-1
0	0	0	0	0	0	0
0	-1	0	0	0	-1	0
0	0	0	-1	0	0	0

Focus 4 (7x7)
Divisor = 3
Offset = 0%

-1	0	0	0	0	0	-1
0	0	0	0	0	0	0
0	0	0	0	0	0	0
0	0	0	7	0	0	0
0	0	0	0	0	0	0
0	0	0	0	0	0	0
-1	0	0	0	0	0	-1

Focus 3 (7x7)
Divisor = 3
Offset = 0%

0	-1	0	-1	0	-1	0
-1	0	0	0	0	0	-1
0	0	-1	0	-1	0	0
-1	0	0	19	0	0	-1
0	0	-1	0	-1	0	0
-1	0	0	0	0	0	-1
0	-1	0	-1	0	-1	0

Focus 5 (7x7)
Divisor = 3
Offset = 0%

Focus filters must be applied carefully, and which filter is applied depends on the amount of blurring that exists in the original image. A small image with minimal blurring may use either the "focus" filter in the upper left or the "detail" variant in the upper right. A larger image or one with more noticeable blurring may benefit from a more wide-ranging focus filter, a few examples of which are shown here. However, applying any filter more than once won't make the image sharper and sharper; the more times the filter is applied the worse the image gets, until it becomes entirely unrecognizable.

Image Processing: Neighborhood Filters (Embossing)

Emboss Light UL (3x3)
Divisor = 1
Offset = 50%

Emboss Heavy UL (3x3)
Divisor = 1
Offset = 50%

Emboss Light LR (3x3)
Divisor = 1
Offset = 50%

Emboss Heavy LR (3x3)
Divisor = 1
Offset = 50%

Emboss Light UR (3x3)
Divisor = 1
Offset = 50%

Emboss Heavy UR (3x3)
Divisor = 1
Offset = 50%

Emboss Light LL (3x3)
Divisor = 1
Offset = 50%

Emboss Heavy LL (3x3)
Divisor = 1
Offset = 50%

Embossing ignores the current pixel and generates the difference between pixels in diagonally opposing corners. Pixel values from the corner containing positive numbers get brightened, the corner containing negative numbers gets darkened, and the current pixel's new value gets the difference. That difference is close to (or less than) zero, so a 50% brightness offset is added (128 for 1-byte systems, 32768 for 2-byte systems). The new image is nearly entirely gray, except where edges in the original image in the direction of the positive corner are slightly brighter and edges in the direction of the negative corner are slightly darker.

If the positive (lighter) corners are in the upper left or upper right, the result will have objects that appear to us to "stick out" from the background, and if the positive corners are in the lower left or lower right the result will have objects that appear to be "pushed in" to the background. This is largely due to us having evolved in an environment where light sources (the sun) come from above.

Image Processing: Dithering

Dithering (also known as **error diffusion**) is the process of reducing the number of unique colors in an image, while preserving the overall look and feel of the original. Simply reducing the colors results in an image that is heavily posterized, but dithering maintains the correct *average* color around each pixel. That is, squinting at a dithered image "fuzzes" the color values together, giving an approximation to the original, full color image. A dithered image tends to appear speckled when examined close-up.

A common, simple technique for dithering is **Floyd-Steinberg** (Robert W. Floyd and Louis Steinberg, 1975-1976), which can be done *in-place on a single canvas*. Starting at the top-left pixel and scanning left-to-right across each raster line, each pixel is converted to its low-color replacement, but the error between the old pixel's value and the new replacement value is distributed to neighbor pixels not yet processed. As the scan progresses left-to-right, top-to-bottom, the adjacent pixels not yet processed are the ones to the right, lower-left, below, and lower-right, as shown here:

The error is distributed fractionally: $7/16$ of the error is added to the right neighbor, $3/16$ of the error to the lower-left neighbor, $5/16$ of the error to the below neighbor, and $1/16$ of the error to the lower-right neighbor. Errors do tend to propagate over the image to the lower-right corner, but since only $1/16$ of the error goes to the lower-right neighbor this effect is minimized. Some algorithms change the scan direction on alternate raster lines: left-to-right on one line, right-to-left on the next (with the weights mirrored as well). This tends to spread out the error.

For RGB images, the process is performed independently on the red, green, and blue information. That is, the red values are dithered, the green values are dithered, and the blue values are dithered all separately.

Care must be taken to avoid referencing pixels off the left, right, or bottom of the canvas (but not the top, as no neighbors above the current pixel need be examined).

Variations in dithering techniques are shown on the next two pages.

Image Processing: Dithering Models

(Robert Floyd, Louis Steinberg, 1975)

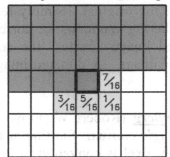

Floyd–Steinberg

(various)

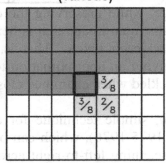

False Floyd–Steinberg

(J. F. Jarvis, C. N. Judice, W. H. Ninke, 1976)

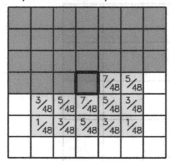

Jarvis–Judice–Ninke (JaJuNi)

(Peter Stucki, 1981)

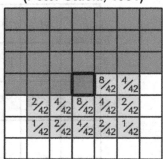

Stucki

(Daniel Burkes, 1988)

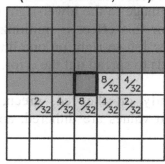

Burkes

(Bill Atkinson, Apple 1980s)

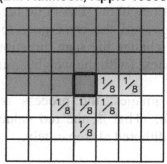

Atkinson

Reduced Color Bleed

Image Processing: Dithering Models (Continued)

(Frankie Sierra, 1989)

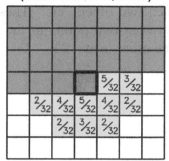

Sierra 3

(Frankie Sierra, 1990)

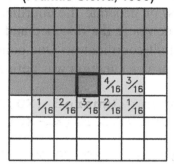

Sierra 2

Two-Row Sierra

(Frankie Sierra, 1990)

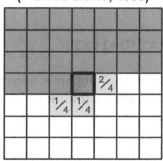

Sierra Lite

Sierra-2-4A

(Zhigang Fan)

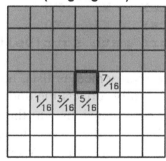

Fan

Custom (Create Your own)

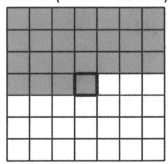

Custom

Custom (Create Your Own)

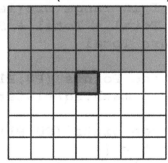

Custom

Python Geometry Functions

In geometric applications, it is important to compute the distance or squared distance between two points, or generate the coordinates of a point in between two others, etc. These first two functions compute the distance and the squared distance between two points in the plane (2D) given explicit coordinates. One point is at (X0, Y0) and the other is at (X1, Y1). Remember that the Square function was defined earlier.

```python
def DistanceSquared (X0,Y0,X1,Y1):
    return Square(X1-X0) + Square(Y1-Y0)

def Distance (X0,Y0,X1,Y1):
    return math.sqrt(DistanceSquared(X0,Y0,X1,Y1))
```

The Distance function can also be written in a completely stand-alone fashion, as follows:

```python
def Distance (X0,Y0,X1,Y1):
    DeltaX = X1 - X0
    DeltaY = Y1 - Y0
    return math.sqrt(DeltaX*DeltaX + DeltaY*DeltaY)
```

If points are represented as lists, however, the argument lists to the functions becomes simpler and more naturally reflects the underlying geometry, but it also allows routines to be written for any number of dimensions. In the following functions, points P0 and P1 are lists, where, for example, P0[0] is the x coordinate of P0, P0[1] is the y coordinate of P0, P1[0] is the x coordinate of P1, and so on. A list contains two elements for 2D, three elements for 3D, four elements for 4D, and so on. Note that P0 and P1 could be tuples instead of lists, but function AveragePoints always returns the intermediate point as a list.

```python
def DistanceSquaredPoints (P0,P1):
    Total = 0
    for I in range(min(len(P0),len(P1))):
        Total = Total + Square(P1[I] - P0[I])
    return Total

def DistancePoints (P0,P1):
    return math.sqrt(DistanceSquaredPoints(P0,P1))

def AveragePoints (P0,P1):
    Result = []
    for I in range(min(len(P0),len(P1))):
        Result = Result + [(P0[I] + P1[I]) / 2.0]
    return Result
```

Python Geometry Functions (Continued)

Points in space often need to become points on a screen with integer coordinates. Function `INTPoint` converts all values in a point (which is a list) into the nearest integer. For example, `INTPoint([7.8, 9.2, 3.1])` returns `[8, 9, 3]`.

Function `INTPointsList` converts a list of points into integer points. For example, `INTPointsList([[2.3,4],[6.6,7],[2,1.4]])` returns `[[2,4],[7,7],[2,1]]`.

```
def INTPoint (P):
    Result = []
    for N in P: Result = Result + [int(round(N))]
    return Result

def INTPointsList (L):
    Result = []
    for P in L: Result = Result + [INTPoint(P)]
    return Result
```

These two functions can also be written to use list comprehensions as:

```
def INTPoint (P):
    return [int(round(N)) for N in P]

def INTPointsList (L):
    return [INTPoint(P) for P in L]
```

This function computes the parametric equations of a line through two points (as in Lagrange interpolation), and evaluates those equations at time *t* to obtain a point on that line. For example, `EvaluateParametricLine([5,7],[10,14],0.5)` evaluates the line through points `[5,7]` and `[10,14]` at *t*=0.5, and returns the value `[7.5,10.5]` as the intermediate point. Point P0 is returned when *t*=0, and P1 is returned when *t*=1. This routine is dimension-agnostic and will work on 2D, 3D, 4D, or other dimension points.

```
def EvaluateParametricLine (P0,P1,T):
    Result = []
    Dimensions = min(len(P0),len(P1))
    for I in range(Dimensions):
        Result = Result + [(P1[I] - P0[I]) * float(T) + P0[I]]
    return Result
```

Parametric Blending

In each function below, the arguments (`T`, `P0`, `P1`, etc.) and the return result are all simple numbers, generally floats. Each one evaluates a particular equation at a parameter `T` (see the Math chapter), where `T=0` returns the first argument (`P0`), `T=1` returns the last argument, and intermediate values of `T` return results somewhere in between.

```
def Blend (P0,P1,T):                          # Linear Blend
    return (P1 - P0) * float(T) + P0

def BlendParabola (P0,P1,P2,T):
    A =  2*P0 - 4*P1 + 2*P2
    B = -3*P0 + 4*P1 -   P2
    C = P0
    T = float(T)
    return A*T*T + B*T + C

def BlendQuadraticSpline(P0,P1,P2,T):
    A = P2 - 2*P1 + P0
    B = 2*P1 - 2*P0
    C = P0
    T = float(T)
    return A*T*T + B*T + C

def BlendCubic (P0,P1,P2,P3,T):
    A = (-9*P0  + 27*P1 - 27*P2 + 9*P3) / 2.0
    B = (18*P0  - 45*P1 + 36*P2 - 9*P3) / 2.0
    C = (-11*P0 + 18*P1 -  9*P2 + 2*P3) / 2.0
    D = P0
    T = float(T)
    return A*T*T*T + B*T*T + C*T + D

def BlendBezier (P0,P1,P2,P3,T):
    A = P3 - 3*P2 + 3*P1 - P0
    B = 3*P2 - 6*P1 + 3*P0
    C = 3*P1 - 3*P0
    D = P0
    T = float(T)
    return A*T*T*T + B*T*T + C*T + D
```

Since these functions operate on numbers and not points, they essentially describe the behavior of *one dimension* of a point traveling through space. That is, if a point P is following a cubic curve through space defined by 3D points P0, P1, P2, and P3, how the *x* coordinate of P changes over time can be described by a single `BlendCubic` working on nothing but the *x* coordinates of the defining points. A different `BlendCubic` working on just the *y* coordinates of the defining points describes how the *y* coordinate of P changes over time, and so on.

Curve Blending (Parametric)

In 2D a point would be a 2-element list $[x, y]$ and in 3D a list $[x, y, z]$, etc. To apply blending to *points of arbitrary dimensions*, all *x*-coordinates from those points must be blended separately from all *y*-coordinates, all *z*-coordinates, etc. The following functions are given points in some number of dimensions, and all use the blending functions from the previous page to return a list of coordinates along the appropriate type of curve. The number of dimensions is determined by the length of point list P0, and all other point lists <u>must</u> have that same length.

```
def BlendPoints (P0,P1,T):
    return [Blend(P0[N], P1[N], T) for N in range(len(P0))]


def GenerateParabolaPoints (P0,P1,P2,Segments=10):
    Result = []
    for I in range(Segments+1):
        T = float(I) / float(Segments)
        P = [BlendParabola(P0[N],P1[N],P2[N],T)   \
                                    for N in range(len(P0))]
        Result = Result + [P]
    return Result


def GenerateQuadraticSplinePoints (P0,P1,P2,Segments=10):
    Result = []
    for I in range(Segments+1):
        T = float(I) / float(Segments)
        P = [BlendQuadraticSpline(P0[N],P1[N],P2[N],T)   \
                                    for N in range(len(P0))]
        Result = Result + [P]
    return Result


def GenerateCubicPoints (P0,P1,P2,P3,Segments=10):
    Result = []
    for I in range(Segments+1):
        T = float(I) / float(Segments)
        P = [BlendCubic(P0[N],P1[N],P2[N],P3[N],T)   \
                                    for N in range(len(P0))]
        Result = Result + [P]
    return Result


def GenerateBezierPoints (P0,P1,P2,P3,Segments=10):
    Result = []
    for I in range(Segments+1):
        T = float(I) / float(Segments)
        P = [BlendBezier(P0[N],P1[N],P2[N],P3[N],T)   \
                                    for N in range(len(P0))]
        Result = Result + [P]
    return Result
```

Bézier and Quadratic Curves (Iterative)

For Bézier and Quadratic Spline curves, there are methods for generating points along the curves that don't depend on their parametric representations (as presented earlier). Instead, a very clever approach called ***de Casteljau's algorithm*** is used, named after its creator Paul de Casteljau (and made popular by Pierre Bézier). The following image shows the tracing of a quadratic spline using this technique.

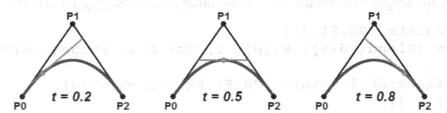

Parameter *t* goes from 0 to 1 in `Segments` steps (generating `Segments+1` points). Parameter *t* is used to linearly blend that proportion of the distance between `P0` and `P1`, creating point `P01`, and then from `P1` to `P2`, creating point `P12`, and finally the proportion of the way from `P01` to `P12`, creating point `P012`, which is on the curve. As *t* increases from 0 to 1, the values of `P012` are successively added to the result list. For the Bézier curve a similar approach is taken, with the understanding that there are now four points that must be considered, not three, with a corresponding increase in the number of intermediate blended points. The de Casteljau approach works well when the number of desired segments is known ahead of time.

```
def GenerateQuadraticSplinePoints (P0,P1,P2,Segments=10):
    Result = []
    for I in range(Segments+1):
        T = float(I) / float(Segments)
        P01 = BlendPoints(P0,P1,T)
        P12 = BlendPoints(P1,P2,T)
        P012 = BlendPoints(P01,P12,T)
        Result = Result + [P012]
    return Result

def GenerateBezierPoints (P0,P1,P2,P3,Segments=10):
    Result = []
    for I in range(Segments+1):
        T = float(I) / float(Segments)
        P01 = BlendPoints(P0,P1,T)
        P12 = BlendPoints(P1,P2,T)
        P23 = BlendPoints(P2,P3,T)
        P012 = BlendPoints(P01,P12,T)
        P123 = BlendPoints(P12,P23,T)
        P0123 = BlendPoints(P012,P123,T)
        Result = Result + [P0123]
    return Result
```

Bézier and Quadratic Curves (Recursive)

This page shows ***recursive*** implementations of de Casteljau's algorithm, which also use a local function inside each curve function (notice the indentation). In the image on the previous page of the quadratic spline curve, the middle case where t=0.5 shows that the curve is split into two equal sections: the section from `P0` to `P01` to `P012`, and the section from `P012` to `P12` to `P2`. Each of these is a complete quadratic spline curve by itself which can be solved independently of the other. Thus, this technique recursively subdivides the curve until the distance between each new point and its endpoints falls below a threshold value (usually 1 for pixel-based graphics systems). The Bézier curve takes a similar approach. The recursive approach adapts well to the size and geometry of the curve, no matter how big or wiggly it becomes.

```python
def GenerateQuadraticSplinePoints (P0,P1,P2,Threshold=1.0):

    def Spline (P0,P1,P2):
        P01   = AveragePoints(P0,P1)
        P12   = AveragePoints(P1,P2)
        P012  = AveragePoints(P01,P12)
        Result = []
        if (DistancePoints(P0,P012) > Threshold):
            Result = Result + Spline(P0,P01,P012)
        Result = Result + [P012]
        if (DistancePoints(P012,P2) > Threshold):
            Result = Result + Spline(P012,P12,P2)
        return Result

    return [P0] + Spline(P0,P1,P2) + [P2]

def GenerateBezierPoints (P0,P1,P2,P3,Threshold=1.0):

    def Bezier (P0,P1,P2,P3):
        P01   = AveragePoints(P0,P1)
        P12   = AveragePoints(P1,P2)
        P23   = AveragePoints(P2,P3)
        P012  = AveragePoints(P01,P12)
        P123  = AveragePoints(P12,P23)
        P0123 = AveragePoints(P012,P123)
        Result = []
        if (DistancePoints(P0,P0123) > Threshold):
            Result = Result + Bezier(P0,P01,P012,P0123)
        Result = Result + [P0123]
        if (DistancePoints(P0123,P3) > Threshold):
            Result = Result + Bezier(P0123,P123,P23,P3)
        return Result

    return [P0] + Bezier(P0,P1,P2,P3) + [P3]
```

Pixel Thinning

Functions such as those used to generate Bézier and Quadratic curves tend to create lists containing a lot of points, far more than are needed to plot pixels on a graphics screen. The Python class described on this page and the next maintains a <u>minimal</u> list of <u>2D</u> pixels to be used in plotting or filling polygons.

In the class, a new object is created by calling the class name `TPixelThinning` as a function. For example, `X = TPixelThinning()` creates a new ***object*** X and calls the `__init__` ***constructor*** to initialize the internal variable `Pixels` to an empty list.

After that, every pixel to be considered is a list of two values (the *x* and *y* coordinates of a 2D point) provided to the object by the ***method*** `AddPixelToList`, as in the examples `X.AddPixelToList([20,30])` and `X.AddPixelToList([72,94])`.

A new pixel is added to the list only if the list is empty or if not empty the new pixel is not the same as the last pixel in the list. If the list does contain two or more points <u>and</u> the new pixel forms a straight line with the last two in the list, the last pixel in the list is replaced by the new pixel, as shown here:

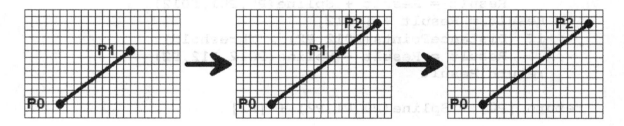

The `getList` method (with no arguments) returns the current value of the internal `Pixels` list, which will be the optimal and minimal list of pixels from all those provided as candidates.

This class requires the presence of the ***greatest common divisor*** function (GCD) as presented earlier. This function is used to reduce slopes to their minimal forms for comparison purposes. For example, slopes $^{15}/_{12}$ and $^{10}/_{8}$ are the same, but this fact can only be determined by dividing the numerator and denominator of each fraction by their GCD to get slopes of $^5/_4$ in each case.

```
def GCD (A,B):
    while (B > 0):
        Temp = B
        B    = A % B
        A    = Temp
    return A
```

Pixel Thinning (Continued)

The class described below has only the __init__ constructor and two methods, one to add a new candidate point to the list, and the other to get the current list.

```python
class TPixelThinning(object):

    def __init__ (self):
        self.Pixels = []
        return

    def getList (self):
        return self.Pixels

    def AddPixelToList (self,P):
        P[0] = int(round(P[0]))
        P[1] = int(round(P[1]))
        if (len(self.Pixels) == 0):                  # Empty list.
            self.Pixels = self.Pixels + [P]
        elif (self.Pixels[-1][0] != P[0]) or  \
             (self.Pixels[-1][1] != P[1]):           # New point.
            if (len(self.Pixels) <= 1):              # List has
                self.Pixels = self.Pixels + [P]      # one point.
            else:
                # Compute the slope of the last two points
                # in the list.
                DX1 = self.Pixels[-1][0] - self.Pixels[-2][0]
                DY1 = self.Pixels[-1][1] - self.Pixels[-2][1]
                G1  = GCD(abs(DX1),abs(DY1))
                DX1 = DX1 // G1
                DY1 = DY1 // G1

                # Compute the slope of the last point in the
                # list and the new point under consideration.
                DX2 = P[0] - self.Pixels[-1][0]
                DY2 = P[1] - self.Pixels[-1][1]
                G2  = GCD(abs(DX2),abs(DY2))
                DX2 = DX2 // G2
                DY2 = DY2 // G2

                if (DX1 == DX2) and (DY1 == DY2):
                    self.Pixels[-1] = P                  # Replace.
                else:
                    self.Pixels = self.Pixels + [P] # Add point.
        return
```

Z-Order

In some problems it is necessary to step through *(x,y)* coordinate pairs in a linear fashion. That is, the first coordinate examined should be *(0,0)*, and as each new item is examined it is in some sense increasingly further and further from *(0,0)*. The problem, then, is to map two integers representing a point in space onto one representing an index into a list.

Z-Order is one mechanism to traverse all possible combinations of two integer values. For a given coordinate in variables X and Y, the technique is to interleave the bits of X with the bits of Y: starting at the right, pick one bit of X, one bit of Y, the next bit of X, the next bit of Y, and so on for as many bits as necessary.

•••	X3	X2	X1	X0	Bits of X
••• Y3	Y2	Y1	Y0		Bits of Y
••• Y3 X3 Y2 X2 Y1 X1 Y0 X0					Interleaved Bits

For example, if X=011 and Y=110, the corresponding interleaved number will be 101101. On the other hand, given 101101, it is as easy to deinterleave the number back into its components 011 and 110. In general, if both X and Y are N-bit numbers, the interleaved value will contain 2N bits, and the total number of coordinates covered will be 2^{2N}. In the table and graphic below, N=3, so X and Y are both 3-bit integers and the interleaved value will contain 6 bits, for $2^6 = 64$ unique locations 0 through 63. As a counter variable counts up from 0 to 63, it is deinterleaved back into its X and Y coordinates, and the traversal follows the patterns below. The graphic shows why this is called a *Z-Order traversal*, which is a type of *fractal* space-filling curve.

	0	1	2	3	4	5	6	7
0	0	1	4	5	16	17	20	21
1	2	3	6	7	18	19	22	23
2	8	9	12	13	24	25	28	29
3	10	11	14	15	26	27	30	31
4	32	33	36	37	48	49	52	53
5	34	35	38	39	50	51	54	55
6	40	41	44	45	56	57	60	61
7	42	43	46	47	58	59	62	63

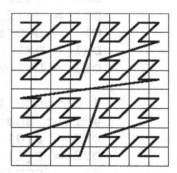

While this example shows the effects for 3 bits in both X and Y and 6 bits in N, the pattern continues onwards for larger numbers of bits. The heavy lines in the table show the results for 1 bit, 2 bits, and 3 bits.

Z-Order (Continued)

This view of the data shows the same table as the earlier version, but this one clearly illustrates the interleaving of the bits of X with the bits of Y:

	000	001	010	011	100	101	110	111
000	000000	000001	000100	000101	010000	010001	010100	010101
001	000010	000011	000110	000111	010010	010011	010110	010111
010	001000	001001	001100	001101	011000	011001	011100	011101
011	001010	001011	001110	001111	011010	011011	011110	011111
100	100000	100001	100100	100101	110000	110001	110100	110101
101	100010	100011	100110	100111	110010	110011	110110	110111
110	101000	101001	101100	101101	111000	111001	111100	111101
111	101010	101011	101110	101111	111010	111011	111110	111111

The functions presented below convert integer coordinates [X,Y] into a single integer N (Interleave), and from N back to [X,Y] (DeInterleave). They both use the Odd function presented earlier, which returns True if its argument is odd and False if it is even.

```
def Interleave (X,Y):
    N    = 0
    Mask = 1
    while (X > 0) or (Y > 0):
        if Odd(X): N = N + Mask
        X    = X // 2
        Mask = Mask * 2
        if Odd(Y): N = N + Mask
        Y    = Y // 2
        Mask = Mask * 2
    return N

def DeInterleave (N):
    X    = 0
    Y    = 0
    Mask = 1
    while (N > 0):
        if Odd(N): X = X + Mask
        N    = N // 2
        if Odd(N): Y = Y + Mask
        N    = N // 2
        Mask = Mask * 2
    return [X,Y]
```

Note that the method can be extended to *any number of dimensions*. That is, in three dimensions three integers X, Y, and Z can be interleaved as easily as two (a bit of X, a bit of Y, a bit of Z, the next bit of X, the next bit of Y, the next bit of Z, etc.).

Computational Geometry: Linear Algebra

Both points in space and vectors, while different concepts, have the same representation in Python: a list of numbers. For example, [3,6,2] can be a point in 3D space or a vector with its tail at [0,0,0]. For these functions it is assumed that V0 and V1 are vectors.

Cross-Product

In the cross product, V0 and V1 are vectors in 3D, and the result is a (pseudo)vector, also in 3D. The direction of the result is at 90° both from V0 and from V1, assuming a left-handed coordinate system. That is, if the fingers of your left hand point in the direction of V0 and they curl to point at V1, your thumb points in the direction of the result.

```
def CrossProduct3D (V0,V1):
    X = V0[1]*V1[2]  - V0[2]*V1[1]
    Y = V0[2]*V1[0]  - V0[0]*V1[2]
    Z = V0[0]*V1[1]  - V0[1]*V1[0]
    return [X,Y,Z]
```

Example: CrossProduct3D([1,0,0], [0,1,0]) gives [0,0,1]
            CrossProduct3D([0,1,0], [1,0,0]) gives [0,0,-1]
            CrossProduct3D([0,0,1], [1,0,0]) gives [0,1,0]

The cross product of two 2D vectors gives a 3D result perpendicular to both. The function below takes two 2D *points* relative to some 2D origin *point*, figures out the appropriate 2D *vectors* from the three points, and returns the magnitude of the *z* component of the resulting normal vector. This function is identical to Z in the previous function when Origin is [0,0].

```
def CrossProduct2D (Origin,V0,V1):
    return (V0[0] - Origin[0]) * (V1[1] - Origin[1]) -    \
           (V0[1] - Origin[1]) * (V1[0] - Origin[0])
```

Dot Product

The dot product is the sum of the products of corresponding elements from two vectors. Geometrically, it also means the product of the length of V0, the length of V1, and the cosine of the angle between V0 and V1. The following function works on vectors in any number of dimensions. If V0 and V1 are the same vector, the cosine is 1.0 (the angle is 0°) and so the dot product is the square of the length of the vector.

```
def DotProduct (V0,V1):
    Result = 0
    for I in range(min(len(V0),len(V1))):
        Result = Result + V0[I] * V1[I]
    return Result
```

Computational Geometry: Linear Algebra (Continued)

Vector Length

The length of a vector is the square root of the dot product of the vector with itself. That is, the dot product is the sum of the squares of the elements, and so the square root of that is the Euclidean length of the vector.

```python
def VectorLength (V):
    return math.sqrt(DotProduct(V,V))
```

Vector Normalization

A non-zero vector has a direction and a length. Vector normalization returns a vector that points in the same direction but has a length of exactly 1.0. This is computed by dividing each element of the vector by the overall length of the vector. In the case of a zero vector, the result of this function is an identical zero vector.

```python
def VectorNormalize (V):
    D = VectorLength(V)
    try:
        Result = [S/D for S in V]
    except:
        Result = [0] * len(V)
    return Result
```

Vector Angle

This function returns the angle (in radians) between two vectors. Since the dot product is the length of V0 times the length of V1 times the cosine of the angle between them, the angle is then the arccosine of the dot product divided by the two lengths. If either vector is a zero vector, the result is zero.

```python
def VectorAngle (V0,V1):
    try:
        Numerator   = DotProduct(V0,V1)
        Denominator = VectorLength(V0) * VectorLength(V1)
        Result      = math.acos(Numerator/Denominator)
    except:
        Result = 0
    return Result
```

Computational Geometry: Distance from a Point to a Line

Given a line segment between P0 and P1 and a point P, what is the distance from the point to the line? What is the closest point on the line to P? Is that closest point inside the segment between P0 and P1? What is the parameter value? Were there any errors? This routine determines all of that information for points of arbitrary dimension, and returns the information in a Python dictionary. This function will work for points in any number of dimensions.

```python
def GeneratePointToLineData (P,P0,P1):
    Result = {}
    Result["Error"] = False
    Dimensions = min(len(P),len(P0),len(P1))

    try:
        T = 0.0
        for I in range(Dimensions):
            T = T + (P[I] - P0[I]) * (P1[I] - P0[I])
        T = T / DistanceSquaredPoints(P0,P1)
    except:
        T = 0.5

    Result["Parameter"] = T
    Result["InsideSegment"] = (T >= 0.0) and (T <= 1.0)

    try:
        Closest = []
        for I in range(Dimensions):
            Closest = Closest + [(P1[I] - P0[I]) * T + P0[I]]
        Result["Closest"] = Closest
        Result["DistanceAway"] = DistancePoints(Closest,P)
    except:
        Result["Error"] = True

    return Result
```

For example, if the line segment is defined by 2D points P0=[2,1] and P1=[10,6], and the test point is P=[5,3], then the function returns the following information:

```
{'InsideSegment': True,
 'DistanceAway': 0.10599978800063638,
 'Closest': [5.056179775280899, 2.9101123595505616],
 'Error': False,
 'Parameter': 0.38202247191011235}
```

Computational Geometry: Intersection of Two 2D Lines

Given two lines in the plane defined by four 2D points (all of which are [X,Y] lists), where do the lines intersect? This function computes the [X,Y] position of the intersection point. (Two values for the intersection are actually returned, one for each line; the two values should be identical.) A parameter is also computed for the relative distance along the segment from P0 to P1 of where the intersection occurs: if less than 0.0 the intersection is outside the segment on the P0 side and if greater than 1.0 it is outside the segment on the P1 side; otherwise it is inside the segment. Similar information for the line through Q0 and Q1 is also computed. An error is returned if the segments are parallel or coincident, or if either segment has zero length.

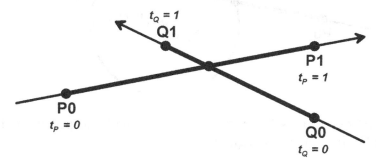

```
def Intersect2D (P0,P1,Q0,Q1):
    Result = {}
    Result["Error"] = False
    try:
        PScaleX = float(P1[0] - P0[0])
        PScaleY = float(P1[1] - P0[1])
        QScaleX = float(Q1[0] - Q0[0])
        QScaleY = float(Q1[1] - Q0[1])
        PQScaleX= float(P0[0] - Q0[0])
        PQScaleY= float(P0[1] - Q0[1])
        Denominator = QScaleY * PScaleX   -   QScaleX * PScaleY
        PNumerator  = QScaleX * PQScaleY  -   QScaleY * PQScaleX
        QNumerator  = PScaleX * PQScaleY  -   PScaleY * PQScaleX
        PParameter  = PNumerator / Denominator
        QParameter  = QNumerator / Denominator
        PIntersectX = PScaleX * PParameter + P0[0]
        PIntersectY = PScaleY * PParameter + P0[1]
        QIntersectX = QScaleX * QParameter + Q0[0]
        QIntersectY = QScaleY * QParameter + Q0[1]
        Result["PIntersection"] = [PIntersectX,PIntersectY]
        Result["QIntersection"] = [QIntersectX,QIntersectY]
        Result["PParameter"] = PParameter
        Result["QParameter"] = QParameter
    except:
        Result["Error"] = True
    return Result
```

Computational Geometry: Intersection of a Line and a Circle

Given a line in the plane and a circle, does the line intersect the circle in two points, graze an edge at one point, or miss the circle entirely? As before, points P0 and P1 define a line in the plane. The circle is defined by point Center and simple number Radius. All three points are in 2D space as lists containing [X, Y] coordinates.

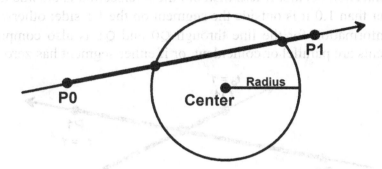

The computation first determines the coefficients to a quadratic polynomial $ax^2 + bx + c$, and then must solve the familiar quadratic equation:

$$x = \frac{-b \pm \sqrt{b^2 - 4ac}}{2a}$$

to obtain information about how many intersection points exist. The discriminant, $b^2 - 4ac$, can be less than zero (the line does not intersect the circle at all), equal to zero (there is one intersection where the line grazes the edge of the circle), or greater than zero (there are two intersections as the line punches through the middle of the circle). The solutions to the quadratic equation, if they exist, are the parameters for the relative distance along the line from P0 through P1 of where the intersection(s) occur. As before, if any parameter is less than 0.0 its corresponding intersection is outside of the segment on the P0 side, but if it is greater than 1.0 the intersection is outside of the segment on the P1 side, and otherwise the intersection is somewhere on the segment in between P0 and P1.

In the code on the next page, the function returns a dictionary where entry "Intersections" is 0, 1, or 2, depending on how many places the line intersects with the circle. For each intersection, there are dictionary entries for both the position in the plane of the intersection itself and the parameter for the relative distance along the line of where the intersection occurs.

An error will be returned if the segment between P0 and P1 has zero length (that is, there is no defined line), or if there are any other numerical problems in the code.

Computational Geometry: Code for Line-Circle Intersection

```python
def IntersectLineCircle2D (P0,P1,Center,Radius):
    Result = {}
    Result["Error"] = False
    try:
        PScaleX = float(P1[0] - P0[0])
        PScaleY = float(P1[1] - P0[1])
        PDiffX  = float(Center[0] - P0[0])
        PDiffY  = float(Center[1] - P0[1])
        A = PScaleX*PScaleX + PScaleY*PScaleY
        B = -2.0 * (PScaleX*PDiffX + PScaleY*PDiffY)
        C = DotProduct(Center,Center) + DotProduct(P0,P0) -   \
            2.0 * DotProduct(P0,Center) - Radius*Radius
        Discriminant = B * B - 4.0 * A * C
        TwoA = 2.0 * A
        if (Discriminant < 0.0):
            Result["Intersections"] = 0
        elif (Discriminant == 0.0):
            PParameter1 = -B / TwoA
            P1X = PScaleX * PParameter1 + P0[0]
            P1Y = PScaleY * PParameter1 + P0[1]
            Result["Intersections"] = 1
            Result["Intersection1"] = [P1X,P1Y]
            Result["PParameter1"] = PParameter1
        else:
            PParameter1 = (-B + math.sqrt(Discriminant)) / TwoA
            P1X = PScaleX * PParameter1 + P0[0]
            P1Y = PScaleY * PParameter1 + P0[1]
            PParameter2 = (-B - math.sqrt(Discriminant)) / TwoA
            P2X = PScaleX * PParameter2 + P0[0]
            P2Y = PScaleY * PParameter2 + P0[1]
            Result["Intersections"] = 2
            Result["Intersection1"] = [P1X,P1Y]
            Result["Intersection2"] = [P2X,P2Y]
            Result["PParameter1"] = PParameter1
            Result["PParameter2"] = PParameter2
    except:
        Result["Error"] = True
    return Result
```

Computational Geometry: Intersection of a Line and a Sphere

As with the intersection of a line in the plane and a circle, the intersection of a line in space and a sphere may also return 0, 1, or 2 intersection points. Indeed, the code for the 3D case is nearly identical to that of the 2D case. Points P0, P1, and Center are all points in 3D space defined as lists containing [X,Y,Z] coordinates. Radius is a simple number describing the size of the sphere.

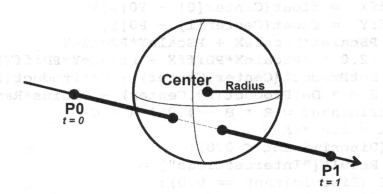

The code still needs to solve a quadratic equation, with the discriminant determining the number of intersections (no intersections if the discriminant is less than zero, one intersection where the line grazes the sphere if the discriminant is equal to zero, and two intersections if the discriminant is greater than zero).

The function returns a dictionary containing the number of intersections, and for each intersection the point in space of the intersection itself and the parameter that determines the relative distance along the line from P0 to P1 that the intersection occurs. If the parameter is less than 0.0 the intersection is outside the segment on the P0 side and if the parameter is greater than 1.0 the intersection is outside the segment on the P1 side; otherwise the intersection is inside the segment.

An error is returned if the distance between P0 and P1 is zero (that is, there is no defined line), or if there are any computational failures.

This type of code is used in ___ray-tracing___, where a ray (line) from the eye through each pixel in a virtual representation of the computer screen is "cast" into a model to see how many objects are hit. The closest intersection point to the eye (that is, the smallest value of the parameter along the line) indicates the intersection that is visible; the color of the pixel is set to the color of that object at that intersection point. (This ignores lighting, shadows, reflections, and refraction.)

Computational Geometry: Code for Line-Sphere Intersection

```
def IntersectLineSphere3D (P0,P1,Center,Radius):
    Result = {}
    Result["Error"] = False
    try:
        PScaleX = float(P1[0] - P0[0])
        PScaleY = float(P1[1] - P0[1])
        PScaleZ = float(P1[2] - P0[2])
        PDiffX  = float(Center[0] - P0[0])
        PDiffY  = float(Center[1] - P0[1])
        PDiffZ  = float(Center[2] - P0[2])
        A = PScaleX*PScaleX + PScaleY*PScaleY + PScaleZ*PScaleZ
        B = -2.0*(PScaleX*PDiffX+PScaleY*PDiffY+PScaleZ*PDiffZ)
        C = DotProduct(Center,Center) + DotProduct(P0,P0) -    \
            2.0 * DotProduct(P0,Center) - Radius*Radius
        Discriminant = B * B - 4.0 * A * C
        TwoA = 2.0 * A
        if (Discriminant < 0.0):
            Result["Intersections"] = 0
        elif (Discriminant == 0.0):
            PParameter1 = -B / TwoA
            P1X = PScaleX * PParameter1 + P0[0]
            P1Y = PScaleY * PParameter1 + P0[1]
            P1Z = PScaleZ * PParameter1 + P0[2]
            Result["Intersections"] = 1
            Result["Intersection1"] = [P1X,P1Y,P1Z]
            Result["PParameter1"] = PParameter1
        else:
            PParameter1 = (-B + math.sqrt(Discriminant)) / TwoA
            P1X = PScaleX * PParameter1 + P0[0]
            P1Y = PScaleY * PParameter1 + P0[1]
            P1Z = PScaleZ * PParameter1 + P0[2]
            PParameter2 = (-B - math.sqrt(Discriminant)) / TwoA
            P2X = PScaleX * PParameter2 + P0[0]
            P2Y = PScaleY * PParameter2 + P0[1]
            P2Z = PScaleZ * PParameter2 + P0[2]
            Result["Intersections"] = 2
            Result["Intersection1"] = [P1X,P1Y,P1Z]
            Result["Intersection2"] = [P2X,P2Y,P2Z]
            Result["PParameter1"] = PParameter1
            Result["PParameter2"] = PParameter2
    except:
        Result["Error"] = True
    return Result
```

Computational Geometry: Triangle Data

Given three points in the plane that form a triangle, this routine can compute the perimeter and area of the triangle, whether the points in the triangle are clockwise or counterclockwise, the position and radius of both the ***incircle*** and ***circumcircle***, and the "sliveriness" of the triangle. The sliveriness is a number between 0 and 1, where 0 means the triangle has no area, and 1 means the triangle is a perfect equilateral. All other triangles will have an intermediate number. If any computational errors are encountered an error flag is returned. This function makes use of the `DistancePoints` function defined earlier.

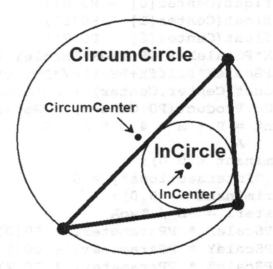

The function takes in three 2D points (lists of two numbers as [X, Y] coordinates), and returns a dictionary containing all the relevant information. This function is too wide to fit on the page, so liberal use is made of line-continuation (\) characters.

A ***triangulation*** is a complete set of non-overlapping triangles formed from a group of points in the plane. A ***Delaunay triangulation*** maximizes the minimum angle of all triangles; no point is inside the circumcircle of any other triangle. This function helps with those determinations.

Computational Geometry: Code for Triangles

```
def GenerateTriangleData2D (P0,P1,P2):
    Result = {}
    Result["Error"] = False

    try:
        Side01 = DistancePoints(P0,P1)
        Side02 = DistancePoints(P0,P2)
        Side12 = DistancePoints(P1,P2)
        Perimeter = Side01 + Side02 + Side12
        Result["Perimeter"] = Perimeter
```

Computational Geometry: Code for Triangles (Continued)

```
    if (Perimeter > 0.0):
        X10 = P1[0] - P0[0]
        Y10 = P1[1] - P0[1]
        X20 = P2[0] - P0[0]
        Y20 = P2[1] - P0[1]
        X21 = P2[0] - P1[0]
        Y21 = P2[1] - P1[1]
        Determinant = X10 * Y20  -  X20 * Y10
        Area = abs(0.5 * Determinant)
        Collinear = (Area < 0.001)
        Result["Area"] = Area
        Result["Clockwise"] = (Determinant < 0.0)
        Result["Sliveriness"] = Area / Square(Perimeter) * \
                            (12.0 * math.sqrt(3.0))
        Result["Collinear"] = Collinear
        if (not Collinear):
            Scale = 0.5 * Perimeter
            DetInverse = 0.5 / Determinant
            Xcc = DetInverse * (Square(Side01) * Y20   -   \
                            Square(Side02) * Y10)
            Ycc = DetInverse * (X10 * Square(Side02)   -   \
                            X20 * Square(Side01))
            Result["CircumCenter"] = [Xcc + P0[0],         \
                                Ycc + P0[1]]
            Result["CircumRadius"] = math.sqrt(            \
                                    Square(Xcc) +     \
                                    Square(Ycc))
            Result["InCenter"] = [(Side12 * P0[0] +        \
                                Side02 * P1[0] +        \
                                Side01 * P2[0]) /       \
                                Perimeter,              \
                                (Side12 * P0[1] +       \
                                Side02 * P1[1] +        \
                                Side01 * P2[1]) /       \
                                Perimeter]
            Result["InRadius"] = math.sqrt(                \
                                (Scale - Side12) *      \
                                (Scale - Side02) *      \
                                (Scale - Side01) / Scale)
    except:
        Result["Error"] = True

    return Result
```

Computational Geometry: Rectangular Beam

This function generates the four points around the periphery of a rectangular beam. Essentially, this allows a graphics program to draw a thick line between two endpoints. When everything works correctly, the function returns a list containing four 2D points. Computational errors that would crash the program (overflows, divide by zero in the case of a zero-width rectangle, etc.) are captured by the try-except structure, returning a line between the endpoints as a result.

```python
def GenerateRectangularBeam (X0,Y0,X1,Y1,Thickness=1.0):
    try:
        D = Distance(X0,Y0,X1,Y1)
        T = float(Thickness) / (D * 2.0)
        XOffset = T * (Y0 - Y1)
        YOffset = T * (X1 - X0)
        P0 = [X0 - XOffset, Y0 - YOffset]
        P1 = [X1 - XOffset, Y1 - YOffset]
        P2 = [X1 + XOffset, Y1 + YOffset]
        P3 = [X0 + XOffset, Y0 + YOffset]
        return [P0,P1,P2,P3]
    except:
        return [[X0,Y0], [X1,Y1]]
```

The image on the left shows the rectangle as it would be drawn on screen for GenerateRectangularBeam(80,250,300,60,60.0). The version on the right shows the same rectangle but annotated to indicate where the input and computed values lie; remember that graphics screens are upside-down from regular Cartesian coordinates.

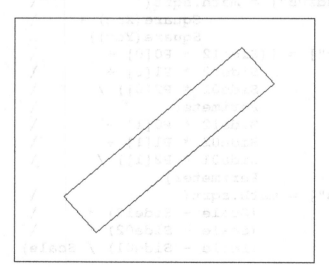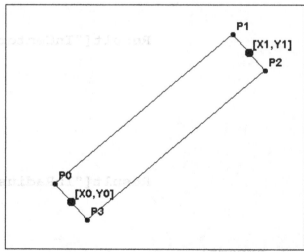

A function that uses 2D point lists is shown below:

```python
def GenerateRectangularBeam2D (P0,P1,Thickness=1.0):
    return GenerateRectangularBeam (P0[0],P0[1],P1[0],P1[1],Thickness)
```

Computational Geometry: Tiled Hexagons

Given the center (X, Y) of a hexagon and its radius R, the locations of the six vertices can be determined by the following function. The cosine of 30° is exactly $\frac{1}{2}\sqrt{3}$, or approximately $0.8660254037844\ldots$, so the literal value can be used here as a constant or as a precomputed variable. It is not necessary to use the expensive cosine function to compute this value over and over. A version that defines the center as a 2D point P is also given here.

```
def GenerateHexagon (X,Y,R):
    r  = R * math.cos(Radians(30))      #  r = R * 0.866025…
    R2 = R / 2.0
    P0 = [X+R,  Y  ]
    P1 = [X+R2, Y+r]
    P2 = [X-R2, Y+r]
    P3 = [X-R,  Y  ]
    P4 = [X-R2, Y-r]
    P5 = [X+R2, Y-r]
    return [P0,P1,P2,P3,P4,P5]

def GenerateHexagon2D (P,R):
    return GenerateHexagon(P[0],P[1],R)
```

To tile a plane with hexagons, the location of one fixed hexagon must be known. The center of each surrounding hexagon relative to that known hexagon can be determined as follows:

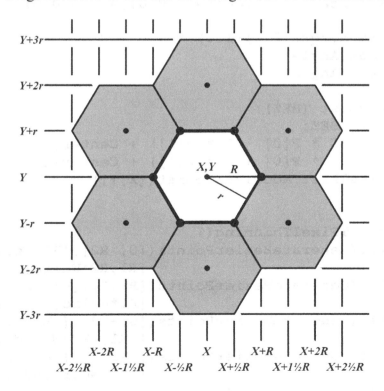

Computational Geometry: Ellipses

Ellipses can be simulated by 2D Bézier curves. For the upper left curve, the distance between P0 and P1 is a fraction of R1, and the distance between P2 and P3 is that <u>same</u> fraction applied to R2; other curves are similar. The fraction (variable Weird in the code) is exactly $\frac{4}{3}(\sqrt{2}-1)$, or approximately 0.5522847498307936… The function generates a basic ellipse from calling the earlier GenerateBezierPoints code for each quadrant, and then rotates the points by Angle and shifts them relative to 2D point Center, using the pixel thinning class TPixelThinning to generate a minimal elliptical polygon for later filling or drawing.

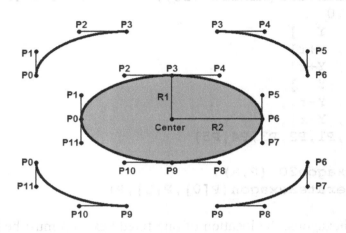

```
def GenerateEllipse (R1,R2,Center=[0,0],Angle=0.0):

    Weird = (math.sqrt(2.0)-1.0) * 4.0 / 3.0
    C = math.cos(Angle)
    S = math.sin(Angle)

    def ProcessList (BEZ):
        for P in BEZ:
            X = (C * P[0] - S * P[1]) + Center[0]
            Y = (S * P[0] + C * P[1]) + Center[1]
            PixelList.AddPixelToList([X,Y])
        return

    PixelList = TPixelThinning()
    ProcessList(GenerateBezierPoints([0, R2],[R1*Weird,R2],   \
                               [R1,R2*Weird],[R1,0]))
    ProcessList(GenerateBezierPoints([R1,0],[R1,-R2*Weird],   \
                               [R1*Weird,-R2],[0,-R2]))
    ProcessList(GenerateBezierPoints([0,-R2],[-R1*Weird,-R2], \
                               [-R1,-R2*Weird],[-R1,0]))
    ProcessList(GenerateBezierPoints([-R1,0],[-R1,R2*Weird],  \
                               [-R1*Weird,R2],[0,R2]))
    return PixelList.getList()
```

Computational Geometry: Rotation of Points

Rotate point *(Xold, Yold)* by angle θ around *(Xc, Yc)* to get new point *(Xnew, Ynew)*:

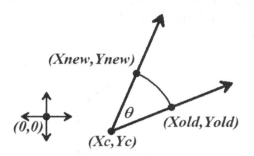

The following functions perform the desired rotations. Variable `Angle` represents θ and is expressed in radians.

```
def RotatePoint (Xc,Yc,Xold,Yold,Angle):
    Sine   = math.sin(Angle)
    Cosine = math.cos(Angle)
    XShift = (Xold - Xc)
    YShift = (Yold - Yc)
    Xnew   = Xc + (XShift * Cosine) - (YShift * Sine  )
    Ynew   = Yc + (XShift * Sine  ) + (YShift * Cosine)
    return [Xnew,Ynew]

def RotatePoint2D (Center,Point,Angle):
    return RotatePoint(Center[0],Center[1],                  \
                   Point[0],Point[1],Angle)
```

When using these functions with a computer graphics screen, remember that the coordinate system of the graphics screen is "upside-down" relative to Cartesian coordinates. This has the effect that rotating a point by any *positive* angle around a center position on the screen actually rotates the point in a *clockwise* manner. To rotate the point around the center in a *counterclockwise* direction to mimic Cartesian coordinates, *negate the angle* in the calls to functions `RotatePoint` and `RotatePoint2D`.

Computational Geometry: Convex Hull

The ***convex hull*** of a set of points is the minimal convex polygon that surrounds all the points. If you envision each point as a nail driven into a sheet of plywood, the convex hull is the shape of a rubber band stretched around all of the nails. Here is a set of 15 points with the convex hull polygon that surrounds them:

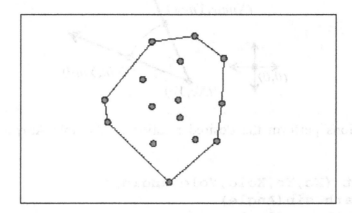

The code on the facing page is a variant of ***Andrew's monotone chain convex hull algorithm*** (A. M. Andrew, 1979). It uses the `Crossproduct2D` function listed earlier: that function is given three points, computes two vectors, and returns the *magnitude* of the *z* direction of the cross product vector. However, that magnitude, positive or negative, determines if there was a left turn or a right turn when going from the origin through the first point to the second point. For example, `CrossProduct2D([0,0],[10,0],[15,10])` returns +100 (a left turn), while `CrossProduct2D([0,0], [10,0], [15,-10])` returns -100 (a right turn).

That is the key to understanding this algorithm. The list of points is sorted by increasing *x* coordinate and then scanned from left to right accepting only those new points that form a left turn relative to the previous two already accepted points. For any case where a right turn is found, previously accepted points have to be deleted back until there are no more right turns in the saved list relative to the new point. When all right turns have been eliminated, the new point is accepted into the list. After this pass, only the lower half of the hull has been determined. The list is then reversed and the process is repeated (equivalent to scanning the points from right to left), generating the upper half of the hull. The two halves both contain the same end points, so the end of each list is deleted to avoid duplicates before the two halves are joined into a single list. By accepting only left turns, the algorithm returns the hull points in counterclockwise order; changing the technique to accept right turns instead returns the hull in clockwise order.

This is one of a number of convex hull algorithms available today, including ***Graham scan*** (R. L. Graham, 1972), ***Jarvis march*** (R. A. Jarvis, 1973), and many others. See also: *Computational Geometry* (F. P. Preparata, M. I. Shamos, 1985). Andrew's algorithm is very elegant when written in Python due to Python's extensive list handling capabilities. It runs in O(N log N) time worst-case because of the need to initially sort the N points by their *x* coordinates. Once the list is sorted, the rest of the algorithm runs in O(N) time, linear in the number of points.

Computational Geometry: Code for Convex Hull

The function shown below will return the convex hull of a list of 2D points, called `P2DList`. Two things to consider: (1) the order of the points in `P2DList` will be changed by this algorithm, first by the `sort` and then by the `reverse`, and (2) the initial list should <u>not</u> contain any duplicate points. Any duplicates must be filtered out before calling this function.

```
def ConvexHull2D (P2DList):
    if len(P2DList) <= 2: return P2DList

    P2DList.sort()
    LowerHull = []
    for P in P2DList:
        while (len(LowerHull) >= 2) and    \
            (CrossProduct2D(LowerHull[-2],LowerHull[-1],P) <= 0):
            LowerHull = LowerHull[:-1]   # Delete last point
        LowerHull = LowerHull + [P]       # Accept new point

    P2DList.reverse()
    UpperHull = []
    for P in P2DList:
        while (len(UpperHull) >= 2) and    \
            (CrossProduct2D(UpperHull[-2],UpperHull[-1],P) <= 0):
            UpperHull = UpperHull[:-1]   # Delete last point
        UpperHull = UpperHull + [P]       # Accept new point

    # Glue together and return the two lists, each minus
    # their last point to eliminate duplicates.
    return LowerHull[:-1] + UpperHull[:-1]
```

Here is an example of a set of eleven 2D points:
```
    L = [[10,10], [12,15], [9,7], [13,9], [9,8], [14,2],
         [13,7], [10,5], [17,1], [15,9], [17,6]]
```

Then `ConvexHull2D(L)` computes the lower and upper hulls:
```
    LowerHull = [[9,7], [10,5], [14,2], [17,1], [17,6]]
    UpperHull = [[17,6], [12,15], [9,8], [9,7]]
```
and returns those lists joined, minus their last elements, with seven points around the hull:
```
    [[9,7], [10,5], [14,2], [17,1], [17,6], [12,15], [9,8]]
```

Afterwards, list `L` still contains the same eleven points it started with, but in a different order:
```
    [[17,6], [17,1], [15,9], [14,2], [13,9], [13,7], [12,15],
     [10,10], [10,5], [9,8], [9,7]]
```

Python Graphics Core Routines (Pixels)

In Python 3 there are no graphics functions built in to the language, but there are graphics libraries available of various complexities. On this and the next few pages are a list of functions that simplify the task of creating graphics images and writing them to a file.

Pixels are three-element lists of red, green, and blue values between 0 and 255, represented as [R,G,B]. For any pixel P, P[0] represents the red component, P[1] the green component, and P[2] the blue component.

A few predefined colors are shown below. Functions getRed, getGreen, and getBlue return the appropriate component of a pixel, while setRed, setGreen, and setBlue change those components to new values.

```
black   = [  0,  0,  0]
blue    = [  0,  0,255]
green   = [  0,255,  0]
cyan    = [  0,255,255]
red     = [255,  0,  0]
magenta = [255,  0,255]
yellow  = [255,255,  0]
white   = [255,255,255]
gray    = [128,128,128]

def getRed (Pixel): return Pixel[0]

def getGreen (Pixel): return Pixel[1]

def getBlue (Pixel): return Pixel[2]

def setRed (Pixel,Value):
    Pixel[0] = Value
    return

def setGreen (Pixel,Value):
    Pixel[1] = Value
    return

def setBlue (Pixel,Value):
    Pixel[2] = Value
    return
```

Python Graphics Core Routines (the Canvas)

The graphics model implemented here uses a Python ***dictionary*** to represent image canvases. The dictionary will always contain entries for the <u>width</u>, <u>height</u>, and <u>default color</u> of the image canvas; all other dictionary entries will be for the colors of individual pixels. The dictionary appears *only* on this page, and these functions insulate the implementation of an image from the functions that "talk" to the image; should a different approach be desired, only these few functions must be rewritten. These functions define a new canvas dictionary, and allow it to be queried for its width, height, and default color, and ask if a location is visible on screen.

```python
def makeEmptyPicture (Width,Height,Color=white):
    return {"Width":Width, "Height":Height, "Default":Color}

def getWidth (Canvas): return Canvas["Width"]

def getHeight (Canvas): return Canvas["Height"]

def getDefault (Canvas): return Canvas["Default"]

def onScreen (Canvas, X, Y):
    X = int(round(X))
    Y = int(round(Y))
    if (X < 0) or (Y < 0): return False
    if (X >= Canvas["Width"]): return False
    if (Y >= Canvas["Height"]): return False
    return True
```

The `setPixel` function ignores any coordinates outside the boundaries of the canvas, and if the desired color is the same as the default background color the corresponding pixel is deleted. Only pixels with colors different from the default are stored, keeping the dictionary size small. The `getPixel` function returns a pixel's color, or the default color if it is not in the dictionary.

```python
def setPixel (Canvas, X, Y, Color=black):
    if not onScreen(Canvas,X,Y): return
    Index = (int(round(X)),int(round(Y)))      # Tuple of <X,Y>
    if Color == Canvas["Default"]:
        if Index in Canvas: del Canvas[Index]
    else:
        Canvas[Index] = Color
    return

def getPixel (Canvas, X, Y):
    Index = (int(round(X)),int(round(Y)))      # Tuple of <X,Y>
    if Index in Canvas:
        Result = Canvas[Index]
    else:
        Result = Canvas["Default"]
    return Result
```

Writing to the BMP File Format

The `.BMP` (***bitmap***) file format is a simple image format developed by Microsoft and used throughout the computing industry. It is ***uncompressed*** (impractical for use on the Web), but many software packages can convert bitmaps into `.JPG`, `.GIF`, or `.PNG` compressed formats. There is a rarely-used ***run-length encoded*** compressed version. Bitmaps support 24 bit-per-pixel (16,777,216 color) images, as well as 1 bit (2 color), 4 bit (16 color), and 8 bit (256 color) images with an associated ***palette***. There have been several revisions to the format since it was introduced. The code presented here generates only simple 24-bit uncompressed `.BMP` files.

The format of a `.BMP` file includes a 14-byte long file header, followed by a (usually) 40-byte image header, and then by the image data. The headers contain information about the image, including its width and height, number of colors, number of bytes per pixel, etc., and since the code here creates only one type of bitmap, many of the options are fixed. For example, "compression" is zero to indicate no compression, "colors used" and "colors important" are both zero to indicate that all colors are important, etc. The "pixels per meter" settings (one for *x* and one for *y*) are usually both zero, but are occasionally 2835 (72 dots per inch times 39.37 inches per meter). Image data are written to the file "upside down" with the bottom-most row of pixels written first and the top-most row written last. Bitmaps have the requirement that each row of pixels occupy a number of bytes evenly divisible by 4, so some "padding" bytes may need to be written at the end of each row. For example, an image 10 pixels wide needs 30 bytes per row, padded to 32 bytes, but an image 16 pixels wide needs 48 bytes per row and no padding.

To support writing to a binary file, the following two functions are necessary, the first to write out a stream of bytes corresponding to the ASCII values of characters in a string, and the second to write out a integer with any desired number of bytes (in little endian order). In both cases, a Python list is converted into a stream of bytes to be written to the file; the file must be opened as a ***binary file*** with `"wb"` file mode. In Python 2 write out the byte values as a stream of characters, but in Python 3 use the `bytes` function (the `bytes` function is specific to Python 3). The code below is set up for Python 3; to change to Python 2 comment out the lines that use the `bytes` function and un-comment the lines that use the `chr` function.

```
def WriteString(Outfile,S):
    L = [ord(CH) for CH in S]
    Outfile.write(bytes(L))                     # Python 3
#   for B in L: Outfile.write(chr(B))           # Python 2
    return

def WriteBytes (Outfile,N,TotalBytes=1):
    L = []
    for I in range(TotalBytes):
        L = L + [N % 256]                        # Little endian
        N = N // 256
    Outfile.write(bytes(L))                      # Python 3
#   for B in L: Outfile.write(chr(B))            # Python 2
    return
```

Writing to the BMP File Format (Continued)

The function shown here writes out a canvas to a simple 24-bit `.BMP` file, as long as the functions `getWidth`, `getHeight`, `getPixel`, `getRed`, `getGreen`, and `getBlue` are available and do the appropriate actions.

```
def WriteBMP (Canvas, FileName):
    Width               = getWidth(Canvas)
    Height              = getHeight(Canvas)
    FileHeaderSize      = 14  # Bytes
    ImageHeaderSize     = 40  # Bytes
    BytesPerPixel       = 3   # Bytes
    BitsPerPixel        = BytesPerPixel * 8
    Pad                 = 4 - (Width * BytesPerPixel) % 4
    if Pad == 4: Pad = 0
    BytesPerRaster      = Width * BytesPerPixel + Pad
    ImageSize           = Height * BytesPerRaster
    Offset              = FileHeaderSize + ImageHeaderSize
    FileSize            = ImageSize + Offset
    Outfile             = open(FileName,"wb")
    try:
        WriteString(Outfile,  "BM")
        WriteBytes (Outfile, FileSize, 4)
        WriteBytes (Outfile, 0, 2)                # Reserved
        WriteBytes (Outfile, 0, 2)                # Reserved
        WriteBytes (Outfile, Offset, 4)
        WriteBytes (Outfile, ImageHeaderSize, 4)
        WriteBytes (Outfile, Width, 4)
        WriteBytes (Outfile, Height, 4)
        WriteBytes (Outfile, 1, 2)                # Planes
        WriteBytes (Outfile, BitsPerPixel, 2)
        WriteBytes (Outfile, 0, 4)                # Compression
        WriteBytes (Outfile, ImageSize, 4)
        WriteBytes (Outfile, 0, 4)                # Pixels per meter
        WriteBytes (Outfile, 0, 4)                # Pixels per meter
        WriteBytes (Outfile, 0, 4)                # Colors Used
        WriteBytes (Outfile, 0, 4)                # Colors Important
        for Y in range(Height-1, -1, -1):
            for X in range(Width):
                Pixel = getPixel(Canvas,X,Y)
                WriteBytes (Outfile, getBlue(Pixel), 1)
                WriteBytes (Outfile, getGreen(Pixel), 1)
                WriteBytes (Outfile, getRed(Pixel), 1)
            if Pad > 0: WriteBytes(Outfile, 0, Pad)
    finally:
        Outfile.close()
    return
```

Drawing Lines Parametrically

Drawing a straight line from *<x1,y1>* to *<x2,y2>* can be done in a number of ways. Here is a version that uses parametric linear equations in both *x* and in *y* to accomplish this. The number of steps is dependent on the Euclidean distance D between the two end points. Parameter T ranges from 0.0 up through and including 1.0 to control the linear equations of interpolation.

```
def addLine (Canvas, X1, Y1, X2, Y2, Color=black):
    D  = int(round(Distance(X1,Y1,X2,Y2))) + 1
    Ax = X2 - X1
    Ay = Y2 - Y1
    for I in range(D+1):
        T = I / float(D)    # Parameter 0.0 ... 1.0
        X = Ax * T + X1     # Parametric Line for X
        Y = Ay * T + Y1     # Parametric Line for Y
        setPixel(Canvas, X, Y, Color)
    return
```

Drawing Lines Recursively

Drawing a line from *<x1,y1>* to *<x2,y2>* can also be done through recursion, although it may not be the best solution in all but a few cases. Locally defined function Recurse does all the work. For any section of the line, the midpoint of the section is computed and Recurse is called on the both first half of the section and on the second half of the section. Recursion stops when the end points of the section are "close enough" and a pixel is drawn. The Threshold value controls the recursion; when it is 1.0 recursion stops when the end points are closer than the width of a pixel, resulting in a solid line, but if it is greater than 1.0 recursion stops much earlier, resulting in a dotted line.

```
def addLine (Canvas, X1, Y1, X2, Y2, Color=black, Threshold=1.0):

    def Recurse (X1,Y1,X2,Y2):
        XM = (X1 + X2) / 2.0
        YM = (Y1 + Y2) / 2.0
        if Distance(X1,Y1,X2,Y2) <= Threshold:
            setPixel(Canvas,XM,YM,Color)
        else:
            Recurse(X1,Y1,XM,YM)
            Recurse(XM,YM,X2,Y2)
        return

    Recurse(X1,Y1,X2,Y2)
    return
```

Drawing Lines with Bresenham's Algorithm

Jack E. Bresenham created a fast algorithm for drawing lines in 1962 that is still in use today. Unlike the two versions on the previous page, this version uses integer arithmetic only (X1, Y1, X2, and Y2, as well as every other variable in this function, are all assumed to be integers, with no floating-point computations), so it can be easily written in assembly language. The bulk of this function configures the line through flipping and mirroring to operate *as if it was in the first octant relative to <0,0>* where DeltaX (the relative displacement along the *x*-axis) is greater than or equal to DeltaY (the relative displacement along the *y*-axis), and then maps each pixel back into its correct octant relative to <*x1,y1*>.

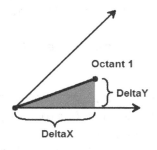

```
def addLine (Canvas, X1, Y1, X2, Y2, Color=black):
    Sign     = [+1,-1]
    DeltaX   = X2 - X1
    DeltaY   = Y2 - Y1
    NegateX = DeltaX < 0
    NegateY = DeltaY < 0
    DeltaX   = abs(DeltaX)
    DeltaY   = abs(DeltaY)
    XYswap   = DeltaX < DeltaY
    if XYswap: DeltaX,DeltaY = DeltaY,DeltaX
    Error    = -DeltaX // 2
    YOffset = 0
    for XOffset in range(DeltaX+1):
        if XYswap:                          # Octants 2,3,6,7
            X = Sign[NegateX] * YOffset
            Y = Sign[NegateY] * XOffset
        else:                               # Octants 1,4,5,8
            X = Sign[NegateX] * XOffset
            Y = Sign[NegateY] * YOffset
        setPixel(Canvas, X1+X, Y1+Y, Color)
        Error = Error + DeltaY
        if Error > 0:
            Error = Error - DeltaX
            YOffset = YOffset + 1
    return
```

Drawing Horizontal and Vertical Lines

The two functions simplify the drawing of horizontal and vertical lines. In `addHorizontalLine` the values of X1 and X2 are sorted (using the multiple assignment technique of Python) so that a line defined from right to left is still drawn; it would not be drawn otherwise. Similarly, Y1 and Y2 are sorted in `addVerticalLine` so that a line defined from bottom to top is still drawn. Horizontal lines above or below the canvas are not painted, nor are vertical lines to the left or right of the canvas. Further clipping could also be performed here to trim lines that are partially on the canvas and partially off so only the visible pixels are painted.

```python
def addHorizontalLine (Canvas, X1, X2, Y, Color=black):
    if (Y < 0) or (Y >= getHeight(Canvas)): return
    if (X1 > X2): X1,X2 = X2,X1
    for X in range(X1,X2+1): setPixel(Canvas,X,Y,Color)
    return

def addVerticalLine (Canvas, X, Y1, Y2, Color=black):
    if (X < 0) or (X >= getWidth(Canvas)): return
    if (Y1 > Y2): Y1,Y2 = Y2,Y1
    for Y in range(Y1,Y2+1): setPixel(Canvas,X,Y,Color)
    return
```

Drawing Boxes and Rectangles #1

The simplest way to draw rectangle outlines (boxes) and filled rectangles makes use of the horizontal and vertical line drawing routines presented above. This approach assumes that pixel coordinates are at the *centers* of each pixel, not at the boundaries between pixels (see the next page).

```python
def addRectangleFilled (Canvas, X1, Y1, X2, Y2, Color=black):
    if (Y1 > Y2): Y1,Y2 = Y2,Y1        # Required
    if (X1 > X2): X1,X2 = X2,X1        # Optional
    for Y in range(Y1,Y2+1):
        addHorizontalLine(Canvas,X1,X2,Y,Color)
    return

def addRectangleOutline (Canvas, X1, Y1, X2, Y2, Color=black):
    if (Y1 > Y2): Y1,Y2 = Y2,Y1        # Optional
    if (X1 > X2): X1,X2 = X2,X1        # Optional
    addHorizontalLine(Canvas, X1, X2, Y1, Color)    # Top
    addHorizontalLine(Canvas, X1, X2, Y2, Color)    # Bottom
    addVerticalLine  (Canvas, X1, Y1, Y2, Color)    # Left
    addVerticalLine  (Canvas, X2, Y1, Y2, Color)    # Right
    return
```

Drawing Boxes and Rectangles #2

The approach on the previous page is simple, effective, and understandable. However, that technique suffers from an interesting problem when dealing with *widths and heights* of rectangles instead of simple pixel coordinates. For example, the call `addRectangleFilled(Canvas,10,10,20,20)` creates a filled rectangle from pixel *<10,10>* up through <u>and including</u> pixel *<20,20>*, which is a rectangle that is 21×21 pixels in size, not 20×20 as the mathematics would imply! A second filled rectangle that starts at *<20,10>* and goes to *<30,20>* of a different color would overlap the rightmost column of pixels from the first rectangle (column 20 of the image). So, for a filled rectangle that starts at *<10,10>* and is both 10 pixels wide and 10 pixels tall exactly, the correct call would have to be `addRectangleFilled(Canvas,10,10,19,19)`, and the 10×10 adjacent filled rectangle that starts at *<20,10>* would be `addRectangleFilled(Canvas,20,10,29,19)` so that the two rectangles do not overlap. This is inconvenient at best and confusing at worst.

For rectangle outlines we actually <u>do</u> want them to overlap so that adjacent rectangles do not show an unusually thick border where they abut. What we want for these functions, then, is to be able to specify the coordinates of the pixel in the upper left corner of a rectangle, along with its width and height, and have them do the right thing.

The functions presented below correctly handle rectangles defined by their upper left corner coordinates `X` and `Y`, their widths `W`, and their heights `H`. This effectively uses the graphics model where pixel coordinates are defined as the *corners* between pixels instead of at their centers, and fits well into the framework where adjacent filled rectangles should not overlap, but rectangle outlines must. Rather than write a lot of new code, we can leverage the existing functions from the previous page.

```
def addRectangleFilledSized (Canvas, X, Y, W, H, Color=black):
    addRectangleFilled(Canvas,X,Y,X+W-1,Y+H-1,Color)
    return

def addRectangleOutlineSized (Canvas, X, Y, W, H, Color=black):
    addRectangleOutline(Canvas,X,Y,X+W,Y+H,Color)
    return
```

It may seem strange that filled rectangles are now one pixel shorter and one pixel narrower than outline rectangles of the same size, but doing so makes the graphics model more closely match the underlying mathematical intuitions than do the versions on the previous page. It must be cautioned that many professional graphics systems use one model or the other (pixel centers or pixel corners, frequently pixel corners), but not both. Sometimes you need one, sometimes the other, and occasionally both at the same time. *Caveat emptor*.

Drawing Circles and Polygons

The General Circle

When a circle of radius R is centered at point (Xc, Yc), then any point (X, Y) on the circumference of the circle can be determined from knowing just the angle θ of the line from the center to that point:

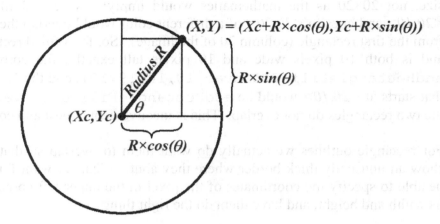

This technique can be used to generate the outline of a polygon. The number of segments can be any number greater than or equal to 3 (triangle), but as the number increases the polygon becomes indistinguishable from a circle. As shown, the functions below paint polygons centered at [Xc, Yc] in *clockwise* order due to the "upside down" nature of graphics screens relative to Cartesian coordinates. To make the function paint polygons in a *counterclockwise* order, mimicking Cartesian coordinates, change the + symbol to a − in the NewY = INT(...) statement.

```
def addPoly (Canvas, Xc, Yc, Radius, Segments=16, Color=black):
    Angle = 0
    Step  = 2.0 * math.pi / Segments       # Radians per point
    OldX  = int(round(Xc + Radius))
    OldY  = int(round(Yc))
    for I in range(1,Segments+1):
        Angle = float(I) * Step
        NewX  = int(round(Xc + Radius * math.cos(Angle)))
        NewY  = int(round(Yc + Radius * math.sin(Angle)))
        addLine (Canvas,OldX,OldY,NewX,NewY,Color)
        OldX  = NewX
        OldY  = NewY
    return

def addCircle (Canvas, Xc, Yc, Radius, Color=black):
    Segments = int(round(math.pi * Radius))    # Pi*Diameter/2
    addPoly (Canvas,Xc,Yc,Radius,Segments,Color)
    return
```

Drawing Circles with Bresenham's Algorithm

Jack Bresenham also created a very fast <u>integer-only</u> algorithm for drawing circles. I've seen a lot of variations on this algorithm, some more efficient than others. This is the one I use. The first version draws a circle outline; the second a solid filled circle. Both depend on functions created earlier to set the color of a pixel or to draw a horizontal line. The code is simple enough to easily write in assembly language.

```
def addBresenhamCircle (Canvas, Xc, Yc, R, Color=black):
    X = R
    Y = 0
    E = -R
    while (X >= Y):
        setPixel (Canvas, Xc - X, Yc + Y, Color)
        setPixel (Canvas, Xc + X, Yc + Y, Color)
        setPixel (Canvas, Xc - X, Yc - Y, Color)
        setPixel (Canvas, Xc + X, Yc - Y, Color)
        setPixel (Canvas, Xc - Y, Yc + X, Color)
        setPixel (Canvas, Xc + Y, Yc + X, Color)
        setPixel (Canvas, Xc - Y, Yc - X, Color)
        setPixel (Canvas, Xc + Y, Yc - X, Color)
        E = E + Y + Y + 1
        Y = Y + 1
        if (E > 0):
            E = E - X - X + 2
            X = X - 1
    return


def addBresenhamFilledCircle (Canvas, Xc, Yc, R, Color=black):
    X = R
    Y = 0
    E = -R
    while (X >= Y):
        addHorizontalLine(Canvas,Xc - X, Xc + X, Yc + Y, Color)
        addHorizontalLine(Canvas,Xc - X, Xc + X, Yc - Y, Color)
        addHorizontalLine(Canvas,Xc - Y, Xc + Y, Yc + X, Color)
        addHorizontalLine(Canvas,Xc - Y, Xc + Y, Yc - X, Color)
        E = E + Y + Y + 1
        Y = Y + 1
        if (E > 0):
            E = E - X - X + 2
            X = X - 1
    return
```

Flood Fill

Irregularly shaped regions on screen of the same color sometimes need to be filled with a new color, without affecting regions that are not "connected" to the region to be filled. There are a number of ways to do this, but the function below is one of the simpler and more effective ones, so long as the region is not especially complicated. Because this function contains a recursive subfunction, it is possible to recurse too deeply and run out of stack space. The location <*x,y*> passed in to the outer function is the "seed" value containing the pixel color to be replaced (`OldColor`). Within the recursive function `Process`, any <*x,y*> location it is given is extended left and right into a horizontal line so long as all pixels in that line have the old color. Those colors are replaced by the new color, and any pixels *adjacent to that line above and below* with the old color are used as the new seed.

```
def addFloodFill (Canvas, X, Y, NewColor):
    if not onScreen(Canvas,X,Y): return
    OldColor = getPixel(Canvas,X,Y)

    def Process (X, Y):
        XLeft = X
        XRight = X

        while (XLeft > 0) and          \
                (getPixel(Canvas,XLeft-1,Y) == OldColor):
            XLeft = XLeft - 1

        while (XRight < getWidth(Canvas)-1) and   \
                (getPixel(Canvas,XRight+1,Y) == OldColor):
            XRight = XRight + 1

        addHorizontalLine(Canvas,XLeft,XRight,Y,NewColor)

        if (Y > 0):
            for I in range(XLeft,XRight+1):
                if getPixel(Canvas,I,Y-1) == OldColor:
                    Process(I,Y-1)

        if (Y < getHeight(Canvas)-1):
            for I in range(XLeft,XRight+1):
                if getPixel(Canvas,I,Y+1) == OldColor:
                    Process(I,Y+1)
        return

    Process(X,Y)
    return
```

Flood Fill (Continued)

The following images show an example of flood fill. The left hand image shows the original graphic, with several yellow blocks among blue and red blocks. The biggest yellow block needs to be changed to cyan. The crosshairs show the location of the seed pixel used for flood fill. By starting there, and flooding all adjacent and connected yellow pixels with cyan, we get the picture on the right. Notice that only the yellow pixels connected to the block containing the seed have been changed; none of the other yellow blocks have been changed, as none of them are connected to the one with the starting seed location.

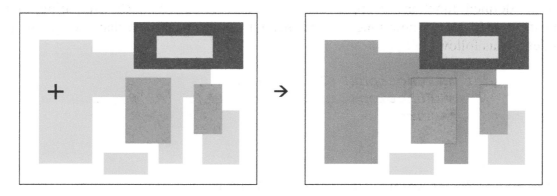

The algorithm on the previous page works best if the region to flood fill is wider than it is tall, and there are not too many "corridors" and "side galleries" to trace. That is, the <u>taller</u> the region to fill, and the <u>deeper</u> the recursion needs to go, the more likely it is that the program will crash due to running out of the stack space needed to handle the recursion.

Graphics Routines that use 2D Points

The functions on this page and the next all operate on 2D points as lists of $[X, Y]$ coordinates, where for any point P the x coordinate is $P[0]$ and the y coordinate is $P[1]$. Without loss of generality, for point P0, P1, P2, Center, etc., the x coordinate is at position 0 in the list and the y coordinate is at position 1 in the list.

All these functions need to do is translate the point lists into individual x and y coordinates to be used with the previously defined functions that have the corresponding name. For example, any previously defined function myFunction(Canvas,X1,Y1,X2,Y2) requiring individual coordinates would have a new function here named myFunction2D that uses points instead, and is defined as follows:

```
def myFunction2D(Canvas,P1,P2):
    myFunction(Canvas,P1[0],P1[1],P2[0],P2[1])
    return
```

```
def setPixel2D (Canvas, P, Color=black):
    setPixel(Canvas,P[0],P[1],Color)
    return
```

```
def getPixel2D (Canvas, P):
    return getPixel(Canvas,P[0],P[1])
```

```
def addLine2D (Canvas, P1, P2, Color=black):
    addLine(Canvas,P1[0],P1[1],P2[0],P2[1],Color)
    return
```

```
def addPoly2D (Canvas, Center, Radius, Segments=16, Color=black):
    addPoly(Canvas,Center[0],Center[1],Radius,Segments,Color)
    return
```

```
def addCircle2D (Canvas, Center, Radius, Color=black):
    addCircle(Canvas,Center[0],Center[1],Radius,Color)
    return
```

Graphics Routines that use 2D Points (Continued)

In these functions, `List2D` is a list of 2D points. That is, a list of three two-dimensional points `[20,10]`, `[50,60]`, and `[35,95]` is represented as `[[20,10],[50,60],[35,95]]` (a list of two-element lists). In both of the functions listed here the variable `PLast` keeps track of the previously processed point (the last `P`), and is updated to the current point `P` after the line between `PLast` and `P` has been drawn.

The `addPolyLine2D` draws a line between each successive pair of points:

```
        Line2D[0]...Line2D[1]        First two points
        Line2D[1]...Line2D[2]
        Line2D[2]...Line2D[3]
        ...
        Line2D[-2]...Line2D[-1]      Last two points
```

```python
def addPolyline2D (Canvas, List2D, Color=black):
    if (len(List2D) >= 2):
        PLast = List2D[0]        # Grab the first point
        for P in List2D[1:]:  # The list without the first point
            addLine2D(Canvas,PLast,P,Color)
            PLast = P
    return
```

The `addPolygon2D` also draws a line between each successive pair of points, but closes the loop from the last point back to the first:

```
        Line2D[0]...Line2D[1]        First two points
        Line2D[1]...Line2D[2]
        Line2D[2]...Line2D[3]
        ...
        Line2D[-2]...Line2D[-1]      Last two points
        Line2D[-1]...Line2D[0]       Closes the loop
```

```python
def addPolygon2D (Canvas, List2D, Color=black):
    if (len(List2D) >= 2):
        PLast = List2D[-1]        # Grab the last point
        for P in List2D:
            addLine2D(Canvas,PLast,P,Color)
            PLast = P
    return
```

2D Polygon Fill

Unlike flood fill, where the region to be colored in is already there but has the wrong color, polygon fill colors in a region defined by a set of 2D coordinates regardless of what is already present. The first half of the algorithm makes a copy of the polygon, determines its extent, and modifies it slightly to make the fill process work well (the modifications are why the polygon has to be copied in the first place). The second half on the next page does all the "heavy lifting" to see how many times each screen line crosses the polygon. For each screen line there will be an even number of crossings: 0 if the line misses (which should not happen), 2 for convex polygons, 4, 6, 8, or more for concave polygons. Each pair of crossings determines one horizontal line to paint for that screen line. `ParameterList2D` is a list of 2D points, such as `[[140,30],[50,160],[140,210],[170,100],[230,210],[310,100]]`.

```
import copy

def addPolygonFill2D (Canvas, ParameterList2D, Color):

    Epsilon = 0.000001
    List2D  = copy.deepcopy(ParameterList2D)

    MinX = List2D[0][0]              # Find the bounding box of
    MinY = List2D[0][1]              # the polygon by scanning
    MaxX = MinX                      # all the points and comparing
    MaxY = MinY                      # their X,Y coordinates to
    for P in List2D:                 # the existing minima and
        X = float(P[0])              # maxima in both X and Y.
        Y = float(P[1])              # This is the only region
        MinX = min(MinX, X)          # of the screen that needs
        MinY = min(MinY, Y)          # any consideration.
        MaxX = max(MaxX, X)          #
        MaxY = max(MaxY, Y)          #
    MidY = (MaxY + MinY) / 2.0       # Vertical middle of polygon

    for I in range(len(List2D)):     # Adjust the Y coordinate
        Y = float(List2D[I][1])      # of any point where its
        if (Y == round(Y)):          # Y value lies exactly on
            if (Y < MidY):           # a scan line, up if it is
                Y = Y - Epsilon      # above the midpoint, down
            else:                    # if is below. This way
                Y = Y + Epsilon      # each line of pixels will
            MaxY = max(MaxY, Y)      # intersect the polygon in
            MinY = min(MinY, Y)      # an even number of crossings.
            List2D[I][1] = Y         #

    MinScan = int(MinY) + 1          # What are the minimum and
    MaxScan = int(MaxY)              # maximum rows of pixels?
```

2D Polygon Fill (Continued)

```
for Yscan in range(MinScan,MaxScan+1):
    XTable = []         # Table of X crossings for current Y.
    P  = List2D[-1]     # Scan pairwise points, starting at
    X1 = round(P[0])    # last one.  Each pair is one line
    Y1 = round(P[1])    # of the polygon to see if current Y
    for P in List2D:    # crosses it at all.
        X2 = round(P[0])
        Y2 = round(P[1])

        # Does the current line cross Y? If so, where?
        # For each crossing found, add it to the list.
        if ((Yscan < Y1) != (Yscan < Y2)):
            XValue = ((Yscan-Y1) / (Y2-Y1)) * (X2-X1) + X1
            XTable = XTable + [int(round(XValue))]

        X1 = X2
        Y1 = Y2

    # Sort crossings by increasing X, then draw a line
    # for the current Y between each pair of crossings.
    XTable.sort()
    for I in range(0,len(XTable),2):
        addHorizontalLine(Canvas,          \
                          XTable[I],        \
                          XTable[I+1], Yscan, Color)
return
```

The left hand image shows the original graphic with the polygon to fill overlaid on top (it is NOT part of the image). The right hand image shows the result of filling that polygon with green, regardless of what was previously inside the polygon.

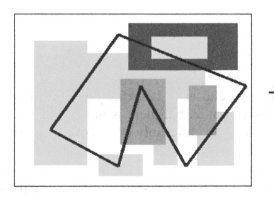 →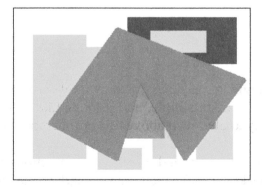

3D Orthographic Projection

There are a number of ways to project points from three dimensions onto a flat, 2D computer graphics screen. The most powerful and flexible involves a proper treatment of perspective. In contrast, the orthographic approach presented here is not as powerful and does not look as good as the perspective approach, but it is considerably simpler to implement.

In this approach, the *x* and *y* axes of the "world" model are flat on the screen, while the +*z* axis is understood to project into the screen away from the viewer. The on-screen left-right distance from the center of the axes to where the point will be drawn is the *x* coordinate of the point, plus the *z* coordinate times the <u>cosine</u> of the projection angle, then the result multiplied by a scale factor which is the number of screen pixels per world unit. Similarly, the up-down distance from the center of the axes is the *y* coordinate of the point, plus the *z* coordinate times the <u>sine</u> of the projection angle, also then multiplied by the scale factor. When viewing the system from a slight angle above and to the right of the 3D origin, the axes appear as follows:

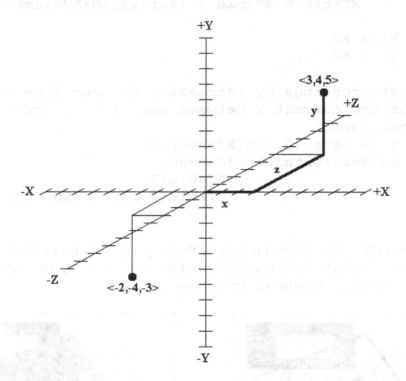

The angle that the *z* axis is drawn relative to the *x* axis is chosen to be exactly 30° here in order to make the math simple, and it looks like a "reasonable" angle, but there is nothing special about it. Any angle much above 45° or much below 20° will have noticeably odd depth artifacts.

The `math.sin` and `math.cos` functions take a very long time to compute. If the angle is always kept at 30°, then the sine and cosine can be computed once and used throughout the code.

Sine(30°) = ½ (exactly 0.5)
Cosine(30°) = ½√3 (approximately 0.8660254037844…)

3D Orthographic Projection (Continued)

In this code block, the `Origin2D` variable is necessary to place the center of the 3D axes on screen, and `Scale2D` maps coordinates from world units to screen units (pixels). They are global to `SetOrigin`, `SetOrigin2D`, `SetScale2D`, and `Project3D`, but to no other functions. Global variables in general are not a good idea, but because of extremely restricted application here we can justify their use to share information between these few functions only.

```
Origin2D = [0,0]            # Pixel location on Screen of Axes
Scale2D = 1.0              # Pixels per World unit

def SetOrigin2D (P2D):     # P2D is an [X,Y] point
    global Origin2D
    Origin2D = P2D         # Set the location on screen of Axes
    return

def SetOrigin (X, Y):
    SetOrigin2D ([X,Y])
    return

def SetScale2D (N):        # Set number of pixels per World unit
    global Scale2D
    Scale2D = N
    return

Cosine30 = math.cos(math.radians(30.0))    # 0.8660254037844…
Sine30   = math.sin(math.radians(30.0))    # 0.5

def Project3D (P3D):
    global Origin2D, Scale2D
    X = Origin2D[0] + (P3D[0] + P3D[2] * Cosine30) * Scale2D
    Y = Origin2D[1] - (P3D[1] + P3D[2] * Sine30)   * Scale2D
    return [X,Y]
```

The `Project3D` function takes in a 3D point as a list of three numbers `[X,Y,Z]` and returns a 2D point `[X,Y]` of where the 3D point appears on screen. The minus sign in the `Y = …` statement adjusts for the upside-down nature of computer graphics screens. We *think* in Cartesian 3D, but `Project3D` compensates for this to plot points correctly on the screen.

```
def addLine3D (Canvas, P1, P2, NewColor=black):
    addLine2D(Canvas,Project3D(P1),Project3D(P2),NewColor)
    return
```

Once the projection from 3D to 2D has been accomplished, all subsequent functions can deal primarily with the 3D world space, rather than the 2D world. For example, `addLine3D` takes in two 3D points and draws a line between them, projected correctly onto the screen.

4D Orthographic Projection

It is also possible to project from 4D into 2D with a similar approach. Yes, it is difficult for 3D creatures such as ourselves to visualize beyond three dimensions, particularly when high-dimensional objects are projected all the way down into 2D. However, the math is consistent no matter the number of dimensions.

In four dimensions there are four orthogonal axes: x, y, z, and w, each of which is at a 90° angle (in 4-space) from the other three axes.

We need a new `Project4D` function to take in a 4D point as a list of four numbers `[X,Y,Z,W]` and return a 2D point `[X,Y]` of where the 4D point must appear on screen. The approach is nearly identical to that of the 3D projection: the x and y axes lie flat on the screen, with the z axis projection at a 30° angle as before, but now also with the w axis at a 60° angle.

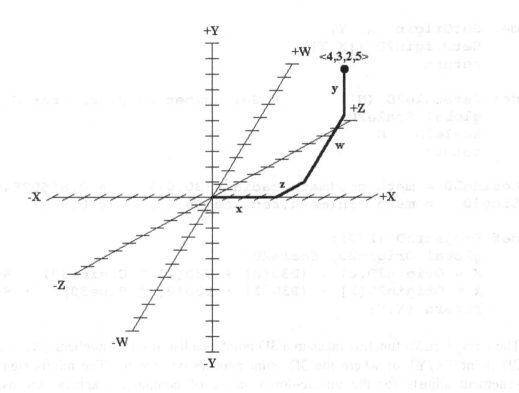

4D Orthographic Projection (Continued)

We can use all the previous code for dealing with coordinates on the screen (variable `Origin2D`, function `SetOrigin`, and function `SetOrigin2D`), and simply add the new `Project4D` function and any new geometry functions such as `addLine4D` to exploit that projection. We can even re-use the `Sine30` and `Cosine30` variables for use with the 4D projection, because the sine of 30° is the same as the cosine of 60° and the cosine of 30° is the same as the sine of 60°.

```
def Project4D (P4D):
    global Origin2D, Scale2D
    X = Origin2D[0] + (P4D[0] + P4D[2] * Cosine30 +            \
                              P4D[3] * Sine30)    * Scale2D
    Y = Origin2D[1] - (P4D[1] + P4D[2] * Sine30   +            \
                              P4D[3] * Cosine30) * Scale2D
    return [X,Y]
```

Once `Project4D` has been implemented, it again is easy to draw lines between any two 4D points in four-dimensional space, as shown with the `addLine4D` function. In `addLine4D`, both `P0` and `P1` are 4D points of the form `[X,Y,Z,W]`.

```
def addLine4D (Canvas,P1,P2,NewColor=black):
    addLine2D(Canvas,Project4D(P1),Project4D(P2),NewColor)
    return
```

With `addLine4D`, we now can draw the edges of a four-dimensional hypercube, called a ***tesseract*** (this is the figure on the front cover of the book):

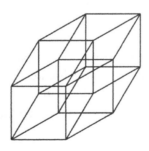

As an aside, the tesseract is a lot easier to visualize when projected into 3D, instead of 2D, by using chenille sticks (pipe cleaners) to build a tactile model.

5D Orthographic Projection

Even higher dimensions are possible, but they do get more complicated as each dimension is added. In the case of 5-dimensional orthographic projections, the five axes *x*, *y*, *z*, *v*, and *w* are projected onto the 2D plane where the *x* axis is at 0 and *y* is at 90, as usual, and then *z*, *v*, and *w* are equally distributed in between at 22.5°, 45°, and 67.5°, respectively (in 5-space they are all at 90° from each other, of course). However, the projection angles for *z*, *v*, and *w* may be slightly altered to prevent or reduce interference of one projected line with another. For example, the 5D hypercube below was plotted with the projection angles for *z*, *v*, and *w* set to 25°, 45°, and 70°, respectively; close enough to their "correct" values to look right, but different enough that no line interfered with any others.

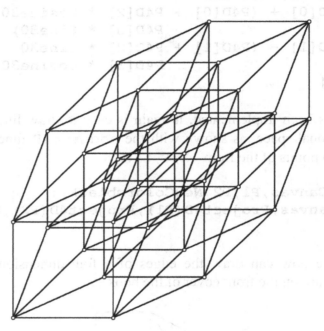

The projection code uses the same framework and approach as before. There is a 2D origin point where the center of the 5D coordinate axes are located on the computer screen, as usual. We need a new Project5D function that takes in a 5D point as a list of five numbers [X,Y,Z,V,W] and returns a 2D point [X,Y] of where the 5D point must appear on screen.

5D Orthographic Projection (Continued)

We can use all the previous code for dealing with coordinates on the screen (variable `Origin2D`, function `SetOrigin`, and function `SetOrigin2D`), and simply add the new `Project5D` function and any new geometry functions such as `addLine5D` to exploit that projection.

```
AngleZ  = math.radians(25.0)   # should be 22.5 degrees (Z)
AngleV  = math.radians(45.0)   # should be 45.0 degrees (V)
AngleW  = math.radians(70.0)   # should be 67.5 degrees (W)
CosineZ = math.cos(AngleZ)
CosineV = math.cos(AngleV)
CosineW = math.cos(AngleW)
SineZ   = math.sin(AngleZ)
SineV   = math.sin(AngleV)
SineW   = math.sin(AngleW)

def Project5D (P5D):
    global Origin2D, Scale2D
    X = Origin2D[0] + (P5D[0] +                          \
                       P5D[2] * CosineZ +                \
                       P5D[3] * CosineV +                \
                       P5D[4] * CosineW) * Scale2D
    Y = Origin2D[1] - (P5D[1] +                          \
                       P5D[2] * SineZ   +                \
                       P5D[3] * SineV   +                \
                       P5D[4] * SineW) * Scale2D
    return [X,Y]
```

Once `Project5D` has been implemented, it again is easy to draw lines between any two 5D points in five-dimensional space, as shown with the `addLine5D` function. In `addLine5D`, both `P0` and `P1` are 5D points of the form `[X,Y,Z,V,W]`.

```
def addLine5D (Canvas, P1, P2, Color=black):
    addLine2D(Canvas, Project5D(P1), Project5D(P2), Color)
    return
```

Writing to the SVG File Format

Bitmaps and other common types of ***raster graphics*** file formats are pixel-based, which leads to ***aliasing*** issues in scaling them up or down in size. In contrast, .SVG (***Scalable Vector Graphics***) files use ***vector graphics***, allowing browsers to scale them mathematically up or down in size without incurring aliasing problems. Here and on the next few pages are Python 3 functions, based on an object-oriented design, that allow for the easy creation of .SVG files.

This page contains the object ***constructor*** (__init__) function, as well as one function to close out the file and another to make sure that any string written to the file always includes a new line character at the end. The constructor opens the output file for writing, and writes out the SVG file prolog.

```python
class TSVG(object):

    def __init__ (self, NewFilename, NewWidth, NewHeight):
        self.Handle = open(NewFilename, "w")
        self.Filename = NewFilename
        self.Width = NewWidth
        self.Height = NewHeight
        self.Write ('<?xml version="1.0"')
        self.Write ('         encoding="UTF-8"')
        self.Write ('         standalone="no"?>')
        self.Write ('')
        self.Write ('<svg')
        self.Write ('     xmlns:svg="http://www.w3.org/2000/svg"')
        self.Write ('     xmlns="http://www.w3.org/2000/svg"')
        self.Write ('     version="1.1"')
        self.Write ('     x="0px"')
        self.Write ('     y="0px"')
        self.Write ('     width="' + str(NewWidth) + 'px"')
        self.Write ('     height="' + str(NewHeight) + 'px"')
        self.Write ('     >')
        self.Write ('')
        return

    def Close (self):
        self.Write ('</svg>')
        self.Handle.close()
        return

    def Write (self, S):
        self.Handle.write(S + "\n")
        return
```

Writing to the SVG File Format (Continued)

Circles and ellipses are defined by the coordinates `Xc, Yc` of the center point, and either one radius `R` (circles) or two radii `Rx` and `Ry` (ellipses). The `StrokeColor` is the color of the outside boundary, and the `FillColor` is the color of the interior. These colors are strings that are either HTML color names or hexadecimal color codes. The `StrokeWidth` value is the thickness in pixels of the outside boundary.

```
def Circle (self, Xc, Yc, R,         \
              StrokeColor="black",   \
              FillColor="white",     \
              StrokeWidth=1):
    self.Write ('<circle')
    self.Write ('    cx="' + str(Xc) + '"')
    self.Write ('    cy="' + str(Yc) + '"')
    self.Write ('    r="' + str(R) + '"')
    self.Write ('    stroke="' + StrokeColor + '"')
    self.Write ('    fill="' + FillColor + '"')
    self.Write ('    stroke-width="'+str(StrokeWidth)+'"')
    self.Write ('    />')
    self.Write ('')
    return


def Ellipse (self, Xc, Yc, Rx, Ry,  \
              StrokeColor="black",    \
              FillColor="white",      \
              StrokeWidth=1):
    self.Write ('<ellipse')
    self.Write ('    cx="' + str(Xc) + '"')
    self.Write ('    cy="' + str(Yc) + '"')
    self.Write ('    rx="' + str(Rx) + '"')
    self.Write ('    ry="' + str(Ry) + '"')
    self.Write ('    stroke="' + StrokeColor + '"')
    self.Write ('    fill="' + FillColor + '"')
    self.Write ('    stroke-width="'+str(StrokeWidth)+'"')
    self.Write ('    />')
    self.Write ('')
    return
```

Writing to the SVG File Format (Continued)

Rectangles are defined by the coordinates X, Y of the upper-left corner of the rectangle, as well as the width W and the height H of the rectangle. As before, StrokeColor and FillColor are HTML color definitions, and StrokeWidth is the thickness in pixels of the surrounding outline.

```
def Rectangle (self, X, Y, W, H,        \
               StrokeColor="black",     \
               FillColor="white",       \
               StrokeWidth=1):
    self.Write ('<rect')
    self.Write ('    x="' + str(X) + '"')
    self.Write ('    y="' + str(Y) + '"')
    self.Write ('    width="' + str(W) + '"')
    self.Write ('    height="' + str(H) + '"')
    self.Write ('    stroke="' + StrokeColor + '"')
    self.Write ('    fill="' + FillColor + '"')
    self.Write ('    stroke-width="'+str(StrokeWidth)+'"')
    self.Write ('    />')
    self.Write ('')
    return
```

Lines require the coordinates of two end points X1,Y1 and X2,Y2, as well as the StrokeColor of the line and the StrokeWidth thickness of the line. As this is not a filled object there is no fill color.

```
def Line (self, X1, Y1, X2, Y2,  \
          StrokeColor="black",   \
          StrokeWidth=1):
    self.Write ('<line')
    self.Write ('    x1="' + str(X1) + '"')
    self.Write ('    y1="' + str(Y1) + '"')
    self.Write ('    x2="' + str(X2) + '"')
    self.Write ('    y2="' + str(Y2) + '"')
    self.Write ('    stroke="' + StrokeColor + '"')
    self.Write ('    stroke-width="'+str(StrokeWidth)+'"')
    self.Write ('    />')
    self.Write ('')
    return
```

Writing to the SVG File Format (Continued)

Writing a text string requires the X, Y coordinates of the <u>lower left corner</u> of the text (text is written out to the right of X and above Y), and the text string S to write out. Options include the FontSize of the text in points (at 72 points per inch), the HTML color in FontColor, and the typeface name in FontName ("Times New Roman", "Arial", etc.). Text may also be Bold or Italic (the values of these options are not written to the file if False).

```
def Text (self, X, Y, S,                    \
            FontSize=12,                     \
            FontColor="black",               \
            FontName="Courier New",          \
            Bold=False,                      \
            Italic=False):
    self.Write ('<text')
    self.Write ('    x="' + str(X) + '"')
    self.Write ('    y="' + str(Y) + '"')
    self.Write ('    font-family="' + FontName + '"')
    self.Write ('    font-size="' + str(FontSize) + '"')
    self.Write ('    fill="' + FontColor + '"')
    if Bold:   self.Write('    font-weight="bold"')
    if Italic: self.Write('    font-style="italic"')
    self.Write ('    >')
    self.Write ('    ' + S)
    self.Write ('</text>')
    self.Write ('')
    return
```

Writing to the SVG File Format (Example)

Here is a complete example of how to use the SVG code on the previous pages. X is the SVG object variable; using the class name as a function calls the constructor to write to test.svg. The result is as it would appear in a Web browser.

```
X = TSVG("test.svg",160,100)
X.Rectangle(0,0,160,100,"black","yellow")
X.Circle(80,50,25,"blue","cyan")
X.Text(10,90,"William T. Verts")
X.Close()
```

18: *Sound and Signal Processing*

This section covers some of the basic concepts and topics behind understanding audio data. Basics include the synthesizing of audio waveforms, issues in quantizing sound for CDs, DTMF telephone tones, tones for audio modems, writing audio data to `.WAV` files, etc.

Code examples are shown in Python due to the simplicity of the language. . Most examples are version agnostic and can be implemented in either Python 2 or Python 3. Where the difference *does* matter, functions will be clearly labeled in red as needing Python 2 or Python 3. Most code examples can be translated into other languages as needed with little difficulty.

Human Audio

Here is an example of an audio waveform of someone speaking. Samples with values that exceed the maximum allowed are clipped, resulting in distortion that can be audible.

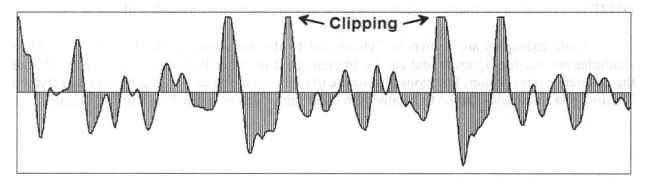

Sine Wave, and Harmonics

Sine waves are pure tones, dependent on the sample angle θ (the sample number times the number of radians per sample), and the multiplier used to scale $sin(\theta)$ to the legal range of sample values.

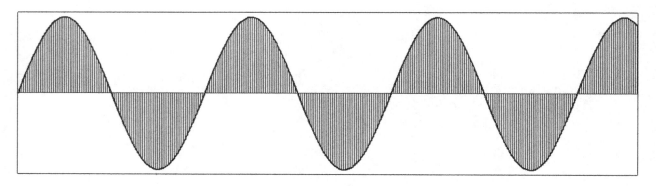

Adding a sine wave plus its 3RD harmonic at $\frac{1}{3}$ the amplitude, plus the 5TH harmonic at $\frac{1}{5}$ the amplitude, the 7TH harmonic at $\frac{1}{7}$ the amplitude, plus the 9TH harmonic at $\frac{1}{9}$ the amplitude results in the following wave form. Continuing the process to infinity gives a square wave.

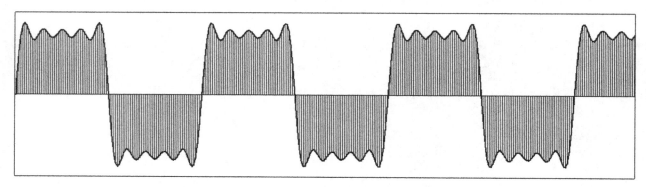

Square

Here is a perfect square wave, where each sample value is either the largest or smallest possible value. Because these waves are essentially an infinite sum of sines, playing them through a speaker results in a heavily distorted sound.

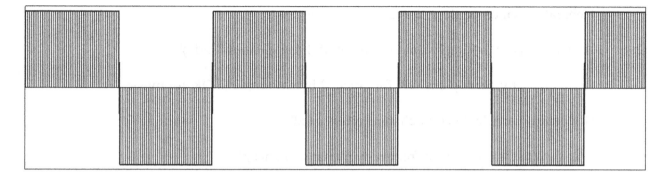

Triangle and Saw Tooth

Triangle (top) and saw tooth (bottom) waves are corresponding easy to synthesize, and have their own audio characteristics. The saw tooth wave may also be inverted, with a gradual ramping-up and sharp drop instead of the ramping-down and sharp rise that you see here.

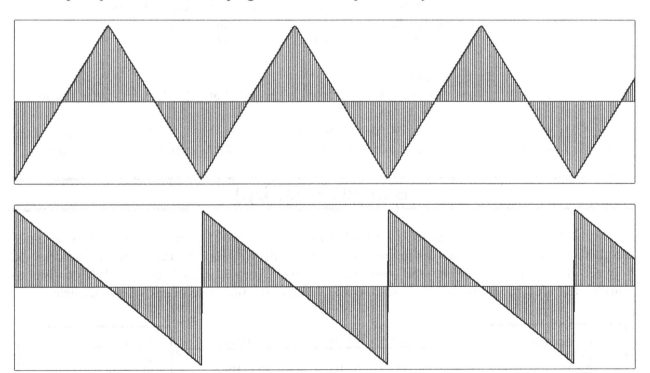

General Audio Issues

Recording audio requires the answers to three major questions:

1.   How many channels of information are required?

Generally 1 (monaural) or 2 (stereo).

2.   How good is each sample (measurement of the audio amplitude)?

Generally 1 byte/sample is OK for voice, 2 bytes/sample is OK for music.

3.   How many samples/second/channel are needed?

    3A.   What is the highest frequency humans can hear?

Around 22 KHz (as infants, upper frequencies tend to drop with age).

    3B.   How does frequency relate to samples/second?

According to the ***Nyquist Sampling Theorem*** (Harry Nyquist, ~1928), you must sample at least twice the rate of the highest frequency to be captured.

22 KHz × 2 = 44,000 samples/second/channel. For compact discs this is actually 44,100 samples/second/channel, as the number 44,100 can be divided evenly by 2, 3, 4, 5, 6, 7, 9, 10, 12, 14, 15, 18, etc. (the factors of 44,100 are 2×2×3×3×5×5×7×7).

Thus, the audio data rate on a CD is:
2 channels × 2 bytes/sample × 44,100 samples/second/channel = 176,400 bytes/second.

Audio CDs may be ripped to .WAV files at the standard rate, but .WAV files may be 1 or 2 channels, 1 or 2 bytes/sample, and at 8000, 11025, 22050, or 44100 samples/second/channel.

Bell 103 (Dial-Up)

Old-style dial-up Bell 103 modems (AT&T Corporation, 1962) used a combination of audio frequencies (sine waves) to distinguish between 0-bits ("space") and 1-bits ("mark"), and between the originating station and answering station. Normally, each end sends a continuous mark signal, interrupted by spaces and marks to indicate the presence of each new character.

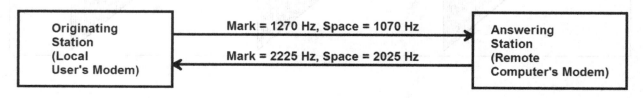

DTMF (Telephone)

Each key on a __*DTMF*__ (Dual-Tone, Multi-Frequency, also known as Touch-Tone™, Bell System 1963) telephone key-pad emits a blend of two sine waves, one unique to the column and the other unique to the row. These frequencies are chosen so that no frequency has any harmonics in common with any of the other frequencies, eliminating the possibility that one key will be misread as another.

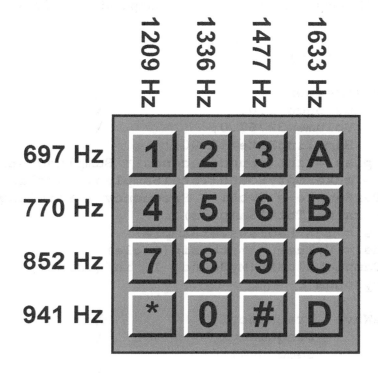

When the 0 key is pressed, for example, a sine wave of 1336 Hz is mixed with a sine wave of 941 Hz, creating the composite that you see below:

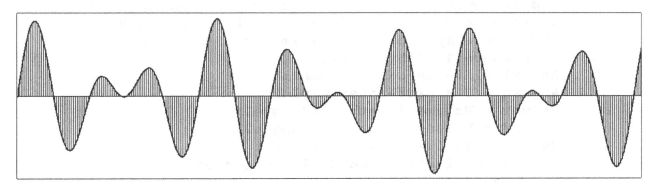

Note: earlier editions of this book had column 3 erroneously defined as 1447 Hz instead of 1477 Hz.

Generating Sine Waves (Python 2, JES)

The Python code below shows how to generate simple single-channel sounds that are comprised of either one or two independent sine waves. This code is specific to the JES Python 2 environment: it uses the `makeEmptySound` function to directly create an empty sound file of the correct length at the specified sampling rate, which by default is always two bytes per sample and one channel. The JES `setSampleValueAt` function sets a particular sample to an integer amplitude value. The range of allowable volumes (amplitudes) is -32768…+32767.

```python
import math
TwoPi = 2.0 * math.pi

def SineWave (Frequency,                            \
              Seconds=1.0,                          \
              Volume=32767.0,                       \
              SamplingRate=44100):
    TotalSamples = int(round(Seconds * SamplingRate))
    MySound = makeEmptySound(TotalSamples, SamplingRate)
    RadiansPerSample = TwoPi * Frequency / SamplingRate
    for I in range(TotalSamples):
        Angle = I * RadiansPerSample
        Value = Volume * math.sin(Angle)
        setSampleValueAt(MySound, I, int(Value))
    return MySound

def DualSineWave (Frequency1,                        \
                  Frequency2,                        \
                  Seconds=1.0,                       \
                  Volume=32767.0,                    \
                  SamplingRate=44100):
    TotalSamples = int(round(Seconds * SamplingRate))
    RadiansPerSample1 = TwoPi * Frequency1 / SamplingRate
    RadiansPerSample2 = TwoPi * Frequency2 / SamplingRate
    MySound = makeEmptySound(TotalSamples, SamplingRate)
    for I in range(TotalSamples):
        Angle1 = I * RadiansPerSample1
        Angle2 = I * RadiansPerSample2
        Value1 = Volume * math.sin(Angle1)
        Value2 = Volume * math.sin(Angle2)
        Value  = (Value1 + Value2) / 2.0
        setSampleValueAt(MySound, I, int(Value))
    return MySound
```

For example, a one-second-long 440 Hz A-above-middle-C tone can be synthesized by `SineWave(440)`, and to generate the DTMF tone for the 0 key on a telephone keypad use `DualSineWave(941,1336)`. In JES sounds can be played with the `play` command.

Generating Sine Waves (Generic)

The Python code here does the same thing as on the previous page in essentially the same way, but instead of relying on special functions that may not be available it generates simple lists of floating-point numbers between -1.0 and +1.0 representing a stream of volumes. Later code can convert these lists into .WAV files with 1 or 2 bytes per sample, and can combine one or two streams into the same audio file. All subsequent examples will use this format. This code will work equally well under Python 2 or Python 3. Use `DualSineWave` to generate DTMF tones.

```python
import math
TwoPi = 2.0 * math.pi

def SineWave (Frequency,            \
                Seconds=1.0,         \
                Volume=1.0,          \
                SamplingRate=44100):
    Result = []
    RadiansPerSample = TwoPi * Frequency / SamplingRate
    TotalSamples = int(round(Seconds * SamplingRate))
    for I in range(TotalSamples):
        Angle = I * RadiansPerSample
        Value = Volume * math.sin(Angle)
        Result.append(Value)
    return Result

def DualSineWave (Frequency1,       \
                Frequency2,          \
                Seconds=1.0,         \
                Volume=1.0,          \
                SamplingRate=44100):
    TotalSamples = int(round(Seconds * SamplingRate))
    RadiansPerSample1 = TwoPi * Frequency1 / SamplingRate
    RadiansPerSample2 = TwoPi * Frequency2 / SamplingRate
    Result = []
    for I in range(TotalSamples):
        Angle1 = I * RadiansPerSample1
        Angle2 = I * RadiansPerSample2
        Value1 = Volume * math.sin(Angle1)
        Value2 = Volume * math.sin(Angle2)
        Value  = (Value1 + Value2) / 2.0
        Result.append(Value)
    return Result
```

By using floating-point numbers between -1.0...+1.0, the audio file can be easily scaled up or down in volume, and then can be checked to see how many samples are out-of-range before creating a .WAV file.

Scaling and Clipping Sounds

Using the model where sounds are lists of floating-point numbers between -1.0 and +1.0, here are a few "helper" functions for managing those lists. The first two functions scale all the sound samples in the lists (called `Data` in each case) by a scale factor. The difference between the functions is that `ScaleSound` returns a new list of scaled samples but does not modify `Data`, and `ScaleSoundInPlace` changes the contents of `Data` directly.

```python
def ScaleSound (Data, Scale=1.0):
    return [Sample*Scale for Sample in Data]

def ScaleSoundInPlace (Data, Scale=1.0):
    for Index in range(len(Data)):
        Data[Index] = Data[Index] * Scale
    return
```

Similarly, `ClipSound` returns a new copy of the list where all samples are guaranteed to be between -1.0 and +1.0 (scaling a sound can easily result in samples outside the range), and `ClipSoundInPlace` changes the contents of `Data` directly.

```python
def ClipSound (Data):
    return [max(-1.0,min(+1.0,Sample)) for Sample in Data]

def ClipSoundInPlace (Data):
    for Index in range(len(Data)):
        Value = Data[Index]
        if    Value > +1.0: Value = +1.0
        elif Value < -1.0: Value = -1.0
        Data[Index] = Value
    return
```

Since scaling a sound can have a result that must be clipped, this function computes the percentage of samples that are out-of-range. It returns 0% if the list is empty, and does not modify `Data` otherwise.

```python
def PercentSoundIsClipped (Data):
    TotalSamples = len(Data)
    if TotalSamples <= 0: return 0.0
    Count = 0
    for Index in range(TotalSamples):
        if abs(Data[Index]) > 1.0:
            Count = Count + 1
    return Count * 100.0 / TotalSamples
```

Blend of two Sine Waves (Linear)

Here is a technique to generate a list of sound samples (using the -1.0...+1.0 model) where the frequency of the sound at the start is `Frequency1` and at the end is `Frequency2`, and the frequency changes linearly from start to finish. That is, halfway through the sound, at $^{Seconds}/_2$ the output frequency is halfway between `Frequency1` and `Frequency2`.

To eliminate any aliasing effects, once a frequency is chosen one full sine wave is generated at that frequency before it is allowed to change. The current frequency is calculated from the parametric linear equation $f(t) = At + B$, where coefficients A and B are computed from the desired starting and ending frequencies, and t ranges from 0 (the start of the sound) to 1 (the end of the sound).

```
import math
TwoPi = 2.0 * math.pi

def SineWaveLinearBlend (Frequency1,          \
                         Frequency2,          \
                         Seconds=1.0,         \
                         Volume=1.0,          \
                         SamplingRate=44100):
    TotalSamples = int(round(Seconds * SamplingRate))
    RadiansPerSample = TwoPi * Frequency1 / SamplingRate
    A = Frequency2 - Frequency1
    B = Frequency1
    Angle = 0.0
    Result = []
    for I in range(TotalSamples):
        Value = Volume * math.sin(Angle)
        Result.append(Value)
        Angle = Angle + RadiansPerSample
        if Angle >= TwoPi:
            Angle = Angle - TwoPi
            T = float(I) / float(TotalSamples-1)
            Frequency = A*T + B
            RadiansPerSample = TwoPi * Frequency / SamplingRate
    return Result
```

Blend of three Sine Waves (Parabolic)

Similar to the linear blending example, this function generates a list of sound samples based on passing a quadratic polynomial through three frequencies, where the output is Frequency1 at the start of the sound, Frequency2 halfway through the sound, and Frequency3 at the end of the sound.

As before, once a frequency is chosen one full sine wave is generated at that frequency before it is allowed to change. The current frequency is calculated from the parametric quadratic (parabolic) equation $f(t) = At^2 + Bt + C$, where coefficients A, B, and C are computed from the three frequencies, and parameter t ranges from 0 (the start of the sound, Frequency1) through ½ (the middle of the sound, Frequency2) to 1 (the end of the sound, Frequency3).

```python
import math
TwoPi = 2.0 * math.pi

def SineWaveParabolicBlend (Frequency1,          \
                            Frequency2,          \
                            Frequency3,          \
                            Seconds=1.0,         \
                            Volume=1.0,          \
                            SamplingRate=44100):
    TotalSamples = int(round(Seconds * SamplingRate))
    RadiansPerSample = TwoPi * Frequency1 / SamplingRate
    A =  2.0 * Frequency1 - 4.0 * Frequency2 + 2.0 * Frequency3
    B = -3.0 * Frequency1 + 4.0 * Frequency2 - 1.0 * Frequency3
    C = Frequency1
    Angle = 0.0
    Result = []
    for I in range(TotalSamples):
        Value = Volume * math.sin(Angle)
        Result.append(Value)
        Angle = Angle + RadiansPerSample
        if Angle >= TwoPi:
            Angle = Angle - TwoPi
            T = float(I) / float(TotalSamples-1)
            Frequency = A*T*T + B*T + C
            RadiansPerSample = TwoPi * Frequency / SamplingRate
    return Result
```

Blend of three Sine Waves (Quadratic Spline)

This code is identical to that of the Parabolic Blend code on the previous page, except that the coefficients of the quadratic polynomial are chosen differently. In this case, the sound starts at `Frequency1` and ends at `Frequency3` as before, but it only approaches `Frequency2` in the same way that a quadratic spline *approaches but does not go through* its control point. Doing this will allow multiple sound lists to be joined in a way that one blends smoothly into the next without abrupt changes in frequency (which are very audible).

```python
import math
TwoPi = 2.0 * math.pi

def SineWaveQuadraticSplineBlend (Frequency1,          \
                                  Frequency2,          \
                                  Frequency3,          \
                                  Seconds=1.0,         \
                                  Volume=1.0,          \
                                  SamplingRate=44100):
    TotalSamples = int(round(Seconds * SamplingRate))
    RadiansPerSample = TwoPi * Frequency1 / SamplingRate
    A =  1.0 * Frequency1 - 2.0 * Frequency2 + 1.0 * Frequency3
    B = -2.0 * Frequency1 + 2.0 * Frequency2
    C = Frequency1
    Angle = 0.0
    Result = []
    for I in range(TotalSamples):
        Value = Volume * math.sin(Angle)
        Result.append(Value)
        Angle = Angle + RadiansPerSample
        if Angle >= TwoPi:
            Angle = Angle - TwoPi
            T = float(I) / float(TotalSamples-1)
            Frequency = A*T*T + B*T + C
            RadiansPerSample = TwoPi * Frequency / SamplingRate
    return Result
```

Blend of four Sine Waves (Cubic)

Similar to earlier examples, this function generates a list of sound samples based on passing a cubic polynomial through four frequencies, where the output is `Frequency1` at the start of the sound ($t=0$), `Frequency2` one third of the way ($t=\frac{1}{3}$) through the sound, `Frequency3` two thirds of the way ($t=\frac{2}{3}$) through the sound, and `Frequency4` at the end of the sound ($t=1$). The current frequency is calculated from the parametric cubic equation $f(t) = At^3 + Bt^2 + Ct + D$, where coefficients A, B, C, and D are computed from the four frequencies.

```
import math
TwoPi = 2.0 * math.pi

def SineWaveCubicBlend (Frequency1,            \
                        Frequency2,            \
                        Frequency3,            \
                        Frequency4,            \
                        Seconds=1.0,           \
                        Volume=1.0,            \
                        SamplingRate=44100):
    TotalSamples = int(round(Seconds * SamplingRate))
    RadiansPerSample = TwoPi * Frequency1 / SamplingRate
    A = ( -9.0 * Frequency1 +           \
          27.0 * Frequency2 -           \
          27.0 * Frequency3 +           \
           9.0 * Frequency4) / 2.0
    B = ( 18.0 * Frequency1 -           \
          45.0 * Frequency2 +           \
          36.0 * Frequency3 -           \
           9.0 * Frequency4) / 2.0
    C = (-11.0 * Frequency1 +           \
          18.0 * Frequency2 -           \
           9.0 * Frequency3 +           \
           2.0 * Frequency4) / 2.0
    D = Frequency1
    Angle = 0.0
    Result = []
    for I in range(TotalSamples):
        Value = Volume * math.sin(Angle)
        Result.append(Value)
        Angle = Angle + RadiansPerSample
        if Angle >= TwoPi:
            Angle = Angle - TwoPi
            T = float(I) / float(TotalSamples-1)
            Frequency = A*T*T*T + B*T*T + C*T + D
            RadiansPerSample = TwoPi * Frequency / SamplingRate
    return Result
```

Blend of four Sine Waves (Bézier)

This code is identical to that of the Cubic Blend code on the previous page, except that the coefficients of the cubic polynomial are chosen differently. In this case, the sound starts at `Frequency1` and ends at `Frequency4` as before, but it only approaches `Frequency2` and `Frequency3` in the same way that a Bézier curve *approaches but does not go through* its control points. Doing this will allow multiple sound lists to be joined in a way that one blends smoothly into the next without abrupt changes in frequency (which are very audible).

```python
import math
TwoPi = 2.0 * math.pi

def SineWaveBezierBlend (Frequency1,              \
                         Frequency2,              \
                         Frequency3,              \
                         Frequency4,              \
                         Seconds=1.0,             \
                         Volume=1.0,              \
                         SamplingRate=44100):
    TotalSamples = int(round(Seconds * SamplingRate))
    RadiansPerSample = TwoPi * Frequency1 / SamplingRate
    A = ( -1.0 * Frequency1 +       \
           3.0 * Frequency2 -       \
           3.0 * Frequency3 +       \
           1.0 * Frequency4)
    B = (  3.0 * Frequency1 -       \
           6.0 * Frequency2 +       \
           3.0 * Frequency3)
    C = ( -3.0 * Frequency1 +       \
           3.0 * Frequency2)
    D = Frequency1
    Angle = 0.0
    Result = []
    for I in range(TotalSamples):
        Value = Volume * math.sin(Angle)
        Result.append(Value)
        Angle = Angle + RadiansPerSample
        if Angle >= TwoPi:
            Angle = Angle - TwoPi
            T = float(I) / float(TotalSamples-1)
            Frequency = A*T*T*T + B*T*T + C*T + D
            RadiansPerSample = TwoPi * Frequency / SamplingRate
    return Result
```

The WAV File Format

The .WAV file format developed by Microsoft and IBM in 1991 and used by a number of platforms since, is a very simple format for handling audio data. While subsequent revisions to the format have been implemented, the discussion here is for the first and simplest version, as shown on the following page. This is one instance of a ***Resource Interchange File Format*** (RIFF), which is a ***container format*** for data in many forms. RIFF files are defined by ***chunks***; each chunk has an eight-byte prefix containing a four-character code (using the numeric ASCII value for each character) that identifies the chunk type and a four byte integer containing the size of the chunk <u>minus the eight bytes of the prefix</u>. The four-character code is case sensitive. All multi-byte integers are stored in ***little endian*** format (least significant byte first).

All RIFF files start with "RIFF" as the first four bytes, and the size of the file minus 8 as the next four bytes. The form name for .WAV files is "WAVE". After the form name comes at least two chunks (actually, <u>sub</u>chunks); the "fmt " and "data" chunks are required, but there may be others. Any programs to read .WAV files <u>must</u> be able to handle all chunk types without error, but are allowed to skip over chunk types that they do not understand. These other chunks may appear anywhere: before the format chunk, before the data chunk, or at the end of the file.

The format chunk ("fmt ") is most often 24 bytes long, where the chunk size is 16 (24 bytes minus the 8 bytes of the prefix), but there are versions which are longer. This chunk contains numbers that indicate the configuration of the audio data. The <u>format tag</u> is usually 1, indicating ***Pulse Code Modulation*** (***PCM***), where every audio sample is stored in the file. Values other than 1 indicate some form of compression, not covered here. There are most often 1 or 2 independent <u>channels</u> of data, 1 for mono and 2 for stereo. The <u>samples per second</u> value may be anything, but is most often 8000, 11025, 22050, or 44100 (CD-quality is 44100 samples per second per channel). The <u>bits per sample</u> value is either 8 or 16 for PCM files. Once these numbers are known, it is then possible to compute the <u>block align</u> value (the size in bytes of a sample block containing one sample for each channel) and the <u>bytes per second</u> value.

The data chunk ("data") is of variable length. Its chunk size is the number of samples in the file times the size of a sample block (the block align value). In special cases where a .WAV file contains <u>only</u> a format chunk and a data chunk, this number is the file size minus 44 (the size of all header information to that point). In sample blocks for two-channel files, the left channel sample comes first, followed by the right channel sample. Two-byte samples (16 bits) are <u>signed values</u> that range from -32768 to +32767, and 0 is the "quiet" value. However, one-byte samples (8 bits) are <u>unsigned values</u> that range from 0 to 255, and 127 is considered the "quiet" value.

For example, in a two-channel file with two bytes per sample (block align = 4), the order of bytes within a single sample block would be at the following offsets:

0:	Left Channel Sample, Low Byte
1:	Left Channel Sample, High Byte
2:	Right Channel Sample, Low Byte
3:	Right Channel Sample, High Byte

The WAV File Format (Continued)

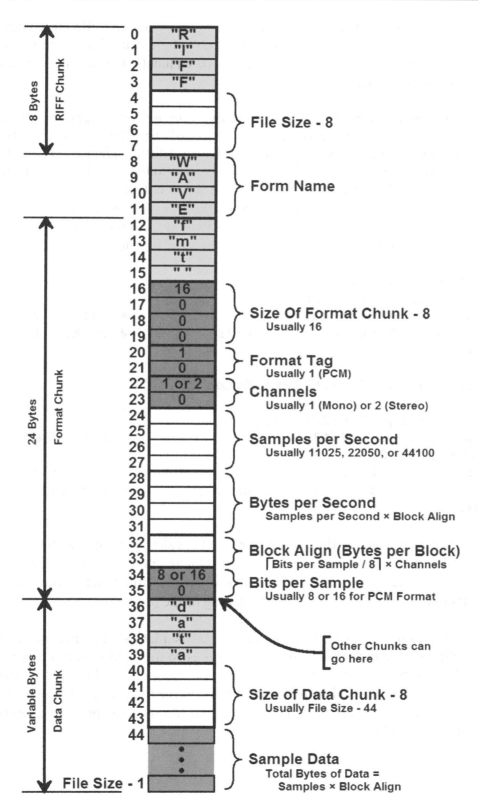

Writing to the WAV File Format

Occasionally it is necessary to write your own code to create a .WAV file, in whatever language is available. In the code on this page and the next, Python is used to write out a binary file containing the bytes for a .WAV file with one or two channels of audio data, at any sampling rate, and with one or two bytes per sample.

To support writing to a binary file, the following two functions are necessary, the first to write out a stream of bytes corresponding to the ASCII values of characters in a string, and the second to write out a integer with any desired number of bytes (in little endian order). In both cases, a Python list is converted into a stream of bytes to be written to the file; the file must be opened as a ***binary file*** with "wb" file mode. In Python 2 write out the byte values as a stream of characters, but in Python 3 use the bytes function (the bytes function is specific to Python 3). The code below is set up for Python 3; to change to Python 2 comment out the lines that use the bytes function and <u>un</u>-comment the lines that use the chr function.

```
def WriteString(Outfile,S):
    L = [ord(CH) for CH in S]
    Outfile.write(bytes(L))              # Python 3
#   for B in L: Outfile.write(chr(B))    # Python 2
    return

def WriteBytes (Outfile,N,TotalBytes=1):
    L = []
    for I in range(TotalBytes):
        L = L + [N % 256]                # Little endian
        N = N // 256
    Outfile.write(bytes(L))              # Python 3
#   for B in L: Outfile.write(chr(B))    # Python 2
    return
```

The function on the next page writes the appropriately scaled and clipped stream of samples in Data0 to the file; to write one channel Data1 must be an empty list, but to write two channels Data1 <u>must</u> contain the same number of samples as Data0 (this function does not check). Do not forget to include import math at the beginning of the program.

The code contains several sophisticated features. Clip is a lambda function that takes in a float and returns it clipped it to the range -1.0...+1.0. This is so too-loud volumes don't have strange numerical values when converted to integers for saving in the file. Similarly, the WriteSample function is local to and uses values defined earlier in WriteWAV. Also, the try-finally block is to make certain that the output file is closed properly even if there were problems writing to the file.

Writing to the WAV File Format (Continued)

```
def WriteWAV (FileName,                          \
              Data0, Data1=[],                   \
              SamplesPerSecond=44100,   \
              BytesPerSample=2):

    Clip          = lambda Sample : max(-1.0, min(+1.0, Sample))
    Samples       = len(Data0)
    Scales        = [127.0, 32767.0]
    Offsets       = [127.0,     0.0]
    Scale         = Scales [BytesPerSample-1]
    Offset        = Offsets[BytesPerSample-1]
    Channels      = 1 + (Data1 != [])
    BitsPerSample = BytesPerSample * 8
    BlockAlign    = int(math.ceil(BitsPerSample / 8) * Channels)
    BytesPerSecond= SamplesPerSecond * BlockAlign
    FileSize      = 44 + Samples * BlockAlign
    Outfile       = open(FileName,"wb")

    def WriteSample (Sample):
        WriteBytes (Outfile,                                    \
                    int(Clip(Sample) * Scale + Offset),  \
                    BytesPerSample)
        return

    try:
        WriteString(Outfile,"RIFF")
        WriteBytes (Outfile, FileSize - 8, 4)
        WriteString(Outfile,"WAVE")
        WriteString(Outfile,"fmt ")
        WriteBytes (Outfile, 16, 4)
        WriteBytes (Outfile, 1, 2)
        WriteBytes (Outfile, Channels, 2)
        WriteBytes (Outfile, SamplesPerSecond, 4)
        WriteBytes (Outfile, BytesPerSecond, 4)
        WriteBytes (Outfile, BlockAlign, 2)
        WriteBytes (Outfile, BitsPerSample, 2)
        WriteString(Outfile,"data")
        WriteBytes (Outfile, FileSize - 44, 4)

        for Index in range(Samples):
            WriteSample(Data0[Index])
            if Channels == 2: WriteSample(Data1[Index])
    finally:
        Outfile.close()
    return
```

Writing to the WAV File Format (Continued)

19: *Coding, Compression, and Encryption*

Information can be encoded, encrypted, and compressed in a number of ways. Here are a few such techniques. This is at best an introduction or survey of the simplest techniques available; there are many more that are outside the scope of this document. It is expected that someone with an interest in any of these topics will use this section as a jumping-off point for their own investigations into the more complex and more interesting topics.

Letter Frequencies

In many of the discussions that follow, codes are based of the frequency of occurrence of letters in some language or block of text. In Morse code, the most commonly used letters use one or two dots and dashes, but less frequently used letters use three or four dots and dashes, while digit characters use five and special characters use six. In attempting to decode a permutation cipher, knowing the language of the original message allows for statistical analysis to make "educated guesses" about what code letters actually mean: the more common a code symbol is in the cipher text the more likely it is to be a common letter in the language. In Huffman compression, part of the process is to first scan the text to be compressed to identify the frequency of occurrence of each letter, and then replace those letters with variable-length codes based on their frequencies.

The basic goal is to use <u>shorter codes for more common</u> letters and <u>longer codes for less frequent</u> ones. This applies to efficiency of sending a message, decoding a hidden message, compressing a message, and a number of other applications.

One place to start is to determine the frequency of occurrence of the letters in some language like English. Many analyses have been performed over the years, but *depending on the source text* used in the analysis the results, while largely congruent, <u>do</u> differ slightly in detail.

An early approach that still works quite well today is that of the Linotype™ keyboard layout. Linotype machines were invented in 1884 by Ottmar Mergenthaler, and were used in newspaper typesetting up through the 1980s. Here is the layout of a typical Linotype keyboard. Although there were many variations from what is shown here, the basic arrangement of the <u>letters</u> is both highly consistent across the variations and what is most important to the current discussion:

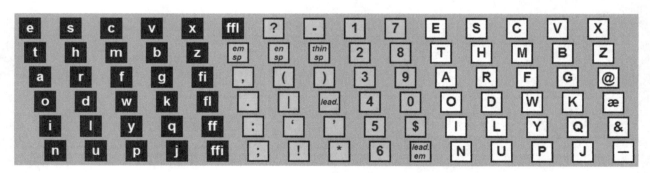

Notice that the most commonly occurring letters run vertically down the left side of the lower case (black keys) and upper case (white keys) block of the keyboard, while infrequently used characters such as the ligatures (fi, fl, æ, etc.) are in the rightmost columns of each block. If you run the letters in each block top-to-bottom, left-to-right you'll get the sequence:

E T A O I N S H R D L U C M F W Y P V B G K Q J X Z

Pronounced "eta-oin-shirdle-ooo," this sequence is a good first approximation to the letter frequencies obtained by experiment, although most of the variations in those experiments come from the U C M F and Q J X Z sequences.

Morse Code

For any transmission speed the basic length of time is a **_unit_**. The lengths of a dot ("dit"), dash ("dah"), and the spacing between them, are all expressed entirely in units. At 20 words per minute (WPM), using a standard test word, a unit is 60ms (milliseconds) in duration. That is:

Unit length (ms) = 1200 / WPM

Units	Item
1	Length of Dot
3	Length of Dash
1	Space between dots and dashes
3	Space between letters
7	Space between words

Character	Morse	Character	Morse
!	-.-.--	A	.-
"	.-..-.	B	-...
$	...-..-	C	-.-.
&	.-...	D	-..
'	.----.	E	.
(	-.--.	F	..-.
)	-.--.-	G	--.
,	--..--	H	....
-	-....-	I	..
.	.-.-.-	J	.---
/	-..-.	K	-.-
0	-----	L	.-..
1	.----	M	--
2	..---	N	-.
3	...--	O	---
4	....-	P	.--.
5	.....	Q	--.-
6	-....	R	.-.
7	--...	S	...
8	---..	T	-
9	----.	U	..-
:	---...	V	...-
;	-.-.-.	W	.--
=	-...-	X	-..-
?	..--..	Y	-.--
@	.--.-.	Z	--..
		_	..--.-

Notice that more common letters (E, T, A, I, M, etc.) have shorter codes than less common letters (X, Y, Z). While the assignment of codes to letters is not optimal, it does show an early attempt to minimize the transmission time of typical messages.

Roman Numerals

Roman numerals are an early form of writing down integers, but unlike the numbers that we use today based on Arabic numerals, Roman numerals are <u>not</u> a positional notation. There are and have been many variations on Roman numerals, but the standard form is shown below.

ROMAN	DECIMAL
I	1
V	5
X	10
L	50
C	100
D	500
M	1000

	0	1	2	3	4	5	6	7	8	9
0		I	II	III	IV	V	VI	VII	VIII	IX
10	X	XI	XII	XIII	XIV	XV	XVI	XVII	XVIII	XIX
20	XX	XXI	XXII	XXIII	XXIV	XXV	XXVI	XXVII	XXVIII	XXIX
30	XXX	XXXI	XXXII	XXXIII	XXXIV	XXXV	XXXVI	XXXVII	XXXVIII	XXXIX
40	XL	XLI	XLII	XLIII	XLIV	XLV	XLVI	XLVII	XLVIII	XLIX
50	L	LI	LII	LIII	LIV	LV	LVI	LVII	LVIII	LIX
60	LX	LXI	LXII	LXIII	LXIV	LXV	LXVI	LXVII	LXVIII	LXIX
70	LXX	LXXI	LXXII	LXXIII	LXXIV	LXXV	LXXVI	LXXVII	LXXVIII	LXXIX
80	LXXX	LXXXI	LXXXII	LXXXIII	LXXXIV	LXXXV	LXXXVI	LXXXVII	LXXXVIII	LXXXIX
90	XC	XCI	XCII	XCIII	XCIV	XCV	XCVI	XCVII	XCVIII	XCIX
100	C	CI	CII	CIII	CIV	CV	CVI	CVII	CVIII	CIX

In its simplest form, Roman numerals are additive: **I + I = II**, **II + I = III**, **X + X = XX**, etc. While some variants do continue this further, as in **III + I = IIII**, **XXX + X = XXXX**, and **CCC + C = CCCC**, the standard today is to use a subtractive method for those multiples of 10 one unit less than the next higher multiple of 5. Thus, instead of writing **IIII** for 4 we would write **IV** (1 less than 5), instead of **XXXX** for 40 we would write **XL** (10 less than 50), and instead of **CCCC** for 400 we would write **CD** (100 less than 500).

Since there is no Roman numeral greater than **M** = 1000, the maximum value representable in standard notation is 3,999 (**MMMCMXCIX** = 3000, plus 100 less than 1000, plus 10 less than 100, plus 1 less than ten, or 3000 + 900 + 90 + 9).

One variation that handles larger numbers is to write the letters with an overline: $\overline{I}$ for 1000, $\overline{V}$ for 5000, $\overline{X}$ for 10000, etc.

It is very difficult to perform basic arithmetic operations on numbers written in Roman numerals. The great innovation of the Arab and Hindu (Indian) mathematicians of thirteen hundred years ago was the positional decimal numeral system, with zero as a placeholder, that we use today, called the **_Western Arabic numerals_** (although there are a number of regional variations on the shapes of those numerals). This system of representing numbers reached Europe in the 10TH Century but did not become popular for some time after that. While Roman numerals are obsolete as a method of representing numerical values, they are still used in a few contexts today, including movie title screens, the carved years on buildings and monuments, and some analog clocks.

American Soundex

American Soundex is a phonetic coding mechanism developed to map surnames onto bins so that similar names go to the same bin (people who are related may spell their last names differently, such as Verts, Virts, and Virtz, or as Tabut, Tabbut, Tibbet, Tibbett, etc.). This algorithm was applied (retroactively) to the United States censuses from 1890 through 1920, but is still in widespread use today.

Every name is converted into a bin code consisting of the first letter of the last name, followed by exactly three digits.

To code a name into a bin, keep the first letter, but discard all vowels (A, E, I, O, U, Y) and soft consonants (H, W). Use the following table to encode all remaining consonants:

CODE	LETTERS
1	B, F, P, V
2	C, G, J, K, Q, S, X, Z
3	D, T
4	L
5	M, N
6	R

If there is a sequence of letters in the original name all with the same digit code, including the first letter, with no separating vowels (or only H and W as separators), then treat the entire sequence as one digit. If that sequence starts the name, retain the first letter as before, and delete the other letters. If there are vowels separating consonants, then the consonants are coded separately, even if they have the same digit code.

This means that the sequences MM and MN are treated as 5, not 55, the sequence SCHK is treated as 2, not 222, and the sequence PHF is treated as 1, not 11. If SCHK starts the name, the S is retained, but the C, H, and K are discarded.

There must be exactly three digits following the leading letter; delete any digits beyond three, and if there are too few then pad the result with zeroes until there are exactly three digits.

NAME	CODE	NOTE
VERTS	V632	Same code as VIRTS and VIRTZ
SCHEIDER	S360	SCH=S, D=3, R=6, one extra 0 needed
LEE	L000	Three extra 0s needed, same code as LE, LI, and LIU
HAMNER	H560	MN=5, R=6, one extra 0 needed, same code as HAMMER
HUMPERDINCK	H516	Code H516352 trimmed to three digits

UPC and EAN-13 Bar Codes

Twelve-digit UPC-A (***Universal Product Code***) and its derivative the thirteen-digit EAN-13 (***European Article Number***) codes both have exactly 95 black and white vertical stripes, some long and some short. At both the left and right ends of the code are long 3-stripe ***guard patterns*** that are always in the order black-white-black. In the middle is a long 5-stripe guard pattern that is always in the order white-black-white-black-white. The guard patterns are there to orient the scanner. Between the left and middle guard patterns are short stripes for <u>six digits</u>, each digit consisting of <u>seven stripes each</u>. Similarly, there are <u>six more digits</u> of <u>seven short stripes each</u> between the middle and right guard patterns. Bar code data are 3 + (6×7) + 5 + (6×7) + 3 = 95 stripes wide. Around the outside of the complete bar code is an additional "quiet zone" that is at least 9 stripes wide; this is to ensure that a scanner isn't confused trying to find the start or end of the code. The entire bar code image is thus 9{quiet zone} + 95{bar code} + 9{quiet zone} = **113 stripes wide**. The length of a **long bar** is 95 stripes, and the length of a **short bar** is 90 stripes. All these values are multiplied by some scale factor to get an appropriate size in pixels.

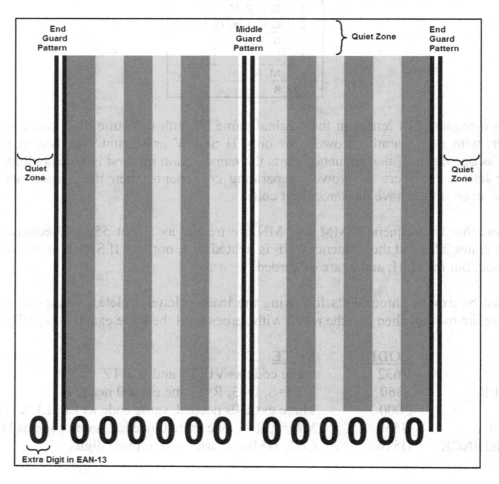

There isn't a reserved set of stripes for the leftmost of the 13 digits in EAN-13; that digit is encoded in a distributed fashion within the region for the left six digits. This is due to the code being reverse-engineered to hold 13 digits instead of 12, and yet still maintain backwards compatibility with UPC-A when that new extra leftmost digit is 0.

UPC and EAN-13 Bar Codes (Continued)

Each of the twelve digits is comprised of exactly seven black (**B**) or white (**W**) stripes. Left of the middle guard pattern all digits start with **W** and end with **B**; right of the middle guard pattern all digits start with **B** and end with **W**. There are always four groups of black and white stripes in any digit, and never more than four adjacent stripes of the same color in each group. For example, **BBWWBBW** is legal, but BWBWBWB is not (more than four groups, start and end with the same color), and neither is BBBBBWB (only three groups, one group longer than four stripes of the same color, start and end with the same color). There are only 40 possible patterns that match these rules, and 30 of them are listed in the L, G, and R code columns below.

Digit	Left Group	Right Group	L Code	G Code	R Code
0	LLLLLL	RRRRRR	WWWBBWB	WBWWBBB	BBBWWBW
1	LLGLGG	RRRRRR	WWBBWWB	WBBWWBB	BBWWBBW
2	LLGGLG	RRRRRR	WWBWWBB	WWBBWBB	BBWBBWW
3	LLGGGL	RRRRRR	WBBBBWB	WBWWWWB	BWWWWBW
4	LGLLGG	RRRRRR	WBWWWBB	WWBBBWB	BWBBBWW
5	LGGLLG	RRRRRR	WBBWWWB	WBBBWWB	BWWBBBW
6	LGGGLL	RRRRRR	WBWBBBB	WWWWBWB	BWBWWWW
7	LGLGLG	RRRRRR	WBBBWBB	WWBWWWB	BWWWBWW
8	LGLGGL	RRRRRR	WBBWBBB	WWWBWWB	BWWBWWW
9	LGGLGL	RRRRRR	WWWBWBB	WWBWBBB	BBBWBWW

In UPC-A, the twelve stripe patterns are chosen solely from the L and R code columns from the table, L for the six digits to the <u>left</u> of the middle guard pattern, and R for the six digits to the <u>right</u> of the middle guard pattern. For any digit value, its L code and its R code are mirror images. For example, the stripe pattern for a 6 is **WBWBBBB** whenever one appears to the left of the middle guard pattern, and **BWBWWWW** whenever one appears to the right.

In EAN-13, the extra digit is encoded by choosing patterns from the Left Group and Right Group, and those patterns indicate for each digit position whether to pick the stripe code from the L, G, or R code columns. In the example here, the leftmost 9 says to use LGGLGL from the Left Group and RRRRRR from the Right Group, so the 7 is chosen from the L code (WBBBWBB), the 8 is chosen from the G code (WWWBWWB), the 1 is chosen from the G code (WBBWWBB), and so on. All of the Right Group patterns are RRRRRR, the same as UPC-A. If the 13TH digit is 0, the Left Group is LLLLLL and the Right Group is RRRRRR, which is backwards compatible with UPC-A.

UUEncoding

Email is by its nature text-only. This becomes a problem when attempting to transmit a binary file via email, as the message may go through any number of intermediate machines with different character sets. However, the printing characters of the 7-bit ASCII character set are fairly universal, and can be used to send email with a reasonable expectation that none of them will be modified in transit. In 1980, Internet pioneer M. Horton used this approach to create the ***uuencode*** and ***uudecode*** programs for UNIX (uuencode means UNIX-to-UNIX encoding) to encode arbitrary files as text or decode them from text, respectively. As an example, here is the first sentence of Lincoln's Gettysburg Address:

> Four score and seven years ago our fathers brought forth on this continent, a new nation, conceived in Liberty, and dedicated to the proposition that all men are created equal.

Here is the uuencoded version of those 178 characters, including the non-printing carriage-return and line-feed characters at the end of the sentence:

```
begin 644 Gettysburg.txt
M1F]U<B!S8V]R92!A;F0@<V5V96X@>65A<G,@86=O(&]U<B!F871H97)S(&)R
M;W5G:'0@9F]R=&@@;VX@=&AI<R!C;VYT:6YE;G0L(&$@;F5W(&YA=&EO;BP@
M8V]N8V5I=F5D(&EN($QI8F5R='DL(&%N9"!D961I8V%T960@=&\@=&AE('!R
K;W!O<VET:6]N('1H870@86QL(&UE;B!A<F4@8W)E871E9"!E<75A;"X-"@``
`
end
```

The first line contains the word `begin`, the UNIX file permissions (usually `644`), and the file name. Subsequent lines each start with a character that indicates the number of bytes encoded on that line, followed by the encoding for those bytes. Every character represents a 6-bit, base-64 digit, where digit values 0…63 are encoded in ASCII as their value plus 32 (except 0 is coded as the grave accent ` because 32 is the ASCII blank). Base-64 digits 0…63 are thus encoded as:

`` `!"#$%&'()*+,-./0123456789:;<=>?@ABCDEFGHIJKLMNOPQRSTUVWXYZ[\]^_ ``

Every three bytes (three groups of 8 bits) are encoded as four groups of 6 bits, each plus 32 to get four new printable characters (except that zero is coded as `` ` ``). This process is shown below:

Source Text	F		o		u		r		blank		s		
ASCII	70		111		117		114		32		115		•••
Binary	0 1 0 0 0 1	1 0	0 1 1 0	1 1 1 1	0 1 1 1 0 1	0 1	0 1 1 1 0 0	1 0	0 0 0 1 0 0	0 0 0 0	1 1 1 0 0 1 1		•••
Base 64	17		38		61		53		28		34		1	51		•••
+32 Offset	49		70		93		85		60		66		33	83		•••
UUencoded	1		F		]		U		<		B		!	S		•••

Most coded lines have a count of `M`; the `M` is ASCII character 77, which is 32+45 (that is, `M` indicates a count of 45 bytes, the maximum allowed per line), so 45 bytes are encoded in 60 characters. The last line in the block may be shorter, and possibly not even contain a multiple of three bytes; if so zeroes are added to fill up the last group as needed. At the end is a line with a count of zero (the `` ` `` by itself) and the word `end`.

Base64 Encoding

Uuencoding is largely obsolete today, although it is still in use. Even though it was designed to be largely character-set agnostic, it still suffers from problems because it contains special characters that have different uses today. For example, HTML uses the <, >, and & characters for special purposes, so a uuencoded file cannot be directly embedded in a Web page without it being misinterpreted by the browser.

One solution is to use a variant of base-64 where every character is guaranteed to be interpreted correctly. This limits characters to the upper case letters, lower case letters, digits, and a few others. With just the 26 upper and 26 lower case letters and 10 digits there are 62 unambiguous characters, requiring just two more to fill out the needed 64. By convention, those last two characters are + and /, so the digit values 0...63 are encoded as:

`ABCDEFGHIJKLMNOPQRSTUVWXYZabcdefghijklmnopqrstuvwxyz0123456789+/`

where digit value 0 is A, value 1 is B, value 2 is C, and so on up to value 63 is /. Coding follows roughly the same process as for uuencoding in that every three input bytes are partitioned into four 6-bit chunks, except that the values of those chunks are used to *directly* look up the appropriate character from the list:

Source Text	F		o		u		r		blank		s		
ASCII	70		111		117		114		32		115		•••
Binary	0 1 0 0 0 1 1 0	0 1 1 0 1 1 1 1	0 1 1 1 0 1 0 1	0 1 1 1 0 0 1 0	0 0 1 0 0 0 0 0	0 1 1 1 0 0 1 1	•••
Base 64	17	38	61	53	28	34	1	51	•••
Character	R	m	9	1	c	i	B	z	•••

The first sentence of Lincoln's Gettysburg Address is base-64 coded as:

```
Rm91ciBzY29yZSBhbmQgc2V2ZW4geWVhcnMgYWdvIG91ciBmYXRoZXJzIGJyb3Vn
aHQgZm9ydGggb24gdGhpcyBjb250aW5lbnQsIGEgbmV3IG5hdGlvbiwgY29uY2Vp
dmVkIGluIExpYmVydHksIGFuZCBkZWRpY2F0ZWQgdG8gdGhlIHByb3Vvc210aW9u
IHRoYXQgYWxsIG1lbiBhcmUgY3JlYXRlZCBlcXVhbC4K
```

The resulting text does not have to be one long unbroken line. The text may have newlines inserted as needed, so that there are no more than a fixed number of characters per line, without affecting the encoded data.

Note that some software uses different characters for positions 62 and 63, such as . or _ or ~ for character 62, and , or - or _ or : for character 63. Be careful.

As with uuencoding, it is possible that the last group not contain a multiple of three bytes; in such cases the = is used as padding to indicate that the extra bytes should be zero during encoding and are not to be included in the output when decoding. Due to the specifics of the format, there will never be more than two = at the end of the encoded data.

For both uuencoding and base-64 encoding, the result is always 33⅓% larger than the source, as every 3 input bytes are converted to 4 output characters.

UTF-8 Encoding

Each of the thousands of text characters used worldwide has an associated number called a ___code point___, defined and maintained by the Unicode Consortium. Writing those code points to a file of bytes presents a number of unique problems. First, any new file format must be able to accommodate 7-bit ASCII text, also used worldwide but specific to English. Second, for any code point requiring a sequence of several bytes, the starting byte of the sequence must be distinguishable from the bytes that follow. Finally, the starting byte of a sequence must also contain information about how many total bytes are in the sequence.

Arguably the most common solution in use today is the 8-bit ___Unicode Transformation Format___, or ___UTF-8___, used extensively for files on the Web. UTF-8 is a variable-length code where each code point takes up 1, 2, 3, or 4 bytes. This mapping is shown below:

UTF-8 (Unicode Transformation Format)

7 Bits, 128 Characters (Standard ASCII)
`0 X X X X X X X`

11 Bits, 2048 Characters
`1 1 0 X X X X X` `1 0 X X X X X X`

16 Bits, 65536 Characters
`1 1 1 0 X X X X` `1 0 X X X X X X` `1 0 X X X X X X`

21 Bits, 2097152 Characters
`1 1 1 1 0 X X X` `1 0 X X X X X X` `1 0 X X X X X X` `1 0 X X X X X X`

If a code point (character) is in the range from 0 through 127, it is a standard ASCII character and is stored as a single byte with a 0 leading bit. Thus, all standard ASCII files are already legal UTF-8 files by default. This satisfies the backwards compatibility requirement.

All code points larger than 127 use sequences of at least two bytes, all of which start with a 1 bit to distinguish them from ASCII characters. The first byte of a multibyte sequence always starts with 11; all remaining bytes of the sequence start with 10. This satisfies the second requirement.

If the starting byte's prefix is 110 then it is a 2-byte sequence, if the prefix is 1110 it is a 3-byte sequence, and if the prefix is 11110 it is a 4-byte sequence. This satisfies the third requirement. All remaining bits of the bytes in that sequence make up the code point. For example, if a starting byte prefix is 1110 then the four remaining bits of that byte and the six remaining bits of each of the two following bytes combine to form a 16-bit code point.

UTF-8 files are self-synchronizing: if a program randomly jumps in to the middle of a UTF-8 file, it can always find the start of a character. For any arbitrary byte, a leading bit of 0 (ASCII) or leading two bits of 11 (multibyte) both indicate the start of a code point and no further action is required. However, if the leading two bits are 10 the program need only search backwards through the file a few bytes to find the one starting with 11.

While not a requirement, it makes sense to assign small code points that take up few bytes to more common characters, and large code points requiring more bytes to less frequent ones.

UTF-16 Encoding

Another code with some similarities to UTF-8 is the 16-bit Unicode Transformation Format, or ***UTF-16***. In this format, code points are represented by one or two 16-bit numbers (rather than 8-bit bytes). Originally, all code points fit into a single 16-bit number, but this limited the number of unique code points to only 65536 distinct values. An extension to make all code points 32 bits (two 16-bit numbers or four bytes) was proposed, but this is extremely wasteful of memory and file space, particularly when using traditional ASCII files. Storing an ASCII file in this format would quadruple its file size. The compromise was to design a format that requires either one or two 16-bit numbers for each code point.

Code points are 21 bits in length, and have values defined to be in the range from 0 up through 1,112,063 (in hexadecimal, **000000** up through **10F7FF**). UTF-16 is *not* backwards compatible with ASCII. The process to convert code points into UTF-16 is complicated, especially when determining if a particular code point will require one or two 16-bit numbers.

Code points in the hexadecimal range **0000** through **D7FF** and the range **E000** through **FFFF** are represented by <u>one</u> 16-bit word with a value identical to the code point. Values **D800** through **DFFF** *never* represent code points, and are used as described below.

All other valid code points are in the hexadecimal range **10000** through **10FFFF** (effectively the same as **10F7FF**) and require <u>two</u> 16-bit numbers in UTF-16. To convert such a code point into UTF-16, the first step is to subtract hexadecimal **010000** (decimal 65536) from the code point, leaving a 20-bit result in the range **00000** through **FFFFF**. This 20-bit number is then split into two 10-bit sections. The left-most 10 bit section has **D800** added to it, giving a result from **D800** through **DBFF** called the ***high surrogate***. The right-most 10 bit section has **DC00** added to it, giving a result from **DC00** through **DFFF** called the ***low surrogate***.

16-bit Value

0000...D7FF	One Number Code Point
D800...DBFF	High Surrogate containing upper 10 bits of Code Point - 65536
DC00...DFFF	Low Surrogate containing lower 10 bits of Code Point - 65536
E000...FFFF	One Number Code Point

Writing 16-bit numbers into a file of bytes is made more complicated in that some processor chips are ***little endian*** (the low byte of a multibyte number comes first in memory) and some are ***big endian*** (the high byte comes first). In some software, text files are stored with an initial 16-bit number called the ***byte order mark***, or ***BOM*** with the hexadecimal value **FEFF**. In little endian systems the first byte will be **FF** and the second will be **FE**, and in big endian systems the **FE** comes first and the **FF** comes second. If the BOM is missing, the recommendation is to assume big endian, but not all software observes this convention. Reading in a little endian file byte-by-byte on a big endian machine, or vice versa, will require that the high and low bytes of each 16-bit number be swapped to make the numbers in the file compatible with the hardware. UTF-16 is used internally in Microsoft Windows, but is rare on the Web.

Caesar Cipher & Rot13

Caesar Cipher, named after Julius Caesar, is a *rotation* of one copy of an alphabet against another copy. Here is a Caesar Cipher of rotation 4. A goes to W, B goes to X, etc. Both sender and receiver have to know the amount of the rotation (the "key").

A	B	C	D	E	F	G	H	I	J	K	L	M	N	O	P	Q	R	S	T	U	V	W	X	Y	Z
W	X	Y	Z	A	B	C	D	E	F	G	H	I	J	K	L	M	N	O	P	Q	R	S	T	U	V

A message such as HELLO THERE maps from the top row to the bottom as DAHHK PDANA. The recipient would map DAHHK PDANA from the bottom row to the top row to get back the plain text message. This is not very secure, as there are only 25 possible encodings, and the message can be broken by brute force.

A rotation of 13 (also called **_Rot13_**) maps letters from the top to the bottom the same way as from bottom to top (A goes to N and N goes to A). Rot13 is used to "lightly encrypt" messages to make them not immediately readable but easily breakable.

A	B	C	D	E	F	G	H	I	J	K	L	M
N	O	P	Q	R	S	T	U	V	W	X	Y	Z

Permutation Ciphers

A **_permutation cipher_** maps one letter from an alphabet onto one of 26! permutations (403,291,461,126,605,635,584,000,000 possibilities). Encoding and decoding work the same way as in the Caesar Cipher, and both sender and recipient must know the permutation (the "key").

A	B	C	D	E	F	G	H	I	J	K	L	M	N	O	P	Q	R	S	T	U	V	W	X	Y	Z
L	C	N	I	Y	D	U	M	T	A	J	X	Q	K	E	Z	P	F	G	R	B	O	S	H	W	V

There are a lot more keys than with the Caesar Cipher, so a brute force attack will take too long. However, this kind of cipher is vulnerable to statistical analysis. Knowing the frequencies of use of the letters in the language of the message means that with enough text it is possible to make educated guesses about what the actual letters are.

XOR Encryption

Here is a single-key encryption technique that works at the bit level instead of the character level. The unencrypted bits of the plain-text message are exclusive-ORed (XOR) with bits from a pseudo-random-number generator. If the recipient XORs the encrypted bits with the same sequence of pseudo-random numbers, the plain-text message will be decoded. This is called a ***stream cipher***.

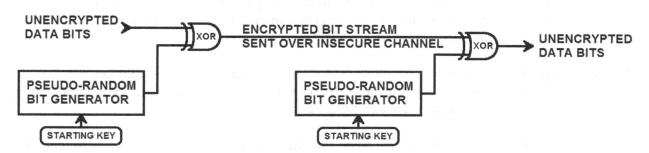

The starting seed to the random-number generators forms the encryption key. Both sender and recipient have to *generate the same random numbers* in the same way, and both need to know the *same starting value* to the random sequence.

Double-Key (Public-Key) Encryption

In ***double-key*** or ***public-key*** encryption, also known as ***asymmetric cryptography*** (Whitfield Diffie and Martin Hellman, 1976) a "key" is comprised of two related parts, generated simultaneously. The mathematics involves the product of two very large prime numbers, and the practical difficulty in factoring that product. One key is kept private; the other is made public. A message can be encrypted with either key, but only can be decrypted with the one not used for the encryption. An early public-key cryptosystem was ***RSA*** (named after authors Ron Rivest, Adi Shamir, and Leonard Adelman, 1977), although an earlier but classified system was based on the same idea (Clifford Cocks, 1973).

People use a public key to encrypt a message that only the holder of the private key can decode. Similarly, people sign messages with their own private key, and others use the corresponding public key to determine the authenticity of the message.

Knowing one part of the key does NOT mean that the other part is easily guessable; to crack the key requires factoring a large number into its two prime factors. If such a number *can* be factored in a reasonable amount of time, larger and larger primes are used. Computationally, it is easier to ask if a number is prime (with reasonable certainty) than it is to determine the actual factors of that number.

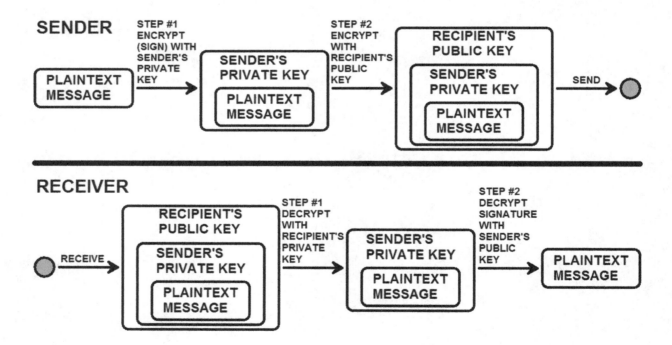

Currently, public key encryption can encrypt only small numeric messages, rather than large streams of text. However, that small number can be the key used in a larger, general purpose single-key encryption technique such as XOR Encryption.

Steganography

Steganography (not stenography) is not encryption, *per se*, but is a way of hiding information in plain sight. There are two common ways to steganographically encode messages, one in images and the other in audio streams.

In images, each bit from the plain-text message is used to set the low-order, least significant bit of the blue channel of one RGB pixel value (one message bit per pixel). Similarly, each bit from the plain-text message is used to set the low-order, least significant bit of one audio sample (one message bit per sample).

Statistically for a "noisy" image of a natural scene or a "noisy" audio file, 50% of the time a 0 is set to 0 and a 1 is set to 1, leaving the pixel or sample unchanged. The other 50% of the time a 0 is set to 1 and a 1 is set to 0, but the effects on the image or sound are too small to be noticed.

Steganography can be used in combination with an encryption technique such as XOR Encryption. Message bits are encrypted before being impressed on the image or audio file. When comparing the original file to the one containing the hidden message, the encoded file looks like a simple statistical noise field has been laid over top of it.

As another example of steganography, consider the obsolete .PCX graphics file format (first, go read the section on run-length encoding a few pages from now, then return back here). The .PCX format allowed for runs of between 0 and 63 repeated pixel bytes. However, it makes no sense for there to be a sequence of no bytes, so a run of length zero would never occur in practice (that is, "repeat the next byte zero times"). Any .PCX image decoders would naturally skip over such bizarre constructions if they were present. That means it is possible to hide information in the data byte of a run of length zero. That information would never be seen normally, but if you knew where to look you could find the hidden message. This, too, is steganography.

Serial Communication

Sending:

Serial communication involves sending the bits of a character one at a time over a single wire. Normally the wire is at logic 1. When the sender is ready to send a character, it first sends out a start bit (logic 0). It then sends out the data bits one at a time, followed by one or two stop bits (logic 1). It can send the next character immediately, or it can wait an arbitrary amount of time. It is the presence of the start bit that synchronizes the receiver to the beginning of the character.

```
Send start bit (usually 0)
Wait 1 bit time
for each data bit:
     Send data bit
     Wait 1 bit time
Send stop bit (usually 1)
Wait 1-2 bit times
```

Receiving:

The receiver listens to the data line, which is resting at logic 1. When it hears the start bit (logic 0), it waits ½ bit time to find the middle of the bit, and measures again to verify that it heard the start bit. It then waits 1 full bit time per measurement so as to measure as close to the middle of the data and stop bit(s) as possible. The duration in time of a bit can differ between sender and receiver by a tiny amount and data will still be read correctly; any "drift" in the clocks between sender and receiver won't affect the receiving process for such a small number of data bits.

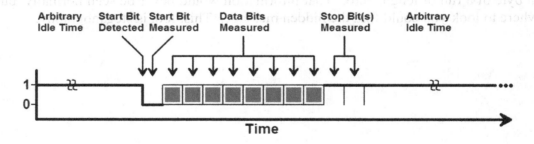

```
Do nothing until start bit detected
Wait ½ bit time
Verify start bit
Wait 1 bit time
for each data bit:
     Read in data bit
     Wait 1 bit time
Read in stop bit
Wait 1-2 bit times
```

Parallel Communication

Unlike serial communication, which sends all data bits over a single wire (or telephone line), parallel communication sends all bits of a bytes simultaneously. Parallel communications are, in general, faster than serial, but many more wires are required. Distances between sender and receiver are often shorter as well (under six to eight feet for some devices). This was the old traditional method for connecting a printer to a computer, where a short, fat cable was acceptable. Parallel communications are very good for connecting two devices that run at greatly different speeds, as well: the process operates at the speed of the <u>slowest</u> device in the system. The diagram below shows a typical connection setup, with a master computer ***unidirectionally*** sending to a slave computer or a printer, although later parallel strategies allowed for ***bidirectional*** communications.

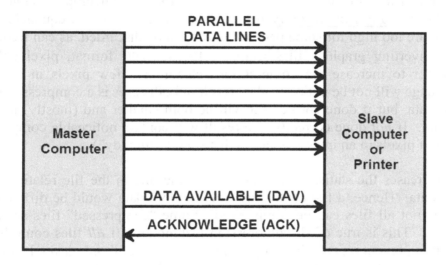

In the "resting state" the data lines have arbitrary values (0 or 1), but both Data Available (DAV) and Acknowledge (ACK) are "low" or 0. The process for sending a byte is called ***handshaking*** and operates as follows:

1:      Sender places new byte value on the data lines, and "raises" DAV from 0 to 1.

2:      Receiver "hears" DAV raise, and then responds (either immediately or some arbitrary time later) by raising ACK.

3:      Sender hears ACK raise and then "drops" DAV from 1 to 0.

4.   Receiver hears DAV drop and knows that the data lines must have stabilized by now to their final values. It captures the data values, and then (either immediately or some arbitrary time later) drops ACK.

5.   Sender hears ACK drop and knows that the receiver has successfully captured the data. DAV and ACK are now both resting at 0. Process repeats.

Lossless vs. Lossy Compression

Compression transforms an input file into a file that, we hope, takes up less space than the original. Compression comes in two forms: *__lossy__* and *__lossless__*. They both have their uses.

__Lossless compression__ reduces the size of a file by replacing regularly-repeating patterns of bits by a shorter sequence, yet encodes those sequences so that the original information can be regenerated from them perfectly. Decompressing a compressed file gives the same bit-for-bit file as the original data.

__Lossy compression__ actually *discards information* as part of the process of making the file smaller. This may seem counterintuitive; why would information be discarded willingly? In converting sound files from `.WAV` to `.MP3` or `.WMA` formats, uncompressed audio signals are decomposed through *__Fourier analysis__* into a set of simultaneous frequencies, where those frequencies that are too high for some people to hear can be discarded, as can frequencies of low volume. In converting graphics files from `.BMP` to `.JPG` format, pixel color values are modified in order to increase the compression (changing a few pixels in a naturally noisy photographic image will not be noticed). The result in both cases is a compressed *approximation* to the original data, but if done correctly it will be both smaller and (mostly) indistinguishable from the original. If *not* done correctly, the result will contain noticeable compression artifacts (blocky groups of pixels in an image, or audio that sounds "muddy").

Compression increases the statistical randomness of the bits in the file relative to the original uncompressed data. Hence, a file containing truly random data would be difficult to compress. Because of this, not all files can be compressed. Some "compressed" files are actually larger than their inputs. This is true of all compression techniques. If *all* files could be compressed, there is nothing to prevent repeatedly compressing the result until only a single bit remains. The goal behind any particular compression algorithm is to reduce the file size on *typical* sets of input values.

Several techniques are used in lossless compression, including *__Run-Length Encoding__* (*__RLE__*), *__Huffman coding__*, *__Lempel-Ziv__* and *__Lempel-Ziv-Welch__* (*__LZW__*) encoding, etc. Techniques differ in number of passes made over the input data, speed, effectiveness of the compression, etc.

There are also several lossy compression techniques, including the *__Discrete Cosine Transform__* (*__DCT__*) used in `.JPG` compression, and the various audio techniques that start with Fourier analysis in order to operate on frequencies instead of on individual samples.

Run-Length Encoding (Compression)

Run-Length Encoding (RLE) replaces long strings (runs) of identical values with a repeat-count plus one copy of that data value. The repeat-count becomes part of the data stream, and *must be uniquely distinguishable* from any possible data values. Data values that can be confused with repeat-counts are hidden behind a repeat-count of 1. This makes the "compressed" version of a short run longer than the original.

As an example, the now-obsolete `.PCX` graphics file format used run-length encoding to compress monochrome bitmaps, where one bit determined if a pixel was black or white (later versions of `.PCX` could handle color). Each byte contained eight pixels, often in patterns such as 01010101 or 00110011 or 10101010, for example, repeated many times. The rule used by `.PCX` was to identify runs of identical data bytes, and then replace the run with 11xxxxxx and <u>one</u> copy of the data byte, where xxxxxx formed a 6-bit number representing a repeat-count between 0 and 63. Runs of up to 63 data bytes could then be replaced by two bytes: one repeat-count byte and one copy of the data byte. If this occurred frequently, the output file would be considerably smaller than the input file, even on images containing complex patterns.

Data bytes that occurred once were inserted into the output file as-is, as long as they did not start with two 1-bits. This neither increases nor decreases the size of the output file.

For those data bytes that <u>did</u> start with 11, a repeat-count of 1 was needed to hide the data byte and keep it from being misunderstood as a repeat-count byte. For example, an input data byte of 11001100 had to be written out as 11000001 11001100 (repeat the byte 11001100 once), thus replacing one byte by two. If the input file consisted of nothing but random data bytes of this form, the "compressed" output file would be double the length of the input file.

Run-length encoding works well on images with large areas of the same color (e.g., cartoons and line art). It does <u>not</u> work well on more-random data such as photographic images or text, where there are few sequences of the same pixel or the same character, respectively.

Huffman Coding (Compression)

Huffman coding (David A. Huffman, 1952) takes <u>two</u> passes over the input file: pass #1 is to gather statistics about the frequency of occurrence of each item (character, byte, whatever), a compression tree is constructed from the statistics, and then pass #2 is to use the tree to replace each item in the file with its code from the tree. Replacement codes will be variable in length; many will be smaller than the original item size, but a few may be larger. The compression is obtained by having many more of the shorter codes than of the longer ones.

To build a compression tree, first *sort the items in descending order* by frequency of occurrence. Take the bottom two items off the list and form a binary tree with one item on the left branch and the other on the right branch. The frequency of occurrence for that new tree will be the sum of the occurrences of the two items. Insert that tree back into the list according to its occurrence number, but put it at the *top* of the group with the same number. Repeat the process until only one tree remains. The path from the root to each leaf (item) forms the replacement code, where following a left branch means to use a 0 bit and following a right branch means to use a 1 bit.

For example, the phrase **MISSISSIPPI RIVER** contains 17 characters including one space (blank). In normal ASCII each of those 17 characters requires a full 8-bit byte, making the total file size 17×8 = 136 bits.

The occurrence counts are shown in the sorted table on the left. The space character is indicated by **SP**. As each step progresses, sub-trees are indicated by parentheses.

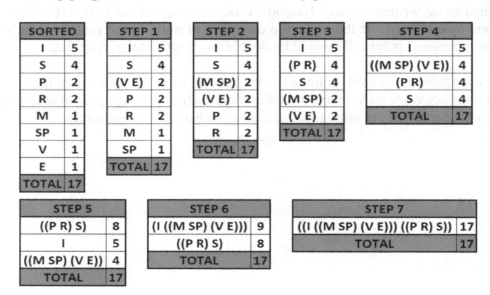

Huffman Coding (Continued)

The final result, **((I ((M SP) (V E))) ((P R) S))**, can be drawn equivalently as an explicit tree as follows:

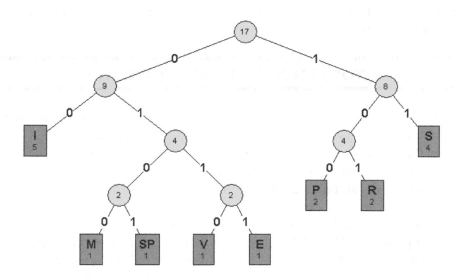

The path from the root to **I** is 00, the path to **M** is 0100, the path to **R** is 101, etc. These are the replacement codes. Each character in the input string is replaced by its new code. As there are 5 occurrences of the **I** character, there will be 5 characters × 2 bits per character = 10 bits required for all the **I** characters in the string.

Source Character	Replacement Code	Bit Length	Character Count	Total Bits
I	00	2	5	10
S	11	2	4	8
P	100	3	2	6
R	101	3	2	6
M	0100	4	1	4
SP	0101	4	1	4
V	0110	4	1	4
E	0111	4	1	4
TOTAL			17	46

The total compressed size will be 46 bits. The original, uncompressed string required 136 bits, so the compressed version is about 34% of the original size.

The downside is that *the compression tree must be stored* along with the compressed data, or it will be impossible to decode the compressed version back into the original text. However, the compression tree could be omitted from the compressed file if used as the encryption key for a single-key encryption technique.

Hamming Distance

The ***Hamming distance*** (Richard Hamming, 1950) between two numbers is the total count of bits that are different. For example, the Hamming distance between 10010 and 10010 is zero, the distance between 10010 and 10100 is 2, and the distance between 10010 and 01101 is five. This measurement is used in error detection and correction, as shown below, as well as in a number of other applications.

Error Detection and Correction

If a bit is sent once, the received bit might not be what was sent due to transmission noise: when a 0 or a 1 is sent, a 0 or a 1 will be received, but there is no information about whether the sent bit is the same as the received bit, or was changed en route. In either case, the receiver will not notice. The Hamming distance between 0 and 1 (the two valid values) is 1. Since both patterns are equally valid, no errors can be detected, much less corrected.

If a bit is sent twice (sending a 0 as 00 and a 1 as 11), the received pattern may be 00, 01, 10, or 11. If the received pattern is 10 or 01 it is known that an error occurred, but because these two patterns have an equal Hamming distance of 1 from <u>both</u> valid patterns, there is no information about whether to correct the error back to 00 or back to 11. If there are two errors, and a 00 sent is received as 11, or 11 is received as 00, the receiver sees valid patterns in both cases and cannot determine that anything went wrong at all. One error can be detected but not corrected, and two errors cannot be detected.

If a bit is sent three times (sending a 0 as 000 or a 1 as 111), the received pattern may be 000, 001, 010, 011, 100, 101, 110, or 111. In the case of 001, 010, and 100, the Hamming distance to 000 is 1 but the distance to 111 is 2, so these patterns can be corrected to 000 (that is, the two 0 bits outvote the single 1 bit). Similarly, the Hamming distance from 011, 101, and 110 to 111 is 1 but the distance to 000 is 2, so these patterns can be corrected to 111. If there are two errors, however, the error will still be detected but the pattern will be *corrected to the wrong value*. If there are three errors (000 is received as 111 or 111 is received as 000), the error is not detected. One error can be corrected, two errors can be detected, but three errors cannot be detected.

These three examples are shown in the following diagram. The line represents a bit sent once, the square represents a bit sent twice, and the cube represents a bit sent three times.

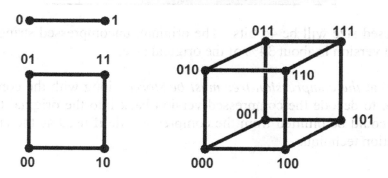

Error Detection and Correction (Continued)

The more times a bit is sent, the more errors can be detected and/or corrected. The 4-dimensional hypercube below shows a bit sent four times (as 0000 or as 1111). There are 16 possible patterns that can be received. Patterns 0001, 0010, 0100, and 1000 get corrected to 0000, and patterns 1110, 1101, 1011, and 0111 get corrected to 1111. Unfortunately, error patterns 0011, 0101, 1001, 0110, 1010, and 1100 all have Hamming distances of 2 from both 0000 and from 1111, so these patterns cannot be corrected. Three errors get corrected but in the wrong direction, and four errors cannot be detected at all. This system can detect one, two, or three errors, but can only correct one error.

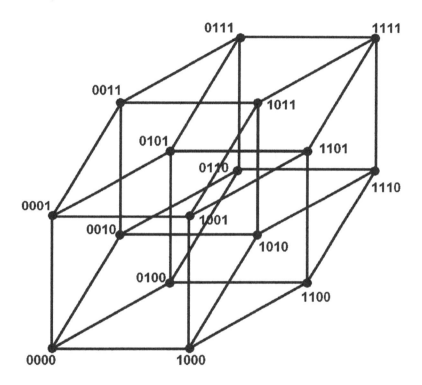

If a bit is sent five times, the system can detect one through four errors, and can correct one or two errors. In general, sending a bit an odd number of times prevents tie votes.

It should be noted that errors in real life tend to be "bursty" (coming in clusters). In any of these strategies, the replicated bits of a group are widely separated in time (and are interleaved with bits from other groups) rather than being sent successively, decreasing the probability that a noise burst damages more than one bit of any group and allowing the remaining undamaged bits to restore the damaged one.

Error Detection and Correction (Continued)

The more times a bit is sent, the more errors can be detected and/or corrected. The 4-dimensional hypercube below shows a bit sent four times i.e. 0000 or 1111. There are 16 possible patterns that can be received. Patterns 0000, 0001, 0010, and 1000 get corrected to 0000, and patterns 1110, 1101, 1011, and 0111 get corrected to 1111. This means that patterns 0011, 0101, 1001, 0110, 1010, and 1100 all have four bits at distance two from both 0000 and from 1111, so these patterns cannot be corrected. These errors get corrected in the wrong direction, and four errors cannot be detected at all. This system can detect one, two, or three errors, but can only correct one error.

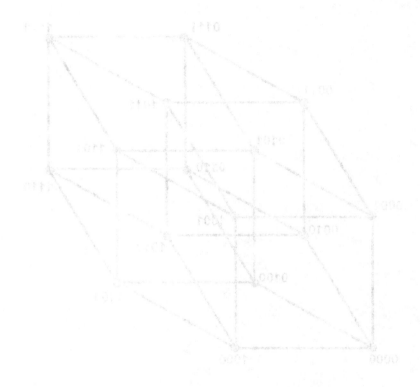

If bits are sent in times, the system can detect one-half the number of errors and correct one or two errors. In general, sending n-bit words number bits represents an error.

It should be noted that errors in real life tend to be random in character. In spite of these strategies, the replicated bits in a group are widely separated — one tends to be hit as well a bit from after group rather than being sent successively. Extending the practice so that noise must damage more than one bit of a group and advancing the technique that spaced bits to restore the data is viable.

20: *Miscellaneous*

Here are a couple of pages of tables that didn't seem to fit anywhere else. Sometimes this happens. The trick is to avoid having everything fall into the "miscellaneous" category, making the reader figure out where things are and what is important. I suppose that if I did everything perfectly there would not be a "miscellaneous" category at all, but considering how short this section is I am well satisfied with the result.

Commonly Misused Words

***Accept	Except***	Accept: Except:	Agree to or receive (I <u>accept</u> my fate.) Special case (All data types <u>except</u> integers.)
***Complement	Compliment***	Complement: Compliment:	Opposite (The one's <u>complement</u> of 1011 is 0100.) Praise (I received a nice <u>compliment</u>.)
***Data	Datum***	Data: Datum:	Plural (These <u>data</u> show a trend.) Singular (This <u>datum</u> shows an exception.) (Note: Despite common usage today, particularly in computing, the phrase "This data…" is always wrong.)
***Infer	Imply***	Infer: Imply:	Guess, you to me (I <u>infer</u> that you are angry.) Hint, me to you (I could <u>imply</u> that I am angry.)
***Its	It's***	Its: It's:	Ownership (The dog bit <u>its</u> owner.) Contraction of "it is" (<u>It's</u> a crying shame.) (Note: this is an exception to the general rule that a possessive is denoted by apostrophe-s appended to the end of a proper noun.)
***Loose	Lose	Lost***	Loose: Lose: Lost:	Untethered (The moose is <u>loose</u>.) Will not win (Fred will <u>lose</u> the game.) Did not win (Fred <u>lost</u> the game.)
***Passed	Past***	Passed: Past:	Movement (The car <u>passed</u> the stop sign.) Earlier Time (The moon landing is in the <u>past</u>.)
***Precede	Proceed***	Precede: Proceed:	Earlier (Earning money should <u>precede</u> spending it.) Continue (We will <u>proceed</u> with the inquisition.)
***Principal	Principle***	Principal: Principle:	Authority/Importance (The <u>principal</u> idea is…) Truth (The <u>principle</u> of maximum hilarity…)
***Stationary	Stationery***	Stationary: Stationery:	Fixed in space (The moose was <u>stationary</u>.) Writing paper (I write notes on <u>stationery</u>.)
***Their	There	They're***	Their: There: They're:	Ownership (This is <u>their</u> dog.) Place (Look over <u>there</u> for the clue.) Contraction of "they are" (<u>They're</u> not happy.)
***To	Too	Two***	To: Too: Two:	Toward (Go <u>to</u> the store for milk.) Excessive/Also (I ate <u>too</u> much ice cream, <u>too</u>.) Number 2 (There are <u>two</u> cookies left.)

Common Cognitive Biases

Argument from Ignorance

This is a bias where an idea is assumed to be true simply because it has not been shown to be false. Conversely, in a choice between two ideas, if one idea is not yet proven to be true or has parts that are not yet understood, the other idea is automatically assumed to be true. Even if the first idea <u>is</u> shown to be false, there is no guarantee that the second idea is true by default; there may be other explanations not yet considered.

Argument from Personal Incredulity

This bias is because someone cannot believe that an idea could possibly be true (or finds it highly unlikely), so therefore it must be false. Sometimes this is coupled with an alternative idea that the person finds compelling, even if there is no proof for that alternative idea.

The Bandwagon Fallacy

An idea is not necessarily true just because a lot of people believe it. Example: A lot of people believed that the Earth was flat. (Conversely, an idea is not necessarily true because of a "lone wolf" who goes against popular opinion or scientific consensus, either. Example: nearly any crack-pot conspiracy theorist.)

Confirmation Bias

This bias comes from someone asserting that a premise is true because they remember only those cases which agree with the premise, and forget all those which do not. Example: "I always have a good game when I wear my lucky shirt." Good games with the shirt and bad games without the shirt are remembered, reinforcing the premise, but all the good games without the shirt and bad games with the shirt are conveniently forgotten.

Correlation vs. Causality

Two events might occur nearby in space or time, but one may not be a *consequent* of the other. It is possible that one caused the other, or that a third event caused both, or they may be completely unrelated coincidence. To quote Randall Munroe of xkcd (`https://xkcd.com/552`): "Correlation doesn't imply causation, but it does waggle its eyebrows suggestively and gesture furtively while mouthing 'look over there'."

Pareidolia

The tendency to extract meaningful patterns from random data. Can be auditory or visual; possibly an evolutionary adaptation. Explains people seeing Jesus in their toast, hearing demonic words in records played backwards, etc.

Common Hayes Modem Commands

Hayes Microcomputer Products, founded by Dennis C. Hayes and active throughout the 1980s, created a series of ***modems*** (modulator-demodulator), devices for communicating between computers over standard telephone lines, or ***dial-up***. In 1981 Hayes introduced a control language for their modems that allowed users to control the modem from their computers or computer terminals directly, rather than by setting switches. A very small subset of that control language is shown below. The company no longer exists.

Modem Command	Meaning
`AT`	"Attention" Gets the modem to respond with "OK"
`ATZ`	Reset the modem to startup defaults
`ATDT`	Dial using tones: `ATDT5453700` dials 545-3700 using tones
`ATDP`	Dial using pulses: `ATDP5453700` dials 545-3700 using pulses
`ATH`	Hang up the phone line
`ATO`	Return to on-line state after an escape using **+++**
(pause) **+++** (pause)	Escape from on-line state back to the modem

Favorite Web Addresses

Site Name	URL (Web Address)
Dr. Bill	http://people.cs.umass.edu/~verts/

21: Jokes

What's better than a good joke or belly laugh? Computer people, mathematicians, and scientists of all stripes have a highly developed, if slightly warped, sense of humor. Here are a few jokes, tall tales, and outright lies told in and around the geek community. Laugh or groan as you will. Don't be afraid to ask for help if you don't understand one, but remember that this is 20% of your final grade.

Dumb Jokes and Weird Sayings

What do you get when you cross a joke with a rhetorical question?

There are 10 kinds of people in the world: those who understand binary and those who don't.

There are 2 kinds of people in the world: those who can extrapolate from incomplete data.

There are 3 kinds of people in the world: those who can count and those who can't.

How many computer programmers does it take to change a light bulb? None; it's a hardware problem.

How do you tell the extroverted computer programmer from the introverted computer programmer? The extrovert stares at *your* shoes.

Did you know that computer programmers can't tell the difference between Halloween and Christmas? That's because 31 OCT = 25 DEC.

Why did the spider cross the road? To get to his Web site!

Age and treachery will always overcome youth and skill.

Time flies like an arrow; fruit flies like a banana.

On a clear disk you can seek forever.

The nice thing about standards is that there are so many to choose from.

To learn about recursion you must first learn about recursion.

Tall Tales and Other Nonsense

The bartender said "We don't serve time-travelers here."
A time-traveler walks into a bar.

At a math conference a bunch of mathematicians got thirsty. The first mathematician walked into a bar and ordered a beer. The second mathematician walked in and ordered a half of a beer. The third ordered a quarter of a beer. The fourth ordered an eighth of a beer. The bartender said "you're all idiots" and poured two beers.

Three statisticians were out hunting, and saw a rabbit. The first fired and missed the rabbit by one foot to the left. The second fired and missed by one foot to the right. The third yelled "We got him!"

There's an old story from back in the days of punched cards about an aircraft being designed that was coming in well over-weight. A manager was hired to investigate and have each design team account for their weight contribution. He was extremely annoyed when the software team reported their contribution as zero. The manager got one of the card decks, and then called a staff meeting. He yelled at the programmers, saying "What are you guys all about? This does not weigh nothing!" The lead software designer calmly picked up a card and showed it to the manager. He said "You don't understand – the software isn't the card, the software is in the holes!"

A Limerick I heard in Grad School:
> Flappity, floppity, flip,
> The mouse on the Möbius strip,
> The strip revolved,
> The mouse dissolved,
> In a chrono-dimensional skip!

The Programmer's Cheer:
> Shift to the Left!
> Shift to the Right!
> Push Down! Pop Up!
> Byte! Byte! Byte!

Tall Tales and Other Nonsense

22: Recipes

Despite the stereotype, not all computer scientists subsist solely on soda, pizza, and junk food. Some of us like to cook, and have gotten pretty good at it. For many students, however, cooking is something that the grown-ups do, and few start out on their own knowing a lot about how to put together a decent, nutritious meal.

When I was first on my own I had to learn to cook the hard way: if I messed up preparing my meal my choice was to eat it anyway, or starve. There wasn't enough in the budget, or the refrigerator, for do-overs. At times, I was down to raisins, ketchup, and spray-cheese as the sum total of my available ingredients. Needless to say, early days on my own were devoted to a lot of culinary experimentation. As I've gotten older, I've had to modify my diet to be relatively low-fat and low-sugar, but that doesn't necessarily mean low-fun. My Dad, a professional biological scientist by training, went through a similar transition, and produced his own cookbook towards the end of his life. He was a terrific cook, who took pride in producing wonderful, solid meals, often with fresh ingredients from his own garden.

The few recipes that I present here are relatively simple, moderately healthy, and flavorful (or, at least I find them so). Some are based on my Dad's recipes; some are of my own design. Good food often acts as a social lubricant – how many problems in this world would be solved if everyone would just sit down at the dinner table together? Besides, when you manage to convince the Awesome Hunk or the Righteous Babe to come pay you a visit, being able to cook them a decent meal gains you lots of street-cred.

In general, most recipes are very forgiving. There are a few that have to be watched carefully, measured precisely, and timed to the second, but most are tolerant of variations of up to ±20% on amounts, temperature, and time. The recipes presented here follow those characteristics.

Measurements

The Europeans measure recipes in grams or milliliters, which is imminently sensible, but in the U.S. measurements follow old baroque English quantities that have very little logic. I don't know too many cooks who can keep all of these entirely straight. The basic units are cups (C), fluid ounces (oz), tablespoons (T), and teaspoons (t), and the abbreviations in parentheses will be used in recipes throughout this chapter.

Many people remember just a couple of conversions, such as eight ounces per cup and four tablespoons per quarter cup, but are there three or four teaspoons per tablespoon? (It's three, which confuses everyone.) The following table shows how to convert between the four basic units.

Liquid Volume Measurements (U.S.)			
Cups (C)	Fluid Ounces (oz)	Tablespoons (T)	Teaspoons (t)
1	8	16	48
$^3/_4$	6	12	36
$^2/_3$	5⅓	10⅔	32
$^1/_2$	4	8	24
$^1/_3$	2⅔	5⅓	16
$^1/_4$	2	4	12
$^1/_8$	1	2	6
$^1/_{16}$	½	1	3

Stovetop

There are four basic types of cook stoves: gas, electric coil, glass top, and induction. Each have their advantages over the others, and each have their advocates and detractors.

Gas

Gas stoves are instant heat: they are up to the proper temperature as soon as you turn them on and ignite the gas (this may be through manual lighting or automatically through an always-burning pilot light). Turning one off immediately stops the heating as well. Gas also has the advantage that it keeps running even if the house electricity fails for any reason. It has the disadvantages that you can burn yourself easily or catch something on fire, and if left on but unlit for any length of time can fill a room with an explosive fuel-air mix. Natural gas is odorless, so a small amount of odor is intentionally added to make detection easier.

Electric Coil

These stoves use a coil of electrically resistive material that heats up when current passes through them. They do not have the inherent dangers of gas, but they take a long time to heat up and cool down. Part of the learning process involves accommodating the inherent thermal inertia. Few of these are made any more, but people who do lots of canning depend on them.

Glass Top and Induction

Glass top stoves are electric, but instead of a coil each burner is covered with a tough glass plate. This makes clean-up easier than other stoves, as spilled food cannot get underneath or inside the burner element. Glass tops can break, however, and badly burnt-on food is hard to scrub off. Induction stoves look similar to glass top stoves, but have an electromagnetic field that directly and quickly transfers energy to a special, compatible pot without greatly heating up a burner.

Cooking with a Hotplate

Never is thermal inertia more apparent than when cooking on a two-burner hotplate. Hotplates generally have a <u>hot</u> side and a <u>medium</u> side, both of which seem to only have settings <u>cold</u>, <u>too hot</u>, and <u>scorch</u>. With practice, however, one can cook many elaborate meals on a hotplate without ruining them, but it does take patience and finesse.

When first starting out, use the hot side only for boiling water, and the medium side for everything else. Thin skillets are NOT recommended as they allow too much heat to be concentrated in too small an area, resulting in scorching of those areas while other areas remain cold. Instead, invest in good cast iron skillets and cookware. Cast iron is thick, and if the temperature is brought up slowly enough (patience!) it will evenly distribute the heat across the bottom of the pan. Even so, when cooking eggs be prepared to have a small layer of overcooked egg stuck to the bottom of the pan – don't dig too deeply! This layer will insulate the rest of the eggs from the perhaps too-hot skillet.

Ovens

Ovens typically have two heating elements, one at the top and one at the bottom, with adjustable racks in between to support the food as it cooks. If you have to guess, a middle rack position is used in the widest range of recipes. Never put plastic or anything that melts in an oven. Always use cookware that is entirely metal or high-temperature ceramic.

Broiling uses the top heating element only and primarily cooks by direct radiant heat. Broiling usually employs a special broiler pan: a deep metal pan with removable stainless steel grill that fits in the top. Heating comes from above, and any fat or other juices from the cooking food will drip from the grill into the pan. Put ½ inch or 1 cm of water in the pan before placing the grill on the pan; this will keep any dripped fat from smoking or burning during the cooking process. There are often two temperature settings for broiling, "low" and "high". Food is cooked on one side at a time only, and must be flipped halfway through the cooking process with a fork or tongs. Be careful; it's hot! Broiling is used for chicken or salmon. Care must be taken to prevent chicken from becoming overcooked on the outside but still raw on the inside; thin cuts may be broiled on the middle rack on high, but thicker cuts may need to be cooked on the lower rack on low for a longer time. For many ovens, broiling works best with the oven door propped open a slight amount by a potholder.

Baking uses both top and bottom heating elements, and primarily cooks by heating the air and the cookware surrounding the food, and although some food items are directly exposed to the heating elements temperatures are usually low enough to reduce broiling effects. Food is placed in a tray, pan, dish, or on a stone, which is often covered with a lid or aluminum foil to keep food from drying out. Temperatures for baking range from 325-350°F for cookies, to 375-425°F for roasting chicken, to 450°F for cornbread, with 350°F a very common setting. Use the lowest setting, often 170°F, to warm a plate to keep cooked food hot. Ovens vary, so monitor an unfamiliar oven until you learn if it runs hotter or cooler than it indicates, and adapt accordingly.

Most recipes that specify oven temperatures, such as "bake at 350°F for 30 minutes," are for conventional consumer ovens with an integrated cook top. However, standalone ***convection ovens*** contain a fan that circulates hot air around the cooking food, which means that food cooks faster and at a lower temperature than does a conventional oven. In general, any recipe calibrated for a conventional oven can be used in a convection oven by dropping the temperature by 25°F and reducing the cooking time by 25%.

English °F		Metric °C	
Conventional	Convection	Conventional	Convection
300	275	149	135
325	300	163	149
350	325	177	163
375	350	191	177
400	375	204	191
425	400	218	204
450	425	232	218

Kitchen Tools

Buy good tools. Life is too short to use inferior tools; good tools may be more expensive than crappy ones, but you will appreciate the difference over time.

I use high-quality cast iron for much of my cooking: a 9-inch ___skillet___, a 12-inch ___skillet with lid___, and a 12-inch round ___griddle___ will cover most cases. Cast iron works well on gas stoves and electric ranges with coil burners, but it might be too heavy for glass-top electric ranges. For those I recommend ___non-stick coated skillets___; be careful to not overheat them as the non-stick coating can degrade badly if scorched. Both types must be cared for. Cast iron often requires "seasoning" by coating with light cooking oil and baking at a low temperature for several hours. Don't put either cast iron or non-stick pans in a dishwasher; wash them lightly by hand and make sure to dry cast iron thoroughly to keep from rusting (re-seasoning may occasionally be necessary).

A set of ___stainless steel saucepans___ is also an asset. A standard set usually contains small, medium, and large pans, with matching lids. These can be used for boiling eggs or potatoes, making sauces and soups, and steaming vegetables. These pans are pretty durable and forgiving, and are dishwasher safe.

Remember when Harry Potter went to Ollivander's to pick out a wand? It is the same with knives. Don't buy knives from a generic department store. Find a cooking store or specialty knife store (they exist!) and find the person equivalent to Ollivander, usually some old grouchy dude in the back. Listen to them carefully. They will help you find a ___chef's knife___ and a ___paring knife___ that fit your hand with just the right balance. They will not be cheap, but if you take care of them they will be tools that you will treasure your entire life. They are yours. Don't let anybody else use them.

Other important tools include a 1-cup glass measuring cup (2-cup and 4-cup are also available), a set of stainless steel measuring cups (¼, ⅓, ½, and 1 cup sizes minimum), and a set of measuring spoons (¼ t, ½ t, 1 t, and 1 T sizes, although ⅛ t and other sizes can be found).

You'll need a spatula for use with the griddle or skillet. Use a metal spatula for cast iron, but a high-temperature plastic spatula on non-stick skillets. Metal on metal, plastic on plastic! High-temperature plastic scrapers are good for cleaning the last bits of food out of a skillet or pan. Get a good (stainless steel) ladle for soups and a big (stainless steel) spoon for large batches of stew or beans.

For baking you will need a pastry blender (get a heavy duty one, lighter-weight ones are garbage), a biscuit cutter, and a large wooden cutting board. Cutting boards are often marked to indicate that one side is used for baking and for cutting vegetables and the other side for processing meats. Raw meat is bacteria-prone so don't get the two sides mixed up!

There are an infinite number of cooking toys that can be purchased, but many are completely unnecessary. Start with the basics as outlined here, and add new items only as needed. You'll get a completely outfitted kitchen soon enough.

Liquid Ingredients

A well-stocked refrigerator or spice cabinet need not have every possible flavoring known to Man, but there are a number of things that should be available to every aspiring cook. The lists on this and the next page(s) are what I consider to be essential, but of course they can be moderated and augmented by individual taste, allergies, cultural preferences, etc.

Olive Oil

A good quality ***extra virgin*** (minimally processed) olive oil has a multitude of uses, and is one of the healthiest oils available. It can be used in sautéing and frying, as the base for a cheese sauce or in a roux (a cooked combination of flour and oil used for stews or gumbos), and as a salad dressing when mixed with a good quality vinegar. It is not as high-heat tolerant as peanut oil for stir frying, but many people are deathly allergic to peanuts in any form. Note that many commercial olive oils are actually blends of olive oil with another oil such as canola or safflower oil; you may have to search on-line for what brands of pure olive oil are available in your area. Pure olive oil is more expensive than blends, but the quality is worth the extra cost. There are also specialty olive oils with infused flavorings such as garlic or rosemary, and while these are good for giving food items an exotic flavor they are not as useful for general cooking purposes as is a pure olive oil.

A Lighter Oil

Olive oil has a distinctive taste, which makes it less than suitable for plain breads or biscuits. For these uses a lighter oil is preferred, such as ***canola*** (rapeseed), ***safflower***, or ***sunflower*** oil. Some people like avocado oil as well. Coconut oil is very high in saturated fats, and both peanut and walnut oils run the risk of severe allergic reactions, so avoid these unless you are absolutely certain they are appropriate.

Sesame Oil

Sesame oil has a very strong flavor, and should be used in moderation. It can really jazz up a stir-fry, a noodle dish, or even a salad, but it is easy to use too much. Warning: some people are allergic to sesame. A little goes a long way, so don't buy too much at once as it can go rancid if left on the shelf too long.

Soy Sauce

While it is primarily associated with stir-fries, soy sauce is very versatile and is a good addition to stews and soups, and is an important component of a marinade for chicken or seafood. Soy sauce can contain a lot of salt; I recommend low-sodium varieties.

Lime Juice

While fresh limes are always better than processed lime juice, having one or the other on hand helps out seafood dishes, marinades, and guacamole, keeps fruit salads fresh, jazzes up orange juice, and of course it is critical for lime pie!

Liquid Ingredients (Continued)

Rice Wine Vinegar

This may be optional for a lot of people, but I have found that rice wine vinegar is a good addition to a marinade for chicken or fish, or added directly to a chicken stew.

Buttermilk

Buttermilk is critical for biscuit, cornbread, and pancake recipes. Cornbread works only with fresh, liquid buttermilk from the dairy, but pancakes and biscuits can also tolerate powdered buttermilk, which keeps well in the refrigerator or freezer.

Vanilla

Use high-quality vanilla, not vanilla flavoring, in cookies, cakes, and other baked treats. Pure vanilla is significantly more expensive than the imitation flavorings, but it is worth the extra expense. Cost is tied primarily to production of vanilla beans in just a few locations in the world, primarily Madagascar and Réunion Island (***Bourbon vanilla***), Indonesia, and others, although it was originally cultivated in pre-conquistador Aztec Mexico.

Maple Syrup

Maple syrup is a staple sweetener in New England and eastern Canada, and comes in several grades. Once, syrup was measured as grade A (light, for the table), grade B (dark, for cooking), and grade C (extra dark), based on when the maple sap was collected and for how long it was boiled. Today, it is measured as Light Amber (mild maple flavor) and Dark Amber (much stronger maple flavor). Dark Amber is good for both cooking and for pouring on pancakes. A New England treat during the winter is to boil maple syrup until it is thick and ropy, and then drizzle it on a plate full of freshly fallen snow to make a chewy candy called ***sugar on snow***. Don't ever get "pancake syrup" as that is most often just brown-colored corn syrup; always go for the real deal!

Molasses

Molasses, a by-product of rendering sugar cane or sugar beets into sugar, is associated with New England as well as the Midwest and South. It is a good addition to cookies and breads, and can be used as a syrup on cornbread, biscuits, or pancakes. A white yeast bread recipe that substitutes cornmeal for some of the flour and molasses for white sugar turns into a savory Anadama bread. Rye breads also commonly use molasses as well. Brown sugar is basically plain white sugar mixed with molasses. Rum is also distilled from fermented molasses. Primarily used for cooking, ***blackstrap molasses*** is thicker and bitterer than regular molasses.

Dried Spices

I've long thought that Simon and Garfunkel got it wrong: instead of "parsley, sage, rosemary, and thyme" it should have been "parsley, sage, rosemary, and oregano" instead, but that doesn't scan as well for popular music.

Salt and pepper should be on everyone's shelf. Other spices can be categorized into two major categories: "savory" spices and "cookie" spices, although there is some overlap (ginger comes to mind). The list below is not complete, and could never be so, but represents a fair average of spices that are used by a lot of cooks. Different ethnic groups will bring their own traditions to bear here, and will add or subtract spices accordingly.

Parsley Sage Rosemary Oregano Thyme Basil Tarragon Garlic Onion Cumin Paprika

Which of these are critical and which can be skipped is largely a matter of personal taste. For me, thyme and basil are probably the spices I use the least. When doing poultry, you cannot go wrong with sage and rosemary (when talking with an acquaintance about Thanksgiving dinner, he replied "Oh, yes, Thanksgiving is all about sage and rosemary"). Sage makes stews just feel right. Tarragon goes very well with broiled salmon and other fish dishes. Paprika, particularly smoked paprika, turns both salmon and poultry into something truly amazing. Oregano and basil give a pasta dish an "Italian" feel, and can be used to jazz up an otherwise lackluster pizza slice. Cumin is a strong spice that goes very well with beans or chili. Parsley is mild, and gives subtle flavors to nearly everything. Of course, garlic and onion goes everywhere; while fresh is always better than dried, garlic powder and onion flakes add depth to a lot of dishes.

Cinnamon Nutmeg Cloves Allspice Ginger

Almost all cookie or muffin recipes call for some combination of these spices. Nutmeg, both in powdered form and freshly grated from whole nutmegs, goes in blueberry pie and is sprinkled on egg nog. Cinnamon and apples go together like they were made for each other (bless the ancient genius who first figured this out). Cinnamon and sugar sprinkled on buttered toast is a treat from a lot of people's childhoods. Cookies for holidays often have a lot of ginger or cloves. Five-spice powder, used in a lot of Asian cooking, is a blend of cinnamon, pepper, cloves, anise seed, and fennel.

There are a few things to be wary of when using any of these spices. First, do not over-salt your dishes. Your diners can always add more to taste, but if something has too much salt it is basically ruined (and too much salt is not healthy anyway). I deliberately under-salt most of my dishes. Second, taste and smell are closely linked; if you do not have much of a sense of smell you may tend to over-spice things. Be careful. Third, some people are "super tasters" where any spice other than salt is extremely jarring and unpleasant. When cooking for a group, you might need to make "regular" and "extra plain" variations of the same dish. Finally, be aware of potential allergy problems. In particular, a lot of people are deathly allergic to nuts, seeds, and related items (particularly peanuts). Calling an ambulance is a poor way to end a dinner party.

Condiments and Dips

While you can always buy specialty condiments and dips, you can make perfectly adequate substitutes with only a handful of ingredients. In particular, most of the items listed here can be made with just a few special ingredients, including the spices and liquids listed earlier, along with **_ketchup_**, **_mayonnaise_** or similar white salad dressing, sweet **_pickle relish_**, and cheap **_yellow mustard_**. If you are on a really tight budget, convenience stores or fast food restaurants often have these basics for free in small single-serving foil containers or pouches. Do buy *something* so you aren't just stealing, but then grab a few extra and stick them in the refrigerator for emergencies. Each of the recipes below is for a single serving, but they all do scale well to as many servings as needed.

Tartar Sauce

In a small bowl mix thoroughly 1 T mayonnaise or white salad dressing with 1 t sweet pickle relish for each expected serving. You may need to adjust the pickle relish up or down to taste.

Cocktail Sauce

In a small bowl mix 1 T ketchup with ¼ t lime juice for each expected serving. Classical cocktail sauce recipes almost always include finely minced horseradish as well, but I find that to be a little too strong for my taste.

Spicy Mayo for Sushi

In a small bowl mix 1 T mayonnaise or white salad dressing with ¼ - ½ t sriracha sauce for each expected serving. A splash of lime juice is optional, but gives a certain depth to the flavor. Spiciness is a very personal setting; you may need to adjust the amount of sriracha sauce up or down to achieve the right balance.

"Secret Sauce" for Burgers

When I was a kid, my favorite burger chain (local only to the Pacific Northwest) had a "secret sauce" that was both absolutely wonderful and truly hideous at the same time. Here is my best approximation to that sauce. In a small bowl mix 1 T ketchup, 1 T mayonnaise or white salad dressing, 1 t yellow mustard, 1 t pickle relish for each expected serving. There may have been some dried onion flakes in it as well. Mix thoroughly until it turns a disgusting orange-pink color. Slather generously on burgers or hot dogs. Let drip down chin.

Simple Guacamole

Peel and core two ripe avocados (cut off and discard any really dark spots). In a medium bowl chop the avocado flesh; a fork or pastry blender works on very ripe avocados, or use a food processor. Optionally add 1 t garlic powder, 1 t dried onion flakes, and/or ½ t red pepper or paprika, to taste. Add 1-2 t lime juice, and mix thoroughly. Alternatively, just mix the chopped avocados with a jar of medium-spicy salsa and call it done!

Breakfast Hash

This recipe takes advantage of having leftover potatoes that have been chopped and steamed, and optionally any leftover fish (cod or salmon), chicken, or sausage.

In heavy skillet, sauté ½ cup leftover cooked potato chunks in 3 T olive oil until hot through and/or browned. Stir occasionally to brown all sides.

When potatoes are hot, optionally add a few ounces of any leftover cooked fish available, such as cod or salmon, broken into flakes. Continue to fry, but do not overdo, as fish will disintegrate if stirred too vigorously. Chunks of leftover chicken or sausage (soy or meat) work well here, too.

Add two whole eggs, or an equivalent amount of egg substitute (1 egg = ¼ C substitute).

Grate about two ounces of cheddar cheese over top (non-fat works OK; sliced American, high fat or no fat, will also work in a pinch).

Add pepper, your favorite seasonings or aromatic spices. Stir and continue to cook until eggs are congealed and cheese is melted.

Salt to taste.

Boiled Eggs

Put two-three eggs into a small sauce pan (metal or glass) and cover with cold water. Heat on medium-high to high. Upon boiling you can reduce heat slightly to avoid splatters as along as the water continues to boil.

Boil for 5 minutes for soft-boiled eggs, 7 minutes for hard-boiled eggs.

At end of time, run cool water into pan to replace boiling water (OK for metal or Pyrex, but not for glass) and to make egg surface cool enough to handle. Remove eggs to paper towel. Residual heat will evaporate the cool water on the surface.

With heavy butter knife, split egg in middle, then scoop out contents taking care to not get any shell fragments in the bowl or on the toast. Yolks may be scooped out and thrown away to reduce the fat load, otherwise scoop out the entire egg. Repeat with other egg(s).

Add butter, salt, or garlic salt to taste.

As comfort food for queasy stomachs, prepare two soft-boiled eggs as above, add 1 T butter or margarine, chop and mix thoroughly, then break 8-10 saltine crackers into fine crumbs into the bowl with the eggs and butter and mix again. The crackers will absorb the extra liquid from the butter and egg yolk. The combination of protein, fat, salt, and starch tends to both satisfy appetite and reduce nausea.

Poached Eggs

With an Egg Poacher

Commercially made egg poachers usually have 3-6 egg cups as part of a frame that fits in a pan, with a lid. With some the cups are removable from the frame; with others the cups are integrated. The frame will have holes to let steam come up from the water underneath.

Fill the bottom of pan with water, ½ inch or 1½ cm. If the cups are separate, put them into the frame without the eggs, then put the frame in the pan. Spray each cup with spray oil (olive or canola). Crack one egg into each cup. Egg whites are OK too: separate egg whites into cups, discard yolks, add a drop of yellow egg substitute if desired (not required). Small eggs may require two whites per cup. Cover the pan with the lid.

Put on medium to medium-low heat. Bring to steam *slowly*. Do NOT put on high heat, as the water will boil over, into the cups and out of the pan, making a froth of egg protein that congeals over everything. Trust me; I know from experience. Steam *gently* for about 5-6 minutes until congealed. Use non-stick scraper to remove cooked eggs from the cups. Eggs will be both slippery AND too hot to handle, so decant them carefully directly onto your plate or onto buttered toast or biscuits.

Without an Egg Poacher

Bring about 2 inches of water in the bottom of a small saucepan to a simmer (not a rolling boil). Carefully crack each egg directly into the water so that it stays localized in a small area. Simmer gently until the egg congeals. Spoon egg(s) onto plate or toast. Do NOT use an aluminum pan: egg proteins will adhere to the metal, making it hard to clean. Use a stainless steel or glass pan.

Fried or Scrambled Eggs

Spray olive or canola oil in the bottom of a small iron skillet or non-stick pan (non-stick pans can still benefit from a little oil). Preheat skillet on medium-low until hot.

Fried

Carefully crack one or two eggs, or three egg whites, into the pan. Covering will speed the process, but it is easy to overcook. Cook until done (sunny side up), flip once and cook for a few seconds to cook the top of the yolk (easy over), or flip once and cook until the yolk is completely solid (over hard). Remove with spatula to plate.

Scrambled

Crack eggs as before, or pour ½ C egg substitute into the hot pan. As desired, add spices (garlic powder, salt, pepper, basil, chives, etc.), or small amount of cheese, crumbled. Continuously scrape eggs with spoon until all the egg has cooked and/or cheese is melted through. Serve.

Pancakes

Yes, there are any number of commercial pancake mixes available, where all you need to do is add water and possibly eggs and you have batter that starts out already tasting like week-old pancakes. Been there, done that. Fortunately, pancakes from scratch are not difficult, and are infinitely customizable according to personal tastes.

Preheat a 12-inch cast iron griddle or skillet over medium low heat (3-4 on a scale of 0 to 10). I prefer iron because it distributes heat evenly. While you <u>can</u> use a thin skillet you have to be careful about hotspots in order to not overcook the pancakes and/or have them stick to the pan in some spots while remaining undercooked elsewhere. Let the griddle heat up as you prepare the batter.

If cooking for more than one person, preheat the oven its lowest setting (usually 170°F) with a large ceramic or metal platter inside. This will keep cooked pancakes hot while later batches are being processed.

For each person, mix the following in a medium bowl (scale by the number of people being fed):
    ½ C white flour (or ⅓ C flour plus 1 T corn meal and/or 1 T oat bran)
    ½ t baking soda
    1 t baking powder
    4 T buttermilk powder if using powdered instead of liquid buttermilk
    Add 1 T light cooking oil (canola or safflower)
    Add 1 egg or ¼ C egg substitute
    Add 1 C buttermilk if using liquid buttermilk, or 1 C water if using buttermilk powder
    Add more buttermilk/water if batter is too stiff.
    Optional: add ¼ t cinnamon, ½ t vanilla, and/or sprinkle of nutmeg
    Optional: add a handful of chocolate chips, chopped bananas, or blueberries.

Spray or wipe the hot griddle with a light film of oil, and with a ¼ C measuring cup dip out a small amount of batter and pour it onto the griddle so it forms a 4-inch round. For a 12-inch round griddle you should be able to put three of these on at the same time so they do not overlap or run together.

Cook until bubbles form or until the bottoms are medium brown. Flip pancakes with spatula, taking care to not have them overlap. Cook second side until medium brown. Remove to plate and eat immediately, or to oven if cooking more than one batch.

When all pancakes are cooked, serve with butter or margarine, maple syrup, honey, or your favorite jam or jelly, as you choose. Don't use "pancake syrup" as it is just colored corn syrup; always use pure maple syrup, the darker the better. Don't forget to turn the oven off!

French Toast

Classic French toast can be quite elaborate, requiring the creation of a complex batter (almost a custard) made up of beaten eggs, milk, oil, cinnamon, sugar, and vanilla. It is fine if you want to go that route, but I generally opt for a much simpler, and thus much faster, approach.

Preheat a 12-inch cast iron griddle or skillet over medium low heat (3-4 on a scale of 0 to 10). I prefer iron because it distributes heat evenly. While you <u>can</u> use a thin skillet you have to be careful about hotspots in order to not overcook the French toast and/or have it stick to the pan in some spots while remaining undercooked elsewhere. Let the griddle heat up as you prepare the bread and the batter.

Depending on the size of your bread, you may have enough space left over on the griddle to also cook a slice of bacon or a sausage patty as desired; if so, start those items on the griddle now as it heats up.

Into a wide shallow dish pour about ½ inch or 1 cm of liquid egg whites or egg substitute. Alternatively, beat 2-3 whole eggs into the dish. (I use liquid egg whites to reduce my fat intake; one-pint or one-quart cartons are usually found in the dairy section of the grocery store.) This is usually enough to handle two pieces of French toast, with some eggs left over for scrambling. If you run out of batter, add more egg substitute or another egg as needed.

Set out one or two slices of bread (for thin store-bought bread you may need two slices, but for the fresh bread I make I cut slices thickly enough that one piece is usually enough for me). French toast is an excellent way of using up stale bread, but it works with fresh bread as well. Note, however, that you do NOT want to soak fresh bread in the egg batter for very long, as the middle of the bread will become soggy and the egg batter will not cook through completely. While edible, it is fairly disgusting. Trust the voice of experience here.

For each piece of French toast, spray or wipe the hot griddle with a light film of oil, quickly dip each side of a slice of bread into the batter, and then drop it onto the griddle. Sprinkle with cinnamon now, if you wish. After a minute or two, lift the edge of the bread with a spatula to see how it is cooking, and flip the bread over when the cooked side is a light to medium brown. If doing bacon or sausage, flip those at about the same time that you flip the bread. Cook the other side until it, too, is light to medium brown, then remove to a plate. Do not overcook (or undercook).

Serve with butter or margarine, maple syrup, honey, or your favorite jam or jelly, as you choose. Pro Tip: pure maple syrup is good on the bacon or sausage, too. Don't use "pancake syrup" as it is just colored corn syrup; always use pure maple syrup, the darker the better.

If you have leftover eggs in the shallow dish, scramble them on the griddle and serve alongside the French toast. Go ahead and turn off the burner as you do this; an iron griddle will retain enough residual heat to cook a small amount of eggs as it cools.

Buttermilk Biscuits

Mix in a medium bowl:

    2 C flour
    ½ t baking soda
    1 T baking powder
    Add 4 T buttermilk powder if using powdered instead of liquid buttermilk
    Add 1 T oat bran if desired
    Add 1 T corn meal if desired
    Add other interesting grains if desired, 1 T each

Cut in very slightly less than ⅓ C light oil with a pastry blender (use a pastry blender with stiff metal cutters, not light wire). An oil such as canola or safflower oil is best – do not use olive oil or the biscuits will be too heavy and have an odd taste.

Mix in 1 C buttermilk, or 1 C water if buttermilk powder is used. Mix thoroughly until all the powder is wet and all the liquid has been mixed in. If using any extra grains, additional liquid (up to ½ C) may be required to completely wet all the dry ingredients.

Tip the dough out onto a clean, floured surface. Add a small amount of flour on top, flour your hands, and then knead into dough. Result should be firm, but neither soupy (too much liquid) nor crumbly (too little liquid). Add a little flour if the dough is too wet; a little water if too dry. Do not over-knead. Roll out flat with rolling pin about 1 cm or ⅜ inch thick. Cut dough into circles or other shapes with a biscuit cutter. Place cut biscuits onto cookie sheet slightly separated from one another.

Bake 10 minutes at 400°, or slightly longer until tops are light brown (particularly if the oven runs cool).

Tactics

Preheat the oven to 400° *before* mixing if you are in a hurry. Otherwise, place the cookie sheet on the back of the stove, and preheat oven only *after* the biscuits have been cut out. This allows the dough to relax and have the biscuits rise before baking.

Powdered buttermilk keeps longer than liquid buttermilk, and can be kept in the refrigerator, or in the freezer indefinitely. You can make richer biscuits by increasing the powder over standard requirements (from 4 T to 5-6 T powder for 1 C water).

None of the extra grains listed (oat bran, cornmeal, etc.) are actually needed to make terrific biscuits, but they do add flavor and texture. If extras are added, slightly more liquid will be needed. Stay away from grains that take a long time to soften, such as cracked wheat, etc.

Don't put sugar in biscuits, unless you are making shortcake. (See the rant about sugar in cornbread on the next page – it's the same deal here.)

Cornbread

I've lived in New England for most of my adult life, and grew up in Oregon, but I come from a long line of Southern stock. One difference I've noted between New England and the South is in how cornbread is prepared. New Englanders typically put sugar in the recipe; Southerners do not. The cornbread recipe presented here does not contain sugar, nor will it ever. This is non-negotiable as it is entirely a matter of religion. Indeed, I have heard tales from my more colorful Arkansas relatives that the American Civil War was fought because the Damn Yankees insisted on putting sugar in the cornbread. No comment.

This cornbread recipe is extremely simple, and is fast to run up, but it does require a 9-inch cast iron skillet, and fresh *liquid* buttermilk. Buttermilk powder works well in biscuits and pancakes, but not here. I've even had poor luck reconstituting buttermilk powder into liquid buttermilk and then using that. Fresh seems to be best.

Put 1-1½ T light oil (safflower or canola) into the 9-inch iron skillet. Spread the oil around so the entire inner surface of the skillet is coated. Place the skillet with the oil <u>into</u> the oven on the middle rack, and start the oven preheating to 450°.

In a medium bowl mix 1 C coarsely-ground corn meal, ½ t baking soda, and ½ t salt. Mix the dry ingredients together. Get one whole egg or ¼ C egg substitute ready to use, and also measure out 1 C fresh liquid buttermilk.

When the oven is ready, things move fast.

With a hot pad, pull the skillet out of the oven and place it onto a burner on the stove. Turn the burner to hot. As the burner heats, quickly add the egg or egg substitute and the buttermilk to the dry ingredients. Mix thoroughly to wet everything.

When the oil in the skillet <u>starts</u> to smoke, **use a hot-pad** to pick up the skillet and pour the extremely hot oil into the batter. Be careful as it will spatter. Place the skillet on a cold burner or trivet (remember that it is deadly hot). Quickly mix the hot oil into the batter, and then pour it into the hot skillet.

Using your hot-pad, place the skillet and batter back into the oven on the middle rack, and bake at 450° for 20 minutes.

With your hot-pad, remove the hot skillet to a cold burner or trivet. Cut into six pie-shaped wedges. Note that if it isn't quite done, there will be a thin liquid band just under the top crust. If this happens, you've added too much liquid, and will need to bake for a few more minutes.

Serve hot with butter, with cream cheese, or as a side dish to chili.

Basic Grits

As someone with a lot of Southern blood in me, I would be remiss if I didn't include a recipe for grits. A lot of people do not like grits, which is made from ground corn without the husk. Admittedly, undercooked grits are pretty nasty, and I've been served grits in the South (a place that should know better) that were inedible. Having said that, when done right corn grits form as tasty a breakfast grain porridge as any other grain, and can be used as a base for many other dishes. Dry ground grits can be found in bulk in most natural foods stores (commercially packaged yellow grits will do in a pinch, but they're too finely ground and I don't recommend it). Buy yellow grits, not white grits. The basic preparation is 4 parts water to 1 part dry grits; this scales up or down easily to any amount.

X dry yellow grits (¼ to ⅓ cup per serving)
4X water
dash salt

Bring water to boil, stir in grits, and reduce heat to low. Grits will want to boil over as heat reduces, so keep stirring (blow air softly at surface to break up starch bubbles). When danger of boil-over is past, cover and cook the remainder of 5 minutes, stirring occasionally.

Serve with butter. Soft-boiled eggs on top is a nice addition.

Modifications:

When basic grits are finished cooking, add cheese (several slices of non-fat American cheese works fine, but an equivalent amount of high-fat cheese will give a richer flavor), spices such as parsley, chives, garlic powder (but not garlic salt), mix through. Serve with butter or eggs.

Cheese Grits Casserole

1 C grits
4 C water
½ t salt
Several slices of non-fat American cheese
½ t Garlic powder
Dash parsley, chives, etc.
1 egg or ¼ C egg substitute

Prepare cheese grits as above.

Add egg or egg beaters and mix through, pour into greased/buttered glass dish, cover with foil, and bake at 350° for 30-35 minutes. This makes an excellent holiday casserole. It is also a great breakfast treat on a cold winter day.

Turkey Chili

Sauté 1 finely chopped white onion in 3-4 T olive oil in medium pot. Add 1 pound 99% lean ground turkey (lean ground beef probably works just as well). Break meat into small bits with a spoon, and continue to sauté over medium heat until both the onion and the meat are cooked through with no pink remaining in the meat.

Add 1 t sage, 1 t parsley, 1 t basil, 1 t garlic powder. Rosemary works well instead of basil.

Add 1 t chili powder if desired (this is not necessary for mild, and I don't add it). Mix through.

Add 1 T soy sauce and 1 small can of tomato paste. Mix thoroughly with the meat, onion, and spices.

Add 1 large can of pinto beans and 1 small can of red kidney beans, or vice-versa. Roman beans and small red beans work OK as well, but don't use chick peas or black-eyed peas. Mix through. Rinse out the bean cans with a small amount of water, then pour the sauce into the pot. Stir through.

Add 1 t to 1 T ground cumin. Mix through. The cumin is a strong spice that gives the chili its distinctive "chili-ness" flavor. It should be added last and not with the other dry spices.

Heat through on medium to medium-low until bubbling. Stir occasionally. Makes approximately six servings.

Basic Rice

Cooking long grain rice is very straightforward: you will need twice as much water by volume as dry rice, plus a little salt. Generally, ½ C rice and 1 C water makes about 1-2 servings, 1 C rice and 2 C water is good for an evening meal of 3-4 people.

In a medium saucepan bring 2X water plus a dash of salt to boiling; add X rice, stir, cover, and drop the heat to low. Cook undisturbed for 19-20 minutes. Rice may boil over before the burner temperature drops; if a boil-over is imminent raise the lid and blow gently to break up the starch bubbles, then re-cover. At the end of the cooking time, stir cooked rice to fluff it up. Serve immediately.

I've had a report from a college student that you can add in one whole egg at the last minute, which cooks as it is mixed in.

While expensive, a good quality rice cooker can make the preparation of rice truly painless. Such machines usually have settings for Jasmine rice, brown rice, and sushi rice.

Cheese Sauce

In a small saucepan cover the bottom with olive oil, 2-3 T flour, and ¼-⅓ C water, then mix. Heat over medium-low heat. If it gets too thick too quickly stir in more water. Add non-fat sliced American cheese (8-10 slices), melt and mix through as each slice is added. Keep stirring, and do not allow the sauce to burn or stick to the bottom of the pan.

Optional: Add 1 T grated Parmesan cheese for taste, allow to mix in and melt. Other non-fat cheeses may be used (cream cheese, Swiss, etc.) as long as hard cheeses are shredded and soft cheeses are broken into small bits so they melt in well. Hard cheddars tend to not work well, but small amounts of Mozzarella, Muenster, or other high-fat soft cheeses do work.

Use in pasta (Mac & Cheese) or over broccoli.

Fast Mushroom Soup

Chop and sauté 1 small white onion, ¼-⅓ of a green pepper in several T olive oil. Add 8-10 slices turkey bacon, chopped, and continue to sauté. Add one large can of mushrooms, 1 small can of Portobello mushrooms, both drained of liquid. Continue to sauté. In large 4 C measuring cup mix ¼ C flour with ½ C water, then add one can condensed/evaporated non-fat milk and mix thoroughly. Add liquid to pot. Stir over medium heat until hot (do not boil) and at desired thickness. Serves three-four. Total run-up time about 20-25 minutes.

Chicken and Rice

In a large skillet place 2 T olive oil, two bunches of scallions cut into about 1 inch lengths or one small white onion chopped, 1 pound of rinsed chicken tenders, and 1 large can of mushrooms. Add several olives, chopped, if available. Sauté covered on medium heat for several minutes until the chicken starts to brown, and liquid appears in bottom of pan. Add ½ to ¾ C white rice, then 1 C chicken broth, completely wetting the rice. Cover until liquid is simmering, then drop heat to low or medium-low, re-cover and continue to simmer 20 minutes or until rice is done. Serves 3-4.

Chicken and Scallions

With a sharp fillet knife slice three boneless chicken breasts into three thin layers each. Put olive oil into a large skillet to mostly cover bottom, then coarsely slice two bunches of scallions. Layer chicken breasts on top of the scallions. Put small can of chopped Portobello mushrooms (drained) on top of the chicken. Drizzle soy sauce over all, then liberally shake garlic powder and/or rosemary over everything. Cover. Heat on medium until done, about 20 minutes. Mix 2-3 T flour with water, pour over all and mix into existing liquid. Cook uncovered a few minutes to thicken gravy.

Quick but Fancy Chicken

Strip the fat from 6-8 boneless chicken thighs, put in bowl. Add some soy sauce and rice vinegar. Marinate for some time (I once saw a TV chef state that marinating was a precise art: somewhere between 15 minutes and two years). Spray olive oil on the bottom of a 12-inch square ceramic or glass dish.

Variation #1

Lay out thighs flat on bottom of dish in one layer. Crush up 8 Club Crackers over top. Add sprinkle of garlic powder, rosemary, pepper, and other savory spices as desired.

Variation #2

In a wide, flat bowl mix ½ C to 1 C cornmeal, 1 t garlic powder, 1 t rosemary, or other savory spices. Add a sprinkle of salt or pepper as desired. Dip thighs in liquid buttermilk, then into cornmeal. Lay thighs flat on bottom of dish in one layer.

Cover dish with foil. Bake at 425° for 30-40 minutes. I usually place glass dishes into a cold oven and then turn it on. This is not as much of a thermal shock on the glass dish as is putting it directly into a hot oven, and it doesn't take most ovens very long to come up to temperature.

Broiling Chicken or Salmon

If you have a broiling pan (a shallow pan with a heavy metal fitted rack), you can make excellent chicken or salmon without a barbeque grill.

Fill the shallow pan with ½ inch of water. This is to keep fat drippings from igniting. Place the metal rack on the pan, and spray it with olive oil.

Put skinless chicken thighs, breasts, legs, etc., or salmon (either steaks or filets) in a bowl with a mixture of soy sauce, lime juice, garlic powder, sage, tarragon (fish) or rosemary (chicken), etc., cover, and refrigerate. Marinate for somewhere between 15 minutes and two years. Place the meat in one layer on the metal rack (skin side down for fish filets). If you are in a hurry, mix the marinade and simply pour it on the meat, taking care to not have too much of it drip through. If you are in a real hurry, dump soy sauce on the meat and sprinkle garlic powder over everything.

Place pan in the oven on the middle rack, and set the oven to broil on high. Some ovens require that you prop the door open a crack with a hot pad; others do not. When the meat is brown and sizzling on top (8-10 minutes), pull the rack out carefully with a hot pad, and flip the meat with a metal spatula. Continue to cook until brown and sizzling, or until the smoke alarm goes off.

Thick chicken might take a little longer to cook than you expect; it must <u>not</u> be pink in the center and any juices must run clear. Salmon can continue to cook skin-side up until the skin is black and crispy; peel it off carefully before serving.

Sautéed Vegetables

Prepare any or all of the following:
> Chop one small white onion.
> Wash and quarter 8-16 ounces of fresh mushrooms.
> Trim the ends from a small zucchini and/or yellow squash and cut into ⅛-inch slices.

In a large skillet add 2-3 T olive oil. Heat on medium to medium high. Depending on which vegetables you have, add in the following order:
> The chopped onion. Sauté until translucent.
> The mushrooms. Sauté until mushrooms are hot through and liquid is rendering out.
> The zucchini/squash. Sauté until soft.

Cover the skillet as the vegetables are cooking. Add a sprinkle of garlic powder, and your favorite savory spices: basil, tarragon, sage, etc. Make sure to not overcook the zucchini or yellow squash – they definitely have to go in last.

When cooking is nearly done, mix 1-2 T flour with water in a small glass, then pour over all. Mix through, then cook until gravy thickens. Serves 3-4 (or just 1 if it's just the mushrooms and my daughter finds out about it).

Steamed Vegetables

A stainless steel steamer basket costs just a few dollars, and is a simple and fast way to make cooked vegetables both tasty and nutritious. They fit into the bottoms of both medium and large saucepans. Regardless of which size you use, fill the bottom of the pan with water to just below the bottom of the steamer basket – you want the veggies to steam, not boil. Place your vegetables in the basket, cover, and heat on medium-high. You can bring the temperature up more quickly by turning the burner on high, but you must reduce the temperature to medium-high to avoid boil-over. Reducing the heat slightly also allows the cooking to last longer without boiling all the water away. Some items take a longer time to cook than others, and if the water boils away they'll scorch. You can cook one type of vegetable or a mixture, but you have to be careful if two different vegetables require different cooking times. Here are some suggestions:

1. Broccoli. Steam 5-10 minutes. You want the result to be bright green, not gray.

2. Corn and peas. Peas are more delicate than corn. They, too, should still be bright green.

3. Carrots (chopped into 1-inch chunks), potatoes (chopped into chunks or quartered), and/or Lima beans. These are harder vegetables; steam 15 minutes or so.

4. Spinach. Fill the pot to overflowing with uncooked spinach, and crunch it in with your hands if you have to. Steam for 5 minutes. The result will be much smaller than what you started with.

Basic Potatoes

Clean 6 to 8 small red, white, or purple potatoes (2 inches or 5 cm in diameter) by cutting out any bad spots or blemishes. Cut into eighths (one cut each along the x, y, and z axes). In a medium saucepan, cover with water, add a dash of salt, and boil with the pot uncovered on medium high. Alternatively, steam them in a steamer basket as described on the previous page (this is the preferred method, as more nutrients are retained than when boiled). They will be done when a fork slides easily into the potato flesh.

Variation #1 – Basic Potatoes

Prepare potatoes as above, drain, serve immediately. These are good with butter or margarine, garlic salt, or ketchup. Leftovers can be refrigerated and used the next day in breakfast hash.

Variation #2 – Mashed Potatoes

Prepare potatoes as above, drain and return to pot. With a hand mixer, start breaking up the potatoes into smaller chunks. Add a tablespoon or two of butter, margarine, or olive oil. Add about a quarter cup of milk, soy milk, or even buttermilk. Optional: add parsley, garlic powder, or shredded cheese, to taste. Continue to beat with the hand mixer until everything is mixed through evenly.

Oven Fried Potatoes

Clean two large russet potatoes by removing bad spots and blemishes, but there is no need to peel them. Alternatively, peel two equivalently large sweet potatoes, or clean one russet and peel one sweet potato. With a very heavy knife or cleaver, chop the potatoes lengthwise into 1 cm square strips (that is 1 cm × 1 cm × the length of the potato). Be careful: sweet potatoes are very woody and take some effort to cut.

Spray cooking oil on a large cookie sheet (even if the cookie sheet is non-stick), then lightly salt the oil. Place the potato strips close together on the cookie sheet but carefully separated so that no two strips touch. Spray the tops of the potatoes with cooking oil and lightly salt once more.

Bake in a 400°F oven about 30 minutes for sweet potatoes, about 40 minutes for russets. Depending on your oven, you may wish to start checking doneness with a fork after about 25 minutes, and adjust the timing appropriately.

Remove cookie sheet to a cooling rack. Serve with ketchup.

Gyoza Soup

This is a fairly light soup that is quick to make and can take advantage of leftover vegetables. It will not be a whole meal, but is a nice appetizer to something larger, particularly stir-fries.

In a medium soup pot, sauté one chopped white onion and one chopped green pepper in 3-4 T olive oil. If using fresh garlic, add two cloves, peeled and chopped. Add one large can, drained, of mushrooms, and continue to sauté until aromatics are soft. Mushrooms can be "generic" or Portobello, sliced or stems-and-pieces. Add 1 C each frozen peas and frozen corn, stir, and continue to sauté until thawed, about 5 minutes or less.

Add 1-2 T dried parsley, ½ t powdered garlic (if not using fresh), ½ t soy sauce. Other spices that may work include cilantro or pepper, but don't overdo. Add 1-2 C chicken broth, 1-2 C of water (you may use only water if there is no broth available, or vegetable broth instead of chicken broth, but the soup will not have as much depth). Add several drops of sesame oil (optional). Bring to a simmer.

We are now at serve minus 15 minutes.

Add one package frozen gyoza dumplings, also known as pot-stickers or dim-sum. Chicken, pork, shrimp, or vegetable will all work, and often come in a package of around 24. Bring soup quickly up to a simmer once more. Do not over-stir or stir vigorously, otherwise the dumplings may disintegrate.

At serve minus 5 minutes add any available leftover cooked vegetables, such as broccoli or pea pods (optional), or uncooked spinach. Bring to a simmer once again.

Serves three with refills, or six without. Soup is very light – I tend to under-salt, but people can add salt to their taste at the table.

Quick Oyster Stew

Unless you are at a seacoast where you can get them fresh, commercial oysters are often sold in half-pint containers. They aren't cheap, but one container will make a fairly decent stew for one person as an occasional treat. If you love oysters as much as I do, this is a good way to stave off the blahs of a cold winter's day. Pick a container where all the oysters are grayish, not brownish.

Empty the oysters and their liquid into a small saucepan, along with about a tablespoon of butter or margarine. Heat on medium to medium high until the oysters are cooked (about 5 minutes). Don't overcook. When hot, open a 12 ounce can of condensed skim milk (or use an equivalent amount of fresh milk or cream), and pour it into the saucepan. Reduce heat, and heat until milk is <u>hot</u> but <u>not</u> boiling. Pour into bowl, then garnish with parsley, butter, paprika, and/or crackers, to taste. Low fat: use margarine and condensed skim milk; high fat: use butter and cream.

For a variation, add a few bay scallops and/or shrimp to oyster stew and heat through.

Quick Barbeque Sauce

This is a basic BBQ sauce that works very well for chicken and other meats. The ingredients, mostly tomato sauce, sugar, and spices, can have their proportions adjusted wildly up or down to get different effects, but the single most critical special ingredient to making this taste like true BBQ sauce brewed by a pit-master is liquid smoke. This is available in small bottles at major grocery store chains, usually in the aisle with the commercial BBQ sauces.

In a medium saucepan, combine one large can (12-15 ounces) of tomato sauce, ½ C vinegar (either apple cider or rice wine), one small can (6 ounces) of tomato paste, ¼ C molasses, 2-3 T Worcestershire sauce (optional), 2 t liquid smoke, 1 t paprika, 1 t garlic powder, ½ t black pepper, ½ t salt, and ½ t onion powder. Other savory spices as desired (sage, parsley, chili powder, etc.). Optional: if the sauce is too tangy, you can add up to ¼-⅓ C of honey or other sweeteners; I find the molasses by itself makes the sauce sweet enough for me.

Bring to a quick simmer, reduce heat until the sauce just simmers, and stir frequently. As the sauce thickens, it will tend to "plop" bubbles like a mud pit at Yellowstone and sling hot BBQ sauce everywhere. Keep stirring; 20-30 minutes. Makes about 4-5 C.

Serve hot, with hot meats. Lasts refrigerated for about a week.

Fry Batters

Frying meats such as chicken or white fish (or even onion rings or other vegetables) in batter is an old Southern tradition. There are a number of approaches that can be taken.

Variation #1

In a wide, shallow bowl, mix together 1 C cornmeal, 1 C flour, 1 t garlic powder, 1 T sage, 1 T parsley, ½ t pepper. Other savory spices as desired. In a second shallow bowl, pour out about a ½ inch layer of fresh buttermilk (can be omitted; see below). Heat a large iron skillet; for each batch heat ¼ inch of vegetable or olive oil in the bottom of the skillet until oil is quite hot.

Dip thin chicken pieces (boneless thighs or breast tenders) or fillets of white fish (cod or pollock) into the buttermilk (can be omitted if desired, as long as meats are first dampened with water), then roll in the cornmeal and flour mixture, and place in the hot skillet. Warning: the hot oil may spatter. When half-cooked, flip the meat with a spatula and finish cooking. Remove to a plate covered in paper towels to absorb excess oil. Serve immediately.

Variation #2

In a bowl mix ½ C flour, ¼ C cornstarch, 1 t baking powder, ¼ t salt, ½ C water, 1 egg or ¼ C egg substitute, and 1 T oil. Optional: add ¼ C cornmeal and increase water to ¾ C. Add slightly more water if the batter seems too thick. Dip meats in batter and fry as described above. Works well for baked meats, too. The cornstarch is what gives the batter its fast-food authenticity.

Fast Chocolate Cake

Preheat oven to 350°. In a medium bowl mix 1 C white sugar, ⅞ C flour, ⅜ C cocoa, ¾ t baking soda, ¾ t baking powder, ½ t salt. Add 1 egg or ¼ C egg substitute, ½ C skim milk or soy milk, ¼ C light vegetable oil, 1+ t vanilla. Mix, then add and mix ½ C boiling (or very hot) water.

Pour batter into greased and floured 9-inch×9-inch metal pan. Bake at 350° for 40 minutes.

Notes

Using Double-Dutch Dark Cocoa for the cocoa is a REALLY good idea!
The finished cake works well with strawberry/blueberry/blackberry jam on top.

Chocolate Pudding

This pudding is fairly low fat, but high in sugar. It runs up very quickly: from start to eat is about 20 minutes.

Whisk together ⅓ C sugar, ¼ C corn starch, 3 T unsweetened cocoa, and a small shake of salt in a medium saucepan. A small shake of cinnamon (optional) can add an interesting depth to the pudding.

Add one can unsweetened condensed/evaporated milk or 2 cups skim milk or soy milk, and then whisk through until the powders have all been wetted. Be careful as you whisk, as cocoa powder is about like lunar regolith: fine, dry, and gets everywhere and into everything.

Heat on stove on medium until boiling, whisk or stir continuously. The phase change from liquid to solid will occur suddenly, so continue to stir to keep the pudding from scorching.

At the end, add a small handful of chocolate chips if desired (not required), and continue to cook and stir about a minute or so. Remove from heat.

Add 1+ t of vanilla, mix through.

Pour or scrape into custard cups (serves 6) or small bowls (serves 3). Can be eaten warm immediately, or chilled and eaten later.

Maple Syrup Cookies

In a medium bowl mix 2 C flour, ½ t baking powder, 1/2 t baking soda, and a dash of salt. Add one egg or ¼ C egg substitute, ½ C butter or margarine, 1 C maple syrup. Mix until the flour is wet and the butter is mixed through. Drop small blobs of batter onto a greased cookie sheet. Bake 10-12 minutes at 400°. You will need two cookie sheets, or will have to bake the cookies in stages.

Cookies come out puffy and chewy, not hard.

If desired you can add chocolate chips or nuts, but it isn't a requirement. I avoid nuts in general as a lot of my friends have severe nut allergies. Blueberries may work as well, if ¼ t nutmeg is added to the dry mix.

I suspect the butter can be reduced by a lot, and the baking powder/baking soda amounts may be adjustable as well. Use grade B or grade A dark amber maple syrup: it is thicker, chewier, and has a much richer flavor than the lighter syrups. Do NOT use a corn-syrup substitute!

Lime Pie

This is an old family recipe that I first made in graduate school along with help from a friend. He shall remain nameless to protect the guilty; suffice it to say that our first attempt involved aluminum foil and a Dremel Moto Tool™. We will speak no more of this.

Crust:

In a bowl crush into dust half of a 1-pound box of graham crackers. Mix in ½ C sugar. Separately melt ½ C butter or margarine, and while still warm mix into the crackers and sugar. Place into glass pie pan. With your fingers form a crust, spread evenly about ¼ inch thick on the bottom, and work up the sides, making a rim above the edge of the pan. Freeze 15-30 minutes.

Filling:

Separate three eggs: whites into one bowl, yolks into another. Don't get any yolk in the bowl with the whites. Extract the juice from three limes, up to ½ C. Mix one can of Eagle Brand™ sweetened condensed milk into the bowl with the yolks, then thoroughly mix in the lime juice. The lime juice will start to "cook" the yolks, so work quickly. Pour the filling into the crust, and put into refrigerator. Preheat the oven to 350°.

Meringue:

Beat egg whites on high for a couple minutes. While continuing to beat, add ¼ t cream of tartar, and slowly add ½ C sugar. Beat until egg whites are stiff. Remove pie from refrigerator, and spread meringue evenly with spatula, poking pie to form peaks. Bake until peaks turn brown, about 10 minutes. Refrigerate for 2 hours before serving.

Simple Upgrades

This section is for those circumstances where cooking space is at a premium (such as in a dorm room) and where meals need to be worked up without a lot of preparation time. In these cases, food choices tend to be quite limited, but pre-packaged commercial products leave a lot to be desired. So, if you are stuck with limited resources, here are a couple suggestions. They won't give you the same experience as with Dad's Home Cooking, but, hey, it's better than nothing.

Canned Soup

The advantage of canned soup is obvious: open a can, heat it up (microwave or stovetop), eat, clean one bowl, and then recycle the can. The problems are that canned soups are woefully limited in their ingredient lists, and are often way too high on their salt content, even the so-called "low sodium" varieties. For example, a popular low-sodium chicken noodle soup contains only chicken chunks, carrots, and noodles, but with 20% of a person's daily sodium requirement.

If you have a freezer, even the one on a dorm fridge, keep in it at all times a bag of frozen corn and/or frozen peas (or a blend). When you open a can of soup, throw in a half-cup or so of the frozen veggies into the pot as it is heating. It'll extend the soup to a couple of bowls worth (thinning out the salt to less per bowl), give you more vegetables, and make the soup much more interesting than it was before. Garnish the soup with Parmesan cheese or fresh parsley, as desired.

Ramen

Like canned soups, ramen noodles are a staple of college students everywhere. That doesn't mean they are good for you, particularly over an extended period of time. As with soups, throwing in a few frozen vegetables helps, and if you have access to fresh veggies through a local grocer or farmer's market, a chopped scallion, clove of garlic, sprig of fresh parsley or basil, or a few leaves of spinach helps enormously. When the noodles have nearly cooked, crack an egg into the soup and let it simmer. I recommend *against* using the "flavor packets" that come with commercial ramen packages, as they are mostly salt and/or monosodium glutamate (MSG), neither of which are desirable.

Eggs and Hot Dogs and Coffee, Oh My!

Often times, dorm rules forbid cooking implements other than a coffee maker and a cube refrigerator. A coffee maker does not have to exclusively make coffee, however. Depending on the type, it may have a stand-alone pitcher on a heating element. If so, the pitcher can heat water to nearly boiling, which makes it suitable for cooking eggs and hot dogs, making ramen, heating soup, and other similar activities. Be careful before using a roommate's coffee maker for non-traditional purposes, as coffee drinkers can get extremely territorial and possessive.

What Not To Do

Here are a couple of culinary mistakes I've made in my life. Learn from my experience.

Don't have a milkshake, followed shortly by ginger ale. The result is roughly hypergolic, and will keep you up all night. It will also have a deleterious effect on your social life, as nobody will want to be within 15 feet of you for several hours. I have it on good authority that ice cream followed by beer has the same effect.

Don't have hot tea with spicy chili. Neither cancels out the other.

Don't use dull knives. You will tend to put too much pressure on them when attempting to cut something, and when (not if) they slip you will do yourself more damage than if the knife was razor sharp. You only need a couple of good quality knives, anyway: a 10-inch chef's knife and one smaller knife will do. Keep them sharp.

Don't walk away leaving the kitchen unmonitored. There is an old saying that goes "a watched pot never boils," which isn't true but just seems so. Unfortunately, the corollary really is true: "an unwatched pot boils over." Keep stirring if there is a chance of something sticking to or burning on the bottom of the pot.

Don't be timid in the kitchen! Cooking can be fun, but don't worry if you make mistakes. Invent new things, blend the best ideas from different cultures, and be open to new tastes. Yeah, you will ruin some stuff, and if you are a poor starving graduate student you might end up having to eat it anyway (the voice of experience here). Don't let that stop you! It is all part of the game.

23: Templates

The following pages contain a few templates for designing your own spreadsheets and tables for databases. After the templates to the end of the book there are plenty of blank pages for adding your own tables, notes, conversion constants, snippets of code, doodles, bad jokes, recipes, or anything else that takes your fancy.

Spreadsheet Template

	A	B	C	D	E	F	G	H
1								
2								
3								
4								
5								
6								
7								
8								
9								
10								
11								
12								
13								
14								
15								
16								
17								
18								
19								
20								
21								
22								
23								
24								
25								
26								
27								
28								
29								
30								

Spreadsheet Template

	A	B	C	D	E	F	G	H
1								
2								
3								
4								
5								
6								
7								
8								
9								
10								
11								
12								
13								
14								
15								
16								
17								
18								
19								
20								
21								
22								
23								
24								
25								
26								
27								
28								
29								
30								

Spreadsheet Template

	A	B	C	D	E	F	G	H
1								
2								
3								
4								
5								
6								
7								
8								
9								
10								
11								
12								
13								
14								
15								
16								
17								
18								
19								
20								
21								
22								
23								
24								
25								
26								
27								
28								
29								
30								

Spreadsheet Template

	A	B	C	D	E	F	G	H
1								
2								
3								
4								
5								
6								
7								
8								
9								
10								
11								
12								
13								
14								
15								
16								
17								
18								
19								
20								
21								
22								
23								
24								
25								
26								
27								
28								
29								
30								

Paradox Database Table Structure Template

	Field Name	Type	Size	Keyed?	Validity Checks			
					Minimum	Maximum	Default	Picture
1								
2								
3								
4								
5								
6								
7								
8								
9								
10								
11								
12								
13								
14								
15								

Paradox Database Table Structure Template

	Field Name	Type	Size	Keyed?	Validity Checks			
					Minimum	Maximum	Default	Picture
1								
2								
3								
4								
5								
6								
7								
8								
9								
10								
11								
12								
13								
14								
15								

Paradox Database Table Structure Template

	Field Name	Type	Size	Keyed?	Validity Checks			
					Minimum	Maximum	Default	Picture
1								
2								
3								
4								
5								
6								
7								
8								
9								
10								
11								
12								
13								
14								
15								

Paradox Database Table Structure Template

	Field Name	Type	Size	Keyed?	Validity Checks			
					Minimum	Maximum	Default	Picture
1								
2								
3								
4								
5								
6								
7								
8								
9								
10								
11								
12								
13								
14								
15								

Access Database Table Structure Template

	Field Name	Data Type	Text Size, or Numeric Sub-Type	Keyed?	Validation Rule	Default
1						
2						
3						
4						
5						
6						
7						
8						
9						
10						
11						
12						
13						
14						
15						

Access Database Table Data Template

	Field #1	Field #2	Field #3	Field #4	Field #5	Field #6
1						
2						
3						
4						
5						
6						
7						
8						
9						
10						
11						
12						
13						
14						
15						

Access Database Table Structure Template

	Field Name	Data Type	Text Size, or Numeric Sub-Type	Keyed?	Validation Rule	Default
1						
2						
3						
4						
5						
6						
7						
8						
9						
10						
11						
12						
13						
14						
15						

Access Database Table Data Template

	Field #1	Field #2	Field #3	Field #4	Field #5	Field #6
1						
2						
3						
4						
5						
6						
7						
8						
9						
10						
11						
12						
13						
14						
15						

Notes

Notes

Notes

Notes

Notes

Notes

Notes

Notes

Notes

Notes

Notes

Notes

Notes

Notes

Notes

Notes

Notes

Notes